EYEWITN

DORDOGNE, BORDEAUX & THE SOUTHWEST COAST

EYEWITNESS TRAVEL

DORDOGNE, BORDEAUX & THE SOUTHWEST COAST

DK

DK

LONDON, NEW YORK,
MELBOURNE, MUNICH AND DELHI
www.dk.com

Produced by Hachette Tourisme, Paris, France
Editorial Director Cécile Boyer-Runge
Series Editor Catherine Laussucq
Project Editor Amélie Baghdiguian
Editor Aurélie Pregliasc
Art Director Éric Laubeuf
Designers Maogani
Cartography Cyrille Suss

Main Contributors Suzanne Boireau-Tartarat, Pierre Chavot, Renée Grimaud, Wilfried Lecarpentier, Santiago Mendieta, Marie-Pascale Rauzier

Photography Philippe Giraud, Pierre Javelle, Éric Guillemot

Dorling Kindersley Limited
Publishing Managers Jane Ewart, Fay Franklin
Project editor Cécile Landau
English Translation Lucilla Watson
DTP Jason Little,Conrad van Dyk
Cartography Casper Morris
Production Louise Daly

Printed and bound in Malaysia by Vivar Printing Sdn.Bhd

First American Edition, 2006

14 15 16 17 10 9 8 7 6 5 4 3 2 1

Published in the United States by DK Publishing,
345 Hudson Street, New York, New York 10014

Reprinted with revisions 2008, 2010, 2012, 2014

Published in Great Britain by Dorling Kindersley Limited.
A catalog record for this book is available from the Library of Congress.

ISSN 1542-1554

ISBN: 978-1-46541-155-6

Floors are referred to throughout in accordance with european usage; ie the "first floor" is the floor above ground level.

Note: The French name of Aquitaine is used to describe the area covered by this guide.

Front cover main image: Château de Monbazillac

MIX
Paper from responsible sources
FSC www.fsc.org
FSC™ C018179

The information in every DK Eyewitness Travel Guide is checked regularly.

Every effort has been made to ensure that this book is as up-to-date as possible at the time of going to press. Some details, however, such as telephone numbers, opening hours, prices, gallery hanging arrangements and travel information are liable to change. The publishers cannot accept responsibility for any consequences arising from the use of this book, nor for any material on third party websites, and cannot guarantee that any website address in this book will be a suitable source of travel information. We value the views and suggestions of our readers very highly. Please write to: Publisher, DK Eyewitness Travel Guides, Dorling Kindersley, 80 Strand, London WC2R 0RL, Great Britain, or email: travelguides@dk.com.

Contents

Decorative panel, the Pink Chamber, Château de Roquetaillade, Gironde

Introducing Aquitaine

Bunches of ripe grapes in a vineyard in Bordeaux

◀ View of the Château de Castelnaud-la-Chapelle, in Castelnaud-la-Chapelle

The port of Hendaye, Pays Basque

Aquitaine Region by Region

16th century building of the Château de Puyguilhem, in the Dordogne

Travellers' Needs

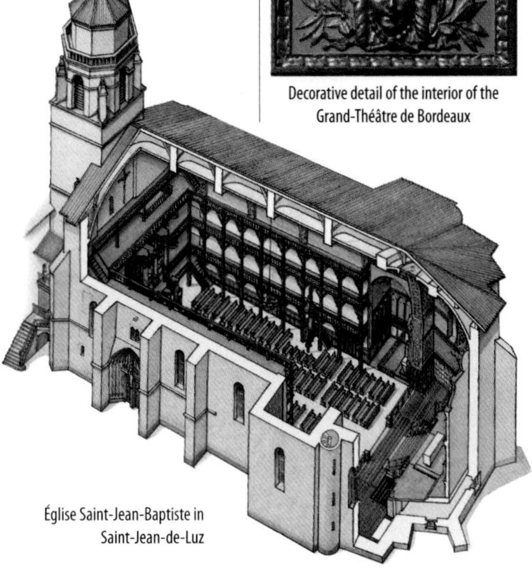

Église Saint-Jean-Baptiste in Saint-Jean-de-Luz

Survival Guide

Traditional dovecote in the Lot-et-Garonne

Decorative detail of the interior of the Grand-Théâtre de Bordeaux

HOW TO USE THIS GUIDE

This Eyewitness Travel Guide helps you to get the most from your stay in Dordogne, Bordeaux & the Southwest Coast. It provides detailed practical information and expert recommendations. *Introducing Aquitaine* maps the entire region, sets it in its historical and cultural context. The six regional chapters describe important sights with the help of maps, photographs and illustrations. The *Travellers' Needs* section gives detailed information about hotels, restaurants, shops and markets, entertainment and sports. The *Survival Guide*, provides practical advice on everything from transport to personal safety.

Aquitaine Region by Region

This region has been divided into six colour-coded areas for easy reference. Each chapter opens with an introduction to the area. This is followed by a regional map showing the most interesting towns, villages and places. Finding your way around the chapter is made simple by the numbering system used throughout. The most important sights and towns are covered in detail in two or more full pages.

1 Introduction The landscape, history and character of each region is described here, showing how the area has developed over the centuries and what it has to offer the visitor today.

A locator map shows the region in relation to the whole of Aquitaine.

Each area of Aquitaine can be quickly identified by its colour coding.

2 Regional Map This gives an illustrated overview of the whole region. All the sights are numbered and there are also useful tips on getting around the area by car and public transport.

Story boxes highlight special or unique aspects of a particular sight.

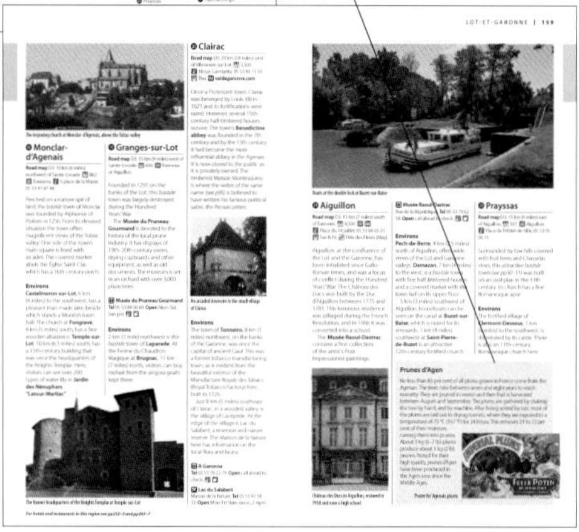

3 Detailed information on each sight All the important towns and other places to visit are described individually. They are listed in order, following the numbering on the Regional Map. Within each town or city, there is detailed information on important buildings and other major sights.

4 Major Towns An introduction covers the history, character and geography of the town. The main sights are described individually and plotted on a Town Map.

Practical Information lists all the information you need to visit every sight such as address, telephone number, open and closed dates.

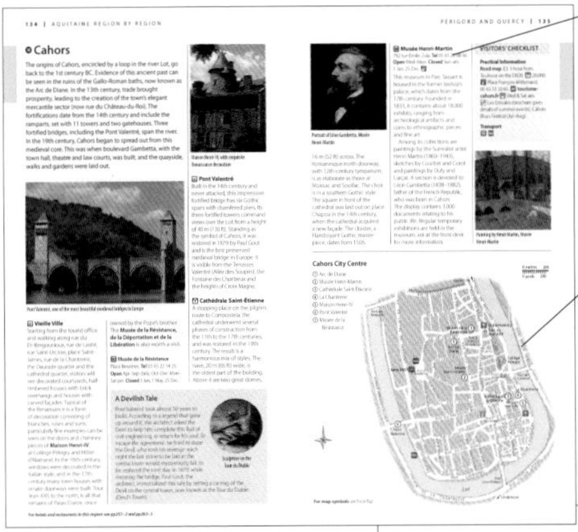

The Town Map shows all main through roads as well as minor streets of interest to visitors. All the sights are plotted, along with the bus and train stations, parking, tourist offices and churches.

5 Street-by-Street Map Towns or districts of special interest to visitors are shown in detailed 3D, with photographs of the most important sights. This gives a bird's-eye view of towns or districts of special interest.

A suggested route for a walk covers the most interesting streets in the area.

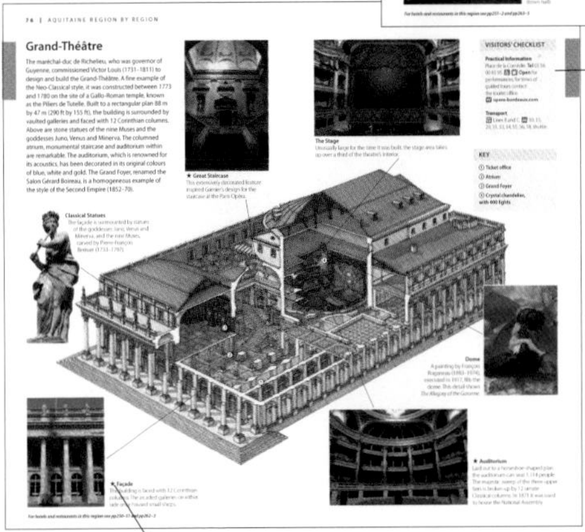

A Visitors' Checklist gives contact points for tourist and transport information, plus details of market days and local festival dates.

6 The top sights These are given two or more pages. Important buildings are dissected to reveal their interiors; museums have colour-coded floorplans to help you locate the most interesting exhibits.

Stars indicate the features no visitor should miss.

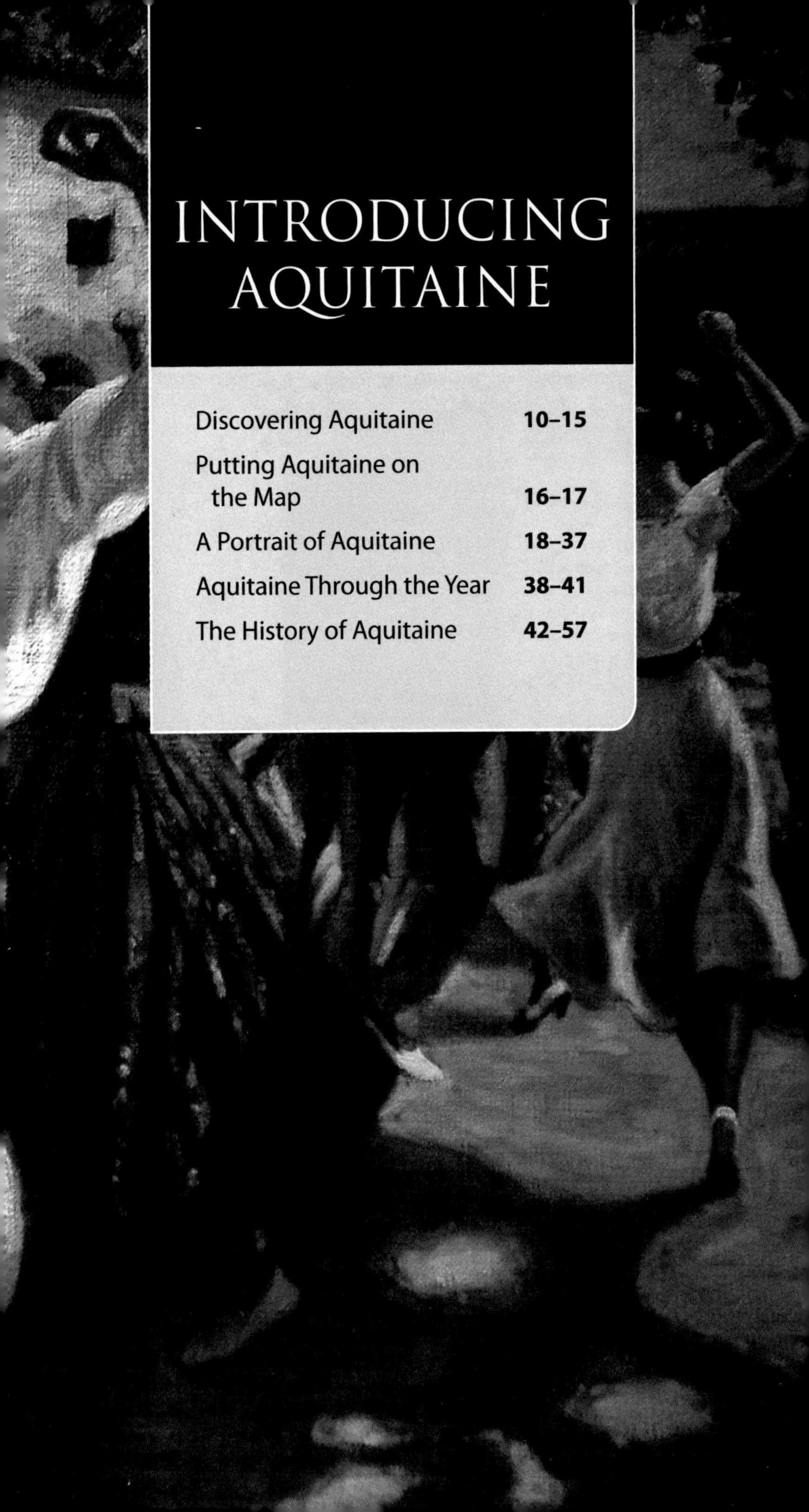

INTRODUCING AQUITAINE

DISCOVERING AQUITAINE

The following itineraries have been arranged to take in the highlights of Aquitaine while keeping travel time to a minimum. The first is a two-day city tour of France's elegant wine capital, Bordeaux. This is followed by two themed itineraries, beginning with a five-day Medieval Tour of the region's outstanding array of castles, medieval villages and Romanesque and Gothic churches. The second is a week-long Gourmet Tour, pinpointing the best food and wine in each area. Finally, two tours cover the main regional highlights, first a week in Western Aquitaine and the second, a week in Eastern Aquitaine and Quercy. These have suggestions for extensions, or could easily be combined for a superb two-week tour of the entire region. Public transport links on the tours are very irregular, if they exist at all; outside of the Bordeaux tour, be prepared to hire a car.

5-day Medieval Tour

- Discover the art of medieval warfare at the **Château de Castelnaud**, then take a river tour on a *gabarre* in pretty **La Roque-Gageac**.
- Find the seven towers of medieval **Martel**, and marvel at the portal of Sainte-Marie in **Souillac**.
- Follow in the footsteps of millions of pilgrims to **Rocamadour**; stroll the medieval lanes of **Figeac**.
- Take in the views over **Saint-Cirq-Lapopie**, and walk over the medieval bridge, the Pont Valentré in **Cahors**.
- Tour the **Château de Biron**, perched over idyllic landscapes, and relax in the square of **Monpazier**.

Dune du Pyla, Gironde
This ever-changing sand dune is France's most moving monument.

Villeneuve-sur-Lot, Lot-et-Garonne
Stradling the Lot river, this is the largest *bastide* town of the Lot-et-Garonne

◀ *Le Fandango*, by Perico Ribera, in the Musée Basque, Bayonne

7-day Gourmet Tour

- Take a wine tasting tour in one of **Bordeaux's** *appellations*, and enjoy oysters in **Arcachon**.
- Try the cured hams in **Bayonne**, and order a Basque seafood soup in **Saint-Jean-de-Luz**.
- Dine on Béarn's sheep cheeses in **Salies-de-Béarn**, and learn the secrets of brandy at **Labastide-d'Armagnac**.
- Trace the story of Agen's prunes in **Granges-sur-Lot** and inhale the aromas of **Lalbenque's** truffle market.
- Savour *foie gras* and *duck confits* in **Sarlat**, and taste Monbazillac wines, near **Bergerac**.

7 days in Western Aquitaine

- Discover the secrets of Médoc wines at the Maison du Vin in **Pauillac**; wade out to the **Phare de Cordouan**.
- Climb Europe's highest sand pile, **Dune de Pyla**; watch or join the surfers at **Hossegar**.
- Stroll past Art Deco villas in chic **Biarritz**, visit the historic pilgrimage town of **Saint-Jean-Pied-du-Port**.
- Walk up the **Gorges de Kakouetta**, and take the train up to **Lac d'Artouste**.
- Stroll along the panoramic **Pau**, and take a trip back in time at **Parc Régional des Landes de Gascogne**.
- Tour the elegant **Château de Cazeneuve**, and marvel at the splendid Gothic Cathedral in **Bazas**.

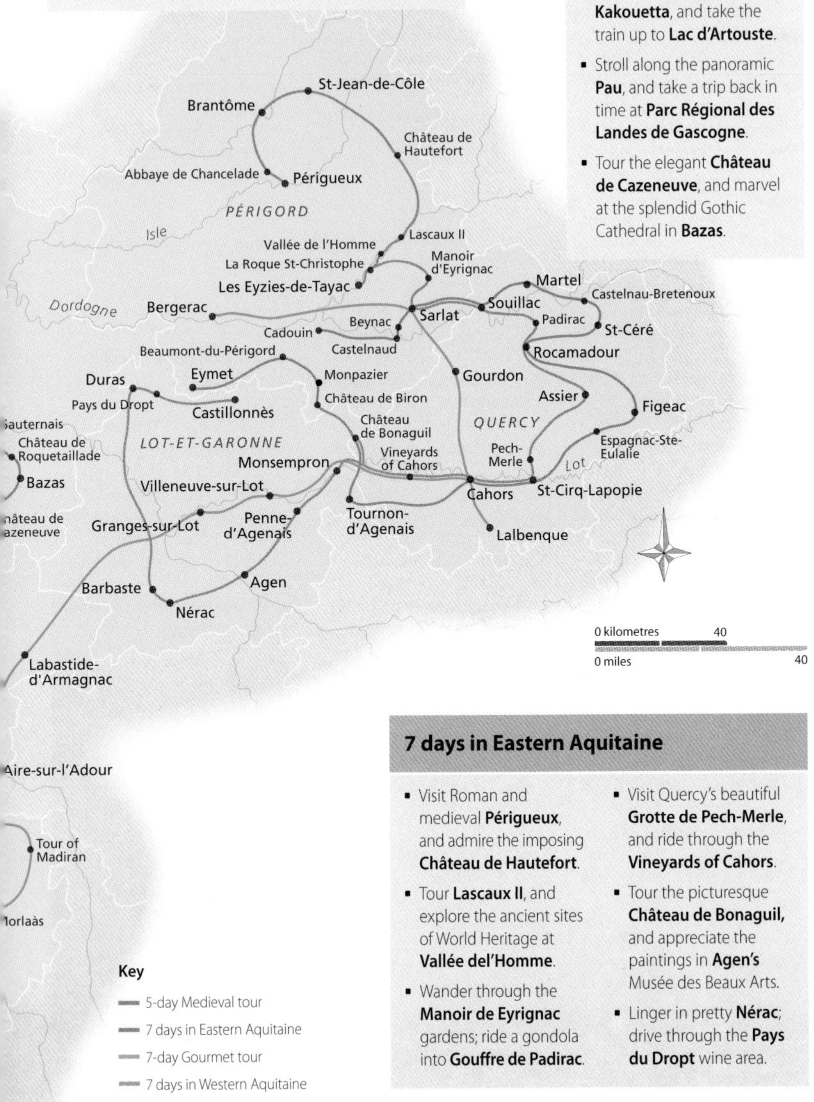

7 days in Eastern Aquitaine

- Visit Roman and medieval **Périgueux**, and admire the imposing **Château de Hautefort**.
- Tour **Lascaux II**, and explore the ancient sites of World Heritage at **Vallée del'Homme**.
- Wander through the **Manoir de Eyrignac** gardens; ride a gondola into **Gouffre de Padirac**.
- Visit Quercy's beautiful **Grotte de Pech-Merle**, and ride through the **Vineyards of Cahors**.
- Tour the picturesque **Château de Bonaguil,** and appreciate the paintings in **Agen's** Musée des Beaux Arts.
- Linger in pretty **Nérac**; drive through the **Pays du Dropt** wine area.

2 days in Bordeaux

France's wine capital has a handsome medieval core, elegant 18th-century architecture and a fascinating collection of museums.

- **Arriving** Bordeaux-Mérignac Airport is 15 km (9 miles) west of the city. Shuttle buses run to the centre every 45 minutes.

Day 1
Morning Start at the majestic **Cathédrale St-André** *(p74)* where Eleanor of Aquitaine married her first husband, French King Louis VII; climb its bell tower, the **Tour Pey-Berland** *(p75)*, for the view. Visit the nearby **Musée des Beaux Arts** *(p78)*, with works by Titian, Delacroix and Matisse, and the **Museé des Arts Décoratifs** *(p78)*, with its new wing of 20th- and 21st-century design.

Afternoon Explore Bordeaux's **Quartier Saint-Pierre** *(p74)*, and its elegant 18th-century architecture; here too is the Gothic **Basilique Saint-Michel** *(pp78–9)* with its towering spire and the iconic medieval gate of the **Grosse Cloche** *(p75)*. Delve into the region's history at the **Musée d'Aquitaine**, and enjoy a night at the opera at the magnificent **Grand Théâtre** *(pp76–7)*.

Day 2
Morning Head to northern Bordeaux, where the city's early Christian roots are tangible at the **Basilique Saint-Seurin** *(pp78–9)*; the nearby **Palais Gallien** *(p79)* is all that remains of Roman Bordeaux. Visit the **Museum d'Histoire Naturelle** *(p78)*, before exploring the picturesque **Chartrons** quarter.

Afternoon Immerse yourself in contemporary art at **CAPC** *(p78)*, stunningly located in a former wine warehouse. Stroll up the Garonne to visit the unique **Musée National des Douanes** *(p74)*. As evening falls, don't miss the beauty of an illuminated **Place de la Bourse** *(p72)* reflected in a massive mirror of water.

To extend your trip...
Visit the Gironde's most beautiful wine town **Saint-Emilion** *(pp84–7)* 40 km (25 miles) from Bordeaux.

5-day Medieval Tour

Northern Aquitaine and Quercy are rich in castles, villages, churches and other buildings that have changed little since the Middle Ages.

- **Airports** Arrive at Bergerac or Bordeaux-Mérignac Airport.
- **Transport** You will need a car. The starting point, the Abbaye de Cadouin, is 37 km (23 miles) from Bergerac or 162 km (100 miles) from Bordeaux.

Day 1: Cadouin, Castelnaud and Sarlat
Start at the peaceful 12th-century **Abbaye de Cadouin** *(p139)*, an important pilgrimage halt with a Flamboyant cloister. It's a stark contrast to the next stop: the stoutly walled **Château de Castelnaud** *(pp140–41)*, home to the Museum of Medieval Warfare. Castelnaud's rival, the **Château de Beynac** *(p138)* looms high over the river. Go for a ride amid castles on a *gabarre* from the picturesque **La Roque-Gageac** *(p123)* before driving to **Sarlat** *(pp120–23)*, one of the most beautiful medieval and Renaissance towns in France.

Day 2: Souillac and Saint-Céré
Stop in **Souillac** *(p124)*, to marvel at the domes and portal of Romanesque Église de Sainte-Marie, then forge east to stroll through **Martel** *(pp124–5)*, the village of seven medieval towers and Carennac, with its ruined fortified monastery. Further east, tour the mighty 12th-century fortress of **Castelnau-Bretenoux** *(p125)* before driving south to **Saint-Céré** *(p129)*, with its pretty medieval streets and 15th-century Château de Montal.

Day 3: Rocamadour and Figeac
It's a pretty drive from St-Céré through the medieval villages of Autoire and Loubressac to **Rocamadour** *(pp126–9)*, hanging on its cliffs and one of the most spectacular medieval pilgrimage sites in Europe. Spend the night in **Figeac** *(p130–31)*, Quercy's second city and a medieval gem.

Day 4: Saint-Cirq-Lapopie and Cahors
Follow the bucolic Célé river past **Espagnac-Sainte-Eulalie** to **Saint-Cirq-Lapopie** *(p131)*, with its medieval houses. Next stop: **Cahors** *(pp134–6)*, the 14th-century tower bridge, the Pont Valentré and the Cathédrale de Saint-Etienne.

Day 5: Bonaguil, Biron and Bastides
Head west to the perched *bastide* village of **Tournon d'Agenais** *(p156)*, then north to the **Château de Bonaguil** *(pp154–5)*, hidden in an idyllic green valley. Take a tour of the mighty **Château de Biron** *(p140)*, then return to Bergerac through the towns of **Monpazier** *(p139)*, **Beaumont-du-Périgord** *(p142)* and **Eymet** *(pp142–3)*.

Château de Castelnaud, with the Dordogne river flowing past

Château de la Rivière and its sunbaked vineyards, near Bordeaux

7-day Gourmet Tour

France's southwest is legendary for its delicious produce, markets, regional cuisine and some of the world's finest wines.

- **Airports** Bordeaux-Mérignac Airport is 15 km (9 miles) west of Bordeaux. Shuttle buses run to the city centre every 45 minutes.
- **Transport** It is essential to hire a car after Day 1.
- **Booking ahead** *Bordeaux:* wine tour

Day 1: Bordeaux

Start with a half (or whole) day wine-tasting tour, operated by the Bordeaux Tourist Office to one of the area's celebrated appellations: Médoc, Margaux, Sauternes, or Saint-Emilion, which take visitors into otherwise inaccessible estates. In Bordeaux, visit the **Musée du Vin et du Négoce** *(p78)*, and snack on Baillardran's *canelés*, the city's famous caramelized pastries.

Day 2: Arcachon and Bayonne

Make a pilgrimage to the nearby **Arcachon Basin** *(pp68–70)* for its delicious fresh oysters, before heading down into Les Landes for an authentic *salade landaise*. Laze on an Atlantic beach along the Côte d'Argent or go for a boat ride on the **Courant d'Huchet** *(p179)*, and end up in **Bayonne** *(pp192–7)*. Bayonne was France's first city to make chocolate and you can learn about the art here.

Day 3: Pays Basque

The Basques boast some of Europe's top chefs as well as traditional dishes such as *piperade* (stewed peppers, onions, tomatoes and eggs), *ttoro* (seafood soup) or *chiperones à l'encre* (baby squid in their own ink). Try them in the seaside resort of **Saint-Jean-de-Luz** *(pp202–203)* in between visits to the **Église Saint-Jean-Baptiste** *(p202)* and **Maison Louis-XIV** *(pp202–3)*. Afterwards drive up the **Nivelle Valley** *(p204)* to the traditional villages of **Ainhoa** and **Espelette** *(p205)*, the latter known for its *piment d'Espelette*. Next, stop at **Itxassou** *(p205)*, famous for its juicy black cherries, which make a delicious jam served with Basque ewe's milk cheese.

Day 4: Béarn

The hearty mountain cuisine of the Béarn is easy to find; restaurants frequently feature specialities such as *garbure* and *poule au pot béarnaise* on their menus, along with the region's white Jurançon and red Madrian wines. In between eating, visit the medieval town of **Salies-de-Béarn** *(p222)*, with its Musée du Sel (Salt Museum), **Orthez** *(p224)* for its iconic tower bridge and **Morlaàs** *(p230)*, with the fascinating Église de Sainte-Foy; take the driving **Tour of Madiran** *(p231)*.

Day 5: Landes and –Lot-et-Garonne

Tour the attractive and fertile **Tursan** *(p186)* and have a memorable lunch in Michel Guerard's restaurant empire in **Eugénie-les-Bains** *(p267)*. Carry on to charming **Labastide-d'Armagnac** *(p189)*, founded in 1291 and famous for brandy. Cross into Lot-et-Garonne, the land of orchards, strawberries, Marmande tomatoes and Côtes-de-Duras and Buzet wines. At **Granges-sur-Lot** *(p158)*, taste and learn all about the prunes d'Agen in the **Musée du Pruneau Gourmand** *(p158)* and spend the night in bustling **Villeneuve-sur-Lot** *(p156)*.

Day 6: Quercy

Follow the river Lot east into Quercy, home of vin de Cahors, the original malbec wine; take the **Vineyards of Cahors** tour *(pp136–7)*, taking in pretty wine villages along the way. In **Cahors** *(pp134–5)*, visit the covered market and dine on succulent duck or lamb dishes, cèpe mushrooms, Rocamador goat cheese and desserts. On Tuesdays in winter, don't miss the truffle market in **Lalbenque** *(p136)*; otherwise carry on to the hilltop market town of **Gourdon** *(pp136–7)*.

Day 7: Périgord

Périgord enjoys a top reputation for *foie gras*, duck and goose dishes, served with *pommes de terre sardalaises*, the speciality of **Sarlat** *(pp120–23)*. **Bergerac** *(pp144–5)* is the centre of Périgord's wine production: taste them at the Maison du Vin and just outside town in the beautiful hilltop **Château de Monbazillac** *(p142)*, source of the sweet golden wine.

Traditional village and lush countryside in the Pays Basque area

7 days in Western Aquitaine

- **Duration** A week – but extends to 10 days with the extra suggestions.
- **Airports** Arrive and depart from Bordeaux-Mérignac Airport.
- **Transport** Hire a car at the airport.

Day 1: Médoc and Soulac-sur-Mer
Drive up the Gironde estuary, past the fabled vineyards and grand châteaux of **Médoc** *(pp80–81)*, stopping at **Pauillac's Maison du Tourisme et du Vin** *(p82)* to learn about the area's *grands crus*. At low tide, wade to the remarkable 17th- and 18th-century **Phare de Cordouan** *(p66)*, the lighthouse nicknamed the 'Versailles of the Sea.' In **Soulac-sur-Mer** *(p65)*, visit the World Heritage Romanesque Basilique-Notre-Dame-de-le-Fin-des-Terres, then head south along the Atlantic coast and the lakes, for a swim or seafood dinner.

Day 2: Arcachon and Hossegar
Take a tour around the charming 19th-century villas in the Ville d'Hiver in **Arcachon** *(p71)* or catch a Transbassin boat on to see the fascinating bird life, oyster huts and huts on stilts in the **Arcachon Basin** *(pp68–9)*, perhaps taking in **Lège-Cap Ferrat's** *(p70)* traditional oyster farming villages. Any time of the year is good for climbing Europe's biggest pile of sand, the **Dune de Pyla** *(p71)*. Then head south again along the "Silver Coast", stopping at one of Les Landes' resorts, either **Biscarrosse** *(p180)*, with its sea plane museum, or **Mimizan** *(p180)*, with its medieval abbey, or trendy, surfing-crazy **Hossegor** *(p181)*.

Day 3: Bayonne and Biarritz
Visit the iconic **Cathédrale Sainte-Marie** *(pp198–9)*, and two excellent museums: the **Musée Basque** *(p196)*, documenting the culture of the Basque lands, and the **Musée Bonnat** *(p197)*, housing works by El Greco, Rubens and Goya. Later, explore the Art Nouveau and Art Deco splendours and the Grande Plage at **Biarritz** *(pp200–201)*.

Day 4: Cambo-les-Bains and Saint-Jean-Pied-du-Port
Explore the beauties of the Basque country: head inland past timbered farmhouses and flocks of sheep to **Hasparren** *(p206)*, then take the scenic Route Impériale des Cimes to **Cambo-les-Bains** *(p206)*, a Belle Époque spa resort. Lunch in the pilgrimage town of **Saint-Jean-Pied-de-Port** *(p210)*, then make the short, dramatic walk up the **Gorges de Kakouetta** *(p217)* and visit the Romanesque chapel **Sainte-Engrâce** *(p217)*.

Day 5: Oloron-Sainte-Marie and Pau
Spend a day in Béarn, starting in **Oloron-Sainte-Marie** *(pp232–3)*, 'the capital of the Haut Béarn, with the Cathédrale de Sainte-Marie. Next, drive up the beautiful **Ossau Valley** *(pp236–9)* with stops at the **Falaise aux Vautours** in Aste-Béon *(p239)* to watch the griffon vultures and take the spectacular train ride up to **Lac d'Artouste** *(p237)*. Spend the night in **Pau** *(pp226–7)*, with its stunning views over the Pyrenees.

The popular, wide beach at Les Landes' resort, Biscarrosse

Day 6: Aire-sur-l'Adour and the Parc Régional des Landes de Gascogne
Loop back north into Les Landes, starting in **Aire-sur-l'Adour** *(p187)*, with its World Heritage Église Sainte-Quitterie. Next, visit the English *bastide* town of **Grenade sure l'Adour** *(p187)*, and **Saint-Sever** *(p187)*, named after its World Heritage Site. In **Mont-de-Marsan** *(p188)*, the Musée Despaiu-Wlérick (the only one in France dedicated to figurative sculpture), may tempt. Round off the day with a trip to the **Parc Régional des Landes de Gascogne** *(pp176–9)*.

Day 7: Château de Cazeneuve and Bazas
Head north into the Gironde for a tour of the Renaissance **Château de Cazeneuve** *(pp98–9)*, where Henri IV's wife Queen Margaret lived in luxurious exile. Next, stop at **Bazas** *(p97)* for its beautiful Gothic cathedral. Another medieval gem is nearby is the restored **Château Roquetaillade** *(pp92–3)*. Then follow the river Garonne back up to Bordeaux, through the **Sauternais** *(p96)* and **Graves** *(p95)* wine-growing areas.

The soaring peaks of the Pic du Midi d'Ossau, Béarn

To extend your trip...
Spend 3 days in Bordeaux and Saint-Emilion *(see p12)*.

7 days in Eastern Aquitaine

- **Duration** A week, or 9 days with extensions.
- **Airports** Arrive at Bergerac or Toulouse-Blagnac Airport.
- **Transport** Hire a car at the airport. The first stop Périgueux is 49 km (30 miles) from Bergerac; if you fly to Toulouse, start the tour on Day 6 in Cahors (114 km/71 miles).
- **Booking ahead** Les Eyzies-de-Tayac, Grotte de Font de Gaume

Day 1: Périgueux and Brantôme
Start in **Périgueux** *(pp104–107)*, with its splendid historic centre dominated by the multi-domed Cathédrale Saint-Front. Visit Vesunna, the Roman villa in a glass building and the Musée d'art et d'archéologie. In the afternoon, see the Romanesque **Abbaye de Chancelade** *(p108)* before heading off to **Brantôme** *(p109)*, the 'Venice of Périgold'.

Day 2: Château de Hautefort and the Vallé du Homme
Start at **Saint-Jean-de-Côle** *(p109)*, one of France's prettiest villages, then visit the mighty **Château de Hautefort** *(pp110–111)* with its formal gardens. Drive south to **Montignac** *(p112)* to visit the reproduction cave, Lascaux II, before exploring the **Vallée de l'Homme** *(pp114–15)*, with a large number of Palaeolithic-era sites.

Day 3: Les Eyzies-de-Tayac, Manoir de Eyrignac and Sarlat
In **Les Eyzies-de-Tayac** *(pp118–19)*, the base for exploring the region, visit (if you have booked ahead) the stunning polychrome Grotte de Font-de-Gaume, the Musée de la Préhistoire, and the fascinating cliff-settlement, **La Roque-Saint-Christophe** *(p115)*. In the afternoon, stroll through the spectacular **Gardens of the Manoir d'Eyrignac** *(pp116–17)*, and spend the evening in beautiful **Sarlat** *(pp120–23)*.

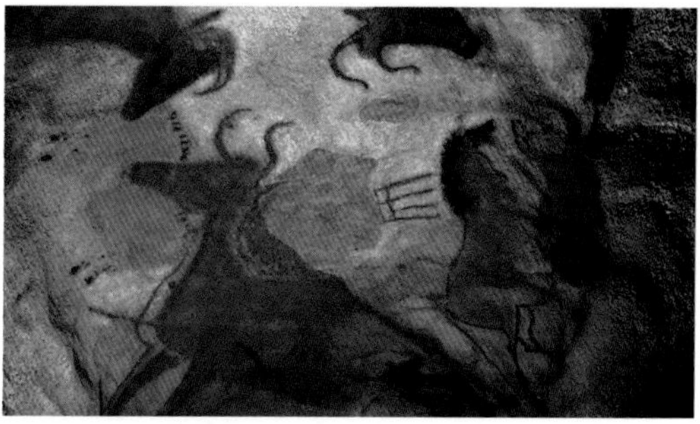

Prehistoric paintings of animals on the walls of Grottes de Lascaux

To extend your trip...
Explore the medieval châteaux and villages along the Dordogne (Medieval Tour Day 1).

Day 4: Souillac, Padirac, Rocamadour
In the morning, visit **Souillac** *(p124)*, taking in its Romanesque Basilique of Sainte-Marie and the Musée de l'Automate, before making your way to the **Gouffre de Padirac** *(p123)* for an amazing gondola trip on a subterranean river into the Great Dome. In the afternoon, visit equally dramatic **Rocamadour** *(pp126–9)*; up in the castle, don't miss the display of raptors and parrots at the Rocher des Aigles.

Day 5: Assier, Pech-Merle and Cahors
Head south to **Assier** *(p129)* to see the elegant Loire-style Château d'Assier, then visit the beautiful Upper Palaeolithic painted cave, the **Grotte du Pech-Merle** *(pp132–3)*. The nearby village of **Saint-Cirq-Lapopie** *(p131)* is one of the most beautiful in France. Spend the evening in handsome **Cahors** *(pp134–7)*, with its famous medieval bridge.

Market in front of the Cathédrale Saint-Etienne, Cahors

To extend your trip...
The medieval *bastide* towns and châteaux (Medieval Tour Day 5).

Day 6: Cahors to Nérac
Take the **Vineyards of Cahors** tour *(pp136–7)*, past rolling vineyards and medieval villages to the striking **Château de Bonaguil** *(pp154–5)*. At **Monsempron** *(p153)*, with its pretty Romanesque church, turn south to **Penne-d'Agenais** *(p156)*, piled under its landmark pilgrimage church. Then aim for **Agen** *(pp164–7)*, capital of Lot-et-Garonne, to visit the Musée des Beaux Arts and handsome Vieille Ville. End up in historic **Nérac** *(p162)*, once a centre of the powerful Albret family, not forgetting a walk in the pretty **Parc de la Garenne** *(p162)*,

Days 7: Duras
Head north, stopping at **Barbaste** *(p163)*, for a look at its Romanesque bridge and fortified mill. Next aim for **Duras** *(p150)*, its 12th-century château and museum, before taking a drive through the **Pays du Dropt** *(pp150–2)*, the centre of the Côte de Duras wine area, not missing the colourful 15th-century frescoes in the church of **Allemans-du-Dropt**. Stroll around the *bastide* town of **Castillonnès** *(p151)* before heading back to Bergerac.

Putting Southwest France on the Map

From the Gironde Estuary in the north to the border with Spain in the south, the southwest corner of France, the region of Aquitaine, covers an area of 41,300 sq km (15,900 sq miles) and stretches out along the Atlantic seaboard for 270 km (170 miles). The region has around 3.1 million inhabitants, with an average of 77 people per sq km (193 per sq mile). Of its five *départements* – the Dordogne, Gironde, Landes, Lot-et-Garonne and Pyrénées-Atlantiques – the Gironde is by far the most densely populated.

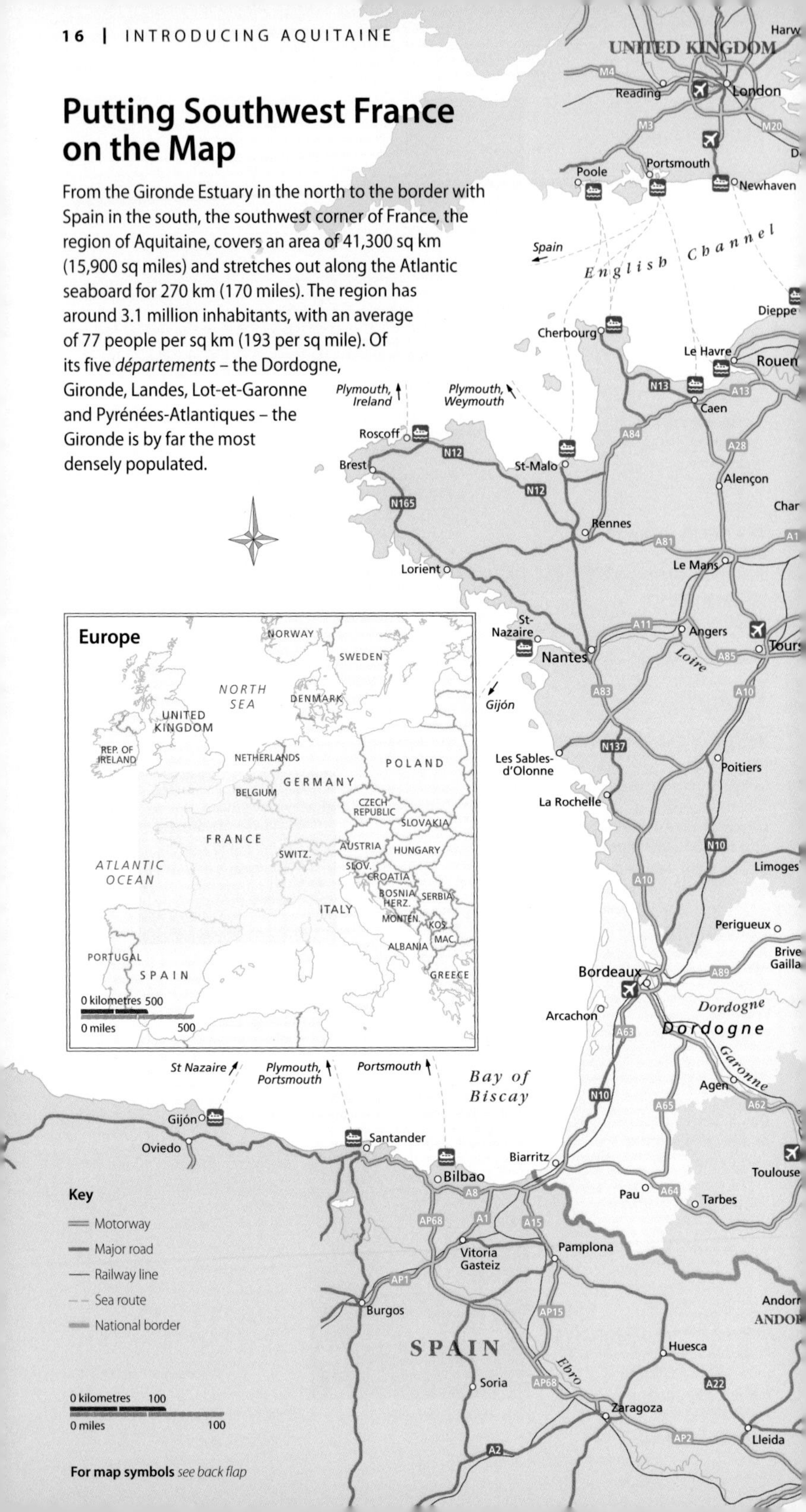

Den Haag
Rotterdam
NETHERLANDS
Essen
Dortmund
Göttingen
Halle
Kassel
Oostende
Antwerpen
Düsseldorf
Dunkerque
Calais
Erfurt
Bruxelles
Köln
Lille
BELGIUM
Bonn
Liège
GERMANY
Abbeville
Douai
Koblenz
Frankfurt
Amiens
LUXEM-
BOURG
Würzburg
Charleville-
Mézièrs
Luxembourg
Nuremberg
Mannheim
Reims
Saarbrücken
Paris
Metz
Karlsruhe
Stuttgart
Rhein
Donau
Nancy
Seine
Strasbourg
Troyes
München
Orléans
Auxerre
Mulhouse
Loire
Bodensee
Basel
Innsbruck
Dijon
Zürich
Bourges
Besançon
AUSTRIA
Bern
FRANCE
SWITZERLAND
Mâcon
Bolzano
Lac Léman
Genève
Clermont-
Ferrand
Trento
Aosta
Bergamo
Lyon
Chambéry
Saint
Etienne
Milano
Grenoble
Torino
Po
Piacenza
Valence
Parma
Gap
Rhône
ITALY
Rodez
Cuneo
Genova
Millau
Savona
Avignon
La Spezia
Nîmes
Montpellier
Nice
Monaco
Pisa
Aix-en-Provence
Livorno
Sète
Carcassonne
Marseille
Narbonne
Toulon
Piombino
Perpignan
Ile Rousse
Bastia
Mediterranean
Sea
Corsica
Girona
Ajaccio
Sardinia
Porto-Vecchio
Barcelona

A PORTRAIT OF AQUITAINE

This culturally diverse region is a mosaic of varied landscapes, bordered by the Atlantic to the west and the Iberian Peninsula to the south. Sited at the crossroads of a number of major routes, it has absorbed many influences over the centuries. Each of its separate areas has its own distinctive heritage, and regional dialects are still heard. Bordeaux, renowned for its wines, is the region's chief city and economic hub.

Aquitaine can be divided into six main areas: Périgord-Quercy (covered by the Dordogne and Lot *départements*) and the Gironde to the north; the Landes and Lot-et-Garonne in the centre; and the Pays Basque and Béarn (together forming the *département* of Pyrénées-Atlantiques) in the south.

In addition to their shared history (particularly in the case of the Dordogne and Quercy), these areas have a great deal in common. They are all wine-producers and are particularly noted for their cultural heritage, sporting achievements and vernacular architecture.

The Romans aptly named the region *Aquitania*, a "land of water". Its abundant rainfall not only accounts for the lush vegetation but has also helped create some of France's most productive farming land.

Extending northward from the Spanish border to the Gironde Estuary, the region covers a total of 41,309 sq km (15,945 sq miles). Its 270-km (170-mile) Atlantic coastline, which stretches from Pointe de Grave in the north to Hendaye at the foot of the Pyrénées, makes it one of France's main tourist attractions, the focal point of which is the Arcachon Basin.

Inland, beyond the wall of dunes that runs parallel to the coast, lie many unspoilt areas, where land-use is tightly controlled. Dotted with lakes and marshes, another

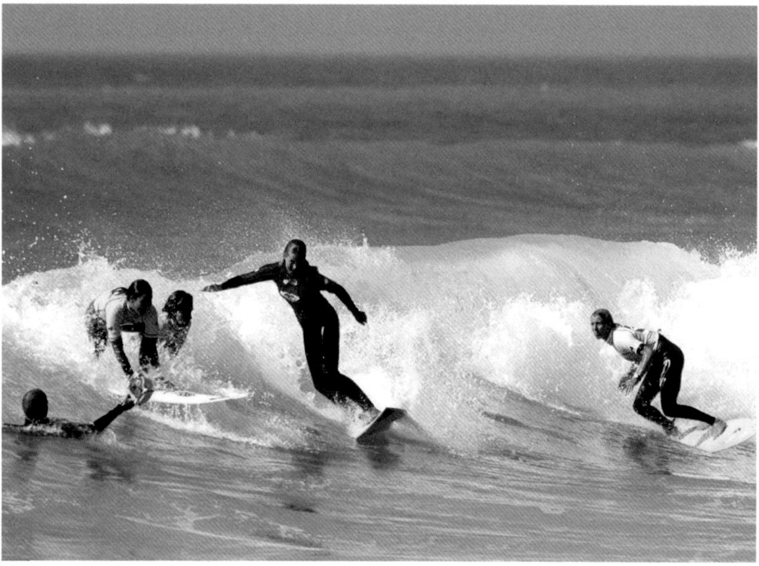

Surfers enjoying the breakers of the Atlantic coastline

◀ A medieval timber frame house in France

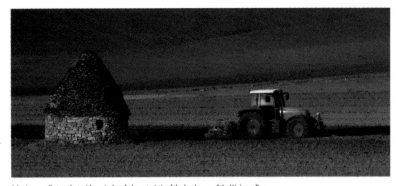

A *borie*, a small stone hut with conical roof, characteristic of the landscape of the Vézère valley

striking feature are the great green valleys carved out by the region's three main rivers, whose rich alluvial deposits continually enrich the soil. In the north, the Garonne meanders across the Agenais to join the Dordogne, flowing out from the Périgord, and spills out into the Gironde Estuary. In the south, the Adour winds through the Pyrénées towards the sea.

The abundance of water has drawn people to Aquitaine since prehistoric times. Sites such as the Lascaux caves in the Dordogne and finds like the Venus

Pottoks, the wild mountain ponies of the Pays Basque

of Brassempouy in the Landes provide ample evidence of this.

Natural Resources

Despite the many features that are common to the region as a whole, its most striking characteristic remains its great diversity. This is most evident in the uneven distribution of the population, nearly 44 per cent of which is concentrated in the largely urban Gironde. Outside the major cities, such as Bordeaux and its suburbs, Libourne, Mont-de-Marsan, Pau, Agen and Bayonne, the population is scattered in small towns and isolated villages.

The extensive areas of highly fertile land support an agricultural economy that still accounts for 5.3 per cent of the region's revenue – slightly ahead of construction – and 83 per cent of the land is given over to farming. In addition to cereals – including maize (the Landes being France's largest producer) – many other crops are now grown. These include kiwi fruit on the banks of the Adour, tobacco around Bergerac and Marmande, walnuts in the Périgord, and plums (the famous *prunes d'Agen*) in the Agenais. Livestock is also important: *jambon de Bayonne* from the Adour valley, lamb from the Pays Basque (also renowned for its cheeses), foie gras and other *confits* from the Dordogne, poultry from Saint-Sever and the Landes, and beef from Chalosse and Bazas are some of the best-known produce. In addition, there is the wine

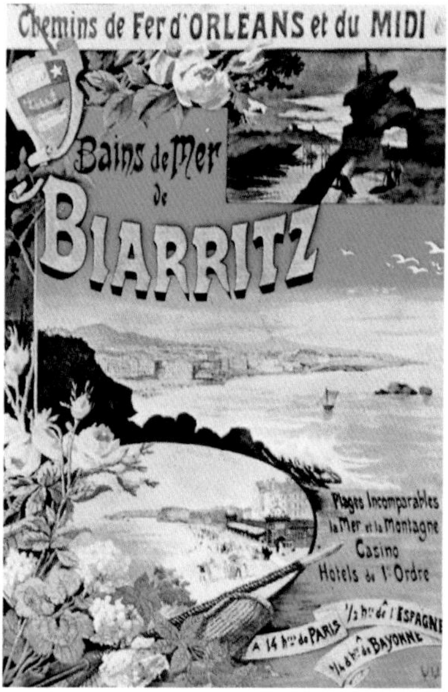

Biarritz, a coastal resort since the 19th century

industry, around three-quarters of which is concentrated in Gironde. The region is one of the foremost producers of quality *(appellation d'origine contrôlée)* wines in France.

Timber is also an important resource. The region contains Europe's largest forested area of around 1.8 million ha (4.4 million acres), which provides pine – for construction and making paper – as well as oak, chestnut and beech. And finally, with four ports, the Gulf of Gascony and the many estuaries and water courses, fishing, along with fish- and oyster-farming, is a key earner too.

Coat of arms at the entrance to Cos d'Estournel

The Role of Industry

Industry accounts for 17 per cent of the region's wealth. The Latécoère aircraft factory was set up at Biscarrosse, in the Landes, in 1930, and the region remains at the forefront of the aeronautics and spacecraft industry. Civil and miltary aircraft, helicopters and onboard systems – notably for the Ariane space rocket – are built either by large industrial consortiums or one of their 600 specialist subcontractors. This sector generally works closely with research scientists and developers, particularly those based at universities. The region contains significant centres of learning, some of European importance. Chemicals, electronics, manufacturing, the canning industry, metallurgy and local crafts such as traditional Basque textiles, are other aspects of this wide-ranging industrial heritage.

However, Aquitaine's main source of wealth is its service sector, which accounts for 72.9 per cent of the economy. It depends largely on tourism and is expanding rapidly. Each year around 6 million visitors, 1 million of them from abroad, come to sample the region's natural attractions and architectural wonders, as well as its many festivals. Yet despite this huge influx, the dynamism and independent spirit of Aquitaine's diverse and distinct cultural heritage has been neither weakened nor compromised.

A Cultural Mosaic

According to the theory advanced in the early 18th century by the philosopher Baron de Montesquieu – one of Aquitaine's most illustrious sons

Pilgrims on the road to Santiago de Compostela

Basque supporters of Biarritz's rugby team

– a region's political system and character are dictated by local, natural and human factors, such as altitude, topography, latitude, distance from the sea, language, and so on. The land of Aquitaine can be seen as a perfect illustration of this theory. Few parts of France boast so many different, deeply rooted cultures.

Even the constant flow of foreign pilgrims, from the 11th century onwards, on route to the shrine of St James at Compostela, did little to dilute this focus on local tradition. As the region lay at the crossroads of the four main pilgrimage routes (from Paris via Tours; from Vézelay; from Le Puy-en-Velay; and from Arles via Toulouse), churches and hostels were built for those that passed through. Many fine examples remain, such as the Cathédrale Saint-André in Bordeaux and the Cathédrale Saint-Étienne in Périgueux. But despite their general Romanesque or Gothic styling, such grand buildings still have a distinctly local look.

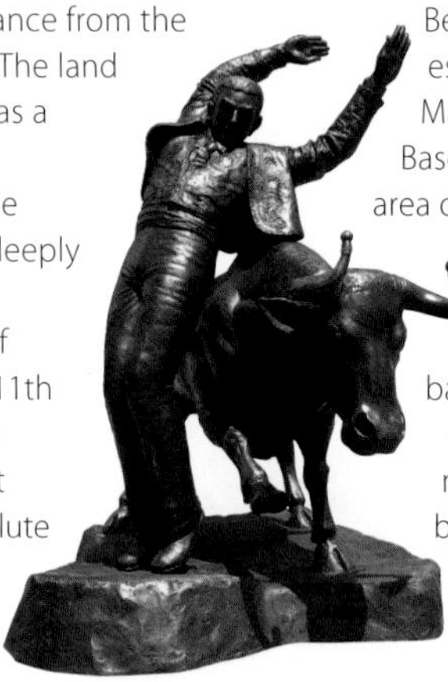
Statue in the Parc Théodore-Denis, in Dax

The Pays Basque, in the south, has a particularly strong sense of identity. This is expressed by the use of its own language, Euskara (taught in all schools), by its characteristic wooden-framed houses or *etxe* *(see p28)* and by its nationalist movement. In Béarn, at the foot of the Pyrénées to the east, Béarnese is spoken, especially in Oloron-Sainte-Marie, the home of the Basque beret. In the central area of the Landes – a mixed landscape of river valleys, expanses of forest and long beaches backed by lakes and streams – local traditions live on most spectacularly in the bull-running festivals that have taken place since 1850. The Agenais, despite its relatively small size, has also preserved its local identity. It is noted for its gastronomic specialities, such as its famous *prunes d'Agen*. The Périgord boasts a number of stately châteaux and

The Stèle de Roland, at the Col d'Ibañeta, erected for Charlemagne's nephew, defeated by the Gascons

The classical and the modern in Bordeaux

prehistoric caves that reflect the area's unique character. It is also bisected by the river Dordogne, along which the traditional craft known *gabares* still sail.

Until well into the 15th century, Gascon was the main language of the the Gironde, and the use of local languages still lingers throughout Aquitaine. You will come across people who speak Occitan, and Bordeaux has its own distinct patois, Bordeluche, although it is beginning to die out.

A "European" Region

But such strong ties to their ancient roots do not mean that the people of Aquitaine have turned their backs on the rest of the world or the future. The A89 motorway joins Bordeaux to Clermont-Ferrand, and there are regular flights from Lyon to Bordeaux, opening up the region to eastern and southeastern Europe. Aquitane also sits at the crossroads of the major trade routes between northern France and the Iberian Peninsula, and the Mediterranean and North Africa to the south. For centuries, people as well as goods have passed through, mostly via Bordeaux or Bayonne, and this traffic continues to enrich the region both economically and culturally. All this places Aquitaine firmly at the heart of modern Europe. However, a measure of the strength of the region's highly distinctive character is that it has always been able to absorb new influences and successfully blend them with the unique traditions of its past.

Château de la Brède, birthplace of Charles, Baron de Montesquieu

Plants and Animals of Aquitaine

The southwest of France lies on the flight path of many thousands of migratory birds. These include barnacle and greylag geese, wigeon, avocets, ringed and grey plovers, knots and curlews. Venture up into the high mountainous areas and you are likely to spot golden (or booted) eagles, and bearded, griffon and Egyptian vultures, along with animals such as chamois and marmots (introduced around 1950). Here too you will find some of the region's most beautiful flowers: gentians, yellow poppies, Pyrenean fritillary, lilies and irises. Down along the coast, sea holly and sea lilies, along with gillyflowers and convolvulus, lie scattered among the dunes, while toadflax, yellow bedstraw, hawkweed and Bayonne vetch appear almost everywhere.

Wood pigeons pass through on their annual migration south over the Pyrenees to spend the winter in Spain. Since the Middle Ages, they have been hunted for food as they fly by.

Sandy Coastline

From Pointe de Grave, south of the the River Adour, sandy dunes stretch for 230 km (140 miles), reaching a height of 105 m (350 ft) at Le Pyla. These dunes support vegetation typical of sandy conditions, including sea holly, sea lilies, golden rod, lucerne, spurge and sometimes shrubby horsetail.

Bayonne vetch grows on the coastal dunes. This rare leguminous plant is now protected.

The Eurasian oystercatcher patrols the beaches in search of the cockles, mussels, winkles and crabs that make up the bulk of its diet.

Estuaries and Coastal Marshland

From November to March, thousands of migratory birds come to the estuaries of the Gironde and the Bidassoa, the marshland of the Blayais and the northern Médoc, the Arcachon Basin, the Arguin sandbank and Txingudi Bay. While most fly on southwards, some spend the winter there.

Greylag geese rest in the region every autumn, on their annual migration south.

The avocet uses its curved beak to search for small crustaceans in the shallow waters of the coastal marshes.

Aquitaine's Fish

Gilt-head bream, black and red sea bream, sea bass, conger eels, blue sharks, bonito, coley, sole, turbot and dabs are found in abundance in the waters along the region's 300-km (190-mile) long coast. Shad, lamprey and eel are taken from the estuaries of the Gironde and the Adour. Tuna and anchovy are a major part of the catch off the shores of the Gulf of Gascony, where today around 2,000 fishermen in more than 400 fishing vessels ply their trade.

Sturgeon swim up river estuaries between March and June, to breed in the spawing grounds of the Dordogne and the Garonne. Some of the eggs will be harvested, then sifted, washed and tossed in salt to produce caviar.

Shad have increased greatly in number since the protection of their breeding grounds on the river at Bergerac, and installations at the Tuillères dam have created spawning areas. The annual catch is around 200–400 tonnes.

Forêt Landaise

Consisting mostly of maritime pines and covering more than 1 million ha (2.5 million acres), this is the largest forest in Europe. The trees were planted in the dunes in the 19th century to help stop sand from them being washed inland. Pine resin, which was tapped until 1990, was once a major source of income in the Landes.

The common crane is a regular visitor to the area around the Bidassoa Estuary. Several hundred overwinter from November to March in the Landes, particularly in the firing ranges at Le Poteau.

Maritime pines have male cones, which are evident in early summer.

Pyrenean Mountains

The rocky outcrops about halfway up the Massif des Arbailles and the Forêts d'Iraty are home to capercaillie, woodpeckers, golden eagles and bearded, griffon and Egyptian vultures. Grouse and marmots can be found in the stony areas. Brown bears, which are becoming increasingly rare, live in the high valleys of the Aspe and the Ossau.

The bearded vulture inhabits the Haute Soule and the high Aspe valley.

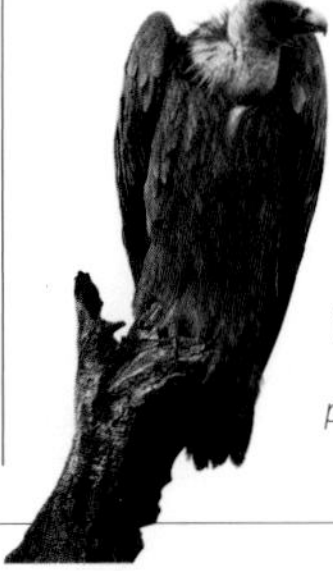

The griffon vulture nests in the Massif de la Pierre-St-Martin, in the Nive valley *(see pp204–205)*, in the Aldudes valley *(see pp208–209)* and in the Forêt des Arbailles *(see p214)*.

Religious Architecture

Four ancient pilgrimage routes to Santiago de Compostela in Spain pass through the southwest corner of France *(see pp212–13)*. This alone has helped to promote a remarkable tradition of religious architecture. Twenty historic buildings across the region lie on the UNESCO World Heritage Site of the Way of St James. Hostelries for the many pilgrims journeying to Compostela, as well as fortified churches and impressive abbeys, were constructed as early as the 7th century. Several were later endowed with majestic cathedrals or great domed churches, fashioned in the Gothic and Renaissance styles.

Façade of the church at Dax, in the Landes

Romanesque (7th–11th Centuries)

The region's Romanesque buildings are of several types. The fortified churches of the Périgord played a defensive role. Others, like l'Hôpital-Saint-Blaise, in the Pays Basque, served as hostels for pilgrims travelling on the route to Compostela. Also typical of the Romanesque architecture of the southwest are great abbeys like those at Cadouin, Moirax, La Sauve-Majeure and Saint-Sever.

Doorway of the 11th-century Église Sainte-Foy, Morlaàs

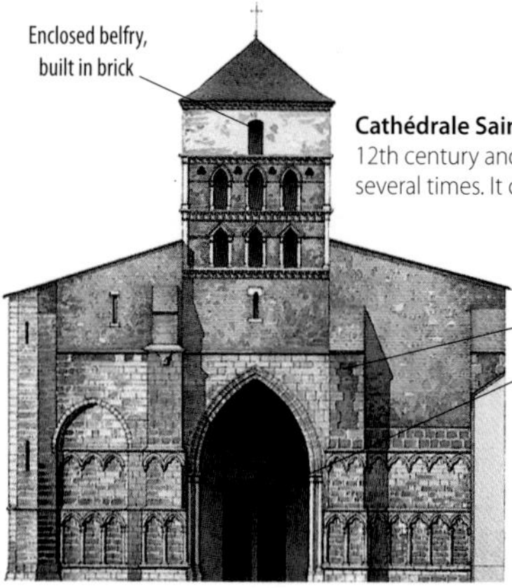

Cathédrale Sainte-Quitterie, in Aire-sur-l'Adour, was built in the 12th century and, up until the 18th century, was remodelled several times. It combines Romanesque and Gothic elements.

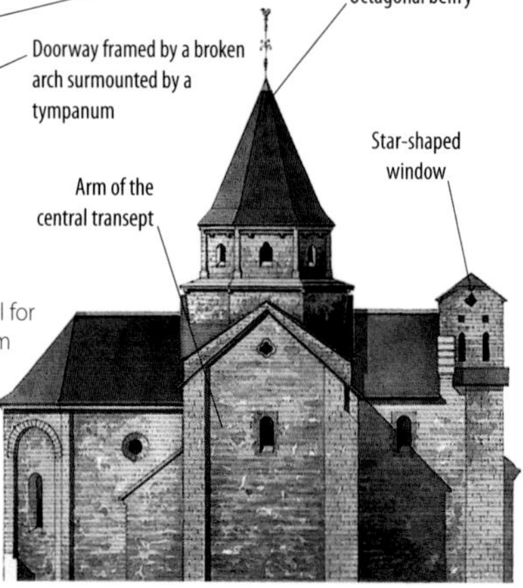

The church of l'Hôpital-Saint-Blaise, a hostel for pilgrims on the route to Compostela, was built from schist and yellow sandstone. Romanesque and Byzantine styles mix at this World Heritage Site.

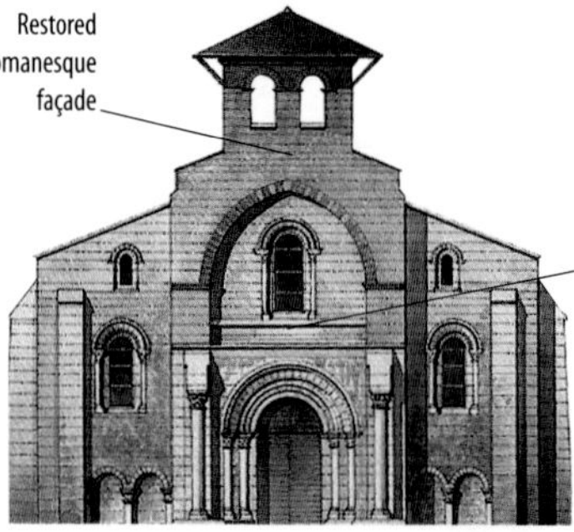

The church at Moirax, in Lot-et-Garonne, formed part of a Cluniac priory. It is a fine example of Romanesque architecture of the 11th and 12th centuries. The central, projecting part of the façade is surmounted by an open belfry, which is in turn crowned by a pointed roof.

Domed Churches (11th–12th Centuries)

From the 11th century, many churches in southwest France, particularly in the Ribérac region, were built with Byzantine-style domes, although they were still laid out to a Romanesque plan. With five domes arranged in the shape of a Greek cross, the Cathédrale Saint-Front, in Périgueux, serves as a good example, despite later alterations. Others are the Église Sainte-Marie in Aubiac and the Église Sainte-Croix in Oloron-Sainte-Marie, which has a Moorish-style ribbed dome.

Domed church in Souillac *(see p124)*

Cathédrale Saint-Front in Périgueux is a typical blend of the Romanesque and Byzantine. The basic 10th-century structure is Romanesque. Five domes, arranged in the shape of a Greek cross, were added in the 12th century.

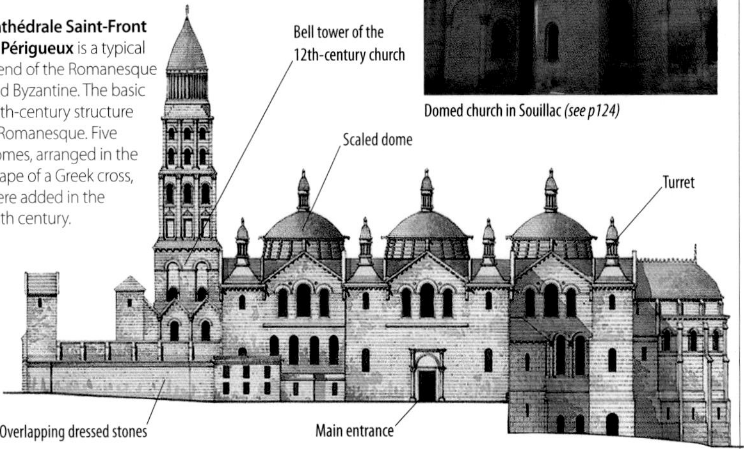

Gothic to Renaissance (13th–16th Centuries)

In Aquitaine, the transition from the Romanesque to the Gothic was gradual. This can be seen in the remodelling of the region's cathedrals, such as the Cathédrale Saint-André in Bordeaux. The Cathédrale de Bazas, built from 1233, was one of the first to use Gothic styling.

15th-century Gothic doorway at Cathédral de Bazas

Cathédrale Saint-André in Bordeaux, consecrated in 1096, has a Romanesque nave with Gothic spires and towers. Renaissance styling can be seen in elements such as the buttresses and the former rood screen.

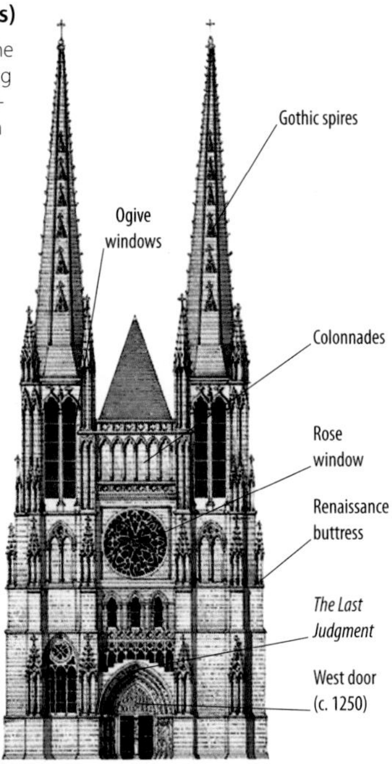

Vernacular Architecture

Because Aquitaine is made up of several, often contrasting, regions, local architecture has evolved to suit a wide range of lifestyles and geographical conditions. The buildings that are typical of Aquitaine range from half-timbered Landes houses and Basque *etxes* to Périgordian farmhouses and dovecotes. While a variety of traditional styles can be seen dotted across the countryside, urban houses such as the *échoppe bordelaise* and Arcachon villa reflect the social and economic development of particular towns and cities.

The bow window, a feature of some Arcachon houses

The Périgordian farmhouse is a highly practical country dwelling. The design varies slightly according to the precise locality, but these sturdily built houses are usually divided up to allow separate areas for human habitation, for keeping animals and for storing crops, allowing family life and farm work to take place all under one roof.

The etche (or *etxe*) is the most common type of house in the Pays Basque. There are several variations, including those typical of Soule and Basse-Navarre. The most typical is the Labourd type *(right)*, which is usually white with coloured half-timbering.

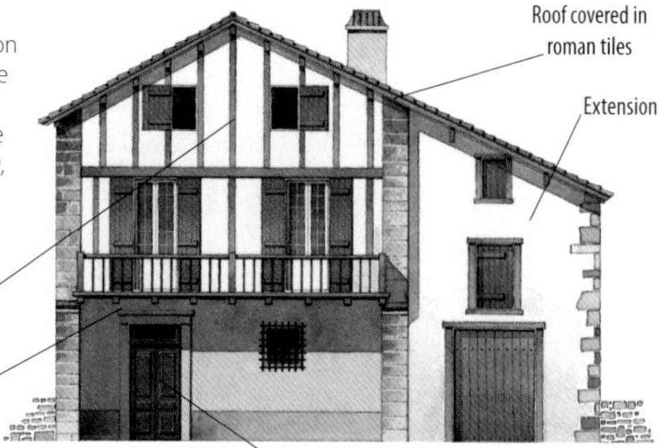

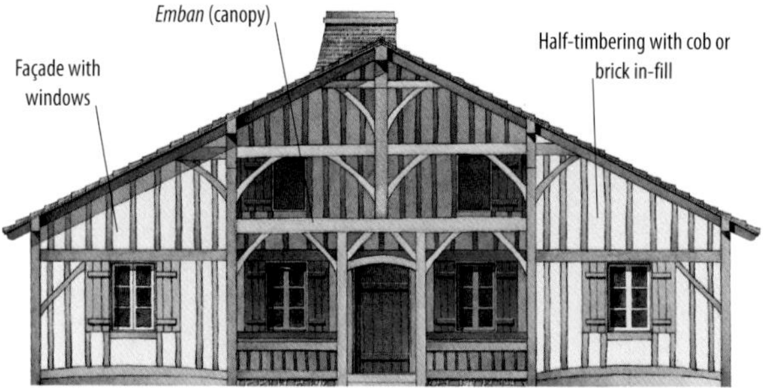

Landes houses have a distinctive outline, with low-pitched roofs and half-timbering. They are often set in an *airial* (a clearing surrounded by pines) and are east-facing for protection against storms coming in off the Atlantic.

Arcachon houses were first built in the mid-19th century in the Ville d'Hiver district of the town, which is now a conservation area *(see p71)*. These houses have either one or two upper floors. The servants lived on the "damp" lower floor. On the first floor, which sometimes has a bow window, were the living rooms. The owners of the house would always sleep on the second floor, under the high-pitched roof.

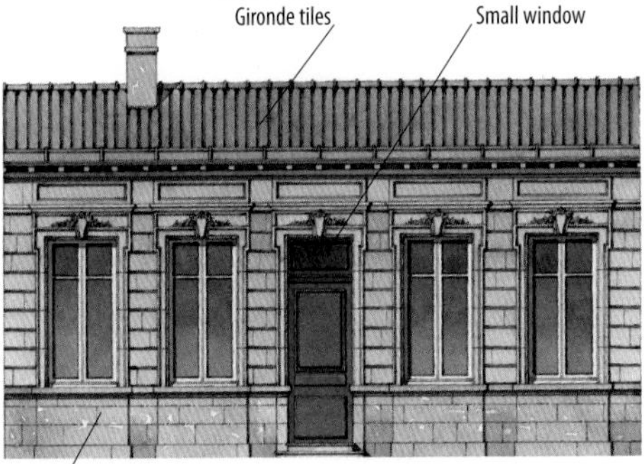

The *échoppe bordelaise* is a single-storey building, sometimes with a small garden at the rear. It is highly typical of Bordeaux and its environs, where there are over 10,000 examples. *Échoppes* were originally relatively humble houses in working-class areas of the city, but later became comfortable middle-class homes.

Dovecotes

Particularly common in the Lot-et-Garonne, *pigeonniers*, or dovecotes, form a distinctive element in the rural architecture of southwest France. A vestige of life in former times, they housed pigeons kept for their eggs and meat; their droppings, known as *colombine* (from *colombe*, meaning "dove"), would be collected and used as fertilizer. Because keeping birds depended on owning a fairly large amount of land, dovecotes also signalled that the owner must be wealthy. They were built in various shapes and sizes, in brick or stone, sometimes with half-timbering and usually with a roof. Constructed either on the ground or set on columns, most were located in open countryside, where the smell and sound of the birds would not offend. Dovecotes were also integrated into other buildings, in the form of large cavities or turrets, and some were built in towns, within *bastides* like Monflanquin.

A dovecote on stilts, for protection against predators

Bastide Towns

Between 1220 and 1370, the counts of Toulouse and King Edward I of England ordered nearly 300 fortified towns *(bastides)* to be built in southwestern France. Laid out to a set plan, they were established for political and economic as well as military reasons. Through them it was possible to bring together local populations and to maximize yields from agricultural land. A reciprocal agreement between the founder of a *bastide* and the owner of the surrounding land safeguarded the rights of each. The *bastide* was governed by a bailiff, who represented the king.

Entrance to the *bastide* of Penne-d'Agenais

The church, an integral element of a *bastide*, served as a refuge during times of danger and as a place of safe-keeping for the relics of saints. With a belfry, small arches, machicolation and corner turrets, some churches were formidable fortresses.

Charretières, wide thoroughfares built especially for carts, served as the main routes into the central main square.

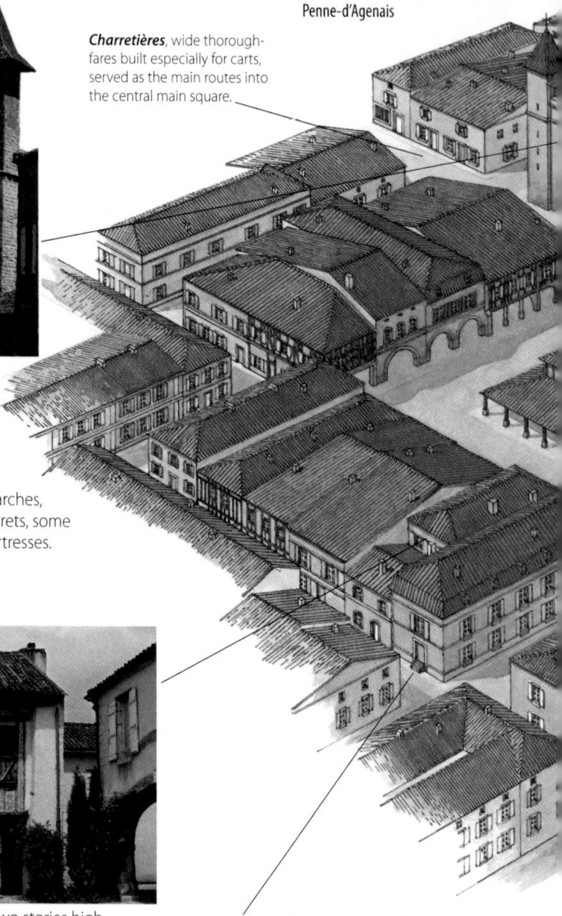

Houses were originally just two stories high, the upper floor providing the living quarters. On the ground floor was a craftsman's workshop or a shopkeeper's store.

Traversières were the smaller streets, set at right angles to the *charretières*.

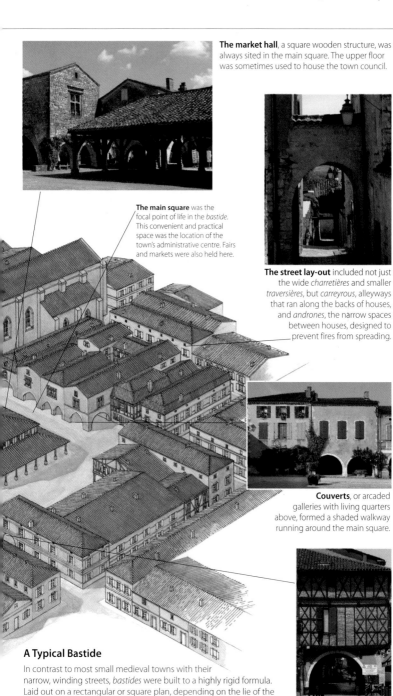

The market hall, a square wooden structure, was always sited in the main square. The upper floor was sometimes used to house the town council.

The main square was the focal point of life in the *bastide*. This convenient and practical space was the location of the town's administrative centre. Fairs and markets were also held here.

The street lay-out included not just the wide *charretières* and smaller *traversières*, but *carreyrous*, alleyways that ran along the backs of houses, and *andrones*, the narrow spaces between houses, designed to prevent fires from spreading.

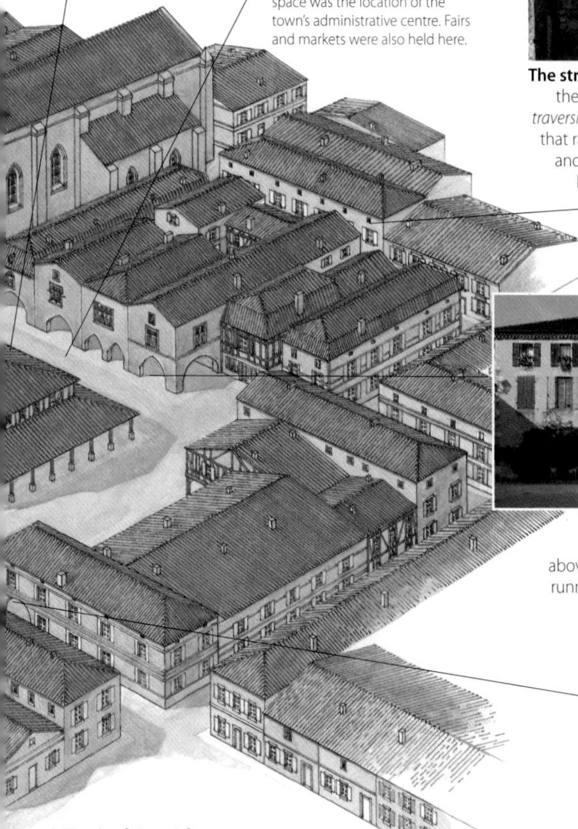

Couverts, or arcaded galleries with living quarters above, formed a shaded walkway running around the main square.

Timber-framed walls of houses were filled in with cob, baked earth or bricks.

A Typical Bastide

In contrast to most small medieval towns with their narrow, winding streets, *bastides* were built to a highly rigid formula. Laid out on a rectangular or square plan, depending on the lie of the land, they have straight streets that intersect at right angles to form a checkerboard pattern. The houses, built on plots of a roughly even size, were generally long and narrow, with a courtyard or a small garden either at the back or front.

Bullfighting and Bull-leaping

For centuries bullfighting has been a popular sport in southwest France, especially in the Landes region where, in the *course landaise*, cows are used in place of bulls and the animals are not killed. Such secular activities were often part of religious festivals, particularly the feast of Saint-Jean in Saint-Sever, and that of Sainte-Madeleine held in Mont-de-Marsan. Although a document dating from 1289 mentions bull-leaping in the streets of Bayonne, it was not until the 19th century that the arena sport of *course landaise*, as it can be seen today, was formalized. The sport of bullfighting arrived in the region from Spain around the same time, with the first French fight taking place in the Saint-Esprit district of Bayonne on 21 August 1853.

Poster for a bullfight in Bayonne in 1897

The *paseo* is the opening ceremony before a bullfight. The matadors parade in the bullring, followed by their assistants and by the picadors.

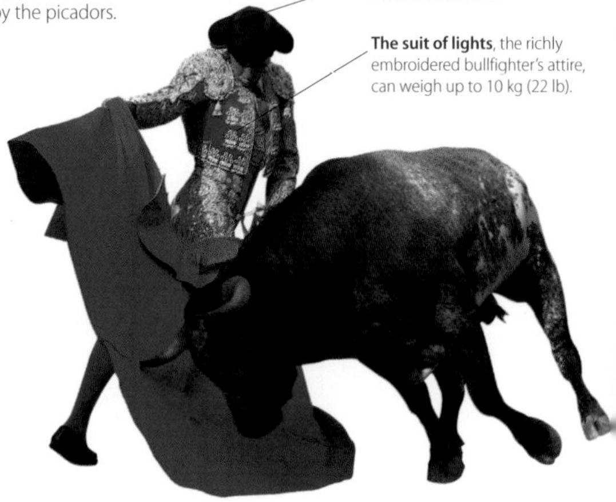

The montera is worn during the first two *tercios*.

The suit of lights, the richly embroidered bullfighter's attire, can weigh up to 10 kg (22 lb).

Inserting the *banderillos* may be done by the *maestro* (the matador) himself, or by a *banderillero*, a member of the *cuadrilla*, the matador's team.

Bullfighting

Pitting a bull against a matador, a bullfight (lidia) *consists of three phases* (tercios). *In the first, the* tercio des piques, *the bull is teased with a cape* (above), *after which the picadors prick the animal with their lances to provoke it to fight. Then come the* tercio des banderilles, *and finally the* faena, *when the matador makes elegant passes at the bull with the* muleta, *a small piece of red fabric that acts as a lure. Finally, the matador kills the bull with a sword.*

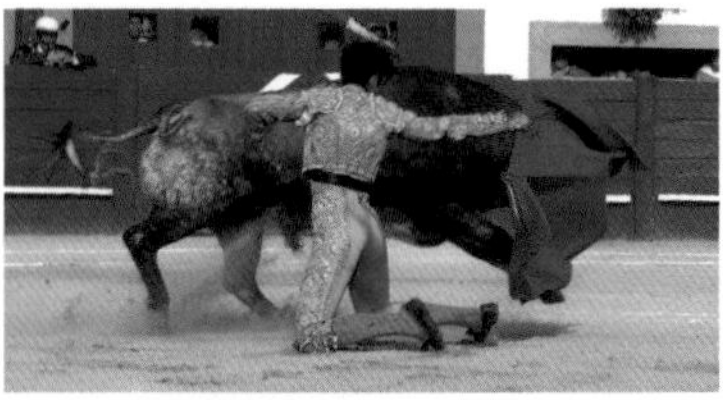

Working with the red cape is the most exciting phase of the bullfight. The bullfighter's skill in using a variety of passes thrills the audience.

The bull is killed by a technique known as *al volapié*, in which the matador leaps onto the bull.

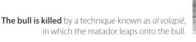

The leap is one of the two main gymnastic moves in *course landaise*. Here it involves a daring backward spiral, an increasingly popular move.

The *écart* or dodge is the other main move. It involves avoiding the charging cow by swerving to one side.

Course Landaise

This colourful spectacle demands both courage and agility. The écarteur *(bull-leaper) avoids the charging cow, the* coursière, *by executing balletic moves of varying complexity; elegance and the degree of risk being highly admired. Today, a rope is attached to the cow to control it more as it charges. The animal's horns are trimmed and the performance does not end with its slaughter.*

The écarteur wears white trousers and a bolero decorated with gold or silver leaf.

One coursière may be used in around 20 bull-leaps a year, over a period of at least 10 years.

The rope is held by the *courdier*, who controls the charging cow.

The *saut périlleux* (daring leap), admired for its technical and artistic qualities, arouses the cow's aggression.

The *saut de l'ange* (angel's leap) over the animal is one of the most widely used moves.

Where to Watch a Bullfight

Most bullfights and bull-leaping spectacles take place from March to October. While bullrunning can easily be seen in many towns and villages in the Landes, there are relatively few bullrings. Some of the most prestigious ones are in the following towns:

Bayonne
Avenue des Fleurs. **Map** A4.
Tel 05 59 46 61 00.

Dax
Bd Paul-Lasaosa. **Map** B4.
Tel 05 58 90 99 09.

Mont-de-Marsan
Bd de la République. **Map** C4.
Tel 05 58 75 39 08.

Saint-Sever
Butte de Morlanne. **Map** C4.
Tel 05 58 76 34 64.

Basque Traditions

The Basque people are fiercely proud of their cultural heritage and ancient language, Euskara, whose origins remain vague. The strength of this sense of national identity can be clearly seen at the many local festivals, such as those held in Bayonne, that involve dancing, singing, music and parades in which traditional red and white Basque costumes are worn and the Basque flag is carried. Jousting and other sports also feature, including trials of strength, boat races – in vessels very similar to ancient whaleboats – and tests of the speed and skill demonstrated in *pelota*, the well-known Basque ball game.

Ikurriña

The Basque flag – the ikurriña *– was designed in the late 19th century in Euskadi, the Basque name for their homeland. Its red background symbolizes the Basque people. On this sits a white cross (symbolizing Christianity), super-imposed over a green cross of St Andrew (symbolizing the law). Along with the Euskara language, the flag is one of the most potent symbols of Basque national pride.*

Weights lifted by Basque strongmen can exceed 200 kg (440 lb).

Basque strongman contests consist of seven separate tests of strength. One of these is stone-lifting. Such contests take place both in the Pays Basque, in France, and in Euskadi, in Spain.

Thigh protectors, pads made of fabric, prevent bruising when the weight-lifter rests heavy stones on his thighs.

Bands of Basque musicians help create the atmosphere at Bayonne's festivals and during bullrunning contests.

Soka-tira is a game of tug-of-war involving two teams of eight to ten people.

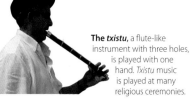

The *txistu*, a flute-like instrument with three holes, is played with one hand. *Txistu* music is played at many religious ceremonies.

Basque Literature

With 790,000 Basque-speakers, 40,000 of whom live in France, Basque literature is enjoying a revival. Some 100 publishers and almost 300 authors have published about 1,500 titles a year since 1975. Authors such as Bernardo Atxaga are keen to keep Basque literature alive and to spread awareness of it around the world. His novel *Obabakoak* has been translated into 25 languages.

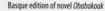

Basque edition of novel *Obabakoak*

The *alarde* is a parade in which hundreds of young people in traditional Basque dress march to the sound of flutes.

The *Zamalzain*, or horseman, is a character in the annual masquerade that takes place in the Basque region of Soule. Hosted by a different village each year, this itinerant carnival in Basque costume begins and ends with brilliantly performed dances.

Basque songs are an aspect of every kind of festivity, from pastoral festivals and masquerades to *bertxulari* contests, when singers improvise on a given theme.

Burial Rites

The circular crosses that were erected to mark graves in Basque cemeteries date back to the Middle Ages. However, they are thought to predate Christianity. These funerary stones, with their disc-shaped heads, are decorated with a square and a circle, which together symbolize the transition from life on earth to the world beyond. They are decorated with religious motifs, inscriptions in Latin or Basque, and tools or implements relating to the trade of the deceased.

Circular crosses over graves in a Basque graveyard

Vineyards in Aquitaine

Bordeaux is widely regarded as the wine capital of the world. The area's fertile soil, gentle climate and age-old methods of production, as well as sea and river trade, have each contributed to this distinguished status. Pauillac, Pessac-Léognan, Pomerol, Saint-Émilion and Sauternes are all wines of international renown. But Aquitaine's vineyards produce other fine wines. These include Bergerac, Buzet, Côtes-de-Duras, Monbazillac, Jurançon and Irouléguy. There is also Armagnac, the famous dry brandy, and the spirit, Floc de Gascogne.

Château Lafite Rothschild at Pauillac, producer of the finest Médoc wines

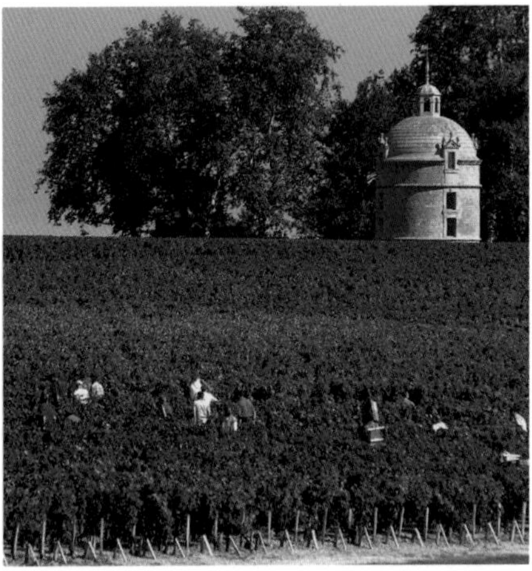

Grape harvest at Château Latour, in the Médoc

Vineyards

The vineyards of Aquitaine fill the region's wide river valleys. While the Garonne flows through the vineyards of Bordeaux and Agen, the Dordogne bisects those of Bergerac. Near the Pyrénées, the vineyards of Tursan, Pacherenc and Madiran are irrigated by the Adour, and those of Jurançon by the Gave de Pau.

The Irouléguy vineyards lie south of Bayonne, around Saint-Étienne-de-Baïgorry and Saint-Jean-Pied de-Port. They produce fruity white, red and rosé wines.

Wine Facts

Location and Climate

The vineyards of Bordeaux have two major advantages: well-drained soil and a temperate climate, with heavy rainfall in winter and plenty of sunshine in summer and autumn. The subsoil, which consists of clay and limestone, is highly suitable for vine-growing.

Grapes

Around Bordeaux, the main grapes are Cabernet-Sauvignon, Merlot and Cabernet Franc for red wine, and Sémillon and Sauvignon for white wine.

Great Vintages

In the 20th century, the years 1945, 1947, 1949, 1953, 1959, 1970, 1988, 1989, 1990 and 1998 produced some exceptional vintages throughout the region. Saint-Émilion and Pomerol vintages of 1998, 2000, 2001, 2005, 2009 and 2010 were outstanding, as were the Médoc and Graves vintages of 1995, 1996, 1999, 2000, 2003, 2005, 2009 and 2010. Sweet white wines like Loupiac, Sauternes and Cérons were excellent in 1996, 1998, 2001, 2003, 2005, 2009 and 2011. Whites like Graves and Pessac-Léognan of 1997, 2000, 2001, 2002 and 2005 were memorable, while vintages from 2006 to 2012 have all proved remarkable.

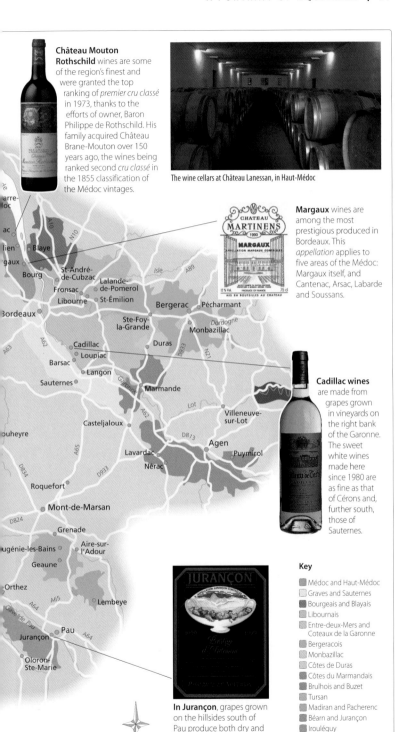

Château Mouton Rothschild wines are some of the region's finest and were granted the top ranking of *premier cru classé* in 1973, thanks to the efforts of owner, Baron Philippe de Rothschild. His family acquired Château Brane-Mouton over 150 years ago, the wines being ranked second *cru classé* in the 1855 classification of the Médoc vintages.

The wine cellars at Château Lanessan, in Haut-Médoc

Margaux wines are among the most prestigious produced in Bordeaux. This *appellation* applies to five areas of the Médoc: Margaux itself, and Cantenac, Arsac, Labarde and Soussans.

Cadillac wines are made from grapes grown in vineyards on the right bank of the Garonne. The sweet white wines made here since 1980 are as fine as that of Cérons and, further south, those of Sauternes.

In Jurançon, grapes grown on the hillsides south of Pau produce both dry and sweet wines.

AQUITAINE THROUGH THE YEAR

In Aquitaine, every season has its attractions. In spring the landscape becomes lush and verdant, and many open-air festivals take place. With traditional as well as modern singing and dancing, these festivals celebrate the region's culture and history. Summer sees the start of the bullfighting and *course landaise* season in the Landes, as well as a number of important sporting events. Autumn and winter are punctuated by festivals showcasing local specialties and marking the grape harvest. This is also when carnivals and masquerades take place in the Pays Basque.

Spring

In spring, and particularly during school holidays, the region's coastal resorts come to life. Many of the region's traditional festivals celebrating local produce also take place at this time of the year.

March

Bi Harriz Lau Xori *(late March)*, Biarritz. Concerts, dancing, theatre and film, celebrating the language of the Pays Basque, Euskara.

April

Fête des Soufflaculs *(early April)*, Nontron. A medieval festival where the town's inhabitants chase each other through the streets, dressed in nightgowns, to ward off evil spirits.

Festival Art et Courage *(late April)*, Pomarez. A major event at the Landes' great mecca for *course landaise*, or bull-leaping *(see p33)*.

Bayonne Ham Fair *(week before Easter)*, Bayonne. Hundreds of local hams are put on display. Music is provided by Basque bands.

Festival des Vallées et des Bergers *(late April–early May)*, Oloron-Sainte-Marie. A two-day festival with groups singing in Béarnais.

May

Wine and Cheese Fair *(8 May)*, Monflanquin. A showcase for growers and producers of southwestern specialities *(see pp258–9)*.

Fête de l'Agneau *(mid-May)*, Pauillac. Wine fraternity procession as well as a lamb lunch and stalls selling local produce on the quays.

Herri Urrats *(mid-May)*. Dancing, singing and other activities, set around the 4-km (3-mile) perimeter of the Lac de St-Pée near Saint-Pée-sur-Nivelle.

Poster advertising Bayonne's programme of festivals

Summer

During the summer, large numbers of visitors flock to the coast. Inland, many towns and villages host festivals. Some of these, such as the grand events that are held in Bayonne, Dax and Mont-de-Marsan, draw huge crowds.

Festival d'Art Flamenco, Mont-de-Marsan

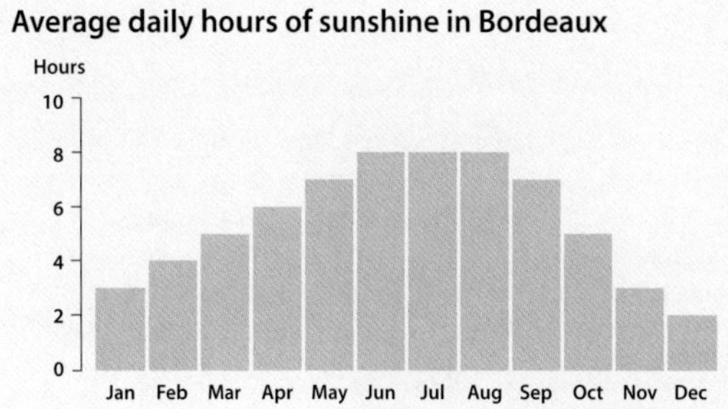

Sunshine Chart
The Gironde enjoys just over 2,000 hours of sunshine a year. The sunniest days are concentrated in the summer months, although winds blowing in from the northwest off the Atlantic help to cool the air. From October to February, parts of the region are often cloaked in fog.

June

Jurade *(3rd Sunday in June)*, Saint-Émilion. A medieval ceremony, revived in 1948, when the season's wine is tasted and given the official Saint-Émilion seal.
Festival d'Art Flamenco *(late June–early July)*, Mont-de-Marsan. Six-day flamenco festival with dancing, music and storytelling.
Internationaux de Cesta Punta Professionel *(June–August)*, Saint-Jean-de-Luz. Professional players compete on open courts.
Fête du Vin *(late June)* and **Fête du Fleuve** *(late June)*, Bordeaux. Two festivals, held in alternate years, with sports, wine tastings and exhibitions.

Transhumance, marked by a festival, in the Ossau valley

July

Fête de la Transhumance *(early July)*, Ossau valley. Traditional singing and dancing, with tastings of cheeses and *garbure* (a soup).
La Félibrée *(early July)*, Dordogne. A celebration of the Occitan language and culture; location varies.
Fêtes de la Madeleine *(mid-July)*, Mont-de-Marsan. A festival with a Spanish flavour, in honour of the town's patron saint.
Les Eclectiques *(mid-July)*, Rocamadour. As the name suggests, a festival that combines different genres of music, theatre and dance.
Festival des Jeux du Théâtre *(mid-July–early August)*, Sarlat. An open-air drama festival.
Bataille de Castillon *(mid-July–mid-August)*. Elaborate reconstruction of this battle of 1453 *(see p47)*.
Fête du Fromage *(late July)*, Aspe valley. The town of Etsaut shows its ewes'-milk cheeses *(see p215)*.
Nuits Atypiques de Langon *(late July)*. A festival of world music, with instruments ranging from *peuhl* flutes to balalaïkas.
Fête de l'Huître *(July–August)*, Arcachon basin. An opportunity to sample the area's famous oysters and see oyster farmers wearing their traditional dress.

An enthusiastic crowd at the Féria de Dax

August

Fêtes de Bayonne *(late July–early August)*. A five-day non-stop fiesta with bull-leaping, Basque orchestras and banqueting in the bodegas, a children's day on Thursday, and a bullfight on Sunday.
Mimos *(1st week)*, Périgueux. World-famous international mime festival.
Féria de Dax *(mid-August)*. With traditional celebrations and bullfighting, this is one of the region's most famous festivals.
Journées Médiévales *(mid-August)*, Monflanquin. Medieval music and dancing.
Festival de Force Basque *(mid-August)*, Saint-Palais. Strongmen of the Pays Basque compete in trials of strength *(see p34)*.
Lacanau Pro Surf *(mid-August)*. World surfing championship.
Festival du Périgord Noir *(throughout August and September)*. Baroque and classical music performed in historic buildings and some more unusual places.

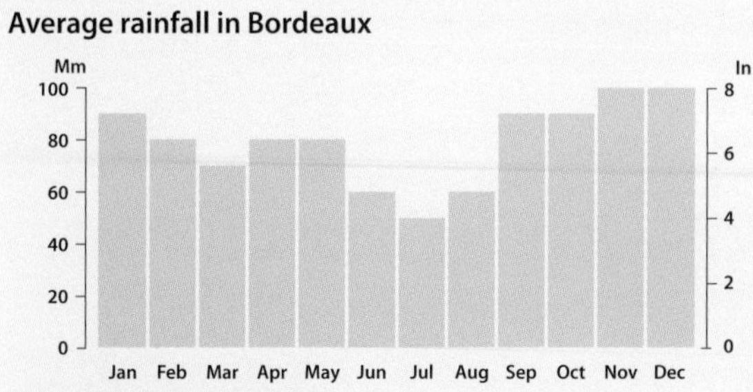

Rainfall
Aquitaine is a fairly wet region, where it generally rains all year round, although it is usually wetter in winter than in summer. Rainfall tends to be gentle rather than heavy. The average annual rainfall in the Gironde area is between 70 cm (27 in) and 100 cm (39 in).

Saint-Émilion's *jurats* (winetasters) at the top of the Tour du Roy

Autumn

In the early autumn, the weather is usually still warm enough for outdoor activities. All over southwest France, the grape harvest is about to begin, and many colourful gatherings take place, celebrating the local wines. Art, dancing and regional specialities also have their own festivals.

September

Académie Internationale de Musique Maurice Ravel *(early September)*, Saint-Jean-de-Luz and Ciboure. Young musicians perform pieces by great French composers, both classical and modern.

Fête du Sel *(mid-September)*, Salies-de-Béarn. A world barrel-lifting championship organized by the *Jurade du Sel (see p223)*.

Hot Air Balloon Festival *(late September)*, Rocamadour. A magnificent gathering of colourful balloons.

Jurade *(late September)*, Saint-Émilion. Linked with the tasting ceremony held in June *(see p39)*, this part of the *Jurade* involves measuring the annual grape harvest.

October

Foire aux Fromages and Marché à l'Ancienne *(first weekend in October)*, Laruns. With street performances, singing, dancing and period dress, the village re-creates the age of Henri IV *(see p49)*.

Championnat de France de Course Landaise *(early October)*. This event, which takes place at a different bullring each year, marks the close of the *course landaise* season.

Fête du Piment *(late October)*, Espelette *(see p205)*. Garlands of the area's famous sweet red peppers are blessed and hung on the façades of houses. Basque strongman contests and enthronings into the local brotherhood also form part of the celebrations.

Pepper motif, Fête du Piment, Espelette

November

Festival du Film *(early November)*, Sarlat. Screenings, awards ceremonies and seminars and training sessions for budding producers and directors given by professional filmmakers.

Festival Novart Bordeaux *(November, biennial)*. A major showcase for all types of contemporary art.

Festivolailles *(late November)*, Saint-Sever. A poultry and *foie gras* fair aimed at gourmets and connoisseurs. Prizes are awarded for the finest fowl and for the best pâtés on show.

Performance at the Temps d'Aimer, a dance festival in Biarritz

Average temperatures in Bordeaux

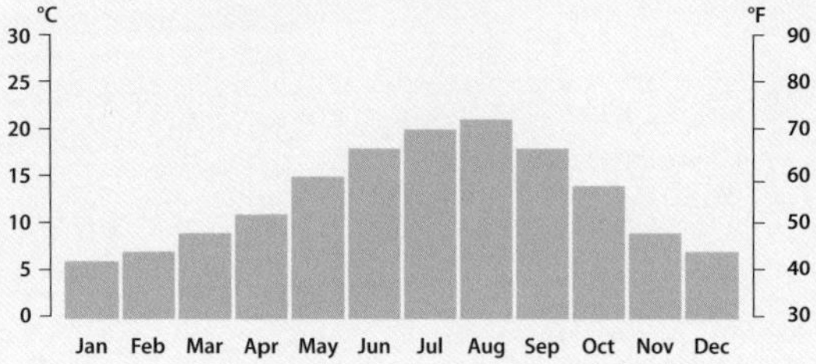

Temperatures
Because of its oceanic climate, the Gironde has relatively mild winters and pleasantly warm summers. The average temperature in January is 5–7 °C (41–45 °F), and in July and August, 19–21 °C (66–70 °F). For about three weeks a year, temperatures can rise as high as 30°C (96°F).

Winter

With Christmas on its way, celebrations begin in earnest. Locally made handicrafts and delicacies fill the many Christmas markets that are held. This is also the season for making *foie gras*, which is honoured with a whole range of festivities.

Masquerade dancer, La Soule

December
Journée Portes Ouvertes en Jurançon *(mid-December)*, Jurançon. Over 40 local wine producers offer wine tastings in their cellars. Exhibitions, music and regional food can be sampled too.
Olentzero *(Christmas)*, Pays Basque. This festival grew out of the pagan practice of marking the winter solstice. Olentzero, a Basque folk character, assumed the status of Father Christmas in the 1960s. According to legend, Olentzero comes down from the mountains, and delivers firewood to towns and villages so that no one should be cold.

January
Masquerades *(first Sun in January to first Thu in Lent)*, La Soule. This ritualized dance carnival takes place on successive Sundays, in a different village each time. The main dance, the *Godalet Dantza* (Glass Dance), is performed around a glass of wine. The festival ends in Tardets, where all masqueraders gather.
Foire aux Pottoks *(last Tue and Wed in January)*, Espelette. A horse fair, where *pottoks* (small Basque horses) are traded *(see p204)*. It takes place twice a year.
Carnivals *(Candlemas to the start of Lent or Easter)*, throughout the Pays Basque and elsewhere, including Pau. Towns and villages come to life with music, dance and colourful parades. A common scene is the ritual awakening of a bear, which heralds the beginning of springtime.

February
Fête des Bœufs Gras *(February–March)*, Bazas. Dating from the 13th century, when Edward I, king of England, ruled Aquitaine, this festival takes place on the Thursday before Shrove Tuesday to mark the end of the carnival season and the approach of Lent. Immaculately groomed oxen, their horns decorated with ribbons and flowers, are weighed, then paraded, before being judged in front of the cathedral. Once the prizes have been awarded, there is an exhibition of winners, followed by a great banquet at which beef is served. All the animals on display are of a local breed that is thought to have originated in Spain.
Jumping International *(early February)*, Bordeaux. Covering everything there is to know about the world of horses, this takes place at the Parc des Expositions, at the same time as the exhibition Chevalexpo. It is a major event in the international showjumping circuit, attracting many famous names, and includes a competition for disabled riders.

The Pyrénées-Atlantiques have several winter sports resorts

Public Holidays

New Year (1 Jan)
Easter Sunday and Easter Monday Ascension (sixth Thursday after Easter)
Labour Day (1 May)
Victory Day (8 May)
Bastille Day (14 Jul)
Assumption (15 Aug)
All Saints' Day (1 Nov)
Armistice Day (11 Nov)
Christmas Day (25 Dec)

THE HISTORY OF AQUITAINE

The Romans gave the name Aquitania to the southwest corner of France, meaning "near the sea" or "water-rich". In the 13th century, the English called it Guyenne. Now known to the French as Aquitaine, its borders have shifted constantly over the centuries. It has served as a melting pot where different peoples have met and intermingled, creating a region marked by sharp contrasts and diversity. Yet the whole region shares a unifying characteristic: a rich cultural heritage stretching back to the beginning of history.

The Dawn of Humanity

Of all regions of France, Aquitaine is by far the most important in terms of prehistory. This is most true of the Périgord, an area with an almost unique cluster of major prehistoric sites.

Around 400,000 BC, the first hunters arrived in the Vézère valley, in the Dordogne, where they lived in rock-shelters in the limestone cliffs and where they made flint tools. Today, traces of their activities have been discovered at over 150 sites and in some 50 decorated caves. Thanks to the discovery of the rock-shelter at Le Moustier, we have an insight into the life and religious rituals of prehistoric hunters from around 80,000–30,000 BC. At the Cro-Magnon site in Les Eyzies, artifacts from 35,000–10,000 BC have revealed the amazingly high level of skill attained by early man. A similar sense of wonder comes from looking at the cave paintings, depicting mammoths, horses and reindeer, at Lascaux, and the female figurines, such as the so-called Venus figures, found at Laussel in the Dordogne and at Brassempouy in the Landes.

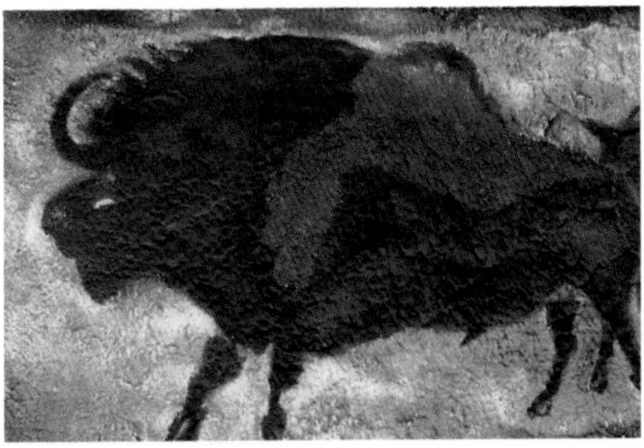

Cave painting of a bison at Lascaux

During the Neolithic period, the population grew. People began to settle in villages and grow crops and domesticate animals. Their craft skills developed. They wove woollen cloth, worked with wood and leather, and made metal tools and weapons, first from copper, then later from bronze. In the Médoc, around 1,500 BC, large bronze axes were being produced.

400,000 BC The first humans settle in the Vézère valley

120,000 BC Tools become markedly more complex and regular in shape

35,000–10 000 BC Cro-Magnon Man makes more sophisticated tools and weapons

400,000 BC | **200,000 BC** | **100,000 BC** | **50,000 BC** | **10,000 BC**

About 200,000 BC Tools designed for a specific purpose, such as scrapers and awls, begin to be made

Venus of Brassempouy

18,000–15,000 BC Cave paintings at Lascaux

◀ The marriage of Louis XIV and Maria Theresa of Austria on 9 June 1660 at Saint-Jean-de-Luz, by Laumosnier

Roman Gaul

In the early 3rd century BC, the Gauls (a Celtic people), began to settle in southwest France, which at the time was sparsely populated. They integrated rapidly with the indigenous population, settling mainly around urban centres such as Burdigala (now Bordeaux) and Aginum (now Agen). Their leaders established trade links with Narbonensis, a Roman province in southern Gaul, and began to import goods from Italy, including wine. But in 52 BC, the Romans defeated the Gauls at the Battle of Alesia. This marked the beginning of Roman dominance in southwest France. Villas with large agricultural estates were established on the banks of the region's great rivers, and a building programme began in the towns, where amphitheatres, aqueducts and temples (a vestige of which is the Tour de Vésone in Périgueux) were constructed. Gallo-Roman civilization was born. However, the end of the 3rd century saw the first of many invasions by Germanic tribes from the east. The population took refuge behind hastily constructed ramparts, and another turbulent period in the history of Aquitaine began.

Marble statue of Diana, Gallo-Roman period

A Dark Age

At the beginning of the 5th century, a series of invasions led to the Visigoths making Aquitaine part of their kingdom in 481. They, in turn, were expelled by the Franks. It was around this time that Christianity was beginning to take hold in the towns and cities, although it did not really become widespread in the region until as late as the 11th century. But this period did see the start of the construction of some of Aquitaine's first great abbeys and churches. After the death of their king, Clovis, in 511, Frankish (Merovingian) control was weakened by the division of the region into separate administrative areas. Taking advantage of this, the Vascons, a people

Roman mosaic in the Musée d'Aquitaine, Bordeaux

Roman Villa at Plassac

From around the 1st century BC, the Romans established agricultural estates all over what is now southwest France. Each centred around a villa complex, which included the owner's house, accommodation for estate workers and various farm buildings. All around was agricultural land, where cereals were cultivated and, from the 1st century AD, vines were also grown. Excavations carried out between 1963 and 1978 at the site of a Gallo-Roman villa near Plassac, at the head of the Gironde Estuary, revealed the foundations of a house built by a wealthy land-owner from Italy in AD 14–20. The house, which was later modified several times, was richly decorated with materials, such as marble, that had been imported from North Africa.

Around 300 BC The first Celtic tribes settle in Aquitaine

Roman sculpture

AD 14–20 The Roman villa at Plassac is built. Vine-growing becomes established in southwestern France

300 BC | 200 BC | 100 BC | AD 1 | AD 100 | 200

56 BC Crassus, Julius Caesar's lieutenant, conquers Aquitaine

284–305 Ramparts are built to defend Bordeaux and Périgueux

Figure of Hercules (3rd century)

from the Pyrenees who are sometimes equated with the Basques, invaded in 580, settling in an area between the Garonne river and the Pyrenees, which became known as Gascony in the 7th century. A hundred years later, the Arabs arrived, but they were repulsed at Poitiers by Charles Martel in 732. Then the Carolingians annexed the territory, but their rule was relatively short-lived. In the mid-9th century, the Normans sailed up the Adour, Dordogne and Garonne rivers, pillaging and ravaging towns, churches and monasteries as they went. Bordeaux was torched in 848. Gallo-Roman civilization was broken and gradually it withered away.

Merovingian buckle

Spread of Christianity

During the 11th and 12th centuries, political stability returned and the population began to increase. Churches and monasteries were now springing up all over the southwest of France. The Abbaye de la Sauve-Majeure was founded by Gérard de Corbie in 1079 and at the time of his death, around 1095, it had more than 300 monks and exercised control over about 20 priories. As religious communities in the region began to multiply, more and more land was being cleared in order to build abbeys and monasteries, especially along the main pilgrim routes going southward through France and the Col de Roncevaux pass over the Pyrenees to Santiago de Compostela. Some religious buildings, like the Cathédrale Saint-Front in Périgueux, were now being built in the Byzantine-Romanesque style. Most churches were also lavishly decorated with ornate mosaics sculptures and frescoes.

But from the 13th century onward, there was a general downturn in religious architecture, although the great Gothic cathedrals of Bordeaux, Bazas and Bayonne were rebuilt in the 14th century, following the devastation of the Hundred Years' War.

Thanks to Philip the Fair, a firm ruler and an accomplished diplomat, Bertrand de Got, Archbishop of Bordeaux, was elected Pope in 1305, as Clement V. His position allowed him to bestow favours on the Gascon clergy. He also initiated the construction of the great châteaux at Roquetaillade, Fargues, Budos and at Villandraut, in the Gironde, where he was a regular visitor.

Bertrand de Got, who became Pope Clement v in 1305

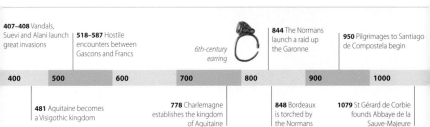

407–408 Vandals, Suevi and Alani launch great invasions

481 Aquitaine becomes a Visigothic kingdom

518–587 Hostile encounters between Gascons and Francs

6th-century earring

778 Charlemagne establishes the kingdom of Aquitaine

844 The Normans launch a raid up the Garonne

848 Bordeaux is torched by the Normans

950 Pilgrimages to Santiago de Compostela begin

1079 St Gérard de Corbie founds Abbaye de la Sauve-Majeure

400 | 500 | 600 | 700 | 800 | 900 | 1000

English Rule in France

In 1137, Eleanor of Aquitaine, daughter and heiress of William X, Duc d'Aquitaine, married Louis VII, later king of France. However, as Eleanor had not only failed to produce a royal heir but also led a life that displeased her husband, the marriage was dissolved in 1152. A few months later Eleanor married Henry Plantagenet who, in 1154, became Henry II of England. Apart from the French enclaves of Armagnac and Béarn, the duchy of Aquitaine was now under English rule. Hostilities between the French and the English in the region began in 1328 and continued until 1453, when the English were soundly defeated at the Battle of Castillon.

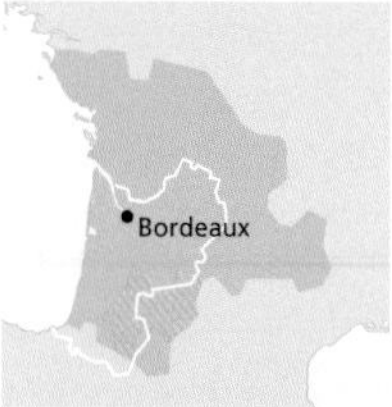

English Aquitaine (1362)

Armagnac and Béarn (p218)

Edward I of England Pays Homage to Philip the Fair

Philip the Fair became king of France in 1285 and, as custom dictated, Edward I, king of England, paid homage to him for the territory that he held within the French kingdom.

King of France

King of England

Arms of Bordeaux

The Grosse Cloche, the bell tower of the town hall in Bordeaux that was built in the 13th century, is surmounted by the three leopards of England. At the foot of the Grosse Cloche, the waters of the Garonne flow by. The crescent motif in the water is an allusion to the port of Bordeaux.

Eleanor of Aquitaine

Eleanor had two daughters by Louis VII of France, and seven children, including Richard the Lionheart and King John, by her second husband, Henry II of England. She eventually left Henry and returned to her native Aquitaine, where she was a patron of the arts, especially of troubadours writing songs and poetry in the courtly love tradition. She was buried in the Abbaye de Fontevraud, near Angers, in 1204.

The Black Prince

In 1337, the King of France claimed Aquitaine, because Edward III of England had refused to pay homage to him. Edward's son, Edward of Woodstock, also known as the Black Prince, took up arms to defend the English position. He even had local support, in Bordeaux, where he had been well received two years earlier for upholding the city's special privileges. Under him, the English triumphed at the Battle of Crécy in 1346 and the Battle of Poitiers in 1356, where the French king, John the Good, was taken prisoner. Aquitaine was made into a principality and granted autonomous powers.

Siege of Duras

The French siege of Duras came to symbolize the numerous attacks that Bertrand du Guesclin launched on the English in Aquitaine. At du Guesclin's death in 1380, the English controlled only Bordeaux and Bayonne.

Battle of Castillon

At the beginning of the 15th century, the English regained part of Aquitaine and, from 1438, major battles resumed. They were brought to an end in June 1451, when the French took Bordeaux, and in 1453, at the Battle of Castillon, when Charles VII finally expelled the English from Guyenne. This marked the end of the Hundred Years' War.

1137 Eleanor of Aquitaine marries Louis VII of France

1360 Treaty of Brétigny. Aquitaine becomes an English possession

1328 Start of the Hundred Years' War

1100 | 1200 | 1300

Late 13th–early 14th century *Bastide* towns are established

1356 Battle of Poitiers. John II, the Good, is taken prisoner by Edward, the Black Prince

1152 Eleanor of Aquitaine marries Henry Plantagenet

1380 After battles fought by Bertrand du Guesclin, the only English enclaves are Bordeaux and Bayonne

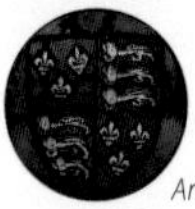

Arms of England

Lords, Peasants and the Bourgeoisie

For much of the Middle Ages, Aquitaine was under English rule. Defending this position against French claims to the territory led to almost continuous conflict and the construction of many castles, particularly in the Périgord, including Beynac and Castelnaud. Each of these great fortresses belonged to a lord, who was either under the protection of the king of France or the king of England. Bertran de Born (born in 1140), the famous troubadour and lord of Hautefort, described this warring, 12th-century society in his writings: men lived for hunting and battle, for finery and for the love of a noble woman. As a castle-owner, Bertran deplored the expansion of farmland: not only did it encroach on woodland, it also allowed new villages to be established and merchants and the bourgeoisie to grow rich, so reducing lordly power. Waging war was thus the foremost occupation of noblemen, who were permanently seeking new ways of maintaining their knightly lifestyle.

Troubadour of Aquitaine

At the same time, the rapid population expansion that occured in the 13th and 14th centuries caused towns and cities to double in size. Large towns like Bayonne, Périgueux and Sarlat, as well as smaller ones like Mussidan and Ribérac, were granted charters that gave their inhabitants certain privileges. Freed from obligations to an overlord, the bourgeoisie could now take part in public life. In the 11th and 12th centuries, with the encouragement of the Church and of enterprising lords, land clearance increased. Peasants were called on to make the land suitable for agriculture, creating what were known as *sauvetés* (as at Sauveterre-de-Guyenne, in the Gironde). In return for this work, they would be granted special favours.

Rebirth of Intellectual Life in the 16th Century

In the 16th century, writers such as Michel Eyquem de Montaigne (1533–92), Étienne de La Boétie (1530–63), Pierre de Bourdeilles, a priest and the lord of Brantôme (1538–1614), Blaise de Lasseran de Massencome, lord of Monluc (1500–77), and Joseph Juste Scaliger (1540–1609) contributed to a

Michel Eyquem de Montaigne (1533–92), author of the *Essays* and member of the Parlement de Bordeaux

1441 The University of Bordeaux is established

1462 The Parlement de Bordeaux is founded

1523 The Generality of Guyenne is created

1450

1500

1453 Battle of Castillon

1498 Printing begins in Périgueux

Arms of Guyenne

rebirth of intellectual life in southwest France. Many of them were well travelled and knew Latin. The introduction of printing to Périgueux in 1498, and the founding of the Collège de Guyenne in 1533, contributed to the diffusion of new ideas. Agen, Nérac and Bordeaux became intellectual centres, where humanism was now the central tenet of philosophical thought. At court, Marguerite of Navarre, queen consort of Henri II and much admired for her intellect, presided over a salon that was dubbed "the new Parnassus".

Jeanne d'Albret, mother of Henri IV

Catholics Versus Protestants

Calvinist doctrine began to spread in Aquitaine from 1532. Marguerite of Navarre and her daughter Jeanne d'Albret, as well as many members of the nobility, such as the Duras, the La Force and the Gramont families, contributed greatly to its diffusion. The towns of Nérac, Oloron, Sainte-Foy, Agen and Bergerac gradually became bastions of Protestantism. The king of France condemned this so-called reformed faith and, from 1562, Catholics and Protestants all over France, and particularly in the southwest, began to attack each other. With the death of Jeanne d'Albret, the crisis deepened. Her son Henri of Navarre (1559–1610), later Henri IV of France, then became leader of the Protestant cause.

Aquitaine and the Kings of France

After the Hundred Years' War, the king of France gradually gained control of the southwest by establishing a range of governing institutions, including the Parlement de Bordeaux in 1462, and the Generality of Guyenne in 1523. Military governors and intendants, acting on behalf of the king, enforced royal power. However, at the end of Louis XIII's reign, strife broke out in the countryside. In Périgord in 1637, *croquants* – peasants who revolted against rising taxes – challenged the

Henri IV

To help bring about reconciliation between Protestants and Catholics, the marriage of Henri, King of Navarre, and Marguerite de Valois took place in Paris on 18 August 1572. But the union was not well received and on 24 August 1572, St Bartholomew's Day, Protestants in Paris for the occasion were massacred by extremist Catholics. Henri of Navarre saved his own life by renouncing his religion. Three years later he returned to Pau, his birthplace in southwest France, where he led the Protestant army in countless battles. Henri became king of France on the death of Henri III. To bring stability to the country, he renounced his Protestant faith again in 1593, issuing the Edict of Toleration in Nantes in 1598, but was assassinated by a Catholic fanatic in 1610.

Henri of Navarre

1550

1559 Birth of Henri of Navarre in Pau

1560 Jeanne d'Albret establishes Calvinism in Pau

1580 Montaigne's *Essays* are published

1598 Edict of Nantes

1600

1610 Henri IV is murdered and Louis XIII becomes king with Marie de Médici as regent

Joseph Juste Scaliger

1620 Béarn becomes part of France

Pierre de Bourdeilles

View of the port of Bordeaux taken from the Chateau Trompette, 1759, by Claude Joseph Vernet

excessive authority and rights of the aristocracy and of the local salt-tax collectors. The *croquants* fought against troops of the Duc d'Épernon, governor of Guyenne, but their efforts were largely overshadowed by the activities of the Fronde (1649–53), a rebellious movement led by aristocrats and parliamentarians seeking to gain more independence from the grip of royal power. *Mazarinades* (pamphlets against Cardinal Mazarin, the effective ruler of France during Louis XIV's minority) flourished. This opposition, known as *l'Ormée* in Bordeaux, was firmly suppressed and Bordeaux's citizens were obliged to submit to greater royal control. To help enforce this rule, Château Trompette (now destroyed) was built at the entrance to the city, on the foundations of the old fortress built by Charles VII. Revolts against rising taxes were also put down.

The Sugar Islands, the Southwest's Eldorado

Between the beginning of the 18th century and the French Revolution, trade with the West Indies boomed. Indigo, annatto, cocoa, coffee, cotton and, most of all, sugar arrived at Bordeaux by boat, to be distributed all over France and throughout Europe. This activity either took the form of two-way trade or, from 1750, as triangular trade: ships would stop on the African coast to pick up slaves, who were then exchanged in the West Indies for exotic goods that

Detail from *The Port of Bordeaux and Foreign Relations* by Frédéric de Buzon (1925)

1610 Assassination of Henri IV

1649–53 The Fronde in Bordeaux

Les Mazarinades, a caricature

1685 Revocation of the Edict of Nantes. Protestants in Béarn, Agenais and Périgord are persecuted

1713 Foundation of the Académie de Bordeaux

1729–55 Place Louis-XV, in Bordeaux, is laid out

1730 Bayor quays renov

1732 The first masonic lodge in Bordeaux is set up

1600 | 1660 | 1700 | 1725

Bordeaux in the 18th century, France's premier port

were brought back to Bordeaux. Many merchants who grew rich from the slave trade built elegant town houses or purchased estates on which they built fine residences in fashionable styles. One such example is the Château de Nairac in Barsac. Bordeaux, as well as the areas further inland, which traded their produce in the West Indies, prospered both from the wealth of goods arriving from the islands and also from expanding trading links with northern Europe. Some merchants opted to buy plantations in Santo Domingo, which would be run by a manager or a younger son. All this trade in the 18th century made Bordeaux into France's foremost port.

The Age of Enlightenment

Intellectual life in southwest France in the 18th century was mainly restricted to academies, learned societies (whose members were scholars and scientists), artists and men of letters. There were academies in Bordeaux, Pau and Agen, and a looser association in Périgueux. It was in such circles, made up of the intellectual elite from the nobility and the bourgeoisie, that new ideas developed, particularly the philosophy of Montesquieu. Certain members of the nobility, such as Sarraut de Boynet et Journu in Bordeaux, Charles de Borda in Dax and the Chevalier de Vivens in Clairac, were as interested in science and medicine as they were in the arts and music. New ideas also took root in masonic lodges, where social divisions tended to be blurred.

At the same time, under the impetus of the aristocracy and public officials, towns and cities in southwestern France underwent a programme of regeneration. Street lighting was installed in Bayonne in the second half of the 18th century. Bordeaux's old city walls were knocked down to make way for ornamental gates and squares, such as Place Louis-XV (better known as Place de la Bourse). Footpaths were created and gardens were laid out.

Bordeaux, the capital of Guyenne, became a beacon for civic improvement in the southwest. In 1780, the Grand-Théâtre, commissioned by the Maréchal Duc de Richelieu, governor of Guyenne, and designed by Victor Louis, was

Montesquieu, writer, politician and native of Bordeaux

Decorative mask, Bordeaux (18th century)

1735 | 1745 | 1775 | 1785

1743–57 Marquis de Tourny, intendant of Bordeaux, lays out the city's elegant squares and boulevards

1748 The first edition of Montesquieu's *Spirit of Laws* appears

1771 Peak of Bordeaux's maritime trade

1780 Inauguration of the Grand-Théâtre, Bordeaux

Trading vessel in Bordeaux

The Grand-Théâtre in Bordeaux, built by Victor Louis and inaugurated in 1780

unveiled, opposite the Allées de Tourny. All over the region, but particulary in Bordeaux, many aristocrats and merchants now owned two houses; they would spend the winter in town and the summer in a château or country residence. Many of them regularly travelled to Paris, bringing back new ideas on land management, on how to entertain and on how to dress, as well new attitudes towards hygiene and new knowledge about medicine. For example, in the second half of the 18th century, the Comte de Lur Saluces brought wallpaper back to Uza and decided to better his estate by installing an ironworks there.

From the Girondins to Napoleon

The southwest's entire economy, which was based on trade with the West Indies, collapsed during the French Revolution. Although highly unpopular with the aristocracy, the fall of the Ancien Régime

The Golden Age of Wine-production in Aquitaine

Comte de Lur Saluces

Between the late 17th and early 18th centuries, the nobility began purchasing wine estates not only in the Médoc, the Sauternes and the Graves, but also outside the Bordeaux area, including Clairac, in the Lot-et-Garonne, and at Monbazillac, in the Dordogne. They turned wine-production into a major industry, building great cellars and, with the help of knowledgeable estate managers, laying down high-quality wines for export to the West Indies, England and northern Europe. The leaders in this enterprise were Monsieur de Pontac in the 17th century, and the Marquis de Ségur, the Comte de Lur Saluces and his wife the Comtesse de Sauvage d'Yquem in the 18th.

Comtesse de Sauvage d'Yquem

1785

1788–9 The Parlement de Bordeaux is exiled to Libourne

1790 Civil Constitution of the Clergy

1793 Defeat of the Girondins

Polling card from the time of the French Revolution

1795

1802 Peace of Amiens. Maritime trade resumes

1805

1806 Continental blockade of Great Britain by Napoleon

1808 Napoleon visits Bordeaux

Emperor Napoleon

was, however, welcomed by a newly created nobility and bourgeoisie that was open to fresh ideas. Members of Bordeaux's parliament had been the first to question royal power by opposing the edict allowing provincial assemblies to be set up. In August 1787, Louis XVI ordered them to be exiled to Libourne. In Bordeaux, this decision marked the beginnings of the French Revolution, as it brought about a short-lived solidarity between the aristocracy and the common people. This soon degenerated as a result of the Civil Constitution of the Clergy (July 1790) and the meagre harvests that blighted the southwest in 1791. The deputies for the Gironde, among whom were several lawyers who were renowned for their eloquence, had the ear of the National Assembly. While the Convention was being drawn up, such Girondins as Vergniaud, Guadet and Ducos rose to prominence, standing up for economic liberalism and decentralization.

However, on 2 June 1792, the Girondins found themselves in the minority, and power passed to their opponents. Several were then arrested, while others escaped and even managed to organize a federalist rebellion. In October 1793, Vergniaud was guillotined, along with other deputies for the Gironde. Guadet fled to Normandy, then hid in Saint-Émilion, his native town, before being arrested and guillotined in June 1794. The Reign of Terror was a painful episode for Bordeaux, where many were killed.

Pierre-Victurnien Vergniaud, a Girondin who was guillotined during the Terror

In other towns and cities in the southwest, the leaders of town councils were often more successful in blurring their differences with the central authorities. After the fall of Robespierre, former federalists who had escaped the Terror were reinstated, and the political situation stabilized under the Directoire, the Consulate and the Empire.

However, the upper classes remained hostile to Napoleon, as the Continental blockade against Britain made trading from Bordeaux yet more difficult. Restricting maritime traffic (most particularly the export of wine), it hampered relations with England and other northern European countries, which

Bordeaux in the 19th century (the Pont de Pierre was completed in 1821)

1815 The Duchesse d'Angoulême makes a triumphal entry into Bordeaux

The painter Goya y Lucentes, who died in Bordeaux

810 | 1820 | 1830

12 March 1814 The English enter Bordeaux

1828 Death of Goya in Bordeaux

Entry of the Duc and Duchesse d'Angoulême into Bordeaux in 1815

were Bordeaux's main trading partners. In March 1814, English troops arriving from Spain were favourably received by Bordeaux's inhabitants, who were now free of the imperial yoke and who welcomed the end of the Napoleonic Wars.

Downturn in the Early 19th Century

After the French Revolution and the Empire, Aquitaine slowly emerged from its torpor. The population gladly returned to monarchic rule, symbolized by the triumphal entry into Bordeaux of the Duc and Duchesse d'Agoulême in March 1815. But the economic outlook remained uncertain. Poor energy sources and a lack of raw materials held back the region's industrial development. Communication channels were still inadequate and underdeveloped, particularly in the Landes, which appeared to have been bypassed by the Industrial Revolution and remained largely rural. With a low birth rate (except in the Pyrenees), the region was also suffering from a shortage of manpower. Many people were also leaving to try their luck elsewhere: large numbers of Basques and people from Béarn left to seek their fortune in the United States, while the inhabitants of the Dordogne and Garonne valleys migrated north, to the Paris region.

The economist and parliamentarian Isaac Pereire, by Léon Bonnat

Expansion During the Second Empire

Thanks to the Pereire brothers, two enterprising financiers, Aquitaine did, however, blossom economically. Their efforts and lobbying had wide-reaching consequences: the pine forests of the Landes were greatly enlarged, fruit- and vegetable-growing and tobacco-farming were introduced in the Garonne valley and, in 1855, Bordeaux wines received their first official classification according to quality. In line with the huge increase in the region's wine exports, the ports of Bordeaux and Bayonne expanded and, with the development of the coastal resorts of Arcachon and Biarritz, tourism grew. Parallel to this economic growth was the rapid expansion of the various networks of communication, most particularly the railways. Whereas in the early 19th century it would take someone travelling from Bordeaux in a sluggish horse-drawn wagon 14 hours to reach the Arcachon

1840 | 1850 | 1860

1841 The region's first railway line, from to Bordeaux to La Teste, opens

1852 Louis-Napoleon gives a lecture in Bordeaux

1852–1870 Empress Eugénie visits the Basque coast and Pyrenean spa resorts

1855 Bordeaux wines are officially classified

1857 Creation of the town of Arcachon

Empress Eugén in Biarritz

1869 Bordeaux's vineyards are attac by the *Phylloxera* vine lc

basin, after the construction of the railway, it took only two. Meanwhile, town planning was going on everywhere. Boulevards were laid out in Bordeaux, Périgueux, Agen and Pau, and railway stations became a standard feature of 19th-century cities. Aquitaine had also become a magnet for an elite who sought to emulate the Emperor and Empress: Eugénie stayed at Biarritz on a number of occasions, and visited the Pyrenean spa resorts several times. The imperial couple also spent time at Arcachon. Finally, in 1857, Napoleon III passed a law making it compulsory to clean up huge tracts of land and plant them with maritime pines. He even set up an experimental plantation at Solférino. In 50 years, the forested areas of Aquitaine increased threefold, exceeding 1 million ha (2,471,000 acres). The vast open expanses of the Landes, which until then had been given over to sheep-farming, disappeared along with the emblematic shepherds on stilts.

Poster for the Exposition Maritime Internationale de Bordeaux, held in 1907

The Third Republic

Bordeaux became the capital of France on three occasions: in 1871, 1914 and 1940, when governments moved there to escape German invasions. At such times, the Grand-Théâtre was requisitioned as a makeshift parliament. In the interwar years, radical ideas spread through the Gironde, particularly in the Dordogne and Lot-et-Garonne. In Bordeaux, Adrien Marquet, its neo-Socialist mayor, was very popular, but tarnished his image by becoming involved with the Vichy regime in 1940. Bordeaux also hosted great exhibitions, such as the renowned Exposition Maritime Internationale of 1907.

Shepherds on traditional stilts in the Landes, before the area was turned over to forestry

1870

1871 Because of the Franco-Prussian War, the Assemblée Nationale sits in Bordeaux

1887 The vineyard fungicide, Bordeaux Mix, is marketed

1900

1907 The Exposition Maritime Internationale is held in Bordeaux

1914 The authorities move to Bordeaux

1925 Frugès, a new town in Pessac designed by Le Corbusier, is completed

1930

1940 Influx of refugees to Bordeaux. Aquitaine is divided by the demarcation line

Railway poster from the early 20th century

German troops outside Bordeaux's Grand-Théâtre, July 1940

The city also benefited from an economic boost created by its thriving food-processing and shipbuilding industries.

Industrial centres began to multiply elsewhere in the southwest, with ironworks established at Le Boucau, on the Adour river, and metalworks in Fumel. One firm, the Compagnie du Midi, started the process of bringing more modern facilities to the region by building hydro-electric dams in the Pyrenees. However, this was brought to a halt by the economic crisis of the 1930s and the looming conflict of World War II.

Général de Gaulle in Bordeaux in 1944

The Dark Years

After the Spanish Civil War, many Republican refugees, fleeing Franco's dictatorship, crossed the border into southwest France. When the country fell to Germany in May 1940, and the Germans occupied northern France, the French government, along with large numbers of French and Belgian refugees, hastily settled in Bordeaux and other towns and cities of the southwest. This influx caused serious hardship. After the Armistice of June 1940, the region was bisected by a demarcation line and, until 1942, Bordeaux and the whole Atlantic coast were occupied by the enemy. The French Résistance gradually came together, but the Gestapo and the French militia harshly cracked down on it. Fearing an Allied landing, the Germans installed a string of military bunkers, known as the Atlantic Wall, all along the coast. When Général de Gaulle returned to France in 1944, he visited Bordeaux in September, where he praised all those whose efforts had helped to liberate the country.

Late 20th Century

After 1945, and until the mid-1970s, severe unrest plagued southwest France. Political life was dominated by Jacques Chaban-Delmas, a Gaullist "baron" who was nicknamed the Duc d'Aquitaine. During the 1950s, the country was severely hit by a rural exodus. The rearing of ducks and cultivation of maize, however, developed in the Périgord and the Landes. Italian immigrants, whose knowledge and experience helped to

Jacques Chaban-Delmas

1945–95 Jacques Chaban-Delmas is deputy and mayor of Bordeaux

1951 Natural gas is discovered at Lacq

1954 Oil begins to be piped at Parentis

1962 French colonists from Algeria settle in Gascony

1967 The Pont d'Aquitaine in Bordeaux opens

1975 Beginning of the economic crisis, which affects Aquitaine particularly badly

1945 | **1955** | **1965** | **1975**

1942 German forces enter the unoccupied zone

1948 Conseil Interprofessionnel du Vin de Bordeaux (CIVB) is set up

Logo of the Parc des Landes de Gascogne

1970 The Parc Naturel Régional des Landes de Gascogne is created

1979 CAPC is founded in Bordeaux

1984 Lascaux II is officially opened by Jack Lang

boost the region's agricultural potential, were especially instrumental in this development. A similar process occurred after 1962 when colonists, returning from the newly independent Algeria, set up fruit- and vegetable-growing farms along the region's main rivers. In the Bordeaux area, the Conseil Interprofessional du Vin de Bordeaux (CIVB), established in 1948, secured foreign markets for the region's wines. By contrast, at the end of the 1960s, there was a downturn in some traditional industries and many firms were forced to close. Shoe factories, metalworks and some food-processing plants were particularly badly affected.

However, the discovery of natural gas at Lacq and of oil deposits at Parentis in the early 1950s helped to boost the economy in the south of the region, turning Pau into a major industrial centre. The aeronautics companies Dassault and SOGERMA, and the car-maker Ford, also set up factories in greater Bordeaux.

In the early 1970s, the global oil crisis drove many factories out of business. Yet the process of modernization continued in towns and cities: certain sites, like Mériadeck in Bordeaux, became important business centres, while Agen became a focus for agricultural production. Communications networks (such as TGV Atlantique) opened up the region, placing it firmly on the European economic stage.

Alain Juppé, French politician, re-elected mayor of Bordeaux in 2006

The 1970s also saw tourism take off around the Arcachon Basin and in the Pays Basque, where it is now the main money-spinner. The opening of the Parc Naturel Régional des Landes de Gascogne and the Parc National des Pyrénées has helped draw in thousands of visitors. And there has been an influx of people buying holiday homes, particularly in the Périgord, drawn by the variety and beauty of the landscape, as well as the mild climate.

A tram, symbol of Bordeaux's modernity, on the city's Pont de Pierre

1999 A violent storm destroys forests in the Landes and the Médoc

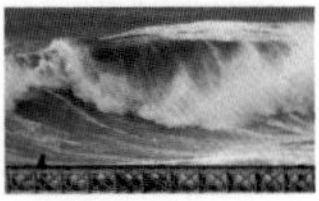

2009 Another violent storm devastates the region

1995 | 2005 | 2015 | 2020

Cave painting at Lascaux II

2003 Inauguration of Bordeaux's tramway

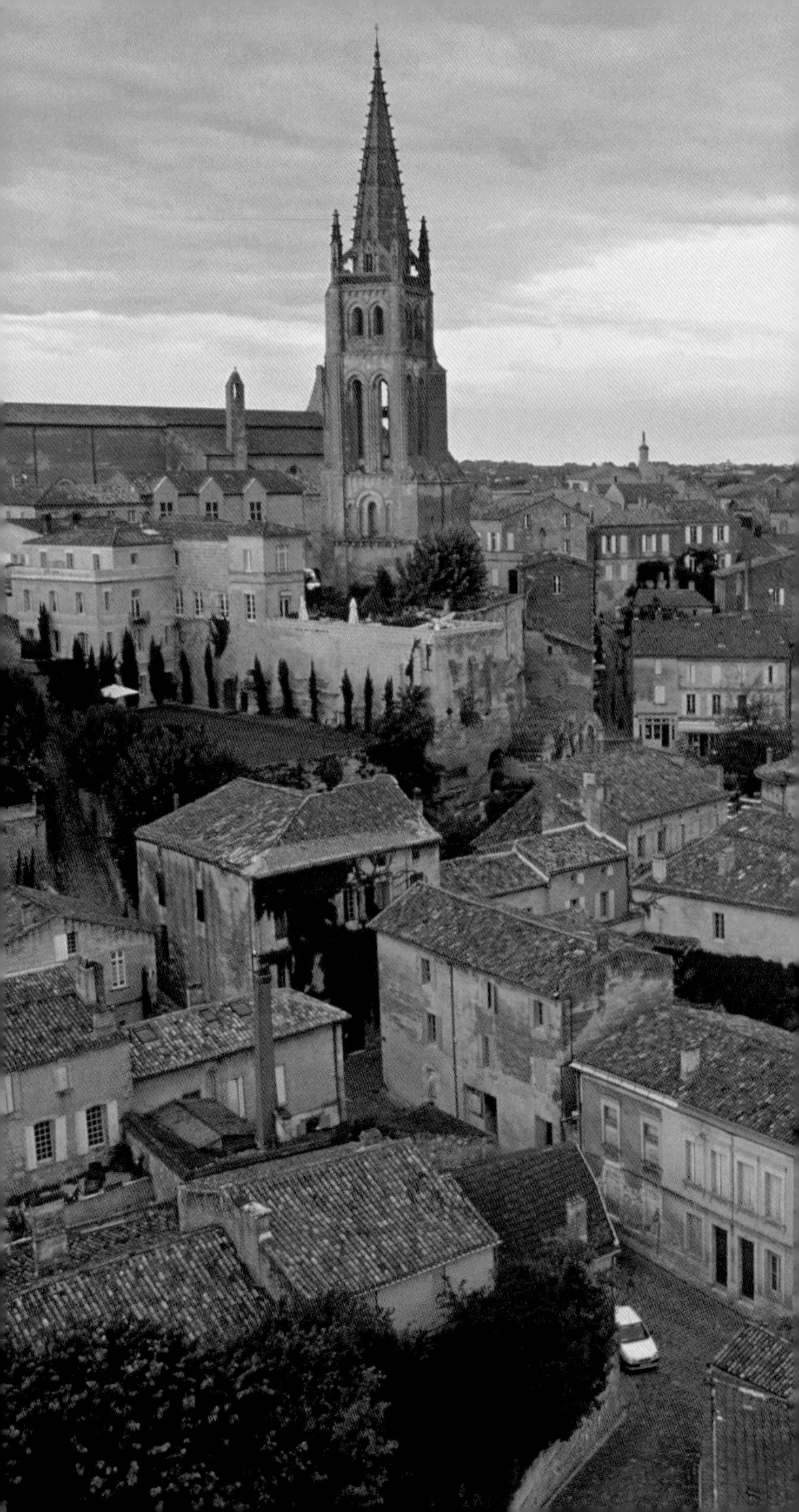

AQUITAINE REGION BY REGION

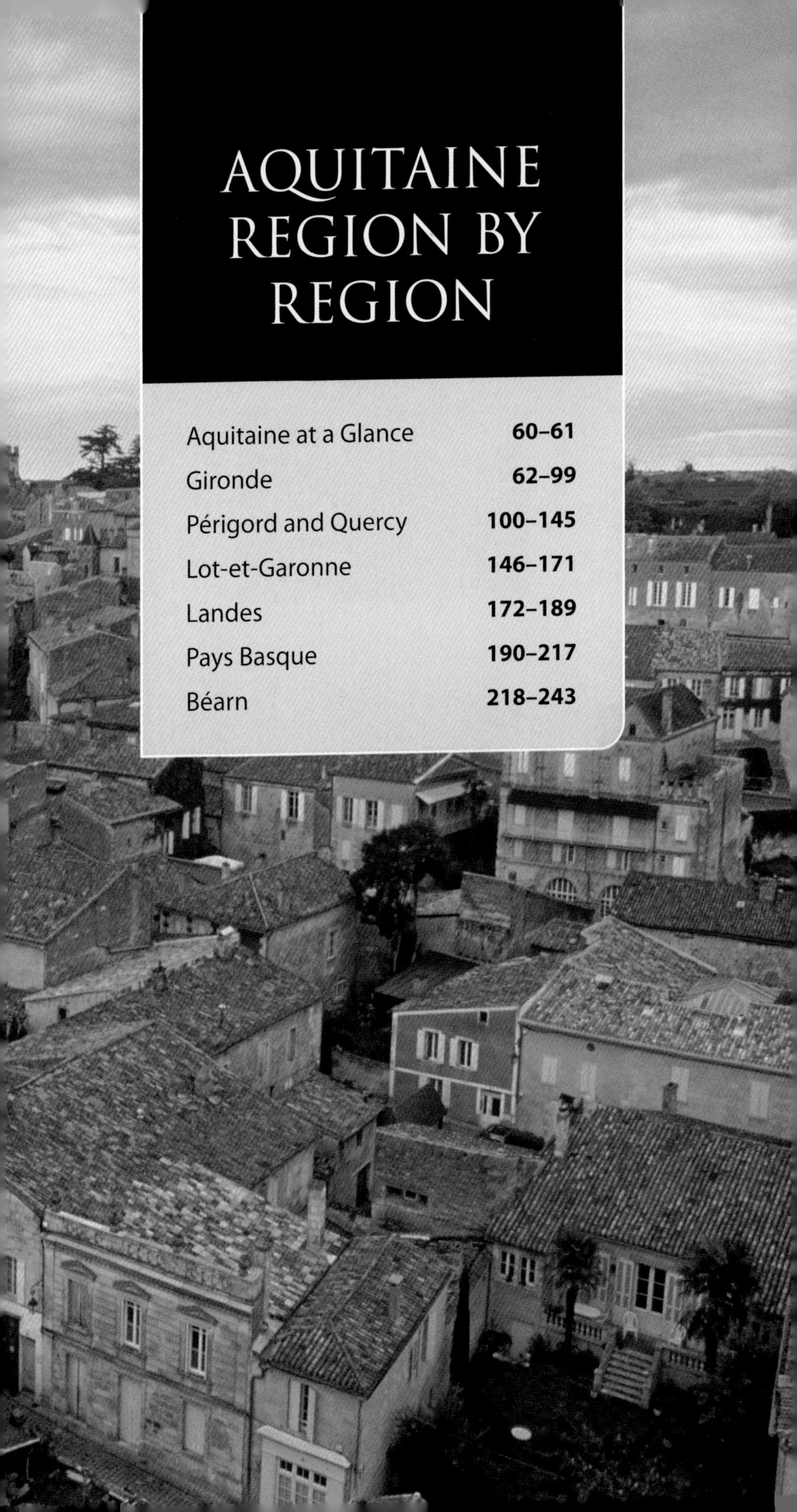

Aquitaine at a Glance

The sandy beaches of Aquitaine, which stretch all along its Atlantic coastline and around the Arcachon Basin, attract large numbers of visitors every summer. In the south, the Pyrenees offer spectacular scenery and mountaineering. And, in addition, the whole region is alive with history, being full of picturesque *bastide* towns, historic fortresses, stately châteaux and majestic abbeys. Bordeaux, the capital, owes its wealth to its local wines. Thanks to their superb quality, the city has become the focus of the most prestigious wine trade in France.

Château Margaux produces one of the world's finest wines. Besides its great vineyards, the estate includes an elegant Neo-Classical château and wine cellars with unusual vaulting.

The Landes coast is a long, more or less straight stretch, lined with sandy beaches that attract many summer visitors. Landes pines are adapted to this soil, covering around 1 million ha (2.5 million acres), Europe's largest forested area.

Basque folk traditions are an important aspect of Aquitaine's cultural identity. The white shirt and trousers, red sash and scarf, and beret, are mostly worn at traditional festivals.

◀ View of Saint-Émilion, in the Gironde

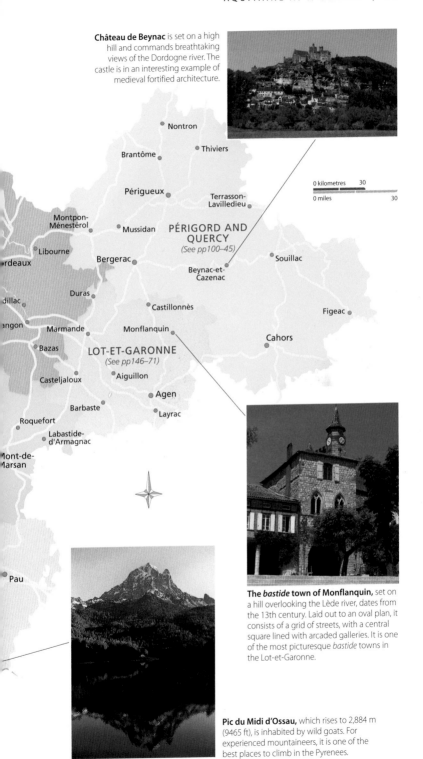

Château de Beynac is set on a high hill and commands breathtaking views of the Dordogne river. The castle is in an interesting example of medieval fortified architecture.

The *bastide* town of Monflanquin, set on a hill overlooking the Lède river, dates from the 13th century. Laid out to an oval plan, it consists of a grid of streets, with a central square lined with arcaded galleries. It is one of the most picturesque *bastide* towns in the Lot-et-Garonne.

Pic du Midi d'Ossau, which rises to 2,884 m (9465 ft), is inhabited by wild goats. For experienced mountaineers, it is one of the best places to climb in the Pyrenees.

GIRONDE

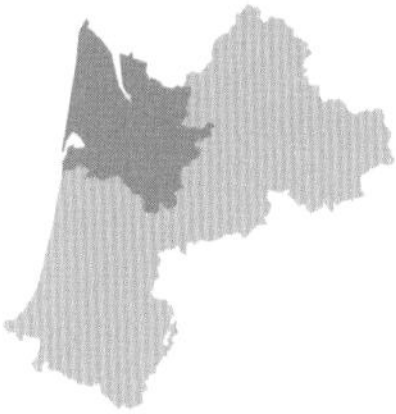

From the banks of the Garonne and the Dordogne to the port of Bordeaux, the capital city, and from Blaye in the north to Bazas in the south, the Gironde's prestigious vineyards cover a substantial part of the region. The Gironde also has a rich and varied cultural heritage, along with a long stretch of sandy coastline that is perfect both for relaxing and for enjoying watersports.

The great waves crashing on to the sandy beaches of Gironde's Atlantic seaboard offer surfers and other watersports enthusiasts near perfect conditions. Similarly, the banks of the Gironde Estuary are a paradise for anglers, and are also lined with a succession of prestigious wine-producing châteaux and some magnificent Romanesque and Gothic architecture. Thanks to its many fine buildings, Bordeaux, the region's largest port in the 18th century, still retains an atmosphere that is both majestic and elegant.

The Romans were among the first to exploit the Gironde's potential. They laid out vineyards on the hillsides, where they built sumptuous villas. Today Bordeaux wines include many world-class *appellations*, from Médoc to Saint-Émilion, and from Graves to Sauternes. Pioneering medieval monks erected prestigious abbeys, such as the Abbaye de Saint-Ferme and Abbaye de Sauve-Majeure. Status was conferred on the region when Pope Clement V laid claim to territory in Uzeste and Villandraut. In their turn, the English rulers established the *bastide* towns such as Monségur and Sauveterre-de-Guyenne.

The late 19th century witnessed the discovery of the health-giving benefits of the sea air at Arcachon and Soulac, and the coming of the railways, making the region accessible. Yet, although the Arcachon Basin is now a prime holiday destination, traditional trades like oyster-farming remain important to the economy.

Finally, the Gironde boasts links to many illustrious Frenchmen, including the philosopher Montesquieu, the writer Montaigne, the painter Albert Marquet and the novelist François Mauriac.

A flat-bottomed fishing smack, typical of the Arcachon Basin

◀ The elegant Place de la Bourse in Bordeaux

Exploring the Gironde

Covering an area of around 10,700 sq km (4,130 sq miles), the Gironde is named after the estuary at the confluence of the Dordogne and Garonne rivers. It is known mainly for its capital city, Bordeaux, and for the Arcachon Basin, but the region also has many vine-growing areas that produce some of the world's most famous wines. Dotted across the landscape are numerous châteaux in a variety of architectural styles, as well as many elegant cathedrals, churches and *bastide* towns. The Gironde's Atlantic coast and its lakesides are ideal for cycling, swimming and other watersports.

The Region at a Glance

1 Phare de Cordouan
2 Pointe de Grave
3 Soulac-sur-Mer
4 Lac d'Hourtin Carcans
5 Lacanau
6 *Arcachon Basin pp68–9*
7 Arcachon
8 Dune du Pyla
9 *Bordeaux pp72–9*
11 Margaux
12 Moulis-en-Médoc
13 Fort-Médoc
14 Pauillac
15 Blaye
16 Bourg
17 Libourne
18 *Saint-Émilion p84*
20 Entre-deux-Mers
21 La Sauve-Majeure
22 Castillon-la-Bataille
23 Rauzan
24 Blasimon
25 Sainte-Foy-la-Grande
26 Sauveterre-de-Guyenne
27 Abbaye de Saint-Ferme
28 Monségur
29 La Réole
30 *Roquetaillade pp92–3*
31 Saint-Macaire
32 Cadillac
33 La Brède
34 Graves
35 Barsac
36 Malle
37 Sauternais
38 Villandraut
39 *Cazeneuve pp98–9*
40 Uzeste
41 Bazas

Tours

10 Tour of the Médoc
19 Vineyards of Saint-Émilion

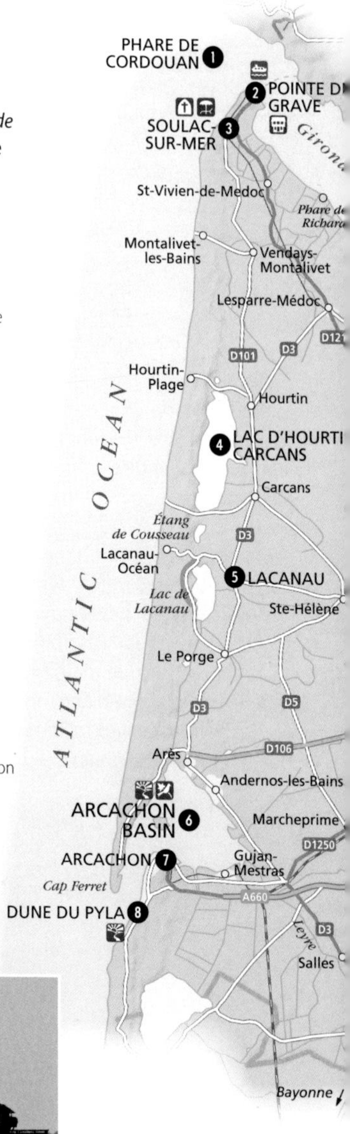

Picturesque fishermen's huts on stilts in the Arcachon Basin

For map symbols *see back flap*

Château Rayne-Vigneau, one of many elegant country residences in the Sauternais

Getting Around

Bordeaux, capital of the Gironde, has an international airport at Mérignac. The TGV (high-speed train) links Paris and Bordeaux in three hours, stopping at Libourne, and continuing to Arcachon (four hours) in the high season. The A10 motorway from Paris to Bordeaux runs through the Gironde. The A63, and its continuation, the A660, connects Bordeaux and the Arcachon Basin to the west. From Bordeaux, the A89 runs to Libourne and continues eastward into the Dordogne.

❶ Phare de Cordouan

The lighthouse's elegant silhouette rises up against the skyline 7 km (4 miles) to the west of Pointe de Grave. Designed by Louis de Foix, work on it began in 1584, although ten years later Henri IV had the original plans altered. In 1611, a Renaissance-style tower was added and, in 1789, the engineer Teulère increased the height to 67.5 m (220 ft). The lighthouse was declared a historic monument in 1862 and, because of its restrained classical style, soon became known as the "Versailles of the Sea".

VISITORS' CHECKLIST

Practical Information
Road map B1. Le Verdon-sur-Mer; 05 56 09 61 78. **Open** Apr–Oct: daily. **Closed** Fri & when keepers change over.

Transport
Pointe de Grave.

Visiting the lighthouse
At low tide, the 260-m (850-ft) long causeway, leading up to the lighthouse, is accessible on foot.

Lantern The beam from the halogen light can be seen from a distance 40 km (25 miles).

Stairwell

Entrance

Doric columns frame the monumental portico.

Parapet

Outer stairway

Chapelle Notre-Dame-de-Cordouan
The stained-glass windows date from the 19th century.

An Engineering Feat

The lighthouse is encircled by an outer wall 41 m (135 ft) long and 8.3 m (27 ft) high. This entire structure is built upon a large, rocky sea plateau.

King's Apartments
In the Renaissance style, these are on the first floor.

An elegant coastal-resort villa at Soulac-sur-Mer

❷ Pointe de Grave

Road map B1. Le Verdon-sur-Mer. Pointe de Grave; 05 56 09 61 78. **littoral33.com**

The lighthouse here, the **Phare de Grave**, houses the Musée du Phare de Cordouan et des Phares et Balises, with exhibits illustrating the daily life of a lighthouse-keeper. The 107 steps to the top of the 28-m (92-ft) tall lighthouse lead to a platform with panoramic views of the Phare de Cordouan out at sea, the beaches along the coast and the port at **Le Verdon**.

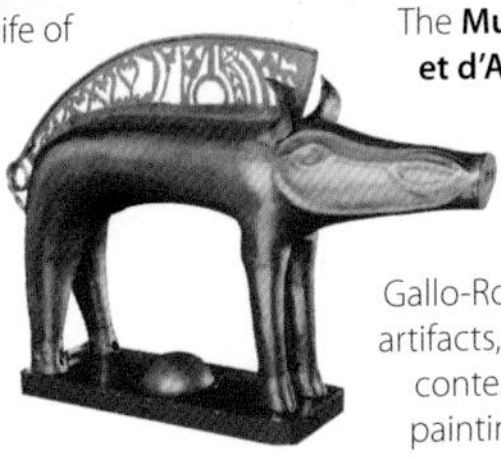
Gaulish cult figure of a wild boar

Environs
About 15 km (9 miles) southeast of Pointe de Grave is the **Phare de Richard**, with its lighthouse and oyster museum.

Phare de Grave
Tel 05 56 09 00 25. **Open** May–Oct: pm Fri–Mon (Jul, Aug: daily).

Phare de Richard
Tel 05 56 09 42 12. **Open** Mar–Jun, Sep, Oct: pm Wed–Mon; Jul, Aug: daily.

❸ Soulac-sur-Mer

Road map B1. 2,714. 68 rue de la Plage; 05 56 09 86 61. daily. **soulac.com**

Backed by a forest and fronted by the ocean, Soulac developed during the Second Empire (1852–70), when a resort served by the railway line was built here. Attractive villas sprang up in the late 19th and early 20th centuries. Soulac has fine sandy beaches, the Plage Amélie and Plage la Négade. The latter is a nudist beach (like the one at Vendays-Montalivet 18 km/ 12 miles away).

A UNESCO World Heritage Site, the **Basilique Notre-Dame-de-la-Fin-des-Terres** lies on the route taken by pilgrims travelling from Britain to Santiago de Compostela. This great 12th-century Romanesque church has superb modern stained-glass windows and carved capitals.

The **Musée d'Art et d'Archéologie** contains exhibits of prehistoric, Gaulish and Gallo-Roman artifacts, as well as contemporary paintings and sculptures.

Basilique Notre-Dame-de-la-Fin-des-Terres
Open daily.

Musée d'Art et d'Archéologie
1 avenue El-Burgo-de-Osma.
Tel 05 56 09 83 99. **Open** Apr–Sep. **Closed** Mon in Apr–Jun & Sep.

❹ Lac d'Hourtin-Carcans

Road map B1. Place du Port, Hourtin-Port; 05 56 09 19 00. **medococean.com**

Some 17 km (11 miles) long and with a surface area in excess of 7,500 ha (18,000 acres), this lake is one of the largest in France. Its shores are a good place to spot wildlife, such as herons, foxes, rabbits and hares. Plants include *Lobelia dortmanna* and several insect-devouring species, such as sundew and pitcher plants.

Environs
The nearby resort of **Carcans-Maubuisson** offers tennis, cycling, horse riding and watersports. It also has a museum of local culture, the Maison des Arts et Traditions Populaires.

❺ Lacanau

Road map B2. 4,381. Place de l'Europe, Lacanau-Océan; 05 56 03 21 01. Wed am. **medococean.com**

With a surface area of 2,000 ha (5,000 acres), the Lac de Lacanau is ideal for sailing and sailboarding. For over 20 years, Lacanau-Océan has hosted a stage of the world surfing championship. It also has a large number of early 20th-century seaside villas, particulary in rue Faugère.

Environs
The **Étang de Cousseau**, 5 km (3 miles) northeast of Lacanau, is a lake with a nature reserve.

Summer visitors on the long sandy beach at Lacanau-Océan

❻ Arcachon Basin

Lying between the Dune du Pilat and the tip of Cap-Ferret, the Arcachon Basin forms a huge triangle more than 100 km (60 miles) long. Being almost completely enclosed, it is like the Gironde's inner sea. At high tide, it holds 370 million cu m (1,300 million cu ft) of water, with a surface area of 156 sq km (60 sq miles). At low tide, only about a quarter of this remains, as the water recedes to reveal sandbanks, mudflats and salt meadows. The basin is an important sanctuary for many birds, including the pied oystercatcher, the common curlew and the great cormorant, as well as for migratory birds, such as sandpipers, avocets and graylag geese, that pass through the nature reserves at the Banc d'Arguin and the Parc Ornithologique du Teich. All around the basin are small oysterfarming communities.

Sailing in the Arcachon Basin

Huts on stilts

These wooden houses on stilts are known as *maisons tchanquées* in Gascon, "*tchanque*" meaning "stilts". They can be seen all around the Arcachon Basin.

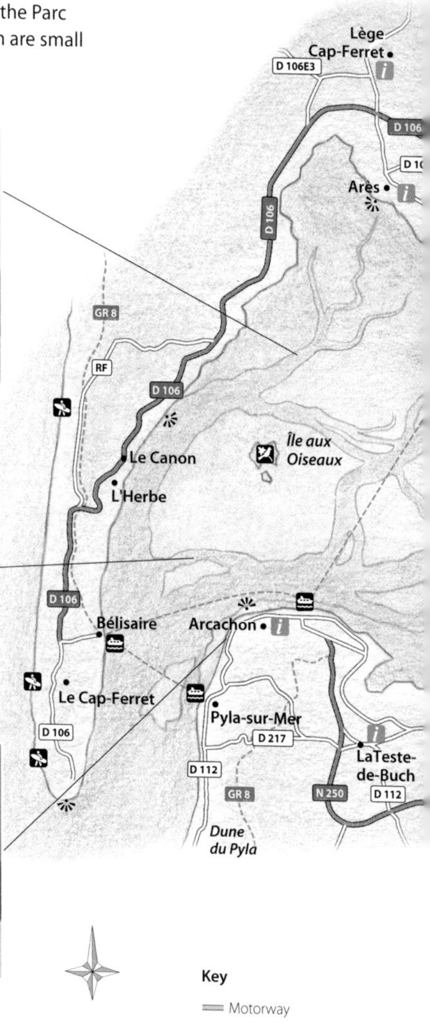

At low tide, the water level in the basin recedes to reveal sandbanks

0 kilometres 1

0 miles 1

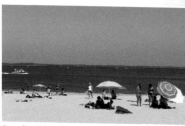

Arcachon's beaches

The soft sand, stretching for several kilometres along Plage Péreire and Plage du Moulleau, two of the Arcachon beaches, makes them a paradise for summer visitors. These safe, family-friendly shores are perfect for swimming.

Key

Motorway

Major road

Minor road

For map symbols *see back flap*

A *pinasse*
Swift and stable, *pinasses* are designed to safely navigate the shallow waters that conceal the basin's sandbanks.

VISITORS' CHECKLIST

Practical Information
Road map B2. Arcachon 05 57 52 97 97; La Teste de Buch 05 56 54 63 14; Gujan-Mestras 05 56 66 12 65; Le Teich 05 56 22 80 93; Biganos & Audenge 05 56 26 95 97; Lanton 05 57 70 26 55; Andernos 05 56 82 02 95; Arès 05 56 60 18 07; Lège-Cap-Ferret 05 56 03 94 49.
arcachon.com

Transport
Arcachon, Andernos, La Teste de Buch. Transbassin, a public ferry sails between Arcachon and Cap-Ferret.

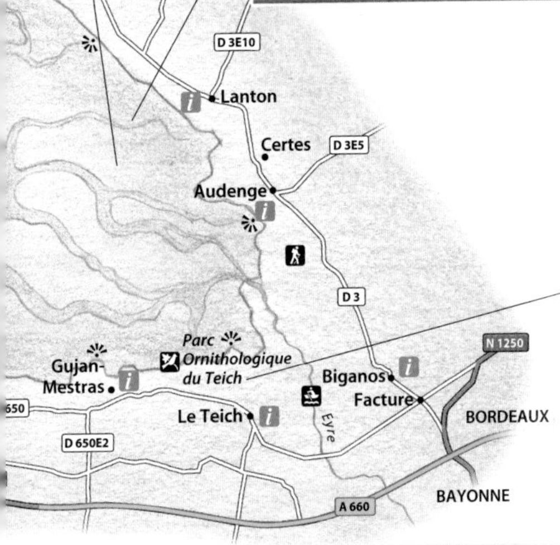

Shipping in the basin
Fishing boats, yachts, *pinasses* and the motor cruisers that provide a regular service between Arcachon and Cap-Ferret are part of the ceaseless traffic that criss-crosses the basin.

Parc Ornithologique du Teich
This bird sanctuary was created in 1971 to preserve a natural habitat and protect a number of bird species.

Oyster-Farming in the Basin

Oyster-farming in the waters here developed in the 1860s, when the first experimental oyster beds were installed by the naturalist J M Coste. It takes several years for oysters to reach maturity. Spat (larval oysters) are grown on lime-washed tiles. In spring, the spat are detached from the tiles and transferred to oyster-beds, about 4–5 km (2.5–3 miles) out to sea, and left to grow. It takes 18 months to three years for the larval oysters to reach maturity. They are then washed and packed into creels, ready to sell. The Arcachon Basin produces around 8–10,000 tonnes of oysters a year.

An oyster-farm worker in the early 20th century

Exploring the Arcachon Basin

This shallow, tidal gulf is surrounded by a variety of different landscapes.

Gujan-Mestras

19 avenue de Lattre-de-Tassigny; 05 56 66 12 65. Wed. Foire aux Huîtres (first two weeks in Aug).

This small town with seven harbours produces 55 per cent of all the oysters farmed in the basin and is the local capital of oyster farming. The **Maison de l'huître**, an information centre, is located in Larros harbour. *Pinasses*, long slender boats made of Landes pine, are anchored in the channels here.

Maison de l'Huître
Tel 05 56 66 23 73. **Open** Jul–Aug: daily; Sep–Jun: Mon–Sat. **Closed** 2 weeks over Christmas.

Lège-Cap-Ferret Peninsula

1 avenue du Général-de-Gaulle; 05 56 03 94 49.

Sandy beaches stretch for 22 km (14 miles) along the western side of this thickly wooded peninsula. On its eastern side, which faces onto the basin, there are sheltered beaches at Claouey, Grand-Piquey, Petit-Piquey and Piraillan. The unspoilt oyster-farming villages of **Canon** and **L'Herbe** can be explored on foot. Most of their tiny cottages are now second homes. The Moorish-style chapel at L'Herbe is all that remains of the Villa Algérienne, a grand residence located between La Vigne and L'Herbe, that was demolished in 1965. The peninsula's smartest resort is at **Phare du Cap-Ferret**. The lighthouse here, with a curious red lantern, looks out over the basin from a height of 53 m (174 ft).

A fisherman's hut, with a square dipping-net

Phare du Cap-Ferret
Tel 05 56 03 94 49. **Open** Apr–Sep: daily; Oct–Mar: pm Wed–Sun. **Closed** Nov–Dec.

Île aux Oiseaux

Lying 3 km (2 miles) north of Arcachon, this island is named for the many sea birds that flock here. The island is also an oyster-farming centre, and is popular with hunters, who lie in wait for their prey in hides. Raised on stilts, these wooden huts are known as *cabanes tchanquées*, from the Gascon word *"tchanque"*, meaning "stilt".

Seagull

Parc Ornithologique du Teich

Maison de la Nature du Bassin d'Arcachon; 05 56 22 80 93. **Open** daily. **parc-ornithologique-du-teich.com**

This 120-ha (300-acre) nature reserve, on the basin's wildest shores along the Eyrre Delta, was created around the brackish waters of abandoned salt meadows. Up to 260 species of migratory birds can be seen here throughout the year. Heron, wild ducks, egrets, storks, swans and bluethroats may be observed in a natural setting, with salt-loving plants such as false willow and tamarisk growing nearby.

Domaine de Certes

Audenge; 05 56 26 95 97. naturalist guides Jul & Aug, organised by Audenge tourist office.

The fish-farming shallows at Certes consist of large expanses of fresh and salt water, covering around 400 ha (990 acres) and interconnected by the odd patch of dry land. Sea bass, grey mullet and sea bream are farmed here. The estate was purchased by the Conservatoire du Littoral in 1984. A footpath runs along the coast, and birdwatchers will be able to see a wide variety of species, including herons, cormorants and ducks, in their natural habitat.

Andernos-les-Bains

Esplanade du Broustic; 05 56 82 02 95.

This family-oriented resort nestles on the northeastern shore of the basin. Although there is no water here at low tide, Andernos is still very popular and is crowded with visitors in summer. When the tide is in, its many small beaches are ideal for relaxing and swimming.

The resort also has an oyster-farm and a marina at Le Bétey, with a 232-m (761-ft) jetty, the longest in France. On the shore stand the ruins of an Early Christian basilica and the Église Saint-Éloi, a charming church with a 12th-century apse.

Audenge, an oyster-farming coastal village, with colourfully painted huts

For hotels and restaurants in this region see pp250–51 and pp262–3

❼ Arcachon

Road map B2. 11,854. (for Cap-Ferret). Esplanade Georges-Pompidou; 05 57 52 97 97. daily (Oct–Jun: Tue–Sun). Le Printemps d'Arcachon (Mar); 18 Heures à la Voile et Tchanquetas (end Jun–beg Jul); Fêtes de la Mer (14–15 Aug). **arcachon.com**

It was thanks to Napoleon III, who fell in love with the place, that Arcachon began to develop as a coastal resort. This process was completed by the arrival of the railway in 1857. Arcachon is one of the most spread-out towns in France, covering 20,000 ha (49,420 acres) and almost merging with the neighbouring La Teste-de-Buch. A marina was built in the 1960s, and the long pier on the busy seafront serves as the town's central meeting place.

In Parc Pereire, modern villas, set in exquisitely kept gardens, look down onto the coast road. At the **Musée-Aquarium**, beside the beach and near the casino, visitors can view exhibits on the local marine life that is found in local waters.

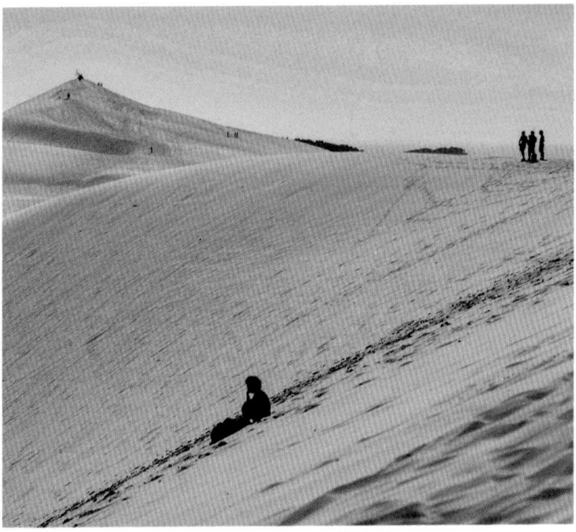

The ever-changing Dune du Pyla, currently 117 m (384 ft) high

Musée-Aquarium
2 rue du Professeur-Jolyet. **Tel** 05 56 54 89 28. **Open** Feb–Nov: daily.

Château Deganne, now Arcachon's casino

❽ Dune du Pyla

Road map B2. Rond-Point du Figuier, Pyla-sur-Mer; 05 56 54 02 22 or 05 56 22 12 85 (summer).

This is literally France's most moving monument. About 3 km (2 miles) long, 500 m (550 ft) wide and 105 m (350 ft) high, the Dune du Pyla is the highest sand dune in Europe. It overlooks the Banc d'Arguin and is covered with beachgrass, sea holly, gilly flowers and convolvulus. It was formed partly by the action of westerly winds, which lift and blow the sand from the banks along the valleys. In 1855, it was only 35 m (114 ft) high, but grows by 1–4 m (3–13 ft) a year. From the top of the dune, there is a splendid view of the Forêt de la Test and the Atlantic Ocean.

Priceless Architectural Heritage

The Ville d'Hiver (Winter Town) at Arcachon was created by the Pereire brothers, bankers who had settled in the region. In 1862, they purchased some 400 ha (988 acres) of wooded dunes above Arcachon, which they divided into plots. They commissioned the architect Régnaud and the landscape designer Alphand to build handsome villas suitable for the visitors who came to Arcachon for health cures – the resinous air was renowned for its therapeutic qualities. Surrounded by pines and sheltered from the wind, the Ville d'Hiver comprised 300 villas. Every one is different: Moorish villas, colonial residences and neo-Gothic manor houses cluster round place des Palmiers. Cornices, corbelling, fretted gables, balconies with pierced wooden balustrades, and semicircular and dormer windows grace these elegant structures. In the 19th century, visitors here included the Italian writer Gabriele D'Annunzio, at Villa Saint-Dominique, and the composer Charles Gounod, who frequently stayed at Villa Faust.

A villa at Arcachon

❾ Street-by-Street: Bordeaux

Built on a curve of the river Garonne, Bordeaux has been a major port since pre-Roman times, but today there is little evidence of this ancient history. Always a forward-looking place, the city underwent a radical transformation in the 18th century. Today its industrial and maritime sprawl is scattered around a mix of grand boulevards and noble, Neo-Classical squares. Facing directly on to the waterfront lies the place de la Bourse, flanked by a row of elegant wine-merchants' houses, originally built to mask the medieval slums that once lay behind. The magnificence of the Esplanade des Quinconces sweeps down to the river, offering a fine view of the lavishly decorated Monument aux Girodins from the quayside. Also striking is the place des Grands-Hommes, near the Église Notre-Dame, a rare example of town planning in Bordeaux at the time of the Revolution.

Église Notre-Dame was begun in 1684 and completed in 1707.

Bar à Vins and Ecole du Vin du CIVB hold professional wine tastings.

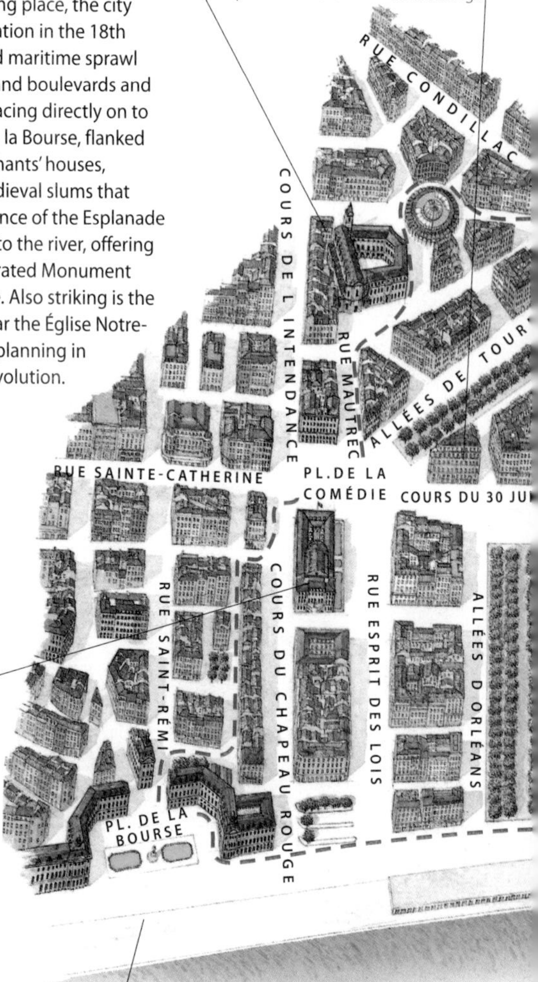

★ Grand-Théâtre
The façade of this building (1773–80) is decorated with statues of the nine Muses, and the goddesses Juno, Minerva and Venus.

Key

— Suggested route

★ Place de la Bourse
A masterpiece of architectural harmony, this square is flanked by two majestic 18th-century buildings, the Bourse (old Stock Exchange) and the Hôtel des Fermes (now housing the Musée des Douanes).

VISITORS' CHECKLIST

Practical Information
Road map C2. 235,890. 12 cours du 30-Juillet; 05 56 00 66 00 & 28 rue des Argentiers; 05 56 48 04 24. Fête Le Fleuve, with food & wine fair (Jun); Fête du Vin (Jun) **bordeaux-tourisme.com**

Transport
10 km (6 miles) west of Bordeaux. Gare Saint-Jean. Esplanade des Quinconces.

Monument aux Girondins
Fountains in the form of statues, symbolizing the Triumph of Concord and of the Republic, flank this monument (1894–1902). It is crowned by a statue of Liberty breaking free of her shackles.

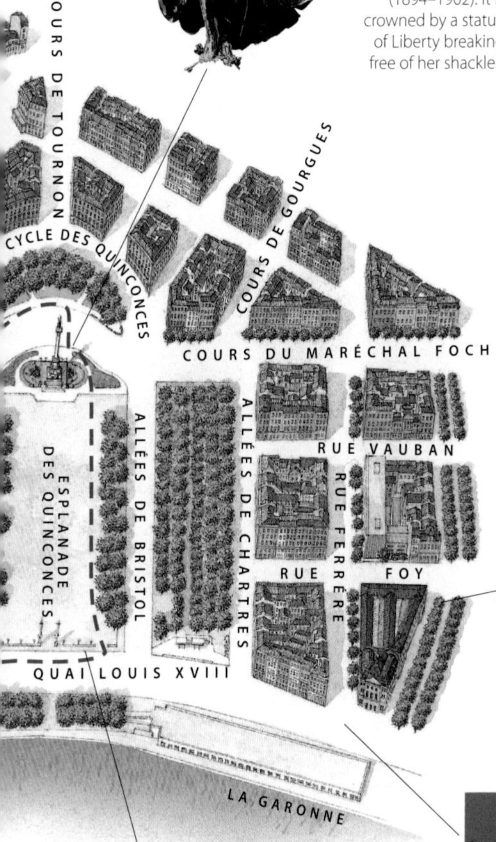

CAPC (Centre d'Art Plastique Contemporain)
The museum of modern art is housed in an early 19th-century port warehouse.

★ Esplanade des Quinconces
Surrounded by trees and set with statues of Montaigne and Montesquieu, this space was laid out in 1827–58.

Les Chartrons
This area, once inhabited by wealthy wine merchants, has been restored. Its fine town houses are highly sought after.

Exploring Bordeaux

Meticulous restoration has enhanced the many splendours of Bordeaux: the richly decorated façades of its majestic buildings; the glorious Gothic churches that hint at its importance in medieval Europe; entire quarters that have been pedestrianized; and quays that offer long riverside walks. All these invite the visitor to explore the city's riches. Particularly impressive is the 18th-century Neo-Classical architecture, dating from a time when Bordeaux began to grow and prosper. The spacious squares, tree-lined avenues and elegant town houses all date from this time.

Quartier Saint-Pierre

Located between the Garonne and the city centre, this quarter was enclosed by walls, which were demolished in the 18th century. Now restored, it is pleasant to explore on foot. What is now **place de la Bourse** was laid out by the Gabriels, a father-and-son team of architects, in 1729–55, when the square was known as place Royale. On its north side is the Bourse and on the south the Hôtel des Fermes, its upper storey set with columns on ornate pediments. Decorative carving covers the majestic façades here, with masks and ironwork on the balconies. In the square's centre is the Fontaine des Trois-Grâces, erected in 1864 to replace a statue of Louis XV. Lined with restaurants and cafés, **place du Parlement**, formerly place du Marché-Royal, commissioned by Tourny in 1754, is a masterpiece of architectural harmony. Louis-XV town houses surround a paved courtyard, containing a neo-Rococo fountain that dates from 1867. On **place Saint-Pierre,** where an organic-food market is held on Thursdays, is the Église Saint-Pierre, built in the 14th–15th centuries and remodelled in the 19th century.

Musée National des Douanes

1 place de la Bourse. **Tel** 05 56 48 82 82. **Open** Tue–Sun. **Closed** 25 Dec, 1 Jan.

Occupying a part of the Hôtel des Fermes that formerly served as a customs house, this museum, the only one of its kind in France, traces the history and work of French customs officers up to the present day. Exhibits include a fine painting by Monet, *La Cabane du Douanier, Effet d'Après-midi* (1882).

Porte Cailhau

Place du Palais. **Open** Jun–Sep: daily pm.

This city gate offers good views of Pont de Pierre and the north bank of the river. The gate was built in 1495 to honour a victory won by the French king, Charles VIII, in Italy. It has both decorative features (small windows and a slated, conical roof) and defensive elements (a portcullis, machicolation and a crenellated gallery).

Carved frieze on the façade of the Musée d'Aquitaine

West door of Cathédrale Saint-André

Cathédrale Saint-André

Place Pey-Berland. **Open** daily.

A UNESCO World Heritage Site, this is the finest of all Bordeaux's churches. It was consecrated in 1096 by Pope Urban II, who had come to the city to preach in favour of the First Crusade. The nave, built in the 11th and 12th centuries, was altered in the 15th century. Depictions of the apostles, bishops and martyrs, and of the Last Judgment, adorn the west and north doors and the entrance to the southern wing of the transept (built in the 13th–14th centuries). The cathedral was restored in the 19th century, having been used to store animal feed during the Revolution.

Fountain on place du Parlement

Musée d'Aquitaine

20 cours Pasteur. **Tel** 05 56 01 51 00. **Open** Tue–Sun. **Closed** public hols.

Built in 1886 as the Faculty of Literature and Science, this building was converted into a museum in 1987. Its four floors display a large archeological collection. Among the prehistoric artifacts are the Venus of Laussel. Gaulish items include an outstanding hoard of gold from Tayac, and Roman pieces include a bronze figure of Hercules *(see p38)*. Also on display is a varied collection of pieces dating from the Middle Ages right up to the 19th century, including regional furniture and everyday objects. Another important aspect of the museum is its African and Oceanic collections.

Tour Pey-Berland

Place Pey-Berland. **Tel** 05 56 81 26 25. **Open** Jun–Sep: daily; Oct–May: Tue–Sun. **Closed** 1 Jan, 1 May, 25 Dec.

Built in the Flamboyant Gothic style (1440–46), this is the cathedral's bell tower. At the top sits a regilded 19th-century statue of Notre-Dame-d'Aquitaine. There are fine views of the city from its two terraces.

Centre National Jean-Moulin

Place Jean Moulin. **Tel** 05 56 10 19 90. **Open** pm Tue–Sun. **Closed** public hols.

This centre, established in 1967, is devoted to the French Resistance, the deportation of France's Jews and the wartime role of the Free French.

Grosse Cloche, vestige of Porte Saint-Éloi

Grosse Cloche

Rue Saint-James.

This clock is the only surviving vestige of Porte Saint-Éloi, the city gate that was built in the ramparts in the 13th century. It was the belfry of the former city hall.

Palais Rohan

Place Pey-Berland.

Wed.

Dating from 1771–83, this was built as the residence of Archbishop Mériadec de Rohan. Since 1937, it has housed the city hall. The building consists of extensive living quarters, flanked by low wings set at right angles to enclose a courtyard. Features of particular note are the lavishly decorated dining-room and grand staircase.

Bordeaux City Centre

1. Centre d'Art Plastique Contemporain (CAPC)
2. Monument aux Girondins
3. Eglise Notre-Dame
4. Grand-Théâtre
5. Musée National des Douanes
6. Porte Cailhau
7. Grosse Cloche
8. Musée d'Aquitaine
9. Cathédrale Saint-André
10. Palais Rohan
11. Musée des Beaux-Arts
12. Musée des Arts Décoratifs
13. Centre National Jean-Moulin

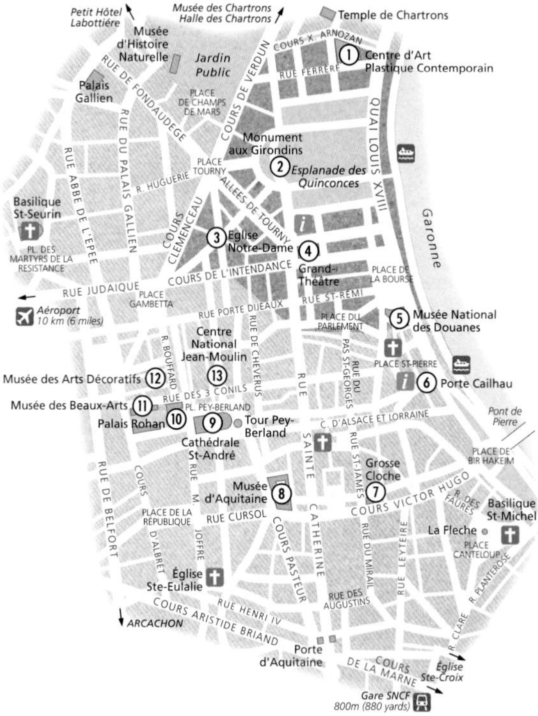

Key

Street-by-Street map *(pp72–3)*

0 metres 800
0 yards 800

For map symbols *see back flap*

Grand-Théâtre

The maréchal-duc de Richelieu, who was governor of Guyenne, commissioned Victor Louis (1731–1811) to design and build the Grand-Théâtre. A fine example of the Neo-Classical style, it was constructed between 1773 and 1780 on the site of a Gallo-Roman temple, known as the Piliers de Tutelle. Built to a rectangular plan 88 m by 47 m (290 ft by 155 ft), the building is surrounded by vaulted galleries and faced with 12 Corinthian columns. Above are stone statues of the nine Muses and the goddesses Juno, Venus and Minerva. The columned atrium, monumental staircase and auditorium within are remarkable. The auditorium, which is renowned for its acoustics, has been decorated in its original colours of blue, white and gold. The Grand Foyer, renamed the Salon Gérard Boireau, is a homogeneous example of the style of the Second Empire (1852–70).

★ Great Staircase
This extensively decorated feature inspired Garnier's design for the staircase at the Paris Opéra.

Classical Statues
The façade is surmounted by statues of the goddesses Juno, Venus and Minerva, and the nine Muses, carved by Pierre-François Berruer (1733–1797).

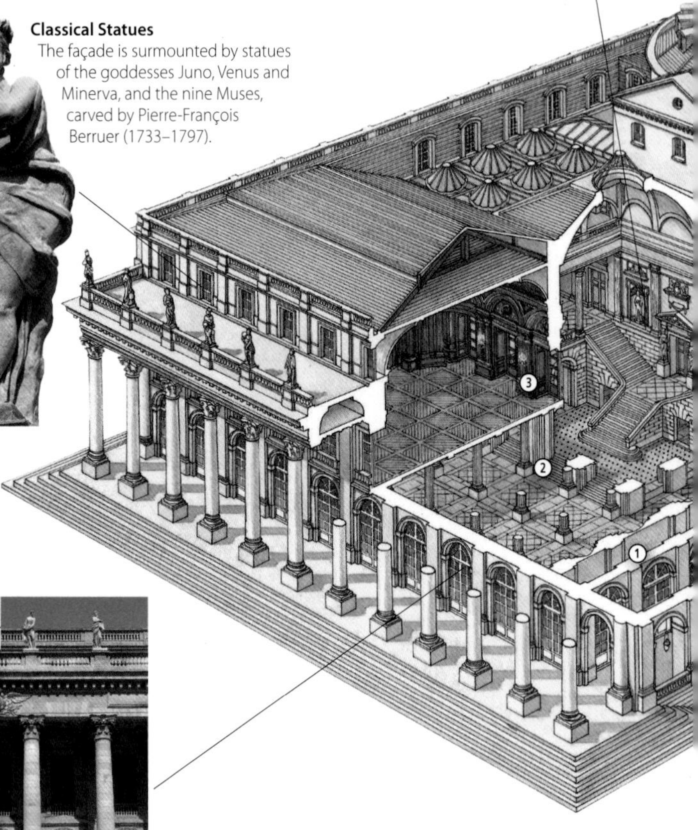

★ Façade
The building is faced with 12 Corinthian columns. The arcaded galleries on either side once housed small shops.

VISITORS' CHECKLIST

Practical Information
Place de la Comédie. **Tel** 05 56 00 85 95. **Open** for performances; for times of guided tours contact the tourist office.
opera-bordeaux.com

Transport
Lines B and C. 10, 15, 29, 31, 53, 54, 55, 56, 58, shuttle.

The Stage
Unusually large for the time it was built, the stage area takes up over a third of the theatre's interior.

KEY

① **Ticket office**

② **Atrium**

③ **Grand Foyer**

④ **Crystal chandelier, with 400 lights**

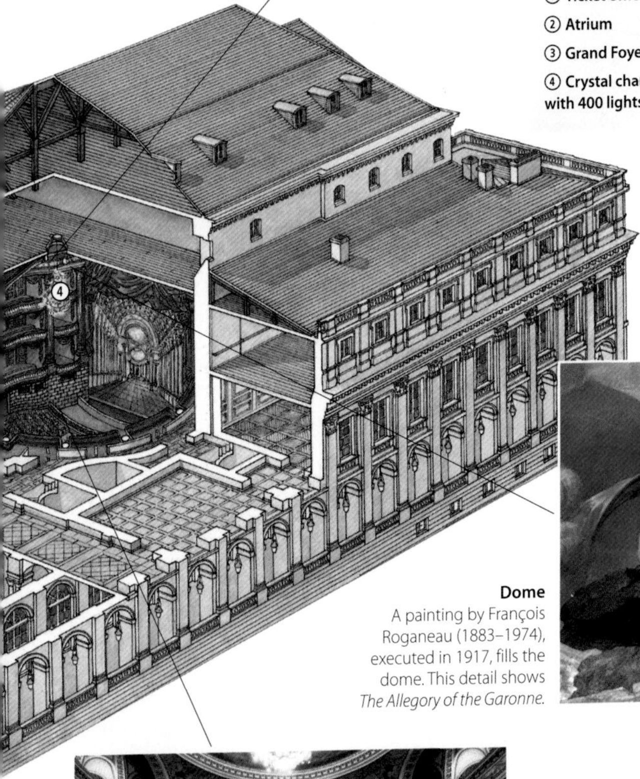

Dome
A painting by François Roganeau (1883–1974), executed in 1917, fills the dome. This detail shows *The Allegory of the Garonne.*

★ Auditorium
Laid out to a horseshoe-shaped plan, the auditorium can seat 1,114 people. The majestic sweep of the three upper tiers is broken up by 12 ornate Classical columns. In 1871 it was used to house the National Assembly.

La Grèce sur les ruines de Missolonghi by Eugène Delacroix

Musée des Beaux-Arts

20 cours d'Albret. **Tel** 05 56 10 20 56. **Open** Wed–Mon. **Closed** public hols.

The north and south wings of the city hall, added to the building by Charles Burguet in 1878–81, now house this museum. Almost the entire history of Western art, from the Renaissance to the late 20th century, is covered by the collection on display. Represented are the Italian School, with works by Perugino and Titian; the Flemish School, with fine offerings by Breughel, Van Dyck and Rubens; Romantic painting, including Delacroix and Corot; Impressionists, such as Boudin; and modern works, including those of Matisse and Kokoschka, as well as Bordeaux artists such as Redon and Marquet.

Musée des Arts Décoratifs

39 rue Bouffard. **Tel** 05 56 10 14 00. **Open** Wed–Mon, Sat–Sun pm only. **Closed** public hols.

This museum is housed in the **Hôtel de Lalande**, a refined town house built by Étienne Laclotte in 1775–9. Several rooms evoke the opulence typical of Bordeaux town-house interiors in the 18th century. On display are paintings, miniatures, prints, sculpture, furniture, ceramics, metalwork and glass from the 18th and 19th centuries.

North of the centre

Although the Quartier des Chartrons and the Quartier Saint-Michel are now fairly industrial, some of the city's greatest religious buildings are here. Stylistically, they range from the Merovingian, as seen in the crypt of the Basilique Saint-Seurin, and the Romanesque, at the Église Sainte-Croix, to the Gothic, displayed by the Basilique Saint-Michel and the Église Sainte-Eulalie. There are also many fine examples of 18th-century architecture, including the handsome town houses along cours Xavier-Arnozan and the small Hôtel Labottière.

Quartier des Chartrons

This is the historic hub of Bordeaux's wine trade, which dates back to Roman times. Here the city's wealth was amassed and dynasties of wine merchants were established.

Musée du Vin et du Négoce de Bordeaux is located in three 18th-century vaulted cellars not far from the quai des Chartrons. The collection relates the history of the wine trade at the Port of Bordeaux through objects, documents, models of *gabares* (freight boats), paintings and film. The **Temple des Chartrons**, a Protestant church, is one the best examples of French Neo-Classical architecture. The **Halle des Chartrons** (market hall), built in 1869, is a highly successful combination of cast iron, glass and stone. The prestigious **cours Xavier-Arnozan**, also known as Pavé des Chartrons, is lined with town houses built by wealthy wine merchants. Their Louis-XVI-style façades have overhanging balconies supported on stone columns. Since 1984 the **CAPC (Centre d'Art Plastique Contemporain)** has occupied a warehouse once used for imports from the colonies. On show here are works by Daniel Buren, Simon Hantaï, Sol LeWitt and other present-generation artists, such as Peter Halley and Robert Combas.

Shell-shaped dish by de Caranza

The **Jardin Public**, once known as Jardin Royal, is a public park laid out by Gabriel. It was completed in 1756 but, a century later, having being ravaged during the French Revolution and Napoleon's Empire, it was relandscaped. A botanical garden, with 2,500 plant species, was also added. The **Muséum d'Histoire Naturelle** is housed in the Hôtel de Lisleferme, which was constructed by the architect Bonfin in 1770.

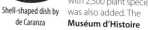

Musée du Vin et du Négoce de Bordeaux

41 rue Borie. **Tel** 05 56 90 19 13. **Open** daily.

Temple des Chartrons

Rue Notre-Dame.

CAPC (Centre d'Art Plastique Contemporain)

Entrepôt Lainé, 7 rue Ferrère. **Tel** 05 56 00 81 50. **Open** Tue–Sun.

Muséum d'Histoire Naturelle

5 place Bardineau. **Closed** for renovations until 2015 .

The old-world charm of a Bordeaux arcade, dating from the 1830s

For hotels and restaurants in this region see pp250–51 and pp262–3

Basilique Saint-Seurin, extensively remodelled between the 12th and the 18th centuries

West of the centre

The **Petit Hôtel Labottière** (1783–8) is a beautiful Neo-Classical town house with a courtyard and a garden. On the side facing the garden, the roof is faced by balusters. The late 2nd-century **Palais Gallien** is the only vestige of ancient Burdigala, as Bordeaux was known in Gallo-Roman times. About 130 m (425 ft) long and 110m (360 ft) wide, this great amphitheatre could seat 15,000 people. Gutted by fire during the barbarian invasions of 276, it was partly destroyed during the Revolution.

The **Basilique Saint-Seurin** stands on place des Martyrs-de-la-Résistance. The west door has early 12th-century capitals and the 11th-century crypt contains several Merovingian tombs. Opposite is the **archeological crypt**, containing an impressive collection of 4th- to 18th-century tombs discovered during excavations in 1910. They include Gallo-Roman and Merovingian sarcophagi and amphorae that were used as tombs for children.

An arch of the Palais Gallien

Petit Hôtel Labottière
13 rue Saint-Laurent. **Tel** 06 75 67 86 21. **Open** by appointment only.

Palais Gallien
Rue du Docteur-Albert-Barraud. **Open** Jun–Sep: pm daily.

Basilique Saint-Seurin
Rue Jean-Burguet. **Open** Tue–Sun.

Archeological Crypt
Open Jun–Sep: pm daily.

South of the centre

The Gothic **Église Sainte-Eulalie** was built in the 14th century and remodelled in the 19th. It contains artifacts from several churches and convents in Bordeaux. Opposite is the **Hôpital Saint-André**, built between 1824 and 1830 by Jean Burguet. Its huge cloister is surrounded by two-tiered arcaded galleries.

The **Porte d'Aquitaine**, in the form of a triumphal arch, is one of eight such gateways into the city. Dating from the 18th century, they replaced medieval postern gates. The Porte d'Aquitaine stands at the head of rue Sainte-Catherine, a pedestrianized thoroughfare and shopping precinct that to the north leads to place de la Comédie, opposite the Grand-Théâtre *(see pp76–7)*.

The Romanesque **Église Sainte-Croix** stands in the restored quarter near the École des Beaux-Arts and Théâtre du Port-de-la-Lune (housed in a former sugar refinery). Its richly carved façade dates from the 12th century, although it was remodelled in the 19th. The hexagonal domes were added in the 13th century. While the north bell tower is Romanesque, the south bell tower was added by Paul Abadie in 1860.

The **Basilique Saint-Michel**, on place Cantaloup, is in a colourful antiques dealers' district, where there is also a lively market on Mondays and Saturdays and a flea market on Sundays. Begun in the 14th century, the church was completed 200 years later in the Flamboyant Gothic style. The Chapelle Saint-Jacques within was built for the use of Bordeaux's brotherhood of pilgrims. The belfry, 114 m (374 ft) high, is known as **La Flèche**. Dating from the 15th century, it was restored by Abadie in the 19th century and separated from the basilica. Beneath the belfry is a 15th-century crypt, which overlies the Carthusian monastery's former cemetery.

Église Sainte-Croix
Open daily.

Basilique Saint-Michel
Open daily pm; La Flèche: Jun–Sep.

Masks of Stone

Many of the façades of Bordeaux's houses are decorated with carved masks. While the earliest date from the 16th century, they are more typical of the 18th century. On place de la Bourse, Mercury, god of trade, surveys the harbour traffic, while the bearded river gods glorify the confluence of the Dordogne and the Garonne, Ceres and Bacchus evoke the wealth that wine brings to the city, and the Zephyrs blow with all their strength. Gods, nymphs, satyrs and monsters wear expressions ranging from angry to brooding or mocking. In the streets round about, these faces take on an earthy wit. Quai Richelieu has faces with features verging on the grotesque, while a saucy pirate looks down from the front of Maison Francia in rue du Mirail.

Masks of Bordeaux

⑩ Tour of the Médoc

The Médoc vineyards produce some of the world's finest wines. The area is located around latitude 45° north and sits between the Gironde Estuary and an extensive forest, with the Atlantic Ocean out to the west. It therefore enjoys a mild, humid climate that is ideal for vines. There is also a good mix of gravel, sand and clay soils. All this, combined with the expertise of local growers, accounts for the subtle wines created from traditional grape varieties, such as Cabernet-Sauvignon, Cabernet-Franc, Merlot and Petit-Verdot.

⑧ Château Cos d'Estournel
This strikingly exotic building dominates the estate's vineyards. The château produces the Saint-Estèphe appellation, a notable *deuxième cru classé.*

⑥ Château Mouton Rothschild
Made a *premier grand cru classé* in 1973, Château Mouton has been owned by the Rothschilds since 1853. Its wine cellars and museum can be visited Mon–Fri by appointment (tel: 05 56 73 21 29).

④ Château Pichon-Longueville
In the 19th century, the vineyards here, a *deuxième grand cru classé*, were divided between two estates, that of the Château Pichon-Longueville-Baron and of the Château Pichon-Longueville-Comtesse-de-Lalande.

③ Château Beychevelle
The name means "lower the sails". As they sailed by, boats were required to do this in homage to the all-powerful Duc d'Épernon, the estate's owner.

0 kilometres 3
0 miles 3

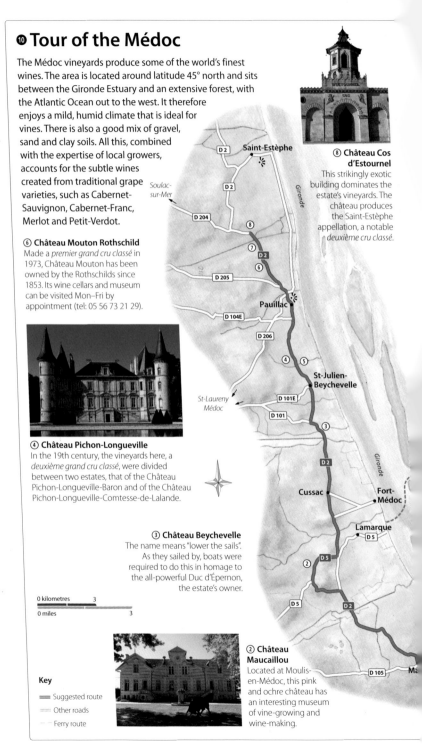

② Château Maucaillou
Located at Moulis-en-Médoc, this pink and ochre château has an interesting museum of vine-growing and wine-making.

Key

- Suggested route
- Other roads
- Ferry route

For map symbols *see back flap*

Tips for Drivers

Tour length: 23 km (14 miles)
Stopping-off points: Château Le Foulon (tel: 05 56 58 20 18), at Castelnau-le-Médoc, is a pleasant guesthouse. Château Guittot-Fellonneau (tel: 05 57 88 47 81), at Macau, is a farmhouse-inn that serves local meals accompanied by good-quality wine.

) Château Lafite-Rothschild
)riginating in the Middle Ages, this hâteau was rebuilt in the 18th entury. Its circular wine cellar was uilt by Ricardo Bofill. Open by ppointment only; tel: 05 56 59 26 83.

) Château Latour
his château dates from the 19th entury. The round tower that looks ut over the vineyards is a vestige of ne fortified building that originally tood on the site.

① Château Margaux
This stately Neo-Classical château was built from 1810 to 1816 by Combes, a pupil of Victor Louis, the architect of the Grand-Théâtre in Bordeaux.

3ordeaux

Façade of Château de Margaux, in a severely Neo-Classical style

⓫ Margaux

Road map C2. 1,358. Château de Margaux: **Tel** 05 57 88 83 83. **Open** Mon–Fri, by appointment only. **Closed** public hols, Aug & grape harvest. book two weeks ahead.

The vineyards around the villages of Arsac, Cantenac, Labarde, Margaux and Soussans produce the wines officially classed as Margaux. Over some 1,200 ha (2,965 acres), vines grow on the gravelly, pebbly soil of the rolling hills. Château Margaux produces one of the great *premier grand cru classé* wines. Its fine oak-beamed cellars are open to the public. The **Maison du Vin et du Tourisme**, on the edge of the small town of Margaux, is an informative visitor centre.

Environs
About 25 km (15 miles) north of Bordeaux is the attractive 17th-century **Château d'Issan**. At the weekend, the small cafés in the little port of Macau serve an assortment of locally caught seafood, including shad, grey mullet, plaice, eel, shrimps and lamprey.

Maison du Vin et du Tourisme
7 place la Trémoille. **Tel** 05 57 88 70 82. **Open** Mon–Sat (daily Jun–Sep).
maisonduvindemargaux.com

⓬ Moulis-en-Médoc

Road map C2. 1,714. La Verrerie, Pauillac; 05 56 59 03 08.

This village has a 12th-century Romanesque church with a Gothic bell tower. The capitals inside are carved with naive depictions of wild animals, monsters and scenes from the Old Testament. The **Maison du Vin de Moulis** here organizes tours of the châteaux within the Médoc *appellation* area.

By taking the D5 northwards, you will come to **Port de Lamarque**, on the Gironde. From here you can take a ferry to Blaye *(see p82)*.

Maison du Vin de Moulis
Tel 05 56 58 32 74. **Open** mid-Jun–mid-Sep: Tue, Thu–Sat; mid-Sep–mid-Jun: Mon, Tue, Thu, Fri.
moulis.com

Port de Lamarque
Tel 05 57 42 04 49.

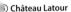

Fortifed Romanesque church at Moulis-en-Médoc, with a Gothic bell tower

Pediment of the Porte Royale at Fort-Médoc

⓭ Fort-Médoc

Road map C2. 16 avenue du Haut-Médoc, Cussac-Fort-Médoc; 05 56 58 98 40. **Open** Daily. **Closed** Dec–Jan.

This fort was built by Vauban in the late 17th century and, together with the citadel at Blaye and Fort-Paté, it formed part of the Gironde Estuary's defences. The Porte Royale, a gateway whose pediment is filled with a relief of the sun, symbolizing Louis XIV, leads through to a courtyard. Beyond are the surviving elements of the fort, which include the guardroom and the battery platform. Based on a rectangular plan, the building is set with four corner bastions. One of these, overlooking the Gironde, offers wide views of the estuary and opposite bank.

Environs

The **Château Lanessan**, 2 km (1 mile) away, welcomes visitors to its wine cellars, where Haut-Médoc wines are matured. It also has a Musée du Cheval (a museum devoted to horses).

Château Lanessan
Cussac-Fort-Médoc. **Tel** 05 56 58 94 80. **Open** daily by arrangement.

⓮ Pauillac

Road map B1. 5,200. La Verrerie; 05 56 59 03 08. Sat. Fête du Nautisme (May), Fête de l'Agneau de Pauillac (May), Marathon des Châteaux du Médoc (Sep).
pauillac-medoc.com

The marina here is a very popular family resort in summer and a stopping-place on the Canal du Midi.
Pauillac, the capital of Médoc wine-making, is famous for its lamb, which is enjoyed all over France. The **Maison du Tourisme et du Vin** here sells local *grands crus* wines and organizes tours of the region's châteaux, with opportunities to meet the growers.

Maison du Tourisme et du Vin
Vinothèque La Verrerie. **Tel** 05 56 59 03 08. **pauillac-medoc.com**
Open daily.

Environs

Some 8 km (5 miles) northwest of Pauillac is **Vertheuil**. The Abbaye des Prémontrés was founded here in the 11th century, but all that remains is an 18th-century building. The **Église Saint-Pierre**, which also dates from the 11th century, is a Romanesque church with a nave flanked by aisles. It has two bell towers, one dating from the 12th century. On the north side, the moulding round a restored doorway is carved with scenes from the life of Christ.

Église Saint-Pierre
Vertheuil. **Open** daily.
Closed Sun pm.

⓯ Blaye

Road map C1. 4,950. (for Lamarque). Allées Marine; 05 57 42 12 09. Wed & Sat. Festival Musique et Theâtre (Jul–Aug); Channel 8 Regatta (Sep).
tourisme-blaye.com

Near the border with the Charente, Blaye is of interest chiefly for its citadel, built by Vauban in 1689 and set with star-shaped bastions.

Overlooking the Gironde, the citadel offers breath-taking sunset views, especially from the Tour de l'Aiguillette. The views make it easy to understand why the Gironde Estuary is so famous for its light.

Entry into Blaye, a town of low houses, covering just 18 ha (44 acres), is through Porte Royale (by car) or Porte Dauphine (on foot). In summer, it is filled with local craftsmen. North of the citadel is the medieval Château des Rudel, which is now a ruin.

The Manutention, a former prison next to Place d'Armes, houses the **Musée de la Boulangerie et Archéologie** as well as two exhibitions, **Estuaire Vivant** ("The Living Estuary") and **Blaye, 7,000 Ans d'Histoire**.

Musée de la Boulangerie et Archéologie
Manutention. **Tel** 06 82 34 72 66 (information from the Conservatoire de l'Estuaire, Place d'Armes). **Open** daily.

Estuaire Vivant
Manutention. **Open** daily.

Blaye, 7,000 Ans d'Histoire
Manutention. **Open** daily.

The citadal at Blaye, a fortress on the Gironde

For hotels and restaurants in this region see pp250–51 and pp262–3

Château du Bouilh, designed by Victor Louis, architect of the Grand-Théâtre in Bordeaux

⓰ Bourg

Road map C2. 2,168. Hôtel de la Jurade, place de la Libération; 05 57 68 31 76. Sun. Foire du Troque-Sel (salt fair) (Aug or Sep).

Built from local limestone, Bourg was a fortified town in the Middle Ages. It once traded in salt from Charente, wines and locally quarried stone. Set on a steep slope, the town offers fine views over the Gironde river below and can only be visited on foot. Today it is known for its local Côtes-de-Bourg wines.

In the upper part of the town is the **Château de la Citadelle**. This elegant folly, built to an elongated plan and surrounded by formal gardens, was once the summer residence of the arch-bishops of Bordeaux. It now houses the **Musée des Calèches**, a museum devoted to the horse-drawn carriage. The upper and lower town are separated by Porte Batailleyre, a 13th-century gate carved out of the surrounding rock.

Near the town are several good viewpoints (*fenêtres* –windows) where you can watch river vessels and the local fishermen at work. There is also a scenic corniche drive from Bourg to La Roque de Thau.

Château de la Citadelle
Parc du Château. **Open** daily.

Musée des Calèches
Tel 05 57 68 23 57. **Open** Jun–Sep: daily; Mar–May & Oct: Sat–Sun. **Closed** Nov–Feb.

Environs

A prehistoric cave, **Grotte de Pair-non-Pair**, is 4.5 km (3 miles) east of Bourg on the D669. Discovered in 1881, its walls are covered with engravings. It is the only decorated cave in the Gironde open to the public. About 10 km (6 miles) southeast of Bourg is **Château du Bouilh**, designed by Victor Louis.

Grotte de Pair-non-Pair
Prignac-et-Marcamps.
Tel 05 57 68 33 40. **Open** Tue–Sun (book ahead). **Closed** public hols.

Château du Bouilh
Saint-André-de-Cubzac.
Tel 05 57 43 06 59. **Open** opening times vary (phone to check)

⓱ Libourne

Road map C2. 23,300. 40 place Abel-Surchamp; 05 57 51 15 04. Tue, Fri, Sun. Fest'Arts (Aug). **libourne-tourisme.com**

Lying at the confluence of the Isle and the Dordogne, this *bastide* town once depended on river trade for its wealth. Portions of the ramparts, as well as a gate, the Porte du Grand-Port, survive. The 15th-century town hall houses the **Musée des Beaux-Arts**.

Musée des Beaux-Arts
42, place Abel-Surchamp. **Tel** 05 57 55 33 44. **Open** Tue pm, Wed–Sat am & pm.

Environs

The **Maison du Pays Fronsadais**, about 10 km (6 miles) northwest of Libourne, documents the workings of the vineyards at Fronsac, which produce robust, full-bodied red wines.

To the north lie the vineyards of **Pomerol**. The fine wines that are produced here owe their smoothness to the iron oxides in the local soil. This is particularly true of Château Pétrus, the most highly prized of them all.

At **Guîtres**, 15 km (9 miles) north, is a large Romanesque abbey, dating from the 11th to the 15th centuries. At the **Musée Ferroviaire**, which has a small railway, visitors can relive the age of steam and diesel trains. The **Train Touristique de Guîtres** operates a steam train service that covers a 14 km (9 mile) circuit of the countryside between Guîtres and Marcenais and stops off at a pleasant rural café-restaurant. Visitors can also do a spot of wildlife-watching on a boat trip up the river Isle, or explore the town using the marked walks. There is also a wine *chai* (warehouse), where local wines can be tasted.

Maison du Pays Fronsadais
Ave Charles de Gaulle, Saint-Germain-de-la Rivière. **Tel** 05 57 84 86 86.
Open Jan–May & Oct–Dec: Mon–Fri; Jun–Sep: Mon–Sat.

Abbatiale de Guîtres
Guîtres. **Tel** 05 57 69 10 34.
Open Jul–Aug: daily pm.

Musée Ferroviaire
Gare de uîtres. **Tel** 05 57 69 11 48.
Open May–Oct: Sun.

Train Touristique de Guîtres
Guîtres. **Tel** 05 57 69 10 69.
Open May–Oct: Sun.

⑱ Street-by-Street: Saint-Émilion

In the 8th century, a hermitage was set up by Émilian, a monk from Vannes in Brittany, on the northern slopes of the Dordogne valley. Fortifications began to be built there in the 12th century, and throughout the Middle Ages, houses, chapels and monasteries were added. The ochre-coloured stone of their walls and the pinkish-red of their roof tiles make St-Emilion a picturesque place. The town's architectural heritage is almost without equal. Saint-Émilion's alliegance oscillated during the Hundred Years' War, but finally rested with the French, and it was granted special privileges by Charles VII.

★ Cloister and Abbey Church
The cloisters are 30 m (98 ft) square. Built originally in the Romanesque style, they were rebuilt in the Gothic period.

Place de l'Église-Monolithe
Once place du Marché, this square is lined with restaurants. The original Tree of Freedom, planted in the centre during the Revolution, died and has been replaced.

★ Bell Tower
One of the finest sights in Saint-Émilion is the bell tower of the Église Monolithe. It is the second-highest in the Gironde after the spire of the Église Saint-Michel in Bordeaux.

0 metres 20

0 yards 20

VISITORS' CHECKLIST

Practical Information

Road map C2. 2,020.
Doyenné (Deanery), Place des Créneaux; 05 57 55 28 28. Sun.
Grandes Heures de Saint-Émilion (Mar–Dec); Jurade (third Sun in Jun and Sep). **saint-emilion- tourisme.com**

Transport

Rooftops of Saint-Émilion, with the bell tower of the Église Monolithe

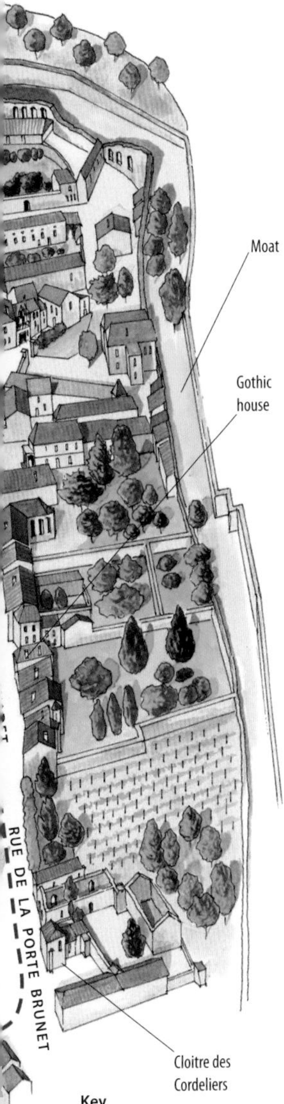

Key

– Suggested route

Exploring Saint-Émilion

The town can only be visited on foot, along steep, narrow **paved streets** known as *tertres* and small **flights of steps** known as *escalettes*, which sometimes offer striking perspectives. Approaching the town by the D243, to the north, visitors will see its great **ramparts**, the remains of the first Dominican monastery that was built here.

Église Monolithe

Place de l'Église-Monolithe.
through the tourist office, pm daily.

This church sits at the heart of the town in the **place de l'Église-Monolithe**, with its ancient covered market and many restaurants. A troglodyte building, it was dug directly out of the surrounding limestone rock in the 11th century, and is unique in Europe. With a nave 12 m (39 ft) high and decorated with relief carvings, it has a 14th-century Gothic doorway with a tympanum containing depictions of the Last Judgment and the Resurrection of the Dead. Excavations have brought to light drainpipes that the monks had installed to channel away rainwater.

Enthroned Christ

Bell Tower of the Église Monolithe

Opposite tourist office. **Open** daily.

The church's tall bell tower rises 133 m (436 ft) above place du Marché. There are breathtaking views of Saint-Émilion and its surrounding vineyards from the top.

Catacombs

Place de l'Église-Monolithe.
through the tourist office, daily.

Beyond the entrance to the Église Monolithe is an underground passage, leading to a space containing several burial niches, dug directly into the rock. Its dome above forms the base of a well whose walls enclose a spiral stair-case. Archeologists studying this area have shown that these catacombs may have been originally used as a funerary chapel.

Chapelle de la Trinité

Place de l'Église-Monolithe.
through the tourist office, daily.

The Chapelle de la Trinité, a Gothic chapel buit in the 13th century, has an apse with four-arched ribbed vaulting and frescoes.

Ermitage de Saint-Émilion

Place de l'Église-Monolithe.
through the tourist office, daily.

The Ermitage de Saint-Émilion is supposed to be where the monk Émilian spent his days. The spring water that flows from the rock nearby is said to have therapeutic powers.

Rue de la Cadène

From Place de l'Église-Monolithe, rue de la Cadène leads to **Porte de la Cadène**, once the access point between the upper and the lower town. A 15th-century wooden house is built onto it.

Tour du Roy in Saint-Émilion, where the Jurade takes place

Abbey Church and Cloisters

Entrance to church off ave de Verdun, to cloisters via tourist office. **Open** daily.

The church's 12th-century nave, in the Romanesque style, has Byzantine-style domes supported by stone pillars. Traces of frescoes remain, including an image of the Madonna and the martyrdom of St Catherine. The choir dates from a later phase of construction in the 14th century. Near the vestry door is a statue of St Valéry, who local vine-growers consider their patron saint. The cloister dates from the 14th century.

Tour du Roy

Open Apr–Sep: daily; Oct–Mar: Sat, Sun & school hols. **Closed** Jan.

A symbol of royal power in Saint-Émilion, this fortress was built in the 13th century. From the top (an 180-step climb) there is a magnificent view. The Fêtes de la Jurade (a committee of wine tasters that release Saint-Émilion wine for global export) takes place here *(see p40)*.

Ramparts

Surrounded by a dry moat, the ramparts encircled the upper part of the town. They were pierced by six gates. The Romanesque **Porte Brunet**, on the southeastern side, the **Tour du Guetteur**, to the south, and **L'Éperon**, a lookout tower at **Porte Bouqueyre**, still stand.

⑲ Vineyards of Saint-Émilion

The vineyards of Saint-Émilion and its surrounding villages enjoy an exceptionally favourable climate and have exceptionally good vine-growing soil. Since 1289, the villages around the town have fallen under Saint-Émilion's jurisdiction, and in 1999 the whole was declared a World Heritage Site. This hilly terrain, covering 7,689 ha (19,000 acres), is dotted with picturesque villages and crossed by narrow roads that wind between vineyards. With colours that change with the seasons, it is strikingly beautiful. The Saint-Émilion appellation consists of 68 *grands crus classés*, the most famous of which are Ausone (after Ausonius, the 4th-century Gallo-Roman consul and poet) and Cheval Blanc.

⑦ **Saint-Laurent-des-Combes** The village nestles in a cluster of wooded valleys, or coombs, which gave it its name. The Romanesque church here is set on the edge of the plateau.

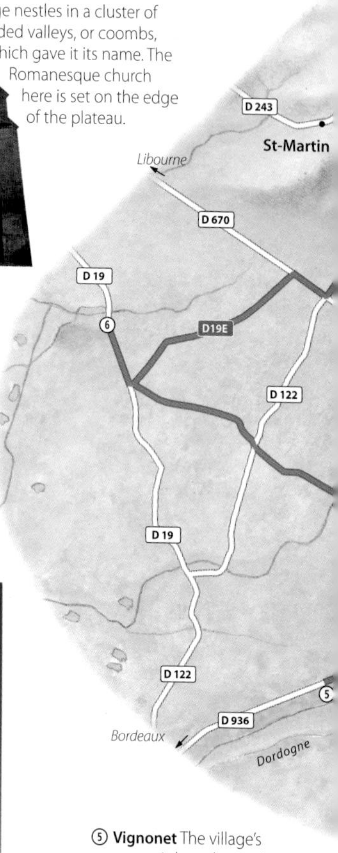

⑥ **Saint-Sulpice-de-Faleyrens** At Pierrefitte, near the village, is a prehistoric menhir. Standing 5 m (16 ft) high, it is made of limestone, widely found on the Saint-Émilion plateau.

⑤ **Vignonet** The village's economy is based entirely on vine-growing, with vineyards right up to the banks of the Dordogne. The village church is in the Romanesque style, but was enlarged in the 18th century.

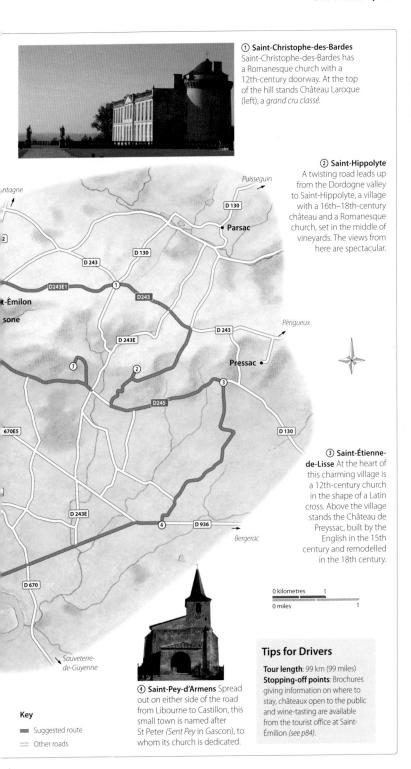

① **Saint-Christophe-des-Bardes** Saint-Christophe-des-Bardes has a Romanesque church with a 12th-century doorway. At the top of the hill stands Château Laroque (left), a *grand cru classé*.

② **Saint-Hippolyte** A twisting road leads up from the Dordogne valley to Saint-Hippolyte, a village with a 16th–18th-century château and a Romanesque church, set in the middle of vineyards. The views from here are spectacular.

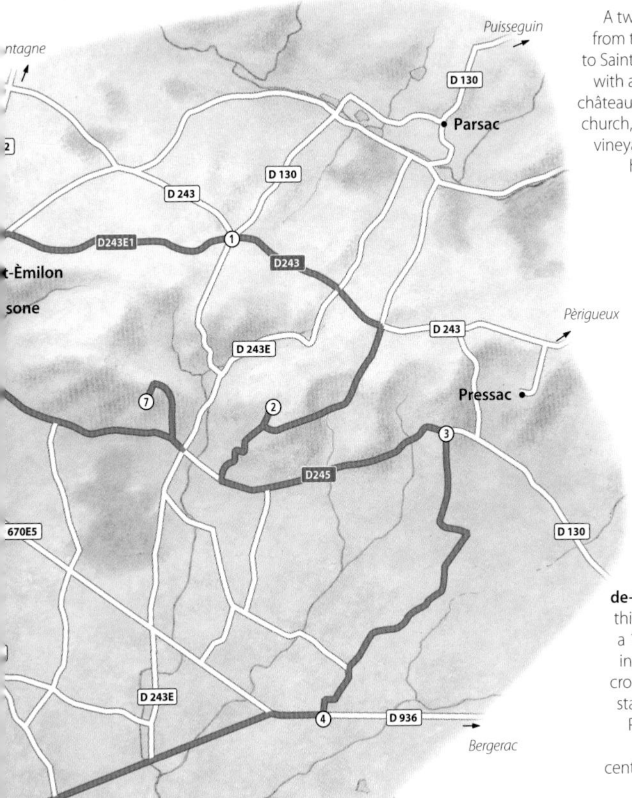

③ **Saint-Étienne-de-Lisse** At the heart of this charming village is a 12th-century church in the shape of a Latin cross. Above the village stands the Château de Preyssac, built by the English in the 15th century and remodelled in the 18th century.

0 kilometres 1

0 miles 1

④ **Saint-Pey-d'Armens** Spread out on either side of the road from Libourne to Castillon, this small town is named after St Peter (*Sent Pey* in Gascon), to whom its church is dedicated.

Tips for Drivers

Tour length: 99 km (99 miles)
Stopping-off points: Brochures giving information on where to stay, châteaux open to the public and wine-tasting are available from the tourist office at Saint-Émilion (*see p84*).

Key

Suggested route

Other roads

Entre-deux-Mers, between the Dordogne and the Garonne, ideal for watersports and relaxation

⓴ Entre-deux-Mers

Road map C2. 4 Rue Issartier, Monségur; 05 56 61 82 73. Fri am. **entredeuxmers.com**

In spite of its name, the area known as Entre-deux-Mers ("Between Two Seas") lies in fact between two rivers, the Dordogne and the Garonne. It consists of a large plateau cut by small valleys that are covered with meadows, fields and woodland. Human settlement here goes back far into prehistory. Entre-deux-Mers also boasts a rich heritage of *bastide* towns, Romanesque churches and fortified mills.

Vayres, set high above the Dordogne, is the gateway to the region.The 13th–17th century **Château de Vayres** was owned by Henri IV. Entre-deux-Mers' vineyards cover 1,500 ha (3,700 acres), with 250 vine growers producing a fruity dry white wine. Visitors can enjoy tastings at the **Maison des Vins de l'Entre-deux-Mers**.

Maison des Vins de l'Entre-deux-Mers
16 rue de l'Abbaye, La Sauve. **Tel** 05 57 34 32 12. **Open** Jun–Sep: Mon–Sat; Oct–May: Mon–Fri. **vins-entre-deux-mers.com**

Château de Vayres
Tel 05 57 84 96 58. **Open** Easter–1 Nov: pm daily.

㉑ La Sauve-Majeure

Road map C2. La Gare, Boulevard Victor-Hugo, Créon; 05 56 23 23 00.

The Benedictine **abbey** of La Sauve-Majeure was founded by Gérard de Corbie in 1079, in an area that the monks gradually cleared of trees. Located on the pilgrim route to Santiago de Compostela, the abbey became a dynamic centre of religion and trade, and counted 70 priories in its sphere of influence.

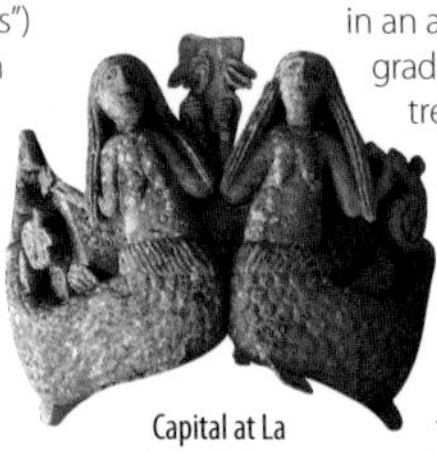

Capital at La Sauve-Majeure

Reduced to ruins by wars and the unrest during the French Revolution, the abbey has undergone several phases of restoration since 1952 and was made a World Heritage Site in 1988.

The abbey's majestic Romanesque and Gothic ruins stand in beautiful, mostly open countryside. The choir has Romanesque capitals carved with strikingly expressive biblical scenes. Next to the church are the remains of the 13th-century cloister, the chapter room and the refectory. A museum displays pieces found during excavations of the abbey.

Fine 13th-century frescoes can be seen in the Église Saint-Pierre, in the village.

Abbey
Tel 05 56 23 01 55. **Open** Jun–Sep: daily; Oct–May: Tue–Sun.

Environs

At **Sadirac**, 10 km (6 miles) west of La Sauve, is **Oh! Légumes Oubliés** ("Oh! Forgotten Vegetables"), a farm-park where neglected delicacies such as nettles and Jerusalem and Chinese artichokes are grown.

The **Maison de la Poterie** here displays a range of pottery, made in a style that has been traditional in Sadirac since antiquity.

Oh! Légumes Oubliés
Château de Belloc, Sadirac. **Tel** 05 56 30 62 00. **Open** Apr–mid-Nov: pm Mon–Sat. **ohlegumesoublies.com**

Maison de la Poterie
Tel 05 56 30 60 03. **Open** pm Tue–Sat (May–Sep: pm Sun).

The ruined abbey at La Sauve-Majeure

For hotels and restaurants in this region see pp250–51 and pp262–3

Ramparts at Castillon-la-Bataille

㉒ Castillon-la-Bataille

Road map C2. 3,360. Place Marcel Paul; 05 57 40 27 58. Mon. Bataille de Castillon (mid-Jul–mid-Aug).

Castillon-la-Bataille is named after the decisive battle fought between the French and the English on the Plaine de Colly in July 1453. General Talbot was killed by Charles VII's troops, under the command of the Bureau brothers, and his 8,000-strong army was decimated. This defeat of the English marked the end of the Hundred Years' War and led to Aquitaine and the southwest being restored to the French crown.

Vestiges of this eventful past include the town's 11th–12th-century gate, the Porte de Fer, a 17th–18th-century Baroque church and the Église Saint-Symphorien. The town hall, a former inn in the form of a rotunda, was built in 1779 with funds provided by Maréchal de Turenne.

The Côtes-de-Castillon wine *appellation*, created in 1989, covers 3,000 ha (7,400 acres) of vineyards and includes about 366 vine growers. It has its own **Maison du Vin**.

Maison du Vin des Côtes-de-Castillon
6 allées de la République.
Tel 05 57 40 00 88.

Environs

At **Petit-Palais-et-Cornemps**, 17km (10 miles) north of Castillon, is the Église Saint-Pierre. It is located just behind the cemetery and its façade is one of the best examples of Romanesque architecture in southwestern France. It has three superimposed arcatures supported by four sets of double columns. The doorway has spectacular carvings of lions and human figures, including a Spinario (a boy removing a thorn from his foot), based on the famous Roman statue.

㉓ Rauzan

Road map C2. 1,130. 12 rue Chapelle 05 57 84 03 88. Sat.

The castle in its present form was built by the Plantagenets in the 14th century. Restored in Gothic style after the Hundred Years' War, it then passed to the Durfort de Duras family. It was acquired by the municipal authorites of Rauzan in 1900. Built on a limestone plateau, the castle still has some impressive features, such as the keep, the main living quarters and the central tower. Access is over a bridge that leads to a massive gateway. The top of the keep, which is 30 m (98 ft) high, offers visitors a wide panorama of the surrounding countryside. The **Grotte Célestine**, an underground river discovered in about 1845, is open to visitors. Boots, protective clothing and helmets with headlamps must be worn and are provided.

Castle
Open Jul–Aug: daily; Sep–Jun: Tue–Sat.

Grotte Célestine
Tel 05 57 84 08 69. **Open** Tue–Sat (phone to reserve visit).

㉔ Blasimon

Road map C2. 725. Mairie; 05 56 71 52 12.

Founded in 1273, Blasimon became a *bastide* town in 1322 on the orders of Edward II of England, when the area was under his rule.

Nestling in a small wooded valley washed by the Gamage river is Blasimon's stately **Benedictine abbey**. Built in the 12th and 13th centuries, it was owned by the abbey of La Sauve-Majeure. The two-tier façade looks particularly beautiful at sunset, when it is bathed in golden light. The doorway and the arches that frame it are decorated with some of the most delicate of all Romanesque carvings in the Gironde. Some of the monastery buildings nearby are now in ruins.

On Wednesday evenings in July and August, there is a market, with local craft items and locally grown produce.

Benedictine Abbey
Quai Pascal Elissalt. **Open** Inner courtyard: all year.

The abbey at Blasimon, set in a small valley washed by the Gamage river

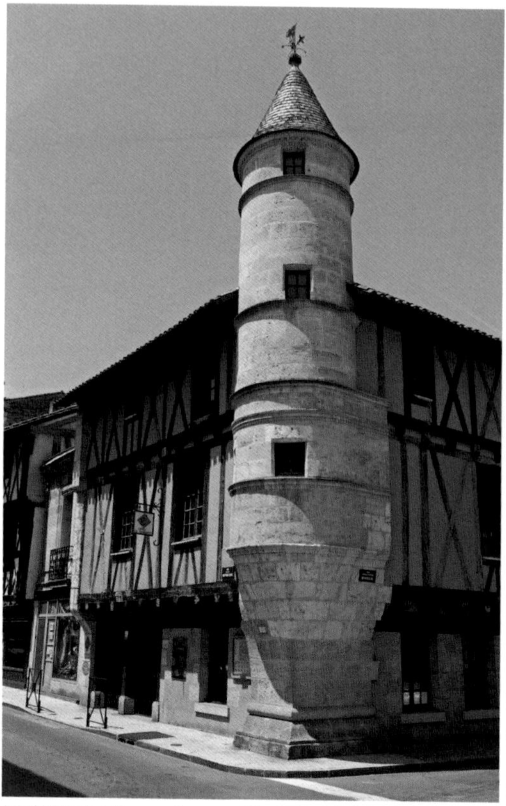

A medieval house with a corner tower, now Sainte-Foy's tourist office

㉕ Sainte-Foy-la-Grande

Road map D2. 2,550. Saint-Jean-de-Luz. 102 rue de la République; 05 57 46 03 00. Sat.

This 13th-century *bastide* town on the banks of the Dordogne was founded by Alphonse of Poitiers, brother of Louis IX. After 1271, it stood in English territory, but was retaken by the French in 1453. In the 16th century, when it had become a major centre of trade, Sainte-Foix was one of most dynamic of all Huguenot towns.

Of the medieval town, only four towers survive, which have been converted into houses. There are also several half-timbered dwellings from the 15th–17th centuries, with towers or carved window surrounds, and a number of fine 18th-century town houses. The tourist office includes the **Musée Charles-Nardin**, a small museum devoted to prehistory and archaeology.

Sainte-Foy-la-Grande is the birthplace of Élisée Reclus (1830–1905), pioneer of modern geography and ecology and author of the great 19-volume *Géographie Universelle*, and of the art historian Élie Faure (1873–1937).

At Port-Sainte-Foy, on the opposite bank of the river, is the **Musée de la Batellerie**. Housed in the Maison du Fleuve, this fascinating museum of river craft has models of *gabares*, wide flat-bottomed boats that sailed down the river as far as the Atlantic.

Musée Charles-Nardin
Tourist office. **Open** Mon–Sat (Jul & Aug: am Sun).

Musée de la Batellerie
Maison du Fleuve. **Tel** 05 53 58 37 34. **Open** Jun–Sep: Tue–Sun pm, Oct–May: Tue–Fri pm, Sat–Sun by appointment only.

㉖ Sauveterre-de-Guyenne

Road map C2. 1,821. Place de la République; 05 56 71 53 45. Tue (since 1530). Fête de la Vigne et de la Gastronomie (last weekend in Jul).

In 1283, Edward VII, king of England, founded the *bastide* town of Selva-Terra. Later known as Sauveterre, it stood on the site of Athala, a small town founded in the 9th century. With its strategic location at the junction of roads running between Libourne and La Réole, and between Bordeaux and Duras, Sauveterre was long an object of dispute between the French and English, until it finally fell to the French in 1451. Sited at the heart of Entre-deux-Mers *(see p88)*, the town no longer has its ramparts, which were destroyed in the early 19th century, though the four gates at the corners of the town remain. A vestige of Sauveterre's days as a defensive town is Tour Saubotte, on its west side, a tower with arrow-slits and a rampart walk.

Environs

Castelviel, situated 4 km (2 miles) southwest of Sau-veterre, has a church with a beautiful Romanesque doorway. The barrel vaulting is decorated with carvings of allegorical figures of the Virtues and Vices.

About 7 km (4 miles) south-west is **Castelmoron-d'Albret**.

One of Sauveterre-de-Guyenne's four medieval gates

With 55 inhabitants, this is one of the smallest villages in France. This former seneschal town of the House of Albret is set on a rocky outcrop with sheer cliffs 80 m (260 ft) high. As it was also surrounded by walls, it could not expand.

㉗ Abbaye de Saint-Ferme

Road map C2. 364. Place de l'Abbaye; 05 56 61 69 92.

The great Abbaye de Saint-Ferme, which seems almost to overwhelm the town, was founded in the 11th century. Being near the Dropt, the river marking the border between French and English territory, it was fortified. This wealthy abbey was run by enterprising monks, who took in pilgrims on the road to Santiago de Compostela *(see pp212–13)*. It was sacked during the Hundred Years' War (1337–1453) and again during the Wars of Religion (1562–1598).

The 12th-century **abbey church** is crowned by a dome, the earliest Gothic-style one in the Gironde. Its Romanesque capitals have magnificent carvings of Daniel in the Lions' Den and other biblical scenes.

Monastery buildings now house the town hall and the small abbey **museum**, with exhibits relating to the abbey, and also a 3rd-century hoard of 1,300 Roman coins that was discovered in 1986.

Abbey church and monastery
Tel 05 56 61 69 92. **Open** Jun–Sep: Tue–Sat pm only; Oct–May: Tue–Fri pm only.

Musée de l'Abbaye
Currently closed for restoration; enquire at the church for reopening date.

㉘ Monségur

Road map C2. 1,454. 33 rue des Victimes-du-3-Août-1944; 05 56 61 89 40. Fri. Foire au Gras (second Sun in Dec and Feb).

This *bastide* town was founded in 1265 by a charter granted by Eleanor of Provence, wife of Henry III of England, who was also Duc d'Aquitaine. It was built on a promontory overlooking the valley of the river Dropt ("Monségur" means "hill of safety"). The surviving medieval buildings include some half-timbered houses, a narrow alley known as the Ruelle du Souley, and a Gothic tower, the Tour du Gouverneur. In the northeast corner of the arcaded square stands the Église Notre-Dame, a late Gothic building that was restored in the 19th century.

The cast-iron and glass market hall dates from late-19th century. It was large enough to store 700 to 800 tonnes of *pruneaux d'Agen*, the famous local prunes *(see p159)*. Today it is the setting for weekly markets and various festivals.

㉙ La Réole

Road map C2. 4,200. 15 rue Armand Caduc; 05 56 61 13 55. Wed, Sat, Sun. Festival Viva Cité (Jul or Aug, along with the Festival International de Folklore).

Double stairway of the priory at La Réole

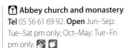

Place du Marché and Église Notre-Dame in Monségur

Because of its strategic location on the banks of the Garonne, not far from the opening of the Dropt valley, this ancient walled town grew rich in the Middle Ages.

The town hall, founded by Richard the Lionheart in about 1200 and superbly well restored, is one of the oldest in France. The 13th-century Château des Quat'Sos is now privately owned.

The town's Benedictine priory is now home to municipal offices. The grille over the central doorway of this jewel of 18th-century architecture was made by the master ironworker Blaise Charlut, who also made the banister of the inner staircase. The building is fronted by an elegant stone double staircase. The Église Saint-Pierre has a Romanesque apse and Gothic vaulting, which was rebuilt during the 17th century.

A signposted walk around the town, with explanatory boards, lets visitors explore its architectural heritage. The town's ramparts were dismantled in 1629 by order of Cardinal Richelieu, but some remains can still be seen, such as the Porte de Sault de Piis with its staircase leading from the quays up to the priory. The suspension bridge that links the town centre to the bank of the Garonne river was designed by Gustav Eiffel when he was still a little known public servant.

㉚ Château de Roquetaillade

Set in extensive parkland full of centuries-old trees, this is one of the most astonishing castles in the Gironde. It perches high over a series of troglodyte caves, a perfect position for striking at would-be invaders. The castle consists of two main parts: the 12th-century Château-Vieux (Old Castle), with its fortified gatehouse, guardroom and keep; and the 14th-century Château-Neuf (New Castle), built by Cardinal Gaillard de La Mothe, nephew of Pope Clement V, in 1306, with the permission of King Edward I of England (then ruler of Aquitaine). Still owned by the Cardinal's family, it boasts six towers and an impressive central keep. In the 19th century, Viollet-le-Duc, the great French exponent of Neo-Gothic architecture, restored the castle, turning it into a highly romanticized medieval jewel.

Monumental Fireplace
This is in the Synod Room, where Pope Clement V held meetings.

★ Pink Room
Like the chapel, the Green Room and the dining room (formerly a stable and barn), this was completely overhauled by Viollet-le-Duc. The decoration and furniture here have been classified as historic monuments.

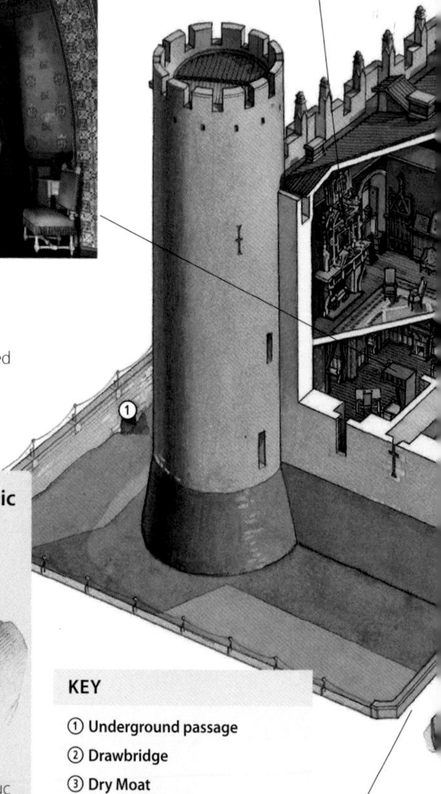

Viollet-Le-Duc, Father of Neo-Gothic

Viollet-le-Duc

The Mauvesin family, who had inherited the castle in 1864, commissioned Eugène Viollet-le-Duc (1814–79) to restore Roquetaillade. This famous architect had already shown his enthusiasm for Gothic styling by restoring medieval buildings in Carcassonne and Vézelay, as well as Notre-Dame-de-Paris and Pierrefonds. Work on Roquetaillade began in 1865, when Viollet-le-Duc started on the exterior. He opened out the ground floor, installed the drawbridge, and created the Grand Staircase and dining room. The Green Room and the Pink Room were decorated with his colleague Edmond Duthoit (1837–89). The castle's decoration, in a style that anticipates Art Nouveau, was never finished.

KEY

① **Underground passage**

② **Drawbridge**

③ **Dry Moat**

④ **Model of the castle**

⑤ **The fountain,** located beneath the Grand Staircase, was installed by Viollet-le-Duc.

⑥ **The keep** has rooms on the first and second floors.

For hotels and restaurants in this region see pp250–51 and pp262–3

Swan Chandelier
Added by Duthoit, it is made of gilded bronze and weighs 350 kg (770 lb).

VISITORS' CHECKLIST

Practical Information
Mazères. **Tel** 05 56 76 14 16.
Open Jul–Aug: daily; Sep–Oct: pm daily; Nov–Easter: pm Sun; Easter–Jun: pm daily. The medieval rooms can be hired.
W chateauroquetaillade.free.fr

Gargoyles
These date from Viollet-le-Duc's restoration.

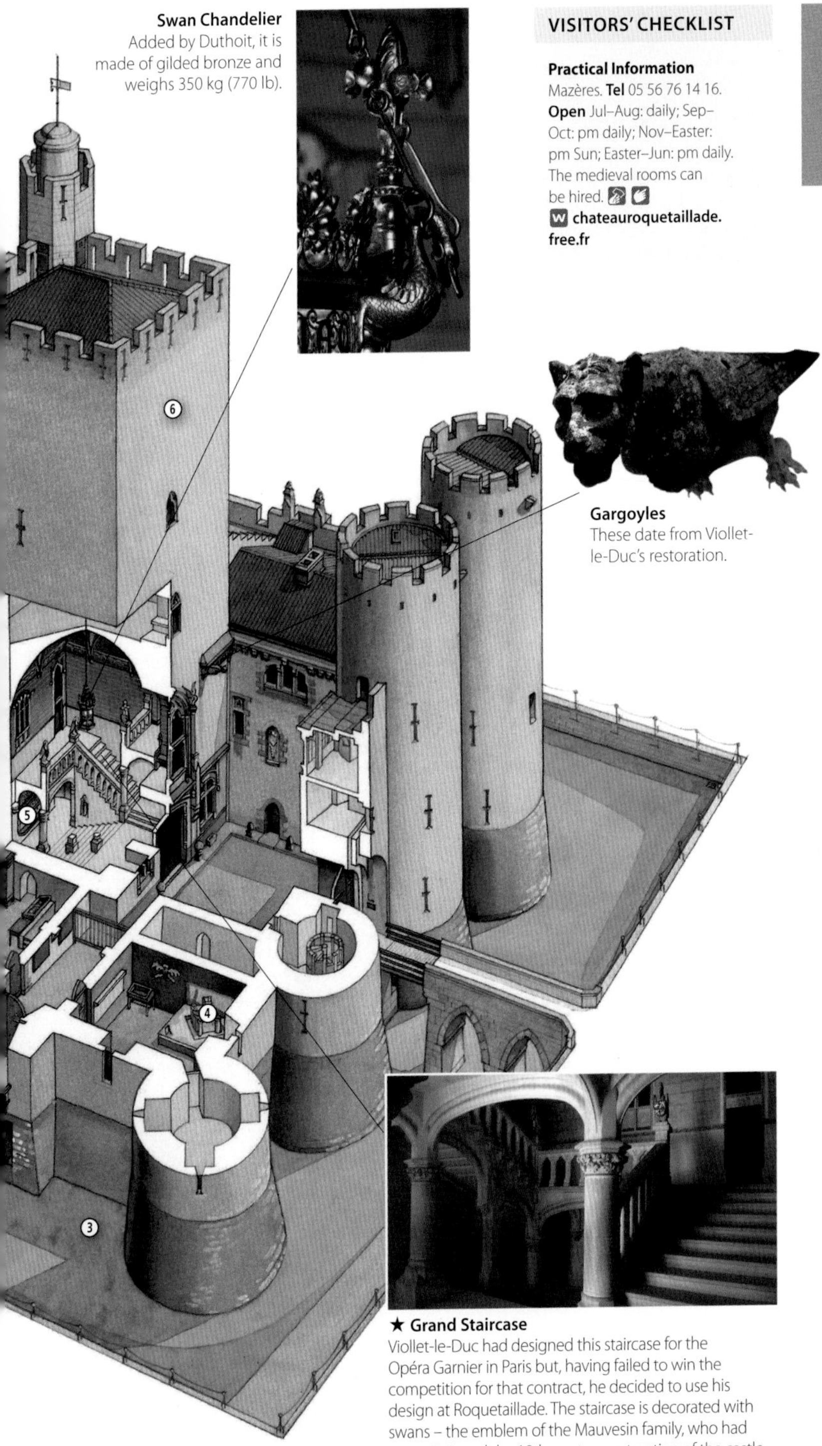

★ Grand Staircase
Viollet-le-Duc had designed this staircase for the Opéra Garnier in Paris but, having failed to win the competition for that contract, he decided to use his design at Roquetaillade. The staircase is decorated with swans – the emblem of the Mauvesin family, who had commissioned the 19th-century restoration of the castle.

Restored 14th-century frescoes in the church at Saint-Macaire

㉛ Saint-Macaire

Road map C2. 1,996. 8 rue du Canton; 05 56 63 32 14. Thu. Les Médiévales (Aug).

This medieval village, on the edge of the Bordeaux region, grew rich from river trade. It boasts some attractive buildings in ochre-coloured limestone. The priory church of Saint-Sauveur, in the form of a Latin cross, contains 14th-century frescoes, as well as a gilded wooden statue of the Madonna and Child. Place du Mercadiou, the ancient market square, is lined with fine 15th- and 16th-century merchants' houses. In summer, the village hosts Les Médiévales, with plays and concerts.

Environs

About 7.5 km (5 miles) northeast of Saint-Macaire, on the D672, is the wine-producing **Château Malromé**, built in the 14th–16th centuries. It was the home of the artist Henri de Toulouse-Lautrec, who died there in September 1901. He is buried in the cemetery at **Verdelais**, 3 km (2 miles) north of Malromé. The inside of the château is not open to the public. Around 3 km (2 miles) to the northwest is **Saint-Maixant**. The **Centre François-Mauriac** here is devoted to the life and work of this French author (1883–1970) and Nobel laureate.

Château Malromé
Saint-André-du-Bois. **Tel** 05 56 76 44 92. **Open** by appointment.
malrome.com

Centre François-Mauriac
Domaine de Malagar, Saint- Maixant. **Tel** 05 57 98 17 17. **Open** Apr–Oct: daily; Nov–Mar: pm Mon–Fri, all day Sat, Sun, public holidays.
malagar.aquitaine.fr

㉜ Cadillac

Road map C2. 2,382. 9 place de la Libération; 05 56 62 12 92. Sat.

Set on the banks of the Garonne, the *bastide* town of Cadillac was established in 1280 to halt the progress of French troops. A gate, the Porte de la Mer, is a reminder of those warlike times.

The town is dominated by the **Château des Ducs d'Épernon**. It was founded in 1599 by one of Henri III's favourites, who demolished the medieval fortress that stood on the site and built a sumptuous residence. Notable features of the interior include the decorated ceiling and eight monumental chimney pieces.

The building was looted in French Revolution, then in 1818 it served as a women's prison. From 1890 to 1952, it was used as a school for young offenders.

Château des Ducs d'Épernon
Tel 05 56 62 69 58. **Open** Jun–Sep: daily; Oct–May: Tue–Sun.

Environs

Rions, 4.5 km (3 miles) north of Cadillac on the D10, is a small town of Gallo-Roman origin and with medieval fortifications. About 11 km (7 miles) northwest on the D10 is the impressive **Forteresse de Langoiran**.

Forteresse de Langoiran
Tel 05 56 67 12 00. **Open** pm daily.

㉝ La Brède

Road map C2. 3,722. 3 place Marcel Vayssière, at Martillac; 05 56 78 47 72.

A wide avenue leads up to the **Château de La Brède**, where Montesquieu was born and lived. This rather austere Gothic building is surrounded by a man-made lake and moats.

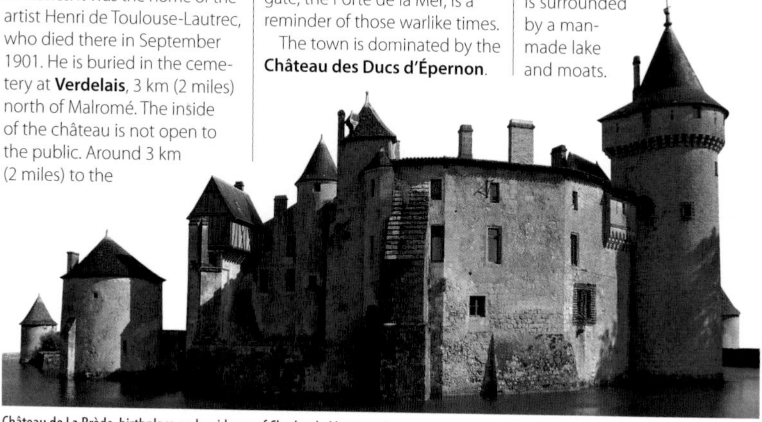

Château de La Brède, birthplace and residence of Charles de Montesquieu

For hotels and restaurants in this region see pp250–51 and pp262–3

While the keep dates from the 13th century, the circular towers, chapel and other buildings date from the 15th century. Inside, Montesquieu's bedroom/study has been preserved. It was here that he wrote *The Spirit of Laws*. His great library, with a barrel-vaulted ceiling, holds 7,000 books. The landscaped grounds in which the château stands were laid out by Montesquieu after a visit to England.

Château de la Brède
Tel 05 56 20 20 49. **Open** Easter–May & Oct–mid-Nov: pm Sat, Sun, public holidays; Jun–Sep: pm Wed–Mon. **Closed** Dec–Mar.

Charles de Montesquieu (1689–1755)

Charles-Louis de Secondat, later Baron de La Brède et de Montesquieu, was born in La Brède in 1689. He became a lawyer but also had a keen interest in science. In 1721, his *Persian Letters*, a political satire on the reign of Louis XIV and a brilliant critique of social mores, were published in Amsterdam, bringing him lasting fame. Elected president of the Parlement de Bordeaux, he also kept in touch with Parisian literary circles. He travelled widely, drawing on his observations to write *The Spirit of Laws* (1748), which laid the foundations of political science. An intellectual, a landowner, and a tireless promoter of the merits of Bordeaux wines, he died in Paris in 1755.

Charles de Montesquieu

34 Graves

Road map C2.

This area stretches along the south bank of the Garonne, south of Bordeaux on the Pessac and Léognan side. The Graves is the oldest wine-producing area in the Bordeaux region. The soil here is gravelly *(graveleux)*, hence its name. There are no fewer than 350 vine-growing estates in the Graves. Both red and white wines are produced, sometimes on the same estate, as at **Château Haut-Brion**. The Graves *appellation* covers an area of 3,700 ha (9,000 acres), which produce about 18,200,000 litres of wine a year.

Podensac, a major port on the Garonne in the 18th century, has some fine houses of this period. *Lillet*, a mixture of wine, fruit liqueur and cinchona bark *(see p260)*, is the traditional aperitif here. The town's **Maison des Vins de Graves** illustrates the history of local wine-making. Podensac is also one of the best places to see the steep wave *(mascaret)* that sweeps up the Gironde Estuary with each incoming tide.

At **Portets**, in the heart of the Graves, stands Château Lagueloup. Its vast 19th-century wine cellars have devices that seem impressively sophisticated for their time. There is also a **Musée de la Vigne et du Vin** here.

Château Haut-Brion
Tel 05 56 00 29 30. **Open** by prior arrangement. **haut-brion.com**

Maison des Vins de Graves
61 cours du Maréchal-Foch, Podensac. **Tel** 05 56 27 09 25. **Open** May–Oct: daily; Nov–Apr: Mon–Fri. **vins-graves.com**

Musée de la Vigne et du Vin
2–4 rue de la Liberté, Portets. **Tel** 05 56 67 18 11. **Open** daily.

Château-Olivier at Léognan, in the Graves area

Altarpiece in the church at Barsac

35 Barsac

Road map C2. 1,964. 1 allée Jean-Jaurès, Langon; 05 56 63 68 00.

From the 18th century, Barsac was an important centre of trade. It owed its wealth not only to wine, but also to the local limestone that was used for building throughout the Bordeaux area. The church, which is dedicated to St Vincent, patron saint of Gironde vine growers, was rebuilt in the 18th century by the architect who designed the Château de Malle *(see p96)*. The Baroque interior features an altarpiece by Vernet and an organ loft by Mollié.

The Barsac *appellation* applies to several châteaux, including Climens and Coutet, *premiers crus classés*.

Maison des Vins de Barsac
Ave Aristide Briand. **Tel** 05 56 27 15 44. **Open** daily.

The central pavilion of the Château de Malle, in the Louis XIV style, and one of the wings

36 Château de Malle

Road map C2. Preignac. **Tel** 05 56 62 36 86. **Open** Apr–Oct: Mon–Fri pm. chateau-de-malle.fr

Encircled by the A62, the RN113 and the Bordeaux-to-Langon railway line, this charming residence was built in the 17th century for Jacques de Malle, a magistrate from Bordeaux. The original parts of the château include the main building and its two wings, which are set at right angles to it, each ending in a circular tower. There is also a two-storey central pavilion, which dates from the 18th century. The balustraded terrace leads to an Italian-style garden, which has an open-air theatre and many stone statues.

The interior contains fine antique furniture and a curious collection of 17th-century trompe l'œil silhouettes that served as "extras" in theatrical productions.

Unusually, the château's vineyards produce two types of wine: fine, top-grade, sweet *cru classé* Sauternes, as well as more basic Graves.

37 Sauternais

Road map C2/C3. 706. 11 rue Principale, Sauternes; 05 56 76 69 13 (Easter–Sep).

Lying along the south bank of the Garonne, 40 km (25 miles) southeast of Bordeaux, the Sauternais area has a mix of siliceous, limestone and gravelly soil. The Ciron river, which flows through the area, gives it a favourable climate. The Sauternais is also dotted with prestigious châteaux, the most famous of which is the **Château d'Yquem cellars**. Rated *premier cru supérieur*, the Sauternes produced there are some of the finest and most expensive wines in the world. Dating from the 15th century, Yquem is also one of the oldest wine estates in the area. Its vineyards cover about 100 ha (250 acres).

The Sauternes *appellation* covers five villages: Sauternes, Bommes, Fargues, Preignac and Barsac. These *grands crus* can be tasted and purchased at the **Maison des Vins de Sauternes**.

Château d'Yquem cellars
Tel 05 57 98 07 07. **Open** request a visit via info@yquem.fr. **Closed** Aug.

Maison des Vins de Sauternes
14 place de la Mairie, Sauternes. **Tel** 05 56 76 69 83. **Open** daily.

Environs
About 4.5 km (3 miles) west of Sauternes, is the fortress at **Budos**, one of Pope Clement V's castles, built in 1308. Ruins of another of his castles lie at **Fargues**, 5 km (3 miles) east.

Sauternes

The grapes used for Sauternes must have been infected by a form of the fungus *Botrytis cinerea*, known as noble rot. This causes them to shrivel and have a very high sugar content, which accounts for the sweetness of the wines. The Sauternes grape harvest is a long and painstaking process, in which every single grape is picked by hand. After fermentation, the wine matures in barrels for two years, before being bottled. Sauternes is served well chilled, but it is not only a dessert wine. It can also be enjoyed as an aperitif, or sipped with *foie gras* or Roquefort cheese.

Barrels of Sauternes, left for two years to mature

38 Villandraut

Road map C3. 935. 9, Place du Général-de-Gaulle; 05 56 25 31 39. Thu.

The impressive **château** here was built in 1305, both as a residential palace and for defensive purposes, on the orders of Pope Clement V (*see p45*), who was born in Villandraut. A huge building with an interior courtyard, it was – like the Château de Roquetaillade (*see pp92–3*) – defended by a rectangular line of ramparts set with six towers. From the top of these, there are fine views of the surrounding landscape.

Château de Villandraut
Tel 05 56 25 87 57. **Open** Apr–Jun: pm daily; Jul–Sep: daily; rest of year by appointment.

Environs
Saint-Symphorien, 10 km (6 miles) west, is the village where the writer François Mauriac grew up, and which inspired his *Thérèse Desqueyroux*.

39 Château de Cazeneuve

See pp98–9.

40 Uzeste

Road map C3. 446. 9, Place du Général-de-Gaulle, Villandraut; 05 56 25 31 39. Festival d'Uzeste (Aug).

Consecrated in 1313 on the orders of Pope Clement V *(see p39)*, the **Collégiale d'Uzeste** is one of the Gironde's finest Gothic buildings. Large in relation to the size of the village, this abbey church was probably built to house the Pope's tomb (sited in the choir). The bell tower, in the Flamboyant Gothic style, stands at the east end.

The imposing Collégiale d'Uzeste

Collégiale d'Uzeste
Tel 06 09 92 20 23. **Open** daily. summer.

41 Bazas

Road map C3. 4,607. Place de la Cathédrale; 05 56 25 25 84. Sat. Fête des Bœufs Gras (Thu before the Feb carnival).
tourisme-bazadais.com

Founded over 2,000 years ago, as the capital of the Roman province of Vasates, the town of Bazas later became a bishopric on the pilgrim route to Santiago de Compostela. Its magnificent Gothic cathedral was built between the 13th and 17th centuries, and has been restored. Particularly striking are the beautiful rose window and a triple Gothic doorway embellished with intricate carvings, both dating from the 13th century. Behind this majestic building lie the chapterhouse gardens.

Place de la Cathédrale is a gently sloping square on which a colourful market has been held for centuries. It is lined with arcaded 16th- and 17th-century houses, which have finely decorated façades.

The **Musée de Bazas** is devoted to the archeology and history of the town. The **Apothicairerie de l'Hôpital Saint-Antoine** contains a fine collection of pottery and glassware. A waymarked walk allows visitors to explore the town's picturesque old streets.

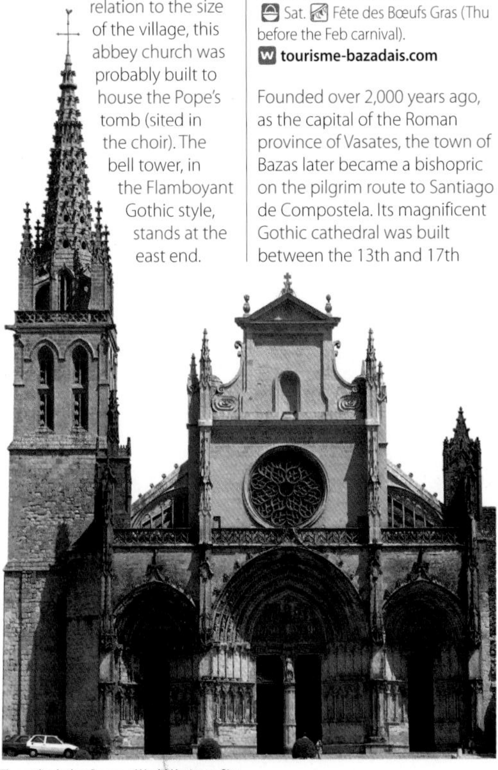

The cathedral at Bazas, a World Heritage Site

Musée de Bazas
Tel 05 56 25 25 84. **Open** Jul–Aug: Tue & Sat.

Apothicairerie de l'Hôpital Saint-Antoine
Tel 05 56 25 25 84. **Open** by appointment only.

Environs
The town of **Captieux** 17 km (10 miles) south of Bazas, is one of the overwintering sites of the migratory common crane. For information about these birds, contact the Ligue de Protection des Oiseaux Aquitaine in Bègles *(tel: 05 56 91 33 81)*.

39 Château de Cazeneuve

Set high above the deep, picturesque gorge carved by the Ciron river, the castle is fronted by 50 ha (120 acres) of wooded parkland. Although this elegant building has a unified look, its appearance today is the result of several successive phases of building. The castle grew out of a simple keep built on a motte in the 11th century. Three hundred years later it had become a fortress and in the 17th century it was converted into a sumptuous residence. The buildings, which are still inhabited, are arranged round the main courtyard. An extensive tour takes visitors through the castle's various stage of development and brings to life famous visitors and inhabitants, including Henri IV of France, who owned it, his queen, Margaret, and the dukes of Albret.

The castle, set high above the gorge of the Ciron river

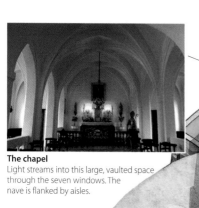

The chapel
Light streams into this large, vaulted space through the seven windows. The nave is flanked by aisles.

The cellars
Dating from the Middle Ages, they are stacked with barrels of highly prized Bordeaux wines.

KEY

① **Merovingian tombs**

② **The lower courtyard** leads to the pool and to the medieval wine cellars.

③ **Study**

④ **Troglodytic caves**

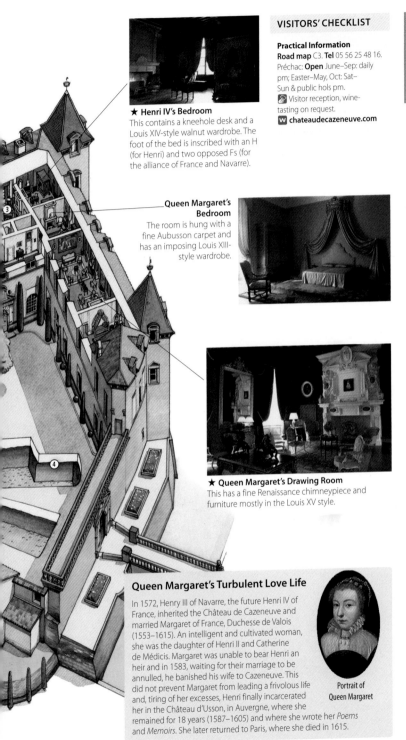

★ Henri IV's Bedroom
This contains a kneehole desk and a Louis XIV-style walnut wardrobe. The foot of the bed is inscribed with an H (for Henri) and two opposed Fs (for the alliance of France and Navarre).

VISITORS' CHECKLIST

Practical Information
Road map C3. **Tel** 05 56 25 48 16. Préchac: **Open** June–Sep: daily pm; Easter–May, Oct: Sat–Sun & public hols pm.
Visitor reception, wine-tasting on request.
chateaudecazeneuve.com

Queen Margaret's Bedroom
The room is hung with a fine Aubusson carpet and has an imposing Louis XIII-style wardrobe.

★ Queen Margaret's Drawing Room
This has a fine Renaissance chimneypiece and furniture mostly in the Louis XV style.

Queen Margaret's Turbulent Love Life

Portrait of Queen Margaret

In 1572, Henry III of Navarre, the future Henri IV of France, inherited the Château de Cazeneuve and married Margaret of France, Duchesse de Valois (1553–1615). An intelligent and cultivated woman, she was the daughter of Henri II and Catherine de Médicis. Margaret was unable to bear Henri an heir and in 1583, waiting for their marriage to be annulled, he banished his wife to Cazeneuve. This did not prevent Margaret from leading a frivolous life and, tiring of her excesses, Henri finally incarcerated her in the Château d'Usson, in Auvergne, where she remained for 18 years (1587–1605) and where she wrote her *Poems* and *Memoirs*. She later returned to Paris, where she died in 1615.

PÉRIGORD AND QUERCY

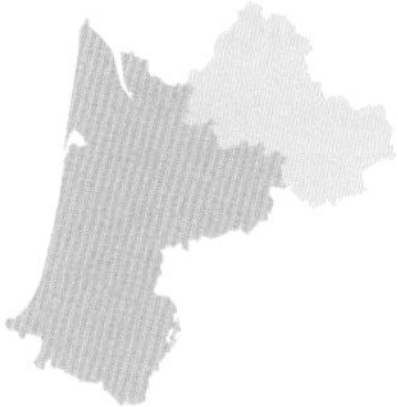

From the deep, narrow gorges of the Vézère to the fertile plains of the wide Dordogne valley, and from the panoramic Cingle de Trémolat to the dense woodland on the edge of the Limousin, the Périgord is a land of contrasts. This varied landscape is also dotted with painted caves, medieval villages and massive castles, traces of human activity that date back to prehistoric times.

Périgord-Quercy stretches across two *départements*, the Lot and the Dordogne – the latter being the third-largest in France, after its Aquitanian neighbours the Landes and the Gironde. The mix of landscapes that make up this region offer something for everyone: to the north, meadows and forests, merging into those of neighbouring Limousin; to the east, rugged limestone plateaux; to the south, vineyards, running down almost seamlessly into those of Bordeaux; and to the west, flatter land, bathed by the pearly coastal light flowing in from the Charentais. Across all of these areas, humans have left their mark, a legacy going back to prehistoric times. The Vézère valley caves, the Gallo-Roman museum in Périgueux, the great castle at Castelnaud that witnessed the Hundred Years' War, the many medieval *bastide* towns, and Sarlat's Renaissance town houses are just a few aspects of a heritage that covers around two-and-a-half million years. From troglodytic cliff-dwellings and fortress towers set high on rocky spurs, to watermills that straddle rivers, and a string of Romanesque churches built in the local ochre sandstone, the architecture sits in perfect harmony with the scenery of this multifaceted yet unified region.

Geese in the Périgord, raised for the production of *foie gras*

◀ The village of Rocamadour at dusk

Exploring Périgord and Quercy

Most of the region lies within the *département* of the Dordogne, the capital of which is Périgueux, set on the banks of the Isle river. The Dordogne divides into four distinct areas. The Périgord Blanc (White Périgord) consists of limestone plateaux, stretching across the centre of the Isle valley, the Vern valley to the east and Forêt de la Double to the west. The Périgord Vert (Green Périgord) covers the north of the *département*, from Ribérac to Hautefort. The picturesque Périgord Noir (Black Périgord) consists of the Vézère and Dordogne valleys, as far as Sarlat and the border with Quercy. And in the southwest is the Périgord Pourpre (Purple Périgord), covered in vineyards and dotted with the *bastide* towns of the Bergerac area.

Getting Around

From Bergerac, which has an international airport, there is a connecting train service to the TGV (high-speed train) at Bordeaux. The railway links Périgueux and Bergerac with Sarlat, Bordeaux and Limoges. The A89 connects Périgueux with Bordeaux. In the opposite direction, the A89 runs as far as Brive-la-Gaillarde. The D6089 runs through the Périgord from east to west, and the N21 from north to south. Périgord is served by a network of roads that run along the main valleys. In Quercy, the A20 links Brive and Cahors, and the D840 provides access to Rocamadour, Padirac and Figeac. There is a bus service between Périgueux and Bergerac, and buses also run between the main towns of the Dordogne.

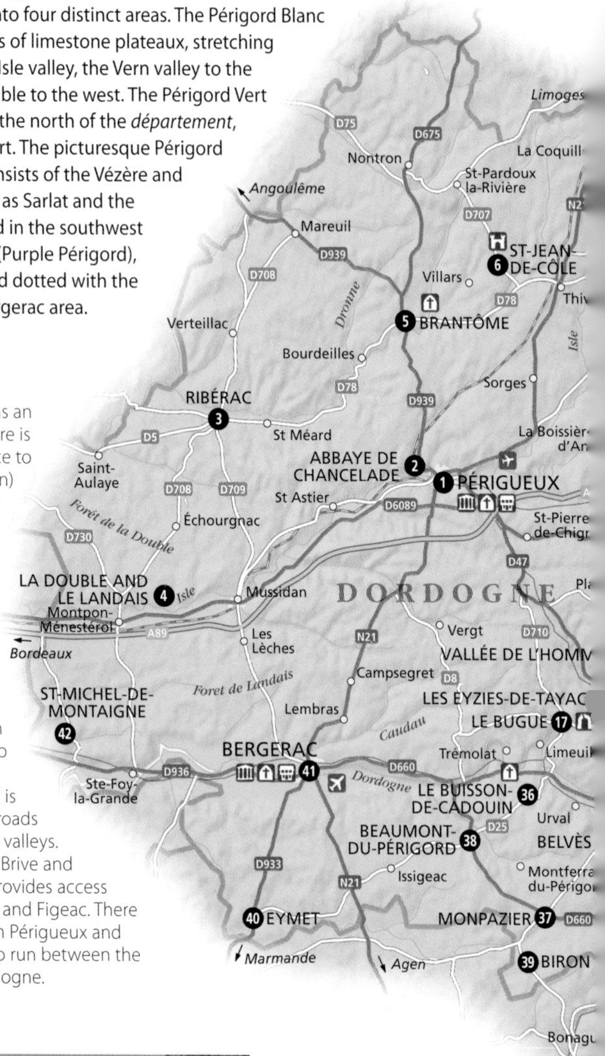

Jardins de l'Imaginaire at Terrasson-Lavilledieu

Key

- Motorway
- Dual carriageway
- Main road
- Minor road
- Main railway
- Minor railway
- Regional border

For map symbols *see back flap*

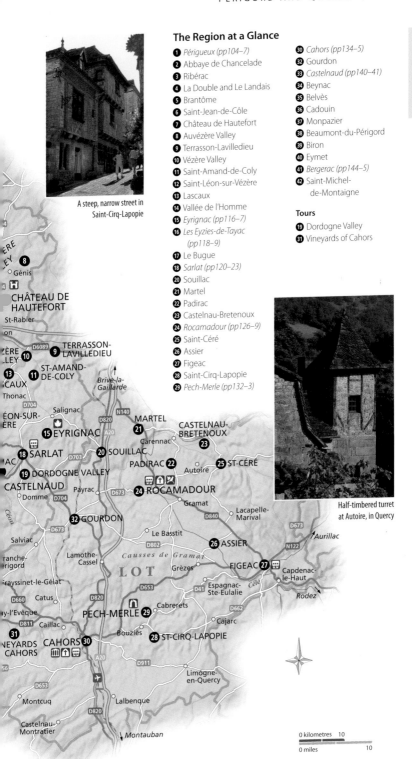

A steep, narrow street in Saint-Cirq-Lapopie

The Region at a Glance

Tours

Half-timbered turret at Autoire, in Quercy

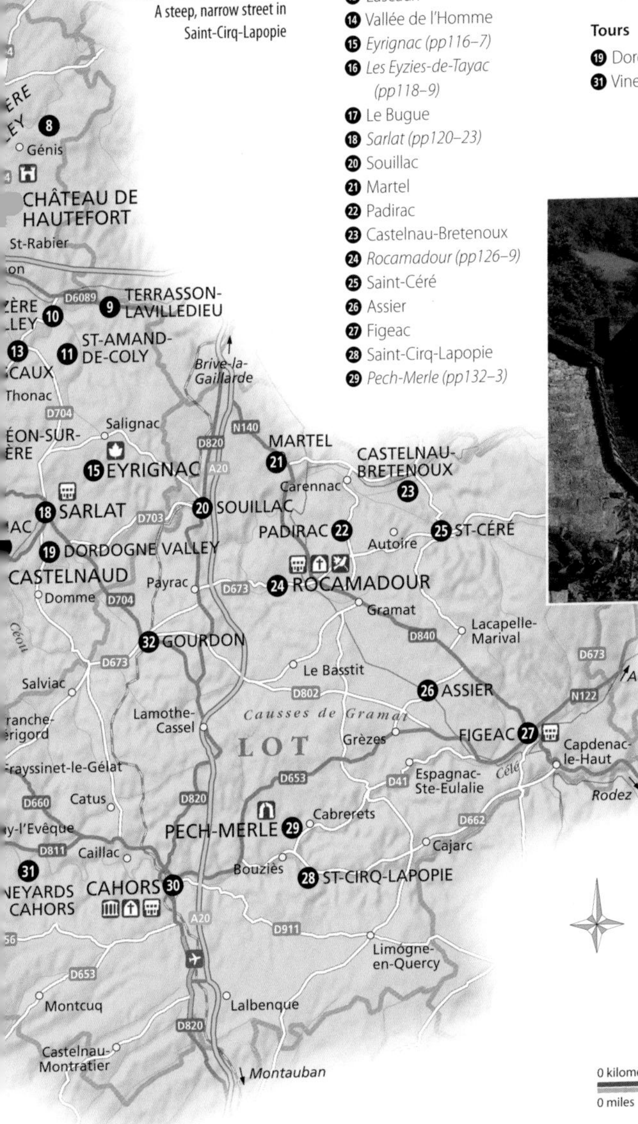

❶ Street-by-Street: Périgueux

The ancient centre of Périgueux is one of the largest urban conservation areas in France. A programme of restoration, which began in 1970, has brought to life the narrow streets that run from the boulevards of the upper town down to the banks of the river Isle, and from the Mataguerre to the Plantier districts. Around the cathedral is the city's pleasant, pedestrianized, medieval area. Place de la Mairie, place du Coderc and place de la Clautre buzz with activity on market days. Place Saint-Louis, not far from rue Limogeanne, and the alleys leading off place de la Vertu make for a pleasant stroll.

Rue Limogeanne, the city's main pedestrian thoroughfare, with shops and Renaissance houses

★ Place Saint-Louis
The finest building on this square is Maison du Pâtissier, or Maison Tenant. This restored 14th-century town house is an important example of Renaissance building in the town. The door was added in the 16th century. Its pediment bears an inscription in Latin.

Hôtel La Joubertie
The town house at 1 rue de la Sagesse has a magnificent Renaissance staircase with coffered vaulting and columns whose capitals are carved with fantasy animals.

Hôtel de Ville

Hôtel Estignard is a town house built in the reign of François I (1515–1547).

Place du Coderc
Périgueux's colourful market stalls fill this square, near the Hôtel de Ville (town hall).

Key

— Suggested route

For hotels and restaurants in this region see pp251–2 and pp263–5

Logis Saint-Front or Hôtel Gamenson
This building, at 7 rue de la Constitution, consists of two 15th-century houses, a 16th-century half-timbered wing and a staircase tower, arranged in a square shape.

Freemasons' Hall
The original masonic symbols on this 1869 building were restored in 1987, having been destroyed under the Vichy government (1940–1944).

VISITORS' CHECKLIST

Practical Information
Road map D1. 29,080. 26 place Francheville, 05 53 53 10 63. Great Market: Wed & Sat am; *foie gras* market: mid-Nov–Mar. Mimos (Festival of Mime) (early Aug); Sinfonia (Sep); Salon International du Livre Gourmand (Nov, even years).

Transport

★ Quayside Houses
These Renaissance buildings include the 17th-century Hôtel Salleton, the 15th-century Maison des Consuls (or Maison Cayla), with its Gothic dormer windows, and Maison Lambert, with its coffered ceilings and carved pilasters.

Jardin du Thouin

Old Mill

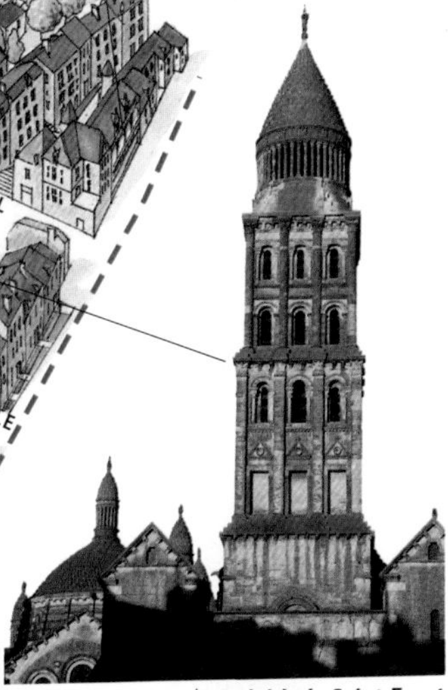

★ Cathédrale Saint-Front
The original roman church was destroyed by fire in 1120, and rebuilt in the form of a Greek cross, like St Mark's in Venice. The plainness of the interior emphasizes its fine proportions. The domes, supported by columns, are 38 m (125 ft) high and 25 m (82 ft) across.

Exploring Périgueux

The modern city of Périgueux sits on the site of ancient Vesunna. Founded in about 16 BC, this Gallo-Roman settlement fell into a decline from around the 4th century onward. During the Middle Ages, a new community sprang up, concentrated around the present Église de la Cité and the Château Barrière, but it was largely overshadowed in importance by Le Puy-Saint-Front to the north, which thrived by serving the needs of pilgrims on the road to Santiago de Compostela. After years of hostility between the two towns, peace was finally made in 1240. During the Renaissance, Périgueux began to grow, spreading out from the area around the cathedral, which remains the hub of the city to this day.

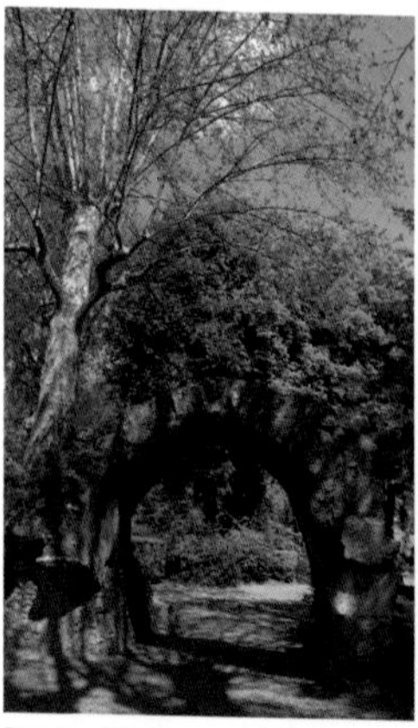

Remains of the Roman amphitheatre in Jardin des Arènes

Vesunna

Parc de Vésone. **Tel** 05 53 53 00 92. **Closed** Jan, Christmas and out of season: Mon.

This museum is named after the ancient city that occupied the site of modern Perigueux. The artworks and everyday objects on show give an insight into daily life in Gallo-Roman times. A building by the architect Jean Nouvel covers the remains of a Roman house discovered in 1959. Nearby is the imposing **Tour de Vésone**. Some 24 m (80 ft) high and with an internal diameter of 17 m (56 ft), it gives an idea of the size of the temple, long gone, of which it formed part. The Jardin des Arènes contains the remains of an amphitheatre that held 20,000 spectators.

Château Barrière

Rue de Turenne, outside only.

For centuries this 12th-century castle served as a fortress for the aristocratic families of the Périgord. It was remodelled in the 15th century and came under attack from Protestant forces in 1575, during the Wars of Religion. The oldest parts – a Gallo-Roman wall and keep – can be seen at the rear. The elegant five-tiered tower and residential quarters date from the Renaissance.

Périgueux City Centre

① Maison du Pâtissier
② Musée d'Art et d'Archéologie du Périgord
③ Quayside Houses
④ Cathédrale Saint-Front
⑤ Logis St-Front
⑥ Musée Militaire
⑦ Tour Mataguerre
⑧ Église de la Cité
⑨ Château Barrière
⑩ Vesunna
⑪ Tour de Vésone

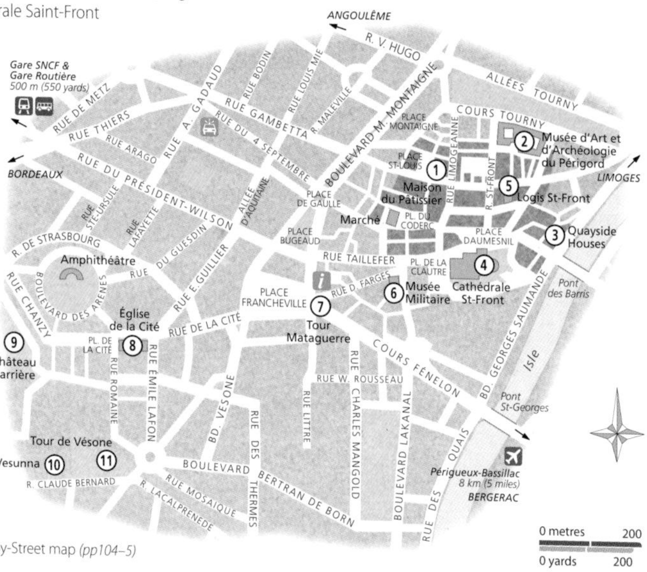

Key

Street-by-Street map *(pp104–5)*

For map symbols *see back flap*

Cathédrale Saint-Front
Place de la Claustre.
The Byzantine-Romanesque elements of Saint-Front, a cathedral since 1669, were added by Paul Abadie, later architect of the Sacré-Cœur in Paris. He added the five domes and installed 17 small steeples. The interior has a magnificent 17th-century Baroque altar-piece and Stations of the Cross by Jacques-Émile Lafon. The remains of the old bell tower are kept in the cloisters. In summer, organ recitals are given, on the 1869 organ.

Église de la Cité
Place de la Cité.
Périgueux's first cathedral, the Romanesque, single-nave Église Saint-Étienne-de-la-Cité, was built in the 11th century and remodelled in the 17th, when it also lost its cathedral status. It still has two of its four original domes.

Tour Mataguerre
Place Francheville. **Tel** 05 53 53 10 63.
Of the 28 towers that once surrounded Le Puy-Saint-Front, only this one still stands. The tourist office next door organizes tours of this vestige of the fortifications that encircled the city from the 12th to the 19th centuries. The top of the tower offers a breathtaking view of Périgueux.

The 15th-century Tour Mataguerre, a vestige of the city's ramparts

A Soul in Heaven (1878) by W A Bouguereau, Musée du Périgord

Some of oldest buildings in the city can be found nearby. Among them are the 12th-century Maison des Dames de la Foi, at 4–6 rue des Farges.

Musée d'Art et d'Archéologie du Périgord
22 cours Tourny. **Tel** 05 53 06 40 70.
Open Wed–Mon, Sat–Sun: pm.
Closed public hols.
This museum, which in some respects resembles a cabinet of curiosities, holds a large and fascinating prehistoric collection. This includes the world's most complete Neanderthal skeleton, found at Régourdou. In addition, beautiful glass, mosaics and earthenware from ancient Vessuna, as well as artifacts from Africa and Oceania, can be seen, along with a display of local paintings, sculptures and pottery, bequeathed by Étienne Hajdu (1907–96). Regular temporary exhibitions are also held here.

Musée Militaire
32 rue des Farges. **Tel** 05 53 53 47 36.
Open Apr–Oct: pm Mon–Sat; Oct–Mar: pm Wed, Sat.
There are around 13,000 exhibits in this museum, the oldest of its kind in France. One room houses a moving series of drawings made in the trenches during World War I by Gilbert-Privat (1892–1965), winner of the Prix de Rome. The colonial and World War II collections, as well as medals, insignia and other wartime memorabilia, help serve as a reminder of the sacrifice of those who fought, and of the need to preserve the peace.

Environs
Sorges, northeast of Périgueux, is the Périgord's truffle capital. The **Écomusée de la Truffe** has displays showing how truffles grow, the methods of finding them and details of some spectacularly large examples.

Écomusée de la Truffe
Sorges. **Tel** 05 53 05 90 11.
Open Tue–Sun (mid-Jun–Aug: daily).

Truffles
The Périgordian truffle, *Tuber melanosporum*, is a highly prized delicacy that, for gourmets, is almost worth its weight in gold. An ingredient of many local specialities, this subterranean fungus is now scarce. In 1870, Sorges' limestone plateau alone produced 6 tonnes of truffles a year, which equals the yield obtained today from the whole of the Dordogne. The main truffle market takes place at Sainte-Alvère, in the Bergerac region. The going price is usually €1,000 per kilogram (about £500 per lb).

A dry-stone truffle-hunter's hut, at the Écomusée de Sorges

For hotels and restaurants in this region see pp251–2 and pp263–5

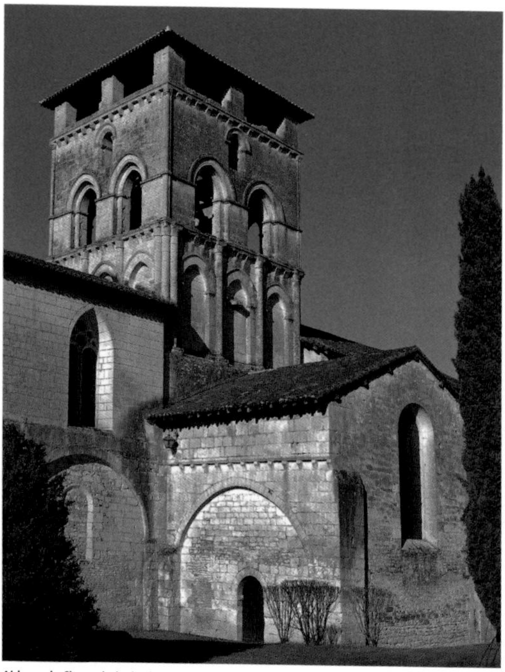

Abbaye de Chancelade, built in the 12th century

❷ Abbaye de Chancelade

Road map D1. 4,174. Périgueux. Maison de la Communauté de Chancelade; 05 53 04 10 46. **Open** daily (access to the exterior only). **abbaye-chancelade.com**

Set in the Beauronne valley, the Augustinian Abbaye de Chancelade was founded in the 12th century and became an important centre of intellectual life. Having survived the Hundred Years' War and the Wars of Religion, it once again became influential in the 17th century. It is remarkably well preserved, with a wash-house, stables, workshops and a mill.

Environs

From the abbey, a marked 14-km (9-mile) long path through woods leads to the old village of **Les Maines**, with a view of the former Templar house at Les Andrivaux.

The **Prieuré de Merlande**, 4 km (3 miles) northeast of Chancelade, is a priory founded by monks from Chancelade.

❸ Ribérac

Road map D1. 4,000. Périgueux. Place du Général-de-Gaulle; 05 53 90 03 10. Fri. Les Musicales (May).

Birthplace of 12th-century troubadour Arnaud Daniel, Ribérac is a town where you are just as likely to hear English as Occitan at the market, because of the large number of English expatriates living in nearby villages. The abbey church, built in the 12th century with later additions, has 17th-century art and a dome above the choir.

Many Romanesque domed churches are dotted around Ribérac: the church at **Siorac-de-Ribérac**, fortified in the 14th century, contains an interesting 18th-century painted and gilded wooden statue; the church at **Grand-Brassac** has a splendid carved doorway as well as three domes supported on stone columns; and the church at **Saint-Privat-des-Prés**, an architectural jewel, has a circular arch with ornate moulding over the entrance.

Environs

30 km (19 miles) northwest of Ribérac are the **Tourbières de Vendoire**, peat bogs where visitors can see extraordinary water-filled plant fossils.

The **Château de Mareuil**, 30 km (19 miles) north of Ribérac, is the only medieval fortress built on a plain. It was once owned by the Talleyrand family, and has 12th-century towers and ramparts, a 15th-century keep with living quarters and a Gothic chapel.

Tourbières de Vendoire
Tel 05 53 90 79 56. **Open** Jul–Aug: Tue–Sun; rest of the year by appointment only.

Château de Mareuil
At junction of D939 & D708.
Tel 05 53 60 46 18. **Open** Apr–Oct: Tue–Sat, Sun pm.

❹ La Double and Le Landais

Road map D2. Between Montpon and Ribérac, via the D708.

The stunning, wild, marshy countryside here is covered with areas of dense forest, dotted with ponds and clearings. At the **Ferme du Parcot** visitors can see

The village of Grand-Brassac and its church, near Ribérac

The covered market and castle at Saint-Jean-de-Côle

local houses made with cob-filled wooden frames. **Saint-Aulaye** is a village known for its church, Cognac museum and a river-side beach along the Dronne. At nearby **La Latière**, a well-attended cattle market has been held since the Middle Ages.

Ferme du Parcot
On the Saint-Astier road, Échourgnac. **Tel** 05 53 81 99 28. **Open** May, Jun & Sep: Sat & Sun pm, Jul–Aug: Tue–Sun .

❺ Brantôme

Road map D1. 2,159. Périgueux. Boulevard Charlemagne; 05 53 05 80 63. Fri am.

The town of Brantôme sits on an island, encircled by a loop of the river Dronne. Its buildings cluster around the 9th-century Benedictine **abbey**. The bell tower, dating from the 11th century, is one of the oldest in France. A 16th-century bridge links the abbey to its gardens. Close by is the Grotte du Jugement Dernier, a cave with a 15th-century carved relief of the Last Judgment.

Abbey
Tel 05 53 05 80 63. **Open** daily. **Closed** Jan.

Environs
10.5 km (6 miles) southwest of Brantôme is the 13th-century **Château de Bourdeilles**. It has an octagonal keep and later Renaissance buildings and ramparts.

The 16th-century **Château de Puyguilhem**, 10 km (6 miles) northeast of Brantôme, has an elegant main house, towers, dormer windows and battlements. The château's interiors are also exceptionally fine.

The **Grotte de Villars**, 15 km (9 miles) northeast of Brantôme, is a network of caves with 13 km (8 miles) of galleries, filled with fascinating rock formations and some prehistoric paintings.

Boat ride through Brantôme, "the Venice of Périgord"

Château de Bourdeilles
Tel 05 53 03 73 36. **Closed** Jan.

Château de Puyguilhem
Villars. **Tel** 05 53 54 82 18. **Open** Apr–Sep: daily; Oct–Mar: Wed–Sun. **Closed** public hols.

Grotte de Villars
Tel 05 53 54 82 36. **Open** Apr–Sep: daily; Oct–mid-Nov: pm daily.
grotte-villars.com

❻ Saint-Jean-de-Côle

Road map D1. 340. Thiviers. Rue du Château; 05 53 62 14 15. Floralies (late Apr or early May).

One of France's prettiest villages, Saint-Jean-de-Côle sits on the banks of the river Côle. Its focal point is a late 11th-century priory, torched by the English during the Hundred Years' War and looted by Protestants in 1569, during the Wars of Religion. It was rebuilt in the 17th century. The 12th-century Byzantine-Romanesque church has an unusual plan: it forms a semicircle around the apse. Wooden carvings in the choir date from the 18th century.

The medieval bridge and the rue du Fond-du-Bourg, lined with 14th-century half-timbered houses, add to the village's picturesque appeal. The 12th-century Château de la Marthonie, on place Saint-Jean, was rebuilt in the 15th century and enlarged in the 17th.

Environs
The **Château de Jumilhac**, 20 km (12 miles) northeast of Saint-Jean-de-Côle, is a 13th-century castle. A magnificent roof set with pepperpot towers and skylights was added in 1600. The outbuildings and ramparts were demolished in the 17th century to make room for luxurious reception areas, including a drawing room based on that at Versailles and a magnificent Louis XIII-style staircase.

Château de Jumilhac
Jumilhac. **Tel** 05 53 52 42 97. **Open** Easter–May & Oct–Nov: daily pm; Jun–Sep: daily.

❼ Château de Hautefort

Closely associated with the warrior-troubadour Bertran de Born, Hautefort was originally a medieval fortress. The imposing residence that later replaced it was built for the Marquis de Hautefort, who envisaged a classic building in the style of a Loire Valley château. Work began in 1630, to plans by Nicolas Rambourg, and was completed in 1670. A drawbridge leads through to the courtyard and main building, with an arcaded gallery and steep slate roof. Baron and Baroness de Bastard began restoring the main building in the 1920s, but this was brought to an abrupt end by a fire in August 1968. All that was saved were the 16th-century tapestries. Photographs showing the devastation of the fire are on view in the 14th-century Tour e Bretagne, the only surviving medieval part of the castle. Further phases of restoration were completed in 1995 and 2005.

★ Grand Staircase
This curves back on itself to lead to the upper floor.

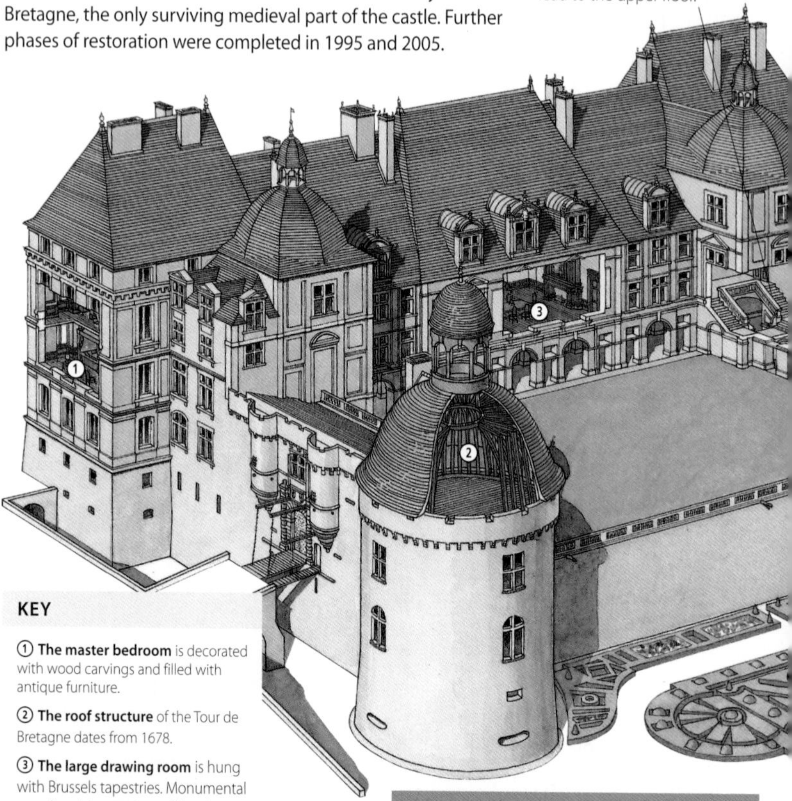

KEY

① **The master bedroom** is decorated with wood carvings and filled with antique furniture.

② **The roof structure** of the Tour de Bretagne dates from 1678.

③ **The large drawing room** is hung with Brussels tapestries. Monumental wooden chimneypieces fill each end of the room.

④ **The formal gardens** are best seen from above, particularly from the main courtyard, which also commands a view of the village on its southern side.

⑤ **The terrace** was rearranged in the 1930s. Box and yew have been clipped into dome shapes to echo the outline of the château and its slate-roofed towers. This formal garden is laid out to give the shape of a gushing fountain, when viewed from above.

The village of Hautefort, with its imposing château above

For hotels and restaurants in this region see pp251–2 and pp263–5

VISITORS' CHECKLIST

Practical Information
Road map E1. **Tel** 05 53 50 51 23.
Open Apr–Oct: daily; Mar & Nov: Sat, Sun & public hols (pm).
Closed mid-Nov–Feb.
chateau-hautefort.com

Transport
Terrasson-Lavilledieu.

★ The Chapel
The ceiling, a trompe l'oeil coffered dome, looks down on a simple clay floor.

The Troubadour of Hautefort

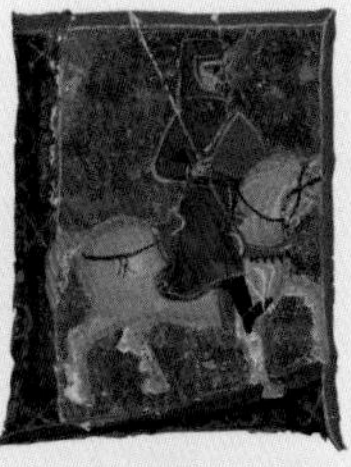

Miniature of Bertran de Born on horseback

Bertran de Born (c.1150–1215), Viscount of Hautefort, is a legendary figure in the Pays d'Oc. Over 40 of his poem-songs survive, many on the theme of courtly love, but some are of a political and warlike nature. On several occasions, he fought both his brother and the English monarchy (then Dukes of Aquitaine) for ownership of Hautefort. This belligerent stance led some to blame him for the conflict between England and France at the time. For this, Dante, in the *Inferno*, portrays him as a sower of discord and places him in hell. He ended his life as a monk at the Abbaye du Dalon.

❽ Auvézère Valley

Road map E1. Périgueux.
Place du Marquis, Hautefort; 05 53 50 40 27. Or 4 place Thomas-Robert-Bugeaud, Lanouaille; 05 53 62 17 82.
Fête de la Noix (Nailhac; Aug), Festival du Pays d'Ans (Jul/Aug).

This valley contains several interesting sights. The **Chapelle d'Auberoche**, with its traditional Périgordiantile roof, perches high on a cliff, offering dramatic views. Moving upriver, the Blâme cascades dramatically into the Auvézère at **La Boissière d'Ans**. Commanding views of the Loue and Auvézère valleys can also be had from the **Colline de Saint-Raphaël**. Two massive columns, in front of the church here, are the remains of a Benedictine priory. **Génis** is also set high up, on a granite plateau, looking down on the gorges of the river Dalon. Upstream from here is an old mill, the **Moulin du Pervendoux**, beyond which are rapids and the **Cascade du Saut-Ruban**. A path (GR 646) leads down to this waterfall from the **Église de Saint-Mesmin**. At Le Puy-des-Âges, set on a quartz-rich spur, is the little chapel of **Notre-Dame-de-Partout**, filled with votive offerings. The hill-top château close to **Savignac-Lédrier** looks down on a 17th-century forge, while at **Payzac** is the former Vaux papermill. Round about, oval, stone barns that were originally thatched, lie dotted across the landscape.

The Auvézère valley, an unspoilt area of hills, woods and pasture

Jardins de l'Imaginaire, on the Vézère river at Terrasson-Lavilledieu

❾ Terrasson-Lavilledieu

Road map E2. On the D6089. 6,218. Rue Jean-Rouby; 05 53 50 37 56. Thu am. Les Chemins de l'Imaginaire (Jul).

At the head of the Vézère valley, which leads down into the Périgord, the town of Terrasson-Lavilledieu grew up around a Merovingian abbey. The Pont Vieux, the town's old stone bridge, dates back to the 12th century, but was damaged during the Hundred Years' War and largely rebuilt in the late 15th century, as were the church and the monastery. Terrasson was also a strategic town during the 16th-century Wars of Religion and also opposed the French Revolution.

The **Jardins de l'Imaginaire**, overlook the old town. These 6 ha (15 acres) include a rose garden, a sacred wood, a water garden, a belvedere and scattered springs, all designed around historical and mythological themes.

Jardins de l'Imaginaire
Place de Genouillac; 05 53 50 86 82. **Open** mid-Apr–Oct.

❿ Vézère Valley

Road map E2. Périgueux. Les Eyzies. 19 Rue de la Préhistoire, Les Eyzies; 05 53 06 97 05. Festival du Périgord Noir (Jul–Oct), Festival du Folklore International (Montignac, Jul)

The valley is dotted with picturesque small towns. **Condat-sur-Vézère**, once a Templar town, stands at the confluence of the Vézère and the Coly. It has a Romanesque church and a castle with a square tower. **Fanlac** clusters round its church and bell tower. The town was the setting for *Jacquou le Croquant*, the film of the novel by Eugène Le Roy. The backdrop to the story was the Forêt Barade and **Château de l'Herm**, nearby. Set in woodland, these highly atmospheric ruins include a polygonal tower with a Gothic doorway that leads to a spiral staircase.

Rouffignac was almost totally destroyed during World War II, athough the church, with a beautiful Renaissance doorway, was spared. Nearby is the **Grotte de Rouffignac**, inhabited around 10,000 BC and open to visitors since the 16th century. A little train takes visitors down 8 km (5 miles) of tunnels, which are covered with paintings and engravings, including 158 depictions of mammoths.

At **Plazac**, the 12th-century keep was converted into a Romanesque church with a square belfry and an adjoining cemetery. The village of **Saint-Geniès** is filled with attractive ochre sandstone houses. The village also has a 15th-century church and a 17th-century château. The Gothic chapel at Le Cheylard, just outside the village, is decorated with 14th-century biblical scenes. The château at **Salignac**, once a walled fortress, is now an elegant residence with a tiled roof. The 16th–17th-century Manoir de Lacypierre at **Saint-Crépin** is worth a detour.

Crossing the Beune, the road leads from **Tamniès**, above a lake, to **Marquay**, a village with a fortified Romanesque church. Further on is the **Château de Commarque**, in a valley that has been settled since prehistoric times. The castle, partly

Tibetan Lamas in the Périgord

In 1977, a hillside close to the village of Le Moustier, near Saint-Léon-sur-Vézère, was chosen by a group of Tibetan Buddhists, under the leadership of HH Dudjom Rinpoche, as the site of a new spiritual community. The emphasis at **Laugeral**, as it was called, is on meditation and the study of the teachings of the Nyingma school of Buddhism by groups of residential students. Anyone, however, is welcome to visit, as long as they come in a spirit of peace. The Dalai Lama is among many distinguished visitors to this unique place.

Buddhist stupa

in ruins, has a 4th-century church. The walk to the keep offers a fine view of the **Château de Laussel**. *Bories*, Périgordian dry-stone circular huts, can be seen around **Sireuil**. A group of these at Bénivès, the **Cabanes du Breuil**, form part of an open-air museum.

The **Château de Puymartin** is almost completely hidden by trees. It was built in the late 13th century, rebuilt in the 15th and restored around 1890. It contains period furniture, tapestries and paintings, including mythological scenes on some ceilings and walls.

Château de l'Herm
Via the D31, Rouffignac-St-Cernin-de Reilhac. **Tel** 05 53 05 46 61. **Open** Apr–Sep: daily. by arrangement.

Grotte de Rouffignac
Via the D32, Rouffignac-St-Cernin-de Reilhac. **Tel** 05 53 05 41 71. **Open** Apr–Oct: daily.

Château de Commarque
On the D48, Sireuil. **Tel** 05 53 59 00 25. **Open** Apr–Oct: daily.

Cabanes du Breuil
Via the D47, Saint-André-d'Allas. **Tel** 06 80 72 38 59. **Open** Mar–mid-Nov: daily; mid-Nov–Feb: pm only.

Château de Puymartin
On the D47, Marquay, midway between Sarlat and Les Eyzies. **Tel** 05 53 59 29 97. **Open** Apr–Sep: daily; Oct–mid-Nov: pm only.

Traditional Périgordian circular huts at Le Breuil, with dry-stone walls

11 Saint-Amand-de-Coly

Road map E2. Off the D704 or D62. 386. Maison du Patrimoine (summer); 05 53 51 47 85. church.

Originally part of a Romanesque abbey founded in the 7th century, the massive, fortified **church** here, with a nave 48 m (158 ft) long, still has defensive elements. Built on the plan of a Latin cross, it is enclosed by 300 m (985 ft) of walls. Its 30 m (98 ft) high belfry-keep is crowned by a garrison. The nave is lit by a stained-glass window set above the three-arched doorway. The floor of the beautifully empty interior slopes gently down towards the choir.

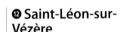

Concerts of classical music, forming part of the Festival du Périgord Noir *(see p39)*, are held here and in the churches of Saint-Léon-sur-Vézère and Auriac. These Romanesque churches provide both a magical setting and fine acoustics.

The Romanesque church at Saint-Léon-sur-Vézère

The imposing church at Saint-Amand-de-Coly

12 Saint-Léon-sur-Vézère

Road map E2. On the D706. 433. Place Bertran-de-Born, Montignac; 05 53 51 82 60. Wed & Sat.

The 11th-century church here is one of the oldest in the Périgord. Its interior is decorated with frescoes, from the 12th to 17th centuries.

The beautifully restored 14th–17th century Château de Chabans has fine stained glass, tapestries and furniture, but is no longer open to the public.

Nearby, at Le Moustier, is a Buddhist centre, **Laugeral**. Founded in 1977, this retreat offers meditation and study, and daily practice for followers.

Laugeral Saint-Léon-sur-Vézère. **Tel** 05 53 70 75 29. **Open** daily. Students by prior appointment.

⓭ Grottes de Lascaux and Lascaux II

Road map E2. Brive & Sarlat.
place Bertran-de-Born, Montignac; 05 53 51 82 60 or 05 53 05 65 65.
Open Jun–Sep: daily; Apr–May & Oct–Dec: Tue–Sun. **Closed** Jan–early Feb.
lascaux.culture.fr

The cave that became known as the "Sistine Chapel of prehistory" was discovered on 12 September 1940 by four young boys who were out walking. Its paintings, which date from around 18,000 BC, provide a glimpse of that remote age. It is now known that the cave was never inhabited, and the precise meaning of the images on its walls remains unclear. The prehistoric artists who created them used the relief of the cave walls to help breathe a sense of life into their depictions of bulls, deer, horses and ibexes that cover every surface from floor to ceiling.

The cave rapidly became a major attraction, drawing in thousands of visitors. But this influx also allowed in a number of harmful micro-organisms, which caused the paintings to deteriorate. It was therefore decided to close the cave in 1963. The local authority then went about creating an exact replica, just 200 m (700 ft) from the original, close to the town of Montignac.

Lascaux II, a remarkable feat of scientific accuracy and artistic skill, opened in 1983. Executed by an artist using the same techniques and materials as her distant ancestors, the paintings are an accurate reconstruction of the originals, around 70 per cent of which have been replicated on the walls of two main cavities, the Diverticule Axial (Central Passage) and the Salle des Taureaux (Hall of Bulls).

Montignac itself is also worth a visit. A bustling town, it contains a number of fine 14th–16th century houses.

Environs

At Thonac, 10 km (6 miles) to the southwest of Lascaux, is the **Château de Losse**, an elegant residence built in 1576 on the ruins of the town's medieval fortress. It was once the residence of Jean II de Losse, the private tutor of Henri IV. The 14th-century Tour de l'Éperon stands on the ramparts and a fortified gatehouse guards the fixed bridge that leads to the main courtyard. A range of interesting 15th- and 17th-century furniture fills the building's Renaissance-style interior. Nearby is the **Tour de la Vermondie**. According to legend, this 13th-century leaning tower was built at this angle in order to make it possible for the young girl who was imprisoned there to lean out and kiss her fiancé as he passed by.

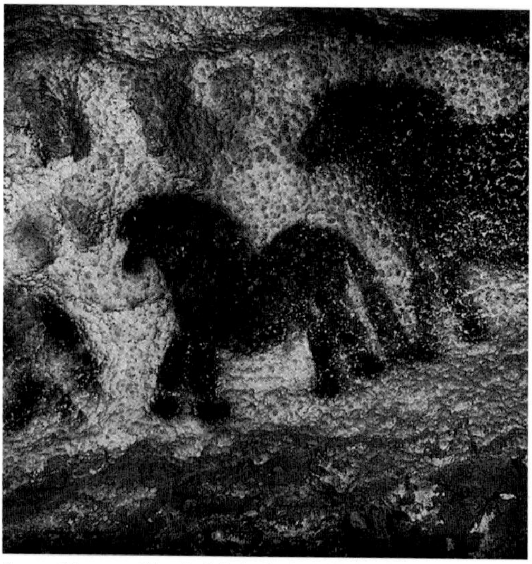
Horses and deer, some of the animals depicted at the Grottes de Lascaux

The 16th-century Château de Losse, near Lascaux

Château de Losse
Thonac. **Tel** 05 53 50 80 08.
Open May–Sep: Sun–Fri.
part of the tour.

⓮ Vallée de l'Homme

Road map E2. On the D706, between Montignac and Les Eyzies.

This section of the Vézère valley, also known as the Vallée de l'Homme ("Valley of Man"), contains a very large number of prehistoric sites.

Le Thot, Espace Cro-Magnon
Thonac. **Tel** 05 53 50 70 44.
Open Jun–Sep: daily; Apr–May & Oct–Dec: Tue–Sun.

The animal park at Le Thot contains species descended from the wild creatures that inhabited the region in the Upper Palaeolithic period, and whose likenesses can be seen on the walls of the prehistoric caves at Lascaux. Among them are reindeer, aurochs (long-horn African cattle) and Przewalski's horses. There are also models of extinct species, such as mammoths and woolly rhinos.

The museum features the re-creation of a prehistoric cave, showing methods used for

A mammoth hunt, one of several reconstructions of prehistoric scenes at Préhisto Parc, Vallée de l'Homme

painting and engraving the walls. An exhibition area and auditorium tells the story of Lascaux II. Four facsimiles of paintings not on view at Lascaux II are displayed: they depict human figures, deer, a cow, horses and bison.

Préhisto Parc

Tursac. **Tel** 05 53 50 73 19. **Open** mid-Feb–mid-Nov: daily.

With reconstructions of daily life in prehistoric times, the family-oriented Préhisto Parc takes visitors on a journey through time, from Neanderthal to Cro-Magnon Man. Flint-knapping, spear-throwing, cave painting and fire-making workshops give visitors a direct insight into prehistoric skills.

Village de la Madeleine

Tursac. **Tel** 05 53 46 36 88. **Open** mid-Feb–mid-Nov: daily.

The rock-shelter at La Madeleine gave its name to the Magdalenian society of hunter-gatherers that lived in the area from around 18,000–10,000 BC. Excavations at this site brought to light a large array of pieces, including a fragment of engraved mammoth ivory. A child's grave, decorated with shells and red ochre, was also discovered here.

From the 8th century, the troglodytic village, cut into the cliff-face over the Vézère, was used as a place of safety.

La Roque-Saint-Christophe

Peyzac-Le Moustier. **Tel** 05 53 50 70 45. **Open** daily. **roque-st-christophe.com**

This sheer rockface above the Vézère is 80 m (260 ft) high and 1 km (0.5 mile) long. It has been inhabited since prehistoric times. The troglodytic fort and town carved in the rock here dates from the 10th century, but additions were made throughout the Middle Ages to increase security. This natural fortress could hold over 1,000 people. Flat, terrace-like areas offer good views out over the valley. A reconstruction of a medieval building site gives a glimpse into the daily life of the period.

Château de Belcayre, between Thonac and Sergeac

Sergeac

Place Bertran-de-Born, Montignac; 05 53 51 82 60.

A 15th-century carved cross stands at the entrance to the village, which was the Knights Templar's main base in the Périgord. Near the commander's residence, a house dating from the 14th–15th centuries, is a fortified church roofed with traditional Périgordian tiles.

Not far from Sergeac is the small valley of **Castel-Merle**, with rock-shelters that were inhabited from the Palaeolithic period to the Iron Age. Between Thonac and Sergac is the splendid Château de Blecayre.

Grottes du Roc de Cazelle

Beyond Les Eyzies, on the D47 to Sarlat. **Tel** 05 53 59 46 09. **Open** daily.

The exhibiton at Roc de Cazelle, one of the many rock-shelters in this area, tells the story of the human habitation of these caves from Upper Palaeolithic times to 1966. The tour includes the reconstruction of scenes from the daily life of the early hunter-gatherers to that of farmers in the 20th century. Other displays show how the rock was made habitable, how a fort was built and houses here were cut out of the living rock.

⓯ Gardens of the Manoir d'Eyrignac

First laid out in the 18th century, the gardens of this manor house form a cool oasis of greenery amidst the dry, rocky limestone of the Périgord Noir. Watered by seven springs, they were made over in the Romantic style in the 19th century, but within 100 years had fallen into such neglect that it took the owners, Gilles Sermadiras and later his son, nearly 40 years to restore them to their full glory. They finally opened to the public in 1987. Today, the gardens are a mix of the more formal French and wilder-looking Italian styles, with rolling lawns and a mass of mature trees and shrubs, such as box, yew, hornbeam and cypress. The French garden, a masterpiece of symmetry and order, with topiary and carefully arranged parterres, stands in stark contrast to the more irregular "jigsaw" of the Italian garden. There are also many surprises to delight the visitor, such as secret nooks and unexpected vistas.

Stonework and greenery sit together in perfect harmony

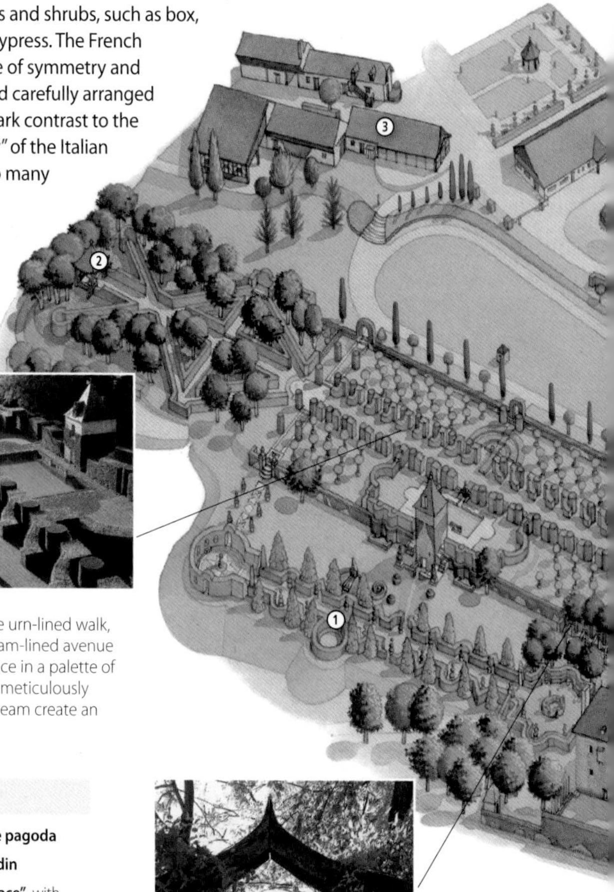

★ Hornbeam Walk
Running parallel with the urn-lined walk, this long, grassy, hornbeam-lined avenue is a geometric masterpiece in a palette of harmonious greens. The meticulously trimmed yew and hornbeam create an impressive perspective.

KEY

① **Red lacquer Chinese pagoda**

② **Restaurant Côté Jardin**

③ **The "enchanted terrace"**, with the rose garden behind, offers a fine view of the manor house and the paddock, and of the formal French garden below.

④ **Le Jardin Fruitier**, with pretty apple and pear trees

⑤ **Potager**

⑥ **The manor house** was built in 1653.

⑦ **Avenue of Vases**

English Arcade
Covered in vegetation that casts subtle patterns of light and shade, this walkway leads from the pavilion, beside the Hornbeam Walk, to a sandy courtyard fronting the manor house.

White Garden
Planted only with white roses, this consists of parterres running along wide, straight avenues. In early summer the flowers fill the air with a delicate scent.

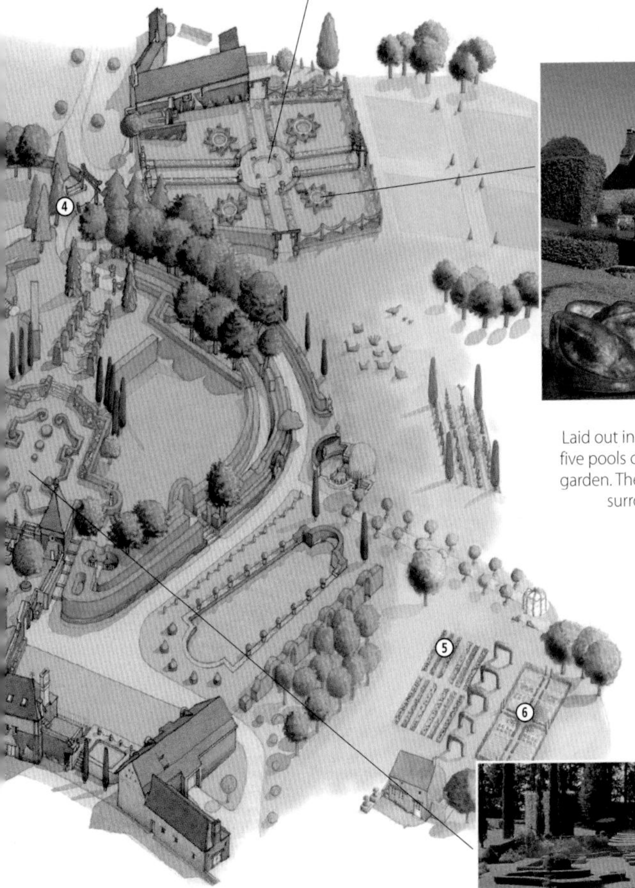

The Pools
Laid out in a geometric pattern, five pools complement the rose garden. The large central pool is surrounded by fountains.

★ French Garden
The terrace, which is laid out with flower-filled parterres, is fronted by a sandy courtyard and a small pond. This garden consists of symmetrical box-tree arabesques and an immaculate lawn.

VISITORS' CHECKLIST

Practical Information
Road map E2. On the D60. Salignac. 1,140. **Tel** 05 53 28 99 71. **Open** daily.
eyrignac.com

Transport
Souillac and Brive-la-Gaillarde.

⑯ Les Eyzies-de-Tayac

At the heart of the Vézère valley, with its prehistoric painted caves and rock-shelters, sits the village of Les Eyzies. Known as "the capital of prehistory", it stretches out along the foot of ochre-coloured cliffs that bear traces of some of the earliest human settlements. The exhibits in the museum cover most of what is known about early man, and would make an ideal preliminary to any visit to the nearby painted caves. A 12th-century, fortified church in Tayac, the hamlet beside Les Eyzies, is also worth a visit.

VISITORS' CHECKLIST

Practical Information
Road map E2. On the D47 between Périgueux and Sarlat. 909. 19 ave de la Préhistoire; 05 53 06 97 05.
tourisme-vezere.com
Apr–Oct: Mon am; Jul–Aug: Fri pm.

Transport
Périgueux, Agen.

Musée National de la Préhistoire

Tel 05 53 06 45 45. **Open** Jul–Aug: daily; Sep–Jun: Wed–Mon.

The museum's collections, which consist mostly of finds from the Vézère valley, include stone tools, burial artifacts, bones of prehistoric animals, ornaments, small sculptures and engravings. The terrace commands impressive views of the valley.

Abri Pataud

Tel 05 53 06 92 46. **Open** Apr–Oct: call in advance for opening times.

The walls of this engraved rock-shelter contain traces of around 40 encampments dating from 35,000 to 20,000 BC, covering the Aurignacian, Gravettian and Solutrean periods. Just below this is another rock-shelter, its ceiling decorated with a splendid relief of an oryx (Solutrean, 17,000 BC). The museum displays finds from the site and gives details of the archeological excavations that have been carried out here to date.

Abri du Cap Blanc

Marquay. **Tel** 05 53 06 86 00. **Open** May–Sep. **Closed** Sat & public hols.

More than 15,000 years ago, prehistoric people carved representations of horses, bison and reindeer on the wall of this rock-shelter. A small display sheds light on daily life during the Magdalenian period, as well as the art that typifies it.

Le Moustier, La Micoque and La Ferrassie

Tel 05 53 06 86 00. **Open** summer; prior booking essential.

The rock-shelter at Le Moustier, where a Neanderthal skeleton was discovered, gave its name to the Mousterian culture (80,000–30,000 BC). La Micoque, the oldest site in the Dordogne, was inhabited from 300,000 BC. The rock-shelter of La Ferrassie, inhabited from 40,000 to 25,000 BC, contained Neanderthal burials. Excavations here also uncovered engraved stone slabs from the Aurignacian period. These are the earliest-known examples of prehistoric art in the Vézère valley.

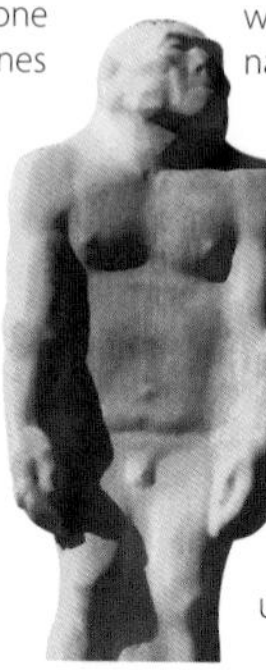
Primitive Man, Musée de la Préhistoire

Abri de Laugerie Haute

Tel 05 53 06 86 00. **Closed** Sat & public hols. prior booking essential.

This huge rock-shelter was inhabited from 22,000 to 12,000 BC. It was abandoned when the ceiling fell in. Flint and bone tools, as well as a large number of harpoons, were discovered here.

Abri du Poisson

Tel 05 53 06 86 00. **Closed** Sat & public hols. prior booking essential.

This small rock-shelter in the valley of the Gorge d'Enfer is named after the relief of a fish that was discovered here. It is of a salmon, 1 m (3 ft) long, carved in about 25,000 BC.

Grotte des Combarelles

Tel 05 53 06 86 00. **Closed** Sat & public hols. prior booking essential.

This cave, used during the

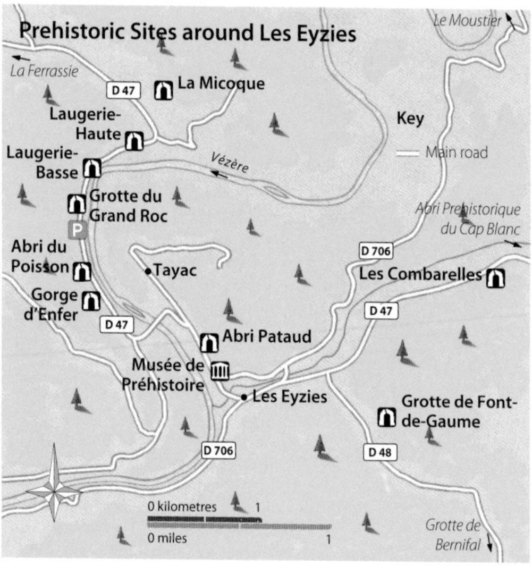

For map symbols *see back flap*

Drawing of a deer in the Grotte de Font-de-Gaume

Magdalenian period (around 15,000 BC), has some 600 engravings and drawings of horses, reindeer, mammoths and woolly rhinoceros, as well as anthropomorphic figures.

Grotte de Font-de-Gaume
Tel 05 53 06 86 00. **Closed** Sat & public hols. prior booking essential.
The walls of this cave are covered with magnificent multicoloured paintings dating from the Magdalenian period. It also has drawings and engravings of almost 200 animals, including 82 bison.

Grotte de Bernifal
Meyrals. **Tel** 05 53 29 66 39. **Open** Jul–Sep: daily, by appointment.
This small cave is reached by walking up through an atmospheric woodland. By torchlight, visitors can see about 100 representations of mammoths and human figures, and signs and symbols, dating from the Magdalenian period.

Abri de Laugerie Basse
Tel 05 53 05 65 60. **Closed** Mon, Jan. special price ticket when combined with a visit to Grand Roc.
This rock-shelter, from the Magdalenian period, contains displays on the life of Cro-Magnon people, covering the tools they made, what they ate, their hunting methods and their artistic skills. Some pieces are replicas because the originals have been taken to other museums around the world. The earliest female figure to be discovered in France, known as the Venus Impudique (Shameless Venus), was found here in 1864 by Marquis Paul de Vibraye.

Grotte du Grand Roc
Tel 05 53 05 65 65 (call ahead for opening times). **Closed** Jan. special price ticket when combined with a visit to Abri de Laugerie Basse.
Lit to reveal its wonders, this cave contains fantastic mineral formations, including stalagmites, stalactites and an assortment of rather weird shapes, some of which are hollow. One of the most amazing forms a cross.

⓱ Le Bugue-sur-Vézère

Road map E2. On the D710. Agen, Périgueux. 2,793. Porte de la Vézère; 05 53 07 20 48. Tue & Sat.

An important tourist centre, this sizeable town offers a variety of attractions, from the **Aquarium du Périgord Noir**, with 6,000 fish, to the **Village du Bournat**, where scenes of rural life in the Périgord in times gone by are re-created in a large open-air museum.

Aquarium du Périgord Noir
Tel 05 53 07 10 74. **Open** mid-Mar–mid-Nov: Sun and pm Mon–Sat (Apr–Sep: all day, daily).

Village du Bournat
Tel 05 53 08 41 99. **Open** Mar–mid-Nov: daily.

Grotte de Bara-Bahau
Le Bugue. **Tel** 05 53 07 44 58.
Open Apr–mid-Nov: daily; mid-Nov–Dec & Feb–Mar: Tue–Sun. **Closed** Jan.
This cave has a large gallery of unusual rock formations.

Son et lumière inside a chasm in the Gouffre de Proumeyssac

The Grand Roc at Les Eyzies, on the banks of the Vézère

This leads to a cavity with engravings of bears, horses and bison, as well as hands, a phallus and other symbols.

Gouffre de Proumeyssac
4 km (2.5 miles) from Le Bugue, on road to Audrix. **Tel** 05 53 07 27 47.
Open Feb, Nov & Dec: pm daily (rest of the year: all day). **Closed** Jan.
The cathedral-like domed interior of this cave contains mineral formations in a huge variety of shapes. There is also a fascinating display on geological formations. By prior arrangement, visitors can descend into the chasm in a cradle suspended on cables, as the first people to explore this cave would have done.

Environs
At the confluence of the Vézère and the Dordogne, 5 km (3 miles) southwest of Le Bugue, is the village of **Limeuil**. It has a pleasant riverside beach and many craftsmen's workshops. Narrow streets lead up to the grounds of the château and an arboretum. Thomas à Becket once visited the elegantly proportioned Chapelle Saint-Martin here.

At Le Buisson de Cadouin, 10 km (6 miles) south of Le Bugue, are the **Grottes de Maxange**. Found in 2000, these caves contain extraordinary rock formations.

Grottes de Maxange
Le Buisson de Cadouin. **Tel** 05 53 23 42 80. **Open** Apr–Nov: daily.

⑱ Street-by-Street: Sarlat

Nestling at the foot of a cluster of *pechs* (small hills), Sarlat has undergone extensive restoration, returning its narrow streets and courtyards to their original splendour. A number of houses here consist of a medieval ground floor with Renaissance floors above. This centre of trade on the road to Santiago de Compostela grew rapidly in the 13th century, and again in the mid-15th century, when its splendid Renaissance houses were built. Rue de la République, laid out in the 19th century and nicknamed "La Traverse", runs between the picturesque medieval district and the town's other ancient streets. Although Sarlat's restored quarter is an architectural jewel, the town's truffle and *fois gras* fairs also attract visitors.

★ Place de la Liberté
The hub of Sarlat, this square is lined with picturesque 16th- and 18th-century house that have featured in a number of films. Th Église Sainte-Marie, in the background, wa restored by the architect Jean Nouvel (194 and is now a covered market.

Rue des Consuls is a street lined with fine 15th- to 17th-century houses.

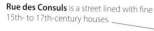

Place aux Oies
This square (Goose Square) was once the venue of Sarlat's live fowl market. This is commemorated by bronze statues of geese by Lalanne. It contains two fine Renaissance buildings: the turreted Hôtel de Vassal and the Hôtel Chassaing.

★ Maison de La Boétie
This beautiful Renaissance house was the birthplace of Étienne de La Boétie, friend Michel de Montaigne *(see p48)*. A shop once filled the ground floor. The ornately decorated upper storeys have mullioned windows with carved surrounds and medallioned pilasters. The building is crowned by an elegant tiled roof.

Cathédrale Saint-Sacerdos
Begun in 1504 and completed in the 17th century, the cathedral lacks stylistic unity. A notable feature of the interior is the overhanging organ loft of 1770.

VISITORS' CHECKLIST

Practical Information
Road map E2. 9,931.
3, Rue Tourny; 05 53 31 45 45.
Apr–Sep. Wed & Sat am; covered market: Fri–Wed Easter–10 Nov; truffle market: Dec–Feb. Festival des Jeux du Théâtre (mid-Jul–early Aug); Festival du Film de Sarlat (second week in Nov); Journées du Terroir (Whitsun).
sarlat-tourisme.com

Transport
Souillac.

0 metres 50
0 yards 50

Lanterne des Morts
Constructed in the 12th century to commemorate St Bernard's visit to Sarlat, this tower offers a fine view of the apse and bell tower of the church.

Chapelle des Pénitents Bleus is the only surviving element of an earlier Romanesque abbey church.

Key

— Suggested route

Bishop's Palace
This building has fine Gothic and Renaissance windows and an upper gallery. It now houses the tourist office, which puts on excellent summer exhibitions.

Exploring Sarlat

In summer, when it is closed to traffic, the heart of Sarlat's old town, with its many architectural jewels, is pleasant to explore on foot. On place de la Liberté is the Hôtel de Maleville (or Hôtel de Vienne), a town house in a combination of French and Italian Renaissance styles. Passage Henri-de-Ségogne, in the restored quarter of the town, is lined with 13th-, 15th- and 16th-century half-timbered corbelled houses with tiled roofs.

Cathédrale Saint-Sacerdos

The cathedral was rebuilt in the 16th and 17th centuries on the site of an early Romanesque abbey church. The interior is arranged around a nave with four ribbed-vaulted sections. A stroll in the vicinity of the cathedral takes in the Cour des Fontaines and the Chapelle des Pénitents Bleus, the remains of the old cloister, and the Jardin des Enfeus, a former cemetery with burial niches carved into the wall. The purpose of the 12th-century Lanterne des Morts (Lantern of the Dead), in which a lamp could be lit, is still unclear.

Traditional Périgordian tiled roofs on houses in Sarlat's old quarter

Eastern Sarlat

The former **Présidial**, in rue Landry, was the seat of the law courts in the 17th century, and is now a restaurant. The façade has a low arch with a loggia, containing a lantern, above. On either side of the **town hall** are 15th- and 17th-century gabled houses. On rue Fénelon,

⑲ Dordogne Valley

Several fine châteaux line this stretch of the Dordogne. They can be admired from the river – in a canoe or *gabare* (local river craft) – or from the road. The hills all around offer extensive views of the landscape. From the esplanade at Domme, the loop in the river at Montfort is a stunning sight. With reflections of sky and sunlight, the river winds like a silver ribbon through cultivated land.

⑤ Château de Beynac

Following the river beyond the attractive village of Envaux, the narrow road sweeps across the plain, bringing into view the imposing Château de Beynac *(see p138)*. From here it is possible to see for miles in all directions.

⑥ Château des Milandes

Built in 1489 and remodelled in the 19th century, the château was once owned by Josephine Baker (1906–75), the singer, dancer, entertainer and philanthropist. Part of the tour of the castle is devoted to her life. Displays of medieval falconry take place in the gardens, against the backdrop of this Renaissance-style setting.

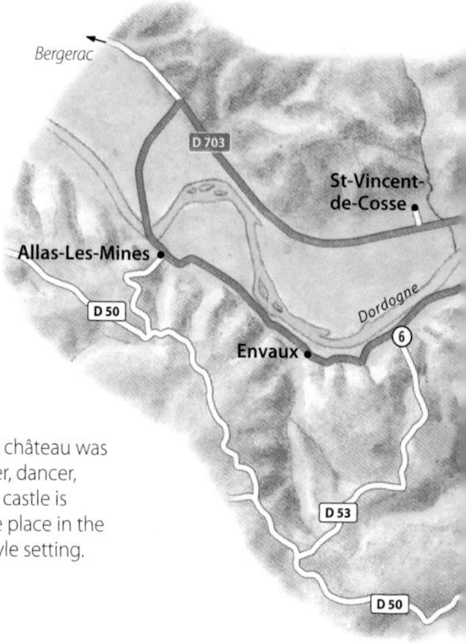

Tips for Drivers

Road map: E2
Tour length: 37 km (23 miles)
Stopping-off places: There are farmhouse-inns and restaurants along the way. Information is available at Sarlat: 05 53 31 45 45.

⑦ Château de Castelnaud

(see pp140–41) Perched on a cliff above the Dordogne river, the château is visible for miles across the countryside.

opposite the alley leading to the 16th-century Hôtel de Gérard, is a doorway framed by four columns decorated with fleur-de-lis. It was once the town hall entrance.

Place de la Liberté

The 15th-century **Hôtel de Gisson**, with tiled roof, is the hub of Sarlat's summer drama festival. Gargoyles stare down from on the bell tower of the **Église Sainte-Marie**, now a covered market.

Rue des Consuls

This street is lined with fine town houses. Among them are the Hôtel Plamon, dating from the 14th to the 17th centuries, and **Hôtel de Mirandol**, near the Fontaine Sainte-Marie. Beyond the arch is the **Hôtel Tapinois de Bétou** with its 17th-century wooden staircase.

Sarlat's old town, ideal for an evening stroll

Western Sarlat

Half-timbered houses line **rue des Armes**, and can be seen from the ramparts. The **Chapelle des Pénitents Blancs** is the remains of a 17th-century convent. Further on is the former **Abbaye Sainte-Claire**, also from the 17th century.

Environs

18 km (11 miles) southeast of Sarlat is **Château de Fénelon**. The theologian and philosopher François de Salignac de la Mothe Fénelon (1651–1715) was born here.

Château de Fénelon
Sainte-Mondane. **Tel** 05 53 29 81 45.
Open Apr–Oct: call ahead.

④ Parc de Marqueyssac
The 6 km (4 miles) of footpaths that wind through these 22 ha (54 acres) of parkland, lead to a stunning belvedere. Fine views can be had, all long this walk, of the many villages and châteaux that dot the surrounding landscape. There are 150,000 finely clipped box trees and cypresses planted here.

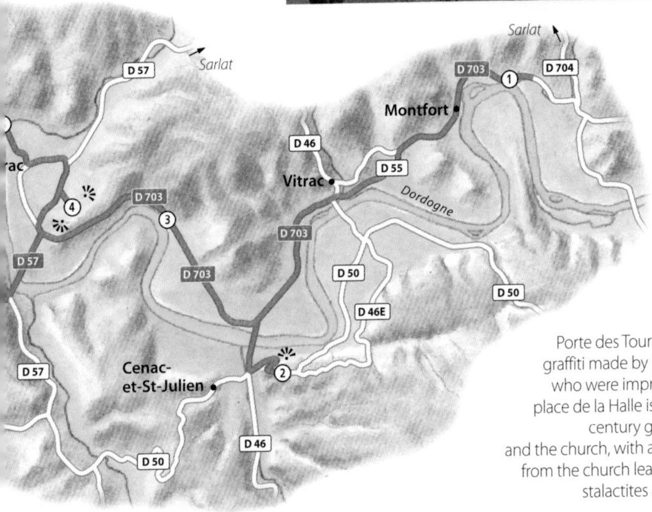

① Cingle de Monfort
A canoe ride along this loop in the river offers good views of the Château de Monfort.

② Domme
Porte des Tours is marked with graffiti made by Knights Templar who were imprisoned here. On place de la Halle is the 15th–16th-century governor's house and the church, with a belfry. A tunnel from the church leads to caves with stalactites and stalagmites.

③ La Roque-Gageac
This village's ochre-coloured houses spread out down to the riverbank. Not far from the church, with its single-wall belfry and the graceful Manoir de Tarde, is a garden of exotic plants. High on the cliffs stands a troglodytic fort. The steep walk up to it is rewarded by a view of the valley, 40 m (130 ft) below.

Key
Suggested route
Other roads

⑳ Souillac

Road map E2. A20 Paris–Toulouse. 3,887. Souillac. Boulevard Louis-Jean-Malvy; 05 65 37 81 56. Fri am. Festival de Jazz (Jul); Les Mercredis du Mime (Weds from mid-Jul to mid-Aug); Musicales de Souillac (Jul). **souillac-sur-dordogne.fr**

The town of Souillac lies between the Dordogne and the Borrèze, in Haut-Quercy. It grew up around a Benedictine monastery that was founded around 655 and that became an abbey in the 16th century. Souillac's influence extended to 150 priories in the area, but it later became a centre of trade, with goods arriving by barge until the installation of the railway in the 19th century.

The **Église Sainte-Marie**, the town's abbey church, was built in the 11th and 12th centuries. Laid out on the plan of a Latin cross and crowned with three domes raised on stone pillars, it is in a splendidly pure Byzantine-Romanesque style inspired by the church of Haghia Sophia in Istanbul. Two notable features of the church are the doorway, which was reversed in the 17th century so as to face inwards, and the 12th-century carvings. These include a column showing animals and humans locked in fierce combat. The Prophet Isaiah is depicted with unusual vigour.

The tourist office occupies a deconsecrated church, the Église Saint-Martin, which has a damaged belfry and Gothic vaulting. Art exhibitions are also held here. The town centre is pleasant to explore on foot, particularly along rue des Oules and rue des Craquelins and in place Roucou and place Benetou.

With 3,000 exhibits, the **Musée de l'Automate**, set up in 1988 in the abbey gardens, is the largest of its kind in Europe. The 19th- and 20th-century collections come mostly from the Roullet-Decamps workshops, which began making automata in 1865. The exhibits, which include a woman powdering her face, a jazz-band and a snake charmer, are very expressive, their movements controlled by finely tuned mechanisms. Designed in collaboration with the Cité des Sciences et de l'Industrie in Paris, the section devoted to robots uses state-of-the-art technology.

Musée de l'Automate

Environs

11 km (7 miles) southeast of Souillac are the **Grottes de Lacave**, caves that were discovered in 1902. Riding on a small train, then taking a lift, visitors travel along 1.6 km (1 mile) of galleries and through a dozen caverns. The sheer variety of weird shapes formed by its stalactites and stalagmites, including some that suggest fantastic animals, makes this the most impressive of all such caves in France.

Musée de l'Automate
Place de l'Abbaye. **Tel** 05 65 37 07 07. **Open** Jan–Mar & Oct–Dec: Wed–Sun pm; Apr–Sep: Tue–Sun; Jul–Aug: daily.

Grottes de Lacave
Tel 05 65 37 87 03. **Open** Apr–mid-Nov: daily. **grottes-de-lacave.com**

㉑ Martel

Road map E2. On the D840, near the A20. 1,579. Quatre-Routes. Palais de la Raymondie, Place des Consuls; 05 65 37 43 44. Wed & Sat am. **martel.fr**

Once the seat of the Vicomte de Turenne, Martel has seven towers, including the bell tower of its fortified Gothic church, which is pierced with arrow slits. Visitors can also see the remains of the 12th–14th-century ramparts, the 13th–14th-century Palais de la Raymondie – which houses a museum of early history, including Gallo-Roman artifacts – and the 18th-century covered market. As well as the regular twice-weekly markets, a truffle market is held here in winter.

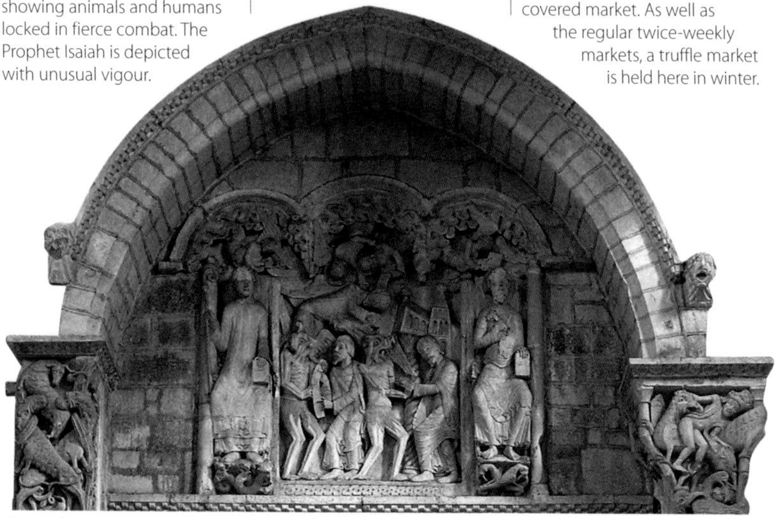

The carved tympanum over the doorway of the Église Sainte-Marie in Souillac

Boat trips on the lake at the bottom of the Gouffre de Padirac

Environs

7 km (4 miles) south of Martel on the N140 is the pre-Romanesque church at **Creysse**. It is unusual in having two identical apses against the straight wall of its east end. The nave follows the rocky spur's convex shape. The church's interior is not open to the public. The village, which has attractive houses roofed in various styles, lies between the course of the Dordogne and walnut orchards.

From 1681 to 1695, the controversial archbishop François Fénelon was prior of the fortified monastery at **Carennac**, 18 km (11 miles) southeast of Martel via the D103, then the D20. All that remains of the monastery are the dean's residence, now a local tourist office, the church, with an arresting depiction of the Last Judgment in the tympanum, and the cloister and chapter room. The village, opposite the Île de la Calypso, an island in the river, is dotted with interesting old houses.

With its lofty setting, the village of **Loubressac**, 20 km (12 miles) southeast of Martel, offers a wide view of the Cère, Bave and Dordogne valleys. From here the Château de Castelnau, Saint-Céré and the towers of Saint-Laurent can be seen. Inside the ramparts, narrow streets wind between the ochre-coloured houses, some of which are covered with cascades of flowers.

Autoire, a village 25 km (15 miles) southeast of Martel, is best approached from the crest of the limestone plateau above a waterfall that crashes down for a sheer 40 m (130 ft). Flanked by majestic cliffs, here the rustic architecture of Quercy rubs shoulders with grand manor houses. The pattern created by the rooftops with their dormers, dovecotes, chimneys, finials and turrets creates an almost mosaic-like effect. It is easy to explore the village on foot, taking in the Chapelle Saint-Roch and the Château des Anglais, which was reduced to ruins during the Hundred Years' War (1337–1453).

㉒ Gouffre de Padirac

Road map F2. Rocamadour-Padirac. Brive–Toulouse. **Tel** 05 65 33 64 56. **Open** Apr–mid-Nov. **gouffre-de-padirac.com**

Detail of the porch at Carrennac

Viewed from above, the huge opening in the earth that forms the entrance to this series of underground caverns, seems almost to be attempting to swallow up the sky. Discovered in 1889 the tunnels inside this geological curiosity were formed at least 1 million years ago, although the gaping hole in the ground that has made them accessible was probably created just 10,000 years ago. Reaching down to about 100 m (230 ft), the caves have a steady temperature of around 13 °C (55 °F). Tours consists of a 400-m (440-yd) walk and a 500-m (550-yd) boat ride. Some 10 m (33 ft) beneath the ground, under the 94 m (300 ft) Great Dome is a spectacular group of giant stalagmites. Beyond this lies a lake, fed solely by water filtering through the rock, that sits "suspended" some 27 m (89 ft) above the level of an underground river. There are also a further 9 km (6 miles) of tunnels that are not generally open to visitors.

㉓ Castelnau-Bretenoux

Road map F2. On the D803. **Tel** 05 65 10 98 00. **Open** daily. **Closed** Oct–Mar: Tue.

With a square keep and seigneurial quarters, this château is a resolutely defensive building. It was founded in the 12th century by the barons of Castelnau, and clear traces of its military past can still be seen in its elegant outline. Remodelled in the 16th and 17th centuries, then abandoned in the 18th, the castle was restored in the late 19th century with funds provided by Jean Mouliérat, the famous tenor. It now contains a fine collection of paintings and furniture.

The impressive fortress of Castelnau-Bretenoux, a fine example of military architecture

24 Rocamadour

Sitting on a rocky plateau high above the Alzou valley, Rocamadour looks as if it is carved straight out of the limestone rock face. The best views are to be had from the nearby hamlet of L'Hospitalet. The village became one of the most famous centres of pilgrimage in France because of the 12th-century statue of the Black Virgin and Child in the Chapelle Notre-Dame that was believed to have miraculous powers. An account dating from 1172 describes the 126 miracles granted by the Madonna, who is still honoured on 8 September each year during the Semaine Mariale (Marian Week). Also, in 1166, an ancient grave was discovreed containing an undecayed body, said to be that of the early Christian hermit St Amadour.

Chapelle Saint-Michel
The chapel is decorated with beautiful 12th-century frescoes.

Great Stairway
This broad flight of steps links the village with the shrines. Pilgrims would climb these on their knees, saying their rosaries as they went.

KEY

① **Crypte de Saint Amadour** is named after the hermit whose reliquary it contains. Pilgrims came here to venerate the saint.

② **The castle** was built against the 14th-century ramparts that defended the shrine from the west.

③ **Ramparts**

④ **Cross of Jerusalem**

⑤ **Basilique Saint-Sauveur**, a late 12th-century sanctuary, backs on to the bare rock face.

⑥ **Chapelle Saint-Jean-Baptiste** faces the fine Gothic portal of the Basilica Saint-Sauveur.

⑦ **Chapelle Sainte-Anne**, from the 13th century, has a fine 17th-century gilded altarpiece.

⑧ **Chapelle Saint-Blaise**

The Village
The 13th-century Porte du Figuier, on the pilgrims' route, leads to the main street, which is now filled with souvenir shops.

VISITORS' CHECKLIST

Practical Information
Road map E2. 677. At L'Hospitalet and in Rocamadour's medieval centre; 05 65 33 22 00. Torchlit procession (Aug); Semaine Mariale (devoted to the Black Madonna; mid-Sep).
vallee-dordogne-rocamadour.com

Transport
Rocamadour.

View of the village
Rocamadour, which almost seems to sprout up from the base of the cliff, is at its most breathtaking at sunrise.

Chapelle Notre-Dame
The remains of St Amadour were found under the floor in front of the chapel. On the altar is the statue of the miraculous Black Virgin and Child.

Exploring Rocamadour

The views from the ramparts of this fortified town are truly breathtaking. Pilgrims climbing on their knees up the 224 steps of the Great Stairway to the shrines could stop at the resting places along the way and gaze for miles across the Alzou valley below. By the 13th century, thousands of them were flocking to Rocamadour every year. The town was pillaged by the English during the Hundred Years' War and desecrated during the Wars of Religion in the 16th century, but the Black Virgin and her miraculous bell survived. Pilgrimages ceased with the Revolution of 1789, but resumed in the 19th century, when the shrine was rehabilitated.

Grand'Rue

The Voie Sainte ("Sacred Way"), used by pilgrims, runs from the hamlet of L'Hospitalet and joins Grand'Rue at the 13th-century Porte du Figuier, one of the eight surviving fortified gates that controlled entry into the town. The 15th-century town hall, in rue de la Couronnerie, close by, has a huge tapestry by Jean Lurçat (1892–1966), which he gave to the town in 1960. It was entirely sewn by hand at Aubusson and depicts the flora and fauna of the region.

Chapelle Notre-Dame

This Flamboyant Gothic chapel was built in about 1476 on the site in the cliff-face that the hermit St Amadour is thought to have inhabited. The object of pilgrimage here is the Black Virgin and Child, a 12th-century walnut statue, 69 cm (27 in) high, covered with silver leaf blackened by candle smoke. According to popular belief, the 9th-century bell above her rang spontaneously whenever the Virgin saved a sailor in peril at sea.

Shrine

Built into the cliff, the shrine consists of seven churches and chapels. While services are held in the Basilique Saint-Sauveur, Chapelle Saint-Blaise is for silent prayer. This Romanesque ensemble was altered in the 19th century.

Chemin de Croix

With its 14 Stations of the Cross, it winds through woodland and leads to the Cross of Jerusalem.

Ramparts

Tel 05 65 33 23 23. **Open** daily.

These are all that remain of the 14th-century fortress which once defended the town and its shrine. The ramparts command extensive views of Rocamadour and the valley below.

Grottes des Merveilles

Tel 05 65 33 67 92. **Open** Apr–mid-Nov: daily. **grotte-des-merveilles.com**

This cave, discovered in 1920, contains a mass of stalactites and stalagmites, and its walls are decorated with paintings that date from the Upper Palaeolithic era. Among the 22 images, which are mostly of animals, including horses and deer, are the outlines of six human hands.

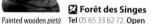

Painted wooden *pietà*

Forêt des Singes

Tel 05 65 33 62 72. **Open** Apr–mid-Sep: daily; mid-Sep–Oct: pm Mon-Fri, Sat–Sun; 1–11 Nov: Sat, Sun.

This animal park is home to 130 macaques, who roam over its 10 ha (25 acres) of woodland. These monkeys, native to the high plateaux of Africa, are endangered.

Rocher des Aigles

Tel 05 65 33 65 45. **Open** Apr–mid-Nov: daily.

The crypt of St Amadour, built into the rock face

Dedicated to breeding birds of prey, this centre has about 100 from all over the world. Displays of falconry are held.

Préhistologia
Lacave. **Tel** 05 65 32 28 28. **Open** Apr–May: pm Mon–Fri, Sat–Sun; Jun–mid-Sep: daily; mid-Sep–mid-Nov: daily pm.

The largest dinosaur park in Europe traces the evolution of the species, from the Big Bang to Neolithic times.

25 Saint-Céré

Road map F2. On the D803/D673. 3,582. Bretenoux. 11 Ave François de Maynard; 05 65 38 11 85. Sat am. Festival Lyrique (late Jul–early Aug). **tourisme-saint-cere.com**

Saint-Céré grew thanks to the traffic of pilgrims visiting the tomb of St Spérie, which stands here. In the 12th century, craftsmen settled and markets were established. The town suffered as a result of epidemics and wars, but regained some of its splendour in the 17th century.

Remains of past prosperity can be seen in rue du Mazel, with the 15th-century Hôtel d'Auzier and the 17th-century Maison Queyssac, and in impasse Lagarouste, with its half-timbered corbelled houses. Hôtel d'Ambert, in rue Saint-Cyr, has turrets and a Renaissance doorway. Rue Paramelle leads to Maison Longueval, a 15th-century turreted house, and the 15th-century Hôtel de Puymule, in the Flamboyant Gothic style. The church contains an 18th-century marble altarpiece and has a Carolingian crypt. On a hill above the town are the Tours de Saint-Laurent, a 13th- and a 15th-century keep, all that remains of the castle. In 1945, they were acquired by Jean Lurçat (1882–1966), the painter and tapestry maker, and are now a **museum-workshop**.

There are also many artists' and craftsmen's studios in Saint-Céré itself.

A tapestry by Jean Lurçat, with colourful and innovative motifs

Atelier-Musée Jean-Lurçat
Tel 05 65 38 28 21. **Open** Apr–Sep: Tue–Sun.

Environs

The **Château de Montal**, 2 km (1 mile) from Saint-Céré, was stripped of its finest architectural elements in the 19th century. However, thanks to the work of Maurice Fenaille (1855–1937), the castle's 16th- and 17th-century tapestries and furniture have been restored to their original setting. The 15th-century circular towers frame a beautiful Renaissance courtyard with a double staircase. A 17th-century Aubusson tapestry hangs in the guardroom. The upper floor rooms have ceilings with exposed beams.

Château de Montal
Saint-Jean-Lespinasse. **Tel** 05 65 38 13 72. **Open** Easter–Sep: daily; Oct–Easter: Wed–Sun. **Closed** public hols.

16th-century dovecote built by Galiot, lord of the manor of Assier

26 Assier

Road map F2. 533. Brive–Toulouse. Causse valley, Place de l'Eglise; 05 65 40 50 60. **otivalleecausse.com**

The remains of the **Château d'Assier** show that this was a Renaissance palace on a par with the finest châteaux of the Loire. It was built by Jacques Galiot de Genouillac (1465–1546), an artillery commander under Louis XII and François I. Of the building completed in 1535, only the entrance wing, with a spectacular portico doorway, survives. The decoration consisted of mythological and classical scenes, Renaissance figures and military emblems. The carved staircase is the finest feature of the interior.

The church contains an effigy of Galiot. Uniquely in France, the dome over the burial chapel has triple groined vaulting that forms an elaborate star pattern.

Château d'Assier
Tel 05 65 40 40 99. **Open** Jul–Aug: daily; Sep–Jun: Wed–Sun. **Closed** public hols.

Environs

The 16th-century **dovecote** on the Lacapelle-Marival road stands 11 m (36 ft) high and holds 2,300 nesting chambers. The birds enter and exit via the open lantern on top.

Near the village are two dolmens known as the **Table de Roux** and **Bois des Bœufs**. There are 11 of these burial chambers, dating from around 1,500 BC, in the vicinity.

For hotels and restaurants in this region see pp251–2 and pp263–5

㉗ Figeac

The town of Figeac, which sits clustered around its 9th-century abbey, grew and prospered as the result of trade. By the 12th century, its growing wealth enabled many inhabitants to build fine houses here. Fortified in the 14th century, the town still has a medieval appearance, reflecting its past importance.

Enlarged replica of the Rosetta Stone, on Place des Écritures

Exploring Figeac

Figeac's most prosperous period stretched from the 12th to the 14th century, and the town boasts exceptionally fine houses from this time. Built of stone and wood, they usually have an *aula* (main living room) on the upper floor, with shops fronted by arcades opening onto the street below. Windows were decorated with finely executed Romanesque carving. Many more fine houses were built in the 15th and 16th centuries, with a *solelho* (open granary) on the top floor. Examples are on place Gaillardy.

Houses were still being built in the medieval style during the Renaissance, but many also had elements such as turrets, arcaded courtyards, spiral staircases and mullioned windows set in an orderly way into the façade. The town houses of the 18th century have monumental staircases. With this rich architectural heritage, Figeac offers a complete panorama of local urban architecture from the 12th century to the present day.

Hôtel de la Monnaie

Place Vival. Museum and tourist office: **Tel** 05 65 34 06 25. **Open** Jul & Aug: daily; Sep–Jun: Mon–Sat.

Although the Ortabadial quarter was partly demolished to make way for place Vival, this 13th-century town house survived. A fine example of a grand Renaissance residence, it has an arcaded ground floor and gemelled windows. It is now the tourist office and, on the first floor, the Musée du Vieux Figeac, housing geological and historical exhibits.

Abbaye Saint-Sauveur

Tel 05 65 34 11 63.

This church is one of the surviving elements of the abbey around which the town grew. The 13th-century chapter room is now the Chapelle Notre-Dame-de-la-Pitié. It is decorated with 17th-century painted panels.

Place Champollion

With place Carnot, this is one of Figeac's two main squares. Formerly place de l'Avoine, it is surrounded by medieval houses. Maison du Griffon, at no. 4, dates from the 12th century and has carved Romanesque decoration. The 14th-century Gothic house at no. 5 has a stone *solelho*.

Musée Champollion: Les Écritures du Monde

Place Champollion. **Tel** 05 65 50 31 08. **Open** Jul & Aug: daily; Sep–Jun: Tue–Sun.

The museum is in the house where Jean-François Champollion (1790–1832), the great Egyptologist, was born. Dating from the 13th and 14th centuries, this large collection focuses on different sorts of writings from around the world, including Egyptian hieroglyphics.

Place des Écritures

This unusual area was laid out by Joseph Kosuth (1945–), a pioneer of conceptual art. Part of his permanent installation here features an enlarged replica of the Rosetta Stone.

Hôtel de Colomb

5 rue de Colomb. **Tel** 05 65 50 05 40. **Open** 10 Jul–19 Sep: daily; Apr–9 Jul & 20 Sep–Oct: Tue–Sun pm.

With a restrained façade and a

View of Figeac from Église Notre-Dame-du-Puy

VISITORS' CHECKLIST

Practical Information
Road map: F2. 10,000.
Hôtel de la Monnaie, place Vival; 05 65 34 06 25. Sat.
Festival Théâtral (late Jul–early Aug). **tourisme-figeac.com**

Transport

highly decorated staircase, this town house is typical of the 17th-century. It contains the town hall and the Espace Patrimoine, an exhibition on Figeac's history and heritage.

Medieval Buildings
Many other buildings in Figeac are worth a view. They include the Hôtel Galiot de Genouillac, with a fine spiral staircase; the 14th-century Palais Balène, arranged round an interior courtyard; the Hôtel d'Auglanat, with a turret on one of its outer corners and a 14th-century decorated doorway; and the Église Notre-Dame-du-Puy, whose 13th-century apse was altered in the 17th century, when a monumental altarpiece of the Madonna was installed.

Environs
Capdenac-le-Haut, 5 km (3 miles) southeast of Figeac, looks down over the Lot. From the esplanade, it is easy to see the strategic importance of this naturally fortified site. The ramparts, keep and former consul's house form a pleasant walk. The Fontaine des Anglais is carved directly into the rock.

The village of **Espagnac-Sainte-Eulalie**, about 20 km (12 miles) west of Figeac, nestles in a bend in the Célé river. It developed around a 12th-century priory. The Église Notre-Dame, which dates from the 13th century, has a half-timbered bell tower.

㉘ Saint-Cirq-Lapopie

Road map E3. 216. Place du Sombral; 05 65 31 31 31.

Its exceptionally picturesque location and ensemble of attractive buildings make Saint-Cirq-Lapopie one of the jewels of the Lot valley. Rising in tiers up the limestone cliff-face, it sits some 100 m (300 ft) above the river. Along its narrow streets are small courtyards and attractive 13th- and 15th-century stone and wooden houses. In the lower village, a 13th-century gate, Porte de la Pélissaria (or Porte de Rocamadour) opens on to Grand'Rue, where the medieval village begins. Places of note include **place du Carol**, with a belvedere-dovecote, where the painter Henri Martin (1860–1943) lived; the 13th-century Maison Vinot; the 14th-century **Maison Médiévale Daura**; **Maison Breton**, once owned by the Surrealist writer André Breton (1896–1966); Maison Bessac, with double corbelling; **place du Sombral** with the 15th-century **Maison Larroque** and **Maison Rignault**, which houses the Musée Rignault; and **Maison de la Fourdonne**, which contains the Maison du Patrimoine. Near the ruined castle, stands a late 16th-century fortified **church**.

The economy of the village, which had 1,500 inhabitants during the Middle Ages, was based on manufacturing, with craftsmen's workshops under the arcades along rue de la Pélissaria and rue de la Peyrolerie. Today, the work of *robinetaïres*, specialist wood-turners who make taps for the Cahors wine barrels, is a craft peculiar to Saint-Cirq-Lapopie.

Environs
From **Bouziès**, 5 km (3 miles) from Saint-Cirq-Lapopie, visitors can take a boat ride on the Lot *(information: 05 65 31 72 25)*.

Cajarc, 15 km (9 miles) east of Saint-Cirq-Lapopie, is a village with narrow medieval streets and fine houses around Maison de l'Hébrardie, a 13th-century former castle.

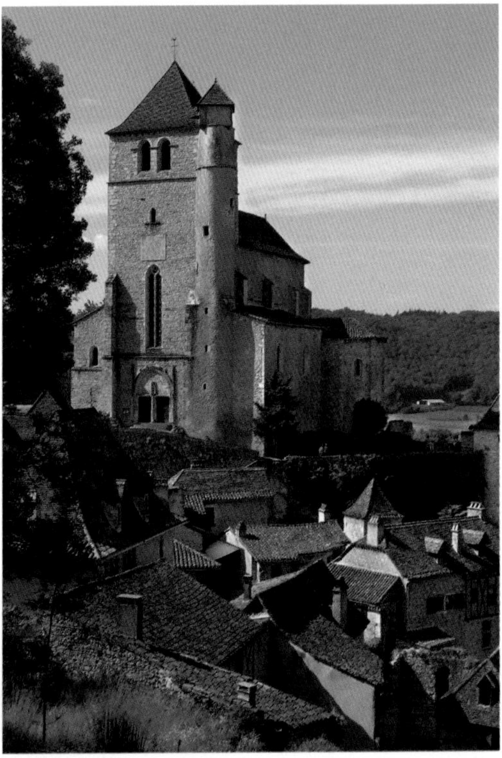

The fortified church at Saint-Cirq-Lapopie

㉙ Grotte du Pech-Merle

To visit this cave is literally to tread in the footsteps of early *Homo sapiens*, entering a mysterious and magical world. About 50 million years ago, a subterranean gallery was carved out by an underground river. This dank space, full of extraordinary natural rock formations, consists of several halls or chambers that contain hundreds of paintings, drawings and engravings of animals, human figures and abstract symbols. Unique to Pech-Merle is the way in which these prehistoric images have been combined with the geological features of the cave. The drawings were executed in charcoal, iron oxide and manganese dioxide. Because it was blocked up by a rockfall around 10,000 years ago, at the end of the Ice Age, the cave remained intact until its discovery in 1922.

Gallery at Pech-Merle, created by an underground river

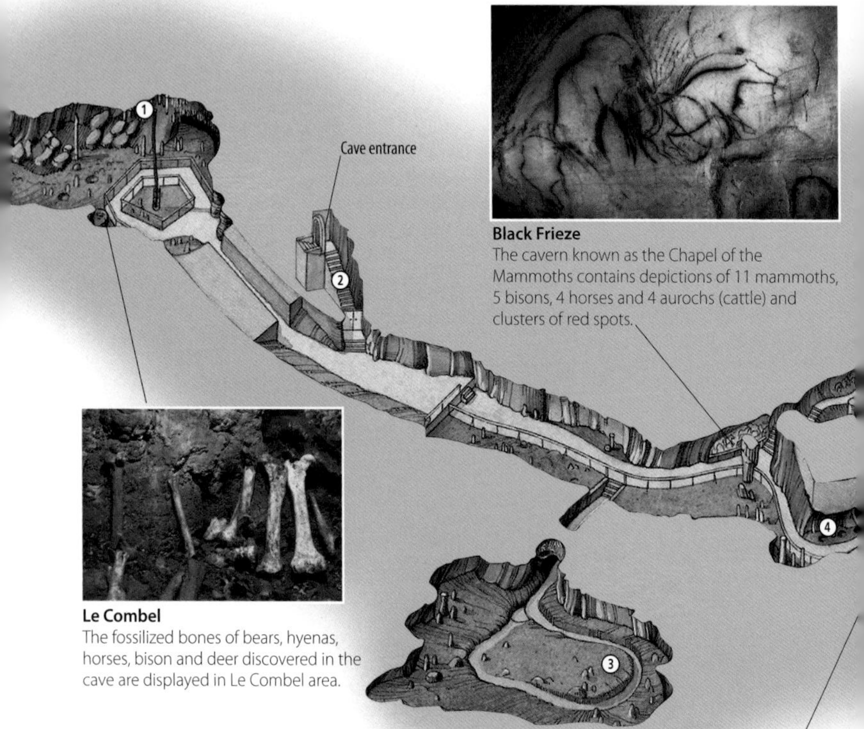

Black Frieze
The cavern known as the Chapel of the Mammoths contains depictions of 11 mammoths, 5 bisons, 4 horses and 4 aurochs (cattle) and clusters of red spots.

Le Combel
The fossilized bones of bears, hyenas, horses, bison and deer discovered in the cave are displayed in Le Combel area.

KEY

① Roots of an oak tree
② Modern stairway
③ Ossuary closed to the public
④ Bear hollow
⑤ Red deer painting
⑥ Beads and top symbol
⑦ Painting of wounded man
⑧ Fossilized human footprints

Frieze of the Dotted Horses
In this 4-m (13-ft) long frieze, the artist has used the unevennesses of the cave wall to give a three-dimensional effect to the paintings. The main subjects are two black horses, back to back, a fish drawn in red, 252 dots and the negative prints of six human hands.

Hall of the Discs
In this cavity, the calcite from the limestone has crystallized in concentric circles, which look like large discs.

VISITORS' CHECKLIST

Practical Information
3 km (2 miles) from Cabrerets.
Road map E3. **Tel** 05 65 31 27 05.
Open Apr–Oct: daily; maximum of 700 visitors per day; in high season book at least 3–4 days in advance. Educational workshops. Joint entry to the cave and museum (Centre de Préhistoire).
pechmerle.com

Transport
Conduché.

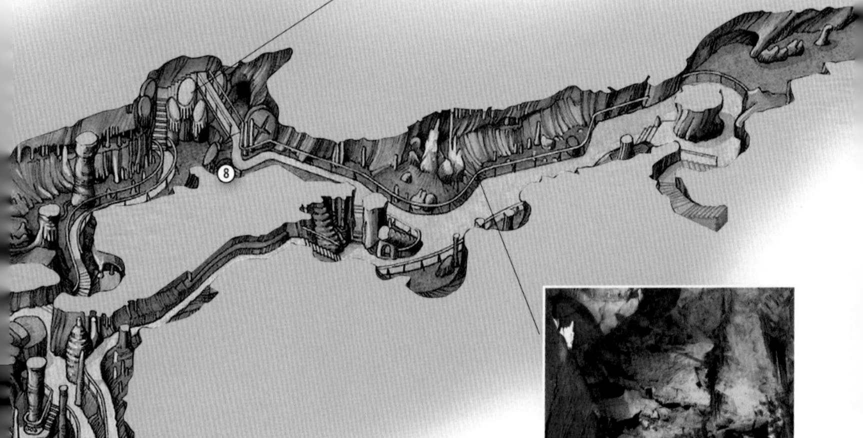

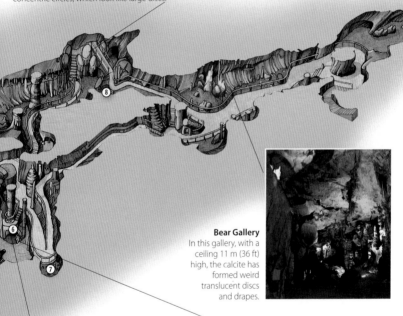

Bear Gallery
In this gallery, with a ceiling 11 m (36 ft) high, the calcite has formed weird translucent discs and drapes.

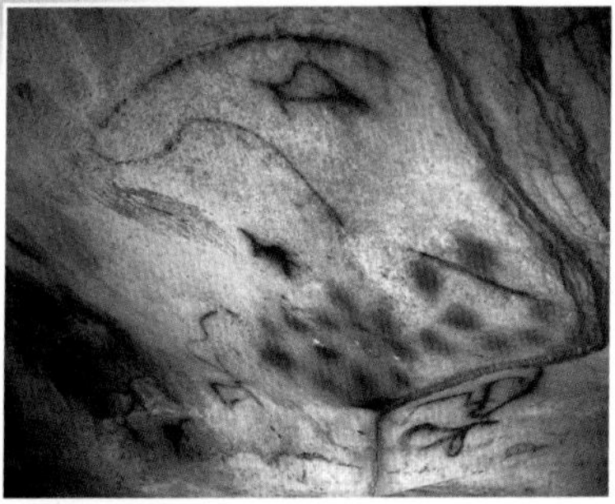

Frieze of the Bison-Women
This small frieze, on the underside of an overhanging rock in the cavern with the Ceiling of the Hieroglyphs, shows a mammoth and stylized female shapes drawn in red.

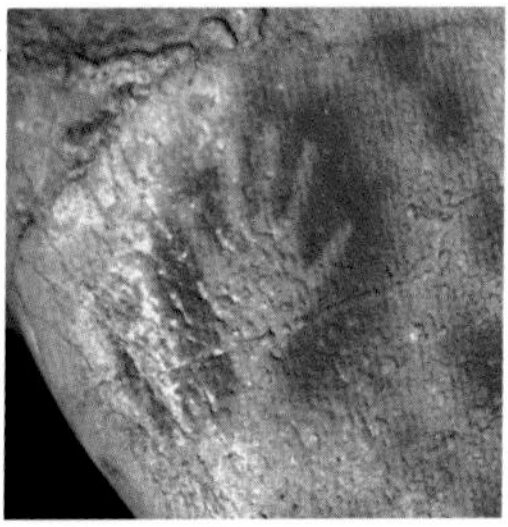

Negative Handprint
Handprints, believed by some archeologists to be those of women, are a rare motif in cave art. To spray the paint onto the wall, the artist is thought to have spat it out of his or her mouth.

30 Cahors

The origins of Cahors, encircled by a loop in the river Lot, go back to the 1st century BC. Evidence of this ancient past can be seen in the ruins of the Gallo-Roman baths, now known as the Arc de Diane. In the 13th century, trade brought prosperity, leading to the creation of the town's elegant mercantile sector (now rue du Château-du-Roi). The fortifications date from the 14th century and include the ramparts, set with 11 towers and two gatehouses. Three fortified bridges, including the Pont Valentré, span the river. In the 19th century, Cahors began to spread out from this medieval core. This was when boulevard Gambetta, with the town hall, theatre and law courts, was built, and the quayside, walks and gardens were laid out.

Maison Henri-IV, with exquisite Renaissance decoration

Pont Valentré, one of the most beautiful medieval bridges in Europe

Vieille Ville

Starting from the tourist office and walking along rue du Dr-Bergounioux, rue de Lastié, rue Saint-Urcisse, place Saint-James, rue de la Chantrerie, the Daurade quarter and the cathedral quarter, visitors will see decorated courtyards, half-timbered houses with brick overhangs and houses with carved façades. Typical of the Renaissance is a form of decoration consisting of branches, roses and suns; particularly fine examples can be seen on the doors and chimney-pieces of **Maison Henri-IV**, at Collège Pélegry and Hôtel d'Alamand. In the 16th century, windows were decorated in the Italian style, and in the 17th century many town houses with ornate doorways were built. Tour Jean-XXII, to the north, is all that remains of Palais Duèze, once owned by the Pope's brother. The **Musée de la Résistance, de la Déportation et de la Libération** is also worth a visit.

Musée de la Résistance

Place Bessières. **Tel** 05 65 22 14 25. **Open** Apr–Sep: daily; Oct–Dec: Mon–Sat pm. **Closed** 1 Jan, 1 May, 25 Dec.

Pont Valentré

Built in the 14th century and never attacked, this impresssive fortified bridge has six Gothic spans with chamfered piers. Its three fortified towers command views over the Lot from a height of 40 m (130 ft). Standing as the symbol of Cahors, it was restored in 1879 by Paul Gout and is the best preserved medieval bridge in Europe. It is visible from the Terrasses Valentré (Allée des Soupirs), the Fontaine des Chartreux and the heights of Croix Magne.

Cathédrale Saint-Étienne

A stopping-place on the pilgrim route to Compostela, the cathedral underwent several phases of construction from the 11th to the 17th centuries, and was restored in the 19th century. The result is a harmonious mix of styles. The nave, 20 m (66 ft) wide, is the oldest part of the building. Above it are two great domes,

A Devilish Tale

Pont Valentré took almost 50 years to build. According to a legend that grew up around it, the architect asked the Devil to help him complete this feat of civil engineering, in return for his soul. To escape the agreement, he tried to dupe the Devil, who took his revenge: each night the last stone to be laid in the central tower would mysteriously fall, to be replaced the next day. In 1879, while restoring the bridge, Paul Gout, the architect, immortalized this tale by setting a carving of the Devil on the central tower, now known as the Tour du Diable (Devil's Tower).

Sculpture on the Tour du Diable

For hotels and restaurants in this region see pp251–2 and pp263–5

Portrait of Léon Gambetta, Musée Henri-Martin

16 m (52 ft) across. The Romanesque north doorway, with 12th-century tympanum, is as elaborate as those at Moissac and Souillac. The choir is in a southern Gothic style. The square in front of the cathedral was laid out on place Chapou in the 14th century, when the cathedral acquired a new façade. The cloister, a Flamboyant Gothic masterpiece, dates from 1506.

Musée Henri-Martin

792 rue Émile-Zola. **Tel** 05 65 20 88 66. **Open** Wed–Mon. **Closed** Sun am, 1 Jan, 25 Dec.

This museum in Parc Tassart is housed in the former bishop's palace, which dates from the 17th century. Founded in 1833, it contains about 18,000 exhibits, ranging from archeological artifacts and coins to ethnographic pieces and fine art.

Among its collections are paintings by the Surrealist artist Henri Martin (1860–1943), sketches by Courbet and Corot and paintings by Dufy and Lurçat. A section is devoted to Léon Gambetta (1838–1882), father of the French Republic, who was born in Cahors. The display contains 3,000 documents relating to his public life. Regular temporary exhibitions are held in the museum; ask at the front desk for more information.

VISITORS' CHECKLIST

Practical Information

Road map: E3. 1 hour from Toulouse on the D820. 20,000. Place François-Mitterrand; 05 65 53 20 65. **tourisme-cahors.fr** Wed & Sat am. Les Estivales (brochure gives details of summer events), Cahors Blues Festival (Jul–Aug).

Transport

Painting by Henri Martin, Musée Henri-Martin

Cahors City Centre

1. Arc de Diane
2. Musée Henri-Martin
3. Cathédrale Saint-Étienne
4. La Chantrerie
5. Maison Henri-IV
6. Pont Valentré
7. Musée de la Résistance

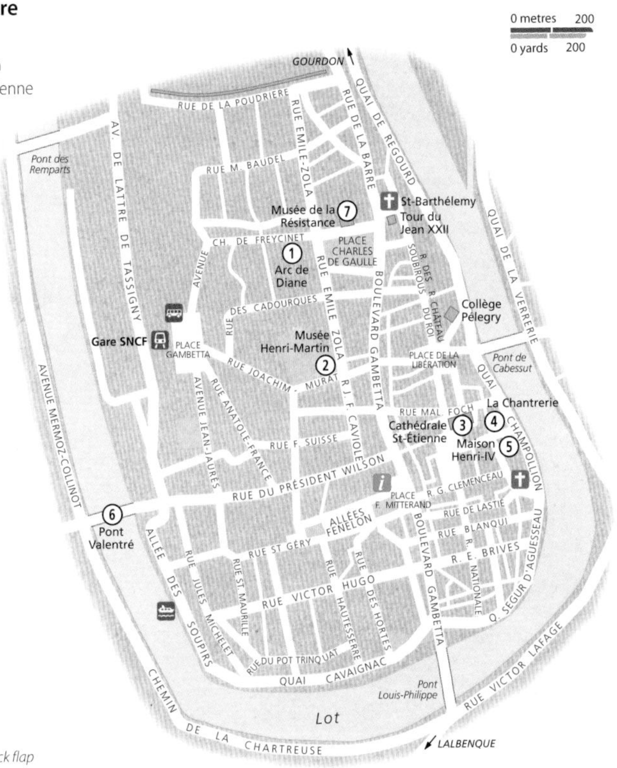

For map symbols *see back flap*

La Chantrerie

35 rue de la Chantrerie. **Tel** 05 65 23 99 70. **Open** Wed–Sat & pm Sun.

Once a washhouse, this historic 14th-century building now hosts regular temporary exhibitions on its upper floor.

Environs

The village of **Lalbenque**, 15 km (9 miles) southeast of Cahors, is renowned for its truffle market, which takes place on Tuesdays from December to mid-March, and for festivities celebrating this "black diamond". The Lot produces 3–10 tonnes of truffles a year. Almost all of Quercy's harvest of black truffles comes from the countryside around Lalbenque. Some 28 km (17 miles) to the southwest of Cahors is the "Capital of Query Blanc", **Montcuq**. The pretty streets are lined with timbered houses and its 17th-century tower is all that remains of the ancient Cathar stronghold, which was plundered and destroyed by the Huguenots. Nearby, there is a tranquil lake with sandy shores, ideal for bathing.

Église Saint-Pierre at Gourdon

32 Gourdon

Road map E2. On the D704. 4,876. 24 rue du Majou; 05 65 27 52 50. Sat am (& Thu am Jul–Aug); 1st and 3rd Tue of month. Les Médiévales (1st weekend in Aug). **tourisme-gourdon.com**

The town of Gourdon, which comes to life on market days, is the capital of Bouriane. In the 16th century it grew rich from its weaving industry. The medieval heart of the town has a 13th-century fortified gate and some fine houses, including the Maison du Sénéchal, Maison Cavaignac and Maison d'Anglars. Two particularly picturesque streets are rue du Majou, which was filled with drapers' shops in the

31 Vineyards of Cahors

The vineyards around Cahors are among the oldest in Europe. Since the Middle Ages, Cahors wine has been noted for its excellent ageing properties, which stem from the high quality vine-growing soil on the limestone plateau of the Causse. Vineyards stretch out for 60 km (35 miles) on either side of the Lot river, mainly in the valley below the city. While an exploration of the region offers many opportunities for wine-tasting, the countryside itself provides a visual feast.

① Montcabrier

This *bastide* town, established in the Thèze valley by Philip the Fair in 1298, has houses with magnificent façades and corbelled corner-tiles.

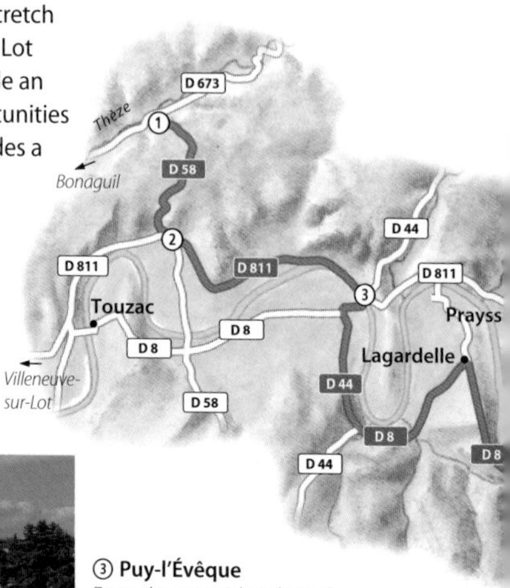

② Duravel

The village grew up around an 11th-century priory. The Romanesque church here contains a sarcophagus with the remains of three saints. The square pre-Romanesque crypt beneath the nave is crowded with pillars and columns that support the roof.

③ Puy-l'Évêque

From the quayside, where there was once a river port, to place de la Truffière, a vantage point with expansive views, the narrow streets of the village wind around medieval houses, passing the massive 13th-century keep and a fortified church, Église Saint-Sauveur, dating from the 14th century.

Middle Ages, and rue Zig-Zag. The Église Saint-Pierre, a Gothic church with asymmetrical towers, has some splendid 16th-century stained-glass windows and Baroque wood carvings. The town is dotted with other religious buildings. Among them are the Église des Cordeliers, built in the 13th century and altered in the 19th, Chapelle Notre-Dame-des-Neiges, Église Saint Siméon and Chapelle du Majou. The medieval castle was destroyed in the 18th century, but the esplanade that fronted it remains and offers good views of the Bouriane river.

Environs

The **Grottes de Cougnac** at Payrignac, 3 km (2 miles) from Gourdon on the D17, are full of stalactites and stalagmites, and other interesting rock formations, which look magical when lit up. The Cro-Magnon people who used the cave 25,000 to 14,000 years ago decorated some walls with paintings of moufflon (wild sheep), human figures and symbols.

Grottes de Cougnac
Tel 05 65 41 47 54. **Open** Easter–Sep: daily; Oct–Nov: pm Mon–Sat.

The team of speleologists who discovered the Grottes de Cougnac

⑥ Luzech

In the shadow of the imposing 12th-century keep, this ancient Cathar fiefdom became one of Quercy's four baronies. A walk around the peninsula leads to the Chapelle Notre-Dame-de-l'Île, a 16th-century chapel. Maison des Consuls, built in the 12th century, houses an archeological museum.

Tips for Drivers

Road map: E3
Tour length: 70 km (43 miles)
Stopping-off places: A good place to stop is Parnac, where you can sample the excellent local wine at the Cave Coopérative du Vignoble de Cahors (Les Côtes d'Olt) (05 65 30 71 86) during the summer months.

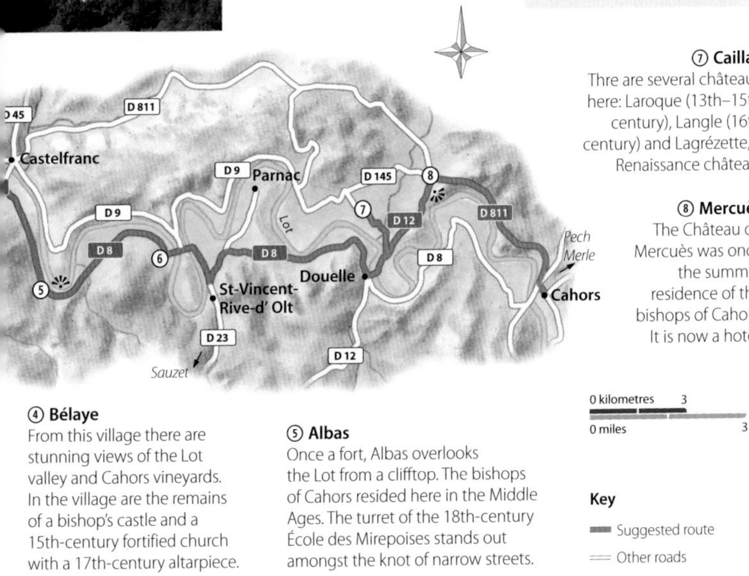

⑦ Caillac

There are several châteaux here: Laroque (13th–15th century), Langle (16th century) and Lagrézette, a Renaissance château.

⑧ Mercuès

The Château de Mercuès was once the summer residence of the bishops of Cahors. It is now a hotel.

④ Bélaye

From this village there are stunning views of the Lot valley and Cahors vineyards. In the village are the remains of a bishop's castle and a 15th-century fortified church with a 17th-century altarpiece.

⑤ Albas

Once a fort, Albas overlooks the Lot from a clifftop. The bishops of Cahors resided here in the Middle Ages. The turret of the 18th-century École des Mirepoises stands out amongst the knot of narrow streets.

❸❸ Castelnaud

See pp140–41.

❸❹ Beynac

Road map E2. On the D703. 516. Sarlat. La Balme; 05 53 29 43 08. **beynac-en-perigord.com**

Beynac, which clings dramatically to a steep cliff-face, has attracted a clutch of artists and writers, including Camille Pissarro (1830–1903), Henry Miller (1891–1980) and the poet Paul Éluard (1895–1952), who spent the last years of his life here. The village is still filled with the artists' studios. The narrow street from the lower village up to the castle passes several ancient houses and offers expansive views.

Perched on a rock 150 m (490 ft) above the river, **Château de Beynac** is visible from afar. The seat of one of the Périgord's four baronies, it occupies a strategic position, like its rival, Castelnaud. The castle repeatedly came under attack during the Hundred Years' War and again during the Wars of Religion in the 16th century. Restoration work began in 1961.

Entry is across a double moat and through a double line of ramparts. The 13th-century keep is flanked by the main building, dating from the same period but remodelled in the 16th century, and another building dating from the 14th and 17th centuries. The great hall, with vaulted ceiling, has a Renaissance chimney-piece. The castle was bought in 1962 by Lucien Grosso, who painstakingly restored the building to evoke life as it was lived here in the past. The exquisite 12th-century chapel, now a parish church, is roofed with traditional Périgordian tiles.

The **Parc Archéologique** at the foot of the castle features the reconstruction of a Bronze Age settlement, creating a vivid impression of the food, clothing, houses and farms of that time. There are also workshops giving visitors an insight into life in the Neolithic period and the Iron Age.

Château de Beynac
Tel 05 53 29 50 40. **Open** daily. by phone appointment.

Parc Archéologique
Tel 05 53 29 51 28. **Open** Jul–mid-Sep: Mon–Fri.

Environs

The delightful, adjoining hamlet of **Cazenac** has a 15th-century church. A walk along the road, running down to the left of it, offers a stunning panorama of the valley below, with the Château de Beynac in the distance.

The village of Belvès, on the site of an ancient hill fort

❸❺ Belvès

Road map D2. On the D710. 1,431. 1 rue des Filhols; 05 53 29 10 20. Sat am. Les 100km du Périgord Noir (ultra-marathon race, Apr); Festival Bach (Jul–Aug); Fête Médiévale (Aug). **tourisme-belves.com**

Set on a hilltop, this village was a fort in the 11th century. Its medieval heart centres on the castle and place d'Armes, where there is a 15th-century covered market. Nearby is the 13th-century Hôtel Bontemps, with a Renaissance façade. The town has seven towers, some of them bell towers. These include one from the 15th-century, the 11th-century keep (known as Tour de l'Auditeur) and the Tour des Frères. Église Notre-Dame, with its Flamboyant Gothic doorway, is all that remains of Belvès's abbey. The troglodytic dwellings cut into the village's medieval fortifications were

Château de Beynac, perched high above the Dordogne

in use from the 13th to the 18th century.

Environs
About 8 km (5 miles) west, on the edge of the Forêt de la Bessède, lies the attractive village of **Urval**. It has a 13th–14th-century communal oven, a rare vestige of medieval village life. Close by is an 11th–12th century fortified Romanesque church.

㊱ Le Buisson-de-Cadouin

Road map D2. 2,115. André Boissière, Le Buisson; 05 53 22 06 09. Wed am.

The village grew up round the 12th-century Cistercian **Abbaye de Cadouin** (a World Heritage Site), on the pilgrim route to Compostela. Until 1932 what was believed to be the Holy Shroud was kept here, and the village grew wealthy from the pilgrims who flocked to this sacred relic. Behind the abbey's imposing buttressed façade is the cloister, built in the 15th and 16th centuries in a mixture of Flamboyant Gothic and Renaissance styles. The carved finials and images, of both biblical and secular subjects, are a masterpiece of stone carving. In the cloister garden stands a tall, pagoda-like bell tower.

Abbaye de Cadouin
Tel 05 53 63 36 28. **Open** Jul–Aug: daily; at other times, call ahead.

Environs
Trémolat, 10 km (6 miles) northwest of Le Buisson-de-Cadouin, was the location where Claude Chabrol shot his film *Le Boucher*. From the belvedere, there are stunning views of the Cingle de Trémolat (the great loop in the Dordogne), and of the fertile plain. The fortified church, with its keeplike bell tower, is arrestingly austere. The village also has some interesting fine houses, dating from the 12th to the 18th centuries.

The covered market in Cadouin

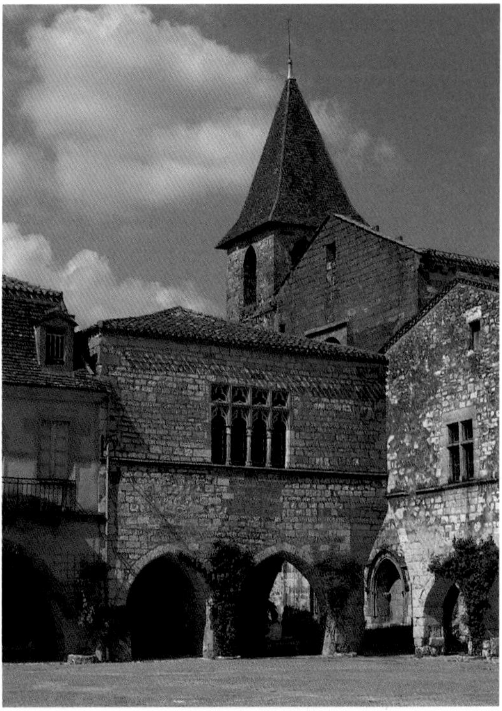
Monpazier, one of the best-preserved *bastide* towns in France

㊲ Monpazier

Road map D2. On the D660. 523. Belvès. Place des Cornières; 05 53 22 68 59. Thu am.

Monpazier is a classic *bastide* town. With a grid of streets and alleyways within its ramparts, it is also one of the most attractive in southwest France. Founded in 1284 by Edward I, king of England, Monpazier has remained almost unchanged for 800 years, although only three of its original six fortified gates still stand. It has been used as a medieval location for several films. Its picturesque central square is lined with arcades that are filled with shops. The square also has a 16th-century covered market, which still contains some antique grain measures. Monpazier is the birthplace of the writer and explorer Jean Galmot (1879–1928).

Environs
17 km (10 miles) southeast of Monpazier, lies **Villefranche-du-Périgord**, a *bastide* town, established in 1261 at the meeting point of the Périgord, Quercy and Agenais. Every autumn, it hosts a famous *cèpes* (boletus) market. This takes place in the town's covered market area, which still has antique grain measures. Attractive arcaded houses stand opposite this market. The oak forests nearby are a pleasant place to take a walk.

A few kilometres further along the D57 lies **Besse**, a village with a splendid fortified church. The single-walled bell tower has an 11th-century doorway, with three archivolts that are covered with carvings of mythological animals.

㉝ Château de Castelnaud

Spread out between its castle and the banks of the river, the village of Castelnaud sits at the intersection of the Dordogne and Céou valleys. In the 13th century, a Cathar lord, Bernard de Casnac, fought Simon de Montfort for control of the castle, which was destroyed by fire but quickly rebuilt. Because the Caumont family, lords of Castelnaud during the Hundred Years' War, sided with the English, the French laid siege to the castle in 1442. During the Wars of Religion in the mid-16th century, Geoffroy de Vivans, a Huguenot, gained control. Abandoned during the French Revolution, the castle gradually fell into ruin. It was bought in 1966 and classed as a historic monument. The museum holds over 200 items of medieval arms, armour and weapons.

Château de Castelnaud, on a cliff overlooking the village

★ Armoury

Decorated daggers, swords, helmets, crossbows, shields and other weapons, such as flails, maces and battle-axes, are displayed in the armoury. It also contains an interesting collection of halberds.

War in the Middle Ages

A formidable arsenal of weapons was developed in the Middle Ages. It included the falconet (a light cannon), the bombard (a stone-hurling contraption) and the arquebus (a long-barrelled gun on a tripod). Various types of catapult were used, often as deterrents that were wheeled out simply to intimidate the enemy. Battles in the 15th century were fought with quite small forces: the cavalry backed up by infantry with knives and lances. From the 16th century, armies were professionally trained and led.

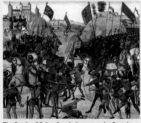

The Battle of Crécy, fought between the French and the English on 26 August 1346

For hotels and restaurants in this region see pp251–2 and pp263–5

The inner courtyard
Sited at the foot of the keep, this contains a 46-m (150-ft) well and a cistern where rain water was collected.

VISITORS' CHECKLIST

Practical Information
Road map E2. On the D57, 10 km (6 miles) from Sarlat. **Tel** 05 53 31 30 00. **Open** daily. in summer. History tour, including heritage workshops, by arrangement; medieval shows & late evening tours for groups.
castelnaud.com

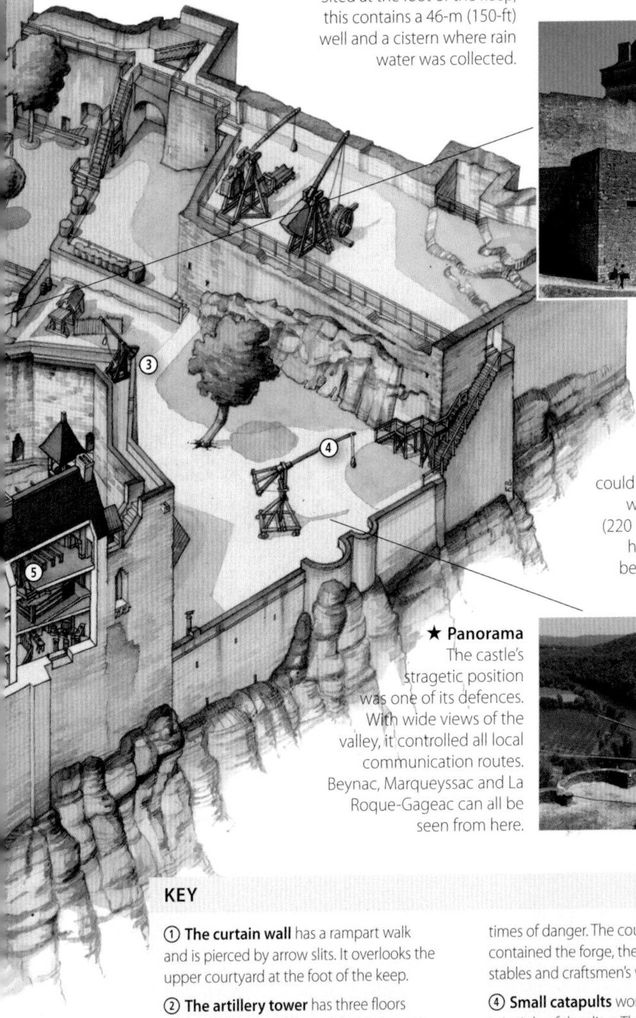

★ Barbican
Pierced with gun-holes on two levels, the barbican defended the castle entrance. The 15th-century bombard opposite could project cannonballs weighing over 100 kg (220 lb), but only one per hour, as it had to cool before being reloaded.

★ Panorama
The castle's stragetic position was one of its defences. With wide views of the valley, it controlled all local communication routes. Beynac, Marqueyssac and La Roque-Gageac can all be seen from here.

KEY

① **The curtain wall** has a rampart walk and is pierced by arrow slits. It overlooks the upper courtyard at the foot of the keep.

② **The artillery tower** has three floors with embrasures, a falconet (light cannon), a bronze hackbut, veuglaires (small cannons) and two organ guns (mounted on wheels).

③ **The outer courtyard**, defended by a low wall and two semicircular towers, was a place of refuge for the villagers in times of danger. The courtyard also contained the forge, the oven, the stables and craftsmen's workshops.

④ **Small catapults** worked on the principle of the sling. They could project stones weighing 5–15 kg (11–33 lb) over distances of up to 60 m (300 ft), at a rate of two per minute.

⑤ **Catapults** were used mostly to repel attacks. As deterrents, they were positioned to be visible, so as to intimidate the enemy.

The fortified church at Beaumont-du-Périgord, dominating the village

38 Beaumont-du-Périgord

Road map D2. On the D25 from Le Buisson. 1,150. Le Buisson-de-Cadouin. 16 Place Jean Moulin; 05 53 22 39 12). Tue & Sat am.

Since its foundation in 1272, Beaumont, a *bastide* town built by the English, has undergone much alteration. Of the 16 gates that once formed part of its fortifications, only one, the Porte de Luzier, remains, forming the present entrance into the town. The central square was remodelled in the 18th century and the covered market no longer exists. There are some fine 13th-, 14th- and 15th-century houses, particularly in rue Romieu and rue Vidal. The town's architectural jewel is its impressive fortified church, the Église Saint-Laurent-et-Saint-Front. One of the finest in southwest France, this huge, severely plain church is in a military Gothic style, with four belfry-like towers, linked by a wall-walk. The church was built from 1280 to 1330 and formed part of the town's defences. The doorway is decorated by a frieze filled with grimacing figures.

Environs

The medieval village of **Saint-Avit-Sénieur**, 5 km (3 miles) east of Beaumont, is visible from afar due to its church. This Romanesque structure was fortified in the 14th century, and a wall-walk connects its two towers.

Some 10 km (6 miles) east of Beaumont lies the village of **Montferrand-du-Périgord**. It has a splendid 16th-century covered market and the ruins of a castle with a 12th-century keep.

The **Château de Lanquais**, 10 km (6 miles) northwest of Beaumont, has a 15th-century circular tower and polygonal staircase tower, as well as residential quarters dating from the 16th and 17th centuries.

Château de Lanquais
Tel 05 53 61 24 24. **Open** Apr–Jun & Sep–Oct: Wed–Mon pm; Jul–Aug: daily.

39 Biron

Road map D2. 183. Place des Cornières, Montpazier; 05 53 22 68 59.

Once the seat of one of Périgord's four baronies, the massive **Château de Biron** straddles the border between the Périgord and the Agenais. With a 12th-century keep, Renaissance living quarters, a Gothic chapel and a small 14th-century manor house, decorated with 16th-century frescoes, it embodies a stunning medley of architectural styles spanning the 12th to the 18th centuries.

Having given asylum to Cathars in 1211, the castle was besieged by Simon de Montfort, and it changed allegiance countless times during the Hundred Years' War, suffering attack and damage as a result. It was largely rebuilt during the Renaissance and now towers over the village of Biron, which has some fine houses around its covered market.

Château de Biron
Tel 05 53 63 13 39. **Open** mid-Apr–mid-Nov: daily; mid-Nov–Dec & Feb–mid-Apr: Tue–Sun.
semitour.com

40 Eymet

Road map D2. 23 km (14 miles) from Bergerac on the D933. 2,552. Bergerac. Place des Arcades; 05 53 23 74 95.

This *bastide* town, built in the Dropt valley in 1270, retains its original square layout. Gargoyles

The Château de Biron, on the border between the Périgord and Agenais

For hotels and restaurants in this region see pp251–2 and pp263–5

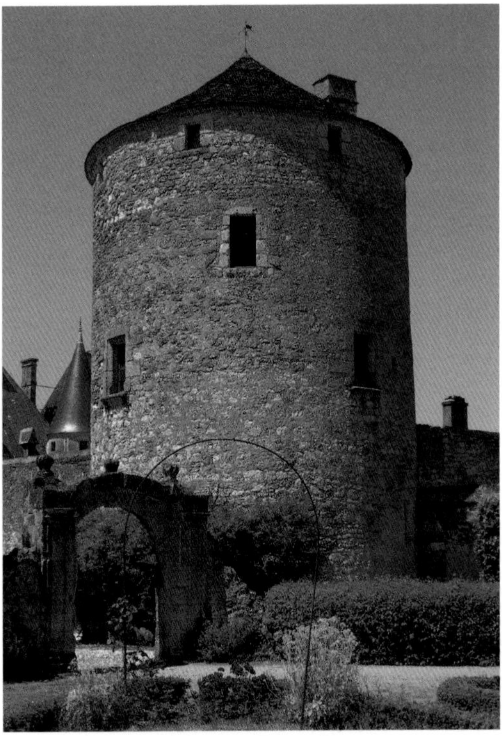
The 16th-century library-tower, all that remains of the time of Montaigne

look down from the 13th-century keep, and the 15th- and 16th-century houses have turrets with mullioned windows. A 17th-century fountain sits in the main square. Once an English stronghold, Eymet now has a large British expatriate community.

Environs
Some 20 km (12 miles) northeast of Eymet is the medieval village of **Issigeac**, with a spiral layout and 13th-century ramparts. The 15th–16th-century Gothic church, with a bell tower over its entrance, stands on the site of a priory. The former bishop's palace, its two pavilions set with corbelled turrets, is now the town hall, while the former tithe barn now houses a tourist office. The main street is lined with fine houses, one of which has 14th-century carved beams.

Arcades in the *bastide* town of Eymet

Montaigne the Humanist

Montaigne

Michel Eyquem de Montaigne was born at the Château de Montaigne in 1533. He studied law and in 1557 became a councillor in Périgueux, then at the Parlement de Bordeaux. From 1572 to 1580, with the Wars of Religion raging around him, he began to consider the nature of human happiness and worked on his famous *Essays*. He led a rather secluded life, but maintained links with powerful people. Elected mayor of Bordeaux in 1581, he led the city with great diplomacy at a time when it was torn between Catholics and Protestants, then hit by plague. He died in 1592.

㊶ Bergerac

See pp144–5.

㊷ Saint-Michel-de-Montaigne

Road map C2. 47 km (29 miles) from Bergerac on the D936. 312. Place Clemenceau, Montpon-Ménestérol; 05 53 82 23 77.

The Romanesque church here has a doorway with columns and four intricately moulded arches. The interior features carved 17th-century furniture and the Stations of the Cross by the artist Gilbert Privat (1892–1969).

Of the château where Montaigne lived, only the 16th-century **tower**, where he had his library and where he wrote, is original, while the rest has been rebuilt. The beams of his study, on the top floor, are inscribed with 57 Greek and Latin sentences and maxims, that represent the Epicurean, Stoic and sceptic ideas that influenced Montaigne. The views from the terrace stretch out over the Lidoire valley.

Tower
Tel 05 53 58 63 93 (call ahead for opening times). **Open** Jul–Aug: daily; Sep–Jun: Wed–Sun. **Closed** Jan.

Environs
About 44 km (27 miles) from Bergerac on the D936 is the village of **Montcaret**. The Romanesque church here has capitals that may have been taken from an earlier Gallo-Roman building. Nearby are the remains of a large Gallo-Roman villa, discovered in 1827. It has fine mosaic flooring, an inner courtyard lined with columns, a 60-sq-m (645-sq-ft) main room with a triple apse, a pool with mosaics of aquatic subjects and baths with a sophisticated heating system. The quality of workmanship suggest that this was a place of luxury. It was built in the 1st century and rebuilt in the 4th. Evidence suggests that the site has been inhabited since antiquity.

41 Bergerac

Bergerac was held alternately by the French and the English during the Hundred Years' War, and later became a stronghold of the Protestant faith. Set on the banks of the Dordogne, it developed as a centre of trade, a stopping point for *gabares* (traditional wooden barges) carrying wood, blocks of stone, paper milled in Couze, wines, locally grown walnuts and chestnuts and other goods between the Périgord and the port at Bordeaux. This Huguenot town once had several harbours of its own. In the 18th century, some 15,000 tonnes of goods and around 1,500 boats passed through every year. The present quayside was built as late as 1838, but was rendered obsolete by the arrival of the railway in the late 19th century. Today *gabares* still set off daily from quai Salvette, although they now carry a cargo of visitors on scenic trips up and down the Dordogne river.

Vieille Ville

The old, half-timbered houses of master-boatmen line place de la Mirpe, where there is a **statue of Cyrano de Bergerac**, Edmond Rostand's long-nosed hero *(see p200)*. Rue Saint-Clar is lined with corbelled houses, with cob, brick and half-timbered walls. Place Pélissière, in a restored area of the town, is named after the skinners whose workshops once stood there. With the Église Saint-Jacques and Fontaine Font-Ronde, once a public wash house, it forms a picturesque enclave. Place Pélissière is the setting for another statue of Cyrano de Bergerac, which was erected in 2005. Rue Saint-James has several interesting houses, including an 18th-century town house, with a shop on the ground floor and bosses on its façade, a 16th-century house with mullioned windows, and 17th- and 18th-century half-timbered houses. Rue des Fontaines has two **medieval houses**.

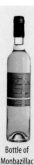

Statue of Cyrano

Église Saint-Jacques

Place Pélissière.

This 12th-century chapel on the pilgrim route to Compostela was enlarged in the 13th century, when it became the medieval town's church, with a single-wall belfry. It was later remodelled on several occasions, the nave being completely rebuilt in the 18th century. The Neo-Gothic organ, built by Aristide Cavaillé-Coll in 1870, is listed as a historic monument.

Bottle of Monbazillac wine

Bergerac Wines

Bergerac wines were highly thought-of in England during the Hundred Years' War, and in Holland when the town was a Protestant stronghold, but their renown goes back as far as the 13th century. Today there are 12,400 ha (306,400 acres) of vineyards in the area, with 13 *appellations*, for red, rosé, and both dry and sweet white wines, including the famous Monbazillac: morning mists and autumn sunshine nurture the *pourriture noble* mould, giving the grapes their extra sweetness. For information on local wine routes, contact the Conseil Interprofessionnel des Vins de la Région de Bergerac (CIVRB): 05 53 63 57 57, www.vins-bergerac.fr.

Restaurant in a pedestrianized street in Bergerac's Vieille Ville

Musée Costi

Access via the inner courtyard of place de la Petite-Mission. **Tel** 05 53 63 04 13. **Open** Jul–Aug: Tue–Sun pm; rest of year by appointment.

This museum fills two cellars of the Presbytère Saint-Jacques. It contains works donated by Costi, a sculptor born in 1906 and who studied under Antoine Bourdelle. They consist of 52 bronzes and seven plaster casts, made between 1926 and 1973.

Maison des Vins-Cloître des Récollets

1 rue des Récollets. **Tel** 05 53 63 57 55. **Open** Jul–Aug: daily; Sep–Jun: Tue–Sat. **Closed** Jan.

The Cloître des Récollets was built in 1630 on the site of the former gardens of the Château de Bergerac. The 16th- and 18th-century galleries look on to the court-yard. For a time the chapel served as a free-mason's hall. It now houses the Maison des Vins de Bergerac, which regulates local wine production and offers tastings. The starting point for the "Route des Vins" is available at the tourist office.

Musée du Vin et de la Batellerie

5 rue des Conférences. **Tel** 05 53 57 80 92. **Open** Tue–Sat (Jun–Sep: pm Sun).

This museum is devoted to the history of river shipping and the local wine trade. The displays include a wide variety of artifacts, models, documents, photographs, and archive materials

The Cloître des Récollets, now home to the Maison des Vins

VISITORS' CHECKLIST

Practical Information
Road map D2. On the N21 Limoges–Agen. 27,201. 97 rue Neuve-d'Argenson; 05 53 57 03 11. Wed am, Sat am. Festival d'Eté (Tue evenings in summer); Fête des Vendanges (early Oct).
bergerac-tourisme.com

Transport

that have been donated by boat-owning and wine-producing families in the area.

Musée d'Intérêt National du Tabac

Maison Peyrarède, place du Feu.
Tel 05 53 63 04 13. **Open** Tue–Sat (mid-Mar–mid-Nov: pm Sun).

Created in 1950 by the Direction des Musées de France, this museum occupies **Maison Peyrarède**, a town house built in 1604 and restored in 1982. The only one of its kind in Europe, the museum traces the history of tobacco over 3,000 years. Its collections illustrate the earliest use of the plant, its spread throughout the world and the ways in which it was smoked, and tackles the anti-smoking lobby. Various smoking implements, with details of their manufacture, are shown. The importance of tobacco-growing in the Dordogne valley is also highlighted.

Bergerac Town Centre

① Église Saint-Jacques
② Musée Costi
③ Musée du Vin et de la Batellerie
④ Statue of Cyrano
⑤ Maison des Vins- Cloître des Récollet
⑥ Medieval houses
⑦ Musée d'Intérêt National du Tabac
⑧ Quai Salvette

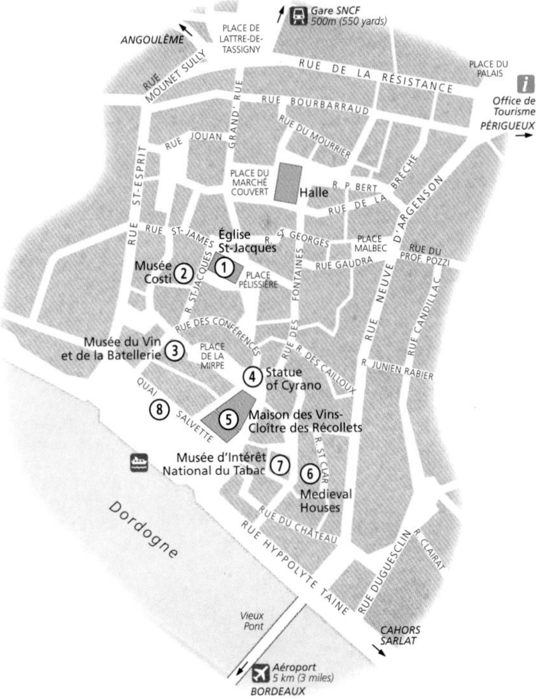

0 metres 200
0 yards 200

For map symbols *see back flap*

LOT-ET-GARONNE

The 19th-century French novelist, Stendhal, likened the sunny, undulating landscape of the Lot-et-Garonne to that of Tuscany. This prosperous and mostly agricultural area also has a rich architectural heritage that reflects its eventful history. Castles, Romanesque churches, *bastide* towns and picturesque villages are everywhere in an area that has much to offer lovers of culture and the countryside.

The Lot-et-Garrone, including what was once the Comté d'Agenais, lies between territories once held by the kings of France and the kings of England (also dukes of Aquitaine), and was the object of bitter dispute until it was finally won by France in 1472. In the 13th and 14th centuries, more than 40 *bastide* towns were built here on the orders of Raymond VII, Comte de Toulouse, of Alphonse de Poitiers, brother of Louis IX of France, and of Edward I of England. With their central arcaded squares and streets laid out to a grid pattern, such towns were built not only as a response to a rapidly growing population, but also to the conflict between France and England that raged over southwest France until well into the 15th century.

With its fertile, rolling hills and valleys, and pine forests that encroach across from the Landes, the Lot-et-Garonne is a region rich in pleasant, rural countryside. Over 200 km (125 miles) of navigable waterways are provided by the Lot, the Garonne and the Baïse rivers, and the canal that runs alongside the Garonne. Once, these were the only means of transporting local produce between Guyenne and Languedoc.

Today, as a prime producer of fruit and vegetables, including its famous prunes *(see p159)*, the Lot-et-Garonne serves as the orchard of Europe. Its fine wines compare favourably with those of neighbouring Bordeaux and are an important element in the bounty of gastronomic specialities to be enjoyed in this corner of France.

A shaded lakeside, near Lauzun

◀ Richly decorated interiors of the Saint-Caprais Cathedral at Agen

Exploring the Lot-et-Garonne

The two great river valleys of the Garonne and its tributary, the Lot, cut right through this varied region. The Lot valley, in the centre, is by turns narrow and steep-sided, and wide and flat. Fruit, including the famous *prunes d'Agen* (a type of plum), and vegetables are grown on the fertile land along its banks. In the southeast are the Agenais and Pays de Serres areas, with their mix of broad plateaux and shallow valleys. In the southwest is the Albret, territory once controlled by the family of Henri IV. To the northwest is the Pays Marmandais, a land of vine-covered hillsides, fruit orchards and vegetable fields. The Pays du Dropt, in the north, and the gentle hills of the Haut-Agenais are dotted with picturesque *bastide* towns. This area is also home to the mighty medieval Château de Bonaguil, in the east, and the grand Renaissance Château de Duras, to the west.

Flower-covered façade of a house in Pujols

The fortified church at Villeréal

Getting Around

Agen, capital of the Lot-et-Garonne, has an airport and a railway station. By TGV (high-speed train), it is 4 hours from Paris and 1 hour from Toulouse and Bordeaux. The A62 runs from the north of Toulouse to Bordeaux, passing through the region from southeast to northwest. The N21 links Agen, Villeneuve-sur-Lot and the north. Following the banks of the Lot, then those of the Garonne, the D911 links Fumel and Marmande. The D813/D1113 follows the Garonne. Direct flights from Agen to Paris Orly West take just 1 hour 20 minutes.

For map symbols *see back flap*

Key

- Motorway
- Main road
- Minor road
- Scenic route
- Main railway
- Minor railway
- Regional border

The Lot near Casseneuil

Dovecote near Poudenas

The Region at a Glance

1 Duras
2 Lauzun
3 Castillonnès
5 Villeréal
6 Monflanquin
7 Gavaudun
8 Saint-Avit
9 Sauveterre-la-Lémance
10 Monsempron
11 *Château de Bonaguil (pp154–5)*
12 Tournon-d'Agenais
13 Penne-d'Agenais
14 Villeneuve-sur-Lot
15 Pujols
16 Sainte-Livrade-sur-Lot
17 Casseneuil
18 Monclar-d'Agenais
19 Granges-sur-Lot
20 Clairac
21 Aiguillon
22 Prayssas
23 Le Mas-d'Agenais
24 Marmande
25 Casteljaloux
26 Mézin
27 Poudenas
28 Nérac
29 Barbaste
30 Vianne
31 *Agen (pp164–7)*
32 Pays de Serres
33 Laroque-Timbaut
34 Beauville
35 Saint-Maurin
36 Puymirol
37 Layrac
38 Moirax
39 Laplume
40 Aubiac
41 Estillac

Tour

4 Pays du Dropt

❶ Duras

Road map D2. 22 km (14 miles) north of Marmande. 1,250. Marmande. 14 boulevard Jean-Brisseau; 05 53 83 63 06. Mon & Wed, in summer. Fête de la Madeleine (Jul); Les Médiévales (Aug). **paysdeduras.com**

Built on the plan of a *bastide* *(see pp30–31)*, this ancient fortified town looks down from a high promontory above the river Dropt. The **Château de Duras** was built in about 1137 and later remodelled several times. By the 14th century, it was a fortress set with eight towers; by the 17th century, it had developed into a grand residential château. During the French Revolution, it was almost reduced to a ruin. The state acquired it in 1969.

The castle is open to visitors, who can walk through almost 35 of its great rooms. These include the Salle des Maréchaux (Marshals' Hall) and a barrel-vaulted ballroom dating from 1740. The tower offers a panoramic view of the Pays de Duras. The museum of local history, in the basement, documents life in Duras, focusing on such aspects of the area as vine-growing, local crafts and other folk traditions.

The 12th-century Château de Duras, once home to the Ducs de Duras, has 35 rooms open to the public

Château de Duras
Tel 05 53 83 77 32. **Open** Apr–Sep: daily; Feb, Mar, Oct & Nov: pm daily.

❷ Lauzun

Road map D2. 26 km (16 miles) east of Duras. 791. Marmande. 5 rue Pissebaque; 05 53 94 13 09. Sat. Gasconnades (2nd Sun in Aug).

The eventful life of the Duc de Lauzun, marshal of France and a courtier of Louis XIV, is conjured up in the rooms of the **Château de Lauzun**, which was built in the 13th century and remodelled in the late 14th century. The listed Renaissance wing has two monumental chimney-pieces with carvings and marble capitals. The Gothic church in the village, opposite a house with caryatids, contains a 17th-century pulpit and altarpiece.

Château de Lauzun
Tel 05 53 94 18 89. **Open** Jul–Aug: pm daily.

❹ Pays du Dropt

Occupying the northwestern corner of the Lot-et-Garonne, the Pays du Dropt is bisected by the Dropt river. It is a region of gentle valleys cov-ered with vines and plum trees, dotted with small, white, stone Romanesque churches. The vineyards of the Côtes de Duras occupy some 2,000ha (4,940 acres), many of them part of small family estates. The Côtes de Duras area was granted its own appellation in 1937.

① Sainte-Colombe-de-Duras
The choir of this small Romanesque church has carved capitals. A fresco shows scenes from the life of St Colomba.

③ Saint-Sernin-de-Duras
The church in this attractive village is picturesquely covered in Virginia creeper. The building was restored in the 15th and 19th centuries.

② Esclottes
The village is named for its *clottes* (boundary stones) that marked the borders of the dioceses of Agen and Bazas. The 11th-century church here has carved capitals showing Christ in Majesty and other scenes.

⑧ Monteton
Set above the Dropt valley, the charming 12th-century Romanesque church here has finely carved capitals, featuring a host of fantasy beasts.

Tips for Drivers

Allemans-du-Dropt; 05 53 20 25 59
Tour length: About 57 km (35 miles)
Stopping-off places: The Étape Gasconne at Allemans-de-Dropt and the table d'hôte at Château Monteton are recommended. Sample M and Mme Dreux's prunes at Esclottes and M and Mme Ros's foie gras at Les Renards, in Saint-Sernin-de-Duras.

For hotels and restaurants in this region see pp252–3 and pp265–7

❸ Castillonnès

Road map D2. 12 km (7 miles) east of Lauzun. 1,442. Villeneuve-sur-Lot or Bergerac. Place des Cornières; 05 53 36 87 44. Tue am.
castillonnestourisme.com

Founded in about 1259, the *bastide* town of Castillonnès perches on a rocky spur. During the Hundred Years' War *(see p47)*, the town passed between the French and the English seven times, but was finally taken by the French in 1451. Two gates are all that remain of the ramparts.

On place des Cornières, the main square, is an unusual 20th-century covered market. On the other side of the square is the former Maison du Gouverneur, with a Renaissance courtyard. The building is now the town hall and tourist office.

The church, which was rebuilt after the 16th-century Wars of Religion, has a 17th-century Baroque altarpiece and stained glass by the master-craftsman Louis Franchéo.

A dovecote at Castillonnès, in a style typical of the Lot-et-Garonne

Environs

About 13 km (8 miles) to the west of Castillonnès is **Miramont-de-Guyenne**. Founded in 1278 by Edward I, this *bastide* town was built on a site that was once used as a look-out post for the Knights Templar. A stroll around Miramont leads to the central square, with its reconstructed covered market and elegant arcades. The town also has a thriving show industry, which started in the 1800s with the creation of a unique, sheepskin clog.

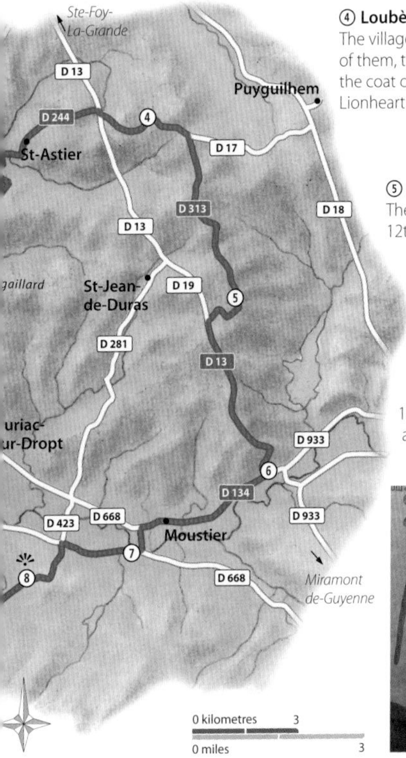

Key

Suggested route

Other roads

④ Loubès-Bernac
The village has four churches. One of them, the Église de Loubès, has the coat of arms of Richard the Lionheart on its doorway.

⑤ Soumensac
There are fine views from the remains of 12th-century ramparts at Soumensac.

⑥ La Sauvetat-du-Dropt
This village, in an ancient *sauve* (area of cleared land), has a large church with a 12th-century choir and a Romanesque bridge.

⑦ Allemans-du-Dropt
The Église Saint-Eutrope is decorated with beautiful, listed 15th-century frescoes. They include depictions of the Last Supper, the Crucifixion, the Resurrection, Hell and the Last Judgment. The choir shows Moorish influence.

The late 14th-century covered market at Villeréal

5 Villeréal

Road map D2. 13 km (8 miles) east of Castillonès. 1,250. Bergerac. Place de la Halle; 05 53 36 09 65. Sat. Bodega (Jul). **villereal-tourisme.com**

Founded in 1265, the *bastide* town of Villeréal is laid out to a regular plan *(see pp30–31)*. The main square, at the centre of the town, is lined with arcades with corbelled houses above. The large, late 14th-century covered market has an upper storey, with half-timbered cob walls, which now houses the town hall. The fortified 13th-century church, which once served as a place of refuge, has two turrets that are connected by a wall-walk. Up to the 17th century access was still by drawbridge.

Environs

There is a cluster of interesting Romanesque churches in the villages around Villeréal. The 12th-century church at Bournel, 6 km (4 miles) to the south, is dedicated to St Madeleine, whose statue can be seen above the arched main doorway. The 12th-century church at **Rives**, 2 km (1.5 miles) north, has an unusual triangular shaped bell tower, with two arches and a round apse. The 14th-century church at **Montaut**, 7 km (4.5 miles) to the southwest, was extremely important, being the seat of the archpriest with around 91 parishes. It has a five-arched bell tower astride two towers, and has two bells.

6 Monflanquin

Road map D3. 13 km (8 miles) south of Villeréal. 2,344. Villeneuve-sur-Lot. Place des Arcades; 05 53 36 40 19. Thu. Foire aux Vins et Fromages (May); Journées Médiévales (Aug). **monflanquin-tourisme.com**

This attractive *bastide* town, officially listed as one of France's prettiest villages, is laid out to an oval plan. It clings to the hillside rising sharply from the Lède valley. Built around 1240, with a grid pattern of streets, the *bastide* developed in 1252 under the leadership of Alphonse de Poitiers, but its defences were dismantled on the orders of Cardinal Richelieu. The streets intersect at place des Arcades, at the top end of the town. The main square is lined with arcaded houses *(see pp30–31)*, including the **Maison du Prince Noir** (House of the Black Prince; *see p47*), with Gothic rib-vaulting and moulded panels. The church, the beautiful **Église Saint-André**, has a single-wall bell tower, whose façade dates from 1927, and a relief-decorated medieval doorway.

Rue de l'Union, rue des Arcades and rue Sainte-Marie are lined with fine stone houses with arcades on the ground floor and 16th-century half-timbered façades above.

Overlooking the town, on a rocky spur, stands the fortified Château de Roquefère (which is only open to the public on Journées du Patrimoines).

The **Musée des Bastides** shows how *bastide* towns were constructed, from the 13th century onward, and how they served their purpose *(see pp30–31)*.

Église Saint-André
Open daily.

Musée des Bastides
Maison du Tourisme, place des Arcades. **Tel** 05 53 36 40 19.
Open Jan–Apr: Mon–Fri; May, Jun, Sep: Mon–Sat, pm Sun; Jul–Aug: daily; Oct–Dec: Mon–Fri.

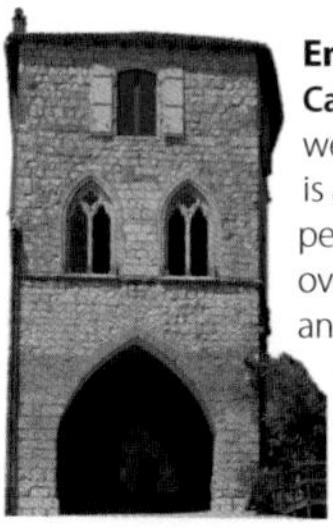

Maison du Prince Noir

Environs

Cancon, 13 km (8 miles) west of Monflanquin, is also a *bastide* town, perched on a hill overlooking Périgord and Quercy. Its old quarter has narrow streets lined by timbered 14th- and 15th-century houses.

Bernard Palissy's "Rustic Figulines"

Bernard Palissy, the famous potter, was born in Lacapelle-Biron around 1510. He made large plates, dishes, ewers and other vessels encrusted with "rustic figulines" in high relief of reptiles, fish, shells and plants, modelled from life and realistically painted. He baked them in a kiln that he reputedly stoked with the furniture and floorboards of his own house. Patronized by the queen, Catherine de Medici and by the Connétable de Montmorency, he became "Inventor of rustic figulines to the King and My Lord the Duc de Montmorency", but was later imprisoned in the Bastille in 1589 for refusing to renounce his Protestant faith. He died in prison a few years later, in 1589 or 1590.

Bernard Palissy

7 Gavaudun

Road map E3. 11 km (7 miles) east of Monflanquin. 327. Monsempron.

Perched high up on a rocky hill, the village of Gavaudun stands proud of the wooded valleys around it. The ruins of its 11th–13th-century fortress, particularly the huge **keep** with its limestone entrance, are very impressive. This stunning setting is regularly used for carnivals and musical events.

Keep
Tel 05 53 40 04 16. **Open** Jul–Aug: daily; out of season: call ahead.

Environs
2 km (1 mile) north of Gavaudun is the small hamlet of **Saint-Sardos-de-Laurenque**, where there is a delightul Romanesque church with a carved doorway.

8 Saint-Avit

Road map D2. 15 km (9 miles) northeast of Monflanquin. 430. Monsempron. Foire à la Poterie (second Sun in Aug).

This attractive hamlet on a hillside in the Lède valley has just one street. The 13th- century Romanesque church is decorated with frescoes. Saint-Avit is the birthplace of Bernard Palissy *(see opposite)*. The **Musée Bernard-Palissy** here is devoted to his life and work, and also displays contemporary ceramics.

Musée Bernard-Palissy
Saint-Avit, Lacapelle-Biron.
Open May–Jun: Sun pm; Jul–Aug: Wed–Mon pm, Sep: Sun–Mon & Wed–Fri pm. **Tel** 05 53 40 98 22.

Château des Rois-Ducs, at Sauveterre-la-Lémance

9 Sauveterre-la-Lémance

Road map E2. 14km (8 miles) east of Saint-Avit. 640. Monsempron.

This village, dominated by the privately owned Château des Rois-Ducs, gave its name to the Sauveterrian, a major period of the Mesolithic age. The small **Musée de la Préhistoire** displays objects found when excavations began in 1920 on a site known as Le Martinet.

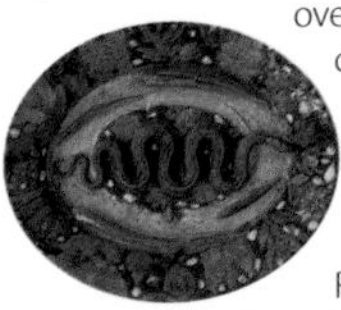

A "rustic figuline" by Bernard Palissy

Musée de la Préhistoire
Tel 05 53 40 73 03.
Open Jan–Apr: Tue–Sat; Apr, Jun, Sep, Oct: Sun–Fri pm; Jul–Aug: daily; Oct–Dec: Wed.

Environs
At **Saint-Front- sur-Lémance**, 2 km (1.5 miles) southwest, there is an interesting 11th–14th-century fortified church.

10 Monsempron

Road map E3. 10 km (6 miles) south of Bonaguil. 2,200. Monsempron. Fumel: Place Georges-Escande. **Tel** 05 53 71 13 70. Thu am. Annual fair & Fête du Printemps (Mar).

Here the imposing outline of the Benedictine priory of Saint-Géraud-de-Monsempron overlooks the confluence of Lot and the Lémance. This fortified village has a beautifully proportioned Romanesque church. Although it was remodelled in the 16th century, it retains some 12th-century elements, including a barrel-vaulted nave with carved capitals, a dome supported on stone columns above the central crossing and a severely plain doorway. The semicircular recesses of the apses overlap one another.

Environs
3 km (2 miles) northeast, **Fumel** has a 12th–16th-century castle, surrounded by formal gardens.

The former Benedictine priory and its Romanesque church, above Monsempron

⓫ Château de Bonaguil

The colossal Château de Bonaguil stands majestically on a rocky spur at the foot of a wooded hill, its towers, ramparts and turrets fleetingly visible from behind lush greenery. Founded in the 13th century on an *aiguille creuse* (hollow peak), it became known as the castle *bona accus, or bonne aiguille*, in French, hence its current name. In 1483, it passed to Bérenger de Roquefeuil (1448–1530), who enlarged it. As the result of inheritance, ownership then changed several times, but in 1761 it was re-acquired by Marguerite de Fumel, who remodelled it. Abandoned during the French Revolution, it was eventually sold to Fumel's municipal authorities in 1860. It is an impressive example of the transition between medieval military architecture and an early Rennaisance noble residence.

The impregnable fortress of Bonaguil, perched on a rocky outcrop

★ Great Tower
The key element of the castle's defences, the Great Tower is ringed by ramparts, which were once covered. It defended the inner courtyard.

Well
Located on the inner side of the main courtyard, the well was dug directly into the rock, its shaft reaching down to the water table below. Behind the well is an elegant Gothic doorway, which leads to the castle's outbuildings.

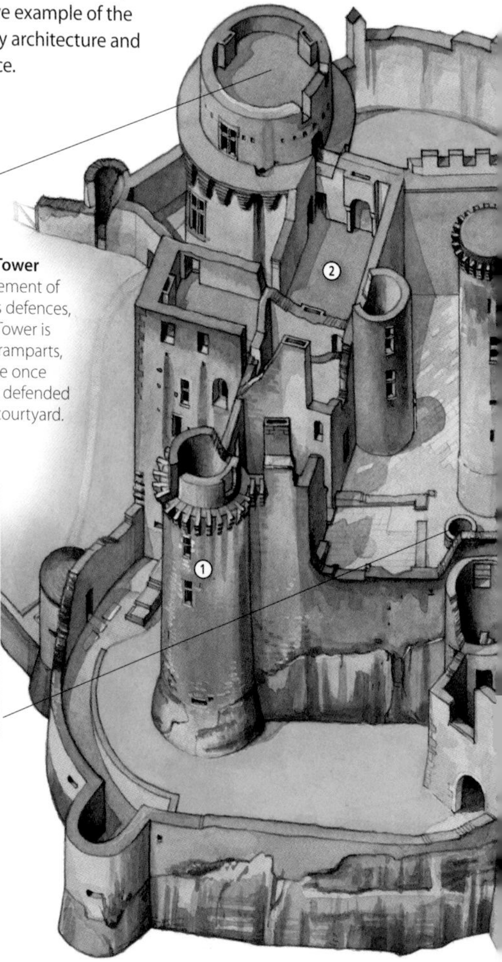

KEY

① **Red Tower**

② **Great hall**

③ **Outer courtyard**

Barbican
This semicircular fortification acted as an area of defence between the inner and outer drawbridges. As one drawbridge was raised, the other was lowered.

VISITORS' CHECKLIST

Practical Information
Road map E3. 6.5 km (4 miles) north of Fumel, near the village of Saint-Front-sur-Lémance. The castle can be reached either by road or on foot from the bottom of the village.
Tel 05 53 71 90 33.
Open Mar–Oct: daily. Festival de Théâtre (Aug).
chateau-bonaguil.com

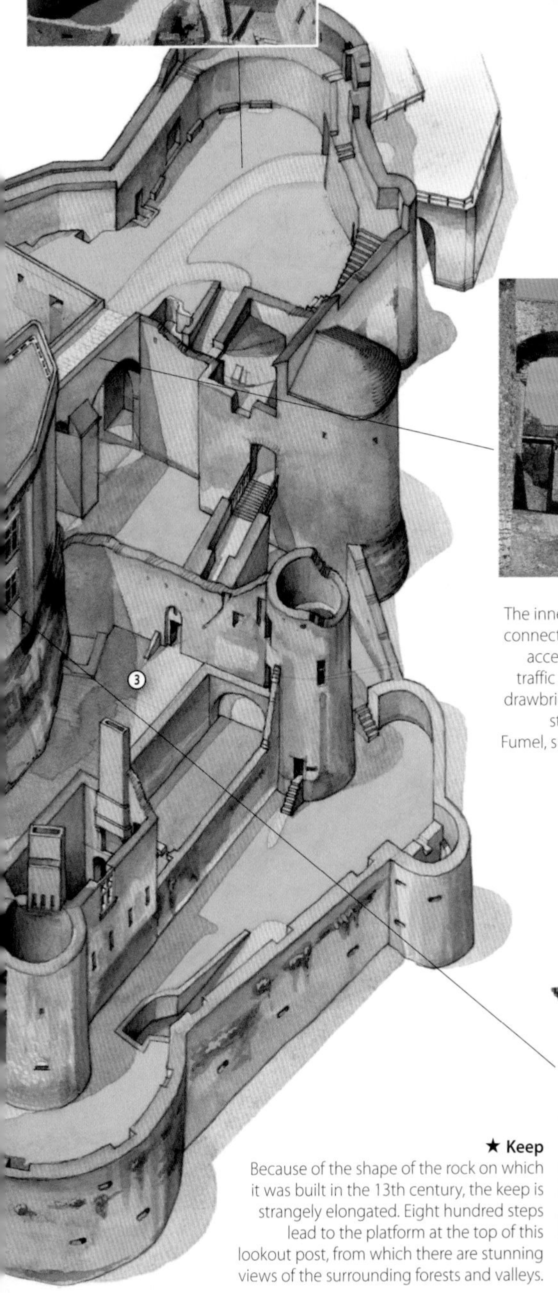

★ Drawbridge
The inner ramparts and the barbican are connected by a drawbridge, which gave access to two gates, one for wheeled traffic and another for pedestrians. The drawbridge, which was converted into a standing bridge by Marguerite de Fumel, spans the castle's wide dry moats.

★ Keep
Because of the shape of the rock on which it was built in the 13th century, the keep is strangely elongated. Eight hundred steps lead to the platform at the top of this lookout post, from which there are stunning views of the surrounding forests and valleys.

The *bastide* town of Tournon-d'Agenais, strategically set on a rocky plateau

⓬ Tournon-d'Agenais

Road map E3. 10 km (6 miles) south of Fumel. 800. Penne-d'Agenais. Pl Hôtel de Ville; 05 53 40 75 82. summer: Fri evening; May: flower market. Fête des Rosières (Aug); Foire à la Tourtière (Aug).
tournondagenais.com

Set on a rocky promontory in the Boudouyssou valley, this *bastide* town was built in about 1270, and soon after came under English control.

Houses built into the ramparts look down from the high clifftop. Constructed from a mix of uncut boulders and dressed stone, some, like those in rue du Bousquet, also have half-timbered walls. The 13th-century Maison de l'Abescat in rue de l'École housed the bishops of Agen during the Middle Ages. The bell tower in the square was built in 1637 and is crowned by a wooden steeple with a fine lunar clock that was added in 1843. Above Place de la Mairie is a municipal garden, laid out on the site of a church that was destroyed in the 16th century during the Wars of Religion.

⓭ Penne-d'Agenais

Road map D3. 16 km (10 miles) west of Tournon. 2,460. Rue du 14-Juillet; 05 53 41 37 80. Sun. Foire à la Tourtière (2nd Sun in Jul).
penne-tourisme.com

By turns a mighty base for the warring Richard the Lionheart, a possession of the counts of Toulouse and of Simon de Montfort's Crusaders, this town was held alternately by the French and the English during the Hundred Years' War, then passed from the Protestants to the Catholics during the Wars of Religion. Filled with picturesque restored houses set on narrow paved streets that run down the hillside, it is crowned by the silvered dome of a great neo-Byzantine basilica, which was built from 1897 to 1947.

Remains of the medieval town include part of the 12th-century walls, as well as fine houses with Gothic doorways, and the square keep of the castle, which was dismantled in the reign of Henri IV (1589–1610). Some houses on the main square have windows with intricate Gothic tracery. A small, restored gateway, the Porte de Ricard, is framed by buttresses. The defence tower on rue des Fossés once formed part of the ramparts. Place du Mercadiel and place Paul-Froment are lined with old arcaded merchants' houses. Beneath the present town hall is the former "royal" prison.

Portrait in the Musée de Gajac

Environs
Port-de-Penne, below the main town on the banks of the Lot, has a 12th-century Romanesque church. A section of its ancient ramparts also survive.

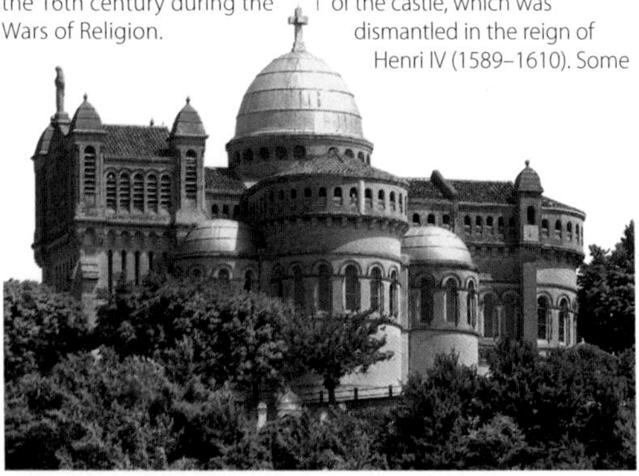

The silvered dome of the Basilique de Peyragude at Penne-d'Agenais

⓮ Villeneuve-sur-Lot

Road map D3. 10 km (6 miles) west of Penne-d'Agenais. 23,600. Penne-d'Agenais. Allée Federico Garcia Lorca; 05 53 36 17 30. Tue & Sat; flower market (Apr). Fête du Cheval (Sep).
tourisme-villeneuvois.com

Straddling the Lot river, Villeneuve was founded by Alphonse de Poitiers in 1264. It is the largest *bastide* town of the Lot-et-Garonne.

The town's symbol is its ancient bridge, Pont Vieux, which was built across the Lot in 1287 and restored in the 17th century. It has five spans and was once set with three fortified towers. On the north bank of the river stands the Chapelle du Bout-du-Pont, built in the 17th century and dedicated to sailors and boatmen. Two majestic gates, Porte de Paris and Porte de Pujols, both 30 m (98 ft) high, once formed

For hotels and restaurants in this region see pp252–3 and pp265–7

Porte de Ville, a fortified gate abutting the Église Saint-Nicolas in Pujols

part of the town's 14th-century ramparts. Colourful markets are still held on place Lafayette, a square lined with arcades.

The Église Sainte-Catherine was built in the 19th century on the site of a demolished earlier building. In the Byzantine-Romanesque style, it has 15th- and 16th-century stained-glass windows and wooden statues. Église Saint-Étienne, on the opposite bank of the Lot, was built in the Gothic style and remodelled in the 16th century.

The **Musée de Gajac**, in a 16th-century disused mill, contains religious and 19th-century paintings.

The **Haras National** (National Stud), established in 1804, has many Arab and Anglo-Arab horses.

In the Quartier d'Eysses, a district in the north of Villeneuve, on the road to Monflanquin, is an archeological site with a 1st-century Gallo-Roman villa. Amphorae and various other objects discovered here are displayed at the site's small **Musée Archéologique**.

Musée de Gajac
2 rue des Jardins. **Tel** 05 53 40 48 00. **Open** Tue & Thu pm.

Haras National
Rue de Bordeaux. **Tel** 05 53 70 46 99. **Open** Mon–Fri & am Sat.

Musée Archéologique
Place Saint-Sernin-d'Eysses. **Tel** 05 53 70 65 19. **Open** Jul–Aug pm.

⓯ Pujols

Road map D3. South of Villeneuve-sur-Lot. 3,657. Penne-d'Agenais. Place Saint-Nicolas; 05 53 36 78 69. Sun; pottery market (Aug). Course du Mont-Pujols (end Feb).

Officially listed as one of France's prettiest villages, this heavily fortified town was dismantled several times in the course of its history.

Porte de Ville, the fortified gate, is the only entrance to this walled town. The gate also serves as the bell tower of the 14th–15th-century Église Saint-Nicolas. The main street is lined with 15th-century half-timbered and corbelled houses. The Église Sainte-Foy, decorated with 16th-century frescoes, hosts temporary exhibitions.

Environs

The nearby **Grotte de Lastournelles** and **Grotte de Fontirou** are caves with interesting natural rock formations.

⓰ Sainte-Livrade-sur-Lot

Road map D3. 9 km (6 miles) west of Villeneuve-sur-Lot. 6,400. Penne-d'Agenais. 2 Place de la Libération, Villeneuve-sur-Lot; 05 53 36 17 30. Fri.

The church in this *bastide* town was built in the 12th to 14th centuries. It has an attractive stone-built Romanesque tiered apse and contains a white marble effigy of a 14th-century bishop. Another interesting feature of Sainte-Livrade is the Tour du Roy, a tower that formed part of a castle built here by Richard the Lionheart.

Roseraie Vicart, situated between Sainte-Livrade and Casseneuil, is a rose garden with some 7,500 rose bushes representing 300 different varieties of rose.

Roseraie Vicart
Sainte-Livrade. **Tel** 05 53 41 04 99. **Open** call ahead to check.

⓱ Casseneuil

Road map D3. 5 km (3 miles) north-east of Sainte-Livrade. 2,500. Penne-d'Agenais. Allée Federico Garcia Lorca, Villeneuve-sur-Lot; 05 53 36 17 30. Wed.

For centuries, this town, set on a peninsula, depended on river transport and river trade for its wealth. In 1214, it held out against the English under Simon de Montfort. Overhanging houses line the riverbank. The **Église Saint-Pierre** contains 13th and 15th century frescoes.

Église Saint-Pierre
Tel 05 53 36 17 30 (tourist office). **Open** call ahead to arrange a visit.

Tour du Roy and its stairway, at Sainte-Livrade-sur-Lot

The imposing church at Monclar-d'Agenais, above the Tolzac valley

⓲ Monclar-d'Agenais

Road map D3. 10 km (6 miles) northwest of Sainte-Livrade. 862. Tonneins. 5 place de la Mairie; 05 53 41 87 44.

Perched on a narrow spit of land, the *bastide* town of Monclar was founded by Alphonse of Poitiers in 1256. From its elevated situation the town offers magnificent views of the Tolzac valley. One side of the town's main square is lined with arcades. The covered market abuts the Église Saint-Clar, which has a 16th-century porch.

Environs

Castelmoron-sur-Lot, 6 km (4 miles) to the southwest, has a pleasant man-made lake, beside which stands a Moorish town hall. The church at **Fongrave**, 8 km (5 miles) south, has a fine wooden altarpiece. **Temple-sur-Lot**, 10 km (6.5 miles) south, has a 15th-century building that was once the headquarters of the Knights Templar. Here, visitors can see over 200 types of water lily in **Jardin des Nénuphars "Latour-Marliac"**.

⓳ Granges-sur-Lot

Road map D3. 15 km (9 miles) west of Sainte-Livrade. 600. Tonneins or Aiguillon.

Founded in 1291 on the banks of the Lot, this *bastide* town was largely destroyed during the Hundred Years' War.

The **Musée du Pruneau Gourmand** is devoted to the history of the local prune industry. It has displays of 19th–20th-century ovens, drying cupboards and other equipment, as well as old documents. The museum is set in an orchard with over 3,000 plum trees.

Musée du Pruneau Gourmand
Tel 05 53 84 00 69. **Open** Mon–Sat, Sun pm.

Environs

2 km (1 mile) northwest is the *bastide* town of **Laparade**. At the Ferme du Chaudron Magique at **Brugnac**, 11 km (7 miles) north, visitors can buy mohair from the angora goats kept there.

The former headquarters of the Knights Templar at Temple-sur-Lot

⓴ Clairac

Road map D3. 29 km (18 miles) west of Villeneuve-sur-Lot. 2,500. 18 rue Gambetta; 05 53 88 71 59. Thu. **valdegaronne.com**

Once a Protestant town, Clairac was besieged by Louis XIII in 1621 and its fortifications were razed. However, several 15th-century half-timbered houses survive. The town's **Benedictine abbey** was founded in the 7th century and by the 13th century it had become the most influential abbey in the Agenais. It is now closed to the public as it is privately owned. The timbered Maison Montesquieu is where the writer of the same name *(see p95)* is believed to have written his famous political satire, the *Persian Letters*.

An arcaded dovecote in the small village of Clairac

Environs

The town of **Tonneins**, 8 km (5 miles) northwest, on the banks of the Garonne, was once the capital of ancient Gaul. This was a former tobacco manufacturing town, as is evident from the beautiful exterior of the Manufacture Royale des Tabacs (Royal Tobacco Factory) here, built in 1726.

Just 8 km (5 miles) southeast of Clairac, in a wooded valley, is the village of Lacépède. At the edge of the village is Lac du Salabert, a reservoir and nature reserve. The Maison de la Nature here has information on the local flora and fauna.

A Garonna
Tel 05 53 79 22 79. **Open** call ahead to check.

Lac du Salabert
Maison de la Nature; **Tel** 05 53 47 18 33. **Open** Mon–Fri: 9am–noon, 2–6pm.

Boats at the double lock at Buzet-sur-Baïse

㉑ Aiguillon

Road map D3. 11 km (7 miles) south of Tonneins. 4,500. Place du 14 juillet; 05 53 64 65 31. Tue & Fri. Fête des Fleurs (May).

Aiguillon, at the confluence of the Lot and the Garonne, has been inhabited since Gallo-Roman times, and was a focus of conflict during the Hundred Years' War. The Château des Ducs was built by the Duc d'Aiguillon between 1775 and 1781. This luxurious residence was pillaged during the French Revolution, and in 1966 it was converted into a school.

The **Musée Raoul-Dastrac** contains a fine collection of the artist's Post-Impressionist paintings.

Château des Ducs in Aiguillon, restored in 1958 and now a high school

Musée Raoul-Dastrac
Rue de la République. **Tel** 05 53 79 62 58. **Open** call ahead to check.

Environs

Pech-de-Berre, 4 km (2.5 miles) north of Aiguillon, offers wide views of the Lot and Garonne valleys. **Damazan**, 7 km (4 miles) to the west, is a *bastide* town with fine half-timbered houses and a covered market with the town hall on its upper floor.

5 km (3 miles) southwest of Aiguillon, houseboats can be seen on the canal at **Buzet-sur-Baïse**, which is noted for its vineyards. 7 km (4 miles) southwest at **Saint-Pierre-de-Buzet** is an attractive 12th-century fortified church.

㉒ Prayssas

Road map D3. 15 km (9 miles) east of Aiguillon. 937. Aiguillon. Place de l'Hôtel-de-Ville; 05 53 95 00 15.

Surrounded by low hills covered with fruit trees and Chasselas vines, this attractive *bastide* town *(see pp30–31)* was built on an oval plan in the 13th century. Its church has a fine Romanesque apse.

Environs

The fortified village of **Clermont-Dessous**, 7 km (4 miles) to the southwest, is dominated by its castle. There is also an 11th-century Romanesque church here.

Prunes d'Agen

No less than 65 per cent of all plums grown in France come from the Agenais. The trees take between seven and eight years to reach maturity. They are pruned in winter and their fruit is harvested between August and September. The plums are gathered by shaking the tree by hand, and by machine. After being sorted by size, most of the plums are laid out in drying tunnels, where they are exposed to a temperature of 75 °C (167 °F) for 24 hours. This removes 21 to 23 per cent of their moisture, turning them into prunes. About 3 kg (6–7 lb) plums produce about 1 kg (2 lb) prunes. Noted for their high quality, *prunes d'Agen* have been produced in the Agen area since the Middle Ages.

Poster for Agenais plums

Gilded woodcarving of the Christ's burial in the church at Marmande

㉓ Le Mas-d'Agenais

Road map D3. 11 km (7 miles) west of Tonneins. 1,425. Marmande or Tonneins. Place de la Halle; 05 53 89 50 58. Wed & Sat.

The village spreads out along the canal that runs parallel to the Garonne. Evidence of Roman occupation has been discovered here, including a marble statue known as the Vénus du Mas, now in the Musée des Beaux-Arts in Agen *(see p166)*. The Collégiale Saint-Vincent, a fine 11th–12th-century abbey church, has 17th-century choir stalls and finely carved capitals. It also contains a painting of *Christ on the Cross* (1631) by Rembrandt. The 17th-century corn market in the square has a fine wooden roof. The wash house nearby is also worth a detour.

Vénus du Mas, from Mas-d'Agenais

㉔ Marmande

Road map D3. 18,000. 11 rue Toupinerie; 05 53 64 44 44). Tue, Thu, Sat. Fête des Fleurs et de la Fraise (May); Fête de la Tomate (Jul); Nuits Lyriques en Marmandais (Aug); Festival du Cheval de Trait (Aug). **valdegaronne.com**

The Marmande area has been a major producer of tomatoes since the 19th century, and now also grows strawberries. Rival factions fought over the town during the Hundred Years' War, but in 1580 it was finally won by France. The **Église Notre-Dame**, founded 1275, has a listed organ built by Cavaillé-Coll in 1859. The church's Chapelle Saint-Benoît contains a 17th-century altarpiece with two carved scenes at the centre. Access to the 16th-century cloister is through gardens.

Rue Labat is lined with half-timbered houses and the old ramparts are decorated with a modern mosaic, depicting major episodes in the town's history.

Église Notre-Dame
Rue de la République. **Open** daily.

Environs
5 km (3 miles) northwest is the **Musée Archéologique André-Larroderie** at the Gallo-Roman site of **Sainte-Bazeille**. It contains artifacts from the Iron Age to the time of Louis XIV, found at various digs in the Marmande area.

Musée Archéologique André-Larroderie
Place René-Sanson. **Tel** 0685 23 60 52. **Open** Jul–Aug: Mon & Wed–Sun pm; Sep–Jun: Sun pm.

㉕ Casteljaloux

Road map C3. 23 km (14 miles) south of Marmande. 4,580. Marmande. Maison du Roy; 05 53 93 00 00. Tue & Sat. Fête de l'Asperge (Apr); Feria (Aug). **casteljaloux.fr**

On the edge of the Landes forests, this spa town is closely associated with the Albret dynasty. Some 40 half-timbered corbelled houses, built in the 15th and 16th centuries, date from the period when the town was the capital of Gascony and a base for Henri IV's hunting expeditions *(see p49)*.

The Maison du Roy (King's House) is a fine 16th-century residence associated with Louis XIII and Louis XIV. Tour Maquebœuf is one of the few surviving vestiges of the town's 14th-century fortifications.

Environs
At **Clarens**, 2 km (1 miles) south of Casteljaloux, is a 17-ha (42-acre) lake surrounded by pine trees and fringed by sandy beaches. Here people of all ages can enjoy a range of watersports. **Bouglon** has a viewpoint that offers fine views of the Landes forests and the Garonne river valley. The **Église Saint-Savin**, 1 km (0.5 mile) south of Villefranche-du-Queyran, is a jewel of Romanesque architecture. Dating from the 11th–12th centuries, it has a beautiful 12-arched choir and some 20 magnificently carved capitals.

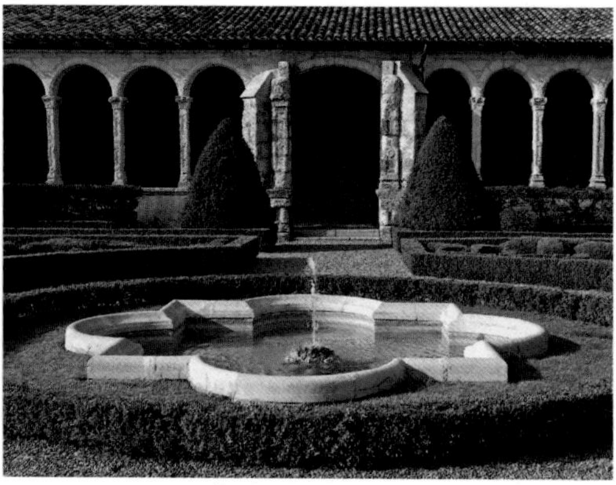

The Renaissance cloister of the Église Notre-Dame in Marmande

The massive 13th-century church at Mézin, which towers over the village

㉖ Mézin

Road map D3. 12 km (7 miles) southwest of Nérac. 1,500. Agen. Place Armand-Fallières; 05 53 65 77 46. Thu & Sun.

The town of Mézin grew up around its medieval monastery, of which nothing now remains, and its church. The main square is lined with picturesque arcades. In the narrow, winding streets all around there are half-timbered houses and a number of fine stone-built residences. The Gothic-arched Porte de Ville, a gateway also known as Porte Anglaise, is a vestige of the town's 13th-century ramparts.

On the square stands the restored 13th-century **Église Saint-Jean-Baptiste**. Despite the ugly, slightly leaning, six columns that flank the nave, the church has an elegant interior. The climb up the bell tower's 90 steps is no longer permitted because it is too dangerous. The wrought-iron cross to the left of the main doorway into the church dates from 1815. It bears the instruments of the Passion, which are surmounted by the cock that crowed when Peter denied Jesus. There are several gardens in the town; it is particularly pleasant to walk around the ramparts, in the rue Neuve quarter and also along the rue des Jardins.

The **Musée du Liège et du Bouchon** is devoted to the cork-making industry, for which the town was famous in the 19th and early 20th centuries.

Église Saint-Jean-Baptiste
Place Armand-Fallières. **Open** daily.

Musée du Liège et du Bouchon
Rue du puits Saint-Côme. **Tel** 05 53 65 68 16. **Open** Apr–May: Tue–Fri & Sun pm; Jun–Sep: Tue–Fri: am & pm, Sat–Mon pm; Oct: Tue–Fri pm.

Environs
Sports-lovers will enjoy the leisure centre 3 km (2 miles) away at **Lislebonne**.

There dozens of interesting Romanesque churches in the area. Those at **Villeneuve-de-Mézin**, 5 km (3 miles) south, **Lannes**, 4 km (2 miles) southeast, and **Saint-Simon-Saint-Pé**, 10 km (6 miles) southwest, are especially fine.

The village of **Moncrabeau**, 10 km (6 miles) to the east, is known as the liars' capital. It won this title in a competition that has been held on the first Sunday in August, every year since the 18th century.

A Century of Cork-Making

At the beginning of the 19th century, when the countryside around Mézin was France's major source of raw cork, cork-making was the Lot-et-Garonne's foremost manufacturing industry. Some 50 factories exported several million corks per day to all parts of the world. The industry's decline began in the second half of the 19th century, with the arrival of maritime pine and imports of raw cork from Spain, Portugal and Algeria. Today only 60 per cent of the raw cork grown around Mézin is used to make corks, and of the cork-oak forests that covered 5,600 ha (14,000 acres) in 1851, only 5,000 trees remain.

Corkmaker in a traditional workshop

The mill at Poudenas, on the banks of the Gélise river

㉗ Poudenas

Road map D3. 4 km (2 miles) west of Mézin. 253. 05 53 65 77 46. Agen. Foire d'Antan (Aug).

This medieval village was once a staging post, where Henri IV was a frequent visitor. The **château** above the village was built by the lords of Poudenas, who were vassals of King Edward I of England.

In the 16th century the castle, which is set in wooded parkland, was converted into a seigneurial residence. It is fronted by arcaded galleries.

Château de Poudenas
Tel 05 53 65 70 53. **Open** groups only, by prior arrangement.

㉘ Nérac

Road map D3. 27 km (17 miles) southwest of Agen. 6,886. Agen. 7 avenue Mondenard; 05 53 65 27 75. Sat. Fêtes du Grand Nérac (May); Festival Musique en Albret (Aug–Oct). **W albret-tourisme.com**

The Baïse, now a navigable river, runs through the centre of Nérac, with the castle and the new town on one bank, and the district of Petit Nérac on the other. In the 14th century, Nérac, capital of the Albret region, was a favourite base of the Albret family. They had settled in the region in the 12th century and married into the Navarrese and the French royal family. Nérac was a Protestant stronghold and, in 1621, its fortifications were dismantled on the orders of Louis XIII.

The **castle**, built above the Baïse in the 14th to 16th centuries, reflects the importance of the Albret family at the height of their power. The castle once consisted of four wings set with circular towers. It was abandoned after the 16th century, and only the north wing now remains. It has an elegant corbelled gallery of twisted columns, built by Alain le Grand d'Albret between 1470 and 1522. Since 1934 the wing has housed the **Musée de Nérac**, with exhibits on the Albret family and life at court in Nérac. A section focuses on local Neolithic and Roman finds.

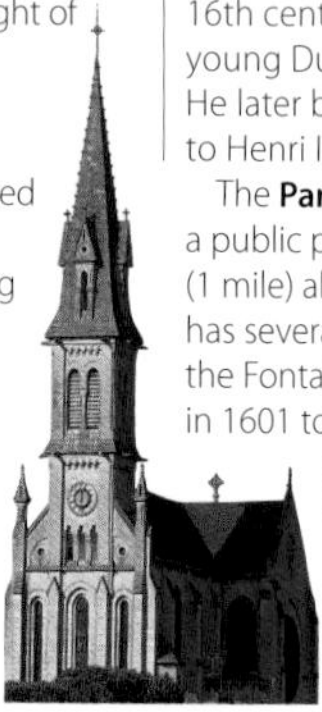

Église de Notre Dame in Petit Nérac

The 18th-century **Église Saint-Nicolas**, with a Neo-Classical façade, is known for its 19th-century stained-glass windows, which show monumental figures of the prophets, and for its frescoes.

The Maison des Conférences, a 16th-century town house on rue des Conférences, has its original tiered galleries and a façade decorated with Renaissance motifs. It is named for the meetings *(conférences)* that Catherine de Medici and Henry of Navarre held here from 1578, to bring about a reconciliation between Catholics and Protestants.

Petit Nérac is full of half-timbered houses. It lies along the Baïse, near the lock (dating from 1835). The district's main feature is the 19th-century Église Notre-Dame. The Maison de Sully, at the other end of the Vieux-Pont, rebuilt in the 16th century, was home to the young Duc de Sully in 1580. He later became first minister to Henri IV.

The **Parc de la Garenne**, now a public park, stretches for 2 km (1 mile) along the river bank. It has several fountains, including the Fontaine du Dauphin, built in 1601 to mark the birth of Louis XIII, and the Fontaine de Fleurette, named after a young girl who drowned herself after being seduced and abandoned by the Prince of Navarre.

Chateau-Musée Henri IV
Impasse Henri IV. **Tel** 05 53 65 21 11. **Open** Apr–Sep: daily; Oct–Mar: Tue–Sat, Sun pm. **Closed** Jan–Feb.

Église Saint-Nicolas
Place Saint-Nicolas. **Open** daily.

Parc de la Garenne
Open daily. via the tourist office.

Half-timbered houses in the district of Petit Nérac, on the Baïse river

For hotels and restaurants in this region see pp252–3 and pp265–7

The ten-span Romanesque bridge at Barbaste

29 Barbaste

Road map D3. 6 km (4 miles) northwest of Nérac via the D930. 1,550. Agen. Moulin des Tours; 05 53 65 09 37. Fête Nationale des Moulins (Jun).

Built in the 13th century and set with four towers, the **fortified mill** here looks out over the Gélise river, onto a ten-span Romanesque bridge. In the mid-19th century, Antonin Bransoulié converted it into a flour mill. He also installed a walkway that linked the towers and mill to the west bank, and built warehouses. In the late 19th century, the building was converted into a cork factory *(see p161)*. It was damaged by fire in 1906 and again in 1937.

Fortified Mill
Tel 05 53 65 09 37.**Open** only in summer; call ahead.

Environs

The *bastide* town of **Lavardac**, 2 km (1 mile) to the northeast, was founded in 1256. The harbour, on the Baïse, was prosperous when river traffic was at its height; it is now a stopping-place for pleasure boats. The 13th-century tower is all that remains of a medieval castle.

Just 6 km (3 miles) west of Barbaste, on the D665, lies the tiny village of **Durance**. This 13th-century *bastide* village is surrounded by pine forest. All that remains of the fortifications is the south gate, next to the ruins of Henri IV's château.

30 Vianne

Road map D3. 8 km (5 miles) northwest of Nérac. 1,260. Agen. Place des Marronniers; 05 53 65 29 54. Jun–Sep: until late eve Fri. Journée des Nations (Jun).

This *bastide* town, which still has its fortifications, was set up in 1284 on the banks of the Baïse. Its focal point is a fine 12th-century church. While the nave, choir and carved capitals are Romanesque, the doorway, the decoration of the apse and the bell tower's fortifications are all in the Gothic style.

The glassmaker's workshop here has closed down, but the tradition is kept alive by local glass blowers and engravers.

Environs

Xaintrailles, 5 km (3 miles) south, has a 15th-century keep. You can see how honey is made at the **Musée de l'Abeille** here. About 12 km (8 miles) west of Vianne lie the remains of Henri IV's castle at **Durance**; to the north is the 13th-century *bastide* town of **Francescas**.

Musée de l'Abeille
Tel 05 53 65 90 26. **Open** Jul–Aug: daily pm; rest of year by appointment.

One of the fortified gateways in the ramparts at Vianne

Women at the Court of Nérac

Jeanne d'Albret, mother of Henri IV

Women at the court of Nérac played an important role in its flowering during the 16th century. Marguerite d'Angoulême (1492–1549), wife of Henry of Navarre and sister of François I, came to Nérac in about 1530, followed by scholars, poets and humanist philosophers such as Lefebvre d'Etaples and Clément Marot. Her daughter, Jeanne d'Albret (1528–72), mother of Henri IV, became a Protestant and devoted herself to spreading Calvinism.

㉛ Street-by-Street: Agen

The French capital of rugby and of prunes – even though the famous *prunes d'Agen* do not in fact come from here – Agen (Aginnum) was originally a Gallo-Roman town. It grew rapidly during the late Roman Empire, but suffered as the result of invasions in the 5th and 6th centuries, and was later incorporated into the Grand State of Aquitaine, formed in 1032. Fought over by the king of England (who was also Duke of Aquitaine) and the king of France, control of the town passed from one to the other during the Hundred Years' War. In the 16th-century Wars of Religion, the town's Protestants were expelled. Agen later became a major manufacturing and trading base, exploiting its position on the river Garonne to export its produce. Today, it is an important administrative centre and university town.

Théâtre Ducourneau
Renowned for its acoustics, this Neo-Classical theatre opened in 1908.

★ Rue Beauville
This well restored thoroughfare is one of the most picturesque in Agen. Both sides are lined with half-timbered houses with an overhanging upper storey.

0 metres 200
0 yards 200

Key

— Suggested route

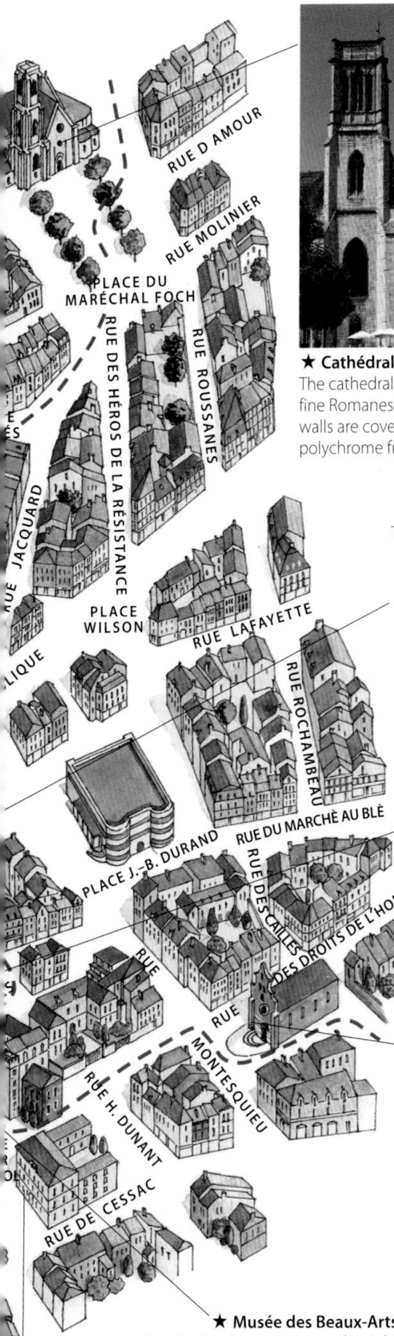

★ Cathédrale Saint-Caprais
The cathedral has an unusually fine Romanesque apse and its walls are covered with stunning polychrome frescoes.

VISITORS' CHECKLIST

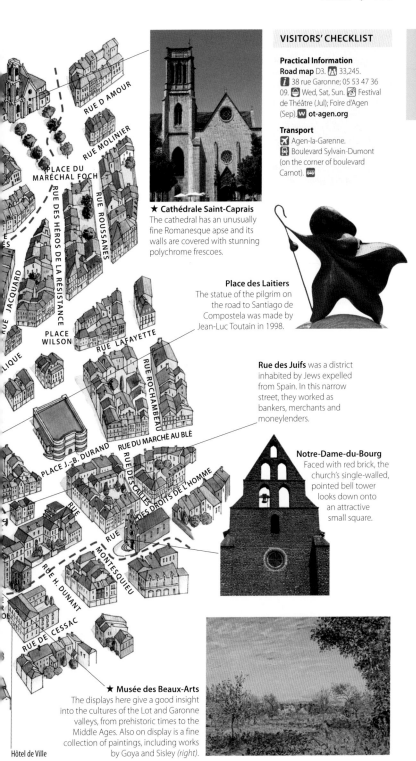

Practical Information
Road map D3. 33,245.
38 rue Garonne; 05 53 47 36 09. Wed, Sat, Sun. Festival de Théâtre (Jul); Foire d'Agen (Sep). **ot-agen.org**

Transport
Agen-la-Garenne.
Boulevard Sylvain-Dumont (on the corner of boulevard Carnot).

Place des Laitiers
The statue of the pilgrim on the road to Santiago de Compostela was made by Jean-Luc Toutain in 1998.

Rue des Juifs was a district inhabited by Jews expelled from Spain. In this narrow street, they worked as bankers, merchants and moneylenders.

Notre-Dame-du-Bourg
Faced with red brick, the church's single-walled, pointed bell tower looks down onto an attractive small square.

★ Musée des Beaux-Arts
The displays here give a good insight into the cultures of the Lot and Garonne valleys, from prehistoric times to the Middle Ages. Also on display is a fine collection of paintings, including works by Goya and Sisley *(right)*.

Exploring Agen

The largest town in the Garonne valley between Toulouse and Bordeaux, Agen still has many fine buildings dating from its periods of prosperity as a manufacturing and trading centre. In the heart of the town, between boulevard Carnot and the Garonne, are narrow streets with restored half-timbered, medieval houses, grand 16th- and 17th-century town houses and arcaded squares. There are also some early 20th-century Neo-Classical buildings and a fine museum. Between esplanade du Gravier, on the Garonne, and the canal running parallel with the river, there are many pleasant areas of greenery.

Renaud et Armide (16th century) by Domenico Tintoretto

Le Plongeur (1877) by Gustave Caillebotte

Musée des Beaux-Arts

Place du Docteur-Esquirol. **Tel** 05 53 69 47 23. **Closed** Tue & public hols.

Founded in 1876, this museum, whose collections cover almost every period from prehistory to the 20th century, is one of the finest in southwest France. The works are displayed in four beautiful 16th- and 17th-century town houses. On show here is the *Vénus du Mas*, a Roman statue from Le Mas-d'Agenais *(see p160)*, as well as Flemish, Dutch, French and Italian paintings of the 16th and 17th centuries and an important collection of 18th- and 19th-century Spanish paintings, including five works by Goya. Paintings by Courbet, Corot and Sisley cover the 19th century, and canvases by Roger Bissière and sculptures by Claude and François-Xavier Lalanne represent the 20th century.

Vieille Ville

This part of town is crammed with many interesting features. These include buildings as diverse as the 13th-century **Chapelle Notre-Dame-du-Bourg**, in rue des Droits-de-l'Homme, which has a single-walled belfry, and one of France's earliest reinforced concrete buildings, the 1906 **Théâtre Ducourneau**, in place du Docteur-Esquirol.

Rue Beauville, a narrow street, is lined with beautiful 15th-century half-timbered houses. The **Église Notre-Dame-des-Jacobins**, once the chapel of a Dominican monastery built here in 1249, is now used for exhibitions. Arcaded galleries line the nearby **place des Laitiers. Ruelle des Juifs**, a narrow alleyway was, until the end of the 14th century, a street of bankers' and merchants.

The canal along the Garonne river, on its course through Agen

Rue des Cornières, on the other side of boulevard de la République, was a major thoroughfare for trade in the 13th century. It is now lined with attractive restored houses, set above rows of arcades in a variety of styles.

Other houses worth seeing are the beautiful 14th-century **Maison du Sénéchal** in rue du Puits-du-Saumon, and the 18th-century **Hôtel Amblard**, at 1 rue Floirac.

Cathédrale Saint-Caprais

Place du Maréchal-Foch. **Tel** 05 53 66 37 27. **Open** daily.

Originally built in the 12th century, the cathedral has been remodelled several times. It has a magnificent Romanesque apse and its walls are covered with richly coloured frescoes.

Place Armand-Fallières

The bishop's palace here, now used as the offices of the local council, was built in 1775 and added to later. A grand staircase, flanked by allegorical statues, fronts the Neo-Classical lawcourts.

Le Gravier

During the reign of Louis XIII, this small island near the river bank hosted regional fairs. The esplanade, laid out in the 18th and 19th centuries, is now a popular place for strolling. On avenue Gambetta is **Hôtel Hutot-de-la-Tour**, an 18th-century, pink brick building that was the tax-collector's house. To its right is the **Tour de la Poudre**, once part of the 14th-century ramparts.

Pont Canal

This 23-span stone bridge is 580 m (1,903 ft) long, one of the longest bridges in France.

Environs

Parc Walibi Aquitaine, 3.5 km (2 miles) west of Agen, has around 20 different rides and other attractions *(see p288)*.

At **Les Serres Exotiques Végétales Visions**, in Colayrac-Saint-Cirq, 6 km (4 miles) to the west of Agen, greenhouses full of rare exotic plants are on display.

Half-timbered houses in rue Richard-Cœur-de-Lion

Parc Walibi Aquitaine

Château de Caudouin, Roquefort. **Tel** 05 53 96 58 32. **Open** mid-Apr–Oct. **walibi.com**

Les Serres Exotiques Végétales Visions

Tel 05 53 67 07 77. **Open** Apr–Jul: Tue–Sun; Aug: daily; Sep–Oct: Tue–Sat. **vegetalesvisions.com**

Agen City Centre

1. Cathédrale Saint-Caprais
2. Hôtel Amblard
3. Maison du Sénéchal
4. Musée des Beaux-Arts
5. Chapelle Notre-Dame- du-Bourg
6. Tour de la Poudre

0 metres 400
0 yards 400

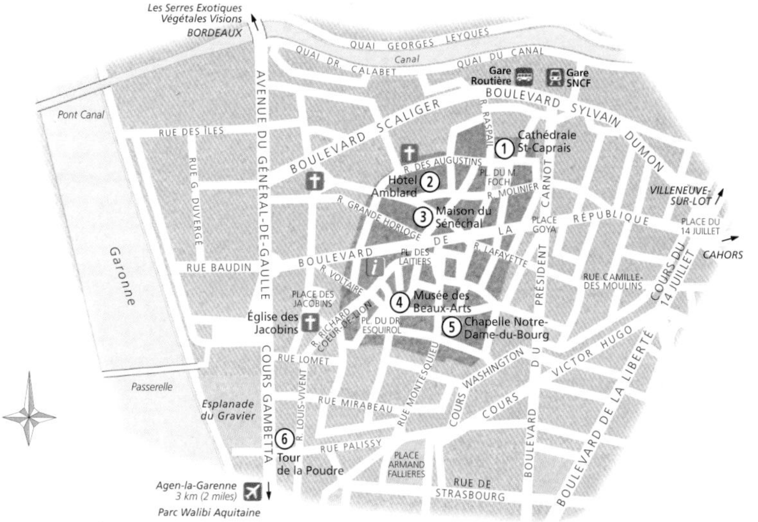

Key

Street-by-Street map *(pp160–61)*

For map symbols *see back flap*

One of the many Romanesque churches in the Pays de Serres

㉜ Pays de Serres

Road map D3.

The steep valleys and plateaux of the Pays de Serres form a geologically distinct area of land, bordered by the river Lot to the north and the Garonne to the south. Narrow bands of limestone, known as *serres* ("long crests") run right across this landscape, which is dotted with villages and old *bastide* towns that perch on the outcrops of rock. There are also many picturesque man-made structures, such as dovecotes, farmhouses and a number of Romanesque churches and chapels, Their typically white stone walls stand out in sharp contrast to the surrounding landscape.

Tuscan columns of the covered market in Laroque-Timbaut

㉝ Laroque-Timbaut

Road map D3. 16 km (10 miles) northeast of Agen. 1,300. Agen. Place de l'Hôtel de Ville; 05 53 95 71 36 (Mairie). Thu am.

The village of Laroque-Timbaut was founded on a rocky outcrop. Its 13th-century covered market has a fine wooden roof, supported on Tuscan columns.

Walking down the pretty rue du Lô, visitors can see the foundations of a 13th-century castle and its old outbuildings. Just outside the village is a memorial to its famous sons, who include the cyclist Paul Dangla (1878–1904) and Louis Brocq (1856–1928), famous for his pioneering work in the treatment of skin disorders.

In the valley is a chapel dedicated to St German, where pilgrims gather on the last Sunday of May each year.

Environs

Hautefage-la-Tour, 7 km (4 miles) to the north, has an unusual hexagonal, tower, built in the 15th century. The 16th-century church has a fine wooden roof. About 6 km (4 miles) northwest of Laroque-Timbaut is the fortified medieval village of **Frespech**. The **Musée du Foie Gras** in nearby **Souleilles** traces the 4,500-year-old history of *foie gras*, a local speciality.

Musée du Foie Gras
Tel 05 53 41 23 24. **Open** Mon–Sat, pm Sun (Jul–Aug: Sun all day). **Closed** Jan.

㉞ Beauville

Road map D3. 11 km (7 miles) east of Laroque-Timbaut. 600. Agen. Place de la Mairie; 05 53 47 63 06. mid-Jun–Aug: Sun.

Sheltering behind a row of trees, the old *bastide* town of Beauville clings to the hillside, commanding an impressive view of the surrounding landscape. The attractive arcaded main square is lined with half-timbered houses. The Château de Beauville was built in the 13th century, with further alterations made in the 16th and 19th centuries. The 16th-century church has a bell tower at the entrance.

Beauville's main square, lined with arcaded houses

㉟ Saint-Maurin

Road map D3. 28 km (17 miles) northeast of Agen. 450. Agen.

This peaceful village, set in a lush valley, developed around an 11th-century Benedictine abbey. The abbey was partly destroyed during the Crusades, then further damage was inflicted by the English in the 14th century. Now all that remains is part of the church and the abbot's house. Built on the plan of a Latin cross, this church has a semicircular choir with six exquisitely carved capitals, including a depiction of the martyrdom of St Maurin. The nave once covered what is now part of the village square. Other vestiges of the abbey lie between newer buildings. The abbot's house contains a **museum**. Designed by the village's inhabitants and with exhibits contributed by them, it documents daily life in the area in the early 20th century. There is also a model of the abbey as it was at the height of its splendour.

On the square in front of the abbot's house are an attractive covered market hall, restored in 1625, a well and several pretty half-timbered houses.

The Église Saint-Martin-d'Anglars, above the village, was founded in the 13th century and rebuilt in the 16th. The furnishings inside it include a 17th-century carved wooden altar and an 18th-century statue of St Joseph.

Abbey museum
Palais abbatial. **Open** Jul–Aug: pm Wed–Mon. **Tel** 05 53 95 31 25 (Mairie, Beauville).

The Église Saint-Martin, Layrac, with a dome over the central crossing

36 Puymirol

Road map D3. 17 km (10 miles) east of Agen. 940. Agen. La Mairie; 05 53 95 32 10.

Founded in 1246, Puymirol was the first *bastide* town to be built in the Agenais. From the heights of the rocky spur on which it perches, the town looks down into the Séoune valley.

Puymirol is surrounded by ramparts with a wall-walk, and entry is via a gate known as Porte Comtale. The main street is rue Royale, and the main square, which is lined with arcades, still has its ancient well. The church, rebuilt in the 17th century, has a 13th-century doorway with a wide carved archway. In the Middle Ages, Puymirol was well known for the fairs held there.

Environs
8 km (5 miles) to the southeast is the hilltop village of **Clermont-Soubiran**, with stunning views of the rolling landscape and woodland all around. It has a 12th-century church with a single-walled belfry. The Château de la Bastide houses the Musée du Vin et de la Tonnellerie, a small museum with exhibits on local wines.

Half-timbered house in Caudecoste

37 Layrac

Road map D3. 10 km (6 miles) south of Agen. 3,450. Agen. 8, place du 11 novembre 1918; 05 53 66 51 53.

Layrac commands stunning views over the Gers and Garonne valleys. The 12th-century Église Saint-Martin is crowned by an 18th-century dome, and it has a particularly fine apse. The capitals on the church's façade are carved with monsters and demons. The church contains a marble altarpiece and on the floor are traces of an 11th–12th-century mosaic, depicting Samson overcoming the lion. The bell tower is all that remains of the older church, which was destroyed in 1792. On place de Salens are a fountain and a washhouse, built against the remains of the ramparts.

Environs
Astaffort, a small town in the Brulhois area, about 11 km (7 miles) south of Layrac, is the birthplace of the singer Francis Cabrel. It has some half-timbered houses and the remains of ramparts. The Romanesque Église Saint-Félix was remodelled in the 17th century.

Caudecoste, on a hilltop, 9 km (6 miles) south of Layrac, was built in 1273. It is one of the few *bastide* towns to have been founded by a religious order. Half-timbered houses on wooden pillars cluster round its small arcaded square. The church, on the edge of the town, is also worth a visit.

The apse of the Romanesque Église Notre-Dame at Moirax

38 Moirax

Road map D3. 7 km (4 miles) south of Agen. 1,100. Agen. Le Bourg; 05 53 87 13 73.

The ancient village of Moirax, which clusters around its majestic Romanesque church, looks out onto the flatlands of the Agenais.

In the mid-11th century, the local baron, Guillaume de Moirax, donated land to the Cluniac order and a monastery was built here. Suffering at the hands of various warring factions, the monastery experienced turbulent times during the Middle Ages. Towards the end of the 17th century, a major programme of rebuilding work was started, but this was brought to an abrupt halt by the outbreak of the French Revolution in 1789.

The **Église Notre-Dame**, which was once part of the monastery, is an exquisite example of Romanesque architecture, and has been superbly restored. An arcaded bell tower now rises above the projecting central section of the façade. This is crowned by a limpet-shaped roof. A double tier of arches lines the buttressed aisles. The arches of the porch are decorated with beading and carved foliated scrolls, and rest on four slender columns. The Gothic arch above frames a semicircular window. Over the choir is a dome decorated with shingles and crowned by a lantern. The arched windows of the apse and side apses are decorated with further beading. The church is laid out to the plan of a basilica, having a nave that is flanked by aisles, a feature which is quite rare in the southwest of France. The only lighting for the nave comes from the window in the west wall.

The strictly symmetrical transept is divided into three equal sections. Each arm of the transept, which is lit by a set of double windows, has steps that lead up to a raised platform or stand. The dome that sits above the central crossing point has been rebuilt in a star-shape.

The choir is lit by arched windows framed by slender columns. Four supporting arches rise up from its square base to the octagonal dome above. Five arched windows illuminate the vaulted apse.

More than 100 ornate capitals decorate the various columns found in this church. As well as abstract geometric and plant motifs, the lion motif features on many of them, while birds, rams and all manner of fantastic monsters also appear. Thirteen of the capitals are carved with Biblical scenes, that include depictions of Adam and Eve in the Garden of Eden, St Michael killing the dragon and Daniel in the lions' den. The aisles are decorated with 17th-century wood carvings, showing various scenes taken from the Old Testament.

Église Notre-Dame
Tel 05 53 67 01 99. **Open** daily. by arrangement with the tourist office.

The 18th-century five-sided wash-house outside Laplume

A picturesque stopping point on the canal at Sérignac-sur-Garonne

39 Laplume

Road map D3. 14 km (9 miles) southwest of Agen. 1,360. Agen. 64 Grande Rue; 05 53 95 16 67.

Once the capital of the small Brulhois area to the southwest of Agen, the village of Laplume looks out across the landscape from its vantage point, high on a rocky outcrop of limestone. Parts of the medieval village survive, including sections of the ramparts and two gates. The 16th-century Église Saint-Barthélemy was restored in the 17th and 18th centuries.

Just outside Laplume is the Lavoir de Labat, a curious five-sided wash-house that dates from the 17th or 18th century.

40 Aubiac

Road map D3. 4 km (3 miles) north of Laplume. 1,000. Agen. 2 place Galard; 05 53 67 81 00. **aubiac-si.com**

Nestling in lush greenery, the beautiful fortified Romanesque Église Sainte-Marie towers over the village. The church was built between the 9th and the 12th centuries on the site of a Merovingian building. Appearing as a square, severely plain fortress from the outside, the church has a contrastingly ornate interior, with rounded arches in the apse and barrel vaulting above the doorway. The dome over the square choir is decorated with 16th-century frescoes depicting the four Evangelists. The 14th-century castle next to the church belonged to a branch of the Galard family. It was rebuilt in the 18th century.

An important archeological find from Aubiac is a Celtic bronze head of a horse, now in the Musée des Beaux-Arts in Agen *(see p166)*.

41 Estillac

Road map D3. 2 km (1 mile) north of Aubiac. 1,700. 08 99 18 41 29 (Mairie).

A stronghold in the 13th century, Estillac was once owned by Blaise de Monluc, the writer and Maréchal de France who led the Catholic armies in the 16th-century Wars of Religion. His white marble effigy lies in the grounds of the privately owned **Château de Monluc**, where he lived. He also distinguished himself in the Franco-Italian wars, and is noted for his *Commentaires*, a treatise on soldiery. The styling of the 16th-century church is typical of architecture in this region.

Effigy of Blaise de Monluc, Estillac

Château de Monluc
Tel 05 53 67 81 83. **Open** Oct–May: Tue–Sun; Jun–Sep: Mon–Sat am & pm; Sun pm. **Closed** Jan.

Environs
Sérignac-sur-Garonne, around 13 km (8 miles) northwest of Estillac, was once a leading *bastide* town. Being on the canal, it is a popular spot for visitors on boating holidays. It has some fine half-timbered houses and an 11th-century church with a Romanesque porch and a spiral belfry, rebuilt in 1922, an exact replica of the 16th-century original.

The imposing fortified Romanesque church at Aubiac

LANDES

Thousands of visitors flock to the Landes region every year, drawn by the beauty of its forests and the long, sandy beaches stretching along its Atlantic coastline, a paradise for surfers. But it is also well worth exploring the picturesque hinterland, with its colourful festivals and many gastronomic treats.

Lying at the heart of Aquitaine, the Landes covers an area of 9,800 sq km (3,800 sq miles). This largely unspoilt region of forests, lakes and rivers enjoys a gentle maritime climate. With its 106 km (66 miles) of golden, sandy beaches and its many rivers (known locally as *courants*), lakes and vast wetlands, the Landes is the perfect setting for watersports. Inland, the pine forests, interspersed with fields of maize, are sparsely dotted with traditional houses. Settlement of the Landes goes back to prehistoric times. The legacy of the Hundred Years' War can be seen in the many *bastide* towns, in strategic locations across the countryside. In this difficult, marshy terrain, life was hard. To keep watch over their sheep, local shepherds used to walk on stilts to make crossing the muddy ground easier. During the Second Empire (1852–1870), the landscape changed, as marshland was drained and extensive pine forests were planted for their resin and timber. Also at this time, the coming of the railways and better roads greatly improved communication between the towns and cities. The creation of the Parc Naturel Régional des Landes de Gascogne, in 1970, has helped to preserve the Landes' traditional way of life. Today, visitors come to the region for its fine Romanesque architecture, mostly sited along the former pilgrim routes to Compostela, as well as the superb surfing and hydrotherapy resorts. Bull-leaping festivals *(see p33)* are also a major attraction. And this beautiful region is a gourmet's paradise. *Foie gras de canard*, free-range chicken, Chalosse beef and sand-grown asparagus, as well as Armagnac and fine Tursan wines, are all on the Landes menu.

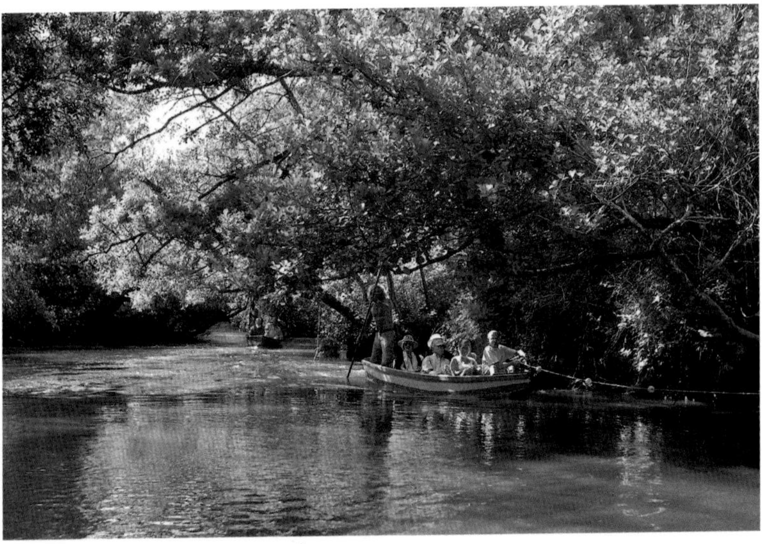

The Courant d'Huchet, plied by boatmen punting their craft along the river

◀ The mouth of the Courant d'Huchet at Moliets-et-Maa

Exploring the Landes

The network of roads that covers this huge region makes it easy to explore. From Biscarosse, in the north, to Capbreton, in the south, the coastline has a succession of long beaches and high-class resorts. Inland, beyond the dunes, is a vast expanse of greenery and unspoiled countryside. A landscape that was once flatlands *(landes)* with a scattering of deciduous trees is now covered in pine forest. The Landes' two major towns are the peaceful Mont-de-Marsan, the regional capital and administrative centre, and Dax, whose thermal springs attract those seeking health cures. The 290,000-ha (716,590-acre) Parc Naturel Régional des Landes de Gascogne is ideal for those who love the great outdoors. Further south lie the gently rolling hills of Armagnac, Chalosse and Tursan, at the foot of the Pyrenees.

Lac d'Aureilhan, near Mimizan, is very popular with amateur sailors

Key

- Motorway
- Dual carriageway
- Main road
- Minor road
- Scenic route
- Main railway
- Minor railway
- Regional border

For map symbols *see back flap*

Pine trees, now the emblem of the Landes

Getting Around

The nearest airports are at Bordeaux, to the north, Biarritz, to the south, and Pau, to the east. The region is also served by the TGV Atlantique (high-speed train) from Paris, which stops at Bordeaux, Mont-de-Marsan and Dax. Two main north–south routes pass through the Landes. In the west between Bordeaux and the Pays Basque is the N10, which passes the Parc Naturel des Landes and gives access to the resorts on the coast. The A65 runs to the east between Pau and Langon, passing close to Aire-sur-L'Adour and not far from Mont-de-Marsan. Use of headlights, as a safety measure, is advisable when travelling along the minor roads, which tend to run in straight lines through the densely forested areas. Some local vehicles are fitted with an ultra-sonic bleeper to frighten wild deer off the roads, as they approach. Bus services also run between towns and villages.

A Landes house in an *airial* (forest clearing)

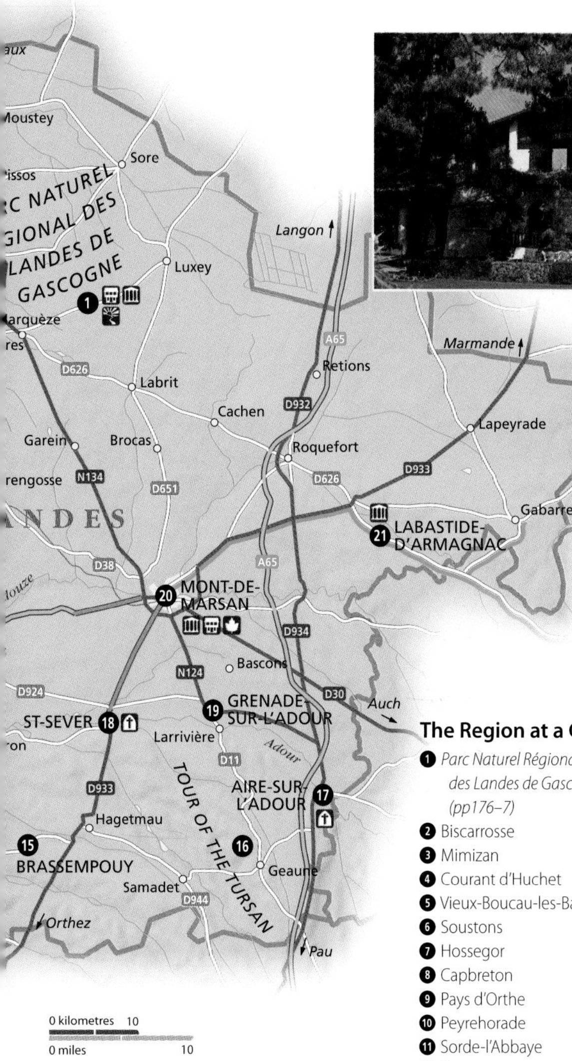

The Region at a Glance

1. *Parc Naturel Régional des Landes de Gascogne (pp176–7)*
2. Biscarrosse
3. Mimizan
4. Courant d'Huchet
5. Vieux-Boucau-les-Bains
6. Soustons
7. Hossegor
8. Capbreton
9. Pays d'Orthe
10. Peyrehorade
11. Sorde-l'Abbaye
12. Dax
13. Monfort-en-Chalosse
14. Pomarez
15. Brassempouy
17. Aire-sur-l'Adour
18. Saint-Sever
19. Grenade-sur-l'Adour
20. Mont-de-Marsan
21. Labastide-d'Armagnac

Tour

16. Tour of the Tursan

❶ Parc Naturel Régional des Landes de Gascogne

This paradise for nature-lovers lies between the Atlantic seaboard to the west, the vineyards of the Gironde to the north and the foothills of the Pyrenees to the south. It was created in 1970 to preserve not only the traditional architecture and culture of the Landes, but also its wildlife, protecting an environment on which around 40,000 people depend for their livelihood. A total of 41 villages, 20 of which are in the Gironde and 21 in the Landes, have benefited. This extensive plateau, which covers over 315,000 ha (778,000 acres), is covered with forests of deciduous trees and evergreen pines, interspersed with large fields of maize. The farmland is irrigated by the river Leyre, which flows all the way through this conservation area. Because the three routes to Santiago de Compostela run through the park, many pilgrims are among the visitors here.

Boating on the river Leyre

Église Saint-Martin, Moustey
Moustey has two churches, the Église Saint-Martin, with fine carving on its doorway, and the Église Notre-Dame, a stopping-off point on the Santiago de Compostela pilgrimage route.

Quartier de Marquèze
At Marquèze, which forms part of the Écomusée de la Grande Lande, there is a reconstruction of a traditional village. Visitors can walk through a group of typical late 19th-century Landes houses.

For hotels and restaurants in this region see pp253–4 and pp267–9

Atelier des Produits Résineux de Luxey
The resin workshop at Luxey is a remnant of an industry that once played a leading role in the Landes' economy. The workshop still holds original machinery. Here also is the Musée de l'Estupr-huc (Firefighting Museum).

VISITORS' CHECKLIST

Practical Information
40 km (25 miles) south of Bordeaux via the N10.
Road map B3/C3. Maison du Parc, 33 route de Bayonne, 33830 Belin-Beliet; 05 57 71 99 99.
Fax 05 56 88 12 72. **Open** Mon–Fri: 8:30am–12:30pm, 1:30–5:30pm. **Closed** public hols.
parc-landes-de-gascogne.fr

Transport
Sabres.

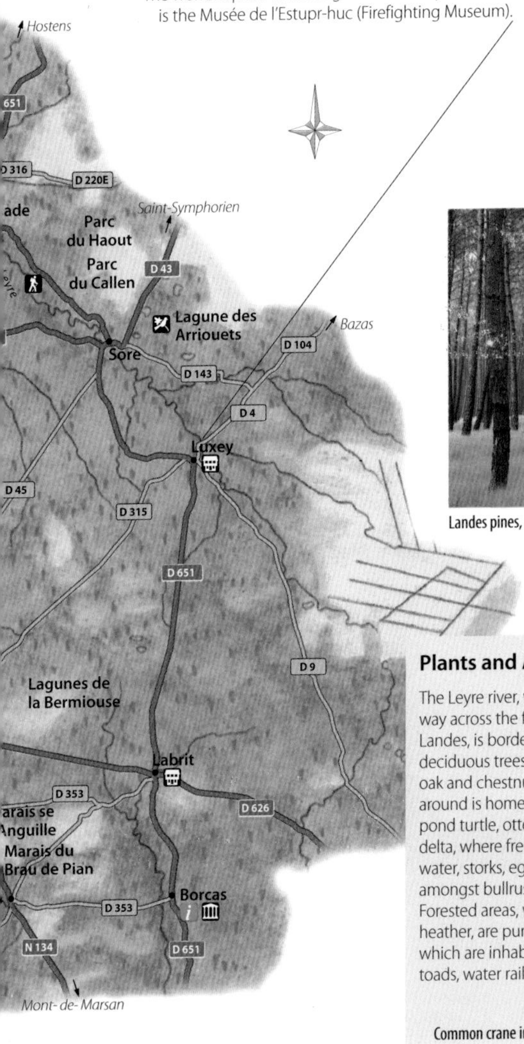

Landes pines, once important for their sap, or resin

Plants and Animals

The Leyre river, which winds its way across the flatlands of the Landes, is bordered by ferns and deciduous trees, such as Pyrenean oak and chestnut. The marshy land all around is home to the European pond turtle, otters and mink. In the delta, where fresh water meets salt water, storks, egrets and cranes live amongst bullrushes and glasswort. Forested areas, with pines, broom and heather, are punctuated by lagoons, which are inhabited by yellow-bellied toads, water rail and warblers.

Common crane in the Parc Régional

For map symbols *see back flap*

Exploring the Parc Naturel Régional des Landes de Gascogne

Located between the Gironde and the Landes, this vast conservation area lies in what was once known as the Grande Lande. Here sheep grazed under the watchful eyes of shepherds, who used stilts to cross the flat, muddy terrain. Most people lived in one of the many small villages, but houses were also built in open countryside, set in *airiaux* – unfenced grassy areas surrounded by deciduous trees. When Napoleon III decided to redevelop the area in the late 19th century, the marshes and pastures gradually disappeared under plantations of pines. Besides these forested areas, the park also contains a number of waterways and small lakes, including the unspoilt banks of the river Leyre, from which visitors can see picturesque villages, ancient farmhouses and splendid Romanesque churches.

Shepherds on stilts, once a common sight in the Grande Landes

Vallées des Leyre

Road map B3. Maison du Parc, 33 Route de Bayonne, 33830 Belin-Beliet. **Tel** 05 57 71 99 99.
Open Mon–Fri. **Closed** public hols.
parc-landes-de-gascogne.fr

The river Leyre, formed by the Grande Leyre and Petite Leyre, flows into the Arcachon Basin. As it is the source of 80 per cent of the basin's water, the river plays a key role in the ecological balance of that watery expanse.

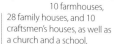

A genet in the Leyre forest

No roads run along its course, so the Leyre can only be explored by canoe or on foot. The forest, through which it flows for 100 km (60 miles), is surrounded by valleys and marshland with a wealth of wildlife. Ancient churches and villages dot the landscape.

Solférino

Road map B3. In the southwest of the park.

The village of Solférino was founded by Napoleon III in 1863. He wanted to create an ideal model of rural life. To populate the region and promote agriculture, the Emperor purchased 7,000 ha (17,000 acres) of flatland on which he built 10 farmhouses, 28 family houses, and 10 craftsmen's houses, as well as a church and a school.

Musée des Forges

Road map C3. Brocas. **Tel** 05 58 51 44 56. **Open** mid-Jun–mid-Sep: Tue–Sun pm.

In the 19th century, Brocas was an important ironworking centre. The museum, in a disused flour mill, shows the tools and techniques that were used in this important industry, and also displays cast-iron objects such as firebacks. Next to the blast-furnace are workshops, a barn and ironworkers' houses.

Quartier de Marquèze

Road map B3. Marquèze, in the northeast of Sabres. 05 58 08 31 31. **Open** Apr–Sep: daily.

The Écomusée de la Grande Lande is an open-air museum with three separate locations: Luxey, which is devoted to resin-tapping; Moustey, which focuses on local religious traditions; and Marquèze, which illustrates daily life in past times, in one area of the Grande Lande. To help create the sense of going back in time, visitors may travel to the town by vintage steam train.

The Ecomusée de Marquèze, which opened in 1969, explores

Harvesting the traditional way, one of the park's many historical re-creations

traditional rural and agricultural life in the Grande Lande, using the reconstruction of a small, local farming community from the late 19th century. Each family would have lived in a house set in an *airial*, a clearing surrounded by deciduous trees; such areas were once the only patches of greenery in the bare flatlands all around. A wide range of different types of building is represented, including a manor house, several tied cottages and sheep barns. Specialist occupations as shepherding, flour-milling and resin-collecting *(see Luxey)*, as well as many other aspects of rural life, are demonstrated in a lively and informative way. The Pavillion de Marquèze features collections on renewable energy development.

One of the few clusters of deciduous trees in the Landes forests

Luxey

Road map C3. In the northeast of Sabres. 05 56 65 06 65 (Bazas).

From the 1850s to the 1950s, the resin industry contributed greatly to the economic prosperity of the Landes. The resin-processing workshop run by Jacques and Louis Vidal at Luxey still has its old buildings, dating from 1859, along with the equipment that was used. Incisions were made in the trunks of the pine trees and, as the sap ran out, it was collected in vessels and transferred to barrels that were taken to the stills. Here the resin and turpentine were separated for use in the chemical industry.

The terrible fires that ravaged the forests of the Landes in 1947 and 1949 severely affected the resin industry. In Luxey, the **Musée de l'Estupe-huc** (meaning "put out the fire" in Gascon) documents the dangerous and difficult task of fighting forest fires in the Landes.

Apse of the 11th-century church at Belhade

La Maison d'Estupe Huc
Luxey. **Tel** 05 58 04 70 70.
Open reservation only.

Moustey

Road map B3.

Moustey has two churches, which stand opposite one another. The late 15th-century parish church of St Martin, to the north, is in the late Gothic style. The Église Notre-Dame, which was connected to a hostel, served pilgrims. It has an interesting 16th-century keystone. The village also has two rivers, which are good for kayaking in summer.

Romanesque churches

Built during the early centuries of the second millennium, the churches of this area were important meeting places for the St Jacques de Compostela pilgrims. Certain sanctuaries were built by the pilgrims themselves, who were almost the only people to cross the marshy flatlands of Les Landes at this period. At **Belhade**, the Eglise St-Vincent de Xaintes de Belhade has an apse, nave and belfry that date from the 11th–12th centuries. The Eglise St-Pierre de Mons, near **Belin-Beliet** was particularly important on the pilgrim route since legend says that followers of Charlemagne who died at Roncesvalles were buried here. Inside there are beautiful wood carvings and sculptured capitals. Eglise St-Michel du Vieux Lugo at **Lugos** is a 12th-century church located in the heart of the forest. A unique apse and nave house painted 15th-century murals. The churches may be closed to the public out of season.

Arnaudin's Priceless Legacy

Berger et Bergerot au Pardéou by Arnaudin

Félix Arnaudin (1844–1921), who lived at Labouheyre (in the southwest of the park), travelled the length and breadth of the Landes, both by bicycle and on foot, with his cumbersome photographic equipment. He recorded a world that was slowly disappearing, photographing shepherds, storytellers and other scenes of country life, as well as the landscape and its architecture. This picture of the late 19th-century Grande Lande, where people lived by planting crops, raising animals and growing timber, on flat expanses that seemed to stretch to infinity, is part of a treasured historical record.

Biscarrosse, one of the most popular resorts on the Landes coast

❷ Biscarrosse

Road map B3. 12,600. 55 place Georges-Dufau; 05 58 78 20 96. Jul–Aug: daily am. Rassemblement International d'Hydravions (May, every two years); Festival de Cirque Rue des Étoiles (Jul); Fête de la Mer (Aug). **biscarrosse.com**

Biscarrosse, with a beach that stretches for 15km (9 miles), as far as the Adour river, marks the beginning of the Côte d'Argent (Silver Coast). Sited between the ocean and the forest, the town has two lakes, which offer a range of watersports. Visitors with an interest in aviation will enjoy the **Musée Historique de l'Hydraviation**, devoted to seaplanes. The museum stands next to the Établissements Latécoère, which produced seaplanes from 1930 to the end of the 1950s. The **Musée des Traditions et de l'Histoire de Biscarrosse** documents the town's history and the lives of resin collectors and shepherds on the Landes.

Musée Historique de l'Hydraviation
332 avenue Louis-Bréguet. **Tel** 05 58 78 00 65. **Open** Jul–Aug: daily; Sep–Jun: pm Wed–Mon.

Musée des Traditions et de l'Histoire de Biscarrosse
216 avenue Louis-Bréguet. **Tel** 05 58 78 77 37. **Open** Jul–Aug: daily (not Sun am); Jun & Sep: Tue–Sat; rest of the year by appointment.

Environs

4 km (2.5 miles) north of Biscarrosse is the **Lac de Sanguinet**. Its 5,600 ha (13,800 acres) of clear, fresh waters are ideal for fishing and watersports. **Sanguinet** itself, on the site of a Gallo-Roman village, has an interesting archeological museum.

Musée Municipale du Lac
Tel 05 58 82 11 82 (Mairie). **Open** mid-Apr–Jun and Sep–Oct: Wed & Sat pm; Jul–Aug: Wed–Mon.

❸ Mimizan

Road map B3. 10,000 (with surrounding villages). Labouheyre or Morcenx. 38 avenue Maurice-Martin; 05 58 09 11 20. Mimizan-Bourg: Fri am; Mimizan-Plage: 15 Jun–15 Sep: Thu am. Fêtes de la Mer (1 May).

The 13th-century bell tower of the abbey church at Mimizan

In summer, Mimizan attracts large numbers of visitors, who come to enjoy its 10 km (6 miles) of beaches, as well as its forests, with their 40 km (25 miles) of cycle tracks. The town has an abbey church whose 13th-century bell tower is listed by UNESCO.

A small museum on the abbey grounds illustrates life here during the Middle Ages. It also explores local geography and history as well as the area's changing relationship with the surrounding forest. Excursions organized by the tourist office, introduces visitors to forestry in the area, with tours of local woodland and forestry businesses.

Clocher Porche du Prieuré de Mimizan
Rue de l'Abbaye. **Tel** 05 58 09 00 61. **Open** by reservation only. Ticket also valid for the local museum.

Environs

At **Saint-Julien-en-Born**, 12 km (7.5 miles) south of Mimizan, a river, the Courant de Contis, flows down to the Plage de Contis, a beach with a lighthouse. At **Lit-et-Mixe**, 4 km (2 miles) further south, is the **Musée "Vieilles Landes"**, which documents local crafts. At **Lévignacq**, 23 km (14 miles) southeast of Mimiza, the 14th-century church has a painted oak ceiling above the nave.

Musée "Vieilles Landes"
Lit-et-Mixte. **Tel** 05 58 42 89 17. **Open** Jul–Aug: Mon–Sat.

For hotels and restaurants in this region see pp253–4 and pp267–9

❹ Courant d'Huchet

Road map B4. Léon. **i** Maison de la Reserve Naturelle du Courant d'Huchet; 05 58 48 73 91.

The coast of the Landes is dotted with watercourses, known as *courants*, that flow into the ocean. The best-known is the Courant d'Huchet, a river with wonderful plants and wildlife. Since 1908, visitors have been able to travel on it in *galupes*, flat-bottomed boats that are propelled along using a *palot* (punt). Starting from the Étang de Léon, the lake from where the *courant* flows, *galupe* tours follow a maze of watercourses, which are inhabited by a variety of birds, including teal, herons and wood-cock. The banks are covered with cypresses, hibiscus, irises, gladioli and bracken, and in summer there are ducks, otters, wild boar, mink, crayfish and eels that come here to spawn from the Sargasso Sea. *Galupes* owned by the Bateliers du Courant d'Huchet *(see p301)* sail down the river for 10 km (6 miles) to the sea.

Statue of Mitterrand

❺ Vieux-Boucau-les-Bains

Road map B4. 1,652. Dax (30 km/19 miles) or Bayonne (35 km/22 miles). **i** 11 promenade du Mail; 05 58 48 13 47. Tue & Sat am. Course landaise (Jun–Sep). **W ot-vieux-bocaux.fr**

Near Vieux-Boucau is the resort of Port-d'Albret, clustered round a 60-ha (148-acre) salt lake. Popular in summer, the resort can only be reached via the leafy Promenade du Mail. The town's arena hosts bull-leaping festivals *(see p33)*.

❻ Soustons

Road map B4. 7,250. Dax. **i** 05 58 41 52 62 (Grange de Labouyrie). Mon am; summer market: Thu am, Fri pm. Fête de la Tulipe (Easter). **W soustons.fr**

The main village of the Marensin district, Soustons stretches out along the banks of a large freshwater lake, which is popular with watersports enthusiasts. In the centre of Soustons is a statue of François Mitterrand, the former president of France, who liked to spend time at his residence, Latché, situated 3 km (2 miles) from here. The **Musée des Traditions et des Vieux Outils** at Château de la Pandelle brings to life local trades such as roofing, carpentry and resin-collecting.

Musée des Traditions et des Vieux Outils
Château de la Pandelle, avenue du Général-de-Gaulle. **Tel** 05 58 41 52 62. **Open** 15 Jun–15 Sep: Wed–Mon pm.

Environs
The Marensin, an area that lies south of Soustons, is cut by rivers and dotted with lakes. These include the **Étang Noir**, a nature reserve, and the Étang Blanc.

Réserve Naturelle de l'Etang Noir
Tel 05 58 72 85 76. **Closed** Sat–Sun.

❼ Hossegor

Road map A4. 3,500. Dax or Bayonne. **i** Place des Halles; 05 58 41 79 00. Sun (also Mon & Wed during Jun–Sep). Les Musicales (Jul–Aug). **W hossegor.fr**

In the early 20th century, a number of writers, including Paul Margueritte and Rosny Jeune, fell under the spell of this picturesque village, surrounded by pine trees. Ever since, Hossegor has drawn a steady stream of visitors. In the 1930s, it became a coastal resort, and the Sporting-Casino was built, along with a traditional *fronton* where the ball game *pelote basque* is still played. The elegant villas around the golf course and the sea lake evoke the resort's heyday in the 1920s and 1930s. Built in a Basque-Béarn style *(see pp28–9)*, they have Basque features, such as white roofs and façades, as well as typical Landes features, such as half-timbering.

Hossegor is now also an international, surfing mecca. The Quiksilver Pro festival that takes place in late August and October attracts the best surfers in the world.

Visitors in a *galupe*, a traditional river craft on the Courant d'Huchet

The Sporting-Casino at Hossegor, a 1930s building in the Basque style

Anglers on the pier at Capbreton

8 Capbreton

Road map A4. 8,000. Avenue du Président-Pompidou; 05 58 72 12 11. Tue, Thu & Sat am. Fête de la Mer (Jun/Jul); Festival de Contes (Aug); Fête du Chipiron (Sep).

Separated from Hossegor by an inlet of the sea, Capbreton became an important port in the Middle Ages and was also a stop on the coastal route of the pilgrimage to Santiago de Compostela. In the 16th and 17th centuries it was known as the "town of a thousand captains", dispatching its whaling and cod-fishing fleets to Newfoundland. Subsequently it lost business to rising Bayonne and sank into decline until Napoleon III ordered the Estacade to be built in 1858. The wooden pier with a lighthouse remains a beloved symbol of the town and a favourite place for promenades. Nowadays Capbreton is still a fishing port as well as a tourist attraction.

The Église de Saint-Étienne-d'Orthe

Environs

The **Marais d'Orx** is a nature reserve covering 800 ha (1,980 acres). Every year, thousands of migratory birds of over 200 species, including the common spoonbill, stop here on their annual journey south.

Marais d'Orx
Accessible from Labenne, 8 km (5 miles) south of Capbreton.
Maison du Marais; 05 59 45 42 46.
Open daily. **Closed** Sat & Sun: am.

9 Pays d'Orthe

Road map B4. Peyrehorade. 147 avenue des Évadés, Peyrehorade; 05 58 73 00 52.
http://tourisme.paysdorthe.fr

South of the Landes lies the Pays d'Orthe, a region that has sat at the crossroads of travellers' routes through southwestern France since prehistoric times. The seat of the Orthe family from the 11th century until the French Revolution, the area has a wealth of magnificent châteaux and religious buildings. The *bastide* town of **Hastingues**, on the pilgrim route to Compostela, not far from where the roads from Le Puy and Vézelay meet, was founded by the English in the 13th century. Its fortified gate once formed part of the town's original ramparts.

The **Centre d'Exposition Saint-Jacques-de-Compostelle**, in a layby on the A64 motorway, documents the pilgrimage to Santiago de Compostela. East of Hastingues and south of Peyrehorade is the **Abbaye d'Arthous**, founded by Premonstratensians in the 12th century and remodelled in the 17th and 18th centuries. The Romanesque church here, built in about 1167, has Gothic elements, including pointed arches in its south aisle and capitals with superb carvings. A ceramics festival with potters from the locality as well as from further afield, takes place in the gardens each summer. Inside, the **Musée d'Histoire** and the regional **Centre Éducatif du Patrimoine** also have interesting displays and exhibits.

Saint-Étienne-d'Orthe, north of Hastingues, is the gateway to the alluvial plains of the river Adour, now a 12,810-ha (31,650-acre) nature reserve. This stretch of land is home to a number of protected species, including white storks, European pond turtles and Landes ponies.

European pond turtle, a protected species in the Landes' lagoons

Château d'Orthe, also known as the Château de Montréal, Peyrehorade

Centre d'Exposition de Saint-Jacques-de-Compostelle
Service area on the A64; also accessible from Hastingues.

Abbaye d'Arthous
About 2 km (1 mile) east of Hastingues. **Tel** 05 58 73 03 89.

Abbey and Musée d'Histoire
Open Apr–Sep: daily; Oct–Mar: pm.
arthous.landes.org

Centre Éducatif du Patrimoine
Open Mon–Fri.

10 Peyrehorade

Road map B4. 3,600. 147 ave des Evadés; 05 58 73 00 52. Wed & Sat am; Nov–Mar: Wed am: foie gras market. Festival des Abbayes (mid-Jun); Festival Nuits d'Été en Pays d'Orthe (late Jul/Aug).

Located in the far south of the Landes, between two rivers, the Gave d'Oloron and Gave de Pau, Peyrehorade is the largest village in the Pays d'Orthe. It is also the youngest, as it was only established in the 14th century as a result of trade between Bayonne and Toulouse. The village is dominated by the **Château d'Aspremont**, built in the 13th century by the Vicomtes d'Orthe on the site of an 11th-century fortress, of which only the ruins of the keep remain. The **Château d'Orthe** (also known as the Château de Montréal), which now houses the town hall, is another splendid building. Dating from the 16th century, it was remodelled by Jean de Montréal in the 18th century. It is not open to the public but, with its four towers which look down on the Gave de Pau, it is an impressive sight.

11 Sorde-l'Abbaye

Road map B4. 665. Mairie; 05 58 73 04 83. Festival des Abbayes (Jun); La Compostellane (late Jul, every two years); Festival Nuits d'Été en Pays d'Orthe (late Jul/Aug).

The spot where Sorde-l'Abbaye now stands has been continuously inhabited since prehistoric times. The Falaise du Pastou, a cliff opposite the Gave d'Oloron, contains four rock-shelters (not open to the public) dating from the Magdalenian period (around 12,000 BC). For thousands of years, a natural fault in the cliff here provided a passage between France and Spain. From the 10th century, it was regularly used by pilgrims on their way to Compostela, and the village became an important stopping-point. In the Bourg-Vieux, the town's historic centre, is the **Abbaye Saint-Jean**, now a World Heritage Site. Benedictine monks, who settled here from around 975, founded it in the 12th century. Destroyed in the 16th century during the Wars of Religion, and rebuilt in the 17th century and again by a Maurist community in the 18th century, the abbey was abandoned during the French Revolution. A medicinal herb garden has been re-created in front of it, which looks down on to the river. Next to the monastery buildings, now in ruins, is a Romanesque church with elements dating from the late 11th century (such as the mosaic floor in the choir) and the 12th century (the apse, doorway and carved capitals). There is also an underground boathouse with a vaulted ceiling, which opens on to the river. This boathouse, the only one of its kind in France, was used for storing cereals.

East of the monastery stands the 16th-century abbot's house, built on the site of a Gallo-Roman villa. Now privately owned, the house is not open to visitors, but the remains of 4th-century baths and mosaic floors can be seen. Sorde-l'Abbaye is now the largest producer of kiwi fruit in France.

Abbaye Saint-Jean
Place de l'Église. **Tel** 05 58 73 09 62. **Open** Mar & Nov: Tue–Sun pm; Apr–Oct: Tue–Sat am & pm, Sun pm.

Ruins of the monastery buildings at the Abbaye Saint-Jean at Sorde

The bullring at Dax, a major bull-running venue, built in 1913

⓬ Dax

Road map B4. 21,500.
11 cours Foch; 05 58 56 86 86.
Sat & Sun (covered market, Halles, place Saint-Pierre).
Festival de la Comédie (Jun); Festival des Abbayes (Jun); Festival Toros y Salsa (Sep). **dax-tourisme.com**

Dax, once a lake settlement, stretches out along the banks of the Adour between flatlands and the Pyrenees. Under Roman rule, the town grew, as it prospered from its thermal springs. In the 19th century, the arrival of the railways made Dax the foremost spa town in France. In the centre, with its narrow medieval streets, the town's famous therapeutic waters gush out of the Fontaine Chaude, also known as the Fontaine de la Nèhe.

The **Musée Jean-Charles de Borda** is housed in the **Chapelle des Carmes**, in the west of the town. The museum traces the town's past from prehistory, through the Middle Ages to present-day Dax. There is also an art exhibition devoted to Landais landscapes, and temporary exhibitions of modern art. The **Musée Georgette-Dupouy** displays paintings by this 20th-century artist. In the north, along Parc Théodore-Denis, are the remains of Gallo- Roman walls and the town's bullring, which was built in 1913.

La Landaise au Chapeau, Musée Georgette-Dupouy

The **Parc du Sarrat** is laid out with an unusual mixture of formal, Japanese and vegetable gardens. Many of the plants and trees in the gardens are rare and protected species. Further south is the **Musée de l'Aviation Légère de l'Armée de Terre**, a museum of light army aircraft where the exhibits include vintage army helicopters. There is also a gallery of aviation photography.

Musée de Borda
La Chapelle des Carmes. **Tel** 05 58 74 12 91. **Open** Tue–Sat pm.

Chapelle des Carmes
11 bis rue des Carmes. **Tel** 05 58 74 12 91.

Musée Georgette-Dupouy
Place de Presidial. **Tel** 05 58 56 04 34. **Open** pm daily.

Parc du Sarrat
Rue du Sel-Gemme. **Tel** 05 58 56 86 86. **Open** Mar–Nov: pm Tue, Thu & Sat. obligatory.

Musée de l'Aviation
Légère de l'Armée de Terre: 58 avenue de l'Aérodrome. **Tel** 05 58 74 66 19. **Open** Jun: Mon–Fri pm; Jul–Aug: Mon–Sat pm.

Environs

The village of **Saint-Paul-lès-Dax**, which lies 2 km (1.5 miles) west of Dax, has an 11th-century church with carved reliefs. Also worth visiting here are the Forges d'Ardy, an old metalworks, and the house of the writer Pierre Benoit (1886–1962), who was a member of the Académie Française. It is now a museum of his life and work.

Musée Pierre-Benoit
650 avenue Pierre-Benoit. **Tel** 05 58 91 09 63. **Open** May–15 Oct: pm Thu. call in advance.

⓭ Montfort-en-Chalosse

Road map B4. 1,200.
55 place Foch; 05 58 98 58 50.
Wed am. Fêtes Patronales (Jul); Festival Music'Arts (Jul); Fête des Vendanges à l'Ancienne (Oct).

This ancient *bastide* town lies in the heart of the Chalosse, a fertile area that produces high-quality beef, as well as ducks that are fed on maize grown on the Landes' flatlands to produce the area's famous *foie gras*. The fact that Montfort was an important stopping place on the route to Compostela can be seen from its church, the Église Saint-Pierre. It has a 12th- century nave and its tower dates from the 15th century. The **Musée de la Chalosse** is housed in a 17th-century estate, the manor house and its outbuildings providing a perfect setting for the re-creation of daily life in 19th-century Chalosse.

Musée de la Chalosse
Domaine de Carcher. **Tel** 05 58 98 69 27. **Open** Apr–Oct: Tue–Fri am & pm, Sat–Sun pm; Nov–Mar: Tue–Fri pm. **Closed** 15 Dec–Jan.

11th-century relief in Église de Saint-Paul-lès-Dax

The 17th-century Château de Gaujacq, near Pomarez

⓮ Pomarez

Road map B4. 1,530.
district tourist office in Amou; 05 58 89 02 25. Mon am.
Fête du Printemps (Mar); Festival Art et Courage (Apr).

Although Pomarez, on the Adour, is an old-established river port, few traces of its history remain. Popularly known as a mecca for *course landaise (see p33)*, the town is a major centre for this sport, which has an enthusiastic following in the Landes.

The town's covered bullring is where the bullfighters parade to music before performing breathtaking feats of agility, as they deftly avoid the charging beasts, which are raised in local *ganaderias* (cattle farms). Working in teams, or *cuadrillas*, and dressed in white trousers and a bolero, they leap, dodge and make their passes, while wind bands, known as *bandas*, play. In order to prevent the bulls from goring the bullfighters, the tips of their horns are sheathed.

Environs
Just 1 km (0.5 miles) west of Pomarez lies the 17th-century **Château de Gaujacq**. The Marquis de Montespan retired to the château to seek solace following his wife's liaison with the king, Louis XIV. The château has a pretty inner courtyard, and the view from the terrace shows the spectacular sweep of the Pyrenean mountain chain. Inside there are several furnished rooms, including the dining room and the Cardinal's bedroom.

Château de Gaujacq
Gaujacq. **Tel** 05 58 89 01 01.
Open Jul–Aug: daily; mid-Feb–Mar, Sep–mid-Nov: Tue–Thu pm.

⓯ Brassempouy

Road map B4. 309. Orthez or Dax. regional tourist office at Amou; 05 58 89 02 25.

Founded in the 13th century, this ancient *bastide* town is associated with the famous Vénus of Brassempouy, a Stone Age figurine of a woman that was discovered in the Grotte du Pape, a prehistoric cave near the town, in 1894. Carved in mammoth ivory more than 20,000 years ago, this figure is the earliest representation of a human face that has so far come to light. It is on display at the Musée des Antiquités Nationales de Saint-Germain-en-Laye, near Paris. A copy of the figure can be seen in the **Maison de la Dame de Brassempouy**, next to the Château de Poudenx, along with other replicas of prehistoric figures from France and elsewhere, dating from 35,000–15,000 BC.

Maison de la Dame de Brassempouy
Tel 05 58 89 21 73. **Open**mid-Feb–Jun & Sep–mid-Nov: Tue–Sun pm; Jul–Aug: daily pm. **Closed** mid-Nov–mid-Feb. Jun–Sep.

Spas in the Landes

The Landes has many spas. The curative powers of the region's thermal waters and warm-mud treatments were already famous in Roman times. Dax is the region's oldest-established spa town, and its warm waters are renowned for their pain-relieving properties. The spring waters and warm mud at Eugénie-les-Bains, Saubusse, Prechacq-les-Bains and Tercis also attract people seeking cures for rheumatism and those wanting to lose weight.

The thermal springs at Dax, enjoyed since Roman times

⑯ Tour of the Tursan

The Tursan is an area of lush green valleys, where maize, grown to fatten geese and ducks for *foie gras*, is the major crop. Tursan wine has been produced for centuries and, in the 11th century, Eleanor of Aquitaine had it exported to the English royal court. Light red, very dry white and rosé wines are made from grapes grown on 460 ha (1,140 acres) of steep, terraced vineyards. The road over these hills follows a scenic route past wine estates, a spa town and some very picturesque buildings.

④ **Eugénie-les-Bains** This spa resort, opened in 1861, is named after Empress Eugénie. Michel Guérard, who has a restaurant here, offers gourmet dishes and special health menus *(see p267)*.

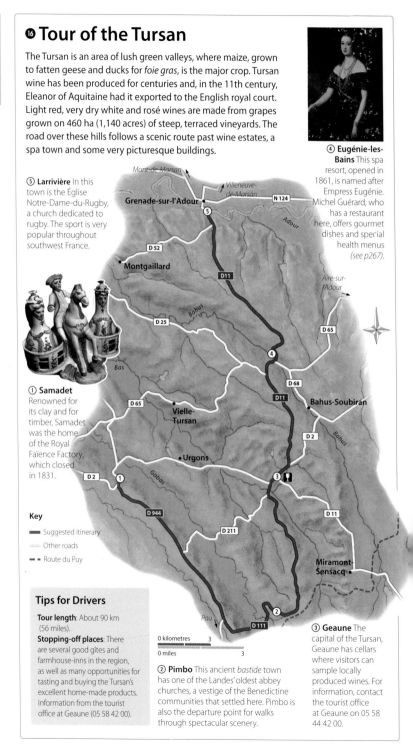

⑤ **Larrivière** In this town is the Église Notre-Dame-du-Rugby, a church dedicated to rugby. The sport is very popular throughout southwest France.

① **Samadet** Renowned for its clay and for timber, Samadet was the home of the Royal Faïence Factory, which closed in 1831.

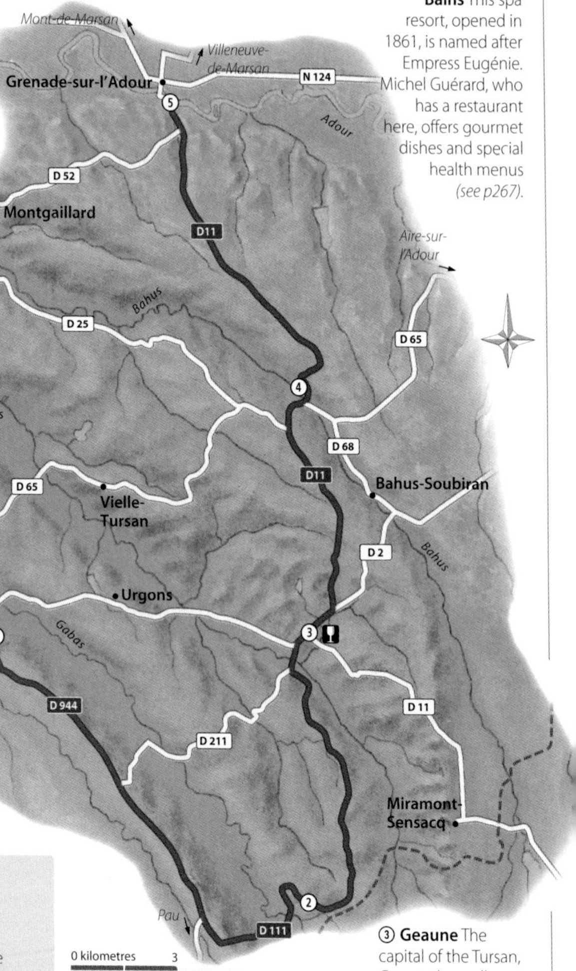

Key

Suggested itinerary

Other roads

Route du Puy

Tips for Drivers

Tour length: About 90 km (56 miles).

Stopping-off places: There are several good gîtes and farmhouse-inns in the region, as well as many opportunities for tasting and buying the Tursan's excellent home-made products. Information from the tourist office at Geaune (05 58 42 00).

② **Pimbo** This ancient *bastide* town has one of the Landes' oldest abbey churches, a vestige of the Benedictine communities that settled here. Pimbo is also the departure point for walks through spectacular scenery.

③ **Geaune** The capital of the Tursan, Geaune has cellars where visitors can sample locally produced wines. For information, contact the tourist office at Geaune on 05 58 44 42 00.

4th-century marble relief on the sarcophagus in Église Sainte-Quitterie

⓱ Aire-sur-l'Adour

Road map C4. 6,650. Mont-de-Marsan. Place 19 mars 1962; 05 58 71 64 70. Tue & Sat: am. Fêtes Patronales (3rd weekend in Jun); Festival de Théâtre (Oct); Festival de la Bande Dessinée (Dec). **aire-sur-adour.fr**

This picturesque town on the banks of the Adour also stands on the pilgrim route to Compostela, and is the gateway to the Tursan. The site was inhabited even before the Romans arrived in 50 BC. The former bishop's palace, built in the early 17th century, now houses the town hall. Next to it stands the 14th-Palais de l'Officialité, the old lawcourts. The Cathédrale Saint-Jean-Baptiste dates from the 12th century, with later alterations. The **Église Sainte-Quitterie-du-Mas**, on the Colline du Mas, is a World Heritage Site. The church's large 11th-century crypt contains the tomb of the patron saint of Gascony. Other notable features are the arches of the 12th-century choir, above which is a brick-built bell tower, and the Baroque pulpit, carved in 1770.

Église Sainte-Quitterie-du-Mas
At the top of rue Félix-Despagnet. **Tel** 05 58 71 64 70. **Open** Jun–Sep: Mon–Sat; by appointment out of season.

⓲ Saint-Sever

Road map C4. 5,000. Mont-de-Marsan, then by bus. Place du Tour- du-Sol; 05 58 76 34 64. Sat am. Festivolailles (Nov); Semaine Taurine (Nov). **saint-sever.fr**

Founded in 993, Saint-Sever is a strategically positioned town with a number of architectural jewels. Remains of the early settlement are clustered on the Plateau de Morlanne, which, with the town's former abbey and its surrounding streets, makes up one of Saint-Sever's two main districts.

The **Abbey de Saint-Sever**, a World Heritage Site, stands on a square lined with fine 18th-century town houses. First established in 988, the abbey was at its full glory in the 11th and 12th centuries. Damaged by fire, earthquakes and wars, the building was restored on several occasions but was abandoned in 1790. In the 19th century, this architecturally important structure underwent some questionable restoration. Built to a Benedictine plan, the church has 150 capitals. Their colourful painted decoration has been restored.

At the **Couvent des Jacobins**, founded in 1280 and later remodelled, the cloister, the church, the chapter room and the old refectory are open to visitors (although some may be closed from time to time). Among the exhibits in the museum of the history of the town is a copy of the *Beatus*, a commentary on the *Apocalypse of St John*, illuminated by Stephanus Garcia. The original is in the Bibliothèque Nationale, Paris.

The *Beatus* of Saint Sever, Bibliothèque Nationale

Abbaye de Saint-Sever
Place du Tour-du-Sol. **Tel** 05 58 76 34 64. **Open** daily.

Couvent des Jacobins
Place de la République. **Tel** 05 58 76 34 64. **Open** daily.

Environs
The ancient *bastide* village of **Montaut**, which is situated 8 km (5 miles) southwest of Saint-Sever on the D32, is well worth a visit.

⓳ Grenade-sur-l'Adour

Road map C4. 2,522. Mont-de-Marsan. 1 place des Déportés; 05 58 45 45 98. Mon & Sat am. Fêtes Patronales (Jun).

A *bastide* town founded by the English in 1322, Grenade-sur-l'Adour has 14th- and 15th-century houses and an attractive church, with a Gothic apse, dating from the late 15th century. The **Petit Musée de l'Histoire Landaise** holds a collection of pieces relating to popular traditions and a display of costumes.

Petit Musée de l'Histoire Landaise
Rue de Verdun. **Tel** 05 58 76 05 25. **Open** Jun–Aug: Tue–Fri pm; rest of year: Wed–Fri pm.

Environs
Bascons, 4 km (2.5 miles) north of Grenade, is a *course landaise* or bull-leaping centre *(see pp32–3)*. It has a chapel and a **museum** with exhibits on the history of this popular regional sport. Displays include 19th-century posters advertising events, and a collection of early 20th-century postcards attesting to the exploits of leading bullfighters.

Musée de la Course Landaise
Bascons. **Open** pm Wed–Fri. **Tel** 05 58 52 91 76.

The 14th-century Donjon Lacataye, with the Musée Despiau-Wlérick

⑳ Mont-de-Marsan

Road map C4. 32,000.
6 place Charles de Gaulle; 05 58 05 87 37. Tue & Sat am.
Festival d'Art Flamenco, Fête de la Madeleine (Jul).

Mont de-Marsan, the Landes' administrative centre since 1790, is set on the banks of the Midou and Douze rivers, which join to form the Midouze. Nicknamed the "Three-River Town", Mont-de-Marsan is a lively centre of trade. Top Spanish bullfighters also come to take part in bullfights here.

Musée Despiau-Wlérick

Donjon de Lacataye, 6 place Marguerite-de-Navarre. **Tel** 05 58 75 00 45. **Open** May–Sep: daily; Oct–Apr: Wed–Mon.

The Musée Despiau-Wlérick, in the Donjon Lacataye, a 14th-century fortress, is the only museum in France that is devoted to French figurative sculpture of the first half of the 20th century. On show here is the work of artists from Mont-de-Marsan, including Charles Despiau (1874–1946) and Robert Wlérick (1882–1944). Other exhibits include works by Alfred Auguste Janniot (1889–1969), a sculptor of the Art Deco period.

Église de la Madeleine

Rue Victor-Hugo.

This Neo-Classical church, built in the early 19th century, contains a high altar created by the Mazetti brothers in the 18th century.

Walking up towards the Douze river, visitors will see two **Romanesque houses** at 6 and 24 bis rue Maubec, built of the local shelly stone.

Apollon by Charles Despiau

Parc Jean Rameau

Entrance on place Francis-Planté.

This 6-ha (15-acre) park is named after Jean Rameau (1858–1942), the Landes novelist and poet. It was created in 1793 and now contains sculptures and Japanese-style gardens.

Mont-de-Marsan Town Centre

① Parc Jean Rameau
② Romanesque house in Rue Maubec
③ Romanesque house in Rue Maubec
④ Église de la Madeleine
⑤ Musée Despiau- Wlérick

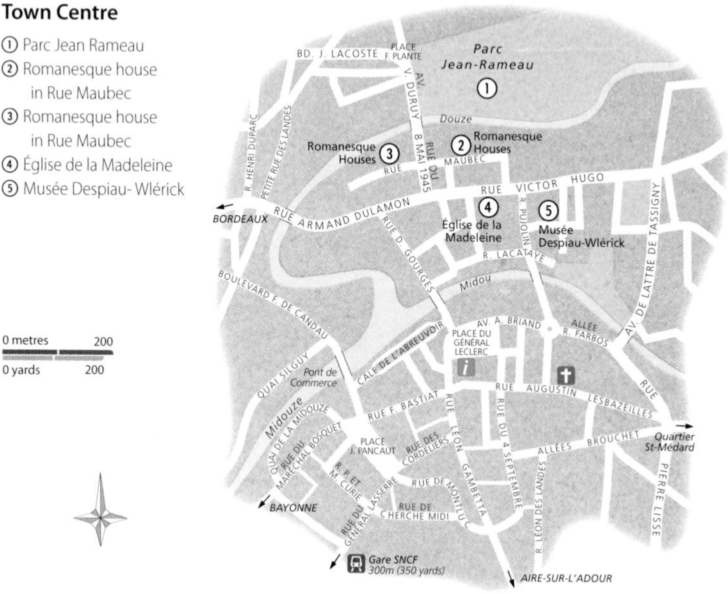

For map symbols *see back flap*

Half-timbered arcaded houses on Place Royale, Labastide-d'Armagnac

Quartier Saint-Médard
East of the centre is a 23-ha (57-acre) zoological garden, the **Parc de Nahuque**. At the end of avenue de Villeneuve. is the **Église Saint-Médard**.

Parc de Nahuques
Route de Villeneuve. **Tel** 05 58 75 94 38. **Open** daily.

21 Labastide-d'Armagnac

Road map C3. 700. Place Royale; 05 58 44 67 56. Local produce market: Jul–Aug: Sun. L'Armagnac en Fête (late Oct).

Set in lush surroundings, this *bastide* town was founded by Bertrand VI, Comte d'Armagnac, in 1291, at a time when the area was held by Edward I of England. The town has 13th-century houses, as well as a 15th-century wash-house. Around place Royale, the town's arcaded central square, are 14th–17th-century half-timbered houses. In the 15th-century Gothic church is a painted wooden *pietà*, which dates from the same period. The fortified bell tower is a sign of the town's turbulent history.

The **Écomusée de l'Armagnac** is an open-air museum that shows how Armagnac is made. It is said to be the oldest style of brandy in the world and has been exported from this area since at least the late 15th century or early 16th century. Also of interest here is **Notre-Dame-des-Cyclistes**, an 11th-century Romanesque chapel dedicated to cycling and bicycle-touring. This unusual chapel has a museum, created by the Abbé Massie in 1959, exhibiting former cycling champions' jerseys and bicycles ridden in the Tour de France. Fête de Notre Dame takes place on Whit Monday with a celebratory mass in the chapel followed by a cycle tour.

Painted *pietà*, Labastide

Écomusée de l'Armagnac
4 km (3 miles) southeast of Labastide. **Tel** 05 58 44 84 35. **Open** Nov–Mar: Mon–Fri; Apr–Oct: daily (Sat–Sun pm only). for groups.

Notre-Dame-des-Cyclistes
Quartier Géou, on the road to Cazaubon. **Tel** 05 58 44 67 56. **Open** May–Jun & Sep–Oct: pm Tue–Sun; Jul, Aug: pm Sun & Mon, Tue–Sat.

Environs
The **Domaine Départemental d'Ognoas**, 10 km (6 miles) northeast of Labastide, is an estate of Armagnac-producing grapes. Visitors can see how Armagnac is distilled by traditional methods using the oldest Alambic in Gascony.

Domaine Départemental d'Ognoas
Arthez-d'Armagnac. **Tel** 05 58 45 22 11. **Open** May–Sep & public hols: daily (Sat–Sun & public hols pm only); Oct–Apr: Mon–Fri, Sat pm only.

Armagnac

Bottles of Armagnac and a wide-bowled brandy glass

Exported since the late Middle Ages, Armagnac is a brandy that has probably been made since ancient Gaulish times. Particular varieties of grape (such as Baco 22A, Colombard, Folle Blanche or Ugni Blanc) are harvested in October. Their juice is extracted and distilled using a copper still. The brandy is aged for two years in oak barrels, from which it acquires its light brown colour and distinctive flavour. It is then bottled. Armagnac should be drunk from a wide-bowled glass.

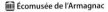

PAYS BASQUE

On the western side of the *département* of Pyrénées-Atlantiques, lies the Pays Basque (Basque Country), between the Adour river and the Pyrenees. From Hendaye northwards to Anglet, it is bordered by the Atlantic Ocean, with a coastline of clean, sandy beaches to which tourists flock year after year. Inland, picturesque villages dot the wide expanses of lush, unspoilt greenery, grazed by flocks of sheep.

Since the early 20th century, when the coastal resorts of the Pays Basque began to develop, most visitors have come to the region for its fine beaches. The attractive hinterland, however, has a rich historical heritage. There is evidence of settlement in this part of France going back to Neolithic times (5000–2000 BC). Later it was invaded by the Celts, then the Romans, who in turn were driven out by Germanic tribes from the east. In 778, the Franks, led by the Emperor Charlemagne, were repulsed, as was an invasion by Louis IX of France (1226–1270) in 824. After this the Pays Basque became part of the newly created kingdom of Pamplona.

In 1530, Charles V (1364–1380) made Basse-Navarre part of France, with Labourd and Soule, the other northern provinces of the region, being added in 1589. Spain retained Biscay, Guipuzcoa, Alava and Navarre. In 1659, the Peace of the Pyrenees brought about a reconciliation between France and Spain, which was consolidated by the marriage of the young Louis XIV of France to the Spanish infanta at Saint-Jean-de-Luz in 1660.

At the end of the 18th century, the Pays Basque entered a period of economic decline, which ended only with the birth of tourism. Today, the region is not only a paradise for watersports enthusiasts, but has also seen a renewal of interest in the ancient pilgrimage routes to Compostela that criss-cross it. These were designated as World Heritage Sites in 1993.

Down the centuries, despite the many changes of government, the Pays Basque has held on firmly to its national identity. Today, this is expressed as much as in the use of Euskara, the Basque language, as in the region's architecture, its religious and secular festivals, and its food specialities.

Partie de Cartes by Ramiro Arrue (1892–1971), showing four men playing *mus*, a Basque card game

◄ View of the sea from Biarritz

Exploring the Pays Basque

The part of the Pays Basque that lies in French territory comprises the three historical provinces of Basse-Navarre, Labourd and Soule. Basse-Navarre has several towns, most notably Saint-Palais and Saint-Jean-Pied-de-Port, that were once major stopping places on the ancient pilgrim routes to Santiago de Compostela. With the Gulf of Gascony to the west, Labourd consists of rolling hills and mountains, such as the Rhune, the Axuria and the Artzamendi, with many scenic villages, such as Ainhoa and Ascain. Soule, the wilder of the three areas, encroaches on the Pyrenean foothills that form part of Béarn. It has some beautiful scenery, including the Forêt des Arbailles and Forêt d'Iraty, and three dramatic limestone canyons: the Gorges de Kakouetta, Gorges d'Holzarté and Gorges d'Olhadubi.

Farm in the Les Aldudes valley, among lush meadows and beech woods

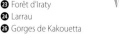

The Region at a Glance

1 *Bayonne (pp194–9)*
2 *Biarritz (pp200–1)*
3 Saint-Jean-de-Luz
4 Ciboure
5 Hendaye
6 Nivelle Valley
7 Ainhoa
8 Espelette
9 Itxassou
10 Cambo-les-Bains
11 Hasparren
12 La Bastide-Clairence
13 Bidache
14 Bidarray
15 Saint-Étienne-de-Baïgorry
17 Saint-Jean-Pied-de-Port
18 Saint-Palais
19 L'Hôpital-Saint-Blaise
20 Mauléon-Licharre
21 Massif des Arbailles
22 Tardets-Sorholus
23 Forêt d'Iraty
24 Larrau
26 Gorges de Kakouetta
27 Sainte-Engrâce

Tours

16 Aldudes Valley
25 Gorges d'Holzarté and Gorges d'Olhadubi

For additional map symbols *see back flap*

ɛtting Around

rritz is the regional airport. There is also a TGV (high-ɜed train) service between Paris and Bayonne. Bayonne ɩccessible via two motorways, the A64 from Toulouse d Pau, and by the A63 from the Landes and Bordeaux. ɱm Bayonne, the D932 leads to Cambo-les-Bains. In the st, the D918 links Espelette, Ainhoa, Saint-Pée-sur-ɣelle and Ascain, in Labourd, then continues southward to Saint-Jean-Pied-de-Port. The D918 leads into the mountains of Soule, where the villages of Larrau and Sainte-Engrâce, and the Gorges d'Holzarté and de Kakouetta are found.

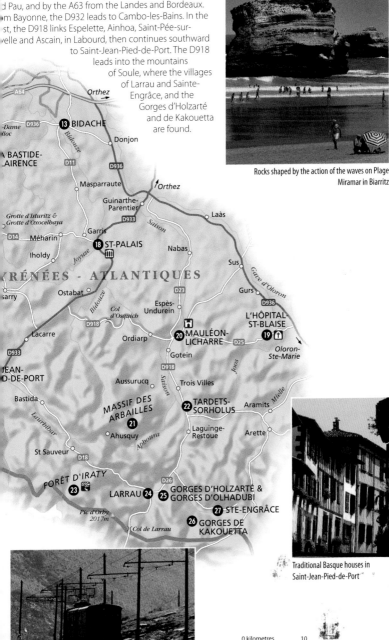

Rocks shaped by the action of the waves on Plage Miramar in Biarritz

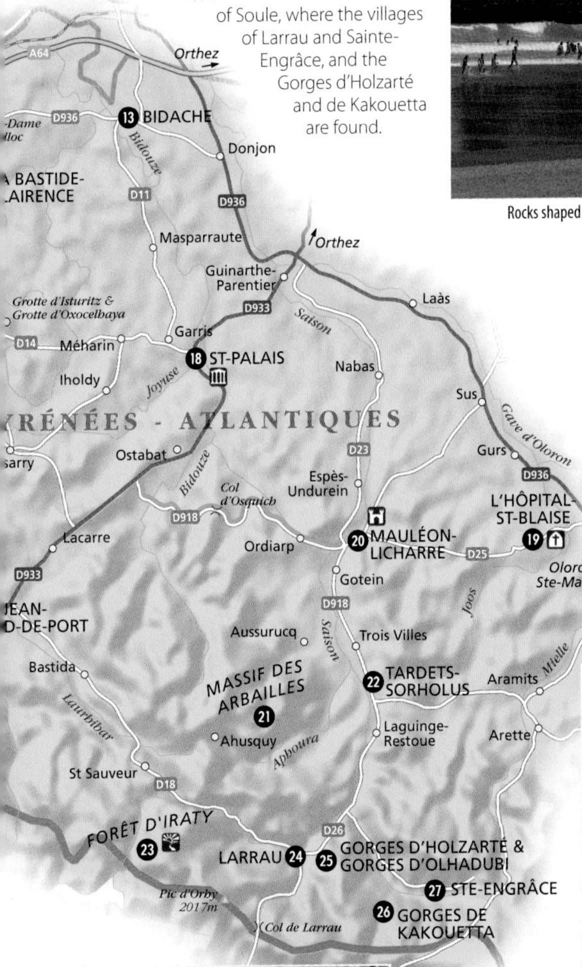

Traditional Basque houses in Saint-Jean-Pied-de-Port

Train on the narrow-gauge railway up the Rhune mountainside

❶ Street-by-Street: Bayonne

The cultural capital of the northern Pays Basque, Bayonne grew and prospered from maritime trade and its strategic position near the border with Spain. It was long held by the English but was finally taken by the French in 1451. In the 16th century Bayonne also opened its gates to many Jewish refugees, who came here to escape persecution during the Spanish and Portuguese Inquisitions. At the confluence of the great Adour, near its estuary, and the smaller Nive, Bayonne has a remarkable architectural heritage. It is also well known for its August festivals and for holding the longest-established bullfighting fiestas in France.

★ Musée Bonnat
The collection of paintings in this gallery includes works by Rubens, El Greco, Degas, Titian, Raphael, Watteau, Delacroix and Goya.

Theatre
Set on the Nive, at the point where it joins the Adour, the theatre was built in 1842. It houses the town hall, from whose balcony Bayonne's festivals are announced.

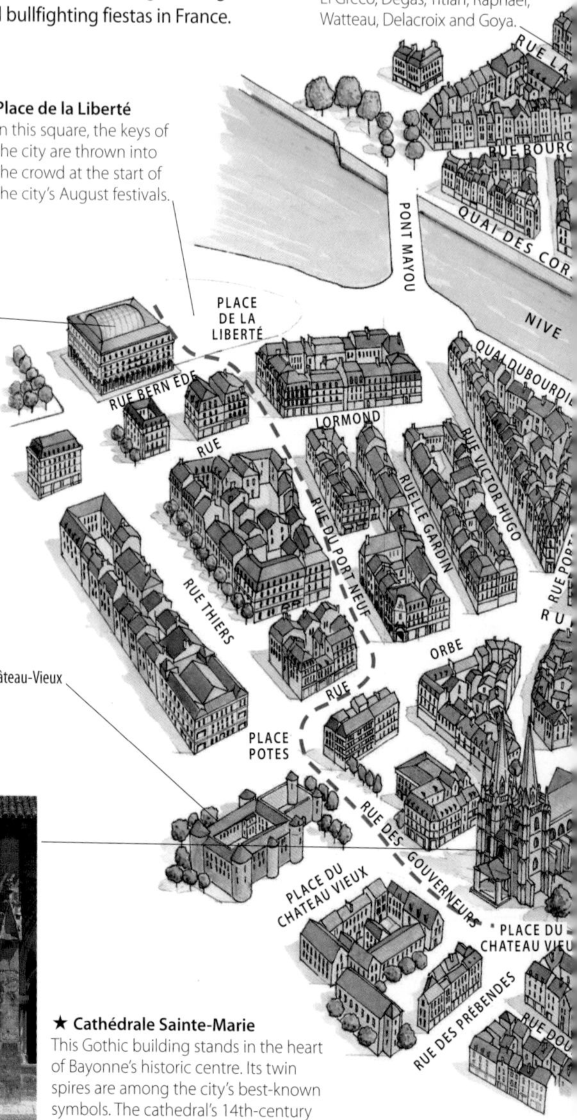

Place de la Liberté
In this square, the keys of the city are thrown into the crowd at the start of the city's August festivals.

Château-Vieux

★ Cathédrale Sainte-Marie
This Gothic building stands in the heart of Bayonne's historic centre. Its twin spires are among the city's best-known symbols. The cathedral's 14th-century cloister is particularly fine.

For hotels and restaurants in this region see pp254–5 and pp269–71

Église Saint-André
Built in the 19th century, this church contains an important painting of the Assumption by Léon Bonnat, and an organ of 1863 presented by Napoleon III.

Key
- Suggested route

VISITORS' CHECKLIST

Practical Information
Road map A4. Baiona in Basque. 45,600. Place des Basques; 0820 42 64 64. daily. Foire au Jambon (mid-Apr), Fêtes de Bayonne (early Aug), bullfights (Aug–Sep).
bayonne-tourisme.com

Transport
Biarritz-Anglet-Bayonne, 8 km (5 miles) south of Bayonne.

★ Musée Basque
This museum, in the late 16th-century Maison Dagourette, documents every aspect of Basque culture.

Nive Embankment
A popular place for a stroll in summer, the embankment along the Nive is filled with music and dancing in the festival season. It is now lined with restaurant terraces, but in the past it was where catches of fish and goods arriving from the Americas were unloaded.

Citizens of Bayonne in festival costume in the old city centre

Exploring Bayonne
The best way to explore the city is to start with the south bank of the Adour, then walk along the Nive. Half-timbered Basque houses line the embankment, their dark red or green shutters giving the place its unique character.

Historic city centre
Until the 17th century, the old city, which clusters round the cathedral, was criss-crossed by canals. Some streets, like rue Port-Neuf, were created when the canals were filled in. Rue Argenterie is named after the goldsmiths and silversmiths who had their workshops here, while rue de la Salie is in the cloth and spice merchants' quarter.

Nive Embankment
Starting at place de la Liberté, the Nive embankment runs past the covered market and open-air marketplace. Quai Jauréguiberry, with its typical Bayonne houses, and rue de Poissonnerie, a little further on, were hives of activity when Bayonne formed a major port for goods from the New World.

Château-Vieux
Rue des Gouverneurs.
Built in the 12th century and extended in the 17th, the castle incorporates elements of a Roman fort. It was once home to Bayonne's English governor, and two French kings, François I and Louis XIV, stayed here. It is not open to public, but visitors can walk into the courtyard.

Musée Basque

Maison Dagourette, 37 quai des Corsaires. **Tel** 05 59 59 08 98. **Closed** Mon & public hols (except Jul & Aug). free for those under 18; combined entry to Musée Bonnat.
musee-basque.com

The museum is in the Maison Dagourette, a superbly restored 16th-century house that is listed as a historic monument. The collections, which have grown since the museum's foundation in 1922, concentrate on Basque culture. Laid out in 20 rooms, they give an insight into the folk art and customs of the Pays Basque. Displays cover a number of different themes, including local farm life and sea and river trade, as well as theatre, music, dance, games and sports, with a room devoted to pelota. There are also sections on everyday clothing and traditional costume, architecture, religious and secular festivals and burial customs. Among the paintings are depictions of typical local scenes and activity.

Place Paul-Bert

In August, during Bayonne's festival season, this square in Petit Bayonne is where young cows are let loose as part of the traditional bull-running events. Nearby is the 19th-century **Église Saint-André**, where mass is celebrated in Basque. Directly opposite the church is **Château-Neuf**, built in the 15th century during the reign of Charles VII. It forms part of the defences that were later built around the city. In summer, the castle is the venue for large-scale temporary exhibitions mounted by the Musée Basque.

Game of Pelota by the Ramparts of Fontarabia, in the Musée Basque by Gustave Colin

Quartier Saint-Esprit

This district on the north bank of the Adour, east of **Pont Saint-Esprit**, is still largely working-class, with quite a cosmopolitan feel. It is where immigrants settled, especially Jews driven out of Spain and Portugal from the mid-16th century onward, helping build up sea trade. A synagogue and a Jewish cemetery are two vestiges of this period.

Environs

The **Croix de Mouguerre**, 8.5 km (5 miles) from Bayonne, commemorates the fallen in a battle fought in 1813, during the Napoleonic Wars, between the English, led by Wellington, and the French, led by Maréchal Soult. From here the views of the Pyrenees, Bayonne, the Adour and the Atlantic Ocean are stunning.

Bayonne City Centre

① Pont Saint-Esprit
② Musée Bonnat
③ Musée Basque
④ Église Saint-André
⑤ Château-Neuf
⑥ Cathédrale Sainte-Marie
⑦ Château-Vieux

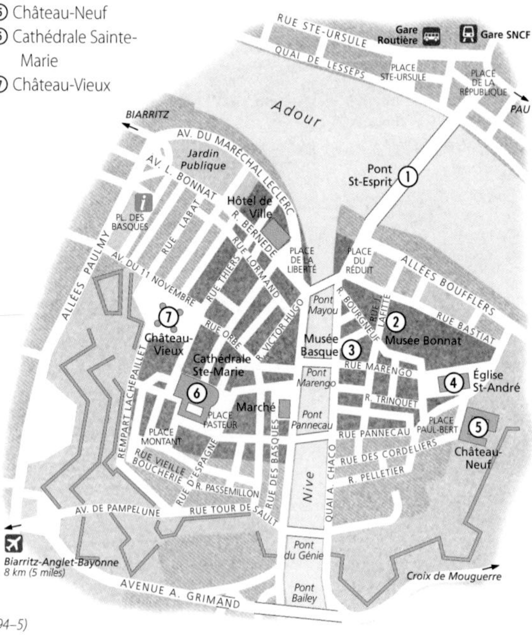

0 metres 200
0 yards 200

Key

Street-by-Street map *(pp194–5)*

For map symbols *see back flap*

Musée Bonnat

Occupying a 19th-century building, the Musée Bonnat (which is closed for restoration until 2014) contains over 5,000 works of art. These date from antiquity right up to the early decades of the 20th century. The galleries are arranged round an inner courtyard and contain paintings, sculpture and ceramics, including works by Goya, Rubens, Ingres, Degas, Van Dyck, Géricault and other major artists. Most of the pieces on display were collected by Léon Bonnat (1822–1922), a painter and native of Bayonne.

Antiquities

The basement contains the museum's collection of Egyptian, Greek and Roman antiquities, among which are some very rare pieces.

Paintings

This eclectic collection of 19th-century pictures contains studies by Géricault, Delacroix, Corot and Degas, as well as Impressionist works. It also includes a dozen paintings and 95 drawings by Jean Auguste Dominique Ingres, amongst which is the museum's most famous painting, *The Bather* (1807).

Portraits by Léon Bonnat

A native of Bayonne, Léon Bonnat painted striking portraits of important people in Parisian high society in the late 19th and early 20th centuries. These included the writer Victor Hugo, society ladies and men from the world of politics. Bonnat's early works are also shown, and in the courtyard there is a large-scale painting by Henri-Achile Zo of Bonnat with his Basque and Béarnese pupils on the hills above Bayonne.

Reserve Collections

In order to show as many works as possible, the museum has six rooms in which an assorted mix of allegorical, animal and figure studies and other genres are hung together. Only a tenth of the museum's holdings can be seen on its three other floors.

Spanish Paintings

Léon Bonnat studied art at the Prado in Madrid and, as a collector, he showed a strong preference for the Spanish Old Masters. This is reflected in the museum's collection of works by Goya – such as *Don Francisco de Borja*, a self-portrait, and *San José de Calasanz's Last Communion* – and by El Greco, such as *The Duke of Benavente* and *Cardinal Don Gaspar de Quiroga*, as well as several paintings by Murillo and Ribera.

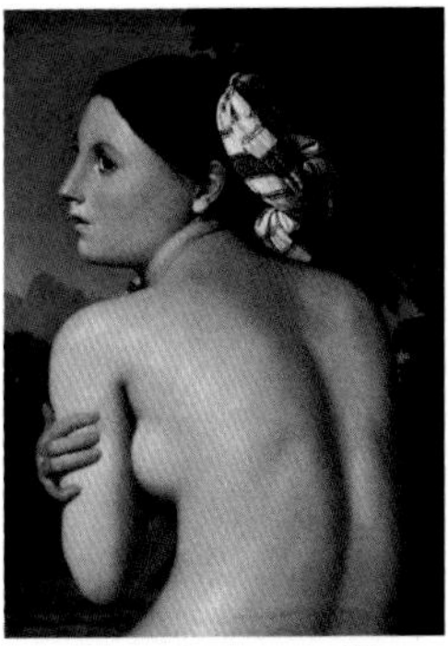
The Bather (1807) by Ingres, one of the Musée Bonnat's finest works

Gallery of Rubens' Sketches

This unique collection consists of preparatory sketches made by Peter Paul Rubens (1577–1640) as designs for tapestries. They depict allegorical themes, created for the king of Spain, and scenes from the life of Henry IV of France. Delicate terracotta sculptures from the Cailleux Collection are also on display here.

Le Carré

In a neighbouring building, Le Carré serves as an extension of the museum. It is used for temporary exhibitions of contemporary art.

The Raising of Lazarus (1853), an early painting by Léon Bonnat

Musée Bonnat
5 rue Jacques-Laffitte. **Tel** 05 59 59 08 52. **Open** currently closed for restoration until 2014. free on first Sun in the month; joint entry to Musée Basque.
museebonnat.bayonne.fr

Le Carré
9 rue Frédéric-Bastiat. **Tel** 05 59 46 61 19. Currently closed for restoration until 2018.

Bayonne Cathedral

Built in the 12th and 13th centuries on the site of a Romanesque cathedral, the Cathédrale Sainte-Marie, also known as Notre-Dame-de-Bayonne, is one of Bayonne's most visible emblems. This imposing structure, in the northern Gothic style, with its tall twin spires, can be seen from afar. Located in the heart of the old city, it was an important stopping-place for pilgrims travelling to Santiago de Compostela in Spain. In the 19th century, it underwent extensive restoration after suffering damage during the French Revolution, making what stands today the result of around 800 years of continuous building work and renovation.

The Flight into Egypt
This biblical scene by Nicolas-Guy Brenet (1728–92) hangs in the Chapelle Saint-Léon. A pupil of François Boucher, Brenet revived the grand manner of painting historical and allegorical scenes in the second half of the 18th century. He executed large-scale religious works for a number of churches in France.

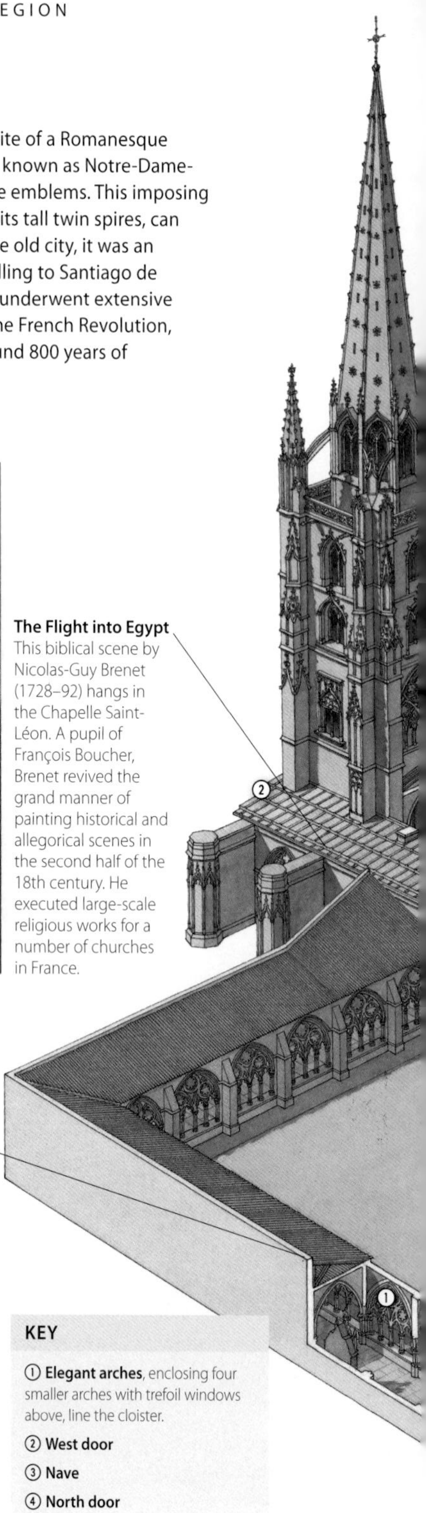

★ Cloister
In the Flamboyant Gothic style, the cloister is on the south side of the cathedral. Three of its arcaded galleries survive. The cloister also served as a burial site and many tombs can still be seen here.

KEY

① **Elegant arches**, enclosing four smaller arches with trefoil windows above, line the cloister.

② **West door**

③ **Nave**

④ **North door**

VISITORS' CHECKLIST

Practical Information
Tel 05 59 59 17 82. Cathedral: **Open** Mon–Sat am & pm; Sun pm. Cloister: **Open** Jun–Sep: am & pm; Oct–May: am & pm. through west door.

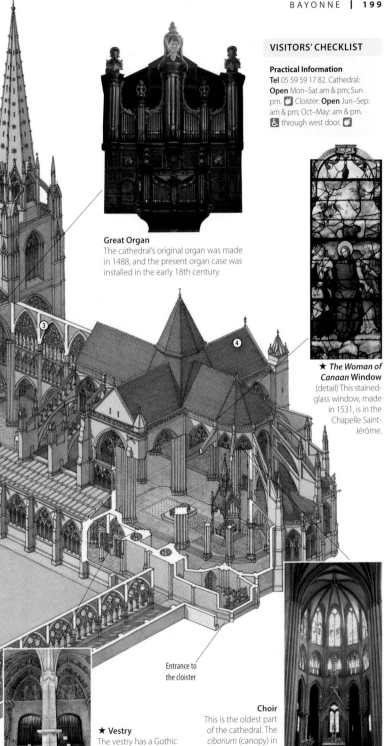

Great Organ
The cathedral's original organ was made in 1488, and the present organ case was installed in the early 18th century.

★ *The Woman of Canaan* Window
(detail) This stained-glass window, made in 1531, is in the Chapelle Saint-Jérôme.

Choir
This is the oldest part of the cathedral. The *ciborium* (canopy) in the centre dates from the mid-19th century.

★ Vestry
The vestry has a Gothic doorway with intricate 13th-century carvings.

❷ Biarritz

Road map A4. Miarritze in Basque. 27,000. 1 square d'Ixelles; 05 59 22 37 00. Jul–Aug. daily. Fête des Casetas (late Jun). **biarritz.fr**

Until the late 19th century, when sea-bathing came into vogue, Biarritz was just a small whaling port. This new trend, fuelled by expansion of the railways and the town's popularity with Napoleon III and Empress Eugénie, led to its discovery by the wider world. Since then, Biarritz, with its elegant villas, has attracted a cosmopolitan crowd, who come to surf and enjoy a little luxury.

Exploring Biarritz

The resort's famous **Grande Plage** (Great Beach) stretches out in front of the **casino**, an Art Deco building dating from 1924. On the right stands the impressive **Hôtel du Palais**, built in the early 20th century on the site of Villa Eugénie, the former imperial residence. In the distance is the **Phare de la Pointe Saint-Martin**. The 248 steps in this lighthouse lead up to the lantern, from where there is a panoramic view, stretching all the way from Anglet to the Landes. **Plage Miramar**, an extension of Grande Plage, is backed by luxurious Belle Époque villas, the finest of which are Villa San Martino and Villa Casablanca. The **Russian Orthodox church** in avenue de l'Impératrice was built in the late 19th century. Fur ther along is an exhibition space known as **Le Bellevue**, in the Empire style, which has an Art Deco rotunda. The **fishing harbour**, created in 1870, sits in a sheltered inlet, above which stands the Église Sainte-Eugénie.

The city's emblem is the **Rocher de la Vierge**, which is connected to the promenade by an iron walkway built by Alexandre Eiffel. The rock is crowned by a statue of the Madonna. The **Villa Belza**, built 1895, looks out to sea. It is an unusual house with a turret and a peaked roof. The **Plage du Port-Vieux**, south of the rocks, leads on to the **Côte des Basques**.

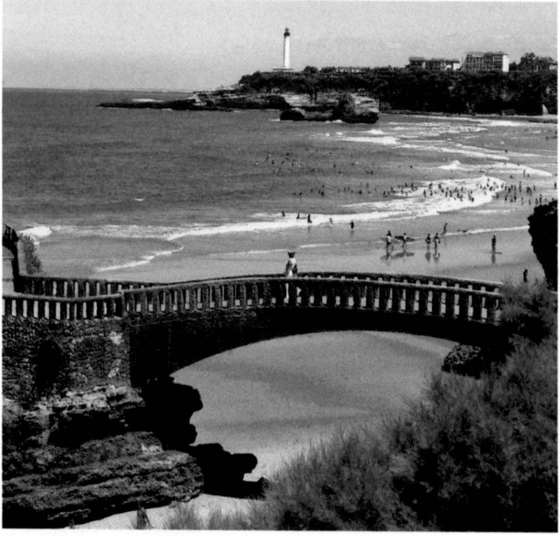

The Grande Plage and lighthouse at Biarritz, from the marina

Chapelle Impériale

Rue Pellot. **Tel** 05 59 22 37 10. **Open** Mar–Jun & Nov–Dec: pm Sat; Jun–Sep: pm Thu & Sat.

This chapel on place Sainte-Eugénie is dedicated to Our Lady of Guadalupe, Mexico's Black Madonna. It was commissioned by Empress Eugénie in 1864. The exterior is in a combination of Byzantine Romanesque and Moorish styles, which were in vogue during the Second Empire. The interior has a painted ceiling, exposed beams and *azulejos* (Moorish-style tiles) made at the Sèvres factory.

Musée de la Mer

Plateau de l'Atalaye. **Tel** 05 59 22 75 40. **Open** Apr–Oct: daily; Nov–Mar: Tue–Sun. **Closed** two weeks in Jan.

In a 1935 Art Deco building, this museum describes the Gulf of Gascony's marine life. It has several aquariums and displays on fishing. Visitors can watch seals swim underwater.

The 19th-century Chapelle Impériale in Biarritz

Musée Historique

Rue Broquedis. **Tel** 05 59 24 86 28. **Open** Tue–Sat.

The history of Biarritz, from small fishing village to high-class resort, is covered by this museum, in a former church.

Phare de la Pointe Saint-Martin

Tel 05 59 22 37 00. **Open** Jul–Aug: pm daily.

Built in 1834, the lighthouse is 73 m (240 ft) high. Climbing the 248 steps to the top is worthwhile for the view.

Environs

Anglet, 4 km (2.5 miles) east of Biarritz, has a long beach, as well as a pine forest, the Chiberta golf course and the legendary Grotte de la Chambre-d'Amour. There are fine views from the Chapelle Sainte-Madeleine at **Bidart**, 5 km (3 miles) south of Biarritz, and at **Guéthary**, 2 km (1 mile) further south, the Musée Municipal Saraleguinea displays contemporary art.

High Society in Biarritz

In the late 19th century, when Napoleon III and Empress Eugénie were putting Biarritz on the map as a coastal resort, the Second Empire gave way to the Belle Époque. It was then that Biarritz became an upper-class resort with a lively nightlife. Full of newly built Art Nouveau and Art Deco buildings, it held great allure for many prominent people, from both France and abroad. President Sadi Carnot and prime minister Georges Clemenceau and the writers Émile Zola and Edmond Rostand spent summer holidays here, and Sissi, or Elizabeth of Austria, came in search of a cure for her world-weariness. In the early 20th century, the town's casinos drew such celebrities as Sarah Bernhardt and the couturier Jean Patou. After World War II, the Marquess of Cueva threw extravagant parties, entertaining royalty and film stars such as Rita Hayworth, Gary Cooper, Bing Crosby and Frank Sinatra.

Edward VII, the king of England, spent many summer holidays in Biarritz in the early 20th century.

Bathing at Biarritz was at its most fashionable in the first half of the 20th century.

Bathing The fashion for sea bathing was born in Biarritz thanks to Napoleon III and Empress Eugénie, who reigned as "Beach Queen" until World War I and again in the interwar period. The heyday of that epoch's seaside holidays was brought to an abrupt end by the Wall Street crash of 1929 and the economic hardship of the 1930s that followed.

Charlie Chaplin was one of a host of internationally famous people who regularly frequented Biarritz's many luxurious hotels, such as the Hôtel Miramar, in 1930s and 1940s.

The British Royal Family, following the lead set by King Edward VII, became regular visitors to Biarritz's sunny shores. This photograph of Edward, Prince of Wales, later the Duke of Windsor, and his younger brother George, Duke of Kent, was taken in 1925, while they were guests at the Villa Hélianthe.

❸ Saint-Jean-de-Luz

Road map A4. Donibane Lohizune in Basque. 14,350. 20 Boulevard Victor Hugo; 05 59 26 03 16. Tue & Fri am. Fêtes Patronales (Jun); Festival International Jeunes Realisateurs (Oct). **saint-jean-de-luz.com**

Once a pirates' stronghold, Saint-Jean-de-Luz lies in a bay with the Fort de Socoa on one side and Pointe de Sainte-Barbe on the other. For centuries the town grew rich from the fortunes of traders and pirates – who were at their most active from the 16th to the 19th centuries – and from whaling and cod, sardine and tuna fishing. The harbour is still a lively place today, and this pleasant resort is popular with surfers.

The coastline northeast of the town has many beaches: Erromardi, Lafitenia, Mayarco and Senix, shared with the neighbouring resort of Guéthary. Place Louis-XIV, opposite the harbour and behind the tourist office, is lined with elegant residences. It is now filled with café terraces, laid out in the shade of plane trees. Rue Mazarin also has beautiful town houses, such as Maison de l'Infante, the Maison des Trois-Canons at no. 10, and Maison de Théophile de la Tour-d'Auvergne at no. 18.

Église Saint-Jean-Baptiste

Rue Gambetta. **Tel** 05 59 26 08 81. **Open** daily.

Having been destroyed by fire in 1419 and then rebuilt in several stages, this sturdy looking church appears plain from the outside, but has a splendid 17th-century interior with a fine altarpiece. It was here that the marriage of Louis XIV and Marie-Thérèse of Austria took place on 9 June 1660 *(see p42)*.

Busy pedestrianized streets in the old quarter of Saint-Jean-de-Luz

Maison Louis-XIV

Place Louis-XIV. **Tel** 05 59 26 01 56. **Open** Apr–mid-Nov: Tue–Sun.

This house was built in 1643 by Johannis de Lohobiague, a shipowner. Cardinal Mazarin (1602–1661), effectively ruler of France during the minority of Louis XIV, stayed here in 1660, as

Église St-Jean-Baptiste

Galleries
As in many Basque churches, the interior is lined with tiered wooden galleries. Here there are three tiers on each side and four behind the organ.

Altarpiece
The elaborate Baroque altarpiece of 1670 features twisted columns, with vine-leaf and acanthus motifs.

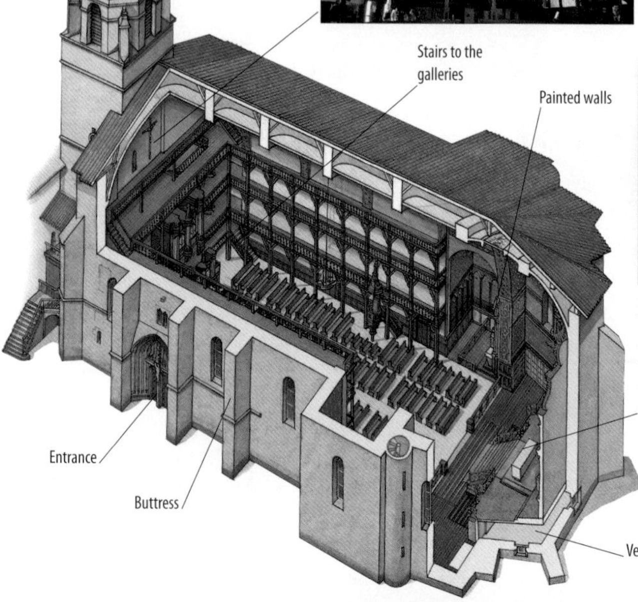

Maison de l'Infante, on the harbour in Saint-Jean-de-Luz

did Anne of Austria and Louis XIV himself, when he came to marry the infanta Marie-Thérèse of Austria, to fulfil the terms of the Peace of the Pyrenees. Next door are **Maison Saubat-Claret**, with carved balconies, and the **Hôtel de Ville** (1654), which contains an equestrian statue of Louis by Bouchardon.

Maison de l'Infante
Quai de l'Infante. **Tel** 05 59 26 36 82. **Open** Jun–mid-Nov: Mon pm–Sat.
This house, also known as Maison Joanoenea and built in about 1640, belonged to the Haraneders, a shipowning family. The future queen of France stayed here in 1660.

Rue de la République
This street leads down to the sea front and **Grande Plage**. Having survived the fire of 1558, Maison Esquerrenea, at no. 17, is the town's oldest house. Like Maison Duplan at no. 10, it has a tower for observing ships entering the harbour. Off place Louis XIV is a pedestrianized street, **rue Gambetta**, with beautiful houses at nos. 18 and 20.

Environs
The town of **Urrugne**, 5 km (3 miles) from Saint-Jean-de-Luz, has an interesting church, the 16th-century **Église Saint-Vincent**. It has a Renaissance doorway, a 45-m (148-ft) bell tower, an organ gallery and 22-m (72-ft) high wooden galleries. The **Château d'Urtubie**, which dates from 1341, was largely rebuilt in the 16th and 18th centuries. Louis XI stayed here in 1463. It is now a hotel.

Château d'Urtubie
RN 10. **Tel** 05 59 54 31 15.
Open Apr–Oct: daily.

❹ Ciboure

Road map A4. Ziburu in Basque. 6,900. Saint-Jean-de-Luz. 27 quai Maurice-Ravel; 05 59 47 64 56. Sun am. Fête du Thon (second Sat in Jul). **ciboure.fr**

Just south of Saint-Jean-de-Luz, on the other side of the Nivelle river, is Ciboure. The town has many fine examples of traditional Basque architecture, with its whitewashed houses, red woodwork and balconies. The **Couvent des Récollets** was built in 1610 and, with the cloisters, it was used as a prison and tribunal during the French Revolution. On the quayside is a 17th-century house with a Dutch-style gabled façade: this is where the composer Maurice Ravel was born, and where the town's tourist office is now located.

The 16th-century **Église Saint-Vincent**, in rue Pocalette, has a fortified octagonal bell tower. The church's interior has wooden galleries arranged in three tiers, an impressive altarpiece and pictures from the Chapelle des Récollets.

The lighthouse here was built in 1936 to a design by the architect André Pavlovsky. The Fort de Socoa, built in the 17th century to defend the whaling port, stands at the tip of the harbour wall.

Couvent des Récollets
Quai Pascal-Elissalt. Cloister: **Tel** 05 59 47 64 56. **Open** daily during exhibitions.

❺ Hendaye

Road map A4. Hendaia in Basque. 14,500. 67b, Boulevard de la Mer; 05 59 20 00 34. Wed & Sat am. Fête Basque (2nd weekend in Aug). **hendaye-tourisme.fr**

The family resort of Hendaye, at the mouth of the Bidassoa river, has two distinct areas, Hendaye-Plage and Hendaye-Ville. The Église Saint-Vincent is notable for its 13th-century crucifix and a 17th-century altarpiece. The two distinctive rocks of Pointe Sainte-Anne mark the entrance to the Baie de Fontarrabie.

Environs
1.5 km (1 mile) from Hendaye lies **Chateau d'Abbadia**, built by explorer Antoine d'Abbadia (1810–1897). Here odd oriental touches mix with the Gothic design.

Château d'Abbadia
Route de la Corniche. **Tel** 05 59 20 04 51. **Open** Jan-Mar & Nov-Dec: Tue-Sun pm; Apr-Oct: daily.

The sturdily built Neo-Gothic Château d'Abbadia at Hendaye

For hotels and restaurants in this region see pp254–5 and pp269–71

Train on the rack railway up the Rhune at Col de Saint-Ignace

6 Nivelle Valley

Road map A4.

Set against the backdrop of three soaring peaks – the Rhune, Mondarrain and Axuria – the landscape of this valley is a mix of rolling hills, open meadows and farmland, enclosed by neat hedges.

Ascain, 6 km (4 miles) from the coast, nestles in the foothills of the Rhune. The village was immortalized by Pierre Loti (1850–1923) in his novel *Ramuntcho*. The old Labourd-style houses on the main square, together with the church, make a picturesque sight. Consecrated in 1626 in the presence of Louis XIII, the church has an imposing west tower. Nearby is **Saint-Pée-sur-Nivelle**, which has 18th-century houses and a church, the Église Saint-Pierre, with tombstones – including one from the 16th century – set in the floor. Behind the church is the **Moulin Plazako Errota**, a 15th-century mill. It is no longer in use, but contains old grain-measures that were used by Basque millers. The state-owned forest has footpaths and bicycle tracks, as well as strangely shaped pollarded oaks. The **Lac de Saint-Pée**, 2 km (1 mile) further on, via the D918, offers watersports activities.

Grottes de Sare, prehistoric caves in the Nivelle valley

The summit of the lofty **Rhune** (905 m/2970 ft) can be reached on foot or by a little train. The mountainsides here are dotted with megalithic monuments dating from the Neolithic period. Visitors will also see shepherds with their sheep, as well as *pottoks* and griffon vultures *(see p25)*.

The old smugglers' village of **Sare** has some fine 17th- and 18th-century Labourd-style houses *(see p28)*. Strolling through its various districts, visitors will come across 14 oratories dedicated to the Madonna and various saints, built in thanksgiving by fishermen from the 17th century onwards.

Maison Ortillopitz, just outside Sare, is a stately 17th-century farmhouse. With half-timbered walls, a fine oak-beamed roof and thick stone walls, it is a typical *etxe*, or traditional Basque house *(see p28)*.

The **Grottes de Sare** lie 7 km (4 miles) south of the village. Bones and flint tools that were discovered here show that these caves were inhabited in prehistoric times.

Moulin Plazako Errota
Tel 05 59 54 19 49. **Open** Jun–Sep by appointment.

Lac de Saint-Pée
Tel 05 59 54 11 69. **Open** Jul–Aug: daily (for watersports).

Petit Train de la Rhune
Col de Saint-Ignace. **Tel** 05 59 54 20 26. **Open** mid-Feb–mid-Nov.
rhune.com

Grottes de Sare
Tel 05 59 54 21 88. **Open** daily. **Closed** Jan. **grottesdesare.fr**

Maison Ortillopitz
Tel 05 59 85 91 92. **Open** Apr–Oct: daily. **ortillopitz.com**

Pottoks

Since prehistoric times, the hills of the Pays Basque have been inhabited by a type of pony known as a *pottok* (pronounced "potiok"), meaning "little horse". *Pottoks* are hardy, having evolved in a harsh environment where food was scarce. They are typically bay or black and pot-bellied, with long manes, dainty legs and small hooves. These tiny horses are endangered but, in the 1970s, certain breeders began to take an interest in them. Once used for farm work or slaughtered for food, they are now protected and treated as the emblem of the Pays Basque.

Pottoks in their natural habitat, the hills of the Pays Basque

❼ Ainhoa

Road map A4. 680. Bayonne, Saint-Jean-de-Luz. Maison du Patrimoine; 05 59 29 93 99.

Said to be one of France's prettiest villages, Ainhoa has rows of splendidly picturesque old houses with red or green woodwork. Some in the main street have carved lintels. The 14th-century church, in the main square, is lined with galleries and contains a gilt altarpiece. It also has a five-tiered bell tower and circular-topped funerary stones in the graveyard *(see p35)*. A further 26 of these traditional Basque gravestones can be found at Notre-Dame-de l'Aubépine, another church, higher up at 450 m (1,477 ft). Views from here take in the Rhune peak, the Atlantic and the frontier district of Dancharia, in Navarre.

Piment d'Espelette

Introduced into the Pays Basque from Mexico in 1650, these sweet red peppers first served as a medicine and only later as a condiment and preservative. They are used whole, either fresh or dried, or in powdered form in many local dishes, and even as a flavouring in chocolate. The Gorria variety, known as *piment d'Espelette*, is grown in ten villages around Espelette. The peppers are picked in late summer, threaded onto string and hung to dry, often across the front of houses. The symbol of Espelette, these peppers have an AOC, and a festival in their honour is held on the last Sunday of October.

Strings of dried *piment*

❽ Espelette

Road map A4. Ezpeleta in Basque. 2,000. Cambo-les-Bains. Château; 05 59 93 95 02. Wed am & Sat (Jul–Aug). Fête du Piment (last weekend in Oct), *pottok* market (last Tue–Wed in Jan).

Famous for its sweet red peppers, this large village is also noted as the birthplace of Father Armand David (1826–1900), who discovered the great panda in China, as well as a species of deer, *Elaphurus davdianus*, which is named after him. A plaque marks Maison Bergara, where he lived. Also worth a visit is the 11th-century **Château des Barons d'Ezpeleta**, which now houses the village hall and tourist office.

The church, just outside, has a painted ceiling, wooden galleries, a 17th-century altarpiece and a large bell tower. In the cemetery are ancient circular-topped funerary stones and the Art Deco tomb of the first woman to become Miss France.

Château des Barons d'Ezpeleta
145 rte Karrika-Nagusia. **Tel** 05 59 93 95 02. **Open** Mon–Fri & Sat am.

White houses and the imposing bell tower at Espelette

❾ Itxassou

Road map A4/B4. Itsasu in Basque. 2,000. Cambo. Mairie; 05 59 29 75 36. Fête de la Cerise (first Sun in Jun); Fête de la Saint Jean (Jun).

Itxassou is set in the heart of a picturesque valley. In the Urzumu quarter of the village stands the 17th-century white-walled Église Saint-Fructueux,

The village of Itxassou, capital of black-cherry cultivation

which is lined with galleries of turned and carved wood. The cemetery contains over 200 circular-topped funerary stones. Black cherries are a speciality of the area and are celebrated at a festival in early June. Either fresh or made into jam, these cherries are delicious with a slice of ewe's milk cheese *(see p215)*.

Environs
1.5 km (1 mile) from Itxassou, a winding road runs alongside the Nive river and the Gorges d'Ateka-Gaitz as far as **Pas-de-Roland**. According to legend, Roland *(see p210)* pierced this great rock with his sword, Durandal. Here **Artzamendi** (Basque for "Bear Mountain") soars up to 926 m (3,040 ft) and is within easy reach, by car or on foot. Another gentle walk along a marked path leads up to the summit of **Mondarrain**, at 750 m (2461 ft), where there are ruins of a Roman fortress that was rebuilt in the Middle Ages.

Villa Arnaga, Edmond Rostand's house in Cambo-les-Bains

⑩ Cambo-les-Bains

Road map A4. Kanbo in Basque. 6,350. Cambo. Avenue de la Mairie; 05 59 29 70 25. Wed & Fri. Festival de Théâtre (mid-Aug); Fête du Gâteau Basque (1st week Oct).
cambolesbains.com

Well known as a spa resort, Cambo-les-Bains is set above the Nive river. Many people, including artists, writers and other famous figures in the 19th and early 20th centuries, have come here to sample the sulphur- and iron-rich waters of its two springs. Amongst them were Napoleon III and the Empress Eugénie, who acquired a holiday home in Biarritz in 1856, the Spanish composer Isaac Albéniz, in 1909, and the painter Pablo Tillac, in 1921.

In clear weather, there are panoramic views of the river valley and the Pyrenees from rue du Trinquet and rue des Terrasses. The Église Saint-Laurent has a late 17th-century, Baroque altarpiece in gilded wood, with a central panel that depicts the martyrdom of St Laurence. In the graveyard are several examples of the circular-topped, Basque-style gravestones *(see p35)*.

Avenue Edmond-Rostand leads to the hillside where Rostand built his home, **Villa Arnaga**, which is set in extensive gardens. Every room is decorated in a different style, including classical elements in the study. Displays relating to the writer's life and work fill the first-floor rooms.

Villa Arnaga
Avenue du Docteur Camino. **Tel** 05 59 29 83 92. **Open** Apr–Oct: daily.

Edmond Rostand

Cambo-les-Bains is closely associated with the writer Edmond Rostand (1868–1918). A member of the Académie Française and the author of the famous verse-drama *Cyrano de Bergerac* (1897), as well as *L'Aiglon* (1900) and *Chantecler* (1910), Rostand was a noted playwright and poet. Suffering from pleurisy, he came to Cambo in 1900 for its curative waters. He soon fell under its spell, and the following year had an elegant residence, the Villa Arnaga, built for himself and his family. Rostand lived here with his wife and two children for almost 15 years.

⑪ Hasparren

Road map B4. Hazparne in Basque. 6,430. Cambo-les-Bains, Bayonne. 2 place Saint-Jean; 05 59 29 62 02. alternate Tue. bullrunning (Jul–Aug); Championnat de l'Irrintzina (Aug).
hasparren-tourisme.com

Hasparren is surrounded by rolling hills and meadows grazed by flocks of sheep, and the landscape is dotted with villages and traditional half-timbered Basque farmhouses with white walls and red shutters. Once a centre for shoe-making and leather goods, Hasparren is now an industrial yet pleasant town.

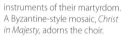

Fresco in Chapelle du Sacré-Cœur

The **Chapelle du Sacré-Cœur**, also known as the Chapelle des Missionnaires, was built in 1933. The walls of the nave are covered in huge frescoes depicting 48 saints, some of whom are shown with the instruments of their martyrdom. A Byzantine-style mosaic, *Christ in Majesty*, adorns the choir.

Maison Eyhartzea, in rue Francis-Jammes, at the entrance to the village, was from 1921 until his death in 1938, the home of the poet Francis Jammes.

Environs

Between Cambo and Hasparren, the D22, known as the **Route Impériale des Cimes** (Mountaintop Road), offers panoramic views of the Nive valley, and of the Rhune, Artzamendi and Mondarrain mountain peaks. Turn off at a junction in the Pachkoenia district to return to Hasparren via Cambo-les-Bains and Bayonne-Saint-Pierre-d'Irube.

About 4 km (2 miles) from Hasparren, at **Ayherre**, there is a panoramic view of the Basque countryside. The Basque name for this village is *Eihera*, which means "mill". There were 14 mills, but now only one is in working order. On the edge of the village stand the ruins of the former Château de Belzance, where the Treaty of Basse-Navarre was signed.

Pleasant countryside near the town of Hasparren

About 13km (8 miles) from Hasparren are the **Grotte d'Isturitz** and **Grotte d'Oxocelhaya**, caves formed by an underground stretch of the Arbéroue river. Paintings and engravings of deer and horses, as well as bones, tools and a musical instrument made out of bone, were found here.

Grotte d'Isturitz and Grotte d'Oxocelhaya
Saint-Martin-d'Arbéroue. **Tel** 05 59 29 64 72. **Open** mid-Mar–mid-Nov. **grottes-isturitz.com**

⓬ La Bastide-Clairence

Road map B4. Bastida in Basque. 1,000. Bayonne. Maison Darrieux, Place des Arceaux; 05 59 29 65 05. pottery market (second weekend in Sep).

This beautiful *bastide* town, on the border with Gascony, was founded in 1312 by the king of Navarre. Its location very near Béarn allowed it to control traffic on the Adour river. In the Middle Ages, the village grew as a result of its weaving and leather-working industries, as well as trade. The town still has its original medieval grid layout, with two main thoroughfares at right angles to six smaller streets, and half-timbered houses and arcades. The 14th-century Église Notre-Dame, in the upper part of the town, stands in a courtyard with gravestones set into it. Further up the hill is a graveyard with about 60 headstones. This was the cemetery of a community of Sephardic Jews who came to the area from Portugal during the 17th century.

Environs
Located 3 km (2 miles) from La Bastide-Clairence is the Benedictine abbey of **Notre-Dame-de-Belloc**. It was founded in 1875 and is inhabited by a community of monks who work the land and who publish books in Basque. The graveyard has a few circular-topped gravestones.

⓭ Bidache

Road map B4. Bidaxune in Basque. 1,240. Puyoô. Bayonne. 1 place Florail; 05 59 56 03 49.

That Bidache was once the seat of a dukedom gives some idea of the town's historical importance. This is also evident from the ruins of the Château de Gramont, built by the duke here in the 13th century. It was remodelled several times up until the 18th century and has both medieval and Renaissance elements. The **Jewish cemetery** in the village is one of the oldest in France.

The Benedictine abbey of Notre-Dame-de-Belloc, near La Bastide-Clairence

⑭ Bidarray

Road map B4/B5. Bidarrai in Basque. 700. Pont Noblia-Bidarray. Cambo-les-Bains. Chemin de l'Eglise; 05 59 37 74 60.

This village is divided into 12 districts, each with typical Basse-Navarre-style houses *(see p28)*. On the square at the top of the hill stands a small 12th-century church with pink sandstone walls. Its graveyard contains circular-topped stones *(see p35)*.

The river Nive here is suitable for watersports, and several local centres organise activities on the river. Being located on the GR10, a long-distance footpath, between Ainhoa and Baïgorry, also makes Bidarray a good starting point for scenic walks up the Iparla and Baygoura mountains and Mont Artzamendi.

Pont-Noblia across the Nive river at Bidarray

Environs

Ossès, 6 km (4 miles) from Bidarray, has fine half-timbered houses, such as Maison Harizmendi and Maison Ibarrondo, and houses with decorated lintels, such as Maison Arrosa and Maison Arrosagaray. On the square stands the Église Saint-Julien, a 16th-century Renaissance-style church with a seven-sided bell tower and a 17th-century Baroque doorway. The interior has carved wooden galleries, a spiral staircase and a magnificent 17th-century Baroque altarpiece.

Saint-Martin-d'Arrosa, 4 km (3 miles) away on the opposite bank of the Nive, has traditional houses with carved lintels. The church, on the promontory here, has a gilded wooden altar and a moulded ceiling. **Irrissary**, a village at the centre of the Pays Basque Nord, has a remarkable 12th-century priory hospital, which was once the seat of a commander of the Knights Templar, St-Jean de Jérusalem.

⑯ Aldudes Valley

At the head of the Aldudes valley lies a region known as the Pays Quint, or Kintoa. Although it belongs to Spain, it is leased in perpetuity to its inhabitants. Like the Baztán, Erro and Valcarlos valleys, over the border in Spain, it is a land of *estives* (summer pastures), beech woods and isolated farmsteads. Flocks of black-faced sheep, known as *manechs*, thrive here.

④ **Kuartela** At a spot near a disused barracks, known as Kuartela, drivers can turn on to the D158 to return to Urepel. This narrow, twisting but scenic route leads through beech woods and lush green meadows.

③ **Venta Baztan** On the Spanish side of the border, shops and supermarkets in the mountain passes are known as *ventas*. They are good places for buying souvenirs or having a quick snack.

The church at Les Aldudes

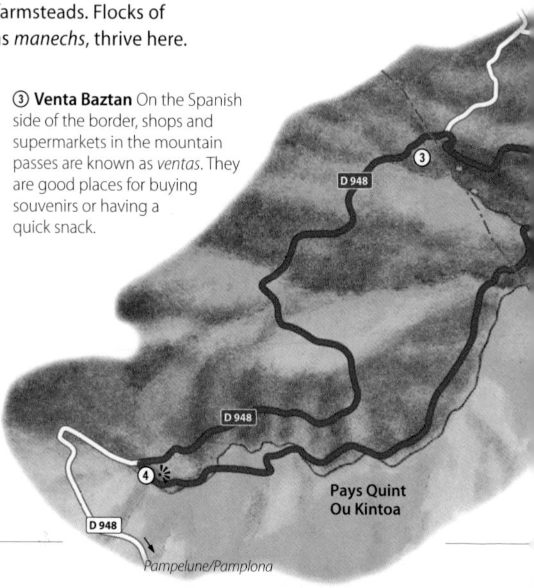

⓯ Saint-Étienne-de-Baïgorry

Road map B5. Baigorri in Basque. 1,650. Ossès. Ossès. Maison Elizondoenea; 05 59 37 47 28. Journée de la Navarre (last weekend in Apr); Euskal Trial (May).

From the central square where the *fronton* (pelota court) is located, there are fine views of Mont Buztanzelai and Mont Oilandoi, and over to Col d'Ispéguy. To the right of the main entrance to the 11th-century Romanesque **church** is the Porte des Cagots, a doorway for Baïgorry's *cagots*, villagers who were set apart for some unexplained reason. Their ghetto was in the Mitchelenea quarter, where there is a single-span bridge. Built in 1661, it is known locally as the **Roman bridge**.

With two medieval towers on its north side and two Renaissance parapets on the south, the **Château d'Etxauz** dominates Baïgorry. Its lord ruled here for 500 years. The castle has a small collection of items associated with Charlie Chaplin, who stayed here.

Environs

The vineyards of **Irouléguy**, 5 km (3 miles) from Saint-Étienne, are the only ones in the northern Pays Basque to have their own **cave co-operative** (wine co-operative).

Just outside **Banca**, 8 km (5 miles) away, are the remains of an 18th-century blast furnace, a vestige of the mines that were once active.

Les Aldudes has Navarre-style houses featuring red sandstone. At Salaisons des Aldudes, a meat-curing factory, visitors can learn about the Basque pork industry and sample its produce. Pierre Oteïza, the owner, has almost single-handedly revived the art of making traditional hams from *pie noir*, a local breed of black-spotted pig.

Large prehistoric stone circles stand on **Argibel**, a mountain west of the village.

Château d'Etxauz
On the D949. **Tel** 05 59 37 48 58.
Open phone for opening times.

Cave Coopérative d'Irouléguy
On the D15. **Tel** 05 59 37 41 33.
Open daily (Oct–mid-Mar: Mon–Sat).
cave-irouleguy.com

Château d'Etxauz in Saint-Étienne-de-Baïgorry

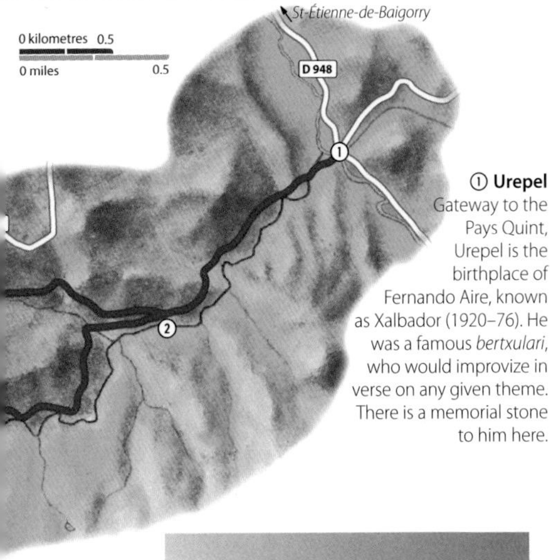

① **Urepel**
Gateway to the Pays Quint, Urepel is the birthplace of Fernando Aire, known as Xalbador (1920–76). He was a famous *bertxulari*, who would improvize in verse on any given theme. There is a memorial stone to him here.

Tips for Drivers

Road map: B5
Tour length: 15km (9 miles), leaving Saint-Étienne-de-Baïgorry on the D948.
Stopping-off places: There is an auberge and a small frontier supermarket at Venta Baztán. The route passes meadows, beech woods and farmsteads, with many convenient stopping-places along the way.

Key
Suggested route
Other roads
Border with Spain

② **Larrategia**
This area is typical of the Basque valleys, where most of the land is only suited to grazing livestock. Here visitors will find isolated farms and shepherds with their flocks.

The Nive river at Saint-Jean-Pied-de-Port, an important stopping-place for pilgrims to Compostela

⓱ Saint-Jean-Pied-de-Port

Road map B5. Donibane Garazi in Basque. 1,750. 14 place Charles-de-Gaulle; 05 59 37 03 57. Mon. game of bare-handed *pelota main* played in the trinquet (Mon); gastronomic fair (Jun); Basque strong-man contests (Jul–Aug).
saintjeanpieddeport-paysbasque-tourisme.com

As the final stopping-place before the dangerous climb over the passes to Roncesvalles, Saint-Jean-Pied-de-Port has been an important commercial town on the pilgrim routes to Santiago de Compostela since the 14th century. Known as the Garden of Navarre, this town switched between sovereigns many times until 1589, when, under Henri IV, it became part of France.

Entry into the old town is from place Charles-de-Gaulle, through Porte de Navarre, a fortified gate with arrow-slits and battlements. Steps lead up to the wall-walk near the Citadelle, built in the 17th century. The attractive 14th century Église Notre-Dame-du-Bout-du-Pont has pink sandstone columns and pillars. Maison Mansart, also built in pink sandstone, houses the town hall.

Rue de la Citadelle is lined with beautiful stone houses, with carved lintels and eaves over richly decorated beams. One of the finest of these houses is Maison Arcanzola, built in 1510, with brick and half-timbered walls in its upper storey. Further up is the Prison des Évêques. In the 19th century it was used as a short-term prison, but the building dates from the times that the town was the seat of a bishopric – three times between 1383 and 1417. **Porte Saint-Jacques**, the gateway at the end of rue de la Citadelle, is a World Heritage Site, and pilgrims still pass through it.

Crossing the Nive by the picturesque Pont Notre-Dame to the rue d'Espagne quarter on the opposite bank, you will come to the ramparts. There is a covered market here, held on Mondays.

Battle of Roncesvalles

15th-century illumination showing Charlemagne before the dead Roland

In 778, having attempted to lay siege to the then Moorish town of Zaragoza, the Christian army of the Holy Roman Emperor, Charlemagne, retreated to the Pyrenean passes. The exhausted rear guard, who were led by Charlemagne's nephew, Roland, were attacked by Vascons, who at the time supported the Moors, in the Roncevaux pass and suffered heavy losses. Roland himself was killed. A stone erected at Col d'Ibañeta stands in memory of these fallen heroes, whose deeds were immortalized in the *Chanson de Roland*, written over 300 hundred years later.

Environs

10 km (6 miles) away, just beyond Arnéguy and Valcarlos, in Spain, is **Roncesvalles** (Roncevaux in Spanish). The town lies below Col de Roncevaux (or Puerto d'Ibañeta), a pass at an altitude of 1,507 m (4946 ft). It has an 18th-century hostel, the 12th-century Chapelle de Sancti Spiritus and the 14th-century Église de Santiago. The town is 800 km (500 miles) from Compostela and, for the pilgrims arriving there, the most arduous part of their journey was over.

For hotels and restaurants in this region see pp254–5 and pp269–71

Traditionally woven Basque linen in a shop in Saint-Jean-de-Luz

Basque Linen

Basque linen is traditionally woven with stripes, which served to identify different families' linen at the village wash-house. Originally woven from flax on wooden handlooms, Basque linen is now made of both flax and cotton, using factory methods. Traditional patterns include variations on the Basque cross, and the ground may be a solid colour, rather than just the traditional white. Linen cloth had a wide range of uses, from tablecloths and napkins to curtains. The largest pieces were used to decorate the interior of Basque houses. Today only a few workshops – Jean Vier in Saint-Jean-de-Luz, Ona Tiss in Saint-Palais and Lartigue in Oloron-Sainte-Marie, in Béarn – keep this ancient skill alive.

⑱ Saint-Palais

Road map B4. Donapaleu in Basque. 2,000. Puyoô. 14 place Charles de Gaulle; 05 59 65 71 78. Fri. Festival de Force Basque (first Sun after 15 Aug); horse fair (Dec); Fête de la Madeleine (Jul).

Founded in the 13th century, the *bastide* town of Saint-Palais later became the capital of the kingdom of Navarre. As it stands at the crossroads of several pilgrimage routes, many markets were held here. It is also where the region's first Estates General met in the 16th century.

The town has some attractive old houses, particularly Maison des Têtes, which is decorated with carvings of heads, set within medallions. The **Musée de Basse-Navarre et des Chemins de Saint-Jacques**, in the courtyard of the town hall, documents local history and the history of pilgrimages to Compostela. The town also has **Ona Tiss**, one of the few remaining traditional Basque linen-weaving workshops.

Musée de Basse-Navarre et des Chemins de Saint-Jacques
Tel 05 59 65 71 78. **Open** daily.

Ona Tiss
23 rue de la Bidouze. **Tel** 05 59 65 71 84. **Open** Mon–Thu.
onatiss.com

Environs
The 16th-century **Château de Camou**, 5 km (3 miles) north of Saint-Palais, has an exhibition on tenant farming and models of Renaissance inventions. At **Garris**, 3 km (2 miles) further northwest, a *pottok* fair takes place on 31 July and 1 August each year. **Ostabat**, 12 km (7 miles) south of Saint-Palais, stands at the junction of the pilgrim routes from Tours, Vézelay and Le Puy. As such it was an important stopping-place for pilgrims.

Château de Camou
Tel 05 59 65 84 03. **Open** Jul–Aug: daily pm.

The 12th-century church at Hôpital-Saint-Blaise

Weaver at Ona Tiss, the Basque linen workshop in Saint-Palais

⑲ L'Hôpital-Saint-Blaise

Road map B5. Ospitale-Pia in Basque. 75. Oloron-Sainte-Marie. Mairie; 05 59 66 11 12. pilgrimage in honour of Saint-Blaise (early Feb).

This tiny village, 13 km (8 miles) northeast of Mauléon-Licharre, lies very close to the border with Béarn *(see p219)*. It was once the seat of a commander of the Knights Templar, and had a hostel where pilgrims would stay and rest, before continuing on their journey up to Col du Somport, via Oloron-Sainte-Marie or Saint-Jean-Pied-de-Port.

The striking 12th-century **Église de L'Hôpital-Saint-Blaise** is in the Romanesque style with Moorish elements. These are particularly noticeable in the stone latticework of the windows and in the capitals of the doorway. Moorish influence is also apparent inside the church: the stone-built dome has groin vaults that intersect to form an eight-pointed star. The interior also has a Baroque altarpiece and traditional Basque-style galleries *(see p202)*. Both these features date from a later period than the church itself.

Église de L'Hôpital-Saint-Blaise
Tel 05 59 66 07 21. **Open** daily.

Pilgrim Routes of Southwest France

The four main pilgrim routes – from Tours, Vézelay, Le Puy-en-Velay and Arles – to Santiago de Compostela run through southwest France. Since the discovery of the supposed tomb of the apostle St James at Compostela in 813, many have embarked on the perilous journey to visit it. James is believed to have preached in Spain, and it is thought that his body was taken there after his martyrdom in Jerusalem in the 1st century AD. Having crossed the Pyrenees via the Col de Somport or Col de Roncevaux, pilgrims still had 800 km (500 miles) to travel before reaching the Cathedral of Santiago. The routes they used were added to UNESCO's World Heritage List in 1993.

Street sign in Bordeaux
Pilgrims arriving from the Médoc and Tours, or by boat along the Garonne, stopped in the city. The shell of St James, emblem of the pilgrimage, is featured.

Backpacks hold the present-day pilgrim's luggage.

Pilgrims cross the Aspe at Oloron-Sainte-Marie, in Béarn.

Book of Hours
Accounts of pilgrimages and guides to the routes were written from the 12th century onwards. Among them was the late 15th-century *Codex Calixtinus*, written by Aymery Picaud, a monk.

The sportelle
This was a badge that pilgrims would sew onto their clothes. In some areas, it served as a kind of pass. Today's pilgrims carry a *credencial*, a passport that is stamped to record their progress and the places where they have stopped.

Map of the pilgrim routes to Compostela
Based on a 17th-century map, this shows the various pilgrim routes and the points at which they converge. Stopping-places are concentrated in the southwest.

Porte Saint-Jacques
Among the many monuments on the route to Compostela that are now listed as World Heritage Sites is this gateway at Saint-Jean-Pied-de-Port *(see p210)*. The town sits at the foot of the Pyrenees, just below the Col de Roncesvalles.

Religious buildings
Many churches, such as that at L'Hôpital Saint-Blaise, shown here, are World Heritage Sites. They testify to the strength of Christian faith in southwest France, as in the rest of Europe, during the Middle Ages.

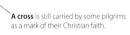

A cross is still carried by some pilgrims as a mark of their Christian faith.

Gîtes and refuges
Along the way there are many gîtes and refuges where pilgrims can spend the night, so long as they can show their *credencial*, which is given to them by their diocese.

Jacquets and Jacquaires

In France, pilgrims travelling to Compostela are known as *jacquets* or *jacquaires*. Although their paths vary according to their point of departure, all pilgrim routes converge in the Pays Basque. Because of the spectacular scenery and the towns and the villages that they pass through, these routes are becoming very popular.

Stèle de Gibraltar
At Ostabat, near Saint-Palais, is a column, that symbolically marks the convergence point of the pilgrim routes from Tours, Le Puy-en-Velay and Vézelay.

Pilgrim sculpture
Sited on the Spanish side of Col du Somport, this marks the route from Arles in France that later converges with four other pilgrim routes at Puente la Reina. From there, a single route, known as the *Camino Francés* (French Road), continues straight to Compostela.

Bell tower with three steeples on the 16th-century church at Gotein, near Mauléon

⑳ Mauléon-Licharre

Road map B5. Maule-Lextarre in Basque. 3,500. Oloron-Sainte-Marie. 10 rue JB Hengas; 05 59 28 02 37 (Mouléon-Soule). Tue & Sat am. Fête de l'Espadrille (15 Aug). **soule-xiberoa.fr**

Capital of the Soule, the smallest and the most sparsely populated of all the provinces of the Pays Basque, Mauléon-Licharre, also known as Mauléon-Soule, stretches out along the banks of the Saison river. In Mauléon, the upper part of the town, stands the 12th-century **Château Fort**. This small fortress, perched on an outcrop of rock that towers over the valley, contains dungeons and old cannons. The old *bastide* town of Mauléon was built in the 13th century, when Edward I of England ruled Aquitaine. Licharre, the lower town to the west, was the province's administrative centre. At the far end of the allées de la Soule, a long esplanade fronts the Hôtel de Montréal, a 17th-century building that now houses the town hall, a bandstand and a *fronton* (pelota court). **Château d'Andurain**, built in the 16th and 17th centuries, has a shingle and slate, keel roof. Still inhabited by the descendants of Arnaud de Maytie, this residence has Renaissance-style decoration, including listed carved mantel-pieces, as well as antique furniture and rare books.

Château Fort de Mauléon
Tel 05 59 28 02 37.
Open Apr–Sep: daily.

Château d'Andurain de Maytie
1 rue du Jeu-de-Paume.
Tel 05 59 28 04 18.
Open Jul–20 Sep.

Environs

Gotein, 4.5 km (3 miles) from Mauléon-Licharre, has a 16th-century church, which contains an 18th-century altarpiece. Its bell tower, with three steeples, each topped by a small cross, is typical of the Soule region.

Ordiarp, 6 km (4 miles) further on, towards Col d'Osquich, was a stopping-place on the route to Compostela. It has several medieval houses, a 12th-century church where mass is said in Basque, and several circular-topped gravestones *(see p35)*. Next to the town hall stands the **Centre d'Évocation de Saint-Jacques de Compostelle**. It documents the Romanesque art and architecture that relates to the history of pilgrimages to Compostela.

At Trois-Villes, 10 km (6 miles) away, is the **Château d'Élizabea**. Built in 1660 and surrounded by gardens, it belonged to the Comte de Tréville, captain of Louis XIII's musketeers. It figures in *The Three Musketeers* (1844), the famous novel by Alexandre Dumas. The route leading to Les Arbailles passes a Soule-style church at **Aussurucq**.

Château d'Élizabea
Tel 05 59 28 54 01. **Open** Apr–May & Jul–Sep: Sat–Mon pm; Aug: Mon am.

Centre d'Évocation de Saint-Jacques-de-Compostelle
Adjoining the town hall. **Tel** 05 59 28 07 63. **Open** mid-Jun–Sep: Mon–Fri.

㉑ Massif des Arbailles

Road map B5. Oloron-Sainte-Marie. Place Centrale, Tardets; 05 59 28 51 28. Transhumance (May, around Ascension); Fête des Bergers, Col d'Ahusquy (first Sun after 15 Aug).

The dense and magical Forêt des Arbailles, which has inspired many Basque legends, covers a mountainous area of limestone rocks. Heavy rainfall there has led to the formation of around 600 rock cavities. Pitted with sinkholes, crevasses and chasms, parts of the area resemble a giant Gruyère cheese. Because the terrain is often so uneven, walkers are advised not to stray off footpaths. From earliest times, the people of Les Arbailles have derived their livelihood from grazing sheep. Shepherds live in huts known as *cayolars* and, from May to October, ewes are milked and cheeses, including Ossau-Iraty, are made.

The D117 leads to **Ahusquy**, where there is a spring whose pure, almost mineral-free waters are thought to have curative and diuretic properties. Ahusquy is a gateway to the Forêt des Arbailles, which is dotted with megalithic monuments, such as the **Cercle de Pierre de Potto** and the Dolmen d'Ithé.

Besides livestock, this fragile, unspoilt environment is inhabited by deer and feral goats, and its cliffs are home to peregrine falcons, eagle owls, bearded vultures and great spotted woodpeckers.

A great spotted woodpecker in the Forêt des Arbailles

Ossau-Iraty

The famous Ossau-Iraty, made by traditional methods

In an area between the Forêt d'Iraty and the Pic du Midi d'Ossau, with the mountains of the Pays Basque on one side and those of Béarn on the other, Ossau-Iraty is made. This unpasteurized ewes' milk cheese has its own AOC. In May, around 2,000 flocks of sheep, with a total of 300,000 ewes, make their way up to high-altitude pastures known as *estives*. Here they graze on the nourishing and diverse greenery that gives the cheese its flavour. After the ewes have been milked, the milk is curdled, and the cheese cut, fermented and pressed into moulds. It is then matured for two to three months. It can be eaten as an appetizer, in salads, or is delicious as a dessert with black cherry jam.

㉒ Tardets-Sorholus

Road map B5. Atharratze-Sohoroluze in Basque. 700. Oloron-Sainte-Marie. Place Centrale; 05 59 28 51 28. Sep–Jun: alternate Mon; Jul–Aug: Mon. Foire aux Fromages; Fêtes de Tardets (third week in Aug).

The origins of Tardets-Sorholus go back to 1289, when it was founded as a *bastide* town. The central square, its focal point, is lined with 17th-century arcaded houses. In the town hall district is a *fronton* where games of pelota are played. Some of the houses along the banks of the Saison river have wooden galleries. The Soule-style farmhouses in the surrounding foothills are similar to the slate-roofed buildings of Béarn.

Environs

5 km (3 miles) from Tardets-Sorholus, in the direction of Barcus, is the 16th-century **Chapelle de la Madeleine**. From here visitors can enjoy stunning views of the Soule and the Pyrenean mountain chain. A Latin inscription inside the church mentions an ancient Basque deity.

㉓ Forêt d'Iraty

Road map B5. 05 59 28 51 28.

Straddling the border between France and Spain, the Forêt d'Iraty covers more than 17,000 ha (42,000 acres). On the French side, altitudes range from 900 to 1,500 m (2,950 to 4,900 ft). The heavy annual rainfall results in luxuriant growth. Both pines and beech trees thrive here – this is Europe's largest beech forest. Like the Massif des Arbailles, the terrain is dotted with the remains of ancient megalithic monuments.

The area also has many peat bogs. Because ancient plant matter is preserved by the airless conditions in the bogs, they act as a record of evolutionary change over thousands of years. The bogs are also home to most of the forest's wildlife, including wild boar, deer, foxes and squirrels.

At Col de Bagarguiac, beyond Col d'Organbidexka, close to a chalet housing a visitor centre, are several marked paths for circular walks of 1.5 to 4 hours, or for cross-country skiing in winter. The GR10, a long-distance footpath, crosses the northern part of the area. You can also drive through Iraty on the D18 from Larrau to Saint-Jean-Pied-de-Port.

Houses in Tardets-Sorholus, a 13th-century *bastide* town

The village of Larrau, beneath the Pic d'Orhy (altitude 2017 m or 6617 ft)

㉔ Larrau

Road map B5. Larraine in Basque. 250. Place Centrale, Tardets; 05 59 28 51 28. Mon, in Tardets.

Larrau, a village of slate-roofed houses, clings to the sides of the Pic d'Orhy, a mountain that figures in local legends. On the edge of the Forêt d'Iraty, the village is the main centre of wood pigeon-hunting, a traditional sport with a lively local following.

Environs

About 12 km (7 miles) from Larrau is **Col de Larrau**, a pass at 1,573 m (5,163 ft). This is a good place to stop on the way up to **Pic d'Orhy**, at 2,017 m (6,619 ft), which is 1.5 hours' walk away. 12.5 km (8 miles) further on is **Col d'Organbidexka**, at 1,284 m (4,214 ft). In the autumn, bird-watchers come here to see migrating birds.

Col d'Organbidexka
Tel 05 59 65 97 13.

㉕ Tour of the Gorges d'Holzarté and Gorges d'Olhadubi

The Gorges d'Holzarté and Gorges d'Olhadubi, near Larrau, are two great canyons cut into the limestone by the action of water. There are dramatic views across the river valleys of both from the Passerelle d'Holzarté, a footbridge over the Gorges d'Olhadubi. Those who suffer from vertigo may find this bridge unnerving, but it is perfectly safe, and there are even picnic places where visitors can stop for lunch.

③ Latsagaborda These restored shelters are now used by hunters of wood pigeons. Dotting the Basque mountains, they were built originally for shepherds.

① Auberge de Loribar
Logibaria lies at the bottom of a valley, amid a verdant mountain landscape. On the GR10 long-distance footpath, this gîte is a good stopping-place for a meal or an overnight stay.

② Pont de la Mouline
This bridge spans the Gave de Larrau. A monument here commemorates a battle between members of the French Résistance and a phalanx of retreating German soldiers during World War II.

⑥ Passerelle d'Holzarté
This footbridge has been strengthened since it was built in 1920. Timber from the Forêt d'Iraty was once carried over it.

⑦ Gorges d'Holzarté
Near the end of their journey, visitors can admire the Gorges Holzarté, a breathtaking chasm carved into the limestone by the swift-flowing water of the river.

0 kilometres 0.5
0 miles 0.5

Key

Suggested route

Other roads

Tips for Walkers

Road map: B5
Tour length: 5 hours for the circular route, 1 hour 30 minutes straight up to the Passerelle d'Holzarté.
Stopping-off places: Visitors can picnic on the Passerelle d'Holzarté, while taking in the grandeur all around. Special care should be taken with young children.

④ **Col d'Ardakhotxia**
This pass commands stunning views of the Larrau valley below. The valley's undulating terrain is typical of the region.

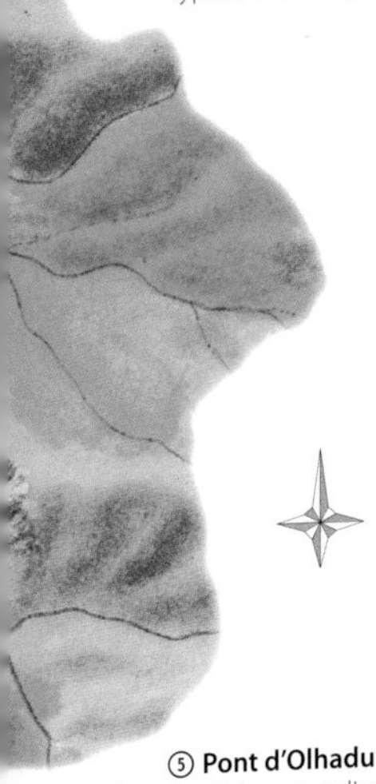

⑤ **Pont d'Olhadubi**
In magnificently wild surroundings laced with small waterfalls, this bridge offers spectacular views. Visitors can bathe in the pools by the bridge and, a little further on, experienced canoeists may wish to attempt an exhilarating descent of the canyon.

The Gorges de Kakouetta, with walkways for visitors

㉖ Gorges de Kakouetta

Road map B5. Sainte-Engrâce. **Open** 15 Mar–15 Nov: daily. **Tel** 05 59 28 60 83 (Mairie). Sturdy walking boots are recommended.

First explored by Édouard-Alfred Martel in 1906, these narrow gorges near Sainte-Engrâce were carved out of the rock by the action of water over thousands of years. You can walk all the way round the canyon in a 6.5-hour trek. You can also walk for 2 km (1 mile) right up into the gorge along metal walkways.

The drop from the clifftops on either side to the bottom of the canyon is about 300 m (985 ft). Some of the narrow passages, including the Grand Étroit, which is one of the most magnificent in France, are no more than a few metres wide, but walking them is a thrilling experience. The moist conditions in these deep gorges allow lush vegetation to thrive.

After walking for about an hour, you will come to a 20-m (65-ft) waterfall, whose source has still not been discovered. About 200 m (220 yds) further on, the walk comes to an end when you reach the Grotte du Lac, a cave with spectacular stalactites and stalagmites.

㉗ Sainte-Engrâce

Road map B5. Santa Graxi in Basque. 250. Oloron-Ste-Mairie. Mauléon. Mairie; 05 59 28 60 83. Patronal festivals (Whitsun).

In the heart of the upper Soule, at 630 m (2,068 ft), the shepherds' hamlet of Sainte-Engrâce lies almost on the border with Béarn and very near Navarre, a province of the Spanish Basque country.

It consists of about 100 farmsteads, and "districts" spread out over a wide area of unspoilt countryside. At the confluence of the Gorges de Kakouetta and Gorges d'Ehujarre, it seems to stand guard over the great amphitheatre of hills all around. The 12th-century Romanesque abbey church is dedicated to Santa Gracia, after whom the village is named. She was a young Portuguese woman who was put to death around 300, when Christians were being persecuted in Moorish Zaragoza. The original chapel on the site was built to house a relic of the saint – her arm, which was miraculously recovered. The chapel was later attached to the monastery at Leyre, in Navarre. It has a wooden pulpit and 21 capitals carved with a wealth of biblical scenes. The wrought-iron rood screen and Baroque altarpieces are also noteworthy. The graveyard has several circular-topped Basque gravestones.

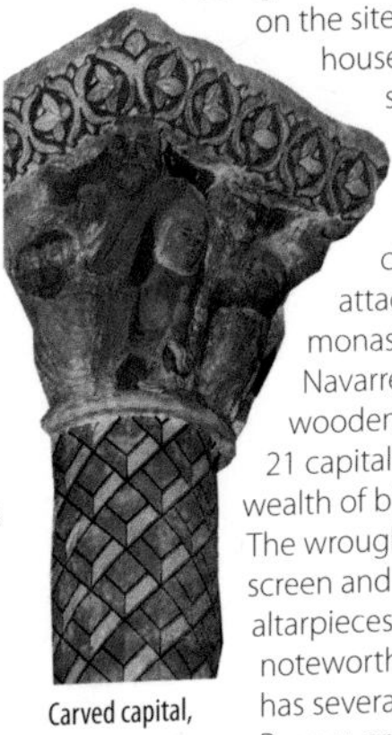

Carved capital, Sainte-Engrâce

BÉARN

With the Pays Basque, Béarn forms part of the *département* of the Pyrénées-Atlantiques. Bordered by Aragón, in Spain, to the south and the Hautes-Pyrénées to the east, Béarn enjoys a gentle climate. The mountains, forests and lush green hills of Haut Béarn contrast with the flatlands of the Gave de Pau and Gave d'Oloron.

With the rugged Pic du Midi d'Ossau in the east and the low-lying plains that merge into the Landes and Gascony to the west, the Béarn has a very varied landscape. Its cultural identity is clearly expressed by the use of its own language, Gascon, and by gastronomic specialities such as *garbure (see p259)*, *confit* of duck, ewes' milk cheese, and wines from Jurançon and Madiran.

Béarn also has a turbulent history. There is evidence of Roman settlement and it was later incorporated into the Spanish kingdom of Aragón. But, by the 9th century, Béarn was under Gascon rule and, by 1290, had passed to the counts of Foix, who ruled it as an independent territory, despite treaties claiming it as part of France. Inheritance led to its inclusion in the kingdom of Navarre and, in 1560, the ruler, Jeanne d'Albret *(see p49)*, declared it a Protestant state, contributing to its bloody role in the Wars of Religion. Her son, Henri IV, was crowned king of France in 1589, but Béarn-Navarre was to remain a separate state until 1620, when Louis XIII brought it under the French crown. After the French Revolution, Béarn was linked with the Pays Basque to create the new *département* of the Basses-Pyrénées, which was renamed the Pyrénées-Atlantiques in 1970.

The modern world seemed barely to touch Béarn in the early 20th century. But it has changed enormously since 1950, thanks to the discovery of gas at Lacq, the intensive cultivation of maize and the expansion of the capital, Pau. Improvements to the road network have also helped to open up this breathtakingly beautiful, unspoilt region, with its unique wildlife.

A herd of *pottoks* in the Soussouéou valley

◄ The Vallée d'Aspe in the Pyrenees

Exploring Béarn

This diverse region, with its rich history and architectural heritage, as well as stunning landscapes, lies within easy reach both of the Atlantic, one hour's drive from Pau, and of the high Pyrenees, just 30 minutes from Pau. In summer, the Aspe, Ossau and Barétous valleys are ideal for hiking, and in winter, skiers come to the resorts of Gourette, Artouste and Pierre-Saint-Martin. Pau, the capital of Béarn and administrative centre of the Pyrénées-Atlantiques, is an elegant city with many green spaces and the château where Henri IV of France, heir of the rulers of Béarn and Navarre, was born.

The Region at a Glance

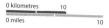

1 Morlanne
2 Salies-de-Béarn
3 Sauveterre-de-Béarn
4 Orthez
5 Navarrenx
6 Monein
7 Lescar
8 *Pau (pp226–7)*
9 Morlaàs
10 Lembeye
12 *Oloron-Sainte-Marie (pp232–3)*
13 Barétous Valley
14 Nay
15 Bétharram
16 *Ossau Valley (pp236–7)*
17 Soussouéou Valley
19 Aspe Valley

Tours

11 Tour of Madiran
18 Pic du Midi d'Ossau

0 kilometres 10
0 miles 10

Rafting on the Gave de Pau, near Bétharram

For additional map symbols *see back flap*

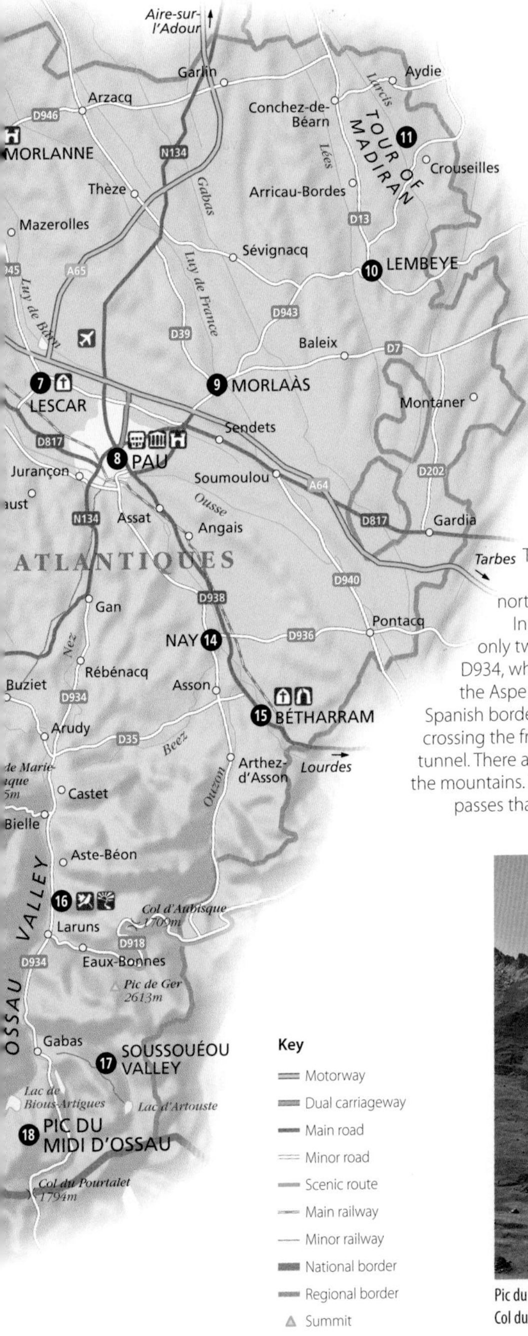

Église Saint-André at Sauveterre-de-Béarn

Getting Around

Pau is served by the airport at Pau-Uzein, and by the Toulouse-Hendaye railway, which crosses Béarn. La Pyrénéenne, the A64 motorway, runs along the foot of the Pyrenees from Toulouse to Bayonne via Pau and Orthez. The A65 runs from Pau northward to Langon and Bordeaux. In the south of the Béarn there are only two main roads, the N135 and the D934, which run north to south up either the Aspe valley or the Ossau valley, to the Spanish border. The N134 is the swiftest route, crossing the frontier by means of the Somport tunnel. There are few east–west connections in the mountains. Those that exist, travel over high passes that are blocked by snow in winter.

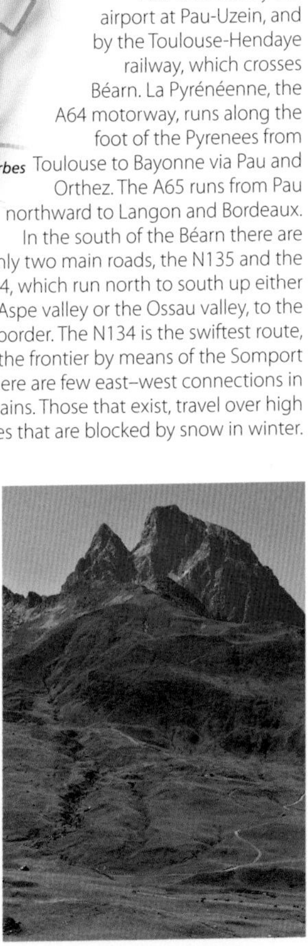
Pic du Midi d'Ossau and Cirque d'Anéou from Col du Pourtalet

The 13th-century Église Saint-Laurent in Morlanne

❶ Morlanne

Road map C4. 550. Orthez. Arzacq. La Grange, Carrère-du-Château, Arzacq; 05 59 81 42 66. Fête de Saint-Laurent (early Aug).

This characterful village has 17th- and 18th-century houses in a style typical of northern Béarn. The **Église Saint-Laurent**, built in the 13th century and fortified in the 14th, is lit by Gothic windows in its west wall and apse. The village's main street runs from Maison Domecq, a 15th-century abbey, to **Château de Morlanne**. Built in 1373 by the half-brother of Gaston Fébus *(see p228)*, this fortress has a 25-m (82-ft) high, brick-built keep. A drawbridge once spanned the moat, which is 6 m (20 ft) deep. The building's original features were restored in the 1960s. On the guided tour of the castle, visitors will see medieval furniture and other pieces, pictures by Fragonard, Nattier, Canaletto and Van de Velde, as well as some fine 16th–18th-century furniture. The grounds feature a formal garden.

Château de Morlanne
Tel 05 59 81 60 27. **Open** Jul–Aug: daily; Apr–Oct: Wed–Mon pm.

Environs
Arzacq, 12 km (7 miles) from Morlanne, is a *bastide* town built by the English. Its focal point is the arcaded place de la République. A local administrative centre, the town is on the pilgrim route to Compostela. The parish church has a stained-glass window with a depiction of St James and a 16th-century painted wood statue of the Madonna and Child. Also in the town is the **Maison du Jambon de Bayonne**, a museum devoted to the history and production and Bayonne ham *(see p258)*.

Château de Momas, 13 km (8 miles) away, dates from the the 14th to the 16th centuries and was the residence of the lords of Momas. The present owner takes visitors on a tour of the garden here, which is planted with rare flowers, shrubs and vegetables.

Maison du Jambon de Bayonne
Route de Samadet. **Tel** 05 59 04 49 35. **Open** Jul–Aug: Mon–Sat; Sep–Jun: Tue–Sat. **jambon-de-bayonne.com**

Château de Momas
Tel 05 59 77 14 71. Apr–Oct: pm Sat–Sun and by arrangement.

❷ Salies-de-Béarn

Road map B4. 5,000. Puyoô. 18 Place de la Trompé; 05 59 38 00 33. Thu; farmers' market: Jul–Aug: Tue. Fête du Sel (second weekend in Sep); Festival Art en Vrac (Easter weekend). **tourisme-bearn-gaves.com**

The town's historic district centres around Place du Bayaà, where stands the Fontaine du Sanglier, named after the legend of the wounded boar that led to the discovery of Salies' famous salt spring *(see p223)*. Flowers hang down the buildings lining the town's ancient narrow streets. The **Musée du Sel et Traditions Béarnaises** is a local history museum that stands among 17th- and 18th-century houses and features a salt-panner's workshop. In front of it is a *coulédé*, a stone trough where water drawn from the fountain was kept before being transferred to reservoirs. The museum showcases traditional costumes and ancient tools of forgotten trades. Historical artifacts and furniture by Salies' cabinetmakers illustrate aspects of local history.

Beyond Pont de la Lune are half-timbered houses on pillars and, opposite, the Maison de la Corporation des

Houses on pillars in the centre of Salies-de-Béarn

Pont de la Légende over the Gave d'Oloron at Sauveterre-de-Béarn, on an ancient route to Navarre

Part-prenants (people who won a legal right to use the salt-water fountain in 1587). The old town ends at the spa quarter. The grand hotels here, such as the Hôtel du Parc (1893), were built during the spa's heyday at the end of the 19th century. Nearby are baths, built originally in 1857 and rebuilt in the Moorish style after a fire in 1888.

Musée du Sel et Traditions Béarnaises
Rue des Puits-Salants. **Tel** 05 59 09 31 99. **Open** May–Oct: Tue–Sat, Thu am.

Salies-de-Béarn's Salt Legend

Fontaine du Sanglier on Place du Bayaà in Salies-de-Béarn

Salt has been panned at Salies-de-Béarn since the Bronze Age. However, according to a medieval legend, the salt-rich waters of the area were only discovered when a boar that hunters had wounded was found in a marsh, covered in salt crystals. In 1587, a law was passed to ensure fair access to this source of salt. The *jurats du sel*, officials who oversaw the drawing of this water, inscribed nine articles of good conduct in the *Livre Noir*. The annual Fête du Sel *(see p40)* features a barrel race in which brine barrels are rolled along. The local salt marshes, which produce 800 tonnes of salt a year, are still in use today.

❸ Sauveterre-de-Béarn

Road map B4. 1,450. Puyoô and Orthez. Place Royale; 05 59 38 32 86. Sat.

Until the end of the Middle Ages, this fortified town helped to defend and preserve Béarn's independence. The 13th-century, 33-m (108-ft) high Tour Monréal was the keep of the viscount's castle and served as Gaston Fébus's hunting lodge. Below the steps to the tower, a path heading down to the river leads to Pont de la Légende, the town's 12th–14th-century fortified bridge. It led to the Île de la Glère, an island covered in lush vegetation. According to legend it was here that a harsh judgment was meted out to Queen Sancie. Accused of murdering her newborn son, she was cast into the river, and was washed up on the island. Entering the old town by Porte de Lester, visitors will come to the town's former arsenal, now restored, and the fortified Porte de Datter. The Église Saint-André is in a transitional Romanesque-Gothic style. The Porte des Cagots, on the south side of the church, was a doorway for people who, for reasons that are still unclear, were forbidden from mixing with the townspeople. They may have been converted Muslims, gypsies, Jews or lepers.

Environs

About 2 km (1 mile) from Sauveterre, on the road to Laàs, is the little **Chapelle de Sunarthe**, a stopping-place on the pilgrim route to Compostela. Inside is a model of medieval Sauveterre, photos and multimedia displays.

Chapelle de Sunarthe
Tel 05 59 38 57 56. **Open** mid-Apr–Jun: pm Sat; Jul–Aug: pm Tue–Sat, or by appointment.

Pont Vieux, with its keep, over the Gave de Pau at Orthez

❹ Orthez

Road map B4. 11 000. Pau. Maison Jeanne-d'Albret, Rue Bourg Vieux; 05 59 38 32 84. Tue; foie gras market: Nov–Mar: Tue. Feria (Jul).

The emblem of Orthez, Béarn's "second capital", is the **Pont Vieux**, built there across the Gave de Pau in the 13th century, under the rule of Gaston VII de Moncade. The tower was added by Gaston Fébus, who inscribed it with a Gascon saying: *Toquey si gaouses* ("Touch it if you dare"). The **Château de Moncade** (or Tour de Moncade) towers above the town. Built in the 13th and 14th centuries, it witnessed the flowering of Fébus's court *(see p228)*, but was torched in 1569 during the Wars of Religion. What remained was sold during the French Revolution. It was finally restored in the 19th century.

The 16th-century house where Jeanne d'Albret *(see p49)* lived has a stair-tower, mullioned windows and a formal garden. It houses the **Musée Jeanne-d'Albret**, which documents the history of Protestantism in Béarn. The **Église Saint-Pierre**, built in the 13th and 14th centuries as part of the town's fortifications, has a nave in the Languedoc Gothic style. **Maison Chrestia**, home of the Béarnese poet Francis Jammes from 1897 to 1907, illustrates his life and work.

Painted keystone, Saint-Pierre d'Orthez

Château de Moncade
Rue Moncade. **Tel** 05 59 69 36 24.
Open Jun–Sep: daily; May: Sat–Sun.

Musée Jeanne-d'Albret
37 rue Bourg Vieux. **Tel** 05 59 69 14 03.
Open Apr–May & Sep: Mon–Sat; Jul–Aug: daily; Oct–Mar: Tue–Sat.
Closed Jan.

Maison Chrestia
7 avenue Francis-Jammes.
Tel 05 59 69 11 24.
Open Mon–Fri.

Environs

The **Monument du Général Foy**, 3.5 km (2 miles) north on the D947, honours the Battle of Orthez and Wellington's victory over the Soult army. The area is dotted with Béarn farmhouses with their steep roofs.

❺ Navarrenx

Road map B4. 1,200. Orthez. 2 place des Casernes; 05 59 38 32 85. Wed. La Saumonade (mid-Jul).

Overlooking the Gave d'Oloron, this fortified town was built in the 16th century by Henri d'Albret. It came under attack during the Wars of Religion and was besieged in 1569. The **Arsenal**, built in 1680, was originally the residence of the kings of Navarre. As its name implies, it later served as an arsenal and also as a provisions store for the viscounts of Béarn. The building is now a cultural centre and tourist office.

In rue Saint-Antoine is a 16th-century house known as Maison de Jeanne-d'Albret, ruler of Béarn in 1555. The 16th-century Église Saint-Germain has arches decorated with carved and painted heads.

Francis Jammes

Born in Tournay in 1838, this poet and novelist took literary Paris by storm. However, he never left his native Béarn, choosing to live a quiet life in Orthez. At the age of 40 he became a devout Catholic. His major works include *De l'Angélus de l'Aube à l'Angélus du Soir* (From the Dawn Angelus to the Dusk Angelus; 1898), *Le Deuil des Primevères* (Primroses in Mourning; 1901), and two novels *Clara d'Ellébeuse* (1899) and *Almaïde d'Étremont* (1901).

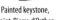

Francis Jammes by Jacques-Émile Blanche

Arsenal
Navarrenx through the Centuries (exhibition). **Open** Jun–Sep: daily.

Environs
4 km (3 miles) from Navarrenx, on the D936 to Oloron, is **Camp de Gurs**. Here Spanish republicans were interned after the Civil War and Jews held before deportation. About 12 km (7 miles) away, at the 17th-century **Château de Laàs**, is a decorative arts museum.

Camp de Gurs
Tel 05 59 83 26 29.

Château de Laàs
Tel 05 59 38 91 53. **Open** Apr, Oct, Nov: Wed–Mon pm; May, Jun, Sep: Wed–Mon am & pm; Jul–Aug: daily).

6 Monein

Road map C4/C5. 4,560. Artix. Mon. 58 rue du Commerce; 05 59 12 30 40.

The town is set in the rolling hills of the Jurançon, a region that produces a renowned wine. A 19th-century building with pillars and stone arches, on place Lacabanne, houses the town hall and covered market.

Église Saint-Girons, built in 1530, is the largest Gothic church in Béarn. A thousand oak trees were needed to build its magnificent hull-shaped roof. The roof beams were originally dowled rather than nailed. A *son et lumière* (sound and light) show explains the roof's unusual construction.

Altarpiece of the Église Saint-Girons in Monein, the largest Gothic church in Béarn

Mosaic in Cathédrale Notre-Dame at Lescar

Église Saint-Girons
Tel 05 59 21 29 28. **Open** Apr–Oct: Tue–Sat (summer: daily); Oct–Apr: Wed & Sat. obligatory.

Environs
10 km (6 miles) southeast of Monein, at Saint-Faust, is **Cité des Abeilles** (Honey-bee City), which is devoted to beekeeping.

Cité des Abeilles
Saint-Faust. **Tel** 05 59 83 10 31. **Open** Apr–Jun & Sep–mid-Oct: pm Tue–Sun; Jul–Aug: pm daily; mid-Oct–Mar: pm Sat–Sun. **Closed** 25 Dec–1 Jan.
citedesabeilles.com

7 Lescar

Road map C4/C5. 10,000. Pau. Place Royale; 05 59 81 15 98. first & third Wed in the month.
mairie-lescar.fr

Now part of the Pau conurbation, Lescar, historically the capital of Béarn, perches on a walled promontory that looks towards the Pyrenees. In the 12th century it became a fortified bishopric, with work on the **Cathédrale Notre-Dame** commencing in 1120. A plaque set into the cathedral floor lists the tombs of some of the kings of Navarre that are buried here. The floor mosaics near the altar depict hunting scenes. The building also has some fine 17th-century sculptures of Christ, the apostles and local saints. Around the cathedral stand the 14th-century Tour de l'Esquirette and two 16th-century towers, the Tour de l'Évêché and Tour du Presbytère.

From the community centre *(salle des fêtes)*, a short walk leads along the ramparts to the upper town. The **Musée Art et Culture** here displays the work of contemporary painters and also has pieces of Iron Age pottery unearthed in excavations at Neandertal, as well as artifacts from a Gallo-Roman villa that was discovered just outside the town.

Cathédrale Notre-Dame
Place Royale. **Open** daily.

Musée Art et Culture
Rue de la Cité. **Tel** 05 59 81 06 18. **Open** May–Sep: pm Wed–Mon.

Environs
About 10 km (6 miles) from Lescar are the **Cave des Producteurs de Jurançon**, at Gan, and the **Maison des Vins de Jurançon**, at Lacommande. At both, visitors can taste and buy local wines. The area's white wine was said to be a favourite of Henri IV, who first tasted it at his Christening.

Cave des Producteurs de Jurançon
53 avenue Henri IV, Gan. **Tel** 05 59 21 57 03. **Open** Mon–Sat. tour of the wine cellars, with wine-tasting.

Maison des Vins de Jurançon
Rue de l'Eglise, Lacommande. **Tel** 05 59 82 70 30. **Open** Apr–May & Oct–Mar: Wed–Sun pm; Jun & Sep: Tue–Sun pm; Jul–Aug: Mon–Sat am & pm, Sun pm. **Closed** public hols.

❽ Pau

The capital of Béarn and seat of the royal court of Navarre, Pau is the birthplace of Henri IV of France and of the Bourbon dynasty. In the first half of the 19th century, the city's gentle climate attracted many visitors, including a number of wealthy English people, who came to spend their winters here. The elegant villas, sumptuous parks and gardens, luxurious hotels and sophisticated town planning from that time help to make Pau a charming and discreetly elegant place.

The 1908 funicular on Boulevard des Pyrénées

Discovering Pau

At the beginning of the 19th century, Pau was discovered by foreign aristocrats, in particular the English gentry, after Alexander Taylor, a Scottish doctor, published an account of the curative properties of the air there. Soon luxurious villas were being built and splendid municipal gardens were laid out. In 1856, the first golf course to be built on the continent of Europe opened in Pau, which also has an Anglican church, the Église Saint-Andrew, on the corner of rue O'Quin and rue Pasteur. Another English-inspired institution is the Pau Hunt, which keeps the British tradition of fox hunting alive in this corner of France.

Villa Saint-Basil's

61 avenue Trespoey. Mairie 05 59 27 85 80.

The **Quartier Trespoey** has several grand houses, almost all of them privately owned. However, **Villa Saint-Basil's**, built between 1885 and 1888 and set in parkland, is open to visitors. There are other privately owned villas north of the castle, beyond rue Gaston-Fébus.

Quartier du Château and Quartier du Hédas

The medieval and Renaissance town clusters around the castle. Remodelled in the 18th century, it has paved streets and several town houses, including **Maison Peyré**, also known as Maison Sully, at 2 rue du Château. Its door knocker, in the shape of a basset hound, is said to be lucky.

Quartier du Hédas, the city's oldest district, has fine 16th-century town houses in rue René-Fournets and at place Reine-Marguerite on rue Maréchal-Joffre.

Boulevard des Pyrénées

This pedestrian promenade was laid out in the late 19th century by Adolphe Alphand, a pupil of the great town planner Baron Haussmann.

About 1,800 m (1 mile) long, it lies on a natural terrace between Parc Beaumont and

For map symbols *see back flap*

Château de Pau, first a medieval fortress, then the Renaissance château of the viscounts of Béarn, and remodelled in the 19th century

Pau City Centre

① Musée des Beaux-Arts
② Parc Beaumont
③ Palais Beaumont
④ Former Hôtel Gassion
⑤ Église Saint-Martin
⑥ Quartier du Hédas
⑦ Musée Bernadotte
⑧ Maison Peyré or Maison de Sully
⑨ Château de Pau *(see pp228–9)*

VISITORS' CHECKLIST

Practical Information
Road map: C5. 85,800.
Place Royale; 05 59 27 27 08.
daily except Sun & public hols. Béarnese carnival (Shrove Tuesday), Grand Prix Automobile (Whitsun), Hestiv'oc, music festival, (Aug), international three-day event (mid-Oct).
pau-pyrenees.com

Transport

Parc du Château, and in clear weather offers both glorious views of the Château gardens below and of the highest peaks of the Pyrenees, which are often snow-capped all year round. Opposite 20 boulevard des Pyrénées there is even an orienta-tion table which names and gives heights of the visible peaks.

The boulevard is lined with the terraces of cafés, restaurants and bars which become lively on summer evenings, spilling out on the pavement. The funicular, installed in 1908, carries passengers from place Royale to the railway station. Nearby is the **Église Saint-Martin**, next to a tree-lined square.

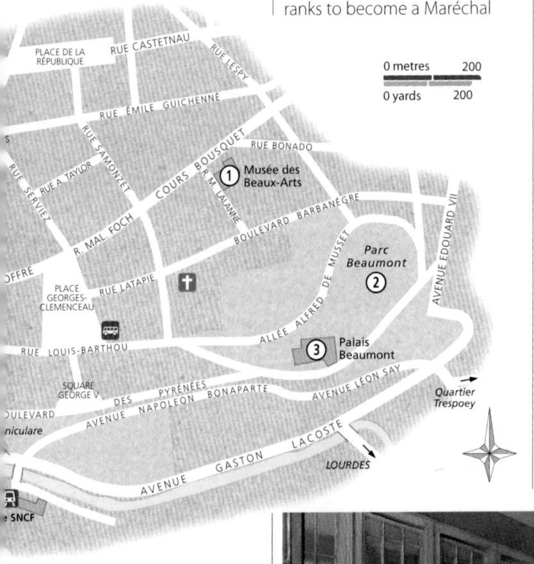

Former Hôtel Gassion

This palace, just beyond boulevard des Pyrénées, was completed in 1872. It stands as a symbol of Pau's heyday in the late 19th century.

Musée des Beaux-Arts

Rue Mathieu-Lalanne. **Tel** 05 59 27 33 02. **Closed** Tue.

In a 1930s building, a stone's throw from the Palais Beaumont and boulevard des Pyrénées, this museum displays some fine examples of painting from the Dutch, Flemish, Spanish, Italian, French and English schools of the 15th to the 20th centuries. Among the museum's most famous works are *Portraits dans un Bureau de La Nouvelle-Orléans* (1873) by Degas, and works by Rubens, Greco, Rodin and Morisot. Major temporary exhibitions are also regularly held at the the museum.

Musée Bernadotte

8 rue Tran. **Tel** 05 59 27 48 42. **Closed** Mon.

The birthplace of Jean-Baptiste-Jules Bernadotte, one of Pau's greatest sons, is now a museum, documenting his phenomenal career.

Having joined the French army as a private in 1780, Bernadotte rose through the ranks to become a Maréchal d'Empire in 1804. With the help of Napoleon, he was created a royal prince of Sweden in 1810, succeeding to that country's throne in 1818, as Charles XIV.

Palais Beaumont

Tel 05 59 27 06 92.

This winter palace, with a Neo-Classical south façade and decorative plasterwork, was built in 1900 to cater for foreign visitors and has since been restored. Set in stunning parkland, it also has a casino and a conference centre.

Parc Beaumont

The variant species of flora growing in the delightful Parc Beaumont, from Californian redwoods to Himalayan cedars, is ample testament to the gentle climate of Pau – just about anything grows here. There is also a lovely rose garden, Pyrenean flowers, a lake and a waterfall.

Portraits dans un bureau de La Nouvelle-Orléans (1873) by Edgar Degas

Château de Pau

As it lay between his territory in Ariège and his court at Orthez, Gaston Fébus, Comte de Foix-Béarn, chose Pau as a strategically located base. The original castle, built in 1370, was a fortress with a triple line of defences. During the Renaissance, it became the residence of the viscounts of Béarn, allies of the Albrets, rulers of Navarre. The birthplace of Henri IV, future king and France's first Bourbon monarch, it served as the centre of a Protestant state created by Henri's mother, Jeanne d'Albret. Later, the castle became a shrine to Henri, and in the 19th century, Louis-Philippe, himself a Bourbon, ordered a major programme of restoration, which was continued by Napoleon III. The château contains many works of art, including some of the finest Flemish and Gobelins tapestries in France.

Henri IV on horseback, by Guillaume Heaulme (1611)

Jeanne d'Albret's Bedchamber
The room is hung with 18th-century tapestries. *Cybèle Imploring Spring to Return* features allegories of Wind and Rain.

Tapestries
The king's bedchamber has some of the richest furnishings of any royal residence in France. This detail is from *Les Mois Arabesques*, designed by Giulio Romano.

★ Chambre du Roi de Navarre
The turtle shell here is supposed to have served as Henri IV's cradle. The embroideries, flags and the plumed helmet were placed in the room in the early 19th century.

For hotels and restaurants in this region see p255 and p271

Statue of Henri IV
With a wreath of laurels, this statue of the king was carved by Barthélemy Tremblay and Germain Gissey in the 17th century, and contributed to the cult of "Good King Henry".

VISITORS' CHECKLIST

Practical Information
Rue du Château. **Tel** 05 59 82 38 02. **Open** daily (guided tours only). **Closed** 1 Jan, 1 May & 25 Dec. (in English or in Spanish by prior arrangement). (free for under-18s & first Sun in the month).
musee-chateau-pau.fr

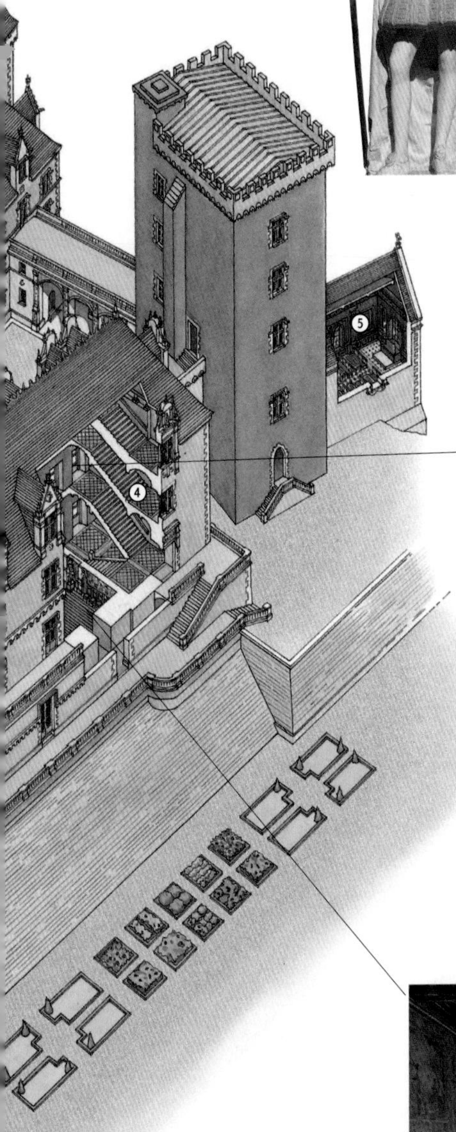

Cupid and Psyche
This 17th-century tapestry with mythological scenes was woven to a design by Raphael.

KEY

① **Statue of Gaston Fébus**

② **Salon de famille**

③ **The main courtyard** is entered via a three-arched portico. The buildings on either side of it have windows with Renaissance-style carving and 19th century decoration.

④ **The main staircase** was one of the first non-spiral staircases to be built in a castle.

⑤ **Chapel**

★ **Salle aux Cent Couverts**
This large room was once the castle's guardroom. It takes its name from the table round which 100 diners can be seated.

9 Morlaàs

Road map C4. 4,500. Place Sainte-Foy; 05 59 33 62 25. Sat, & Fri am (twice a month).

Capital of Béarn from 1080 to 1260, and a stopping-place on the pilgrim routes to Compostela, Morlaàs was once an important stronghold of Gaston Fébus *(see p228)* and had its own mint. Most of the town was destroyed during the Wars of Religion in the 16th century, and very little remains of its prestigious past other than the Église Sainte-Foy. This church, built in 1080, has a Romanesque doorway, restored in the 19th century, carved with a depiction of St John's vision of the Apocalypse. The capitals in the apse are carved with scenes from the life and martyrdom of St Foy. The church is in a similar style to other buildings on the pilgrim route, particularly those in Jaca in the Spanish province of Aragon, on the other side of the Pyrenees.

Like Orthez, Salies-de-Béarn and other towns in the area, Morlaàs is also noted for traditional furniture-making.

10 Lembeye

Road map C4. 690. Pau, 35 km (22 miles). Place du Marché; 05 59 68 28 78. Thu am. Les Médiévales (Montaner, Jul).

The Last Judgment fresco in the Église Saint-Michel, Montaner

Set on a steep hillside, Lembeye was founded by Gaston VII of Béarn in 1286, and became the capital of Vic-Bilh ("Old Villages"), an area adjoining Bigorre and Gascony. Not far from place Marcadieu, near some old arcaded houses, is a fortified gate, known as Tour de l'Horloge ("Clock Tower"). Lembeye's large Gothic church has an interesting carved doorway.

Environs

About 17 km (11 miles) from Lembeye is the **Château de Mascaraas**, with 17th-and 18th-century decoration. 21 km (13 miles) away, at **Montaner**, is the 14th-century **Château**, built on the order of Gaston Fébus, and the **Église Saint-Michel**, a church with remarkable frescoes from the 15th and 16th centuries.

Château de Mascaraas
Tel 05 59 04 92 60. **Open** Apr–Sep: Wed–Mon; Oct–Mar: Sat & Sun. compulsory.

Château de Montaner
Tel 05 59 81 98 29. **Open** Apr–Jun and Sep–Oct: Tue–Sun pm; Jul–Aug: daily.

Église Saint-Michel
Tel 05 62 31 42 33. **Open** Jul–Aug: daily pm; Apr–Jun, Sep–Oct: Wed–Mon pm. Jul–Aug: Wed–Mon.

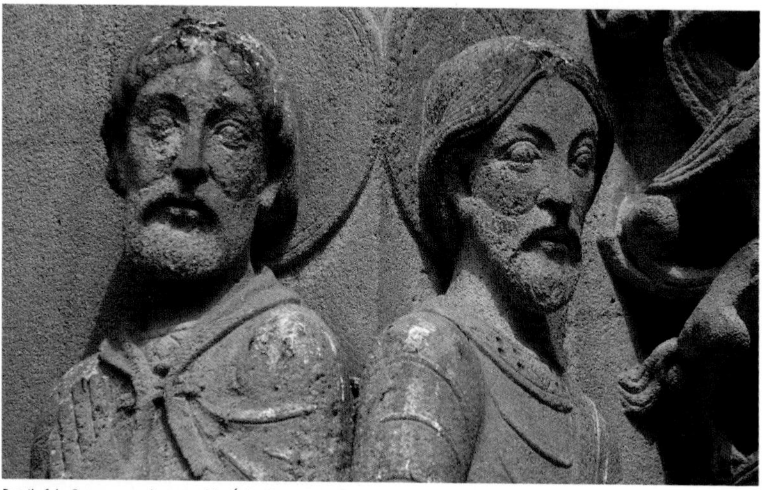

Detail of the Romanesque doorway of the Église Sainte-Foy in Morlaàs

⓫ Tour of Madiran

The vineyards of Madiran and Pacherenc du Vic-Bilh lie at the intersection of Béarn, the Gers and the Hautes-Pyrénées. Madiran's robust, dark red wine acquired an AOC in 1948. Long used as a communion wine, it became known to the wider world thanks to pilgrims who passed through the area on their way to Compostela. Since then, as the quality of Madiran wine has improved, it has become even better known. The lesser-known Pacherenc vineyards produce both a dry and a sweet, white wine.

Tips for Drivers

Road map: C4
Tour length: 38.5km (24 miles)
Stopping-off places: Two pleasant places to stop are the Château d'Aydie on the Domaine Laplace 05 59 04 08 00, and the priory in the village of Madiran, where there is a Maison des Vins 05 62 31 90 67.

④ **Aydie** Between Béarn, Bigorre and the Landes, Aydie is a major centre for the production of Madiran wine, as well as the wines of five other estates. The village is also associated with the writer Joseph Peyré, who lived in a villa here.

③ **Conchez-de-Béarn** From the 16th century, Conchez was the home town of Béarn's aristocracy. It also has some more bourgeois 16th- and 17th-century houses.

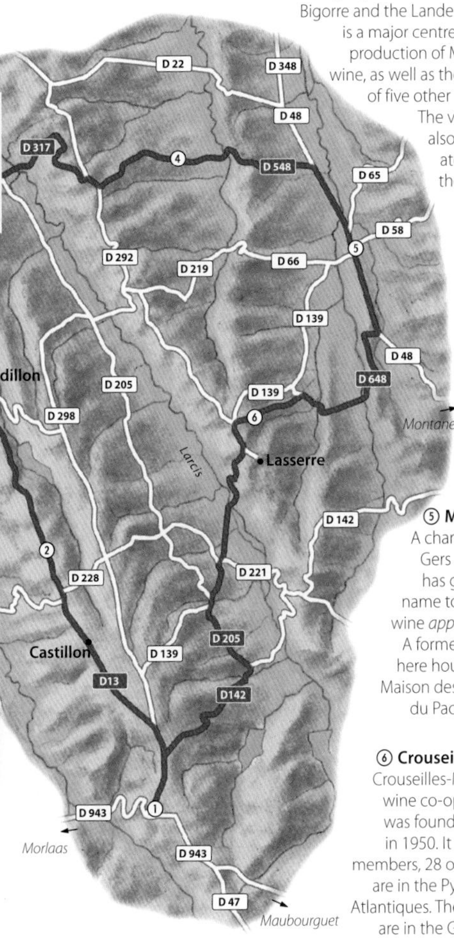

⑤ **Madiran** A characterful Gers town, it has given its name to a local wine *appellation*. A former priory here houses the Maison des Vins et du Pacherenc.

② **Arricau-Bordes** Although the magnificent château here is closed to the public, visitors are welcome to explore the wine cellars, in the former stables. They can also participate in tutored wine tastings. The 25 ha (62 acres) of Arricau-Bordes vineyards produce a very fine wine.

① **Lembeye** In the 17th century, this *bastide* town, 35 km (22 miles) from Pau, was the sixth largest in Béarn.

⑥ **Crouseilles** The Crouseilles-Madiran wine co-operative was founded here in 1950. It has 162 members, 28 of whom are in the Pyrénées-Atlantiques. The others are in the Gers and the Hautes-Pyrénées The co-operative is open to visitors.

0 kilometres 2
0 miles 2

Key

Suggested route

Other roads

⑫ Oloron-Sainte-Marie

Situated at the confluence of the Gave d'Aspe and Gave d'Ossau, Oloron-Sainte-Marie is the capital of Haut Béarn and the gateway to the Aspe valley. In the 11th century, Oloron and the neighbouring bishopric of Sainte-Marie began to expand and merge, becoming a strategic point of trade with the Spanish kingdom of Aragon, as well as a major textile-weaving centre. The two were officially united to create one city in 1858. The most notable feature here is the magnificent 12th-century Romanesque carved doorway of Cathédrale Sainte-Marie. Covered by a porch, it is certainly the finest and best-preserved such doorway in Béarn and features on UNESCO's World Heritage List.

Detail of the doorway of Cathédrale Sainte-Marie

Carving detail
One of the 24 Elders of the Apocalypse is shown holding a mandolin.

Christ in Majesty
Crowned by a halo, symbol of divine power, Christ is shown appeasing two lions, which sit on either side of Him.

Salmon panel
A series of scenes show salmon-fishing in the Gave d'Oloron, with the fish being cut up and smoked.

Doorway capital
Bowed down by an invisible burden and grimacing with pain, these figures symbolize human suffering.

The 12th-century Romanesque doorway of Cathédrale Sainte-Marie

Back-to-Back Atlantes
This carving is also known as "The Chained Saracens".

Monster Swallowing the Damned
The hideous monster shown swallowing two heads is next to a bearded grape-picker.

Quartier Sainte-Croix

The Quartier Sainte-Croix is set above the lower part of Oloron-Sainte-Marie. It stands on the site of a former Roman settlement, known as Iluro. The Église Sainte-Croix, built in the 11th century, has an unusual tower-like belfry. With its Moorish design, the interior of the dome is unique in France. Opposite the church is an attractive group of medieval buildings. The 17th-century Maison Marque houses the **Maison du Patrimoine**. As well as artifacts from ancient Iluro, the museum has an exhibition on the French concentration camp that was set up at Gurs during World War II.

Quartier Notre-Dame

Of interest here are the 19th-century Église Notre-Dame, a former **Capuchin monastery,** and **Marcadet** on place Gambetta, which comes to life when the Friday morning market takes place. It is also pleasant to stroll along the mills in the fountains district, next to the village of Estos.

Contemporary Sculptures

Oloron's streets and parks are graced with eight contemporary sculptures. These refer to the artistic activity that was associated with the traditional pilgrim routes to Compostela. Oloron is a stopping-place on the pilgrim route to Santiago via Col du Somport. The city's tourist office is especially geared to catering to the needs of pilgrims.

VISITORS' CHECKLIST

Practical Information
Road map B4/B5. 11,800.
Allée du Comte-de-Tréville; 05 59 39 98 00. Fri am; traditional fair on 1 May.
Garburade (first Sat in Sep).
tourisme-oloron.com

Transport

Lartigue 1910

2 Avenue Georges-Messier. **Tel** 05 59 39 50 11. **Open** Mon–Fri. Jul–Aug: Mon–Sat or by request.

Along with Nay, Oloron is the major manufacturing centre of the traditional Basque béret. Textiles are still important to the town, although Lartigue 1910, in Quartier Sainte-Marie, is the only surviving weaving workshop that still uses traditional methods.

Oloron-Sainte-Marie, on the Gave d'Aspe

The mountain pastures of Col de la Pierre-Saint-Martin, dotted with outcrops of white limestone

⓭ Barétous Valley

Road map B5. Oloron-Sainte-Marie. Arette 05 59 88 95 38, or La Pierre-Saint-Martin 05 59 66 20 09. Sun in Aramits. Junte du Roncal (13 Jul); Fête des Bergers d'Aramits (third weekend in Sep).

Near the border between the Pays Basque, in France, and Navarre, in Spain, the Barétous valley is a region of sharp contrasts. Woodland, green hillsides and *estives* (summer pastures), grazed by sheep, mix with steep gorges, the lofty, 2,504-m (8218-ft) high Pic d'Anie and the Col de la Pierre-Saint-Martin, a long, arid limestone chasm, thought to be the deepest in the world, that is a paradise for cave-explorers.

Aramits, once the valley's administrative centre, is the birthplace of the fictional Aramis, one of Alexandre Dumas' famous three musketeers. In 1221, the *jurats* (municipal officers) for the Barétous area, met at the Maison de la Vallée here.

Musée du Béret, Nay

Lanne-en-Barétous, birthplace of Porthos, another of Dumas' fictional musketeers, stands near the border with the Pays Basque. Here, a footpath leads to a set of suspended nets that are used to trap passing wood pigeons, on their migratory route over the Pyrenees.

Arette, with 1,135 inhabitants, is the valley's largest town. On 13 August 1967, it was hit by an earthquake. The Centre Sismologique here (tours can be arranged through the tourist office) registers earth tremors in the region. The **Maison de Barétous**, at the tourist office, has an exhibition on life in the valley, and a feature on the Junte du Roncal.

At **Pierre-Saint-Martin**, on Col du Roncal, is an enormous limestone chasm where water rushes through underground caverns and galleries.

Junte Du Roncal

On 13 July each year, at the Col de la Pierre-Saint-Martin, the Junte du Roncal, also known as the *Tribut des Trois Génisses* (Gift of Three Heffers), commemorates a peace treaty that has been in force since 1375, between the inhabitants of the Barétous valley and those of the Roncal valley, in the Spanish province of Navarre. The mayors of each valley take an oath and, to mark it, the Béarnese present the Navarrese with three heffers. In exchange, they can graze their sheep on the *estives* (summer pastures) of their neighbours in the Roncal.

Mayors' oath of agreement

⓮ Nay

Road map C5. 3,600. Place du 8 Mai 1945; 05 59 13 94 99. Coarraze-Nay. Tue & Sat. Festival du Conte (Jul); Fêtes de Nay (last weekend in Aug).

At the beginning of the 12th century, monks from Sainte-Christine in Gabas founded Nay (pronounced "Nye") to provide food and shelter for pilgrims travelling to Compostela. This small town, on the edge of the Hautes-Pyrénées, stands on the Gave de Pau, which becomes swollen with meltwater in spring. In 1302, Marguerite de Moncade made Nay a fortified *bastide* town. It began to prosper during the Middle Ages, thanks to the growth of the weaving industry, reaching the height of its prosperity in the 18th century

For hotels and restaurants in this region see p255 and p271

with the manufacture of Basque bérets and textiles. In 1543, Nay was severely damaged by fire. The Église Saint-Vincent, a single-nave church in the Languedoc Gothic style, originally from the 15th–16th-century, was remodelled when the rest of the town was rebuilt.

The 16th-century **Maison Carrée**, built by Pedro Sacaze, a rich merchant from Aragon, is a Renaissance-style town house with Italian loggias and an inner courtyard. It fell into ruin in the 18th century but has been restored. The upper floors house the **Musée Béarnais**, which features a display on industry in Nay through the ages, with sections on local metalwork, weaving and quarrying.

The **Musée du Béret**, in a former industrial building, traces the history of the béret and shows the stages in its manufacture. Despite being associated with the Pays Basque, this famous type of headgear in fact originates in the Ossau valley. From the industrial revolution onwards, its manufacture was a major source of income in Nay and Oloron-Sainte-Marie. However, béret-making is now in decline.

The Four Evangelists on the façade of the Chapelle Notre-Dame, Bétharram

Maison Carrée and Musée Béarnais
Place de la République. **Tel** 05 59 13 99 65. **Open** Jul–Aug: daily; rest of the year: Tue–Sat.

Musée du Béret
36 Rue Léon Gambetta. **Tel** 05 59 61 91 70. **Open** check website for opening times. **grottes-de-betharram.com**

Vintage poster advertising the Grottes de Bétharram

⓯ Bétharram

Road map C5. 1,035.
Coarraze-Nay. Fête de la Saint-Jean (usually 24 June).

The town's main attraction is a series of caves, the **Grottes de Bétharram**, on five levels, that visitors explore on foot, by boat and on a small train. An amazing array of draped, fringed and lace-like rock formations hang from the walls and ceilings of these great caverns, which have names such as *Le Chaos* and *La Salle des Lustres* (Hall of the Chandeliers).

Bétharram also has a Baroque chapel, the **Chapelle Notre-Dame**, built in the 17th century on the orders of Louis XIII and the counts of Béarn. According to legend, the original chapel here was built in the 14th century after the Madonna had appeared on the banks of the Gave de Pau. A second chapel was destroyed by fire in 1569. The west front of the present chapel is of grey marble, with statues of the Four Evangelists and the Madonna and Child. The interior is unusually opulent: it has black marble pillars, a 17th-century altarpiece, paintings and gilded wooden sculptures.

The chapel is associated with Michel Garicoïts (1797–1863), a priest who is buried here. Founder of the Society of the Priests of the Sacred Heart of Bétharram, he was canonized in 1947.

Grottes de Bétharram
Saint-Pée-de-Bigorre. **Tel** 05 62 41 80 04. **Open** 8 Feb–25 Mar: Mon–Fri; 26 Mar–Oct: daily.
grottes-de-betharram.com

Chapelle Notre-Dame de Bétharram
Lestelle-Bétharram. **Tel** 05 59 71 92 30. **Open** As for the grottoes.

⓰ Ossau Valley

After the Aspe and Barétous valleys, the Ossau valley is the third-largest in Béarn. Beginning south of Pau, it lies at right angles to the Pyrenees and runs right up to Col du Pourtalet, at 1,794 m (5,888 ft), on the border with Spain. Glaciers covered this whole area during the last Ice Age. The lower part of the valley stretches between the towns of Arudy and Laruns. In the upper valley, villages such as Eaux-Chaudes, Gabas and Bious are sited in basins, amid deep gorges and broad plateaux, such as those at Cezy, Soussouéou and Aule, encircled by the rocky outcrops, like the Cirque d'Anéou, below Le Pourtalet. The highest peak in this majestic landscape is the 2,884-m (9,465-ft) high Pic du Midi d'Ossau. The collapsed cone of an extinct volcano, it serves as the emblem of the Haut Béarn.

★ Falaise aux Vautours
This centre at Aste-Béon *(see p239)* is dedicated to the observation of the griffon vulture. Hides set into the cliffside allow visitors to watch these carrion birds in flight, as well as when attending to their nesting chicks.

Eaux-Chaudes
The village takes its name from the hot springs that made it famous and that were very popular in the 19th and early 20th centuries. Various health treatments are still available here.

Haut Ossau
Throughout the summer, flocks of sheep graze on the high-altitude pastures here, watched over by shepherds.

Key
- Main road
- Minor road
- Border with Spain
- Railway line

For map symbols *see back flap*

★ Col d'Aubisque
The road over this pass, which is open from June to September, offers stunning views of the Cirque de Gourette and Cirque du Litor.

VISITORS' CHECKLIST

Practical Information
Road map C5. From Pau, take the N134 to Gan, then the D934 to Laruns. At Col du Pourtalet, the road crosses into Spain, then leads down the Tena valley, in Aragón. Place de Laruns, Laruns; 05 59 05 31 41, or Maison du Parc National des Pyrénées, Avenue de la Gare, Laruns; 05 59 05 41 59.
ossau-pyrenees.com

Transport
Oloron-Sainte-Marie.

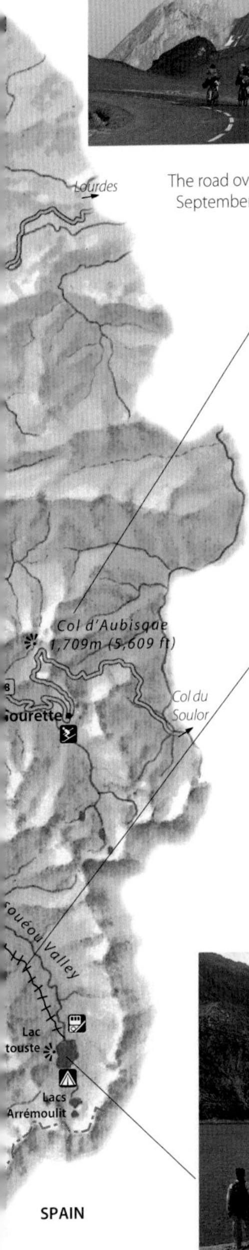

Train to Lac d'Artouste
Running along a narrow-gauge track laid out in 1924, when the dam at Artouste was being built, a little train takes visitors to Lac d'Artouste (May–Sep). This scenic journey, at an altitude of 2,000 m (6,564 ft), takes 50 minutes.

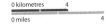

0 kilometres 4
0 miles 4

★ Lac d'Artouste
The departure point for several good walking routes, the lake can also be reached in about 3 hours, along a footpath that starts near the hut at Soques, at the bottom of the valley.

For hotels and restaurants in this region see p255 and p271

Exploring the Ossau Valley

The Ossau valley, which is divided into the Bas Ossau (lower valley) and the Haut Ossau (upper valley), has a strong cultural identity. This is expressed through traditional songs and dances and the continuing use of the Gascon dialect. Life here is centred around the raising of livestock, the main source of income in the area. Until the French Revolution, every village elected *jurats*, municipal officers who took care of the community's welfare and defended its rights and customs. Being governed by such democratic principles gave the valley a certain degree of independence from the central government of France.

Gothic doorway of Église Saint-Vivien in Bielle

Arudy

Place de l'Hôtel-de-Ville; 05 59 05 77 11. Wed & Sat. Fête Locale (1st Sun of Jun).

Arudy is famous for its fine marble. This ranges from a blueish-grey variety, the most common, to the rarest, which is veined with red or a mix of several colours. The Église Saint-Germain, dating from the 16th and 17th centuries, has a pointed dome and capitals carved with bears and cows, the emblems of Ossau.

The 17th-century abbey now houses the **Maison d'Ossau**. This is a visitor centre with displays on the plants and wildlife of the Parc National des Pyrénées and a museum of prehistory. A prehistoric site was discovered here that gave its name to the Arudyan period of the Magdalenian era (14,000–7,500 BC). The village also has some 50 engraved lintels, dating from 1674 to 1893.

Maison d'Ossau
Rue de l'Église. **Tel** 05 59 05 61 71. **Open** Jan–Jun & Sep: Sun–Fri pm; Jul & Aug: daily; Oct–Dec: Sun pm.

Sainte-Colome

2 km (1 mile) east of Arudy. 05 59 05 77 11.

This was a stopping-place on the stretch of the pilgrim route to Compostela that passed through the foothills of the Pyrenees. The town has a 12th–13th-century fortified house, some sturdily built, Ossau-style decorated houses and the Église Saint-Sylvestre, a 15th-century church.

Louvie-Juzon

2.5 km (2 miles) southeast of Arudy. Place de la Mairie; (05) 59 05 61 70. Estives Musicales Internationales (classical music festival), Jul.

The 16th-century **Église Saint-Martin** here is in a very late Gothic style. Its capitals are beautifully carved with depictions of the four ages of man, and with angels, devils and a bestiary. The church also has some interesting furnishings and an 18th-century organ.

Castet

4.5 km (3 miles) southeast of Arudy. 05 59 05 79 51 (Mairie).

This attractive village takes its name from the castle here, the valley's only fortification. Built on a rocky outcrop in the 13th century, it was dismantled by the valley's inhabitants in 1450, and all that remain are two towers. There is also a Romanesque church, the Église Saint-Polycarpe. A road leads down to the harbour, beside a lake on the Gave d'Ossau. Here there are marked pathways and an "espace naturel" devoted to the wildlife living in and around these waters.

Bielle

6 km (4 miles) south of Arudy. 05 59 82 60 36 (Mairie).

As the town where the *jurats* sat, Bielle was the valley's political capital. It remained autonomous until the French Revolution in 1789. The records of the community's legal business were stored in a triple-lock chest, now displayed in the **Église Saint-Vivien**. The tympanum of this 16th-century church is carved with a bear and a cow, emblems of Ossau. Among the town's richly decorated 15th–18th-century houses are Maison Trille and the former convent, which has a square pavilion and a circular tower, with an arched doorway.

Workshop in Nay, making the bells worn by sheep in the Ossau valley

For hotels and restaurants in this region see p255 and p271

Bilhères
6 km (4 miles) southwest of Arudy.
05 59 82 60 92 (Mairie).

Bilhères lies on the D294, which connects the Ossau and Aspe valleys via **Col de Marie-Blanque** at 1,035 m (3,397 ft). The doorways of some of the 16th- and 17th-century houses here are carved with keys. The **Église Saint-Jean-Baptiste** has a painted wooden canopy.

Falaise aux Vautours d'Aste-Béon
Tel 05 59 82 65 49. **Open** Jul–Aug: daily; Apr–Jun & Sep: pm daily.

The cliffs at the villages of Aste and Béon are a protected nature reserve. The visitor centre at the foot of the cliffs displays information about the griffon vulture. Hides in the cliffs allow these birds to be observed at close quarters.

Laruns
Place de Laruns; 05 59 05 31 41. Maison du Parc National des Pyrénées: Avenue de la Gare. **Tel** 05 59 05 41 59. "Noste Dama" fete (15 Aug); Cheese fair (first weekend in Oct).

Laruns is home to the Ossau's tourist office and the **Maison du Parc National**. Here the valley's traditional culture is kept alive at the festival of music and dancing that takes place on 15 August each year. The Pon quarter, in the south of the town, has 16th- and 17th-century houses.

Laruns's municipal district includes the spa town of **Eaux-Chaudes**, about 5 km (3 miles) to the sourth, which was at its peak during the 19th century. There are seven hot springs near the baths.

Dancing in traditional dress at the Laruns festival on 15 August

Route de l'Aubisque
This pass, which leads through stunning mountain scenery, lies beyond Laruns on the D918 to Gourette. Empress Eugénie instigated the construction of this "spa route" and encouraged the development of the health spa of **Eaux-Bonnes** along it.

Béost
2 km (1 mile) northeast of Laruns.
05 59 05 31 93 (Mairie).

A narrow street in this high-set hamlet leads to a 12th-century castle and a church with a fine 14th-century doorway. Some of the 16th-century houses here have their original bread-ovens.

Louvie-Soubiron
4 km (3 miles) northeast of Laruns.
05 59 05 37 09 (Mairie).

White marble from here was used at La Madeleine in Paris and for statuary on Place de la Concorde, and also at the Palais de Versailles. The Romanesque church has a 12th-century font and baptistry.

Brown bears in the mountains between the Ossau and Aspe valleys

⓱ Soussouéou Valley

Road map C5. Beyond Laruns, towards Gabas.

The breathtakingly beautiful, high Soussouéou valley is about 10 km (6 miles) long. Information on hiking here is available from the tourist office at Laruns. If you intend to walk in the valley, drive out of Laruns on the Gabas road, follow it to the Miégebat power station and, 2 km (1 mile) from there, take a left turn to Pont de Goua, a bridge by which you can park your car. From here a footpath leads through the undergrowth. A 30-minute walk brings you to the GR10, a long-distance path. From here, a day's walk along this irregularly signposted but well-used track will take you to Lac d'Artouste.

An alternative route up the valley is to drive through Gabas and park at the **Lac de Fabrèges cable-car** car park, 4 km (3 miles) further on. From here, a 12-minute ride will take you up to **Col de la Sagette**, where you can catch the **Artouste train**, which follows a track up the side of the valley. The journey, in open carriages, takes 55 minutes and offers splendid views of the Pic d'Ossau. From the terminus, it takes about 15 minutes to reach Lac d'Artouste on foot.

You can also walk down from Col de la Sagette to the Soussouéou plateau and, in summer, you can ride up again on a chair lift, the **Télésiège de l'Ours**.

⑱ Pic du Midi d'Ossau

Standing out like a giant shark's tooth, the Pic du Midi d'Ossau soars up to a height of 2,884 m (9,465 ft). Climbing to the top is safe only for experienced mountaineers, but its lower slopes are more easily accessible and offer pleasant walks as well as a number of family attractions. From the lakes and passes around the peak there are spectacular views of Béarn's mountains. Hikers, however, should never set out without a good map and suitable equipment.

One of the many varied landscapes in the Pic du Midi d'Ossau

① **Lac de Bious-Artigues (1,422 m /4,667 ft)** This artificial lake in Haut Béarn is a gateway to the Parc National des Pyrénées. The peaceful, shaded lakeside is a perfect place to relax and, from here, the distinctive shark's-tooth outline of the Pic du Midi d'Ossau is in full view.

② **Pont de Bious (1,500 m/4,923 ft)** This bridge over the Gave de Bious is an intersection and landmark on the GR10 footpath.

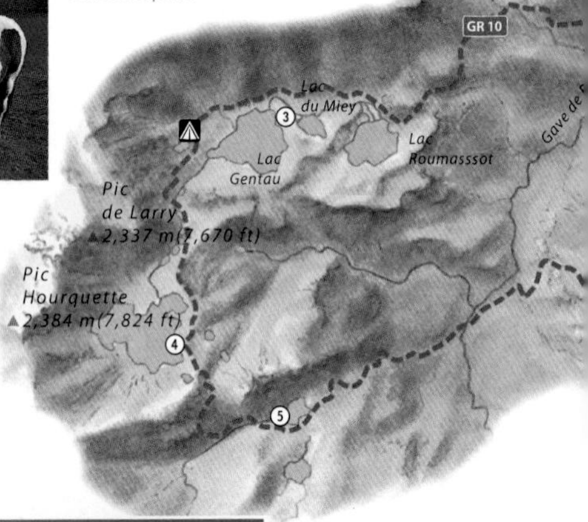

③ **Lacs d'Ayous (1,947 m/6,390 ft)** This lake is one of the most beautiful and best-known sights in the Haut Ossau. From the staffed refuge, where you may spend the night, you can see the rays of the setting sun reflected on the water and the mountainside.

④ **Lac Bersau (2,083 m/ 6,836 ft)** This lake was formed when glaciers melted at the end of the last Ice Age. It is one of the largest glacial lakes in the Pyrenees.

⑤ **Lac Castérau** A little way beyond Lac Bersau, the footpath branches off to the left, leading due east down to the hut at Cap de Pount. Lac Castérau, which is well known to mountaineers, is frozen in winter, but in summer its cool water is perfect for a paddle, to help reinvigorate tired feet.

Key

- Suggested route
- Other roads

0 kilometres 1

0 miles 1

⑧ Col Long de Magnabaigt (1,698 m /5,573 ft) The 11 cromlechs and two tumuli at Magnabaigt show that the area was inhabited in Neolithic times. From the pass there is a gentle walk down to Lac de Bious-Artigues. The footpath leads through more thickly wooded landscape, with dense beech forests.

Lac de Pombie and its staffed refuge, where hikers can have a meal and spend the night

⑦ Col de Suzon (2,127 m /6980 ft) This ascent is relatively gentle, and on this stretch, via the Pic Saoubiste, you will see another aspect of the Pic du Midi. You can either spend an extra night at the refuge at Pombie or walk back down to Bious-Artigues, just a few hours away.

⑥ Col de Peyreget (2,208 m/7,247 ft) From Col de Peyreget, there is a clear view of the four peaks of the Pic du Midi d'Ossau. They each have a name: Petit Pic, Grand Pic, Pointe Jean Santé and Pointe d'Aragon, which is the nearest to Spain.

Tips for Walkers

Road map: C5
Tour length: In good weather the whole tour takes 2 days. The refuges at Lac d'Ayous 05 59 05 37 00 and Lac de Pombie 05 59 05 31 78 are open Jun–Sep. The walk round Lac de Bious-Artigues takes 1 hour, and round both Lac d'Ayous and Lac Bious-Artigues, it takes 5 hours.
Access: To reach the Pic du Midi d'Ossau, take the D934 out of Laruns, then follow the D231. The road from Gabas to Bious-Artigues is open May–Nov, depending on weather conditions.

The Romanesque chapel at Jouers, in the Bedous valley

⓳ Aspe Valley

Road map C4/C5. 2,800. Place Sarraillé, Bedous; 05 59 34 57 57. Oloron-Sainte-Marie. Oloron–Canfranc route. Thu in Bedous; Sun in Etsaut (Jul–Aug). cheese fair at Etsaut (late Jul). **tourisme-aspe.com**

The Aspe valley, south of Oloron-Sainte-Marie, is washed by the Gave d'Aspe. The railway viaduct here was built in 1910 to carry the now-defunct Pau–Canfranc line. Notre-Dame-de-la-Pierre, at **Sarrance**, is the first of four stops along a trail that makes up the **Écomusée de la Vallée d'Aspe**, the valley's open-air museum. This stop focuses on the legend of Sarrance and its pilgrims. Visitors can then see the 17th-century church and cloister. At **Lourdios Ichère**, the open-air museum's next stop, an audiovisual presentation explains the daily life of the inhabitants of this mountain village. **Bedous** is the valley's commercial centre. The GR65, a long-distance path known as the Chemin de Saint-Jacques, runs from Bedous to **Accous**. Here visitors can taste cheeses made by local farmers. The imposing Église Saint-Martin d'Accous suffered severe damage twice in its history, first in 1569, then again in 1793. The **Cirque de Lescun**, at the head of the valley, is a huge green plateau dotted with barns and surrounded by peaks, the Pic Billare, Pic d'Anie and Aiguilles d'Ansabère. **Cette-Eygun** has a fine 12th-century church, the Église Saint-Pierre.

The **Maison du Parc National des Pyrénées at Etsaut** has an exhibition about the Pyrenean brown bear. About 2 km (1 mile) beyond Etsaut, a track joins the **Chemin de la Mâture**. This stretch of the GR10 is dug into the rockface above a sheer drop. In the mid-18th century, pine trunks to be used as masts *(mâture)* for French navy ships were dragged through here. The Chapelle Saint-Jacques at **Borce** once took in pilgrims. Inside are 16th-century frescoes as well as graffiti by Napoleon's soldiers. The main street has picturesque 15th- and 16th-century houses with mullioned windows, Gothic doorways and bread-ovens. The striking **Fort du Portalet** (1860), above the Gorge d'Enfer and its river, was used as a state prison during World War II.

Écomusée de la Vallée d'Aspe (Sarrance)
Tel 05 59 34 57 65. **Open** daily at Accous & Borce; Jul–Sep: daily; Jun: daily pm; Oct–May: Sat–Sun pm at Sarrance & Lourdios. **Closed** Accous: Sun mid-Sep–Jun; Sarrance & Lourdios: Jan. free at Accous.
ecomusee.vallee-aspe.com

Maison du Parc National des Pyrénées
Etsaut. **Tel** 05 59 34 88 30.
Open May–Oct: daily.

Pic de Billare (2,309m/7578ft) and Pic d'Anie (2,504m/8,218ft) from the Labérouat refuge, above Lescun

For hotels and restaurants in this region see p255 and p271

Livestock in Béarn

The shepherds and stock breeders of the mountains of the Haut Béarn earn their living largely from the production of fine cheeses, mostly made from unpasteurized ewe's milk. The shepherds who take their flocks up to the *estives* (high-altitude summer pastures) of the Aspe, Ossau and Barétous valleys not only help to preserve this beautiful landscape, but also keep alive traditional way of life that survives almost nowhere else in the Pyrenees, except in the Pays Basque. Some of Béarn's highest *estives* are difficult and often dangerous to reach. In the more remote pastures, flocks may be attacked by bears, who sometimes take ewes for food.

The Yearly Round
When the snow begins to melt, herds of cows and flocks of sheep return to the high-altitude pastures, or *estives*. Over the summer shepherds live in huts, close to their flocks, although with such modern equipment as radios and solar power, their lives are now much easier. Cheeses made in the mountains are carried down to the villages by donkey.

A small reconstructed farmstead, high up in the mountains

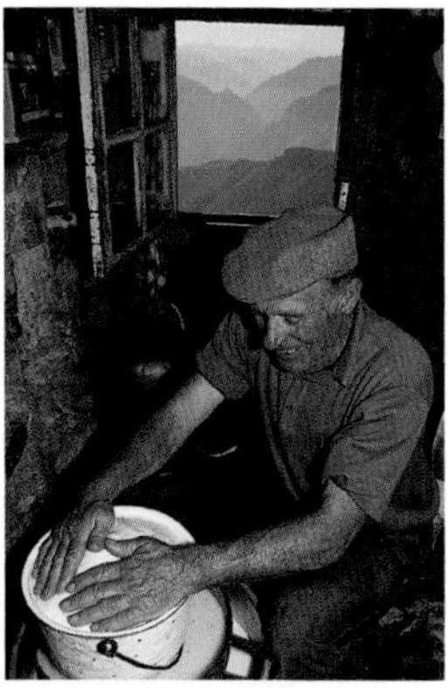

Ossau customs are vigorously kept alive, particularly through traditional music and local dancing.

Ewe's milk cheese is made in the summer. For this, the ewes are milked twice a day.

Traditional instruments are still used today. The most common are a three-hole flute and a stringed tambourine known as a *ttun-ttun*.

Sheep shearing is always done in spring, before the flocks are driven up to the *estives*. However, these fleeces now fetch relatively low prices.

Sheep-rearing in Béarn survives thanks to demand for the cheeses that are made on the *estives*, and to subsidies that allow breeders to live in the mountains. Although a younger generation continues to take up this traditional way of life, it is still in danger of dying out.

IZZERIA
Le Glacier
CHAMBRES

TRAVELLERS' NEEDS

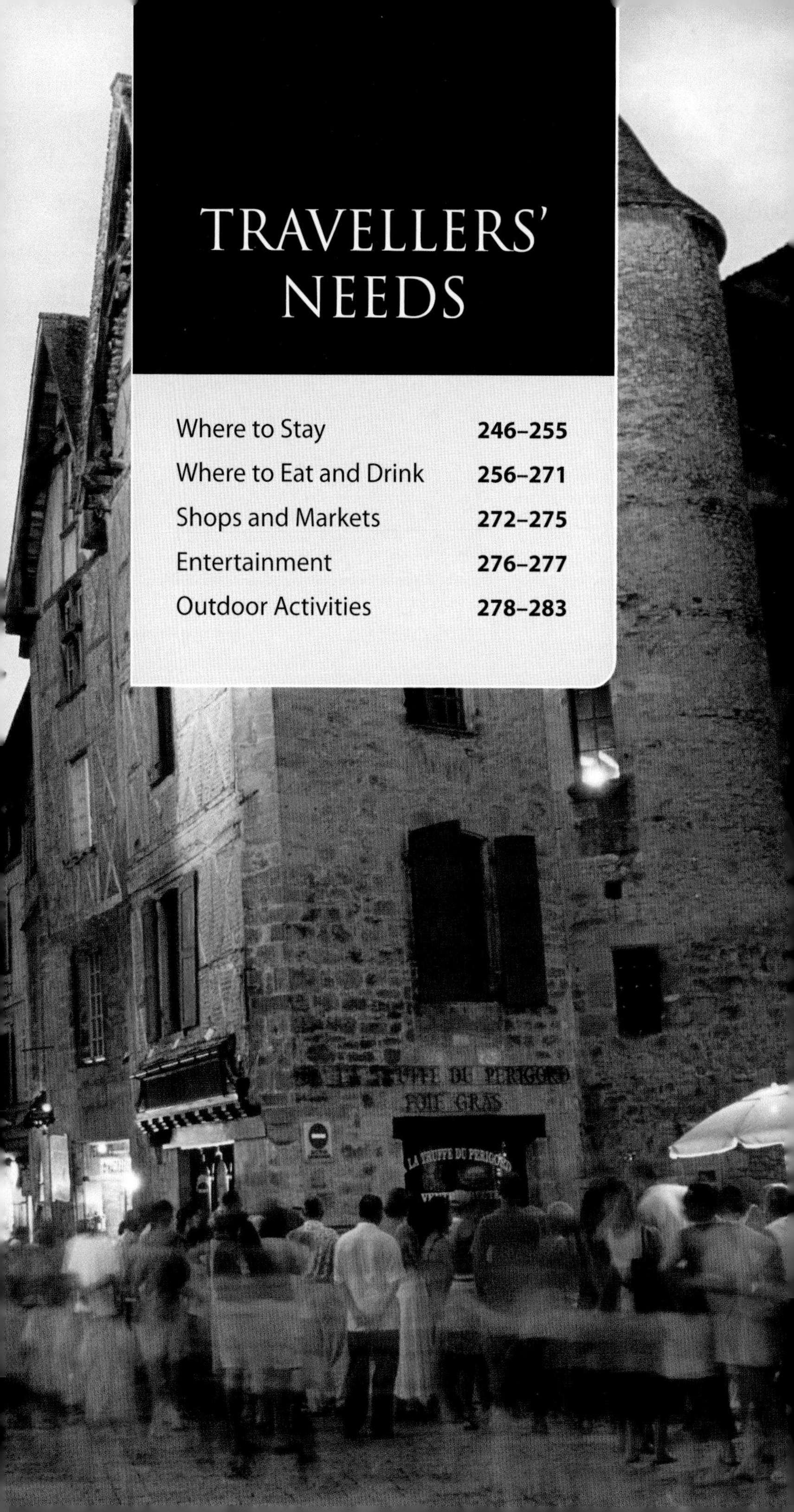

WHERE TO STAY

From Château De Cordeillan-Bages in Pauillac, to Château d'Urtubie in Saint-Jean-de-Luz, the region is dotted with attractive hotels, many of them rich in history. Several grand 18th- and 19th-century townhouses and country residences have been converted into comfortable *chambres d'hôte* (B&Bs), while numerous gîtes, holiday homes and campsites offer affordable options. In small villages, many B&Bs will offer half board, which is a good way to experience French family cooking.

Reservations

In summer, it can be difficult to find a hotel room without booking several months in advance, particularly from mid-July to mid-August, the peak holiday season. Outside this period, hotels are also likely to be fully booked for the duration of major regional events such as Vinexpo, Bordeaux's biennial wine fair, and the world surfing championships at Lacanau in early August. Even hotels and B&Bs at a considerable distance from such events often have no vacant rooms.

Generally, however, the further away from the coast you go, the greater your chances of finding a room, especially in large towns and cities, which are quieter in summer. Check websites for special early booking offers, and compare the hotel's own best price with aggregators such as www.hotels.com, www.lastminute.com or www.booking.com. Town hotels often offer special weekend deals *("Bon week-end en ville")*. Many hotels close in winter, usually between November and February. For more information, contact the regional tourist board, **Comité Régional de Tourisme d'Aquitaine**.

Simple decor at the Peyraguey Maison Rouge in Bommesr *(see p251)*

Les Hortensias du Lac, a hotel at Hossegor *(see p254)*

Hotel Gradings

All accommodation, from simple gîtes to luxurious hotel suites, is graded by the French Ministry of Tourism. Various levels of comfort are indicated by stars, daggers, keys and other symbols. Be aware, however, that the classification may not take into account considerations such as the general appeal of a place or an attractive setting. By contrast, the more up-market hotel associations such as **Relais et Châteaux, Relais du Silence** and **Châteaux et Hôtels Collection** do take such factors into account. Each of these has a website and a central booking system.

Prices

By law, hotels must clearly display their charges, and these should include service and taxes. You may, however, be able to negotiate a lower price outside the peak summer season. Many offer rates for half-board or for full-board, even for stays of just one night *(soirée étape)*. Sometimes these can be excellent value, especially if the hotel has a good restaurant, with local produce on the menu. Nearly all guest houses include breakfast in the price of the room.

Luxury Hotels

All large towns and cities in Aquitaine have top-class hotels, including Biarritz's glamorous seaside Hôtel du Palais. Some of the most luxurious are located in the countryside or in small villages, such as the Relais de la Poste in Soustons *(see 254)*, the Médoc's Château de Cordeillan-Bages *(see p250)*, and Les Prés d'Eugénie *(see p254)*; others, such as the Château de Brindos *(see p254)*, near Biarritz, and the Château de la Treyne in Lacave *(see p251)* enjoy stunning lake-side and river-side locations. The websites of Châteaux et Hôtels de France and Relais et Châteaux list many such establishments.

Historic Hotels

Southwestern France is especially rich in historic buildings that have been converted into hotels, where guests can immerse themselves in the region's rich past. Examples include the antiques-filled Château Camiac *(see p250)*, located amid the vines in Creon, the fairytale Château de la Côte in Brantôme *(see p251)* and the elegant Château d'Urtubie *(see p255)*, in Saint-Jean-de-Luz, where guests are welcomed by the count himself. Others are located in more

◀ Street cafes on the Place de la Liberté

humble yet charming structures, such as mills (the Moulin de la Beune in Les Eyzies, *see p251*); while still others have been inns for centuries (the 17th-century Ithurria, in Ainhoa, *see p254*).

Interiors of Les Pres d'Eugenie at Eugenie-Les-Bains *(see p254)*

Boutique Hotels

Increasingly popular are the region's well-equipped, chic boutique hotels. Perhaps the best known is Bordeaux's Hauterives & Restaurant St James *(see p250)*, designed by Jean Nouvel and set in four pavilions around a 17th-century vinegrower's house. Many others are along the coast: one of the most stylish is Lège-Cap-Ferret's Coté Sable. Others, like the Maison de la Halle near Duras *(see p252)*, are tucked away in tiny villages.

Classic Hotels

This category encompasses most purpose-built hotels from the mid-19th century on, which are generally a good choice for families. Many of these, like the L'Oyat in Lacanau-Océan *(see p250)*, are by the beach. Establishments marked "Station Kid" are particularly suitable for families with very young children.

Many good, moderately priced, independent, family-run hotels belong to the **Logis de France** association, whose members offer accommodation with charm and character. The **Fédération Nationale des Tables et Auberges de France** provides information on hotels that take special pride in their restaurants; the Relais du Silence concentrates on hotels located in peaceful rural settings.

This category also includes chain hotels, which do provide a guaranteed standard of comfort, although they often can seem rather impersonal. Exceptions are some of the hotels of the **Sofitel** or **Best Western** chains.

Chambres d'Hôtes (B&Bs)

Bed and breakfasts *(chambres d'hôte)* offer comfortable accommodation, often in quiet or out-of-the-way places. Prices vary according to the degree of comfort and the facilities – many in the southwest are in châteaux or other historic buildings and are quite luxurious. Some may have a room especially equipped for families. Breakfast is frequently included in the price and is often very filling. French *chambres d'hôte* associations include **Gîtes de France** *(see p249)* and **Fleurs de Soleil**.

Indoor swimming pool at the spa town of Salies-de-Béarn *(see p255)*

Spas & Thalassotherapy

Most of Aquitaine's health and fitness centres are in the Landes and Pays Basque. There are high-class establishments near Biarritz, such as the thalassotherapy centre at the Grand Hôtel Loreamar in Saint-Jean-de-Luz (*see p255*). There are also several spa resorts in the Pyrénées-Atlantiques, including Cambo-les-Bains, Les Eaux-Bonnes, Les Eaux-Chaudes and Salies-de-Béarn. With its 17 spa centres, Dax *(see p254)* is the Landes' health-treatment capital, although none matches the luxurious setting of Les Prés d'Eugénie spa in Eugénie-les-Bains *(see p254)*, with its famous restaurant. There are also several thalassotherapy centres in the Gironde, including Les Sources de Caudalie *(see p250)*, the pioneer of vinotherapy treatments using vine and grape extracts. For others, check listings on the **Chaîne Thermale du Soleil** website. City hotels increasingly offer spas and well-being centres, such as the glamorous facilities in the Grand Hôtel in Bordeaux *(see p250)* or the Grand Hôtel Loreamar in St-Jean-de-Luz.

Gîtes & Holiday Rentals

A country gîte *(gîte rural)* is a house, or furnished detached building, with one or more bedrooms, a dining-sitting room, a kitchen or kitchenette and a bathroom. Gîtes can be rented for a few days or for a weekend, but are most often rented for a minimum of one week. Gîtes de France is an association that guarantees certain well-defined levels of comfort (indicated by 1–5 blades of wheat symbols). All the gîtes in this association are regularly checked and graded by Gîtes de France, which has five agencies in Aquitaine.

Another reliable organization is **Clévacances**, whose members offer high quality accommodation with a personal touch. This applies both to rented accommodation and to individual rooms in B&Bs. There are five grades of comfort.

The website of **Aquitaine Location Vacances** is also useful for people who want to rent a house of character. Most local tourist offices also issue lists giving full details of all rentable accommodation in their area.

Youth Hostels

Youth hostels offer inexpensive accommodation to anyone, regardless of their age. However, to stay in a youth hostel, you must have a membership card, the Carte de la Fédération Unie des Auberges de Jeunesse **(FUAJ)**, which can be obtained from any youth hostel. Although Bordeaux and Arcachon each have a youth hostel, most are concentrated in the region between the coast of the Pays Basque and its hinterland.

Château d'Urtubie, a fortified castle, at Urrugne *(see p255)*

Campsites

Aquitaine has a large number of campsites, many belonging to **Camping Qualité Aquitaine**. Members of this association must display, and adhere to, a clear pricing structure, and maintain high standards of hygiene and cleanliness. The Féderation Française de Camping et Caravaning has a useful website with a guide to campsites and their facilities (www.ffcc.fr).

Disabled Travellers

Many hotels in southwest France (especially the newer ones) and many B&Bs have at least one or two rooms especially designed to accommodate visitors who are physically challenged. Information on these is available from **Tourisme et Handicap** and **Association des Paralysés de France (APF)**, from **Mobility International USA** and the UK-based **Tourism for All**. The APF has teamed up with Gîtes de France to recommend country gîtes, B&Bs and other places to stay that are suitable for people with physical disabilities. These places appear in the on-line listings for each *département*.

Recommended Hotels

The hotels and B&Bs recommended in this guide have been chosen from across five categories: Luxury, Historic, Boutique, Classic and B&B. These have been selected for the

The 18th-century Auberge du Moulin de Labique in Saint-Eutrope-de-Born, near Villeréal *(see p253)*

quality of accommodation they offer, for their location in some of Southwest France's most popular destinations and in some cases, because they offer value for money.

Among the listings you'll find hotels or B&Bs that have been designated DK Choices for one or more outstanding feature. This could be exceptional facilities, the beauty of the location, the views, or anything that lifts it and sets it apart from others in its category.

Swimming pool at the Eskualduna campsite, near Hendaye *(see p203)*

DIRECTORY

General Information

Comité Régional de Tourisme d'Aquitaine
4/5 Place Jean Jaurès, 33074 Bordeaux
Tel 05 56 01 70 00.
W tourisme-aquitaine.fr

Chain Hotels

Best Western
W bestwestern.com

Sofitel
W sofitel.com

Classic Hotels

Fédération Nationale des Tables et Auberges de France
W tables-auberges.com

Logis de France
W logishotels.com

Relais du Silence
Tel 01 70 23 81 63 (central booking).
W relaisdusilence.com

Luxury Hotels

Châteaux et Hôtels Collection
Tel 01 72 72 92 02 (central booking number from abroad); 08 11 74 17 40 in France.
W chateaux hotels.com

Relais et Châteaux
Tel 0825 82 51 80 (central booking). Freephone 00 800 200 000 02 UK, Freephone 1 800 735 2478 USA
W relaischateaux.com

B&BS

Fleurs de Soleil
W fleursdesoleil.fr

Gîtes de France
59 rue Saint-Lazare, 75439 Paris Cedex 09
Tel 01 49 70 75 75
W gites-de-france.fr

Thalassotherapy & Hydrotherapy

Chaîne Thermale du Soleil
Tel 0800 05 05 32.
W chainethermale.fr

Country Gîtes

See Gîtes de France, above

Fédération Nationale des Locations de France Clévacances
54 boulevard de l'Embouchure, BP 22361, 31022 Toulouse.
Tel 05 32 10 82 30 .
W clevacances.com

Rented Accommodation

Aquitaine Location Vacances
W aquitaine-location-vacances.com

Youth Hostels

Fédération Unie des Auberges de Jeunesse (FUAJ)
9 rue Pajol, 75018 Paris.
Tel 01 44 89 87 27.
W fuaj.org

Campsites

Camping Qualité Aquitaine
Contact using website
W campings-aquitaine.com

Disabled Travellers

Association Tourisme et Handicap
43 rue Marx Dormoy, 75018 Paris.
Tel 01 44 11 10 41.
W tourisme-handicaps.org

Association des Paralysés de France
17 bd Auguste Blanqui, 75013 Paris.
Tel 01 40 78 69 90.
Tel 05 56 08 67 30. (Gironde: Le Bouscat)
Tel 05 58 74 67 92. (Landes: Dax)
W apf.asso.fr

Mobility International USA
132 E Broadway, Eugene, Oregon 97401.
Tel (541) 343 12 84.
W miusa.org

Tourism for All
7A Pixel Mill 44 Appleby Road, Kendal, Cumbria LA9 6ES.
Tel (0845) 124 99 71.
W tourismforall.org.uk

Where to Stay

Gironde

ARCACHON: Hôtel Le Dauphin €€
Classic **Map** B2
7 avenue Gounod, 33120
Tel *05 56 83 02 89*
W dauphin-arcachon.com
Bright and comfortable rooms in a 19th-century villa-hotel.

ARCACHON BASIN: La Guérinière €€
Boutique **Map** B2
18 cours de Verdun, Gujan Mestras, 33470
Tel *05 56 66 08 78*
W laguerinière.com
Contemporary decor, a garden and pool, as well as a Michelin-starred restaurant.

BLAYE: Villa Prémayac €€
B&B **Map** C1
13 rue de Prémayac, 33390
Tel *05 57 42 27 39*
W villa-premayac.com
Rooms in this 18th-century villa have a chic, Bohemian ambience.

BORDEAUX: Acanthe €
Classic **Map** C2
12–14 rue St-Remi, Quartier St Pierre, 33000
Tel *05 56 81 66 58*
W acanthe-hotel-bordeaux.com
Bright, soundproof rooms, some with balconies and views of the Garonne. Friendly staff.

BORDEAUX: La Maison du Lierre €
Classic **Map** C2
57 rue Huguerie, 33000
Tel *05 56 51 92 71*
W maisondulierre.com
Enjoy the warm atmosphere at this restored 20th-century mansion.

BORDEAUX: Best Western Bordeaux Bayonne Etche-Ona €€
Classic **Map** C2
15 cours Intendance, 33000
Tel *05 56 48 00 88*
W bordeaux-hotel.com
Two 18th-century mansions: the contemporary Bayonne and the Basque-inspired Etche-Ona.

BORDEAUX: La Maison Bordeaux €€
Boutique **Map** C2
113 rue de Docteur Albert Barraud, 33000
Tel *05 56 44 00 45*
W lamaisonbordeaux.com
An 18th-century mansion with ultra modern decor. Delightful bar.

BORDEAUX: Hauterives & Restaurant St James €€€
Boutique **Map** C2
Place Camille-Hostein, Bouliac, 33270
Tel *05 57 97 06 00*
W saintjames-bouliac.com
Four pavilions with minimalist, high-tech rooms and superb city views, designed by Jean Nouvel.

DK Choice

BORDEAUX: Le Grand Hôtel Bordeaux €€€
Luxury **Map** C2
2-5 Place de la Comedie, 33000
Tel *05 57 30 44 44*
W ghbordeaux.com
Designer Jacques Garcia's fabulous overhaul of this historic hotel has been part of Bordeaux's revival. The rooms, even though the standard ones are a little small, have been beautifully redone. The Bain de Léa spa is grand and the rooftop Jacuzzi bar just great.

BOURG: Château de la Grave €
B&B **Map** C2
2km (1 mile) from Bourg centre, 33710
Tel *05 57 68 41 49*
W chateaudelagrave.com
This 16th-century château has charming, antique-decorated rooms, stunning vineyard views and wonderful wines.

CAP-FERRET: La Maison du Bassin €€
Boutique **Map** B2
5 rue des Pionniers, 33950
Tel *05 56 60 60 63*
W lamaisondubassin.com
Ultra-chic, with a laid-back colonial ambience, complete with rum cocktails and verandah dining.

Simple and bright decor at Château Cordeillan-Bages in Pauillac

Price Guide
Unless specified, price categories are for a standard double room per night during the high season, including breakfast and taxes.

€	up to €100
€€	€100 to 200
€€€	over €200

CREON: Château Camiac €€€
Historic **Map** C2
Route de la Fôret, D121, 33670
Tel *05 56 23 20 85*
W chateaucamiac.com
A 19th-century château amid the vineyards, with antique-filled bedrooms, a fine restaurant, pool and a cheaper annexe.

LACANAU-OCEAN: Best Western Golf Hôtel Lacanau €
Classic **Map** B2
Domaine de l Ardilouse, 33680
Tel *05 56 03 92 92*
W golf-hotel-lacanau.fr
Modern rooms and spa over-looking the forest. Special packages, bike hire avaiilable.

LEGE-CAP-FERRET: Côté Sable €€€
Boutique **Map** B2
37 Boulevard de la Plage, 33970
Tel *05 57 17 07 27*
W cotesable.fr
Elegant, individually decorated rooms with views over forests and the bay; Clarins spa.

LIBOURNE: Château de la Rivière €€
B&B **Map** C2
8km (5 miles) northwest of Libourne, La Rivière, 33126
Tel *05 57 55 56 51*
W chateau-de-la-riviere.com
Renaissance period château surrounded by vineyards and gardens.

MARTILLAC: Les Sources de Caudalie €€€
Luxury **Map** C2
Chemin Smith Haut Lafitte, 33650
Tel *05 57 83 83 83*
W sources-caudalie.com
Idyllic setting with enchanting rooms, gourmet restaurant and a spa that invented vinotherapy.

PAUILLAC: Château Cordeillan-Bages €€€
Luxury **Map** B1
Route des châteaux, 33250
Tel *05 56 59 24 24*
W cordeillanbages.com
Once a 17th-century Carthusian monastery, now a sophisticated hotel amid the vines with a renowned restaurant.

Peyraguey Maison Rouge, set in pretty natural surroundings in Sauternes

SAINTE CROIX DE MONT: Château Lamarque €
B&B **Map** C2
6km (4 miles) east of Cadillac, 33410
Tel *05 56 62 01 21*
W ch-lamarque.com
Two suites, pretty pool, and home-made jams for breakfast.

SAUTERNES: Peyraguey Maison Rouge €
B&B **Map** C3
2km (1 mile) from Sauternes, Bommes-Sauternes, 33210
Tel *05 57 31 07 55*
W peyraguey-sauternes.com
Ancient house of a winemaker with three elegant bedrooms. Can organize wine-tastings.

SOULAC-SUR-MER: Hôtel Michelet €
Classic **Map** B1
1 rue Bernard Baguenard, 33780
Tel *05 56 09 84 18*
W hotelmichelet.fr
Cheerful family-run hotel, a short walk from the beach.

ST-ÉMILION: Au Logis des Remparts €€
Classic **Map** C2
18 rue Guadet, 33330
Tel *05 57 24 70 43*
W logisdesremparts.com
Charming hotel with wooded grounds on the village ramparts.

ST-ÉMILION: Hostellerie de Plaisance €€€
Luxury **Map** C2
Place du Clocher, 33330
Tel *05 57 55 07 55*
W hostellerie-plaisance.com
Overlooking St-Emilion. Great service, superb restaurant.

ST-MACAIRE: Hôtel Les Feuilles d'Acanthe €
Historic **Map** C2
5 rue de l'Eglise, 33490
Tel *05 56 62 33 75*
W feuilles-dacanthe.com
Simple and elegant rooms in a 16th-century merchant's house. Has a Jacuzzi and indoor pool.

Périgord and Quercy

ANNESSE-ET-BEAULIEU: Château de Lalande €€
Historic **Map** D1
Route de Saint-Astier, 24430
Tel *05 53 54 52 30*
W chateau-lalande-perigord.com
In a park with ancient trees; classic French wallpapered rooms.

BERGERAC: Château des Merles €€
Boutique **Map** D2
12km (7 miles) east of Bergerac, Tulières, Mouleydier, 24520
Tel *05 53 63 13 42*
W lesmerles.com
Neo-Classical château with stylish rooms and a wellness centre.

BEYNAC: Hôtel du Château €
Classic **Map** E2
La Balme, 24220
Tel *05 53 29 19 20*
W hotel-beynac-dordogne.com
Attractive rooms, a good restaurant, and friendly service.

BRANTÔME: Château de la Côte €€
Historic **Map** D1
5km (3 miles) south of Brantôme, Biras-Bordeilles, 24310
Tel *05 53 03 70 11*
W chateaudelacote.com
One of Périgord's most enchanting Renaissance-era château hotels.

CAHORS: Le Grand Hotel Terminus €
Historic **Map** E3
Avenue Charles de Freycinet, 46000
Tel *05 65 53 32 00*
W balandre.com
Elegant 1920s mansion, comfortable rooms and great restaurant.

CHANCELADE: Château des Reynats €€
Historic **Map** D1
Avenue des Reynats, 24650
Tel *05 53 03 53 59*
W chateau-hotel-perigord.com
Endearing 19th-century château with smart rooms, a top restaurant and a cheaper bistro.

DOMME: L'Esplanade €€
Classic **Map** E2
Esplanade de la Barre, 24250
Tel *05 53 28 31 41*
W esplanade-perigord.com
Elegant rooms, some with four-poster beds. Clifftop location.

FIGEAC: Hôtel des Bains €
Historic **Map** F2
1 rue du Griffoul, 46100
Tel *05 65 34 10 89*
W hoteldesbains.fr
A 19th-century bathhouse; great rooms, pretty garden terrace.

LA ROQUE GAGEAC: Auberge de la Plume d'Oie €
B&B **Map** E2
Le Bourg, 24250
Tel *05 53 29 57 05*
W aubergelaplumedoie.com
Charming stone-built inn with stylish rooms and gourmet food.

DK Choice

LACAVE: Château de la Treyne €€€
Historic **Map** E2
Route de Souillac à Rocamadour, 46200
Tel *05 65 27 60 60*
W chateaudelatreyne.com
This 14th-17th-century château, surrounded by acres of woodland, overhangs the Dordogne River. Rooms are irresistibly romantic and the Michelin-starred restaurant is truly exceptional. Summer dining under the stars on the riverside terrace is unforgettable.

LES EYZIES-DE-TAYAC: Le Moulin de la Beune €
Historic **Map** E2
2 rue du Moulin-Bas, 24620
Tel *05 53 06 94 33*
W moulindelabeune.com
Light, airy rooms in a tastefully converted old mill with lush riverside gardens.

MARTEL: Relais Ste-Anne €€
Historic **Map** E2
Rue du Pourtanel, 46600
Tel *05 65 37 40 56*
W relais-sainte-anne.com
Former girls' boarding school now has beautifully appointed rooms and a heated pool.

MAUZAC: La Métairie €€
Luxury **Map** D2
Millac, 24150 Mauzac et Grand Castang
Tel *05 53 22 50 47*
W la-metairie.com
Graceful 19th-century manor with well appointed, individually decorated rooms and a large pool.

MERCUES: Château de Mercuès €€€
Luxury **Map** E3
Mercuès 46090
Tel *05 65 20 00 01*
W chateaudemercues.com
Princely rooms, gourmet dining, and extraordinary cellars distinguish this 13th-century château.

MOISSAC: Le Moulin de Moissac €
Classic **Map** E3
Esplanade du Moulin, 82200
Tel *05 63 32 88 88*
W lemoulindemoissac.com
Former riverside mill with well-equipped rooms, spa and restaurant in a tranquil setting.

MONTPAZIER: Edward 1er €€
Historic **Map** D2
5 rue Saint Pierre, 24540
Tel *05 53 22 44 00*
W hoteledward1er.com
Exquisite 19th-century château; elegant bedrooms with antiques and canopied beds.

NONTRON: Le Grand Hôtel Pélisson €
Classic **Map** D1
3 place Alfred Agard, 24300
Tel *05 53 56 11 22*
W hotel-pelisson-nontron.com
Friendly, unassuming hotel, family-run for generations.

PERIGUEUX: Ibis Périgueux Centre €
Classic **Map** D1
8 Boulevard Georges Saumande, 24000
Tel *05 53 53 64 58*
W ibis.com
Great views of the many-domed cathedral. Big buffet breakfast.

PUY L'EVEQUE: Domaine du Haut Baran €€
B&B **Map** E3
5km (3 miles) west of Puy l'Evêque, Duravel, 46700
Tel *05 65 24 63 24*
W hautbaran.com
Stone farmhouse with charming rooms in secluded woodland.

ROCAMADOUR: Amadour €
Classic **Map** E2
L'Hospitalet, 46500
Tel *05 65 33 73 50*
W amadour-hotel.com

Tasteful and elegant interiors at the Chateau-de-Cambes, Agen

Delightful budget option with simple but modern and comfortable rooms.

SARLAT: Clos la Boëtie €€€
Luxury **Map** E2
97 avenue de Selves, 24200
Tel *05 53 29 44 18*
W closlaboetie-sarlat.com
Magnificent mansion; romantic rooms and private grounds.

ST JULIEN DE CREMPSE: Manoir du Grand Vignoble €
Historic **Map** D2
St Julien de Crempse, 24140
Tel *05 53 24 23 18*
W manoirdugrandvignoble.com
A 17th-century manor set in forest and parkland. Lots of activities.

TREMOLAT: Le Vieux Logis €€€
Historic **Map** D2
Route des Champs, Le Bourg, 24510
Tel *05 53 22 80 06*
W vieux-logis.com
Farm dating from the 16th century, with elegant rooms and apartments and a fabulous restaurant.

Lot-et-Garonne

AGEN: Le Colombier du Touron €
Classic **Map** D3
6km (4 miles) west of Agen, 187 avenue des Landes, Brax, 47310
Tel *05 53 87 87 91*
W colombierdutouron.com
Family-run hotel in an 18th century building. Nice, shady terrace and good restaurant.

AGEN: Château de Cambes €€
B&B **Map** D3
6km (4 miles) from Agen, in Cambes, 47480 Pont-du-Casse
Tel *05 53 95 38 73*
W chateau-de-cambes.com
Renaissance château. Lovely rooms with unusual themes.

AGEN: Hôtel Château des Jacobins €€
Historic **Map** D3
1 place des Jacobins, 47000
Tel *05 53 47 03 31*
W chateau-des-jacobins.com
Peaceful little château with period rooms in a walled garden. Parking available.

AIGUILLON: Moulin de Rocquebert €
B&B **Map** D3
8 miles (12km) from Aiguillon, Route de Verteuil, Grateloup-Saint-Gayrand, 47400
Tel *05 53 93 78 22*
W moulinderocquebert.fr
Old mill, with a glass floor over the river. Lovely rooms.

ASTAFFORT: Fondragon les Cedres €
B&B **Map** D3
Astaffort, 47220
Tel *05 53 67 06 39*
Art Deco residence in the middle of a huge garden. Offers an excellent sit-down breakfast.

CASTILLONNES: Hôtel Restaurant Les Remparts €
Classic **Map** D2
26 rue de la Paix, 47330
Tel *05 53 49 55 85*
W hotelrestaurant-lesremparts.com
Attractive 17th-century manor with spacious rooms and a romantic restaurant.

CASTILLONNES: La Maison Prideaux €€
B&B **Map** D2
10km (6 miles) east of Castillonnès, Le Bourg, Parranquet, 47210
Tel *05 53 49 01 19*
W gites-dordogne.com
Well-furnished stone-built farmhouse offering golf and cookery weekends. Charming rooms and gîtes.

DURAS: La Maison de la Halle €€
Boutique **Map** D2
7km (4 miles) south of Duras, Lévignac-de-Guyenne, 47120
Tel *05 53 94 37 61*
An 18th-century mansion with rooms in rustic-chic modelled by the interior designer owners. Wonderful views.

LAPLUME: Château de Lassalle €€
Historic **Map** D3
12km (7 miles) southwest of Laplume, Brimont, 47310
Tel *05 53 95 10 58*
W chateaudelassalle.com
Tranquil 18th-century residence with a relaxed, country house atmosphere and a gourmet restaurant. Parking available.

Key to Price Guide *see page 250*

LAUZUN: Château de Péchalbet €
B&B **Map** D2
6km (4 miles) west of Lauzun, Agnac, 47800
Tel *05 53 83 04 70*
W pechalbet.free.fr
Peaceful rooms in a beautiful 17th-century stone manor; table d'hôte by request.

MARMANDE: Château de Malvirade €€
B&B **Map** D3
8km (5 miles) south of Marmande, Grézet-Cavagnan, 47250
Tel *05 53 20 61 31*
W malvirade.com
Splendid Renaissance château with striking period guest rooms.

MONCLAR D'AGENAIS: Château de la Seiglal €
B&B **Map** D3
2km (1 mile) from Monclar, 47380
Tel *05 53 41 81 30*
W chateau-de-la-seiglal.fr
Country-style rooms in a 19th-century château, set among ancient cedars.

MONFLANQUIN: Les Bourdeaux €
B&B **Map** D3
2km (1 mile) from Monflanquin, 47150
Tel *05 53 49 16 57*
W lesbourdeaux.com
Comfortable rooms with extra long beds, magnificent views, boules, and a giant chess set.

NERAC: Auberge du Vieux Pont €
Historic **Map** D3
19 rue Séderie, 47600
Tel *05 53 97 51 04*
W vieux-pont.com
Appealing old inn on the River Baise with a waterfront restaurant. Balconies have delightful views.

DK Choice

PENNE D'AGENAIS: Le Relais de Roquefereau €€
B&B **Map** D3
Roquefereau, 47140
Tel *05 53 41 40 62*
W lerelaisderoquefereau.com
Enjoy stunning views over a lush valley at this elegantly restored 13th-century inn. Besides two gorgeous guest rooms, Le Relais offers a romantic yurt and two family gîtes sleeping up to seven.

PUJOLS: Hôtel des Chênes €
Classic **Map** D3
4km (2 miles) southwest of Pujols, Lieu dit Bel-Air, 47300
Tel *05 53 49 04 55*
W hoteldeschenes.com
Cheerful rooms, some family, in a peaceful atmosphere, with panoramic views of Pujols.

PUYMIROL: Michel Trama €€€
Luxury **Map** D3
52 rue Royale, 47270
Tel *05 53 95 31 46*
W aubergade.com
Aristocratic medieval residence with gorgeous rooms, courtyards, and Michelin-starred restaurant.

SERIGNAC-SUR-GARONNE: Le Prince Noir €
Historic **Map** D3
6 route de Menjoulan, 47310
Tel *05 53 68 74 30*
W le-prince-noir.com
Family-run hotel in a 17th-century monastery; gourmet restaurant.

TOURNON D'AGENAIS: Château de l'Hoste €
Historic **Map** E3
10km (6 miles) southwest of Tournon d'Agenais, St-Beauzeil, 82150
Tel *05 63 95 25 61*
W chateaudelhoste.com
Warm, welcoming 18th-century manor with a huge park.

VILLEREAL: Auberge du Moulin de Labique €
B&B **Map** D2
8km (5 miles) south of Villeréal, Saint-Eutrope de Born, 47210
Tel *05 53 01 63 90*
W moulin-de-labique.net
Rustic chic on an enormous 18th-century estate. Delicious regional home cooking.

Landes

AIRE-SUR-L'ADOUR: La Maison du Bos €
B&B **Map** C4
9km (6 miles) southwest of Aire-sur-l'Adour, Miramont-Sensacq, 40320
Tel *05 58 79 93 18*
W maisondubos.com
Ancient farmhouse, lovingly restored. Private entrance to each room. Kitchen available to guests.

BISCAROSSE: La Caravelle €
Classic **Map** B3
3km (2 miles) north of Biscarosse, Route des Lacs, Ispe, 40600
Tel *05 58 09 82 67*
W lacaravelle.fr
Tranquil, old-fashioned hotel right on the lake. Half board in summer.

BISCAROSSE: Hype Hôtel €€
Boutique **Map** B3
40 rue du Lieutenant de Vaisseau Paris, 40600
Tel *05 58 07 36 35*
W hypehotel.fr
Beautifully decorated, modern rooms, great service and an exceptional breakfast.

CAPBRETON: Hôtel Aquitaine €
Classic **Map** A4
66 avenue du Marechal Delattre De Tassigny, 40130
Tel *05 58 72 38 11*
W hotelaquitaine-capbreton.com
Spacious rooms and a flower-filled garden, a short stroll from the beach. Great for families.

CAPBRETON: Baya Hotel & Spa €€
Classic **Map** A4
85 avenue de Maréchal de Lattre de Tassigny, 40130
Tel *05 58 41 80 00*
W bayahotel.com
Modern beachfront hotel and spa offering many sporting activities.

CASTETS: Les Bruyères €
Classic **Map** B4
Route André Dupuy Z.A.C. de Cazalieu - 40260 Castets
Tel *05 58 55 05 30*
W hotel-lesbruyeres.com
Modern hotel with a good restaurant, ideally based to explore Landes.

CASTETS: La Bergerie St Michel €€
B&B **Map** B4
4km (2 miles) west of Castets, 50 Chemin Plomb, St Michel-Escalus, 40550
Tel *05 58 48 74 04*
W bergeriestmichel.fr
Ancient farmhouse, stylishly furnished with country antiques.

CREON D'ARMAGNAC: Le Poutic €
B&B **Map** C3
Route de Cazauban, 40240
Tel *05 58 44 66 97*
W lepoutic.com
Beautiful stone farmhouse with contemporary furnishings.

Stylish exteriors at the Hype Hotel in Biscarosse

For more information on types of hotels *see page 248*

Garden seating in the romantic grounds of Les Prés d'Eugénie, Eugenie-Les-Bains

DAX: L'Espace Thermal €
Classic **Map** B4
1 Boulevard Albert Camus, 40104 Dax
Tel *05 58 56 50 00*
W espacethermal.fr
Central and affordable self-catering apartments for one to four people. Buffet breakfast.

EUGENIE-LES-BAINS: La Maison Rose €€€
Boutique **Map** C4
334 rue René Vielle, 40320
Tel *05 58 05 06 07*
W michelguerard.com
Delightful country guest house, part of illustrious chef Michel Guérard's mini hotel chain.

DK Choice

EUGENIE-LES-BAINS: Les Prés d'Eugénie €€€
Boutique **Map** C4
334 rue René Vielle, 40320
Tel *05 58 05 06 07*
W michelguerard.com
This 19th-century manor is the most luxurious of Michel Guérard's hotels, where guests are thoroughly pampered. The restaurant is famed for its unique "cuisine minceur": delectable, yet lighter versions of some of France's finest cooking.

HAGETMAU: Hôtel des Lacs de l'Halco €€
Boutique **Map** C4
Route de Cazalis, 40700
Tel *05 58 79 30 79*
W hotel-des-lacs-dhalco.com
Sleek contemporary structure of glass, steel, wood and stone set between forest and lake.

HOSSEGOR: Les Fougères €€
Classic **Map** A4
91 Avenue de Gaujacq, 40150
Tel *05 58 43 78 00*
W lesfougeres.e-monsite.com
Modern rooms, most with terrace or balcony, a short walk from the beach. Popular with surfers.

HOSSEGOR: Hotel 202 €€€
Boutique **Map** A4
202 Avenue du Golf, 40150
Tel *05 58 43 22 02*
W hotel202.fr
Hip design hotel; modern rooms in neutral shades with balconies, parking and sauna.

HOSSEGOR: Les Hortensias du Lac €€€
Luxury **Map** A4
1578 avenue du Tour du Lac, 40150
Tel *05 58 43 99 00*
W hortensias-du-lac.com
Magnificent hotel, surrounded by fragrant pinewoods; has direct access to the beach.

LABASTIDE ARMAGNAC: Domaine de Paguy €
B&B **Map** C3
2km (1 mile) east of La Bastide, Betbezer-d'Armagnac, 40240
Tel *05 58 44 81 57*
W domainedepaguy.com
Large comfortable rooms at a 16th-century manor, overlooking vines. Makes its own armagnacs.

MIMIZAN: Hôtel Le Plaisance €
Classic **Map** B3
10 rue des Cormorans, 40200
Tel *05 58 09 08 06*
W leplaisance.com
Simple, warm and welcoming family-run hotel near the beach; excellent breakfast.

MONT-DE-MARSAN: Maison d'Agès €
B&B **Map** C4
12km (7 miles) northwest of Mont-de-Marsan, Ousse Suzan, 40110
Tel *05 58 51 82 28*
W hotes-landes.fr
Ivy-clad house with antique-filled bedrooms tucked away in the pines. Equestrians welcome.

MONTFORT-EN-CHALOSSE: Aux Tauzins €
Classic **Map** B4
Route de Hagetmau, 40380
Tel *05 58 98 60 22*
W auxtauzins.com
Most rooms at this warm, family-run hotel have balconies affording superb views over the countryside.

PEYREHORADE: Maison Basta €
B&B **Map** B4
335 chemin de Basta, Ortheveille, 40300
Tel *05 58 73 15 01*
W maison-basta.com
Pretty, family-friendly rooms on a 17th-century farm. Good table d'hôte dinners as well.

RENUNG: Domaine de Benauge €
B&B **Map** C4
20 chemin de Benauge, 40270
Tel *05 58 71 77 30*
W benauge.com
Five rooms in a 15th-century country house with geothermal heating. Family friendly.

SABRES: Auberge des Pins €
Boutique **Map** B3
Route de la Piscine, 40630
Tel *05 58 08 30 00*
W aubergedespins.fr
Deep in the forests of Landes Regional Park, this farmhouse has quiet, comfortable country rooms.

SEIGNOSSE: La Villa de l'Etang Blanc €€
Boutique **Map** A4
2265 route de l'Etang Blanc, 40510
Tel *05 58 72 80 15*
W villaetangblanc.com
Small hotel on the idyllic Etang Blanc. Minimalist romantic rooms.

SOUSTONS: Relais de la Poste €€€
Luxury **Map** B4
10 km (6 miles) south of Soustons, 24 ave de Marenne, Magesq, 40140
Tel *05 58 47 70 25*
W relaisposte.com
This 19th-century staging post is now an inn with a fitness centre and Michelin-starred restaurant.

Pays Basque

AINHOA: Ithurria €€
Historic **Map** A5
Place du Fronton, 64250
Tel *05 59 29 92 11 28*
W ithurria.com
Pretty rooms in a 17th-century Basque inn steeped in character.

ANGLET: Château de Brindos €€€
Luxury **Map** A4
1 allée du Château, 64600
Tel *05 59 23 89 80*
W chateaudebrindos.com
Picturesque country house on green lawns alongside a lake.

BARCUS: Hôtel Chilo €
Classic **Map** B4
Le Bourg, 64130
Tel *05 59 28 90 79*
W hotel-chilo.com
Located in the Vallée de Soule with beautiful mountain views.

BAYONNE: Best Western Le Grand Hôtel €€
Classic **Map** A4
21 rue Thiers, 64100
Tel *05 59 59 62 00*
W bw-legrandhotel.com

Key to Price Guide *see page 250*

Conveniently located 19th-century mansion with modern rooms. Original antique lift.

BIARRITZ: Hôtel Maïtagaria €
Classic **Map** A4
34 avenue Carnot, 64200
Tel *05 59 24 26 65*
W hotel-maitagaria.com
Art Deco rooms overlook the ocean or gardens at this friendly hotel in a 19th-century building.

BIARRITZ: Hôtel du Palais €€
Luxury **Map** A4
1 avenue de l'Impératrice, 64200
Tel *05 59 41 64 00*
W hotel-du-palais.com
Opulent Belle Epoque palace with a heated seawater pool.

BIARRITZ: Hôtel Windsor €€
Boutique **Map** A4
Grande Plage, 64200
Tel *05 59 24 08 52*
W hotelwindsorbiarritz.com
Trendy town house hotel, with stylish seafront café-brasserie.

BIDARRAY: Auberge Ostapé €€€
Historic **Map** B5
Bidarray, 64780
Tel *05 59 37 91 91*
W ostape.com
Luxurious suites in a traditional Basque house with a *hamam*.

LARRAU: Etchemaïté €
Classic **Map** B5
Larrau, 64560
Tel *05 59 28 61 45*
W hotel-etchemaite.fr
Family-run auberge at the foot of the Pic d'Orhy, with lovely views.

SARE: Ttakoinenborda €
B&B **Map** A5
Route de Lizarrieta, 64310
Tel *05 59 47 51 42*
W chambredhotebasque.fr
Sensitively modernized and maintained 17th-century farmhouse; idyllic location.

ST-ETIENNE-DE-BAÏGORRY: Hôtel Arcé €€
Boutique **Map** B5
Route Col d'Ispeguy, 64430
Tel *05 59 37 40 14*
W hotel-arce.com
Traditional family-run inn by the River Nive with contemporary rooms and great ambience.

ST-JEAN-DE-LUZ: Château Urtubie €€
Historic **Map** A4
Rue Bernard de Coral, Urrugne, 64122
Tel *05 59 54 31 15*
W chateaudurtubie.fr
Elegant 14th-century castle in which Wellington, Louis X and Louis XVI stayed. Grand bedrooms.

ST-JEAN-DE-LUZ: Grand Hôtel Loreamar €€€
Luxury **Map** A4
43 boulevard Thiers, 64500
Tel *05 59 26 35 36*
W luzgrandhotel.fr
Classy Belle Epoque seaside hotel, with an excellent spa-thalasso-therapy centre. Great restaurant.

DK Choice

ST-JEAN-PIED-DE-PORT: Hôtel les Pyrénées €€
Classic **Map** B5
19 place du Général-de-Gaulle, 64220
Tel *05 59 37 01 01*
W hotel-les-pyrenees.com
On the route to Compostella, this 18th-century coaching inn belongs to the Arrambide family. Now a Relais & Châteaux, it offers contemporary rooms, some of which overlook the gardens. Enjoy Phillippe Arrambide's creative cuisine, served on the lovely terrace.

Béarn

Arthez-de-Bearn: Domaine de la Carrère €€
B&B **Map** B4
54 La Carrere, 64370
Tel *05 24 37 61 24*
W domaine-de-la-carrere.fr
Stunning restoration of a 17th-century family abode; gorgeous antique furniture.

DK Choice

LASSEUBE: Maison Rancèsamy €
B&B **Map** C5
Quartier Rey, 64290
Tel *05 59 04 26 37*
W missbrowne.com
Set amid lush gardens with enchanting views of the pristine countryside and the Pyrenees, this stone farmhouse from 1727 has been lovingly restored by owners Isabelle and Simon Browne. Don't miss their excellent table d'hôte meals, prepared from their own organic produce.

MONEIN: Maison Canterou €
B&B **Map** C4
Quartier Laquidée, 64360
Tel *05 59 21 41 38*
W gites-de-france-64.com/maison-canterou/
Traditional farmhouse with an enclosed courtyard. The owners produce Jurançon wines.

OLORON-STE-MARIE: Alysson Hôtel €€
Classic **Map** B5
Boulevard Pyrénées, 64400
Tel *05 59 39 70 70*
W alysson-hotel.fr
Well-designed modern rooms, spa, terrace-bar and top-notch restaurant, not far from the Pyrenees and Basque coast.

ORTHEZ: Inter Hôtel La Reine Jeanne €
Classic **Map** B4
44 rue Bourg Vieux, 64300
Tel *05 59 67 00 76*
W inter-hotel.com/en
Small guest rooms around a sheltered courtyard in an 18th-century building. Also has a modern wing.

PAU: Hôtel Continental €
Classic **Map** C5
2 rue Maréchal Foch, 64000
Tel *05 59 27 69 31*
W bestwestern-continental.com
Opened in 1912, this hotel offers a mix of old-world charm and modern facilities.

PAU: Hôtel du Parc Beaumont €€€
Boutique **Map** C5
1 avenue Edouard VII, 64000
Tel *05 59 11 84 00*
W hotel-parc-beaumont.com
Smart, luxurious rooms with views of the Pyrenees; indoor pool and excellent spa.

SALIES-DE-BEARN: Hôtel Hélios €
Classic **Map** B4
Chemin de Labarthe, 64270
Tel *05 59 38 37 59*
W golfsalies.com
Pleasant little hotel, scenically located with its balconies over-looking a beautiful golf course. Snack bar open for lunch.

Extravagant Belle Epoch detailing at the Hotel du Palais in Biarritz

For more information on types of hotels *see page 248*

WHERE TO EAT AND DRINK

The art of cooking is deeply rooted in the culture of Aquitaine, and the wealth of fine produce, specific to the region, is reflected in the wide range of superb local dishes. Some specialities, including beef from Bazas, black cherries from Itxassou and, of course, truffles from the Périgord, are celebrated at the many food festivals that punctuate the year here. Wherever you go, from the Médoc to the Pays Basque, and from the Arcachon Basin to the high Pyrenees, you are sure to enjoy excellent food, not only in the area's many famous restaurants, but also at more informal bistros and brasseries.

Claude Darroze restaurant in Langon *(see p263)*

Types of Restaurants

Aquitaine offers a wide variety of places where you can enjoy good food. These range from top-class gastronomic to contemporary restaurants, serving creative dishes based on local ingredients. Along the coast, seafood restaurants, from simple oyster bars to lavish haute cuisine temples, reign supreme, while inland, farm restaurants *(ferme auberges)* usually feature traditional duck, foie gras, lamb and beef dishes. At classic restaurants, you'll find French favourites such as steak or *moules frites*, or escargots and *tournedos Rossini* at more up-market places. There is also a range of reasonably-priced bistros, brasseries, wine bars, tapas bars and pizzerias.

A good gauge of quality is often the display of a badge or logo, indicating membership of an association, such as the **Fédération Nationale des Tables et Auberges de France** *(see p249)*, the **Maîtres Cuisiniers de France** or **Restaurateurs de France**. One group, **Toques du Périgord**, accepts as members those restaurants in the Dordogne where professional chefs produce authentic dishes by traditional methods.

Local Produce

Besides its world-famous wines, Aquitaine is an abundant source of top-quality produce, such as lamb from Pauillac, ducks and geese from the Landes, beef from Bazas and capons from Grignols. All along the rivers Garonne and Dordogne, shad and lamprey, two species of migratory fish, are highly prized for their fine flavour; sturgeon has made a comeback after decades, along with caviar d'Aquitaine. The region is also noted for its magnificent crayfish, bred from an imported New World variety, as the indigenous species is now protected. Oysters are gathered in the Arcachon Basin and on the Arguin sand-bank, as are shellfish, including piddock, which is eaten both raw or cooked. Hake is fished in the Gulf of Gascony and sardines in the waters off Saint-Jean-de-Luz.

Among the region's finest fruit and vegeta-bles are prunes and melons from the Agenais, tomatoes from Marmande and asparagus from Blayais. Walnuts from the Périgord are a wonderful addition to *salade landaise*, made with gizzard confit. In the Pays Basque, strings of bright red, Espelette peppers, which add a touch of spice to many local dishes, are often hung up to dry across the fronts of houses. Several hundred different species of edible mushroom also grow in Aquitaine, including cèpes and the highly prized truffle – the "black diamond" of the Perigord.

Specialities

With every season, certain specialities come into their own. Autumn is the time to enjoy game and wild mushroom dishes; in winter, look for scallops sautéed with shallots and parsley, truffles in various forms and wood pigeon, eaten either roasted or as *salmi* (a rich stew). If you like freshwater fish, try the elvers, popularly known as "the white gold of the Adour". Foie gras *(see p258)*, lightly cooked or fried as escalopes and served with fruit, is probably the region's most famous delicacy; *garbure (see p259)*, a hearty Béarnese vegetable soup made with confit of goose is more homely. Aquitaine's cuisine also features a host of pork products, such as Bayonne ham *(see p258)*.

Restaurant de la Poste, in Parentis-en-Born *(see p269)*

Empress Eugénie's former summer palace in Biarritz, now the Hôtel du Palais *(see p270)*

In Basque auberges, you will be served tasty dishes in which colourful, sweet red Espelette peppers frequently feature. These range from *chipirons* (small stuffed squid) and *marmitako* (tuna casserole) to *txanguro* (stuffed crab) and *piperade* (a type of ratatouille). Some restaurants organize courses that aim to introduce visitors to the art of cooking, with the emphasis on the traditional preparation of local produce.

Cheeses and Desserts

The most popular cheese in Aquitaine is *tomme de brebis*, a ewe's milk cheese from the Ossau valley, that is served with black cherry jam *(see p259)* or quince jelly. This is closely followed in popularity by *cabécou*, a creamy goat's cheese.

Traditional desserts include *cannelés de Bordeaux* (small fluted cakes with a soft, moist centre and caramelized shell), *tourtière aux pruneaux* (a crisp, flaky layered cake made with prunes), served flambéed in Armagnac, *gâteau basque (see p259)*, and *touron*, a specialist Basque confectionery *(see p275)*.

Eating Out

The enjoyment of food in convivial surroundings is of central importance right across France. In inexpensive places, bread and a carafe of water will be brought automatically to your table and included in the price of the meal, as is service, though it is still customary to leave a tip. It is always advisable to book a table in advance, especially for dinner. In the low season, particularly in rural areas, many restaurants close for periods of a few weeks to several months.

Most establishments (except *ferme auberges*) accept major credit cards, especially Visa and Mastercard.

Wheelchair Access

Any establishment that displays a "Tourisme et Handicap" sticker will have wheelchair access and facilities for people with disabilities. Brochures issued by tourist offices also give details of establishments part of the Tourisme et Handicap scheme.

Children

Almost all restaurants in Aquitaine welcome children, and most have special, cheaper children's menus. Very few, however, provide high chairs for very young children.

Ma Maison, at La Sauvetat-du-Dropt *(see p266)*

Recommended Restaurants

The restaurants listed in this guide include some of the best in Southwest France. They have been chosen for their reliably good food and service, with the aim of presenting a wide range of cuisine and price ranges in the region's most visited cities, towns, villages and countryside. Many country restaurants are attached to hotels but serve a predominantly non-residential clientele. These offer good value for money and are often the focus of local social activity.

Among the listings, you will also find DK Choice restaurants. These have been selected for one or more exceptional feature, whether it is the superb quality of cuisine, the atmosphere, a beautiful setting or spectacular views.

DIRECTORY

Les Toques du Périgord
W toques-perigord.com

Restaurateurs de France
W restaurateursdefrance.com

Maîtres Cuisiniers de France
W maitrescuisiniersde france.com

Ferme auberges: Bienvenue à la Ferme
W bienvenue-a-la-ferme.com/ aquitaine

The Flavours of Aquitaine

Southwestern France fulfils the requirements of the most demanding gourmet. The Atlantic coast supplies fine seafood, while inland forests are a rich hunting ground for game, truffles and wild mushrooms. Geese and ducks provide the fat that is key to local cuisine, as well as meat and *foie gras*. The Pyrenees offer beef and lamb grazed on mountain pastures, and the Basque country adds the spicy notes of red peppers and fine chocolate. Charcuterie and cheeses abound. Garlic, saffron and walnut oil contribute yet more flavour and colour. Bordeaux's world-class wines *(see pp260–61)* are the perfect accompaniment.

Black truffles

Fishermen opening oysters at a maritime festival in Arcachon

Meat, Game & Seafood

Ducks and geese, fattened to produce *foie gras* and confit meat (preserved in fat), are highly prized, as are flavourful rosy *agneau de Quercy* lamb, raised on the grasslands of the Causses de Quercy, and milk-fed veal *(veau sous la mère)*. Regional charcuterie (preserved meat, usually pork but also game) is superb, notably the sweet, salted and dried ham of Bayonne. Pork also features in the *boudin blanc* and *boudin noir* of Quercy and is used with duck or goose liver in pâtés. The woodlands of the Dordogne and Lot are rich in game: *sanglier* (wild boar), *chevreuil* (roe deer), *faisan* (pheasant), *lièvre* (hare) and *perdrix* (partridge).

The pure, clear waters of the Arcachon Basin enhance the flavour of its oysters. They need no accompaniment other than lemon or shallot vinegar, but the citizens of Bordeaux like to eat them with little sausages. Mussels are also raised on the coast, and the sea yields a variety of fish. Eels, lamprey and sturgeon are caught in the Gironde Estuary.

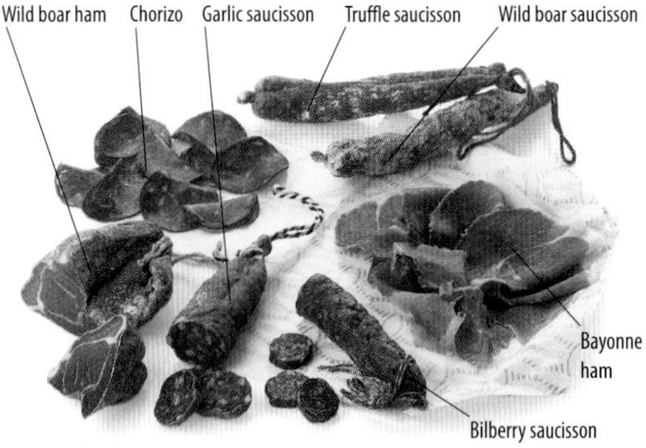

Selection of traditional southwestern charcuterie

Regional Dishes and Specialities

Pink garlic

As a starter, duck or goose *foie gras* may be served with a jelly of sweet Monbazillac wine. On the coast, a seafood soup such as *chaudrée* (with white wine and garlic) might be offered. In the Pays Basque, there could be a dish of *chipirons* (little peppers stuffed with spicy salt cod). *Salades quercynoise, périgordienne* and *landaise* are all variants on salad with *foie gras*, smoked *magret* (duck breast fillet), *confit de gésiers* (preserved gizzards) and perhaps stuffed goose neck *(cou farci)*. Meat may be served with a *sauce Périgueux* (shallots, truffle shavings and Monbazillac) or *à l'Agennaise* (with prunes and Armagnac). Rocamadour goat's cheese is often served with a salad, dressed with walnut oil, while *fromage de brébis* (ewe's milk cheese) comes with cherry or quince jam *(pâte de coings)*. Desserts tend to be based on local fruits.

Salade landaise, featuring *foie gras*, duck confit and gizzards, makes a good main meal in a bistro.

Fattened Périgord geese, the source of *foie gras*

Fruit, Nuts & Vegetables

The fruit that best characterizes the region is the plum or, rather, two plums: the round, green *reine-claude* (greengage) and the larger, purple plums that become *pruneaux d'Agen*, succulent black prunes used in tarts and patisserie or enveloped in chocolate. Other fruits include *fraises du Périgord* strawberries and the black cherries of Itxassou. Walnut trees are abundant in the Dordogne and Lot, where plantations hug the river valleys. Walnuts are served raw with cheese, as well as going into many traditional recipes, from sauces to bread, cakes and tarts. Walnut oil is never used in cooked dishes, but is delicious simply drizzled over lettuce.

Basque cuisine gets its spicy identity from the red Espelette pepper *(see p205)*, which is dried and powdered for use in dishes such as *piperade*. Vegetables such as asparagus and early carrots thrive in the sandy soil of the Landes.

Walnuts are harvested in Dordogne between October and November

Truffles

The oak forests that cover much of the Périgord region conceal one of its most prized treasures, the black truffle or *truffe du Périgord*, also dubbed the "black diamond", which goes to flavour many luxury dishes. Truffles grow on the roots of oak trees and are located with the help of trained pigs or dogs. During the season, from November to March, truffles sell for astronomical prices at markets in villages such as Lalbenque and Limogne-en-Quercy.

ON THE MENU

Chipirones à l'encre Baby squid cooked in their own ink

Civet de lièvre Jugged hare

Entrecôte à la bordelaise Steak in a sauce of red wine, shallots and bone marrow

Garbure béarnaise Vegetable soup with confit of duck or goose and red wine

Matelotte d'anguilles Eel stewed in wine sauce

Pommes sarladaises Potatoes sautéed in goose fat with chopped garlic and parsley

Poule au pot béarnaise Chicken stuffed with giblets, garlic, onion, breadcrumbs and egg, stewed with vegetables

Ttoro Rich fish and shellfish stew with tomatoes, onions and Espelette peppers

Omelette aux truffes is a simple dish transformed by its luxurious garnish of shaved black truffle.

Piperade is a Basque dish of stewed peppers, onions and tomatoes with eggs. Bayonne ham may be laid on the top.

Croustade, thin pastry layered with butter and sliced apples, is perfumed with Armagnac and vanilla.

What to Drink in Aquitaine

For centuries, the vineyards of Aquitaine have been producing excellent wines and other alcoholic drinks, most notably the world-renowned wines of Bordeaux and the great Armagnacs. The fine wines produced in areas such as Bergerac, Cahors, Côtes-de-Duras and Jurançon are also recognized internationally for their high quality. Modern wine-making techniques, allied with age-old methods, are now widely used, resulting in an almost unequalled level of expertise. Eaux-de-vie is made by a dwindling number of travelling home-distillers, and the region is also noted for its spring and mineral waters and for its locally produced fruit juices.

Poster advertising Lillet, an aperitif

Bergerac

Côtes-de-Duras

Saint-Émilion

Red Wines

Wines produced in the Bordeaux region have several *appellations*: Haut-Médoc, Margaux, Saint-Estèphe, Graves, Fronsac, Saint-Émilion and Pomerol. Aquitaine has some famous wine châteaux and several *grands crus*, such as Mouton Rothschild. The CIVB (Conseil Interprofessionnel des Vins de Bordeaux; 05 56 00 22 66), and the *maisons du vin* that have been set up in many vine-growing areas, work to promote the region's wines, and growers often open their cellars to visitors. Not far from the Bordeaux area are other, equally renowned wine-producing regions, including Buzet, Madiran, Bergerac and Côtes-de-Duras, one of the oldest AOCs in France. Thanks to a few enthusiasts, some lesser-known areas are returning to prominence. These include Estaing, in the Lot, and Domme, in the Périgord. Cahors wines, which are already well known, are going from strength to strength.

White Wines

Bottle of Pacherenc

The region's best-known dessert wine is undoubtedly Sauternes, whose producers include the legendary Château d'Yquem. Other excellent dessert wines include Sainte-Croix-du-Mont, Loupiac and, of course, Monbazillac. The two smooth, white wines of the Dordogne, Saussignac and Rosette, are both excellent accompaniments to fish and white meat, but they can also be enjoyed dessert wines. The dry white wines Entre-Deux-Mers, Tursan and Chalosse, go particularly well with cheese. Tariquet, between the Landes and the Gers, is a large estate well known for its Côtes de Gascogne *vins de pays* and for its brandies. The vineyards of the Jurançon area, at the foot of the Pyrenees, produce distinctive dry, sweet and dessert wines.

Wine-tasting

Certain inter-professional organizations, including INAO (Institut National des Appellations d'Origine), have designed a set of glasses that allow the drinker to fully appreciate the colour, nose and other characteristics of each type of wine. For example, a brandy glass is wider than a red wine glass and has a shorter stem. A white wine glass is taller and narrower.

INAO red wine glass

INAO white wine glass

Brandy glass

Liqueurs and Brandies

Aquitaine produces many different types of apéritif, including plum or walnut liqueurs and red or white Kina Lillet, a mixture of Peruvian quinine and local wine, made in the Bordeaux region since 1887. Armagnac is the oldest French eau-de-vie, and 6 million bottles of it are sold each year. Floc de Gascogne is an apéritif version of Armagnac. Izarra, a liqueur made from a blend of Pyrenean and Oriental plants, has been made in the Pays Basque since 1835. Pacharan, from Basse-Navarre, is an aniseed-flavoured liqueur in which wild sloes are macerated. Like Izarra, Pacharan is served either before or after a meal.

Lillet, an apéritif from Bordeaux

Bottle of Armagnac

Floc de Gascogne

Prune-based apéritif

Perifruit orange juice

Non-alcoholic Drinks

With its well-preserved natural environment, southwestern France has several sources of pure spring and mineral water. Although the Lot's spa has closed, its spring is the source of Miers-Alvignac water. Being rich in beneficial minerals and having diuretic properties, this is available from chemists. Ogeu mineral water, from the Pyrénées at Ogeu les Bains, is ideal for everyday drinking. Drinks made from pure fruit juices, such as prune and apple, are produced by several makers, including Perifruit in Le Bugue, in the Périgord.

Café terrace in Mézin

Reading a Wine Label

Wines are mainly classified according to their country and region of origin, their category (AOC or *vin de pays*), their alcohol content and their vintage. Choosing a wine will depend on the type of dish it is to accompany, on price in relation to quality, and on age. You can invest in young wines for laying down or buy those that are ready to drink. The choice in Aquitaine ranges from little-known *vins de pays* to some of the world's greatest vintages.

Estate

Vintage (the year when the grapes were harvested). Some labels also show the wine's alcohol content.

"Mis en bouteille au château" ("estate-bottled") is a guarantee of the wine's authenticity.

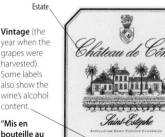

The château is sometimes shown on the label.

Appellation d'Origine Contrôlée indicates the area of production.

Classification

Bottle's capacity

Where to Eat and Drink

Gironde

ARCACHON: Café de la Plage €€
Traditional **Map** B2
1 Boulevard Veyrier-Montagnères, 33120
Tel *05 56 22 52 94*
A beach bar and fine restaurant (Chez Pierre) combination. Offers crêpes, sandwiches, and ice cream as well as gourmet seafood.

ARCACHON BASIN: Chez Eliette €
Seafood **Map** B2
19 avenue Commandant-Allègre, Andernos-les-Bains, 33510
Tel *05 56 82 16 77* **Closed** *Mon, Tue*
Former oyster shop, now a good value restaurant featuring fresh seafood and irresistible desserts.

ARCACHON BASIN: La Guérinière €€€
Gastronomic **Map** B2
18 cours Verdun, Gujan-Mestres, 33470
Tel *05 56 66 08 78*
Relaxed, Michelin-starred restaurant serves creative cuisine (seafood and much else) around a pool. Good value set menus.

ARCACHON BASIN: Pinasse Café €€€
Seafood **Map** B2
2 bis Avenue de l'Océan, Lege-Cap-Ferret, 33970
Tel *05 56 03 77 87* **Closed** *12 Nov–first weekend of Mar*
Fashionable waterfront eatery serving exquisite seafood (try mussels cooked in pine needles).

ARCINS: Le Lion d'Or €
Bistro **Map** C2
Place de la République, 33460
Tel *05 56 58 96 79* **Closed** *Sun, Mon, Jul*
Order the menu *du jour*, featuring regional dishes at this animated institution in the Médoc.

BAZAS: Les Remparts €€
Contemporary **Map** C3
49 Place de la Cathédrale, 33430
Tel *05 56 25 95 24* **Closed** *Mon*
Innovative cuisine such as pork Duroc with aubergines, cèpes, and plantains. Its terrace overlooks the cathedral garden.

BORDEAUX: Café Maritime €
Contemporary **Map** C2
1 quai Armand-Lalande, Hangar G2, Bassin à Flot (berth) No 1, 33000
Tel *05 57 10 20 40* **Closed** *Sun*
Smart restaurant in a converted dockside boatshed; mix of French and exotic dishes (sushi).

BORDEAUX: L'Autre Petit Bois €
Bistro **Map** C2
12 Place du Parlement, 33000
Tel *05 56 48 02 93*
Popular bistro amid a forest of real and artificial trees, offers light meals, salads, and wines.

BORDEAUX: Vinset €
Wine Bar **Map** C2
27 rue des Bahutiers, 33000
Tel *09 52 19 09 37* **Closed** *Sun–Wed*
Range of Bordeaux wines, served by the glass, with plates of cheese, tapas, charcuteries and other finger foods.

BORDEAUX: Fernand €€
Bistro **Map** C2
7 quai de la Douane, 33000
Tel *05 56 81 23 40*
In what was a printers' shop, this bistro offers regional produce such as Pauillac lamb, lamprey, and Blonde d'Aquitaine beef.

BORDEAUX: L'Oiseau Blue €€
Gastronomic **Map** C2
127 Av Thiers, 33100
Tel *05 56 81 09 39* **Closed** *Sun, Mon*
Former police station with some of the most tantalizing fusion cuisine in southwest France.

BORDEAUX: Les Sens Ciel €€
Gastronomic **Map** C2
59 Rue du Palais Gallien, 33000
Tel *05 56 81 43 51* **Closed** *Sun*
Gourmet food with unusual fruits and vegetables. Choose a wine – chef will cook dinner to match.

BORDEAUX: L'Estacade €€€
Contemporary **Map** C2
Quai des Queyries, 33000
Tel *05 57 54 02 50*
Elegant restaurant offering great views of Place de la Bourse. Serves imaginative seafood dishes.

Price Guide
The following price categories are for a three-course meal for one, including half a bottle of house wine, service and tax.

€	up to €35
€€	€35 to 50
€€€	over €50

BORDEAUX: Le Chapon Fin €€€
Gastronomic **Map** C2
5 rue Montesquieu, 33000
Tel *05 56 79 10 10* **Closed** *Sun, Mon, Aug, holidays*
Remarkable Belle Epoque décor and delectable gastronomic cuisine by chef Nicolas Frion.

FRONSAC: Le Bord d'Eau €€
Southwestern **Map** C2
4 Rue Poinsonnet, 33126
Tel *05 57 51 99 91* **Closed** *Mon*
Riverside restaurant offering freshwater fish, aromatic meat stews, and *lamprey à la bordelaise*. Great list of Fronsac wines.

GRADIGNAN: Au Comté d'Ornon €
Classic **Map** C2
Allée de Mégevie, 33170
Tel *05 56 75 26 85* **Closed** *Sun*
Traditional restaurant with a buffet selection of starters and desserts. Play facilities for kids.

LA REOLE: Aux Fontaines €
Contemporary **Map** C2
8 rue de Verdun, 33190
Tel *05 56 61 15 25* **Closed** *Sun, Mon*
Outstanding, innovative seasonal menu served on a lovely terrace.

LACANAU OCÉAN: L'Imprèvu €€
Contemporary **Map** B2
Front de Mer, 33680
Tel *05 56 03 11 11* **Closed** *Nov–Apr*
Stylish hotel restaurant and ocean-front terrace, featuring inventive cuisine, like fresh tuna with mango.

Belle Epoque decor at La Chapon Fin, Bordeaux

DK Choice

LANGON: Claude Darozze €€€
Contemporary **Map** C2
95 cours du Général-Leclerc, 33210
Tel *05 56 63 00 48* **Closed** *Mid Oct–first week Nov, and two weeks in Jan*
Enjoy superb seasonal cuisine at this unassuming hotel-restaurant with a charming leafy terrace. Depending on the time of year, try the *carpaccio de thon rouge* (red tuna), exquisite scallops, and endives with *foie gras* cream. Save room for Darroze's famous, light as air, Grand Marnier soufflé.

Plush seating at Claude Darroze, Langon

LIBOURNE: Chez Servais €
Southwestern **Map** C2
14 Place Decazes, 33500
Tel *05 57 51 83 97* **Closed** *Mid May, last half of Aug*
Generous portions of some of the most tasty food in the area.

Martillac: La Grand'Vigne €€€
Gastronomic **Map** C2
Chemin de Smith-Haut-Lafitte, 33650
Tel *05 57 83 83 83* **Closed** *Mon, Tue*
Chef Nicolas Masse presents one of Bordeaux's top gastronomic experiences at this beautiful lakefront restaurant.

MONSEGUR: La Ferme Gauvry €
Ferme-auberge **Map** C2
10km (6 miles) west of Monségur, D16, Rimons, 33540
Tel *05 56 71 83 96*
Working farm with ducks, cattle, and vineyards, offers authentic home-made dishes and picnic lunches. Reservations required.

MONTAGNE ST-EMILION: Le Vieux Presbytère €€
Contemporary **Map** C2
Place de l'Eglise, 33570
Tel *05 57 74 65 33* **Closed** *Tue, Wed, two weeks in Jun*
Stylish restaurant in an ancient presbytery with a lovely terrace, serves dishes based on regional ingredients. Good for families.

PAUILLAC: Château Cordeillan-Bages €€€
Gastronomic **Map** B1
61 rue Vignerons, 33250
Tel *05 56 59 24 24* **Closed** *Mon, Tue; mid-Dec–early Feb*
Michelin-starred elegance: Pauillac lamb and Aquitaine caviar as signature dishes. Extraordinary wine list.

PYLA-SUR-MER: l'Authentic €€€
Gastronomic **Map** B2
35 boulevard de l'Océan, 33115
Tel *05 56 54 07 94* **Closed** *Wed*
Gourmet sea and land food with a contemporary twist. Wonderful lobster ravioli. Bordeaux wines.

SAUTERNES: Le Saprien €
Contemporary **Map** C3
14 rue Principale, 33210
Tel *05 56 76 60 87* **Closed** *Mon; mid-Feb–early Mar*
The local favourite, with good value menus; a mix of meat and seafood dishes, some grilled.

SOULAC-SUR-MER: Le Grill Océan €
Bistro **Map** B1
2 Esplanade des Girondins, 33780
Tel *05 56 09 89 64* **Closed** *15 Nov–15 Feb*
Seaside setting with good food featuring duck as well as fish.

ST-EMILION: L'Envers du Décor €
Bistro **Map** C2
11 rue du Clocher, 33330
Tel *05 57 74 48 31* **Closed** *Two weeks in Jan*
With tables in the intimate courtyard garden, this bistro and wine bar offers salads, omelettes, *foie gras*, and chalkboard daily specials.

Château Cordeillan-Bages, set amidst vines in Pauillac

ST-EMILION: Hostellerie de Plaisance €€€
Gastronomic **Map** C2
Place du Clocher, 33330
Tel *05 57 55 07 55* **Closed** *Sun, Mon*
Philippe Etchebest creatively uses top ingredients from around the world at this culinary temple.

Périgord and Quercy

BERGERAC: L'Imparfait €€
Contemporary **Map** D2
8 rue des Fontaines, 24100
Tel *05 53 57 47 92*
Lively, cheerful place near the Musée du Vin combines fresh traditional ingredients with contemporary flair.

BERGERAC: Le Vin'Quatre €€
Contemporary **Map** D2
14 rue St-Clar, 24100
Tel *05 53 22 37 26* **Closed** *Wed*
Popular for its creative cuisine featuring old Périgourdin favourites and the chef's own creations.

BOURDEILLES: Les Griffons €€
Southwestern **Map** D1
Bourdeilles, 24310
Tel *05 53 45 45 35* **Closed** *Mid-Oct–Apr*
Gracious old establishment that serves a wide choice of Périgourdin favourites.

BRANTÔME: Les Frères Charbonnel €€
Southwestern **Map** D1
57 rue Gambetta, 24310
Tel *05 53 05 70 15* **Closed** *Mid-Nov to mid-Dec*
Consistently plating first-rate cooking, this local favourite offers a wide range of dishes and menus.

BRANTÔME: Le Moulin du Roc €€€
Gastronomic **Map** D1
Le Pont, Champagnac de Belair, 24530 (7km northeast of Brantôme)
Tel *05 53 02 86 00* **Closed** *Tue, early Nov–Mar*
Michelin-starred restaurant, in a gorgeous 17th-century mill on the Dronne, has lavish dishes, loaded with truffles and *foie gras*.

CAHORS: Le Lamparo €
Brasserie **Map** E3
76 rue Georges-Clémenceau, 46000
Tel *05 65 35 25 93* **Closed** *Sun*
Huge choice of pizzas, pastas, salads, grills, crêpes, and ice cream desserts. Very popular.

CAHORS: La Table de Haute-Serre €€€
Gastronomic **Map** E3
9km (5 miles) south of Cahors at Cieurac, 46230
Tel *05 65 20 80 20* **Closed** *Wed, Thu*
Excellent creative cuisine at this renowned Cahors wine château. Don't miss the all-truffle Toques n' Truffes menu from January to March.

DOMME: L'Esplanade €€
Southwestern **Map** E2
Le Bourg, 24250
Tel *05 53 28 31 41* **Closed** *Mon*
Great Périgourdin menu of truffles, *foie gras*, pigeons, and game dishes, against the unbeatable panorama of the Dordogne valley.

FIGEAC: La Dînée du Viguier €€
Gastronomic **Map** F2
4 rue Boutaric, 46100
Tel *05 65 50 08 08* **Closed** *Mon*
In a medieval château by the Musée Champollion, this elegant restaurant offers amazing cuisine and particularly delightful seafood.

Elegantly decorated interiors at La Table de Haute-Serre, Cahors

Outdoor tables at La Roseraie, Montignac-Lascaux

DK Choice

FRAYSSINET-LE-GELAT: La Serpt €
Ferme-auberge **Map** E2
La Serp, 46250
Tel *05 65 35 62 07* **Closed** *Mon*
Located near Villefranche-du-Périgord, this working family-run duck farm offers farm-lunch made with its own products. Its traditional menu has rich patés, *foie gras*, maigrets and confits, as well as Quercy sautéed potatoes and the house Cahors wine. Reservations essential.

GREZELS: La Terrasse €
Classic **Map** E3
Le Bourg, 46700 (on the D8 south of Puy l'Évêque)
Tel *05 65 21 34 03* **Closed** *Mon*
Set menu with no choices, but generous portions of exceptional cooking. Tremendous bargain.

LA ROQUE-GAGEAC: La Belle Étoile €€
Southwestern **Map** E2
Le Bourg, 24250
Tel *05 53 29 51 44* **Closed** *Mon; early Nov–Mar*
Refined establishment overlooking the Dordogne that works wonders with duck and *foie gras*.

LACAVE: Le Pont de l'Ouysse €€€
Gastronomic **Map** E2
Lacave, 46200
Tel *05 65 37 87 04* **Closed** *Mon*
Two celebrated chefs, with their own truffle farm, do magic with traditional ingredients.

LES EYZIES-DE-TAYAC: Au Coup de Silex €
Southwestern **Map** E2
4 rue du Musée, 24620
Tel *05 53 05 14 29* **Closed** *Wed; Nov–Mar*
Unpretentious restaurant that offers exceptional cooking: *foie gras* with roast apples, *ris de veau*, and beef with wild mushrooms.

MEYRONNE: La Terrasse €€
Gastronomic **Map** E2
Le Bourg, 46200
Tel *05 65 32 26 93*
Delectable cuisine with plenty of duck, sturgeon, rabbit and *ris de veau*.

MONBAZILLAC: La Tour des Vents €€
Gastronomic **Map** D2
Moulin de Malfourat, 24240
Tel *05 53 58 30 10* **Closed** *Mon, Jan-early Feb*
Michelin-star cuisine with a fruity touch, served in a stylish setting, high above the Dordogne valley.

MONTIGNAC-LASCAUX: La Roseraie €€
Contemporary **Map** E2
11 place d'Armes, 24290
Tel *05 53 50 53 92* **Closed** *Nov–Easter*
Elegant place for lunch after visiting the caves. Rich meat dishes and great desserts.

PÉRIGUEUX: Café de la Place €
Bistro **Map** D1
7 place du Marché au Bois, 24000
Tel *05 53 08 21 11* **Closed** *none*
Popular, retro café with excellent cooking: French and Périgourdin classics, salads, and sandwiches.

PÉRIGUEUX: Le Clos Saint-Front €€
Contemporary **Map** D1
5 rue de la Vertu, 24000
Tel *05 53 46 78 58* **Closed** *Mon*
Rare creativity: duck with figs, cannelloni with smoked haddock, scallops and wild mushrooms.

PÉRIGUEUX: L'Essentiel €€€
Gastronomic **Map** D1
8 rue de la Clarté, 24000
Tel *05 53 35 15 15* **Closed** *Sun, Mon*
Gourmet experience of southern tastes and colours: *foie gras* with pear, roast pigeon and lobster.

PÉRIGUEUX: L'Oisan €€€
Gastronomic **Map** D1
Château des Reynats, 15 avenue des Reynats, Chancelade (6km east of Périgueux), 24650
Tel *05 53 03 53 59* **Closed** *Sun, Mon; first week Jan-first week Feb*
Majestic château salon, where the elite of Périgord gather for a Michelin-starred treat.

RIBERAC: Le Chabrot €€
Southwestern **Map** D1
8 rue Gambetta, 24600
Tel *05 53 91 28 59* **Closed** *Wed*
Lots of duck and *foie gras* on the menu along with some

Key to Price Guide *see page 262*

imaginative surprises. Good cooking, friendly service and great bargain menus.

ROCAMADOUR: Jehan de Valon €€
Southwestern **Map** E2
Cité Médiévale, 46500
Tel *05 65 33 63 08* **Closed** *Mid-Nov-mid Feb*
The Lot's duck, *foie gras* and lamb at their best – on the edge of Rocamadour's dramatic gorge.

SARLAT: Le Bistro de l'Octroi €
Southwestern **Map** E2
111 avenue de Selves, 24200
Tel *05 53 30 83 40* **Closed** *none*
This stone-built 1830s toll house with outdoor tables brings new life to the old Périgord favourites.

SARLAT: Le Couleuvrine €€
Southwestern **Map** E2
1 place de la Bouquerie, 24200
Tel *05 53 59 27 80* **Closed** *Mon*
Charming oak-beam space with a big fireplace and robust cooking offers duck, veal, boar, and *foie gras*. And terrines.

SARLAT: Lo Gorissado €€€
Contemporary **Map** E2
7km (4 miles) west of Sarlat at Le Pontou 24200 Saint-André-d'Allas
Tel *05 53 59 34 06* **Closed** *Mon-Thu in low season; Mid Dec-mid Feb*
Creative chef produces unusual fusion dishes using exquisite local ingredients such as saffron and Dordogne sturgeon.

SORGES: Auberge de la Truffe €€
Southwestern **Map** D1
Le Bourg, 24420
Tel *05 53 05 02 05* **Closed** *none*
This deceptively modest village inn, in Périgord's truffle capital, features sophisticated cooking, and an all-truffle menu.

Peaceful, countryside setting of Lo Gorissado in Sarlat

Sophisticated decor at Auberge De La Truffe, Sorges

ST-CÉRÉ: Les Trois Soleils de Montal €€
Gastronomic **Map** F2
3 km (2 miles) east of St-Céré, Les Près de Montal, St-Jean-l'Espinasse, 46400
Tel *05 65 10 16 16* **Closed** *none*
This top-rated restaurant is known for its rich main dishes, especially the Quercy lamb.

ST-CIRQ-LAPOPIE: L'Oustal €
Southwestern **Map** E3
Le Bourg, 46330
Tel *05 65 31 20 17* **Closed** *Nov-late Mar*
Great value at a tourist destination, and good food: try duck and rabbit with Quercy potatoes or cassoulet.

ST-MEDARD DE CATUS: Le Gindreau €€€
Gastronomic **Map** E4
Le Bourg, 46150
Tel *05 65 36 22 27* **Closed** *Mon, Tue*
One of the Lot's best – effortless blending of tradition and modern styles, in a village schoolhouse.

TREMOLAT: Le Vieux Logis €€€
Gastronomic **Map** D2
Le Bourg, Trémolat, 24510
Tel *05 53 22 80 06* **Closed** *Wed and Thu from mid Oct-mid Apr*
Michelin-starred cuisine in a delightfully lavish dining room. Less-expensive bistro, too.

Lot-et-Garonne

AGEN: Le Cauquil €
Bistro **Map** D3
9 avenue du Générale-de-Gaulle, 47000
Tel *05 53 48 02 34* **Closed** *Sun*
Tasty, daily-changing menu made from fresh produce. Generous portions and relaxed atmosphere.

AGEN: Osaka €
Japanese **Map** D3
38 Boulevard Sylvain Dumon, 47000
Tel *05 53 66 31 76* **Closed** *Sun, Mon*
Relaxed atmosphere, and some of the best Japanese food in southwest France: tempura, sushi, maki, grilled meats and sashimi platters.

AGEN: L'Atelier €€
Contemporary **Map** D3
14 rue Jeu de Paume, 47000
Tel *05 53 87 89 22* **Closed** *Sun*
Lively restaurant set in a carpenter's workshop, with a great menu that features marinated salmon and roast duckling.

AGEN: Margoton €€
Classic **Map** D3
52 rue Richard-Coeur-de-Lion, 47000
Tel *05 53 48 11 55* **Closed** *Sun, Mon*
Bare bricks and wooden floors set the ambience for deftly prepared classics: sautéed scallops, beef filet in *foie gras* sauce, and profiteroles.

AGEN: Philippe Vannier €€
Contemporary **Map** D3
66 rue Camille-Desmoulins, 47000
Tel *05 53 66 63 70* **Closed** *Sun*
Stylish restaurant decorated with contemporary art offers delicious classics with a twist. Try the sea bass *(tranche de bar)*.

AGEN: Mariottat €€€
Southwestern **Map** D3
25 rue Louis-Vivent, 47000
Tel *05 53 77 99 77* **Closed** *Mon; two weeks in Jan*
The *assiette tout canard* (duck) is what makes this elegant town house restaurant famous. Its creative dishes and delightful desserts are also good.

ASTAFFORT: Auberge du Brulhois €
Traditional **Map** D3
3, Avenue d'Agen, 47220 Astaffort
Tel *05 53 66 04 79* **Closed** *Sun eve, Mon; last ten days in December, first week in January.*
Popular rustic restaurant with fixed-price menus. Specialities include chicken with apricot sauce and prune-based sweets.

Tables on the covered terrace at Le Moulin de Dausse, Dausse

ASTAFFORT: Cochon Canard et Compagnie €
Southwestern **Map** D3
9 faubourg Corné, 47200
Tel *05 53 67 10 27* **Closed** *Wed*
Regional dishes, some unusual (hamburger with onion confits and sheep cheese), and good, affordable southwestern wines.

BUZET-SUR-BAISE: Au Bord de l'Eau €
Southwestern **Map** D3
Halte Nautique, 47160
Tel *05 53 84 53 31* **Closed** *Wed, Nov-Mar*
Watch the boats pass by while lunching on *magret de canard aux prunes et vin rouge*, salads, and Buzet wines.

CASTELJALOUX: La Vieille Auberge €€
Southwestern **Map** C3
11 rue Posterne, 47700
Tel *05 53 93 01 36* **Closed** *Mon*
Cosy restaurant serving south-western favourites: warm pan-fried *foie gras* with apples, deboned pigeon stuffed with cèpes, and more.

CASTILLONNES: Les Remparts €€
Contemporary **Map** D2
26 rue de la Paix, 47330
Tel *05 53 49 55 85* **Closed** *Mon*
Attractive hotel restaurant serves original fare: duck confit profiteroles with caramelized onions, and crêpes Suzette with *foie gras*.

CLAIRAC: Auberge de Clairac €€
Southwestern **Map** D3
12 route de Tonneins, 47320
Tel *05 53 79 22 52* **Closed** *Tue, Wed*
Family-friendly restaurant with a lovely terrace; excellent steaks, duck, and fish stew.

DAUSSE: Le Moulin de Dausse €€
Contemporary **Map** D3
Route d'Anthe, 47140
Tel *05 53 41 26 00* **Closed** *Mon–Wed, Nov–Mar*
Talented Dutch couple prepares a delightful array of seasonal hors d'oeuvres and delectable desserts to match the delicious mains.

DURAS: Le Cabri €
Classic **Map** D2
Route de Savignac, 47120
Tel *05 53 83 81 03* **Closed** *Variable*
Short menu of well prepared classics: steaks, veal escalope, poached salmon, and salad Niçoise. Nice terrace.

DURAS: Le Don Camillo €
Italian **Map** D2
Rue Paul Persil, 47120
Tel *05 53 83 76 00* **Closed** *Tue (except Jul and Aug)*
Family-orientated eatery offering delicious home-made lasagne, garlic prawns, pizzas, and salads. Shady terrace for summer dining.

FRANCESCAS: Le Relais de la Hire €€
Gastronomic **Map** D3
11 rue Porte-Neuve, 47600
Tel *05 53 65 41 59* **Closed** *Mon*
Delicious dishes that make good use of herbs and flowers; desserts that are works of art; together with great wines, armagnacs and cigars.

LA SAUVETAT-DU-DROPT: Ma Maison €€
Contemporary **Map** D2
10 Avenue Grammont, 47800
Tel *05 53 94 33 42* **Closed** *Mon; Nov-Mar*
Try the limited but superb menu of fresh cuisine at this delightful courtyard restaurant in a private residence. Reservations are essential.

LAPLUME: Château de Lassalle €€
Gastronomic **Map** D3
3km (2 miles) from Laplume, Brimont, 47310
Tel *05 53 95 10 58* **Closed** *Sat, Sun in winter*
Situated in an 18th-century *orangerie*, this eatery has wonderful seasonal cuisine, with some unusual offerings such as salmon sausage with leeks.

MARMANDE: Auberge L'Escale €
Southwestern **Map** D3
Pont des Sables, Fourques sur Garonne, 47200
Tel *05 53 93 60 11* **Closed** *Mon*
A 1683 canal-side farmhouse with a pretty terrace; serves grilled meats, duck breast with figs, and stuffed Marmande tomatoes.

MARMANDE: Boat aux Saveurs €€
Contemporary **Map** D3
36-38 av. Jean-Jaurès, 47200 Marmande
Tel *05 53 64 20 35* **Closed** *Mon, Tue lunch, Sunday evening*
Modern restaurant set up in an old convent; has refreshing variations on traditional cuisine, affordable fixed menus, and an inexpensive wine list.

MEILHAN-SUR-GARONNE: Le Font d'Uzas €
Contemporary **Map** C3
1 avenue de la Font d'Uzas, 47180
Tel *05 53 89 62 97* **Closed** *Mon*
Nice manor house near the canal. The menu lists plenty of sea and land food, home-made profiteroles, and good house wine.

MOIRAX: Auberge du Prieuré €€
Contemporary **Map** D3
Le Boug, 47310
Tel *05 53 47 59 55* **Closed** *Mon, Tue; Feb*
Imaginative and traditional fare along with some unusual

Bright, colourful facade of Ma Maison, La Sauvetat-du-Dropt

Key to Price Guide *see page 262*

desserts (like poached apricots with curry and cucumber) in a quiet village.

NERAC: Le Vert Gallant €
Contemporary **Map** D3
11 rue Séderie, 47600
Tel *05 53 65 31 99* **Closed** *none*
Traditional dishes served with home-made ice cream in unique flavours: fruits, flowers, spices, cheese, and vegetables. Beautiful views over the river.

PENNE D'AGENAIS: La Maison sur la Place €€
Classic **Map** D3
10 place Gambetta, 47140
Tel *05 53 01 29 18* **Closed** *Mon*
Former grocery store, now a rustic chic restaurant serving tasty salads, duck, and seafood dishes. Home-made pastries too.

PUJOLS: Villa Smeralda €€
Mediterranean **Map** D3
Le Bourg, 47300
Tel *05 53 36 72 12* **Closed** *Mon*
Popular family restaurant offering huge servings of antipasti, salads, pasta, and seafood. Specialty: lamb baked for eight hours.

PUJOLS: La Toque Blanche €€€
Classic **Map** D3
Pujols, 47300
Tel *05 53 49 00 30* **Closed** *Sun, Mon*
Classic French haute cuisine such as roast partridge with cabbage and *foie gras*, great desserts, and an extensive wine list.

DK Choice

PUYMIROL: Michel Trama €€€
Gastronomic **Map** D3
52 rue Royale, 47270
Tel *05 53 95 31 46* **Closed** *Mon*
A medieval hilltop lodge built by the Counts of Toulouse and given a wonderfully theatrical décor by Jacques Garcia (think Baroque drapes, chandeliers, and a gorgeous Italianate courtyard), provides the perfect backdrop for top chef Michel Trama's culinary works of art: truffled potatoes, the famous *foie gras* hamburger, and exquisite desserts.

ST-ETIENNE-DE-FOUGERES: Auberge de Feuillade €
Ferme-auberge **Map** D3
Feuillade, 2 km (1 mile) outside St Livrade-sur-Lot, 47380
Tel *05 53 01 09 84* **Closed** *Wed*
Farmhouse fare with *foie gras*, duck confit, classic poule farcie, and home-made desserts. Lunch only on weekdays. Book ahead.

Beautiful interiors at the Michel Trama restaurant in Puymirol, known for its refined cuisine

VILLENEUVE-SUR-LOT: La Table des Sens €€
Gastronomic **Map** D3
8 rue de Penne, 47300
Tel *05 53 36 97 04* **Closed** *Mon, Tue*
Pretty and creative seasonal cuisine from a young, talented team. Intimate atmosphere. Reservations essential.

VIRAZEIL: Le Moulin d'Ané €
Southwestern **Map** D3
Route de Gontaud - Moulin Dane, Virazeil, 47200
Tel *05 53 20 18 25* **Closed** *Mon, Tue*
Excellent seasonal cuisine in an 18th-century watermill. Try the succulent Blonde d'Aquitaine beef and apple tart.

Landes

CAPBRETON: MB Restaurant €€
Contemporary **Map** A4
17 avenue Georges Pompidou, 40130
Tel *05 58 72 12 02* **Closed** *Mon*
Stylish restaurant with small menu that changes every month, oysters holding pride of place.

La Maison sur la Place, located at the top of a hill in Penne d'Agenais

CASTETS: Ferme-Auberge Lesca €
Ferme-auberge **Map** B4
428 chemin des Tucs, 40260
Tel *05 58 89 41 45* **Closed** *Mon; Nov-Apr*
Landes' oldest farm restaurant features duck in every form, including five different *foie gras* prepartions. Reservations only.

DAX: La Table de Pascal €€
Bistro **Map** B4
4 rue Fontaine-Chaude, 40100
Tel *05 58 74 89 00* **Closed** *none*
Very popular Parisian-style, bistro with delicious, mostly southwestern, dishes. Reserve in advance.

DAX: Le Moulin de Poustagnacq €€€
Gastronomic **Map** B4
3km (2 miles) north of Dax, Rue René Loustalot, Saint Paul lès Dax, 40990
Tel *05 58 91 31 03* **Closed** *Mon*
Overlooking a pond in the woods, this restaurant has an innovative menu based on the finest regional produce. Good selection of wines too.

EUGENIE-LES-BAINS: La Ferme aux Grives €€€
Southwestern **Map** C4
111 rue Thermes, 40320
Tel *05 58 05 05 05* **Closed** *Wed*
One of Michel Guérard's more "rustic" restaurants, featuring country cuisine such as roast suckling pig and Landaise chicken baked in fig leaves.

EUGENIE-LES-BAINS: Les Prés d'Eugénie €€€
Gastronomic **Map** C4
Le Bourg, 40320
Tel *05 58 05 05 05* **Closed** *Mon*
At this, the headquarters of French culinary genius Michel Guérard, everything is outstanding: both gourmand and the famous *minceur* (diet) menus.

For more information on types of restaurants *see page 257*

HOSSEGOR: Le Surfing €
International **Map** A4
6 Place des Estagnots, 40510
Tel *05 58 47 99 76* **Closed** *Oct-Apr*
Varied menu of tapas, burritos, Thai fish cakes and Moroccan couscous; favoured by surfers.

HOSSEGOR: Lou Casaou De Le Ma €
Oyster Bar **Map** A4
Fond Du Lac, 40150
Tel *06 19 78 21 88* **Closed** *Nov-Mar*
Super fresh oysters: served with lemon, shallot sauce, bread and butter, white wines, and big smiles.

DK Choice

HOSSEGOR: Jean des Sables €€€
Seafood **Map** A4
121 Boulevard de la Dune, 40150
Tel *05 58 72 29 82* **Closed** *Mon; Jan-early Feb*
Welcome addition along the Landaise coast, this oceanfront restaurant is run by Coussaus of Magesq's Relais de la Poste. Its seafood is exquisitely prepared and full of flavour-packed surprises. Try the Fish & Chic menu, or the bargain weekday lunch menu, which includes wine and coffee.

MAGESQ: Bistrot le Quillier €
Bistro **Map** B4
Avenue de Marenne, 40140
Tel *05 58 47 79 50* **Closed** *none*
Just 20m (20 yards) from the Relais de la Poste, this bistro serves a tasty meal and is more pocket-friendly. It has a terrace and garden. Ideal for families.

MAGESQ: Relais de la Poste €€€
Gastronomic **Map** B4
24 avenue de Marenne, 40140
Tel *05 58 47 70 25* **Closed** *Mon, Tue*
Delightful setting for Jean Coussau's classic French cuisine such as Adour salmon and white Magesq asparagus. Superb wines. Panoramic terrace.

Welcoming exterior of Les Clefs d'Argent in Mont-de-Marsan

MIMIZAN: Hôtel Atlantique €
Seafood **Map** B3
38 avenue de la Côte d'Argent, 40200
Tel *05 58 09 09 42* **Closed** *Sat, Sun; 3 weeks in Jan*
Very popular for its excellent and affordable seafood. Meat choices for those who don't eat fish.

MIMIZAN: L'Orchestra Bar €
Wine Bar **Map** B3
16 rue du Casino, 40200
Tel *06 29 05 98 25* **Closed** *Mid-Oct-mid Mar*
Wine and tapas bar, with tasty nibbles and an excellent list of wines and cocktails. A perfect stop after the beach.

MOLIETS ET MAA: La Cave aux Moules €
Seafood **Map** B4
Av d'Océan, 40660
Tel *05 58 48 54 05* **Closed** *Mon; Nov-Mar*
Informal spot with wooden benches, specializing in mussels, pasta dishes, and pizza. Arrive around 7pm or be prepared to queue.

Casual and relaxed ambience at the Relais de la Poste, Magesq

MONT-DE-MARSAN: Auberge de la Pouillique €
Southwestern **Map** C4
Chemin de la Pouillique, Mazerolles 40900
Tel *05 58 75 22 97* **Closed** *Mon*
Charming farmhouse that offers traditional seasonal dishes. Try the *tourtière Landaise aux pommes.*

MONT-DE-MARSAN: Gandhi €
Indian **Map** C4
28 bis, Place Joseph-Pancaut, 40000
Tel *05 58 85 97 97* **Closed** *Wed*
A nice change of pace; excellent naans, tandoori and curries. Ask if you like it spicy.

MONT-DE-MARSAN: Un Air de Campagne €€
Contemporary **Map** C4
3 Rue Thérèse Clavé, 40000
Tel *05 58 06 05 41* **Closed** *Mon*
Refined cuisine in a beautiful setting. Inspired *menu du jour,* and truly scrumptious desserts.

MONT-DE-MARSAN: Les Clefs d'Argent €€€
Gastronomic **Map** C4
333 avenue des Martyrs de la Résistance, 40000
Tel *05 58 06 16 45* **Closed** *Mon, 3 weeks in Aug*
Gourmet creations made from local produce that have surprising undertones inspired by the African roots of the chef's wife.

MUGRON: Ferme Auberge Marquine €
Ferme-auberge **Map** B4
Route d'Hagetmau Marquine, 40250
Tel *05 58 97 74 23* **Closed** *none*
Atmospheric farm with truly delicious fare: duck, Chalosse beef, and more. Reservations only.

PARENTIS-EN-BORN: Chez Flo €
Contemporary **Map** B3
9 rue St-Barthélémy, 40160
Tel *05 58 78 40 21* **Closed** *Mon*
Warm, friendly restaurant, enthusiastic young chef, and

truly excellent dishes, simply prepared. Great for families, and excellent value for money.

PARENTIS-EN-BORN: Restaurant de la Poste €
Southwestern **Map** B3
12 Avenue du 8 mai 45, 40160
Tel *05 58 78 40 23* **Closed** *none*
Laid back restaurant, popular for its *planchot*: an array of delicacies served on a wooden board. Outstanding Landaise salad.

PISSOS: Café de Pissos €
Southwestern **Map** B3
42 rue du Pont-Battant, 40140
Tel *05 58 08 90 16* **Closed** *Wed*
On a pleasant terrace, this eatery serves timeless dishes such as duck with cep mushroom sauce.

ROQUEFORT: Le Logis de Saint Vincent €€
Southwestern **Map** C3
76 rue Laubaner, 40210
Tel *05 58 45 75 36* **Closed** *Sun*
The 19th-century *hôtel particulier*, has an exotic garden, and a sophisticated menu combining tradition with creativity.

SABRES: Auberge des Pins €€
Southwestern **Map** B3
Route de la Piscine, 40630
Tel *05 58 08 30 00* **Closed** *Mon*
Attractive farmhouse serving Landaise cuisine: try its boned pigeon stuffed with *foie gras*.

SAUBUSSE: Villa Stings €€
Contemporary **Map** B3
Rue du Port, 40180
Tel *05 58 57 70 18* **Closed** *Mon*
19th-century house on the Adour river; has updated classics such as bass spiked with smoked eel.

SEIGNOSSE: Le Loom €
Basque **Map** A4
1, avenue Jean Moulin - 40510
Tel *05 58 43 31 39* **Closed** *Jan*
Unassuming, but has a great wine list, amazing pintxos (Basque tapas), and excellent seafood. Themed nights at the bar.

SEIGNOSSE: Les Roseaux €
Southwestern **Map** A4
Route Louis de Bourmont, 40510
Tel *05 58 72 80 30* **Closed** *Tue*
Good value Basque and Landaise menus plus lovely views over the Etang Blanc. Boats for hire. Reservations recommended.

SEIGNOSSE: Villa de L'Etang Blanc €€
Gastronomic **Map** A4
2265 Route de L'Etang Blanc, 40510
Tel *05 58 72 80 15* **Closed** *Mon, Tue; Nov–Feb*
Enchanting location for refined, innovative dining. Short menu, but each dish perfect.

SOUSTONS: La Storia €
Southwestern **Map** B4
29 rue Emile Nougaro, 40141
Tel *05 58 41 22 66* **Closed** *Sun*
Something for every taste: steaks, seafood, duck dishes, grilled fresh fish, pasta, omelettes and pizza.

SOUSTONS: Marinero €
Seafood **Map** B4
8km (5 miles) east of Soustons, 15 Grand Rue, Vieux Boucau, 40480
Tel *05 58 48 14 15* **Closed** *Mon, Tue, Oct-Apr*
Seafood prepared with a Spanish touch *(sea bass a la plancha)*. Excellent value fixed menus.

Pays Basque

ASCAIN: Cidrerie Txopinondo €
Basque **Map** A4
Zone artisanale Lan Zelai, Sagarnotegi Bidea, 64310
Tel *05 59 54 62 34* **Closed** *Tue, Wed*
While serving huge steaks and pintxos, this cider microbrewery practices *txotx*: the art of keeping glasses full.

Charming and delightful interiors at the Auberge des Pins, Sabres

BARCUS: Chilo €€
Contemporary **Map** B5
Le Bourg, 64130
Tel *05 59 28 90 79* **Closed** *none*
Long-established gourmet address near Mauléon. A culinary world of its own: local lamb, duck, and game.

BAYONNE: Auberge du Cheval Blanc €€
Contemporary **Map** A4
68 rue Bourgneuf, 64100
Tel *05 59 59 01 33* **Closed** *Mon*
The chef here is truly creative with trout, scallops, pigeon and wild mushrooms. The restaurant has been managed by members of the same family for 50 years.

BAYONNE: Le Bayonnais €€
Basque **Map** A4
38 quai des Corsaires, 64100
Tel *05 59 25 61 19* **Closed** *Mon*
Modest restaurant famous for its generous dishes: duck, rabbit, game, langoustines and scallops. Tables outside by the river.

Wooden cider barrels at the unique Cidrerie Txopinondo in Ascain

BAYONNE: Le Bistrot Itsaski €€
Basque **Map** A4
43 quai Amiral Jaureguiberry, 64100
Tel *05 59 46 13 96* **Closed** *Wed*
Good for tapas, quick lunch, or full meal with lovely seafood entrees, oysters, grilled meats, and fish. Right on the river.

BAYONNE: Rôtisserie de Roy Léon €€
Southwestern **Map** A4
8 rue du Coursic, 64100
Tel *05 59 59 55 84* **Closed** *none*
Medieval approach, with plenty of spit-roast meats: venison, beef, duck. Also *seafood a la plancha*.

BIARRITZ: Le Clos Basque €
Basque **Map** A4
12 rue L. Barthou, 64200
Tel *05 59 24 24 96* **Closed** *Mon*
Cheerful tavern offers good value creative cooking that blends Basque and southwestern French influences. Always packed.

BIARRITZ: Chez Albert €€
Seafood **Map** A4
51bis Port des Pêcheurs, 64200
Tel *05 59 24 43 84* **Closed** *Wed*
Outdoor dining on the fishing port at this eatery reputed for great seafood and excellent grills.

BIARRITZ: La Table d'Aranda €€
Gastronomic **Map** A4
87 av de la Marne, 64200
Tel *05 59 22 16 04* **Closed** *Sun, Mon*
Far from the city's tourist traps, this remarkable, though slightly eccentric place, has exceptional cooking at reasonable prices.

BIARRITZ: Villa Eugénie (Hôtel de Palais) €€€
Classic **Map** A4
1 avenue de l'Impératrice, 64200
Tel *05 59 41 64 00* **Closed** *Mon, Tue; Feb-mid Mar*
Sumptuous classic cuisine, as it used to be in Eugénie's day, is brought up to date in this majestic salon built to match the tastes of an empress.

Pretty terrace of Auberge Ostapé in Bidarray, known fot its Basque cuisine

Rustic decor at Etchémaïté in Larrau

DK Choice

BIDARRAY: Auberge Ostapé €€
Basque **Map** B4
Domaine de la Chatahoa, 64780
Tel *05 59 37 91 91* **Closed** *Tue; late Nov-early Mar*
An endearing space, with a flowery terrace that overlooks lush green hills. The talented chef introduces you to the best of Basque cuisine, with colour, imagination, and a touch of Espelette pepper: trout, *txangurros* (spider crab, a favourite in the Basque region), beef with ceps, and roast pigeon.

BIDART: Les Frères Ibarboure €€€
Gastronomic **Map** C4
Chemin de Ttaliénèa, near Guéthary, 64210
Tel *05 59 54 81 64* **Closed** *Mon, Wed; 2 weeks in Nov, 2 weeks in Jan*
One of the region's top-rated restaurants offers a unique combination of taste and colour with memorable shellfish starters, lobster, grouse and partridge.

CAMBO-LES-BAINS: Chez Tante Ursule €
Basque **Map** B4
fronton du Bas-Cambo, 64250
Tel *05 59 29 78 23* **Closed** *Tue*
Enjoy Basque cooking with *foie gras* and Aunt Ursule's formidable desserts right on the fronton, where they play *pelota*.

CIBOURE: Chez Mattin €€
Basque **Map** A4
63 rue Evariste Baignol, 64500
Tel *05 59 47 19 52* **Closed** *Sun, Mon*
Traditional Basque dishes without the modern frills: *ttoro* (fish soup), grilled brochettes and authentic *tripes basquaise*.

ESPELETTE: Euzkadi €€
Basque **Map** A4
285 Karrika Nagusia, 64250
Tel *05 59 93 91 88* **Closed** *Mon; Nov-mid Dec*
Many of the area's noble AOC peppers, find their way into the duck, salt cod, and charcuterie of this elegant address.

HENDAYE-PLAGE: La Cabane de Pecheur €
Seafood **Map** A4
Quai de la Floride, 64700
Tel *05 59 20 38 09* **Closed** *Mon*
Unpretentious restaurant overlooking the fishing port; fish soup, prawns and squid, mussels, and grilled steaks at friendly prices.

LARRAU: Etchémaïté €€
Basque **Map** B5
Larrau, 64560
Tel *05 59 28 61 45* **Closed** *Jan-mid Mar*
Sophisticated mountain cooking at this family-run inn, with roast pigeon, *ris d'agneau* with ceps, and a terrace with views.

ST-JEAN-PIED-DE-PORT: Hôtel Andreinia €
Basque **Map** B5
8km (5 miles) south of St Jean, Le Bourg, Esterençuby, 64220
Tel *05 59 37 09 70* **Closed** *2 weeks in Nov*
Choose from salt cod with piquillo peppers, *foie gras*, Basque

salads, wild mushrooms, and grilled chops at this simple mountain inn.

ST-JEAN-PIED-DE-PORT: Les Pyrénées €€€
Gastronomic **Map** B5
19 place Charles de Gaulle, 64220
Tel *05 59 37 01 01* **Closed** *Tue; mid Nov-mid Dec, 3 weeks in Jan*
Refined, Michelin-starred cooking, at this very chic and modern reworking of a Basque inn up in the mountains.

ST-JEAN-DE-LUZ: Chez Maya-Le Petit Grill Basque €
Basque **Map** A4
2 rue St-Jacques, 64500
Tel *05 59 26 80 76* **Closed** *Wed*
Excellent Basque home cooking with good fish soup, stuffed peppers, and great grilled squid. An institution in St-Jean.

ST-JEAN-DE-LUZ: Le Kaïku €€
Gastronomic **Map** A4
17 rue de la République, 64500
Tel *05 59 26 13 20* **Closed** *Tue, Wed out of season*
This gracious establishment, in St-Jean's oldest house, welcomes you to experience the creativite freedom offered by modern Basque cuisine. Reasonable prices.

ST-JEAN-DE-LUZ: Pilpil Enea €€
Seafood **Map** A4
3 Rue Sallagoity, 64500
Tel *05 59 51 20 80* **Closed** *2 weeks in Nov, 2 weeks in Jun-Jul*
Highly popular and usually crowded, this unpretentious restaurant is known especially for its *parillada* (mixed grills) and *hake pil-pil*.

Béarn

AUDAUX: Auberge Claverie €
Southwestern **Map** B4
2 Place de l'Estanquet 64190
Tel *05 59 66 03 80* **Closed** *Mon; 2 weeks in Oct*
Family-run country inn, packed with locals enjoying its delicious traditional food, and home-made desserts. Book on weekends.

BOSDORROS: Auberge Labarthe €€
Gastronomic **Map** C5
Rue Pierre Bidau, 64290
Tel *05 59 21 50 13* **Closed** *Mon, Tue*
Classic dining room with Michelin-starred cuisine: seafood, vegetables, and farm-raised meats. Good set menus.

JURANÇON: Le Cas du Pont d'Oly €€
Contemporary **Map** C5
2 avenue Rausky, 64110
Tel *05 59 06 13 40* **Closed** *none*
Pretty place to lunch on seafood salad with smoked salmon and pork confits by the pool.

OLORON-STE-MARIE: Le Chaudron €
Southwestern **Map** B5
18 avenue Lattre-de-Tassigny, 64400
Tel *05 59 39 76 99* **Closed** *Sat; one week in May, all Aug*
Traditional cuisine in generous portions. Specialities include *Tournedos Rossini* and *assiette repas* (duck or fish assortments).

PAU: Le Bistro a Coté €
Bistro **Map** C5
1 Place Gramont, 64000
Tel *05 59 27 98 08* **Closed** *Sun*
Cool jazzy bistro with tasty and affordable dishes (T-bone steak *a la plancha*), frequent concerts, and a little bit of Paris.

PAU: Le Majestic €
Contemporary **Map** C5
9 Place Royale, 64000
Tel *05 59 27 56 83* **Closed** *Mon*
Lovely food served on a pleasant terrace under the trees, especially the fish. Excellent value for high quality of cuisine.

DK Choice

PAU: Marc Destrade €€
Contemporary **Map** C5
30 rue Pasteur, 64000
Tel *05 59 27 62 60* **Closed** *Mon*
This 17th century building is located next to Pau's covered market. Sit in the intimate dining room with its open fire, and enjoy chef Marc Destrade's delicious modern takes on traditional French dishes – for instance, monk fish with passion fruit vinegar, and the rack of lamb with pistachios. The set lunch menu offers excellent value.

SALIES-DE-BEARN: La Belle Auberge €
Classic **Map** B4
9km (5 miles) west of Salies in Castagnede, 64270
Tel *05 59 38 15 28* **Closed** *Jan, 2 weeks in Jun*
Join the crowd for delicious favourites that include garbure, *moules marinieres*, and chocolate profiteroles, in a charming rural setting. Be sure to book ahead.

Intimate dining at the Auberge Labarthe, Bosdorros

SHOPS AND MARKETS

Aquitaine is a mainly agricultural region, with an abundance of food specialities. These are often sold by the producers themselves at local markets. Here you will find *foie gras* from the Périgord or the Landes, oysters from Arcachon, strawberries and prunes from the Lot-et-Garonne, goat's cheese from Quercy, wines from the Bordeaux area, and Armagnac. Many local artists and craftspeople offer their work for sale, and some open their studios to visitors. There are also numerous antiques shops and flea markets.

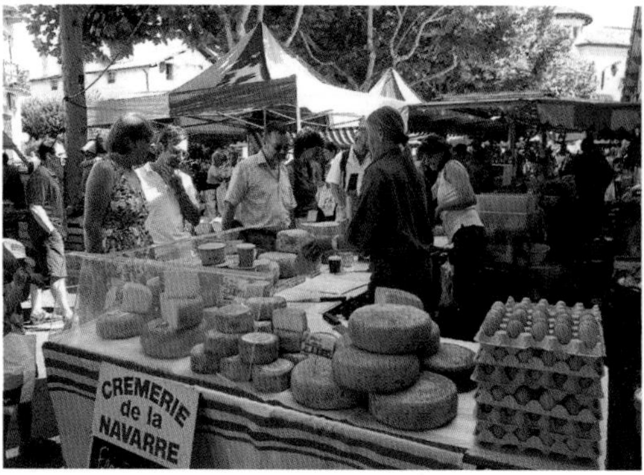

A lively market in Saint-Jean-de-Luz, selling local produce

Markets

Markets are friendly, lively places, where all sorts of tempting delicacies are on offer. Small producers set out their home-grown vegetables and fruit, which may include some vineyard peaches and old-fashioned varieties of apple. Other stalls are loaded with charcuterie, jars of *foie gras* and jams, such as those made by **Francis Miot**, and a range of local specialities, many of them made with organic produce. Markets vary according to season and to the area, and there are frequent speciality events, such as the cèpes market in Villefranche-du-Périgord, the truffle market in Lalbenque, various *foie gras* markets, and fish auctions in coastal towns. The Fête du Piment, devoted to sweet red peppers, takes place in Espelette in October, after the harvest. Powdered red pepper is available from **Ttipia** and **Xavier Jauregui's** farm, both in Espellete. Farmers' markets usually start at around 7am and most are over by about 12.30pm.

Wine

Wine-producers whose estates are on official wine routes open their cellars to visitors, as do several Maisons des Vins and wine co-operatives. Here visitors may taste the wine and buy direct from the producer.

Local wine merchants stock such regional wines as Bordeaux, Bergerac (particularly **Julien de Savignac**, in Le Bugue), Cahors, Côtes-de-Duras and Jurançon, and spirits such as eau-de-vie and Armagnac. Information is available from **Bordeaux Tourist Office**, with details of **wine tours** at www.winetravelguides.com.

Shops and Crafts Studios

Besides outlets for gastronomic specialities, the southwest has a host of shops selling handicrafts and traditional health and beauty preparations. Some local produce has surprising uses. Both walnuts and salt from Salies-de-Béarn are used in cosmetics, and grape extracts feature in the treatments offered by **Les Sources the Caudalie** *(see p251)*.

Crafts stalls are often found at produce markets in certain villages, particularly in summer. Hatters, metalworkers, stringed-instrument makers, potters, enamellers and glass-blowers at **La Poterie Landaise** welcome visitors to their studios. Individual events are also devoted to certain crafts. There are pottery fairs, weaving and basketry markets, and cutlery fairs. A craftworkers' festival takes place in July at La Bachellerie, in the Dordogne. Aquitaine also has a long pottery-making tradition. **Cazaux**, in Biarritz, is one of several outlets where original pieces can be found. **Madilar**, in Bayonne, is one of several Basque jewellers who use traditional designs. *Makhilas*, Basque shepherd's crooks with decorative finials, are custom-made by Ainciart Bergara. Boxwood-handled knives, made in Nontron, are another Périgordian classic. Traditional makers include **Coutellerie Nontronnaise**.

Jam produced by Francis Miot

Regional Produce

Aquitaine produces a wide variety of fine foods. This includes the beef from Chalosse, ham from Bayonne and caviar from **Sturia**, the Périgordian fish-farming

Interior of Confiserie Pierre Boisson, a confectioner's in Agen

business, as well as poultry, cheese, such as ewe's milk cheese from Ossau-Iraty, and fruit and vegetables, such as chasselas grapes from Prayssas, tomatoes from Marmande and black cherries from Itxassou. While some producers have roadside stalls, others have joint outlets in certain villages.

The region is also known for its sweet delicacies, such as prunes, produced by **Pierre Boisson** in Agen; *cannelés*, baked by **Baillardran** in Bordeaux; and the famous *Les Pyrénéens* chocolates, made by Lindt in Oloron-Sainte-Marie. Macaroons, the speciality in Saint-Jean-de-Luz, are made at **Maison Adam** and the confectioner **Pariès**.

Linen

Colourfully striped Basque linen *(see p211)* is sold in interior decoration shops such as **Tissages Moutet**, who use leading designers. Rope-soled espadrilles, everyday footwear in the Pays Basque, are made in fashionable versions by **Fabrique Prodiso**.

At **Béatex**, in Oloron-Sainte-Marie, Basque bérets are still made from Pyrenean wool. This is especially warm, like the mohair that is woven at **Ferme du Chaudron Magique**, in Brugnac.

Largely because of the popularity of surfing, sportswear is now another speciality of the region. T-shirts by the Spanish Kukuxumusu label are in popular demand.

Ducks at the Musée du Foie Gras in the Lot-et-Garonne

Window display at a Basque linen shop in Saint-Jean-de-Luz

Farm Shops

The popularity of countryside holidays has benefited many farms in Aquitaine. All over the region you will see "Bienvenue à la Ferme" signs by the roadside. Farms displaying this have campsites or rooms to let, and they also provide open-air activities, meals and tasty snacks for children.

Many farmers sell their produce by opening their premises to visitors and giving free tastings. At these farms, you are likely to find everything from fruit juice, wine, honey and walnut cake, to goat's cheese, free-range eggs and chickens, preserves and aromatic and medicinal herbs.

DIRECTORY

Specialities

Gironde

Baillardran
Galerie des Grands-Hommes, Bordeaux.
Tel 05 56 79 05 89.

Bordeaux Tourist Office
12 cours 30 juillet, Bordeaux.
Tel 05 56 00 66 01.

Sturia
21 rue de la Gare, 33450 St Sulpice & Cameyrac.
Tel 05 56 30 27 94.
W caviar-sturia.com

Wine tours
W winetravelguides.com

Périgord-Quercy

Julien de Savignac
Avenue de la Libération, 24260 Le Bugue.
Tel 05 53 07 10 31.

Lot-et-Garonne

Confiserie Pierre Boisson
20 rue Grande-Horloge, Agen.
Tel 05 53 66 20 61.

Pays Basque

Xavier Jauregui
Ferme Erreka, Espelette.
Tel 05 59 93 80 29.

Maison Adam
6 rue de la République, Saint-Jean-de-Luz.
Tel 05 59 26 03 54.

Pariès
14 rue du Port-Neuf, Bayonne.
Tel 05 59 59 06 29.

Ttipia
Merkatu Plaza, Espelette.
Tel 05 59 93 97 82.

Béarn

Les Confitures (Francis) Miot
48 rue Joffre, Pau.
Tel 05 59 27 69 51.

Clothes & Handmade Items

Gironde

Les Sources de Caudalie
Chemin de Smith Haut-Lafitte, Bordeaux-Martillac. **Tel** 05 57 83 83 83.

Périgord-Quercy

Coutellerie Nontronnaise
Place Paul-Bert, Nontron.
Tel 05 53 56 01 55.

Lot-et-Garonne

Ferme du Chaudron Magique
Brugnac.
Tel 05 53 88 80 77.

Landes

La Poterie Landaise
Allée des Vergnes, 40140, Soustons.
Tel 05 58 41 14 81.

Pays Basque

Cazaux
10 rue Broquedis, Biarritz.
Tel 05 59 22 36 03.

Madilar
58 ave Maréchal-Soult, Bayonne.
Tel 05 59 63 38 18.

Béarn

Béatex
Rue Rocgrand, Oloron-Sainte-Marie.
Tel 05 59 39 12 07.

Fabrique Prodiso
Zone Artisanale, Mauléon-Licharre.
Tel 05 59 28 28 48.

Tissages Moutet
Rue du Souvenir Français, Z.A. de Salignes, Orthez.
Tel 05 59 69 14 33.

What to Buy in Aquitaine

Aquitaine will tempt you with a great range of souvenirs, from Basque linen and Médoc confectionery to Périgord *foie gras* and studio ceramics. Small shops in villages all over the region offer a wide variety of local products and specialities. Also, the farmers' markets, craftsmen's workshops and farm shops are particularly good places to buy, as producers are always happy to pass on a little of their knowledge and to explain their methods.

Espadrilles

Basque Items

Besides espadrilles, berets and woollen items, linen is one of the finest of all Basque items. Woven from flax, it has seven coloured stripes for the seven Basque provinces. T-shirts made by Kukuxumusu are very fashionable in the Pays Basque, and the popularity of surfing has given sportswear by Quiksilver, 64 and other makers a fresh cachet.

T-shirts made in the Pays Basque

Basque berets

Basque linen

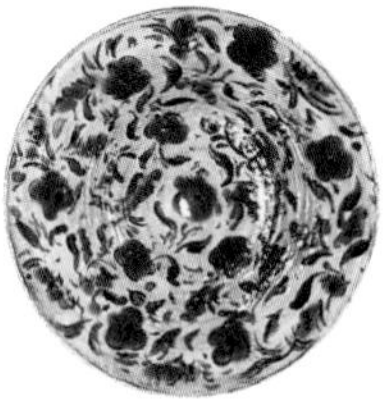

Painted plate

Basque crockery

Most Basque crockery consists of white porcelain decorated in green and red, the traditional colours of the Pays Basque. The principal manufacturers are located on the Adour river.

Ceramic vase

Key fob with Basque cross

Brooches and pendants featuring traditional motifs

Silver bracelets

Basque jewellery

The Basque cross is a motif that appears on rings, chokers, bracelets and many other items. An ancient sun symbol, it is known all over the world, and its four scrolled arms symbolize the movement of the stars. Basque crosses, known as *Lauburu* (Four Heads), are supposed to be good-luck charms.

Natural Products

A vinotherapy spa centre, with hot springs and health treatments using grape extracts, was established in Bordeaux in the 1990s. It now produces a range of cosmetics based on these spring waters and grape extracts. Other spas in Aquitaine also produce many of their own health products, such as salt and clay extracts, for use at home.

Honey soaps from La Cité des Abeilles, Saint-Faust, Béarn

Fine salt from Salies-de-Béarn

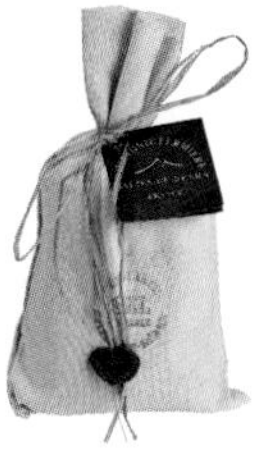

Coarse salt from Salies-de-Béarn, for hydrotherapy

Caudalie health product

Regional Specialities

Aquitaine has a great gastronomic tradition. Its many specialities include Périgordian truffles and *foie gras*, Arcachon oysters, Agen prunes, Bayonne ham, Béarnese ewe's milk cheese, Espelette red peppers, Basque cakes and Bordeaux wines. Besides such factory-made products as Lindt chocolate, a wide range of traditionally made products are available, straight from the maker.

Box of Basque macaroons

Stuffed Agen prunes

Walnuts in liqueur

Agen prune purée

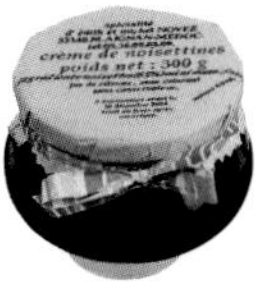

Chocolate and Médoc hazelnut spread

Lindt chocolate, made in Oloron-Sainte-Marie

Lindt's famous *Les Pyrénéens* chocolates

Médoc hazelnut chocolates

Almond sweets made by Francis Miot

Tourons, traditional Basque confectionery

ENTERTAINMENT

A festive spirit pervades many aspects of daily life in Aquitaine. Basque *bandas* play in the streets, and even enjoying a drink in a local *bodega* is likely to be enlivened by music. From jazz and film to bullfighting and Basque choral singing, the region offers a wide choice of entertainment all year round. The many dance and drama festivals, as well as concert halls and art galleries, also play an important part in this vibrant cultural scene.

General Information

Regional daily newspapers, local radio stations and tourist organizations *(see pp287 and 288)* are good sources of up-to-date information about cultural events. **Clubs et Concerts**, a free fortnightly events bulletin published in Bordeaux, also has a useful website.

A production of the ballet *Sleeping Beauty* at Opéra National de Bordeaux

Buying Tickets

Tickets for most mainstream events are available from outlets such as **FNAC**, the large books and music store, and hypermarkets, including **Carrefour. France Billet**, an online ticket agency, allows you to purchase tickets either over the Internet or from one of the region's agencies.

Theatre and Dance

One of the region's leading cultural attractions is the **Opéra National de Bordeaux**, at the city's Grand Théâtre *(see pp76–7)*, with a regular programme of opera, operetta, classical ballet and contemporary dance. Outside large towns, a large number of **festivals** take place throughout the summer. These include Jeux du Théâtre, in Sarlat *(see p39)*, and the major international contemporary mime festival, Mimos, in Périgueux, *(see p105)*. Dance companies come to Biarritz to take part in Le Temps d'Aimer, and to Mont-de-Marsan for the Festival d'Art Flamenco *(see p39)*. The Festival de Pau *(see p39)* features drama, music and dance.

Traditional Basque fanfare at the Fêtes de Bayonne

Music

The region's concert halls cater to every musical taste. The **Scène Nationale de Bayonne et du Sud Aquitain**, among others, hosts a wide range of events, but it is in the **Zénith de Pau**, the region's largest concert hall, that the biggest stars usually perform.

Classical recitals take place in the Médoc's vine-growing châteaux and Romanesque churches, and jazz is played at various festivals in the Gironde (at Uzeste and Monségur, for example) and at **Comptoir du Jazz** in Bordeaux. The Festival de Musique Baroque du Périgord Noir takes place in some of the area's finest churches. Les Nuits Lyriques en Marmandais *(see p160)* is a concert series, given by top soloists.

Cinema

The regional daily newspaper *Sud-Ouest (see p287)* provides information about films throughout the region. Art-house films are also shown at **Utopia**, in a deconsecrated church. The **Jean-Eustache** cinema in Pessac hosts a festival of films on historical themes. **Ciné-Passion** is a mobile cinema that shows films at venues around Brantôme, in the Périgord, with open- air showings during the summer months. The Festival des Jeunes Réalisateurs, held in Saint-Jean-de-Luz in October, is a showcase for films by young directors.

Utopia, a cinema in Bordeaux

Casino de la Plage, in Château Deganne, in Arcachon

Art Galleries and Craft Studios

Bordeaux has about 30 art galleries, including **Arrêt sur l'Image**, which is devoted to photography. Art studios in Monflanquin (Lot-et-Garonne) are highly sought after, and some major European artists have set up studios in the **Domaine d'Abbadia** in Hendaye. Art galleries on the south coast are filled with paintings with a strong regional character.

The **Route des Métiers d'Art** was created to help promote the region's crafts studios. A guide to workshops along it is published by the regional tourist authority *(see p287)*.

Casinos

Several towns, including **Arcachon, Biarritz, Saint-Jean-de-Luz, Pau** and Hossegor, have grand houses that have been converted into casinos, with slot machines and roulette.

DIRECTORY

General Information

W **clubsetconcerts.com**

Tickets

Carrefour
W **carrefourspectacles.com**

FNAC
W **fnac.com**

France Billet
Tel 0892 692 694.
W **francebillet.com**

Theatre, Dance & Music

Comptoir du Jazz
Le Port de la Lune, 58 quai de Paludate, 33800 Bordeaux.
Tel 05 56 49 15 55.

Festivals d'Aquitaine
Aquitaine en Scène.
W **festivals.aquitaine.fr**

Opéra National de Bordeaux
Grand Théâtre Place de la Comédie, 33000 Bordeaux.
Tel 05 56 00 85 95.
W **opera-bordeaux.com**

Scène Nationale de Bayonne et du Sud Aquitain
1 rue Edouard Doucerė, 64100 Bayonne.
Tel 05 59 59 07 27.
W **snbsa.fr**

Zénith de Pau
Boulvevard du Cami-Salié, 64000 Pau.
Tel 05 59 80 77 50.
W **zenith-pyrenees.fr**

Cinemas

Cinéma Jean-Eustache
Place de la 5ème-République, 33600 Pessac.
Tel 05 56 46 00 96.
W **webeustache.com**

Ciné-Passion en Périgord
La Fabrique. Rue Amiral-Courbet, 24110 Saint-Astier. **Tel** 05 53 02 64 97.
W **cine-passion24. com**

Utopia
5 place Camille-Jullian, 33000 Bordeaux.
Tel 05 56 52 00 03.
W **cinemas-utopia.org**

Art Galleries & Craft Studios

Aprasaq
Association pour la Promotion de Métiers d'Art en Périgord.
Tel 05 53 35 87 00.
W **artisanat24.com**

Domaine d'Abbadia
64700 Hendaye.
Tel 05 59 20 37 20.
W **abbadia.fr**

Galerie Arrêt sur l'Image
Quai Armand-Lalande, 33300 Bordeaux.
Tel 05 56 69 16 48.
W **arretsurlimage.com**

Website for the arts and art galleries of the southwest
Lists galleries, art festivals and exhibitions.
W **articite.com/aquitaine/galeries_dart/galeries_aquitaine.htm**

Casinos

Arcachon
163 boulevard de La Plage. **Tel** 05 56 83 41 44.
W **casinoarcachon.com**

Biarritz
1 avenue Édouard-VII
Tel 05 59 22 77 77.
W **lucienbarriere.com**

Pau
Parc Beaumont.
Tel 05 59 27 06 92.

Saint-Jean-de-Luz
Place Maurice-Ravel.
Tel 05 59 51 58 58.

OUTDOOR ACTIVITIES

For visitors, both rugby, in which Aquitaine excels, and Basque pelota are likely to be spectator sports. However, the region offers a range of other sporting and outdoor activities. In summer, the Pyrenees are ideal for hiking, hanggliding and mountaineering and, in winter, they offer superb skiing and snow-walking. The coastline, the flat expanses of the Landes and the gentle hills of the region's vineyards are pleasant to explore by bicycle or on horseback, the leisurely pace enabling you to take in the spectacular scenery. Aquitaine is also a top destination for golfing enthusiasts, being home to several of the finest courses in Europe.

Hiking in the Massif de la Rhune, in the Pays Basque

Walking

From the coast to the Pyrenees, through the vineyards of Bordeaux and across the Landes, more than 6,000 km (3,730 miles) of waymarked footpaths criss-cross Aquitaine. For example, the GR653 and GR65 are two good, long-distance paths on the ancient pilgrim routes to Compostela. They are all managed by the **Association de Coopération Interrégionale**.

In the Pyrénées-Atlantiques, the legendary GR10, from Hendaye to the Cirque de Litor, and the GR8, from Urt to Sare, lead through pristine valleys and tracts of unspoilt countryside. Information can be obtained from the **Fédération Française de la Randonée Pédestre**. Official footpaths in Aquitaine also include those known as the Sentiers d'Émilie, and guides to these are available from bookshops. Some organizations offer hiking trips with a donkey to carry your luggage. Full information about this is available from departmental tourist authorities *(see p288)*.

Cycling

Aquitaine has a total of 2,000 km (1,240 miles) of cycle tracks and mountain-biking routes, which are graded by level of difficulty. The disused railway lines along the coast and around the Arcachon Basin have been made into cycle tracks. These are particularly good, with the densest network between Pointe de Grave and Bayonne. With their gentle hills and picturesque *bastide* towns, the Périgord, the Lot-et-Garonne, the Pays Basque and Béarn are all perfect for leisurely cycling. In the more mountainous areas, cycling is of course more arduous, although steep climbs are rewarded by exhilarating descents. *À Vélo*, a brochure issued by the regional tourist authority *(see p287)*, gives details of various short cycling circuits and longer tours. Another source of information is the **Fédération Française de Cyclotourisme**.

Horse Riding

One of the best ways of exploring the countryside is on horseback. There are several thousand kilometres of official bridleways in the region and a good number of riding centres. Escorted rides, on horses, ponys or *pottoks* (small Pyrenean horses), follow the many picturesque bridleways. In the Pyrenees, there are also escorted rides along the routes used by local shepherds and their flocks. Covering over 1 million ha (2471,000 acres), the forests of the Landes offer ideal terrain for horses. Information about opportunities for horse riding in the southwest is available from the **Comité Régional**.

Cycling on a quiet country road in the Dordogne

An escorted ride in the Pays Basque, one of the best ways to see the country

Golf

The first golf course on the Continent was built at Pau in 1856. Since then, about 50 others, including several putting greens, have been created. The diversity of the region's landscape has made it possible to build golf courses with widely different terrain. Most are in set beautiful surroundings, in the heart of verdant countryside in Pau and Arcangues, or in the midst of vineyards in the Médoc. The Chiberta golf course at Anglet, just a few hundred yards from the beaches, is one of the finest golf courses on the Basque coast. Chantaco, at Saint-Jean-de-Luz, is another. The well-known courses at Hossegor, Seignosse and Moliets are regarded as being among the 50 best in Europe. The Bordeaux-Gironde Golf-Pass and Biarritz Golf-Pass allow visiting golfers to play on several courses in one zone at preferential rates. The **Ligue d'Aquitaine de Golf** provides information on all aspects of golfing in the region.

Winter Sports

With several Pyrenean mountain resorts, the south-west has much to offer winter sports enthusiasts. There is downhill skiing at La Pierre-Saint-Martin, Artouste and Gourette, at an altitude of 2,400 m (7,877 ft), and cross-country skiing at Issarbe, Le Col du Somport and the Forêt d'Iraty. The **Comité Régional** offers detailed information.

Hanggliding

Hanggliding can offer spectacular views of the Pyrenean valleys. Centres at Accous and Saint-Jean-Pied-de-Port welcome beginners, but they may prefer to go to the Dune du Pyla. Here you only need to run a few yards to take off and float high above the Arcachon Basin. Several hanggliding schools are members of the **Fédération Française de Vol Libre**.

Golf course at the Château de Montal, in the hills of Quercy

Disabled Visitors

Various organizations promote sport for people with disabilities. While **Handisport** has a special interest in people with restricted mobility or impaired sight, the **Ligue du Sport Adapté d'Aquitaine** is concerned with mentally handicapped people. **Tourisme et Handicap** is a useful source of information on wheelchair access. Through APF Évasion *(see p249)* the **Association des Paralysés de France** organizes holidays for people with disabilities.

DIRECTORY

Walking

Association de Coopération Interrégionale
Les Chemins de Saint-Jacques-de-Compostelle, 4 rue Clémence-Isaure, 31000 Toulouse.
Tel 05 62 27 00 05.
W chemins-compostelle.com

Fédération Française de la Randonée Pédestre
64 rue du Dessous des Berges, 75013 Paris.
Tel 01 44 89 93 93.

Cycling

Fédération Française de Cyclotourisme
12 rue Louis Bertrand, 94207 Ivry-sur-Seine.
Tel 01 56 20 88 88.
W ffct.org

Horse Riding

Comité Régional de Tourisme Equestre d'Aquitaine
Hippodrome du Bouscat, BP 80095, 33492 Le Bouscat Cedex.
Tel 05 56 28 01 48.
W cheval-aquitaine.com

Golf

Ligue d'Aquitaine de Golf
16–18 rue Hermite 33520 Bruges, Gironde.
Tel 05 56 57 61 83.
W ffg-aquitaine.org

Mountain Sports

Comité Régional du Club Alpin Français
8 bis rue Francis Jammes, 64300 Orthez.
Tel 05 59 69 12 62.
W clubalpinorthez.fr

Comité Régional de la Montagne et de l'Escalade
12 rue Garrigou Lagrange, Pau. **Tel** 05 59 30 18 94.
W ffme.fr

Fédération Française de Vol Libre
4 rue de Suisse, 06000 Nice.
Tel 04 97 03 82 82.
W federation.ffvl.fr

Disabled Visitors

Association des Paralysés de France
W apf.asso.fr

Association Tourisme et Handicap
W gihpnational.org

Comité Régional d'Aquitaine Handisport
Maison Départmentale des Sports, 153 rue David Johnston, 33000 Bordeaux.
Tel 05 56 48 56 59.
W handisport.org

Ligue du Sport Adapté d'Aquitaine
(as for Handisport)
Tel 05 57 22 42 18.

Watersports

The beaches of southwest France, which stretch for over 250 km (155 miles), are renowned for having the best breakers in Europe. This makes them very popular for surfing, although the sea here is also ideal for other watersports. Sheltered by dunes and pine forests, the lakes of the Landes and Gironde are perfect for sailing. The white-water rivers of the Pyrenees, the Périgord and the Leyre, as well as their calmer stretches, offer excellent opportunities for canoeing. Sea fishing and angling in streams or lakes, are other options.

Canoeing in the lower Vézère valley

Sea-kayaking and Surf-kayaking

The whole of the region's coastline is suitable for sea kayaking. In "frenzy", a more energetic form of surf-kayaking, a light unsinkable craft is used to skim along the crest of breakers at exhilarating speed. While the slow-moving waters of the Dordogne and lower Vézère rivers are perfect for novice canoeists, the Auvézère, upper Dronne and upper Isle present a suitable challenge for the more experienced. The **Fédération Française Canoë-Kayak** co-ordinates information, and some organizations, such as **Vallée de la Vézère** and **Explorando**, rent canoes and arrange themed routes.

Sailing, Windsurfing and Sand-yachting

La Teste-De-Buche, **Arcachon** and **Hendaye** are coastal resorts identified as *stations voile* (windsurfing, sailing and sand-yatching centres) by the Fédération Française. The region's many natural and man-made lakes also offer superb watersports facilities and, unlike coastal resorts, they are not affected by the tide. Carcans-Hourtin, Lacanau, Cazaux, Sanguinet, Parentis, Soustons, Hossegor and Biscarrosse are resorts that offer ideal conditions for catamaran sailing, as well as for windsurfing and funboarding. Surrounded by maritime pines, these sheltered lakes are also ideal for bathing, and young children can play at the water's edge in complete safety. The Gironde Estuary also offers opportunities for watersports enthusiasts. Each year, between March and late November, the **Club Nautique Bourquais** organizes regattas. Aquitaine's wide Atlantic beaches offer vast spaces for sand-yachting, particularly in autumn, when the wind is most favourable. Information about these sports is posted on the **Ligue d'Aquitaine** website.

Windsurfer on the Étang de Léon, in the Landes

Deep-sea Diving

Between the Pays Basque and the Arcachon Basin, there are several diving centres. Those on the Arcachon Basin, where the **Fédération Française d'Etudes Sports Sous-marin** is based, are very popular. Diving in the shallow waters off the coast is organized from the jetty at La Croix des Marins, while diving in deeper waters, further out at sea, is organized from the marina. Off the Plage des Gallouneys, the water is up to 15–18m (50–60ft) deep, and here old World War II blockhouses, now covered with sea anemones, have become home to a variety of marine life. You can also go diving in the Étang de Sanguinet, which is 7–8m (23–26ft) deep. It harbours a wreck, half buried in sand, that is home to freshwater fishes. For several years now, the Association de Défense et d'Études Marines de la Côte has installed the Adremca, an artificial reef, 25 m (80 ft) down in the sea off Mimizan. Degraded by over-fishing and oil pollution, this area of the seabed is rapidly recovering, and is being recolonized by marine plants and animals.

A twin-hulled sailing dinghy

Kite-surfers at Lacanau, one of the region's greatest surfing resorts

Surfing

More than simply a sport, surfing in this part of France is almost a way of life. The waves hitting the beaches here are at their highest and most powerful in the autumn. **Anglet, Biarritz**, Hossegor and **Lacanau** are major venues for international competitions, and each of them has a number of surfing clubs. One of the best centres for surfers, however, is **Capbreton**, which is also well known as a diving spot because of the Gouf, an underwater canyon, more than 3,000 m (9,846 ft) deep.

There are also a large number of surfing schools dotted along the coast, that offer instruction for both beginners and experienced surfers. Many of these are members of the **Fédération Française de Surf**.

Surfer on breakers at a beach in the Pays Basque

You can hire surfing equipment at almost any resort. Information on all aspects of surfing in the southwest, including competitions, regional surfing schools and events, is given by the **Comité Régional d'Aquitaine de Surf**. The waves here are also perfect for bodyboarding, in which you ride the waves lying on a surfboard, and for kite-surfing, in which you skim along the waves, towed, and sometimes lifted, by a kite. Kite-surfing is especially popular at Arcachon, Biscarrosse and Lacanau. **Surf Report**, accessible by telephone or via the Internet, gives daily reports on the best surfing spots and on weather conditions. Other websites provide information on conditions along the whole of the region's coastline.

Pupils from one of the region's many surfing schools

DIRECTORY

Where to Surf

Comité Régional d'Aquitaine de Surf
1 avenue de Fray, 40140 Soustons Plage.
Tel 05 58 49 31 37.
W **surfingaquitaine.com**

Fédération Française de Surf (FFS)
123 bvd de la Dune, 40150 Hossegor. **Tel** 05 58 43 55 88.
W **surfingfrance.com**

Anglet Surf Club
5 Espace de l'océan, 64600 Anglet.
Tel 05 59 03 01 66.
W **angletsurf.com**

Biarritz Surf Club
Centre de Glisse de la Milady, 64200 Biarritz.
Tel 05 59 23 24 42.
W **surfingbiarritz.com**

Capbreton Surf Club
Plage de la Savane, 40130 Capbreton.
Tel 05 58 72 33 80.
W **capbretonsurfclub.com**

Lacanau Surf Club
Boulevard de la Plage, 33680 Lacanau-Océan. **Tel** 05 56 26 38 84.
W **surflacanau.com**

Surf Report
Tel 0892 68 13 60.
W **surf-report.com**

White-water rafting on the Gave de Pau, near Bétharram

White-water Rafting and Canyoning

Many clubs and other organizations have special programmes tailored for beginners, as well as for experienced enthusiasts. In Béarn, the rivers that rush down the Pyrenean valleys offer a thrilling challenge to skilled rafters and canyoners. Also, the Nive river, close to the Basque coast, is an excellent site, and offers opportunities for a host of other watersports as well.

Whether you choose a demanding or a more gentle descent, you must be able to swim and must obey your guide at all times.

Many organizations, including **Eaux Vives, Canoë-Kayak de Mer** and **Loisirs 64**, will provide all the essential information.

Canal Boating

The Canal de Garonne, the continuation of the Canal du Midi, as well as the Lot, Dordogne and Baïse rivers are either partly or wholly accessible by motor boat. Those who enjoy exploring a region off the beaten track will be interested in the choice of options available *(see pp300–301)*. These range from a short trip on the river to a cruise in a hired boat. Sailing down the Leyre, which winds through the forests from the Landes in Gascony to the Arcachon Basin in the Gironde, offers a voyage of discovery at a leisurely pace. There are 12 boat-hire centres along this river, which has been aptly nicknamed "the little Amazon". You can enjoy trips of just a few hours or of several days, accompanied by a qualified leader.

Fishing

The region's lakes and rivers offer fishermen almost limitless opportunities to indulge their passion. They are divided into three grades. The best waters are home to trout and salmon. In the second- and third-grade waters, carp, tench, roach, pike and black bass can be found.

Fishing is controlled by law, so as to protect fish stocks across all species and preserve the environment. To fish in Aquitaine, you must purchase a licence, which is available from fishing-tackle shops and other outlets. Fishing licences are available for one day, for two weeks *(forfait vacances)* or for a year.

There are a huge number of lakes in this region of France. Among the best for fishing are the large ones along the coast of the Gironde and the Landes. The Garonne and the Dordogne are rich in such migratory species as salmon, shad and meagre. The still waters of the Lot-et-Garonne, the canal parallel with the Garonne and many lakes are also good fishing spots.

Whether using a rod and reel or fly-fishing, the more active anglers will usually head for the Pyrénées-Atlantiques, which has some of the best fishing waters in Europe. The Gave d'Oloron is one of the finest salmon-rivers in France.

On the coast, anglers can catch turbot, sole and bream. Boats taking visitors further out on tuna- and shark-fishing expeditions leave from Saint-Jean-de-Luz and Biarritz. A more unusual kind of fishing is surf-casting. This is done from beaches at night or at dawn, using 4.50-m (15-ft) rods to cast into the surf.

Every *département* in France has a **Fédération de Pêche** (fishing association), to which approved fishing clubs and organizations belong.

Barge on the Baïse, below the lock at Lavardac

Anglers on the jetty leading to the lighthouse at Capbreton

Safety at Sea

Every year, accidents in the Atlantic happen as the result of holidaymakers disregarding basic safety rules. The main danger to swimmers is being swept out to sea by the strong currents that form in large bays as the tide turns. To be safe, swimmers should bathe only on beaches that are supervised (from June to September). Swimming is forbidden outside areas marked by blue pennants. Surfing and bodyboarding are only permitted outside bathing areas, and some beaches have specially marked surfing and bodyboarding zones, where swimmers are not allowed. If you want to go sailing, you should always check the **sea forecast** *(météo marine)* before setting out, as weather conditions at sea can change rapidly. Inexperienced sailors should always be supervised by professionals. **CROSS** (Centre Régional Opérationnel de Surveillance et de Sauvetage) will come to the rescue of sailors or swimmers in difficulty.

Green flag, the signal for safe bathing

Watersports for Disabled People

Some beaches in the Pays Basque have been made accessible to people with disabilities thanks to **Handiplage**, an association that also publishes *Handi Long*, a guide for visitors with disabilities. Among the outdoor activities that have been especially adapted through **Handisport** *(see p279)* are surfing (contact Handisurf), canoeing and deep-sea diving.

DIRECTORY

Useful Numbers

CROSS Atlantique
Tel 112.
W netmarine.net

Sea Forecast
W plages-landes.info

Visitors with Disabilities Handiplage
Tel 05 59 50 08 38.
W handiplage.fr

Canoeing

Canoës Vallée de la Vézère
1–3 promenade de la Vézère, 24620 Les Eyzies-de-Tayac.
Tel 05 53 05 10 11.
W canoesvalleevezere.com

Explorando
24250 Grolejac.
Tel 05 53 28 13 84.
W canoedordogne.com

Fédération Française de Canoë-Kayak
Bordeaux.
Tel 06 28 80 51 32. Mont de Marsan.
Tel 05 58 85 93 06. Périgueux.
Tel 05 53 04 24 08.
W ffck.org

Rafting

Canoë-Kayak de Mer
Maison de la Nature du Bassin d'Arcachon, 33470 Le Teich.
Tel 05 56 22 80 93.
W parc-landes-de-gascogne.fr

Eaux Vives
W eauxvives.org

Loisirs 64
21 rue de Hirigogne, 64600 Anglet.
Tel 05 59 93 33 65.
W loisirs64.com

Sailing

Ligue d'Aquitaine
Tel 05 56 50 47 93.
W ligue-voile-aquitaine.com

Cercle de Voile d'Arcachon
Marina (port de plaisance), 33120 Arcachon.
Tel 05 56 83 05 92.
W voile-arcachon.org

Club Nautique Bourquais
2 bis quai des Verreries, 33710 Bourg-sur-Gironde.
Tel 05 56 36 45 24.
W bourg-voile.com

Centre Nautique d'Hendaye
Bd de Txingundi, 64700 Hendaye. **Tel** 05 40 39 85 43. **W centrenautique.hendaye.com**

Sand Yachting

Ligue d'Aquitaine
Tel 06 26 90 54 19.
W charsavoile.com

Deep-sea Diving

Comité Interrégional Atlantique-Sud
119 bd Wilson, 33200 Bordeaux-Caudéran.
Tel 05 56 17 01 03.
W plongee-cias.org

Club d'Exploration Sous-marine d'Aquitaine
69 avenue d'Arès, 33000 Bordeaux.
Tel 05 56 99 46 26.
W cesma.free.fr

Fédération Française d'Etudes Sports Sous-marin
209 rue 14 juillet, 33400 Talence.
Tel 05 56 96 67 52.
W ffessm.fr

Fishing

Fédérations Départementales de Pêche

Dordogne
16 rue des Prés, 24000 Périgueux.
W federation-pechedordogne.fr

Gironde
299 cours de la Somme, 33800 Bordeaux.
W peche33.com

Landes
102 allée Marine, 40400 Tartas.
W peche-landes.com

Lot-et-Garonne
44 cours du 9 ème de Ligne, 47006 Agen.
W federationpeche.fr/47/

Pyrénées-Atlantiques
12 bd Hauterive, 64000 Pau.
W peche64.com

SURVIVAL GUIDE

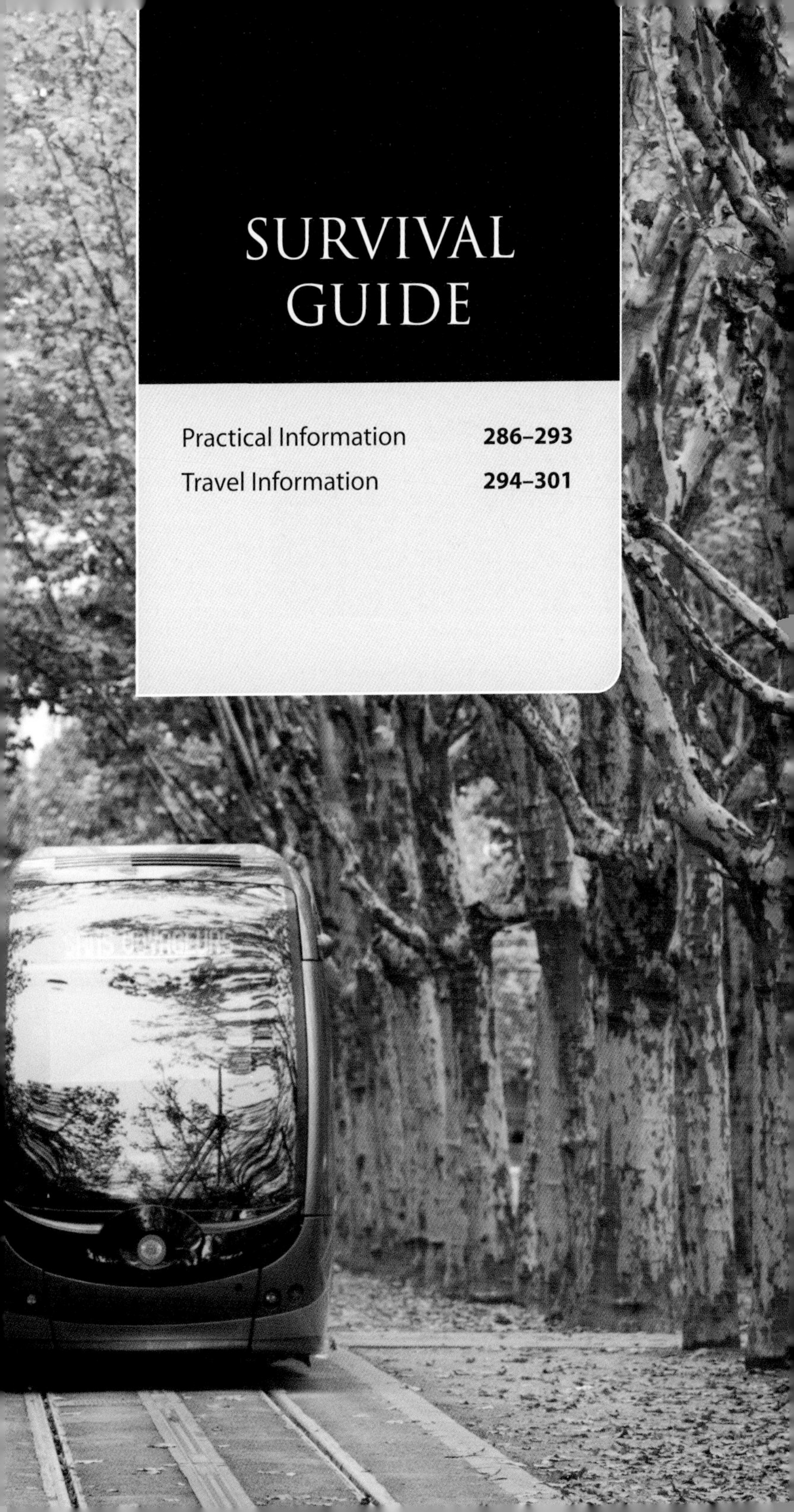

PRACTICAL INFORMATION

Because of its gentle climate, southwest France attracts tourists all year round. But it is during the summer, particularly in the coastal resorts, that it sees the largest number of visitors. Covering an area as large as the Netherlands, the region offers many different types of scenery, including mountains, a beautiful coastline, forests and vineyards, as well as a wide choice of activities. It also has a rich cultural heritage, with several major prehistoric sites, many grand, imposing châteaux, and numerous picturesque, medieval towns and villages.

Beach and Fort de Socoa at Saint-Jean-de-Luz, in the Pays Basque

When to Go

During summer, southwest France welcomes a constant stream of visitors, and the areas along the coast become particularly crowded. The whole of Aquitaine is enlivened with festivals and fairs, and it is also the high season for watersports.

Autumn is the best time of year for golf, surfing, hunting and fishing, and is also when truffles and cèpes are gathered, and grapes harvested in the vineyards. By contrast to the coastal resorts, which are now fairly quiet, large towns and cities remain lively places. In Bordeaux, for example, theatre, concerts and exhibitions are in full swing, shops are busy and just taking a stroll in the streets is pleasant.

In the Pyrenees, between November and Easter, the snow-covered peaks draw winter-sports enthusiasts. The resorts are particularly busy during school holidays.

Visas

Whether you need a visa to visit France depends on your nationality and length of stay. Citizens of European Union countries do not need one. Citizens of the USA, Canada, Australia and New Zealand do not need a visa for stays of up to three months. All foreign visitors need an identity card or valid passport.

Animals

There is no bar to bringing pets to France, so long as the animal is at least three months old, has microchip identification and has been vaccinated against rabies. A certificate of vaccination, issued by a qualified, registered vet must be shown.

Some beaches have a no-dogs policy. In coastal resorts, it is an offence to allow your dog to foul pavements and other public areas, and transgressions are likely to be punished by a €70 fine. Particularly "aggressive" dogs, such as pit bull terriers, are outlawed in France.

Tax-free Goods

Visitors from outside the European Union can reclaim most of the sales tax TVA (VAT) paid on certain goods through the Global Refund Scheme if the total value of purchases on a single day in one shop is more than €175. A portion of the tax is withheld as an administration fee. TVA is slightly lower on some items in Spain and many people in Béarn and Pays Basque cross the border to shop, especially for alcohol and cigarettes.

Customs Duties

If you are travelling within the European Union, there is no limit to the amount of goods you can buy so long as they are for your personal use. (This does not apply to new vehicles.) However, you should not take home more than 800 cigarettes, more than 10 litres of spirits or more than 90 litres of wine. Plants, ivory, counterfeit items and works of art are subject to particular restrictions. If you

One of the region's many important museums and galleries

◀ Tram passing through the Esplanade des Quinconces park in Bordeaux

A tourist office in a historic building

have doubts about anything, it is advisable to check with the **Service des Douanes**.

Admission Charges

Admission charges for most museums, monuments and archaeological and other sites range from €2 to €7. There are reductions for children up to 12 years old, and usually no charge for children under six. Students under the age of 26 and people over 65 are also entitled to reductions. Consult **Centres d'Information pour la Jeunesse** for further details of the range of concessions available to young people.

A student ID card entitles visitors to many discounts

Tourist Information

Information on everything, from the region's coast and countryside to its villages, towns and cities, as well as the passes of the Pyrenees and local wine routes, is available from the **Comité Régional du Tourisme**. This organization can also give advice on where to go, what to do and where to stay.

Each *département* has a **Comité Départemental du Tourisme**, which coordinates information from all local business involved in tourism, and which can also help you book accommodation. To contact a **tourist office**, no matter where you are in France, dial 3265 and you will be put through to the relevant branch. The **Maison Aquitaine** in Paris is another good source of information for planning your stay.

Opening Times

Most archaeological sites, museums and other visitor attractions are closed on Mondays or Tuesdays. In summer, however, museums open every day, and shops are likely to stay open at lunchtime or later in the evenings. Out of the high season, shops open from 9am to 7:30pm, and close at lunchtime. Hypermarkets are open all day and many also open on Sunday mornings.

Apart from those in major coastal resorts, large towns and on motorways, most petrol stations close on Sundays. In restaurants, it can sometimes be difficult to order a meal after 2pm at lunchtime and after 10pm in the evening.

Media

The principal French national daily newspapers, such as *Le Monde*, go on sale at news-agents from opening time every morning. The best way of getting the feel of local life in Aquitaine (for French speakers) is to read *Sud Ouest* (www.sudouest.fr), a regional daily that claims to have more than 1 million readers, published in 21 local editions.

Many kiosks, especially in larger towns, also sell a wide range of foreign newspapers, though they will cost considerably more than at home, and most 3-, 4- and 5-star hotels provide news-papers for their foreign guests. Bars and bistros also put out a copy of the local newspaper for customers to read.

The best-known and most widely read regional magazine is the bimonthly *Pyrénées Magazine* (www.pyrenees-magazine.com), which carries lots of interesting features on mountain hiking and local culture. Other magazines include *Pays Basque Magazine* (www.paysbasquemagazine.com) and *Le Festin* (www.lefestin.net), an art journal devoted to the cultural heritage of the region. Both are published quarterly.

Logo of TV7 Bordeaux and France Bleu

Aquitaine also has a number of radio stations. Among them is France Bleu, which has local stations in the Gironde, the Périgord, Béarn and in the Pays Basque.

Local television stations include FR3 Aquitaine and TV7, which covers the area in and around Bordeaux. Satellite channels, including a wide range of foreign channels, are also usually available in 3-, 4- and 5-star hotels.

The daily newspaper *Sud Ouest* and the magazine *Pyrénées*

A ride at the Parc d'Attractions Walibi

Travelling with Children

Children are welcome almost everywhere in southwest France, including hotels, campsites and gîtes. The time when there is most on offer for children is, of course, during school holidays.

Besides its many activity and entertainment centres, the region has several theme parks. These include the **Parc Oceafaunia** in Capbreton, the **Haras National de Gelos** (horse-breeding centre) near Pau, the **Parc d'Attractions Walibi** *(see p167)* near Agen, and the **Parc Préhistorique Prehistologia**, with the largest exhibit devoted to prehistoric animals anywhere in Europe.

As in other countries, children in cars are legally required to travel in child car seats. Swimming pools in public places should also be fenced. On the beach, parents should protect children from strong sun and obey safety rules imposed by lifeguards. If you would prefer to avoid beaches with large waves, keep to the Arcachon Basin, the bay at Saint-Jean-de-Luz or any of the large coastal lakes *(see pp280–81)*.

Smoking

Smoking is forbidden in public places, such as cinemas, museums, galleries, historical monuments and buildings that are open to visitors, and on public transport. The same is true for restaurants and bars but many provide outdoor terraces, heated in winter, where smoking is permitted.

Disabled Travellers

Two websites, **APF** and **Handitec-Handroit**, offer detailed information about the legal provision in France for disabled travellers, and other practical details. They also provide useful information and relevant addresses that will help you to plan your trip and make the most of your stay. For details on sport for people with disabilities, *(see p279)*.

Electricity

As elsewhere in Europe, the current in France is 220v-AC. Two-pin plugs, with rounded prongs, are used.

DIRECTORY

Tourist Information

Centre d'Information Jeunesse Aquitaine (CIJA)
125 cours Alsace-Lorraine, 33000 Bordeaux.
Tel 05 56 56 00 56.
W info-jeune.net

Maison Aquitaine
21 rue des Pyramides, 75008 Paris. **Tel** 01 55 35 31 42.

Service des Douanes
Tel 0811 20 44 44.
W douane.gouv.fr

Comité Régional du Tourisme
Cité Mondiale, 23 parvis des Chartrons, 33074 Bordeaux Cedex.
Tel 05 56 01 70 00.
W tourisme-aquitaine.fr

Disabled Travellers

APF
W apf.asso.fr

Handitec-Handroit
W handroit.com

Comités Départementaux Du Tourisme

Périgord
BP2063, 24002 Périgueux.
Tel 05 53 35 50 24.
W dordogne-perigord-tourisme.fr

Gironde
21 cours de l'Intendance, 33000 Bordeaux.
Tel 05 56 52 61 40.
W tourisme-gironde.fr

Landes
4 rue Aristide-Briand, BP 407,
40012 Mont-de-Marsan Cedex.
Tel 05 58 06 89 89.
W tourismelandes.com

Lot-et-Garonne
271 rue Péchabout, BP 30158,
47005 Agen Cedex.
Tel 05 53 66 14 14.
W tourisme-lotetgaronne.com

Béarn-Pays Basque
4 allées des Platanes BP 811,
64100 Bayonne.
Tel 05 59 30 01 30.
W tourisme64.com

Children

Haras National de Gelos
1 rue du Maréchal Leclerc, 64110 Gelos.
Tel 05 59 35 06 52.
W haras-nationaux.fr

Parc Oceafaunia
Avenue de l'Océan, 40530 Labenne (south of Capbreton).
Tel 05 59 45 43 93.

Parc d'Attractions Walibi
Château de Caudouin, 47310 Roquefort.
Tel 0820 426 420.
W walibi.com

Parc Préhistorique Prehistologia
46200 Lacave (near Rocamadour).
Tel 05 65 32 28 28.

Personal Security and Health

Its well-run local authorities and public services make Aquitaine a generally safe place to visit. But you should always guard against petty crime by taking a few simple precautions, such as locking your car and not flaunting valuable personal possessions. Pharmacies are almost everywhere, and all large towns have modern, well-equipped hospitals, such as the CHU in Bordeaux.

Personal Security

If you are involved in an accident, call the **police**, and take statements from witnesses. This may be useful if you need to provide a report. If you are the victim of assault or robbery, contact the nearest police station. Your country's consulate or embassy may also be able to help you. If you lose your passport or other important documents, report this to the nearest police station. If your credit card is lost or stolen, you must notify the police of this too *(see pp290–91)* and, of course, contact the card issuer.

Emergencies

In an emergency, dial 15 for **SAMU** (Service d'Aide Médicale d'Urgence) or 18 for the **Sapeurs Pompiers** (fire brigade). Unless they are in immediate danger, do not try to move someone who is injured before medical help arrives. If you are involved in an emergency in the mountains, call **PGHM** for the Pyrénées-Atlantiques (Béarn and Pays Basque). This is the police force in charge of high mountain areas. You can summon help by dialling 112, the central, European-wide number of the **emergency service**. For difficulties at sea, contact **CROSS**, which will notify the lifeguard and lifeboat organizations.

Medical Care

No vaccinations are needed to visit France. If you come from a European country, apply for a European Health Insurance Card (EHIC). You can do this online or at post offices in the UK, before you leave. It will enable you to claim for state health service treatment in European Union countries, should you need it. You can receive hospital treatment, consult a doctor at a surgery or even ask one to visit. Outside normal hours, there will always be a doctor on call and a duty pharmacy that is open. Details of these services are posted outside surgeries and published in local papers, and are also available from police stations. While some medicines can be obtained by prescription only, others are sold over the counter.

Pharmacy sign

Outdoors

Every summer the ocean claims more lives. On beaches, always heed lifeguards' safety instructions and only swim in supervised areas. If the red pennant is flying, the sea is dangerous and you should not enter the water.

Never venture off into the mountains alone, and always check conditions first with the **local weather station**. A mobile phone, good map and sturdy boots are essentials.

Lifeguards on a beach, along the Atlantic coast

DIRECTORY

Emergency Numbers

CROSS Étel Atlantique
Tel 112.

PGHM for Pyrénées-Atlantiques
Quartier Saint-Pée, 64400 Oloron-Sainte-Marie.
Tel 05 59 10 02 50.

SAMU (Medical emergencies)
Tel 15.

Police and Gendarmerie
Tel 17.

Sapeurs Pompiers (Fire)
Tel 18.

Emergency Service
Tel 112 (Europe-wide number).

France Meteo
Tel 3250 for all weather, including sea and mountain forecasts.
W **meteo.fr.**

Main Hospitals

Bordeaux
Place Amélie-Raba-Léon.
Tel 05 56 79 56 79.

Périgueux
80 avenue Georges-Pompidou.
Tel 05 53 45 25 25.

Mont-de-Marsan
Avenue Pierre-de-Coubertin.
Tel 05 58 05 10 10.

Agen
21 route de Villeneuve.
Tel 05 53 69 70 71.

Bayonne
13 avenue Interne Jacques-Loëb.
Tel 05 59 44 35 35.

Pau
4 boulevard Hauterive.
Tel 05 59 06 45 22.

Consulates

UK
353 blvd du Président Wilson, Bordeaux.
Tel 05 57 22 21 10.

USA
89 quai des Chartrons, Bordeaux.
Tel 05 56 48 63 85.

Banking and Local Currency

Because of the large number of tourists it attracts, the southwest of France is well served by banks and bureaux de change, where visitors can change travellers' cheques or foreign currency. It is also possible to obtain euros at post offices and to withdraw cash from automatic cash machines, which can be found in all towns and many villages. Those who come from a country where the euro (€) is the national currency, can also withdraw cash from any bank.

Currency

Visitors from countries outside the Eurozone can change currency in banks and post offices, and at bureaux de change in department stores in cities, as well as at railway stations, airports and around tourist resorts. A commission is usually charged when changing currency, even if the rate is fixed, and this should be clearly displayed. It is always advisable to look around for the most favourable rates. You may like to consult an internet currency converter, which uses the most up-to-date exchange rates to make its calculations. Changing banknotes is as economical as changing travellers' cheques, but if you use a debit card to obtain cash, you may have to pay an additional charge of 1per cent of the amount drawn.

Travellers' Cheques

Travellers' cheques from **Travelex** or **American Express** are a safe and convenient way of carrying large amounts of cash. Travellers' cheques can be cashed at any bank or bureau de change and, subject to certain conditions, their value is refundable in case of loss or theft. Remember to keep a record of your cheques' serial numbers in a safe place, separate from the cheques themselves, as you will be asked to provide these should you need to claim a refund. You must countersign each cheque when you exchange it for cash or use it to make a purchase.

Bank Cheques

Paying by bank cheque when you are abroad is not a viable option. Most bureaux de change do not accept bank cheques in exchange for currency.

Credit Cards

Credit and debit cards are accepted in many shops, hotels and restaurants. However, some establishments will not accept cards for amounts below a certain figure, and this policy should be displayed. The most commonly used cards are **Visa** and **Eurocard-Mastercard**, although hotels and restaurants also accept **American Express** and **Diner's Club**.

There are ATMs (automatic teller machines) in every town in the region. Bear in mind, however, that ATMs may run out of cash over a long weekend, such as Easter, or when a public holiday falls on a Friday or a Monday.

Some banks are located in historic buildings

Banking Hours

Most banks in France are open for business from 9am to 12:30pm and from 1:45pm to 4:45pm, Tuesday to Sunday. Remember that on the eve of public holidays, such as Bastille Day (14 July) and Assumption (15 August), banks close early. The major French banks have branches in most towns in Aquitaine.

DIRECTORY

Bureaux De Change

American Express Bordeaux
11 cours de l'Intendance.
Tel 05 56 00 63 33.

Change Plus, Biarritz
9 rue Mazagran.
Tel 05 59 24 82 47.

ICE, Bordeaux airport
Hall A, 33700 Mérignac.
Tel 05 56 34 03 40.

CCCO Périgueux
11 Bd Montaigne.
Tel 05 53 35 67 00.

Current Exchange Rates in France

Le Monde
W bourse.lemonde.fr

Internet Currency Converters

W xe.com/ucc
W x-rates.com/calculator.html

Lost Cards and Travellers' Cheques

Eurocard-Mastercard
Tel 0800 90 13 87.
W mastercard.com

Visa
Tel 0892 70 57 05.
W visa-europe.fr

Diner's Club
Tel 0820 820 536.
W dinersclub.fr

American Express
Tel 01 47 77 72 00 (cards & cheques).
W americanexpress.fr

Travelex
Tel 0800 905 190.
W travelex.com

The Euro

France was one of the twelve countries taking the euro (€) in 2002, with the original currency, the franc, phased out on 17 February 2002.

EU members using the euro as sole official currency are known as the Eurozone. Several EU members have either opted out or have not met the conditions for adopting the single currency.

Euro notes are identical throughout the Eurozone countries, each one including designs of fictional monuments and architectural structures, and the 12 stars of the EU. The coins, however, have one side identical (the value side), and one side with an image unique to each country. Both notes and coins are exchangeable in any of the participating Euro countries.

Banknotes

Euro bank notes have seven denominations. The €5 note (grey in colour) is the smallest, followed by the €10 note (pink), €20 note (blue), €50 note (orange), €100 note (green), €200 note (yellow) and €500 note (purple). All notes show the stars of the European Union.

5 euros

10 euros

20 euros

50 euros

100 euros

200 euros

500 euros

2 euros

1 euro

50 cents

20 cents

10 cents

Coins

The euro has eight coin denominations: €1 and €2; 50 cents, 20 cents, 10 cents, 5 cents, 2 cents and 1 cent. The €2 and €1 coins are both silver and gold in colour. The 50-, 20- and 10-cent coins are gold. The 5-, 2- and 1-cent coins are bronze.

5 cents

2 cents

1 cent

Communications

French telecommunication systems are reliable and efficient. Most public telephones are now operated using pre-pay cards that are available from post offices and tobacconist-newsagents. The mobile phone network has also expanded. With the growth of the Internet, Wi-Fi hotspots are widespread, offering access to the web and allowing users to check their email. La Poste, the French postal service, is reliable and relatively inexpensive, and there are post offices all over Aquitaine, even in remote rural areas.

Distinctive yellow French mailbox

Telephoning in France

All French telephone numbers have 10 digits. The first two digits indicate the region: 01 indicates Paris and the Île de France; 02 the northwest; 03 the northeast; 04 the southeast (including Corsica); and 05 the southwest. When phoning from outside France, dial 00 33 and omit the initial zero from the 10-digit number (for example, 00 33 3 45 67 89 10).

Numbers beginning 080 (also called *numéro vert*) are free to the caller; 0810 (*numéro azur*) are charged at the cost of a local call; all other 08 numbers are charged at premium rates, with 0898 and 0899 being the most expensive. To call another country from France, dial 00, followed by the country code, then the number. All call charges and country codes are printed in telephone directories and also appear on the website of France Télécom. In case of difficulty, you can be connected by an operator.

A good way to save money on phone calls is to use a service such as **TeleRabais**, which allows you to call abroad at greatly reduced call charges. The company's website lists one or more access numbers for each country.

A useful place to search for international phone numbers is the independent online directory **www.numberway.com**.

Public Telephones

To use a payphone (*cabine téléphonique*), you usually need a phone card (*télécarte*). These are available in 50 or 120 telephone units. **Travelex** sells an International Telephone Card that provides good value for money. All types of phonecards (from pre-pay cards to top-up cards for mobile phones) are available at post offices and at most newsagents, supermarkets and tobacconists.

When you enter a phone box, the phone display will say "*Decrochez*", your signal to pick up the phone, followed by "*Introduisez votre carte*", for you to insert your card. The display will then say "*Patientez SVP*", followed by "*Numérotez*", at which point you dial the number you wish to call. For local calls, one unit lasts up to six minutes. Don't forget to take your card with you when you finish the call.

Mobile Phones

Mobile phone coverage is generally good throughout southwest France, although signals may be weak in some mountain areas. French mobiles use the European-standard 900 and 1900 MHz frequencies, so UK mobiles work if they have a roaming facility enabled. North American mobile phones will only operate in France if they are tri- or quad-band. Always check roaming charges with your service provider before travelling, as making and receiving calls can be very expensive. Some companies offer "packages" for foreign calls which can work out cheaper. If you expect to use your phone frequently, it can be more economical to get a cheap pay-as-you-go French mobile from one of the main local providers such as **Orange France**, **Bouygues Télécom** or **SFR**. You can insert a local SIM card into your own phone, but this will only work if your phone has not been blocked by your service provider.

A *télécarte*

Internet Access

The Internet is widely used in France, but surprisingly, Internet cafés are much less common than in most of Europe. Also, privately owned cybercafés tend to have a short lifespan. In rural areas, there may be a publicly provided "cyber-base" with free or fairly cheap Internet access. The best way to find the nearest place to go online is to ask at the tourist information office. It is often much easier to get online if you travel with a laptop. Look out for free Wi-Fi in airports, motorway service areas, stations, public libraries and cafés. Many hotels and even *chambres-d'hôtes* now offer Wi-Fi connections.

French Wi-Fi servers often use different frequencies to those common in the UK and North America, so you may need to manually search for the network. For more information on how to do this, see the Orange Wi-Fi website. If you need to use a cable connection, note that the French modem socket is incompatible with US and UK plugs. Adaptors are available, but it is often cheaper and easier to buy a French modem lead.

Using La Poste

To send a letter, use one of La Poste's distinctive yellow mailboxes. These are found in the street and also outside every post office. Collection times are indicated on the front of the box.

Stamps are available from post offices, newsagents and tobacconists. They are sold individually or in books *(carnets de timbres)* of 10 and 12. Postage rates vary according to the weight of the letter or parcel and its destination. The postal service is fast and reliable. A letter to a destination within France will arrive in 24 to 48 hours; from France to another country allow one to five days, unless you have paid for express delivery.

Some post offices have facilities that obviate the need to queue. These include stamp machines, franking machines and cash dispensers.

Poste Restante

French post offices, right across the country, also provide a mail-holding service *(poste restante)*, so that you can receive mail while travelling, without the need for a fixed address. Letters and parcels sent to you at a *poste restante* should be addressed with the name of the addressee, the words *"poste restante"*, the name of the relevant post office, the town and the postcode. To collect mail, you will need some form of identification.

You can also arrange to have your mail forwarded to an address of your choice, when you are away from home. There is a charge for this service, and you should allow about four days for it to come into effect.

Post office in Périgord

La Poste also provides banking services. You can withdraw cash and change foreign currency, but as elsewhere, you will need identification to complete both of these transactions.

Express Parcels

Two courier companies, Colissimo and Chronopost, work in conjunction with La Poste to deliver express parcels. These services are very efficient. They guarantee delivery within 12 to 48 hours, and you can track your parcel on the Internet by using a number that you will be given when you consign it. However, using them is much more expensive than sending parcels by ordinary post.

Stamp with Eleanor of Aquitaine

Postcodes

Each district of Aquitaine has a five-digit postcode. In an address, this number should appear in front of the name of the town or village, and should be on the same line. The first two digits correspond to the number of the *département*, and the three others to the relevant sorting office. The postcode 24 corresponds to the Dordogne, 33 to the Gironde, 40 to the Landes, 46 to the Lot (part of Quercy), 47 to the Lot-et-Garonne, and 64 to the Pyrénées-Atlantiques.

DIRECTORY

Useful Numbers

Country codes
UK: 44.
Ireland: 353.
USA and Canada: 1.
Australia: 61.
New Zealand: 64.

Directory enquiries for France
118 712.
W **118712.fr**
W **118218.fr (mobiles)**
Yellow Pages:
W **pagesjaune.fr**

International directory enquiries
W **numberway.com**

Low-cost calls
Telerabais: W **telerabais.com**
Travelex: W **travelex.com**

Mobile operators
Bouygues:
Tel 3106.
W **bouyguestelecom.fr**
Orange France:
Tel 0800 364 775.
W **orange.fr**
SFR:
Tel 1026.
W **sfr.fr**

Wi-Fi Hotspots

W **hotspot-gratuit.com**

Postal Services

La Poste
Tel 3631.
W **laposte.fr**

Chronopost
W **chronopost.com**

Colissimo
W **colissimo.fr**

TRAVEL INFORMATION

It is easy to travel to and around Aquitaine. There are major international airports at Bordeaux and at Toulouse (in the neighbouring region of Midi-Pyrénées). Smaller airports with international flights are at Biarritz, Bergerac, Brive and Pau. The TGV (high-speed, long-distance train) and the TER (the regional express train) services, together with the seaports at Bordeaux and Bayonne and an excellent network of major roads and motorways, also provide speedy access to most parts of the region, as well as links with Spain.

Bordeaux airport, serving 3 million passengers a year

Airports

Several international, national and regional airlines operate flights to airports in Aquitaine. Average flight times are about one hour from a destination within France, and about two hours from any European city. Passengers from North America will change at Paris for frequent connections to the region's airports. **Bordeaux-Mérignac airport** handles 3 million passengers a year and about 200 aircraft a week take off and land there. From Bordeaux, there are around 20 international connections to destinations such as Athens, Lisbon, London, Montreal and Prague, and daily internal flights to about 10 French cities, as well as many charter flights. The national French airline, Air France, operates direct flights to Spain, Belgium and Portugal from Bordeaux.

A shuttle service operates between Bordeaux airport and the city centre. There are departures every 45 minutes, and the journey time is about 30–45 minutes.

Biarritz airport handles 1 million passengers a year, with direct flights from Paris, Lyon, Geneva and other European cities. Buses run into central Biarritz and Bayonne, and to the coastal towns of Hendaye and Saint-Jean-de-Luz. **Pau airport** is used by Air France. There is also a good shuttle bus service into the city centre.

Bergerac airport, in the Dordogne, handles flights to a number of destinations in Britain, including London, Southampton, Birmingham, Liverpool, Exeter and Bristol. **Brive airport** is a smaller alternative.

Airport	Information	Distance from City	Getting into Town
Dordogne			
Bergerac	05 53 22 25 25 **bergerac.aeroport.fr**	5 km (3 miles) SW of Bergerac	€12–15 by taxi to the centre of Bergerac
Brive Vallée de la Dordogne	05 55 22 40 00 **aeroport-brive-vallee-dordogne.com**	5 km (3 miles) W of Brive	€30 by taxi to Brive; €80 to Sarlat; €140 to Périgueux
Gironde			
Bordeaux	05 56 34 50 50 **bordeaux.aeroport.fr**	15 km (9 miles) W of Bordeaux	€25–30 by taxi; Jet Bus from arrivals Hall B or bus line 1
Pyrénées-Atlantiques			
Biarritz	05 59 43 83 83 **biarritz.aeroport.fr**	2 km (1 mile) SE of Biarritz	€13–20 by taxi to Biarritz, Anglet or Bayonne; buses to Biarritz and Bayonne
Pau-Pyrénées	05 59 33 33 00 **pau.aeroport.fr**	7 km (4 miles) N of Pau	€25–30 by taxi to the centre of Pau; Idelis Line Proxilis 20 to railway station

Pau-Pyrénées airport by night

Connections

Many regular airlines, as well as the low-cost airlines Ryanair, Easyjet, Flybe and bmibaby, operate flights to southwest France. Most flights from Paris (Roissy-Charles de Gaulle and Orly Sud) are provided by the national carrier **Air France**, which also operates flights from the southwest to Geneva, London, Madrid, Barcelona and Amsterdam.

Most of the foreign airlines that serve the region provide flights to Bordeaux. The low-cost airlines serve a wide range of destinations. **Ryanair** operates flights from London-Stansted to Biarritz, Bergerac and Lourdes, and also from the cities of Bristol and Liverpool to Bergerac. **Flybe** operates flights from Southampton, Leeds, Birmingham, Exeter and Newcastle to Bergerac; and **Air France** has flights to Brussels and Lisbon from Bordeaux.

Air Fares

The low-cost airlines have dramatically reduced the price of travelling by plane. A number of websites, such as **cheapflights.co.uk**, allow travellers to compare fares offered by several different airlines. In general, the further in advance you buy your ticket, the cheaper it will be. However, low-cost airlines do not offer all the comforts and facilities that are usually provided by the regular airlines. There may also be additional charges for luggage; limitations on the dimensions and weight of hand luggage are strictly enforced at all airports.

Regular airlines also offer reduced fares, mainly for families, and people under 25 and over 60. Children under two travel free, although they are not allocated a seat. Bear in mind that certain types of ticket are not exchangeable or refundable, and that others are valid only for return journeys or require your stay to include a Saturday night.

Cheap flights to internal and international destinations are available from Air France, which offers last-minute cut-price tickets from midnight on Wednesdays.

Formalities

Check-in for passengers and their luggage usually closes 30 minutes before the flight's departure, but it is best to arrive at the airport two hours before boarding time. Each passenger usually has a baggage allowance of 20 kg (44 lb) in economy class, and 30 kg (66 lb) in business class. Special rates apply to golfing and winter-sports equipment. Passengers are allowed one piece of hand luggage each. Anything that can be used as a weapon, such as a sharp or pointed object, cannot be carried in hand luggage. New security measures should be consulted as restrictions change frequently.

Passengers in the hall at the Pau-Pyrénées airport

Children between the ages of 4 and 12 can travel alone with the majority of airlines, provided they have their own passport and wear some form of identity. Airlines will take good care of them for their complete journey.

Animals usually travel in the hold. Those weighing less than 5 kg (11 lb) may travel with their owner, in a carrier (at the airline's discretion). Assistance dogs are also usually permitted to travel with the owner.

DIRECTORY

Airline Companies

Air France
France **Tel** 3654.
W **airfrance.com**

British Airways
France **Tel** 0825 825 400.
UK **Tel** 0844 493 0787.
USA **Tel** 1-800-247-9297.
W **britishairways.com**

Low-cost Airlines

Easyjet
France **Tel** 0899 650 011.
UK **Tel** 0905 821 0905.
W **easyjet.com**

Flybe
W **flybe.com**

Ryanair
UK **Tel** 0871 246 0000.
W **ryanair.com**

Airline Tickets on the Internet

Cheapflights
W **cheapflights.co.uk**

Travelling by Train

Thanks to an excellent rail network, whose backbone is the high-speed TGV Atlantique service, the region forms a key link in Europe's north–south transport axis. By train, Bordeaux is now less than three hours from Paris, Lille five hours and Brussels under seven. Quick, convenient and comfortable, the high-speed train service, along with an efficient network of regional express trains (the TER), offers an ideal way of exploring Aquitaine, especially in high season, when roads can be congested.

The concourse at Bordeaux's TGV station

Rail Services

French trains are generally punctual and reliable. The timetables for TGV and TER services are available at all stations, including the main southwestern regional ones at **Agen, Bayonne, Bordeaux, Mont-de-Marsan, Périgueux** and at **Pau**.

The SNCF, French national railways, offers a **luggage-delivery service** *(service d'enlèvement des bagages à domicile)*, which is particularly useful to older people. This allows travellers to arrange for their luggage, including cases, pushchairs, bicycles and other items, to be taken directly to wherever they are staying.

Most trains have a bar or a restaurant car. For passengers who want to take their car on the train, an **auto-train** service runs between Paris and Bordeaux (all year), and to Biarritz (in summer) and to Toulouse. SNCF also offers special **Train + Location voiture** rates for rail travellers who need to hire a car at their destination. Similar deals apply to bicycle hire. Further information can be obtained from station concourses.

High-speed Trains

About 20 high-speed train services run between Paris and Bordeaux every day, with an average journey time of 3 hours. There are also 12 daily Paris–Agen services (4 hours), four Paris–Pau services (5 hours), and seven to the Basque coast (4.5 hours), including a sleeper service. Planned improvements to the Tours–Bordeaux stretch of the TGV Atlantique route should cut the journey time from Paris to Bordeaux down to two hours by 2017. Smoking is pro-hibited on all TGV trains and all seats must be pre-booked.

Regional Express Trains

Aquitaine's network of regional express (TER) services covers 2,647 km (1,645 miles). There are 163 stations and 26 lines, for a total of 360 towns and villages. Whether you are off to Pau for a major sporting event or simply want to get away for a relaxing break on the Arcachon Basin, regional express trains allow you to travel economically, with no worries about congested roads or parking problems.

A TER regional express train

Twenty return services run between Arcachon and Bordeaux every day, and the journey time is 45 minutes. From Bordeaux, the journey takes 1 hour 15 minutes to Périgueux, 1 hour 20 minutes to Dax, 1 hour 30 minutes to Agen, and 2 hours to Pau.

Tickets

Tickets can be purchased at railway stations, from SNCF-approved travel agents, and from automatic machines. A telephone information line, that is open seven days a week, provides details of train times and allows you to buy a ticket, which will be sent to you free of charge, and is valid for two months.

You can also reserve a seat, buy an electronic ticket, book a hotel and arrange car hire by visiting SNCF's website.

Fares

A reduction of 25 to 50 per cent on rail fares is available for children under the age of 12, people between the ages of 12 and 25, and those over 60. This applies to TGV train journeys so long as seats are still available, and on Corail and TER trains out of peak times *(périodes bleues)*. When your tickets are checked, you may be asked to show proof of your age. For frequent rail travellers, there are special passes (such as Enfant+ and Senior) that allow cheaper travel. If you buy your ticket two months to two weeks in advance, this will be a

The SNCF railway station at Biarritz

"Prem" ticket, with a reduction of 30 to 40 per cent.

Special tickets are also available to foreign visitors. An essential first stop before setting out on a trip around France is **Rail Europe**, an SNCF agency which gives advice and makes reservations online, by phone or in person at its offices in London and New York. It sells a range of rail passes valid for 3–9 days, consecutive or not, within a one-month period.

Animals

For an extra €5, you can take a small dog or a cat with you on a train. However, dogs must be muzzled and cats must not weigh more than 6 kg (13 lb), and must be carried either in a bag or a basket.

For animals that weigh more, you will have to pay half the cost of a second-class ticket. This also applies to first-class travel. Be sure that fellow-travellers do not object to your pet, as they can refuse to share a carriage with any animal. Guide dogs travel for free.

Bicycles

On main rail routes and on TER trains, bicycles are carried free. On TGVs, they must be dismantled, placed in a carrying bag and stored in luggage spaces.

On trains other than TGVs, bicycles can be carried in the guard's van or other designated places, and do not need to be dismantled. If your bicycle is stored in a guard's van, you will be responsible for lifting it in, securing it and lifting it out at your destination.

Disabled Travellers

To help plan their journey, people with disabilities can call the free phone number for the **SNCF Accessibilité Service**. As well as giving practical help and information, this service can arrange to have tickets sent to your home address. To ensure that the help you need is available at the appropriate time and place, it is best to make any arrangements at least 24 hours in advance.

Les Compagnons du Voyage is an association that can provide a suitable companion to travel with you on any train journey outside the Paris area.

Scenic Journeys

The most scenic journey by tourist train is the ride up to Lac d'Artouste *(see p237)*, which offers spectacular views of the highest peaks in the Pyrénées-Atlantiques. The rack railway up the Rhune *(see p204)* also offers breathtaking mountain views. SNCF also runs *trains touristiques* on particularly scenic sections of its regional network.

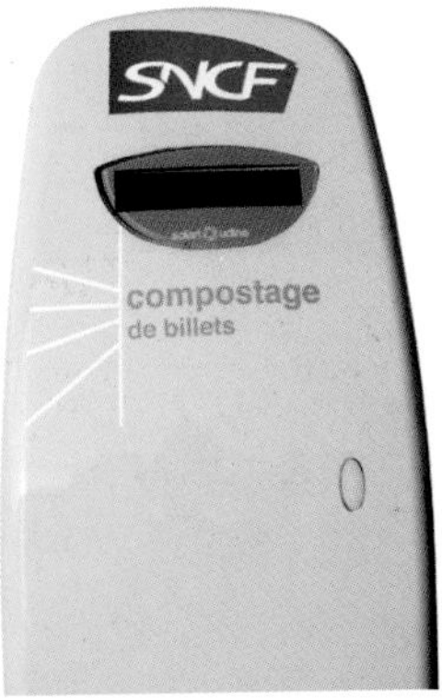

DIRECTORY

Useful Numbers

Auto-Train
Tel 0892 353 533.

Disabled Travellers SNCF Accessibilité Service
Tel 0890 640 650.
W accessibilite.sncf.com

Eurostar (London–Paris)
Tel 08705 186 186.
W eurostar.com

Information and Reservations
Tel 3635.
W sncf.com

Les Compagnons du Voyage
Tel 01 58 76 08 33.

Rail Europe
UK: 1 Regent St, London W1.
Tel 08448 484 064.
USA & Canada: 44 South Broadway, White Plains, NY.
Tel 1-800-622-8600 (USA); 1-800-361-RAIL (Canada).
W raileurope.com

TER Aquitaine
W ter-sncf.com

Railway Stations

Agen
Tel 3635 and say "gares".

Bayonne
Tel 3635 and say "gares."

Bordeaux
Tel 05 47 47 10 00.

Périgueux
Tel 3635 and say "gares".

Scenic Journeys

Train d'Artouste
Village de Fabrèges.
Tel 05 59 05 36 99.
W train-artouste.com

Train de la Rhune
Col de Saint-Ignace.
Tel 05 59 54 20 26.
W rhune.com

Composteur Machine
Yellow *composteur* machines *(left)* are located in station halls and at the head of each platform. Insert tickets and reservations separately, printed side up. The *composteur* will punch your ticket and print the time and date on the back. A penalty may be imposed by the inspector on the train if you fail to do this.

Travelling by Road

The extensive network of roads and motorways that serve Aquitaine include some of the main routes between Paris and Spain, and the Atlantic and Mediterranean coasts. Both major and minor roads in the southwest are well maintained, well sign-posted and generally pleasant to drive along. Some pass through stunning countryside.

Driving

Drivers should carry a registration certificate, insurance documents and a valid driving licence. At peak times on the roads, or at the start of major holiday periods, town centres and ringroads are likely to be congested. For information on traffic conditions, go to the "Wily Bison" website (**Bison Futé**), tune into to *Autoroute FM* on 107.7, or contact **CRICR**.

Distances by Road

The most direct road route from Paris to Bordeaux is the A10 motorway. From there, the N10 and the A63 motorway lead south to Biarritz, Saint-Jean-de-Luz and Hendaye. The A62, meanwhile, connects Bordeaux and Agen. A branch off it, the A65, leads to Pau.

The journey from Paris to Bordeaux is 584 km (363 miles); Bordeaux to Pau, 200 km (124 miles); Bordeaux to Bayonne, 190 km (118 miles); Bayonne to Périgueux, 317km (197 miles); Dax to Agen, 179km (111 miles); Arcachon to Villeneuve-sur-Lot, 200 km (124 miles); and Paris to Bayonne, 736 km (457 miles).

Road signs in French and Basque

Speed Limits

The speed limits are 50 km/h (30 mph) in towns; 90 km/h (55 mph) on open roads, but 80 km/h (50 mph) if it is wet or foggy; 110 km/h on dual carriageways, but 90 km/h (55 mph) when wet or foggy; and 130 km/h (80 mph) on motorways, but 110 km/h (70 mph) if wet or foggy.

Speed-limit sign

Road Safety

Seat belts must be worn by everyone travelling in the car. Before you set off on a long journey, check your tyre pressure. Children must travel in child carseats, and the use of mobile phones while driving is prohibited. Driving with over 0.05 per cent alcohol in the blood is illegal. You must carry spare light bulbs, a red warning triangle and a luminous reflecting jacket. If you plan to drive in the Pyrenees in the ski season, you must carry snow chains. On motorways and major roads, beware of heavy trucks travelling at speed. As much of the region is inhabited by wild animals that may jump out onto the road, be especially vigilant wherever you see warning signs.

A minor road in the Ossau valley, in Béarn

Trunk roads through open countryside are a pleasure to drive on

Fuel

Fuel stations on motorways clearly display their prices. There is little variation between them, and they are relatively high. Supermarkets such as Carrefour, Géant and Hyper U sell fuel cheaper. In rural areas few fuel stations open late, and often close Sunday to Monday and on public holidays.

Breakdown

Breakdown services, such as the **AA** and **RAC**, sell policies that provide 24-hour cover in Europe. Some insurers also offer a 24-hour breakdown service. Toll-charging motorways in France are privately managed, and if you break down on them you will not be covered by your normal insurance. You must call the official assistance provider and get the vehicle towed off the motorway first.

Tolls

At the entrance to a stretch of motorway where there is a toll (*péage*), you must collect a ticket, which you hand in at

A pay-and-display parking area in a town square

the motorway exit, when you pay the toll. This varies according to the type of vehicle and distance travelled. Automatic toll booths accept credit cards. Information on motorways is available on www.autoroutes.fr.

Hiring a Car

To hire a car you must be at least 21 years old and have a valid driving licence, which you must have held for at least a year. The main car-hire companies have offices in major railway stations, at airports and in town centres. Charges vary according to mileage and hire period and whether you return the car to another office. Car-hire companies in France that have a comprehensive network of offices and pick-up sites, include **ADA**, **Avis**, **Hertz** and **Europcar**.

Parking

Few town car parks are free. When you park, you must buy a ticket from a machine and place it in full view on the dashboard. Most towns have underground car parks.

Camper Vans

The overnight parking of camper vans is tightly regulated. In some districts there are special areas for camper vans, with water and other facilities. *Camping-Car Magazine* give details of 17,000 such areas in France.

Road Maps

You will find a road map of the region on the inside covers of this guide. If you want to drive on minor roads or go touring off the beaten track, the more detailed Michelin or IGN maps are recommended. The **Michelin** and **Mappy** websites are also useful for planning routes.

Buses

The region is served by a network of bus routes, operated by several different companies. **CITRAM**, for example, covers the Pyrénées-Atlantiques as well as 365 towns and rural areas in the Gironde. **RDTL** operates in the Landes, and **CFTA** in the Dordogne. Information on bus routes and timetables is available at all bus stations.

Eurolines is a long-distance coach company that runs regular services between Britain and the Continent.

Hitching and Car-sharing

If you would like to give a hitch-hiker a lift, contact **Allostop Bordeaux**, which gives useful information. You are entitled to a contribution to cover fuel costs, and this is a maximum of 20 centimes per km (about 15p a mile) for each passenger you carry. **123envoiture.com** organizes car-sharing all over the region.

DIRECTORY

Traffic Information

Bison Futé
W **bison-fute.equipement.gouv.fr**

CRICR (Centre Régional d'Information Routière)
Tel 0800 100 200.

Breakdown

AA
Tel 0800 072 32 79.
W **theaa.com**

RAC
Tel 0800 942 044.
W **rac.co.uk**

Car Hire

ADA
Tel 0825 169 169.

Avis
Tel 0821 230 760.
W **avis.fr**

Europcar
Tel 0825 358 358.
W **europcar.fr**

Hertz
Tel 0825 861 861.
W **hertz.fr**

Planning Routes

W **viamichelin.com**
W **mappy.com**

Hitching and Car-sharing

W **allostop.net**
W **123envoiture.com**

Bus Companies

Eurolines
W **eurolines.co.uk**

Gironde CITRAM-Aquitaine
Tel 0974 500 033.
W **citram.fr**

Dordogne CFTA Centre-Ouest
Tel 05 53 08 43 13.
W **cfta.co.fr**

Landes RDTL
Tel 05 58 05 66 00.
W **rdtl.fr**

Pyrénées-Atlantiques CITRAM-Pyrénées
Tel 05 59 27 22 22.
W **citrampyrenees.fr**

Travelling by Boat

The Arcachon Basin, the Gironde Estuary and the lakes of the Landes and the Gironde are all excellent places for sailing. Also, cruising along the extensive network of navigable waterways formed by Aquitaine's rivers and canals is a perfect way to explore the unspoilt countryside of the region. You may hire a boat to enjoy these calm waters and their beautiful scenery, even without a sailing licence.

Salako, one of many ferries in the Arcachon Basin

Capbreton, a sea port and coastal resort in the Landes

Marinas

The marina at **Arcachon** is the second-largest in western France, after the marina at La Rochelle. It has 2,600 moorings, including 250 for visitors, on 28 fully equipped pontoons.

Hendaye, where boats can put in whatever the weather conditions, has 850 pontoon moorings, including 120 for visitors. **Capbreton**, which is unuseable in rough seas, has 950 pontoon moorings, including 61 for visitors.

Sailing and Boating

You need a licence to sail a pleasure boat with an engine more powerful than 6HP. Three types of licence are available: *permis mer côtier* (coastal licence), *carte mer* (sea licence) and *permis mer hauturier* (ocean-going licence). Further information is available from the website of the **Ministry for Ecology, Sustainable Development, Transport and Housing**.

Every evening, the port authority posts the weather forecast for the following day, and the outlook for the next few days. The website of the **Fédération Française de Voile** gives times of high water at each harbour as well as contact details for boat trips and boat hire.

For boating on canals and rivers, you do not need a licence, and hire companies will show you the basics of navigating a boat, as well as how to go through a lock. The regional tourist authority issues a brochure with details of navigable waterways, boat trips and boat-hire companies.

Boat Trips at Sea

The Arcachon Basin, with its oyster farms, huts on stilts, Cap-Ferret, the Île aux Oiseaux (Bird Island) and the Leyre delta, offers a great deal to explore by boat, either aboard a fishing smack or on one of the cruisers run by the basin's boatmen. On some trips a meal is included.

Boats from the jetty at Thiers and Eyrac, or from Le Pyla or Le Mouleau, take you to Banc d'Arguin, where you spend the day (bring a picnic). Another memorable trip is to the Phare de Cordouan *(see p66)*, in the open sea between Le Verdon-sur-Mer and Royan. Boats for this lighthouse, which include the cruiser **La Bohême**, leave from Pointe de Grave.

Ferries

Two useful car ferry links from the Médoc peninsula to the other side of the Gironde Estuary are from **Verdon-sur-Mer to Royan** and from **Lamarque to Blaye**. **Bateliers Arcachonnais** provides convenient sea links between Arcachon and Cap-Ferret, Le Mouleau and Cap-Ferret, and Arcachon and Andernos. The Arcachon–Cap-Ferret service runs all year, with services from 9am to 1am in the high season.

From Hendaye, ferries run between the Spanish port of **Hondarribia** all year round, every half-hour out of season and every 15 minutes during the summer. The fares are very reasonable.

The ferry on the upper Gironde Estuary, at Blaye

River and Canal Cruises

The Dordogne, Baïse, Isle and Adour rivers, the Gironde Estuary and the Canal Latéral à la Garonne can all be explored on short boat trips, or on cruises aboard hired boats. A useful source of information about getting around on France's inland waterways is **Voies Navigables de France**.

Sailing along the Canal du Midi (which, with the Canal Latéral à la Garonne, forms the Canal des Deux-Mers) you can make frequent stops to visit the many historic monuments and other places of interest, or to swap the peace of the river for the bustle of a picturesque town. You will also pass through several locks. Boat-hire companies include **Bateau Ville de Bordeaux**, **Croisières Les Caminades** in the Périgord, **Gabare Val-de-Garonne**, and **Croisadour** in Peyrehorade. You can hire a barge or cabin cruiser by the week (no licence is needed) from **Aquitaine Navigation** or **Le Boat**. Prices are €900–€3,500 a week for a six-berth boat. You can also hire boats by the day. **En Péniche** is a company that runs upmarket barges, with all the facilities of a good hotel or guest house, including really comfortable berths.

Gabare (sailing barge), on the Dordogne

For day trips through magnificent scenery, you can also book a ride on traditional river craft, such as the *gabares* (local sailing boats) that still cruise along the Dordogne. **Bateliers du Courant d'Huchet** take visitors on trips to the stunningly beautiful nature reserve at the Courant d'Huchet *(see p181)*, aboard a *galupe*, a local type of flat-bottomed craft.

DIRECTORY

Marinas

Arcachon
Tel 0890 711 733.
w port-arcachon.com

Capbreton
Tel 05 58 72 21 23.
w port-capbreton.com

Hendaye
Tel 05 59 48 06 00.
w hendaye.com

Ferry Services

Les Bateliers Arcachonnais
Arcachon Basin.
Tel 05 57 72 28 28.
w bateliers-arcachon.com

Hondarribia (Spain)
Bateau Marie-Louise, 764700 Hendaye.
Tel 06 07 02 55 09.

Lamarque-Blaye car ferry
Tel 05 57 42 04 49.

Verdon-Royan car ferry
19 avenue du Phare de Cordouan, 33123 Le Verdon-sur-Mer.
Tel 05 56 73 37 73.

Boat Trips

Bateliers du Courant d'Huchet
Courant d'Huchet Rue des Berges-du-Lac, 40550 Léon.
Tel 05 58 48 75 39.
w bateliers-courant-huchet.fr

Vedette La Bohême
Chemin du Tourq Le-Verdon-sur-Mer, 33123
Tel 05 56 09 62 93.
w vedettelaboheme.com

General Information

Fédération Française de Voile
w ffvoile.net

Ministry for Ecology, Sustainable Development, Transport and Housing
w mer.gouv.fr

Voies Navigables de France
w vnf.fr

Canal-boat Hire

Aquitaine Navigation
47160 Buzet-sur-Baïse.
Tel 05 53 84 72 50.
w aquitaine-navigation.com

Le Boat
47430 Le Mas-d'Agenais.
Tel 05 53 89 50 80.
w leboat.com

Barges

En Péniche
Tel 04 67 13 19 62.
w en-peniche.com

River Cruises

Bateau Ville de Bordeaux
2 quai des Chartrons, 33000 Bordeaux.
Tel 05 56 52 88 88.
w bateauxbordeaux.com

Croisadour
102 quai du Roc, 40300 Peyrehorade.
Tel 05 58 73 25 87.
w croisadour.com

Croisières Les Caminades
24250 La Roque-Gageac.
Tel 05 53 29 40 95.
w gabarrecaminade.com

Gabare Val-de-Garonne
47200 Fourques-sur-Garonne.
Tel 05 53 89 16 85.
w emeraude-navigation.com

General Index

Page numbers in **bold** refer to main entries.

D

Acknowledgments

Main Contributors

Suzanne Boireau-Tartarat

Suzanne Boireau-Tartarat is the director of communications for Périgueux city council, and has contributed to many publications about the Dordogne. She is the author of the chapters on the Périgord and Quercy.

Pierre Chavot

Pierre Chavot, who lives near Bordeaux, is a freelance writer. He contributed to the chapter on the Landes for this guide, and has also written for several travel guides published by Hachette.

Renée Grimaud

Renée Grimaud, who lives in Bordeaux, is the author of several illustrated books and of travel guides to various regions of France. She is also a regulator contributor to Hachette's *Guides Voir*. She wrote the chapter on the Gironde.

Santiago Mendieta

Santiago Mendieta is a freelance journalist and writer. With the photographer, Étienne Follet, he has produced several illustrated books on the Pyrenees. He is the author of the chapters on the Pays Basque and Béarn.

Marie-Pascale Rauzier

A historian and journalist, Marie-Pascale Rauzier has written many books and travel guides, including the *DK Eyewitness Guide* to Morocco. She wrote the chapter on the Lot-et-Garonne.

Marguerite Figeac

Dr Marguerite Figeac has a PhD in history from the Sorbonne and teaches at the Institut de Formation des Maîtres d'Aquitaine in Bordeaux. She wrote the chapter on the history of Aquitaine.

Wilfried Lecarpentier

Wilfried Lecarpentier is the French correspondent of the *Los Angeles Times* and a member of the Association Professionnelle des Critiques et Informateurs Gastronomiques. He wrote the Travellers' Needs and Survival Guide chapters.

Gaëtan du Chatenet

Entomologist, ornithologist, member of the Muséum National d'Histoire Naturelle de Paris, draughtsman and painter, Gaëtan du Chatenet is the author of many works published by Delachaux & Niestlé and Gallimard.

Other Contributors

Xavier Becheler, Marie-Christine Degos, Isabelle De Jaham, Natacha Kotchetkova, Paulina Nourissier, Lyn Parry, Nicolas Pelé, Natasha Penot, François Pinassaud, Adam Stambul, Roger Williams.

For Dorling Kindersley

Douglas Amrine (Publisher), Jane Ewart, Fay Franklin (Publishing Managers), Uma Bhattacharya, Mohammad Hassan, Jasneet Kaur, Casper Morris (Cartography), Vinod Harish, Vincent Kurien, Jason Little, Azeem Siddiqui (DTP), Louise Abbott, Emma Anacootee, Karen Fitzpatrick, Anna Freiberger, Laura Jones, Delphine Lawrance, Jude Ledger, Carly Madden, Dora Whitaker (Editorial), Nick Inman, Lyn Parry (Factchecker), Julie Bond, Sonal Modha, Marisa Renzullo (Design), Rachel Barber, Rhiannon Furbear (Picture Research).

Editor

Cécile Landau.

Proofreader

Cate Casey.

Photography

Philippe Giraud.

Studio Photography and Additional Photography

Pierre Javelle, Éric Guillemot, Andrew Holligan, Roger Moss, Ian O'Leary.

Picture Research

Marie-Christine Petit.

Cartography

Cyrille Suss.

Illustrations

François Brosse

Architectural drawings pp 60, 86–7, 92–3, 110–11, 126–7, 134–5, 148–9, 196.

Jean-Sylvain Roveri

Architectural drawings pp24–5, 70–71, 104–05, 192–3, 222–3.

Éric Geoffroy

Illustrations on "Exploring" and "At a Glance" maps, on small town plans and tour maps.

Emmanuel Guillon

Façades and perspectives on pp20–21 and 22–3.

Rodolphe Corbel

Street-by-street maps pp78–9, 98–9, 158–9, 188–9.

Index

Marion Crouzet.

Revisions Team

Madhura Birdi, Dana Facaros, Rupanki Kaushik, Priyanka Kumar, John Malathronas, Deepak Mittal, Susie Peachey, Ellen Root, Ajay Verma

Special Assistance

The publishers would like to thank the following people and institutions, whose assistance has made the preparation of this book possible: Mme Cappé and M. Caunesil, at the tourist office in Verdon-sur-Mer; M. Laurent Croizier and Mme Valentina Bressan at the Grand-Théâtre de Bordeaux; M. Alain Gouaillardou at the Château de Pau; Mmr Marie-Lou Talet at the town hall in Fumel; M. Yves-Marie Delpit at the Château de Bonaguil; Mme Patricia Fruchon at the Château de Castelnaud; Mme Yvette Dupré and Mme Sophie Maynard at the Jardins du Manoir d'Eyrignac and at the Château de Hautefort; M. Serge Roussel and M. Bertrand Defois at the Grotte du Pech-Merle; Mme Larralde of the parish of Saint-Jean-de-Luz; Mme Anne Mangin-Payen at SDAP 64; M. François Caussarieu and Mme Christiane Bonnat at CDT Béarn Pays Basque; the municipal authories of the Tursan; Mme Cécile Van Espen at the town hall in Lescar; the tourist office at Lescar; M. Gérard Duhamel at CAUE Dordogne; M. Roger Labiano at Kukuxumusu; M. Jean-Sébastien Canaux at the tourist office in Monflanquin; M. Christophe Pichambert at CLS Remy Cointreau; M. Daniel Margnes and M. Jean-François Gracieux at Maison Aquitaine; M. Éric Badets at the tourist office in Parentis-en-Born; Mme Anne Pregat at the Musée des Beaux-Arts de Pau; Mme Françoise Henry-Morlier at the Château de Cadillac; the Centre des Archives Historiques du Lot-et-Garonne; Mme Maïté Etchechoury at the Archives Départementales de Dordogne; M. Louis Bergès and Mme Detot at the Archives Départementales de Gironde; Mme Caroline Féaud at France 3 Rhône-Alpes-Auvergne; Mme Anne Le Meur of *Guide Hachette des Vins*.

For their hospitality and helpfulness, the publishers would like especially to thank Mme la Vicomtesse and M. le Vicomte Sébastien de Baritault du Carpia, owners of the Château de Roquetaillade, and Mme and M. Élséar de Sabran-Pontevès, owners of the Château de Cazeneuve. The publishers also extend their thanks to all those who sent in regional produce; they are too numerous to acknowledge individually.

Photography Permissions

The publisher would like to thank the following owners, curators, guides and other site staff, transport networks, shops, organisations and institutions who have given permission to photograph on their premises:

Phare de Cordouan and boat *La Bohême II*; the animal park *La Coccinelle* at La Hune; Parc Ornithologique du Teich; Grand-Théâtre de Bordeaux; Hrottes de Pair-Non-Pair; Château de Vayres; the tourist office at Saint-Émilion; Abbaye de la Sauve-Majeure; the Gallo-Roman villa at Loupiac; Château de La Brède; Mme Valérie Lailheugue at Château d'Yquem; M. Max de Pontac at Château Myra; M. Dominique Befve at Château Lascombes; Château Margaux; M. Philippe Dourthe at Château Maucaillou; M. Éric Derluyn at Château de Mascaraas; the tourist office at Lescar; the Musée de l'Abeille at Monein; the Maison du Jambon de Bayonne at Arzacq; Château de Morlanne; the Musée du Béret in Nay; the Musée des Beaux-Arts de Pau; the Artouste train; the Musée Basque in Bayonne; the Réserve du Pottock at Bidarray; the Comité des Fêtes d'Espelette; Château d'Abbadia; the Grottes de Kakouetta; Prodiso, the espadrille factory in Mauléon; Ona Tiss, the weaving workshop in Saint-Palais; the Rhune train; Château de Ravignan; the Musée de l'Hydraviation in Biscarosse; the Comité des Fêtes de Gabarret et de Roquefort; the Musée de l'Aviation Légère de l'Armée de l'Air in Dax; the Musée de Borda in Dax; the boatmen on the Courant d'Huchet; the Musée de la Chalosse at Monfort-en-Chalosse; the Écomusée de la Grande Lande; the Atelier Jacques et Louis Vidal in Luxey; the Musée de l'Estupe-huc in Luxey; the Musée de la Dame de Brassempouy; the Musée de la Faïence in Samadet; Château de Duras; Château Molhière; M. Bertrand de Boisseson at Château de Montluc; the Musée du Pruneau in Granges-sur-Lot; Mme Valérie Duguet-Parickmiler at Château de Nérac; M. Jean de Nadaillac at Château de Poudenas; M. Michel Trama de l'Aubergade in Puymirol; Mme Geneviève and M. Yves Boissière at the Musée du Foie Gras in Souleilles; M. Joël Gallot, glass-maker in Vianne; the national stud at Villeneuve-sur-Lot; Mme Hélène Lages at the Musée de Gajac in Villeneuve-sur-Lot; M. Bruno Rouable de Caudecoste and St-Nicolas-de-la-Balerme; the Musée du Tabac in Bergerac; M. Jean-Max Touron at Grotte du Roc de Cazelle and La Roque-Saint-Christophe; M. Patrick Sermadiras at the Château de Hautefort; M. Armando Molteni at Grotte du Grand-Roc; Mme and M. Jean-Luc Delautre at Château de Fénelon; Grotte de Proumeyssac; Mme Angélique de Saint-Exupéry at Château des Milandes; Château de Montal; M. François Gondran at the Gallo-Roman villa in Montcarret; Grotte du Pech-Merle; Château de Puyguilhem; Mme Nicole de Montbron at Château de Puymartin; Mme Nadia Lincetto at the Musée d'Art Sacré Francis-Poulenc in Rocamadour; Château de Montaigne; Les Jardins de l'Imaginaire in Terrasson-Lavilledieu; the Préhisto Parc in Tursac; Mme Marie and M. Dominique Palué at Château de l'Herm.

Picture Credits

The publisher would also like to thank the following individuals and institutions who have given their permission for their photographs to be used in this guide:

a - above; b - below/bottom; c - centre; f - far; l - left; r - right; t - top.

4Corners Images: SIME/Giovanni Simeone 13tl.

Bordeaux Airport: Nihat Akgoz 294cla.
Pau Airport: Studio Vu 295tl and 295bc.
AFP: 56cl, 56crb.
AKG-Images: 55br; British Library 45crb and 47tl; Jean-François Amelo 46bl; Jean-Pierre Verney 48br.
Alamy Images: A la poste 292tr; Andy Arthur 293tr; Jon Arnold Images Ltd 58-9; Cephas Picture Library/Hervé Champollion 12br; John Kellerman 62, 146; M@rcel 172; nagelestock.com 14bl; Sébastien Baussais 297bc; Tony Kwan 18.
Archives de Villeneuve-sur-Lot: R. Delvert 57bc, 114bl.
Auberge de la Truffe: 265tr.

Auberge des Pins: 269tr.
Auberge Labarthe: 271bc.
Biarritz Culture: Ballet de Lorraine-Laurent Philippe.
BNF Paris: 46-47, 47ca, 48tl, 111bc, 140bl, 187bc.
Bridgeman Art Library: Archives Charmet 32tr; Giraudon/Lauros 42, 44clb, 49br, 53tc abd 54br; Giraudon 9bc; Sally Greene 210cb; Bridgeman Art Library 49crb, 55tr.

Casino d'Arcachon: Marcel Partouche 277cla.
Caudalie: 279tr.
Cave des producteurs de Jurançon: 37bc.
CCIP Bordeaux: Selva/Leemage 53crb.
Céramiques Cazaux & Fils: 274c, 274cr.
La Chapin Fin: 262br.
Château de Cambes: 252tc.
Château de Côme: 261br.
Château Cordeillan-Bages: Sébastien Cottereau/Bordeaux Code 01 250bc, 263bc.
Château de Fargues: Archives Familiales de Lur Saluces 52clb, 52crb.
Château Martinens: 37ca.
Cidrerie Txopinondo: 269bc.
Cinéma Utopia: 277tl.
Restaurant Claude Darroze: 256cla, 263tr.
Le Clefs d'Argent: 268tr.
Conseil général du Lot: Nelly Blaya 129tr.
Corbis: Tibor Bognar 244-5; Robert Harding World Imagery 13br; Jose Fuste Raga 2-3.

G. Dagli Orti: 43clb, 51br, 52bl, 212cl.
F. Desmesure: 276cra.
Domaine des Cassagnoles: 261tcr.
Dorling Kindersley: 121crb, 126bl, 127br, 283cra 289ca, 291, 298cr, 299ct, 299cc, 299cb.
Dreamstime.com: Davidmartyn 218; Ericlefrancais 10ca; Francisco Javier Gil Oreja 100.

Éditions Clouet: 21tl and 260tr.
Etchemaite: 270tr.
Festival Art Flamenco de Mont-de-Marsan: Sébastien Zambon/CG40 38b.
E. Follet: 34bc, 34crb, 34–5, 35cl, 35cra, 35bl, 35br, 39cra, 41c, 41bc, 61bl, 215tl, 234bl, 236ca, 238br, 239bl, 239tr, 240tl, 240tr, 240clb, 240bc, 241tr, 241cr, 241bl, 243cra, 243cl, 243c, 243crb, 243bl, 243bc.
France Bleu Gironde: 287cr.
France Telecom: 292bl: 1998 PhotoDisc, Inc. All rights reserved. Images provided by: 1998 Nick Rowe - France Telecom.

Gaïa Images: A. Senosiain 214br; Marlène Meissonnier 177cr.
Gamma: Politique Image/Gamma 57tr.
Getty Images: Walter Bibikow 284-5; Shaun Egan 190; James Warwick 24bc.
Lo Gorissado: 265bl.
Gouffre de Padirac: Cliché POUX, SES Padirac 125tl.
Grottes de Bétharram: 235bl.
Grottes Préhistoriques de Cougnac: 137tr: Francis Jach.

Robert Harding Picture Library: Daniel P. Acevedo/age fotostock 207tc.
Hemisphere Images: Pierre Jacques 14tr; Patrice Thomas 10bl.
Hoa-qui: Andre le Gall/Jacona 24tr; JA Jimenez/Age/Hoa-Qui 182cr; J. Cancalosi/Nature Pl/Jacana 25br; Mike Wilkes/Nature Pl/Jacana 24br, 24crb; Morales/Age/Hoa-Qui; 25clb; Philippe Prigent/Jacana 25bl; Pierre Petit/Jacana 24clb; S. Raman/Age/Hoa-Qui 25crb; Rodriguez 179tr; U. Walz Gdt/Age/Hoa-Qui 25crb; W. Bollmann/Age/Hoa-Qui 177br; Jose B. Ruiz 178clb.
Hotel du Palais: 255br.
Hype Hotel: 253bc.
Jardins d'Eyrignac: D. Reperant 117br; J.-B. Leroux 116cl and 117tl.
P. Javelle: 36cr, 37cr, 144bl, 260fcl, 260cl, 260c, 260bl, 260bc, 260br, 260fbr, 261cla, 261ca, 261cra, 272crb, 274cra, 274cla, 274tr, 274clb, 274bl, 275tl, 275cla, 275cra, 275cr, 275clb, 275cra, 275crb, 275cbcl, 275bcb, 275cbcr, 275bl.

Keystone-France: 51cb.
Kharbine-Tapabor: 50bc, 69br, 161bc, 178tr.
Leemage/Selva: 201cra, 201cr.
Librairie Megadenda: Éditions Erein 35tr
Ma Maison: 257bc, 266br.
Mairie de Dax: Philippe Salvat 39bl.
Mairie de Soulac: 67cl.
Maison Pariès: 275br.
La Maison sur la Place: 267bc.
Michel Trama: 267tr.
Le Moulin de Dausse: 266tl.
Mouton Rothschild: 37tl.
Musée basque et de l'histoire de Bayonne: 8-9, 191b, 195c, 196c.
Musée d'Aquitaine: : DEC, Bordeaux-B. Fontanel 44crb, 50cb; DEC, Bordeaux-B. Fontanel & L. Gauthier 44br; DEC, Bordeaux-Hugo Maertens, Bruxelles 44ca; DEC, Bordeaux-J.-M. Arnaud 45tc, 45cb; DEC, Bordeaux-J. Gilson 46clb, 47bl; CAPC-Frédéric Delpech 73cr.
Musée d'Art Sacré de Rocamadour: J.-L. Nespoulous 212bl.
Musée de Cahors Henri Martin: 135cr: J.-C. Meauxsoone.
Musée de Gajac de Villeneuve sur Lot: 156cr.
Musée des Arts Décoratifs de Bordeaux: DMB-L. Gauthier 78cr.
Musée des Beaux-Arts d'Agen: 166tr; Hugo Maertens, Bruges 160cl, 165br, 166cl.
Musée des Beaux-Arts de Bordeaux: M.B.A. Bordeaux-Lysiane Gauthier 51tr and 54tl.
Musée Despiau-Wlérick: 188crt: Studio Ernest, Mont-de-Marsan.
Musée du Périgord de Périgueux: B. Dupuy 107tr.
Musée du Pruneau de Lafitte: 159br.
Musée Georgette-Dupouy: S. Dom Pedro Gilo 184cl.
J.-B. Nadeau: J.B. Nadeau/Appa 86bc and 87bc.

Office de Tourisme d'Espelette: 40c.
Office de Tourisme de Soule: 216clb.
Ostape: 270bl.

Parc Naturel Régional des Landes de Gascogne, Belin-Beliet: 55cb, 56bc, 179bl.
Parc Walibi Aquitaine: 288tl.
Peyraguey Maison Rouge: 246bl, 251tl.
PERIFRUIT S.A: 261cl.
Photothèque Hachette: Hachette Livre 49cr, 52t, 52br, 92bl, 119tl, 206bc; Hachette Livre-Lacoste 53br.
Photothèque Ville de Cahors: Nelly Blaya 134br.
C. de Prada: 216br, 217cla.
Les Pres d'Eugenie: 247tr, 254tl.
Presse-Sports: 19b, 22tl.
Pyrénées Magazine: Étienne Follet-Milan 287br.
Relais de la Poste: 268bl; **REUTERS**: Regis Duvignau 57bc.
RMN: A. Danvers 50tl, 78tl, 95tr, 153cr, 186tr; Bellot/Coursaget 227br; Bulloz 224br; D. Arnaudet et J. Schormans 47crb; Franck Raux 163bc; Gérard Blot 48cr, 54cb, 99br, 135tl, 152bc; J. G. Berizzi 49tc; R. G. Ojéda 194tr, 197tr, 197bl, 228tr, 228cla, 229cr; V. Dubourg 228clb.
Roger-Viollet: Lapi 201br; 56tl; Lipnitzki 201bl; Branger 201cla; **La Roseraie:** 264tc.
SIBA: Brigitte Ruiz 28tr and 71br.
SNCF: 296cla; CAV-Patrick Leveque 296br; CAV-Philippe Fraysseix.
SNTP: 293cl.
STA TRAVEL GROUP: 287clb.
Studio Vidal: Cyrille Vidal. 33c, 33bl
Sud-Ouest: 287crb.
Superstock: Hemis.fr 15tr; Jean-Daniel Sudres/Hemis.fr.
Syndicat Viticole de Saint-Émilion: 40cla:
La Table de Haute-Serre: 264bl.
S. Tartarat: 140cl.
TV7: 287cr.

Front Endpaper
Alamy Images: John Kellerman Ltl, Rbr; M@rcel Rbc; **Dreamstime.com:** Davidmartyn Rbl; Francisco Javier Gil Oreja Rcr; **Getty Images:** Shaun Egan Lcl.

Jacket
Front and Spine - **AWL Images:** Doug Pearson.

Phrase Book

In an Emergency

Help!	**Au secours!**	*oh sekoor*
Stop!	**Arrêtez!**	*aret-ay*
Call a doctor!	**Appelez un médecin!**	*apuh-lay uñ medsañ*
Call an ambulance!	**Appelez une ambulance!**	*apuh-lay oon oñboo-loñs*
Call the police!	**Appelez la police!**	*apuh-lay lah poh-lees*
Call the fire department!	**Appelez les pompiers!**	*apuh-lay leh poñ-peeyay*
Where is the nearest telephone?	**Où est le téléphone le plus proche?**	*oo ay luh tehlehfon luh ploo prosh*
Where is the nearest hospital?	**Où est l'hôpital le plus proche?**	*oo ay l'opeetal luh ploo prosh*

Communication Essentials

Yes	**Oui**	*wee*
No	**Non**	*noñ*
Please	**S'il vous plaît**	*seel voo play*
Thank you	**Merci**	*mer-see*
Excuse me	**Excusez-moi**	*exkoo-zay mwah*
Hello	**Bonjour**	*boñzhoor*
Goodbye	**Au revoir**	*oh ruh-vwar*
Good night	**Bonsoir**	*boñ-swar*
Morning	**Le matin**	*matañ*
Afternoon	**L'après-midi**	*l'apreh-meedee*
Evening	**Le soir**	*swar*
Yesterday	**Hier**	*eeyehr*
Today	**Aujourd'hui**	*oh-zhoor-dwee*
Tomorrow	**Demain**	*duhmañ*
Here	**Ici**	*ee-see*
There	**Là**	*lah*
What?	**Quoi?**	*kwahl*
When?	**Quand?**	*koñ*
Why?	**Pourquoi?**	*poor-kwah*
Where?	**Où?**	*oo*

Useful Phrases

How are you?	**Comment allez-vous?**	*kom-moñ talay voo*
Very well, thank you.	**Très bien, merci.**	*treh byañ, mer-see*
Pleased to meet you.	**Enchanté de faire votre connaissance.**	*oñshoñ-tay duh fehr votr kon-ay-sans*
See you soon.	**A bientôt.**	*byañ-toh*
That's fine	**C'est parfait**	*say parfay*
Where is/are…?	**Où est/sont…?**	*oo ay/soñ*
How far is it to…?	**Combien de kilomètres d'ici à…?**	*kom-byañ duh keelo-metr d'ee-see ah*
Which way to…?	**Quelle est la direction pour…?**	*kel ay lah deer-ek-syoñ poor*
Do you speak English?	**Parlez-vous anglais?**	*par-lay voo uñg-lay*
I don't understand.	**Je ne comprends pas.**	*zhuh nuh kom-proñ pah*
Could you speak slowly please?	**Pouvez-vous parler moins vite s'il vous plaît?**	*poo-vay voo par-lay mwañ veet seel voo play*
I'm sorry.	**Excusez-moi.**	*exkoo-zay mwah*

Useful Words

big	**grand**	*groñ*
small	**petit**	*puh-tee*
hot	**chaud**	*show*
cold	**froid**	*frwah*
good	**bon**	*boñ*
bad	**mauvais**	*moh-veh*
enough	**assez**	*assay*
well	**bien**	*byañ*
open	**ouvert**	*oo-ver*
closed	**fermé**	*fer-meh*
left	**gauche**	*gohsh*
right	**droit**	*drwah*
straight ahead	**tout droit**	*too drwah*
near	**près**	*preh*
far	**loin**	*lwañ*
up	**en haut**	*oñ oh*
down	**en bas**	*oñ bah*
early	**de bonne heure**	*duh bon urr*
late	**en retard**	*oñ ruh-tar*
entrance	**l'entrée**	*l'on-tray*
exit	**la sortie**	*sor-tee*
toilet	**les toilettes, les WC**	*twah-let, vay-see*
free, unoccupied	**libre**	*leebr*
free, no charge	**gratuit**	*grah-twee*

Making a Telephone Call

I'd like to place a long-distance call.	**Je voudrais faire un appel interurbain.**	*zhuh voodreh fehr uñ appel añter-oorbañ*
I'd like to make a collect call.	**Je voudrais faire une communication PCV.**	*zhuh voodreh fehr oon komoonikah-syoñ peh-seh-veh*
I'll try again later.	**Je rappelerai plus tard.**	*zhuh rapel-eray ploo tar*
Can I leave a message?	**Est-ce que je peux laisser un message?**	*es-keh zhuh puh leh-say uñ mehsazh*
Hold on.	**Ne quittez pas, s'il vous plaît.**	*nuh kee-tay pah seel voo play*
Could you speak up a little please?	**Pouvez-vous parler un peu plus fort?**	*poo-vay voo par-lay uñ puh ploo for*
local call	**la communication locale**	*komoonikah-syoñ low-kal*

Shopping

How much does this cost?	**C'est combien s'il vous plaît?**	*say kom-byañ seel voo play*
I would like …	**je voudrais…**	*zhuh voo-dray*
Do you have?	**Est-ce que vous avez?**	*es-kuh voo zavay*
I'm just looking.	**Je regarde seulement.**	*zhuh ruhgar suhlmoñ*
Do you take credit cards?	**Est-ce que vous acceptez les cartes de crédit?**	*es-kuh voo zaksept-ay leh kart duh kreh-dee*
Do you take traveler's checks?	**Est-ce que vous acceptez les chèques de voyage?**	*es-kuh voo zaksept-ay leh shek duh vwayazh*
What time do you open?	**A quelle heure vous êtes ouvert?**	*ah kel urr voo zet oo-ver*
What time do you close?	**A quelle heure vous êtes fermé?**	*ah kel urr voo zet fer-may*
This one.	**Celui-ci.**	*suhl-wee-see*
That one.	**Celui-là.**	*suhl-wee-lah*
expensive	**cher**	*shehr*
cheap	**pas cher, bon marché**	*pah shehr, boñ mar-shay*
size, clothes	**la taille**	*tye*
size, shoes	**la pointure**	*pwañ-tur*
white	**blanc**	*bloñ*
black	**noir**	*nwahr*
red	**rouge**	*roozh*
yellow	**jaune**	*zhohwn*
green	**vert**	*vehr*
blue	**bleu**	*bluh*

Types of Shops

antiques shop	**le magasin d'antiquités**	*maga-zañ d'oñteekee-tay*
bakery	**la boulangerie**	*booloñ-zhuree*
bank	**la banque**	*boñk*
book store	**la librairie**	*lee-brehree*
butcher	**la boucherie**	*boo-shehree*
cake shop	**la pâtisserie**	*patee-sree*
cheese shop	**la fromagerie**	*fromazh-ree*
dairy	**la crémerie**	*krem-ree*
department store	**le grand magasin**	*groñ maga-zañ*
delicatessen	**la charcuterie**	*sharkoot-ree*
drugstore	**la pharmacie**	*farmah-see*
fish seller	**la poissonnerie**	*pwasson-ree*
gift shop	**le magasin de cadeaux**	*maga-zañ duh kadoh*
greengrocer	**le marchand de légumes**	*mar-shoñ duh lay-goom*
grocery	**l'alimentation**	*alee-moñta-syoñ*
hairdresser	**le coiffeur**	*kwafuhr*
market	**le marché**	*marsh-ay*
newsstand	**le magasin de journaux**	*maga-zañ duh zhoor-no*
post office	**la poste, le bureau de poste**	*pohst, booroh duh pohst*
shoe store	**le magasin de chaussures**	*maga-zañ duh show-soor*
supermarket	**le supermarché**	*soo pehr-marshay*
tobacconist	**le tabac**	*tabah*
travel agent	**l'agence de voyages**	*l'azhoñs duh vwayazh*

Sightseeing

abbey	**l'abbaye**	*l'abay-ee*
art gallery	**la galerie d'art**	*galer-ree dart*
bus station	**la gare routière**	*gahr roo-tee-yehr*

cathedral	la cathédrale	*katay-**dral***
church	l'église	*l'ayg**leez***
garden	le jardin	*zhar-**dañ***
library	la bibliothèque	*beeb**leeo**-tek*
museum	le musée	*moo-**zay***
tourist information office	l'office de tourisme, le syndicat d'initiative	*loff-**ees** de too-**reesm**, sandee-ka d'eenee-sya**teev***
town hall	l'hôtel de ville	*l'oh**tel** duh veel*
train station	la gare (SNCF)	*gahr (es-en-say-ef)*
private mansion	l'hôtel particulier	*l'oh**tel** partikoo-**lyay***
closed for	fermeture	*fehrmeh-**tur***
public holiday	jour férié	*zhoor fehree-**ay***

Staying in a Hotel

Do you have a vacant room?	Est-ce que vous avez une chambre?	*es-kuh voo-**zavay** oon shambr*
double room, with double bed	la chambre à deux personnes, avec un grand lit	*shambr ah duh pehr-**son** avek un gronñ lee*
twin room	la chambre à deux lits	*shambr ah duh lee*
single room	la chambre individuelle	*shambr indivi-**joo-ell***
room with a bath, shower	la chambre avec salle de bains, une douche	*shambr avek sal duh bañ, oon doosh*
porter	le garçon	*gar-**soñ***
key	la clef	*klay*
I have a reservation.	J'ai fait une réservation.	*zhay fay oon rayzehrva-**syoñ***

Eating Out

Have you got a table?	Avez-vous une table libre?	*avay-**voo** oon tahbl leebr*
I want to reserve a table.	Je voudrais réserver une table.	*zhuh voo-**dray** rayzehr-**vay** oon tahbl*
The check please.	L'addition s'il vous plaît.	*l'adee-**syoñ** seel voo **play***
I am a vegetarian.	Je suis végétarien.	*zhuh swee vezhay-**tehryañ***
Waitress/ waiter	Madame, Mademoiselle/ Monsieur	*mah-**dam**, mah-demwah**zel**/ muh-**syuh***
menu	le menu, la carte	*men-**oo**, kart*
fixed-price menu	le menu à prix fixe	*men-**oo** ah pree feeks*
cover charge	le couvert	*koo-**vehr***
wine list	la carte des vins	***kart**-deh vañ*
glass	le verre	*vehr*
bottle	la bouteille	*boo-**tay***
knife	le couteau	*koo-**toh***
fork	la fourchette	*for-**shet***
spoon	la cuillère	*kwee-**yehr***
breakfast	le petit déjeuner	*puh-**tee** deh-**zhuh-nay***
lunch	le déjeuner	*deh-**zhuh-nay***
dinner	le dîner	*dee-**nay***
main course	le plat principal	*plah prañsee-**pal***
appetizer, first course	l'entrée, le hors d'oeuvre	*l'oñ-**tray**, or-duhvr*
dish of the day	le plat du jour	*plah doo zhoor*
wine bar	le bar à vin	*bar ah vañ*
café	le café	*ka-**fay***
rare	saignant	***say**-noñ*
medium	à point	*ah **pwañ***
well-done	bien cuit	*byañ **kwee***

Menu Decoder

l'agneau	l'an**yoh**	*lamb*
l'ail	l'eye	*garlic*
la banane	ba**nan**	*banana*
le beurre	burr	*butter*
la bière,bière	bee-**yehr**, bee-**yehr**	*beer, draft*
une pression	oon pres-**syoñ**	*beer*
le bifteck, le steack	beef-**tek**, stek	*steak*
le boeuf	buhf	*beef*
bouilli	boo-**yee**	*boiled*
le café	kah-**fay**	*coffee*
le canard	kan**ar**	*duck*
le chocolat	**shoko**-lah	*chocolate*
le citron	see-**troñ**	*lemon*
le citron pressé	see-**troñ** press-**eh**	*fresh lemon juice*
les crevettes	kruh-**vet**	*prawns*
les crustacés	**kroos**-ta-**say**	*shellfish*
cuit au four	kweet oh foor	*baked*
le dessert	deh-**ser**	*dessert*
l'eau minérale	l'oh **meeney**-ral	*mineral water*
les escargots	leh zes-kar-**goh**	*snails*
les frites	freet	*chips*
le fromage	from-**azh**	*cheese*
le fruit frais	frwee freh	*fresh fruit*
les fruits de mer	frwee duh mer	*seafood*
le gâteau	gah-**toh**	*cake*
la glace	glas	*ice, ice cream*
grillé	gree-**yay**	*grilled*
le homard	om**ahr**	*lobster*
l'huile	l'weel	*oil*
le jambon	zhoñ-**boñ**	*ham*
le lait	leh	*milk*
les légumes	lay-**goom**	*vegetables*
la moutarde	moo-**tard**	*mustard*
l'oeuf	l'uf	*egg*
les oignons	leh zon**yoñ**	*onions*
les olives	leh zo**leev**	*olives*
l'orange	l'oroñzh	*orange*
l'orange pressée	l'oroñzh press-**eh**	*fresh orange juice*
le pain	pan	*bread*
le petit pain	puh-**tee** pañ	*roll*
poché	posh-**ay**	*poached*
le poisson	pwah-**ssoñ**	*fish*
le poivre	pwavr	*pepper*
la pomme	pom	*apple*
les pommes de terre	pom-duh **tehr**	*potatoes*
le porc	por	*pork*
le potage	poh-**tazh**	*soup*
le poulet	poo-**lay**	*chicken*
le riz	ree	*rice*
rôti	row-**tee**	*roast*
la sauce	sohs	*sauce*
la saucisse	soh**sees**	*sausage, fresh*
sec	sek	*dry*
le sel	sel	*salt*
la soupe	soop	*soup*
le sucre	sookr	*sugar*
le thé	tay	*tea*
le toast	toast	*toast*
la viande	vee-**yand**	*meat*
le vin blanc	vañ **bloñ**	*white wine*
le vin rouge	vañ **roozh**	*red wine*
le vinaigre	vee**naygr**	*vinegar*

Numbers

0	**zéro**	*zeh-**roh***
1	**un, une**	*uñ, oon*
2	**deux**	*duh*
3	**trois**	*trwah*
4	**quatre**	*katr*
5	**cinq**	*sañk*
6	**six**	*sees*
7	**sept**	*set*
8	**huit**	*weet*
9	**neuf**	*nerf*
10	**dix**	*dees*
11	**onze**	*oñz*
12	**douze**	*dooz*
13	**treize**	*trehz*
14	**quatorze**	*ka**torz***
15	**quinze**	*kañz*
16	**seize**	*sehz*
17	**dix-sept**	*dees-**set***
18	**dix-huit**	*dees-**weet***
19	**dix-neuf**	*dees-**nerf***
20	**vingt**	*vañ*
30	**trente**	*tront*
40	**quarante**	*kar**oñt***
50	**cinquante**	*sañk**oñt***
60	**soixante**	*swas**oñt***
70	**soixante-dix**	*swasoñt-**dees***
80	**quatre-vingt**	*katr-**vañ***
90	**quatre-vingt-dix**	*katr-vañ-**dees***
100	**cent**	*soñ*
1,000	**mille**	*meel*

Time

one minute	**une minute**	*oon mee-**noot***
one hour	**une heure**	*oon urr*
half an hour	**une demi-heure**	*oon **duh-mee** urr*
Monday	**lundi**	*luñ-**dee***
Tuesday	**mardi**	*mar-**dee***
Wednesday	**mercredi**	*mehrkruh-**dee***
Thursday	**jeudi**	*zhuh-**dee***
Friday	**vendredi**	*voñdruh-**dee***
Saturday	**samedi**	*sam-**dee***
Sunday	**dimanche**	*dee-**moñsh***

DATE DUE			

Road map of Dordogne, Bordeaux and the Southwest Coast

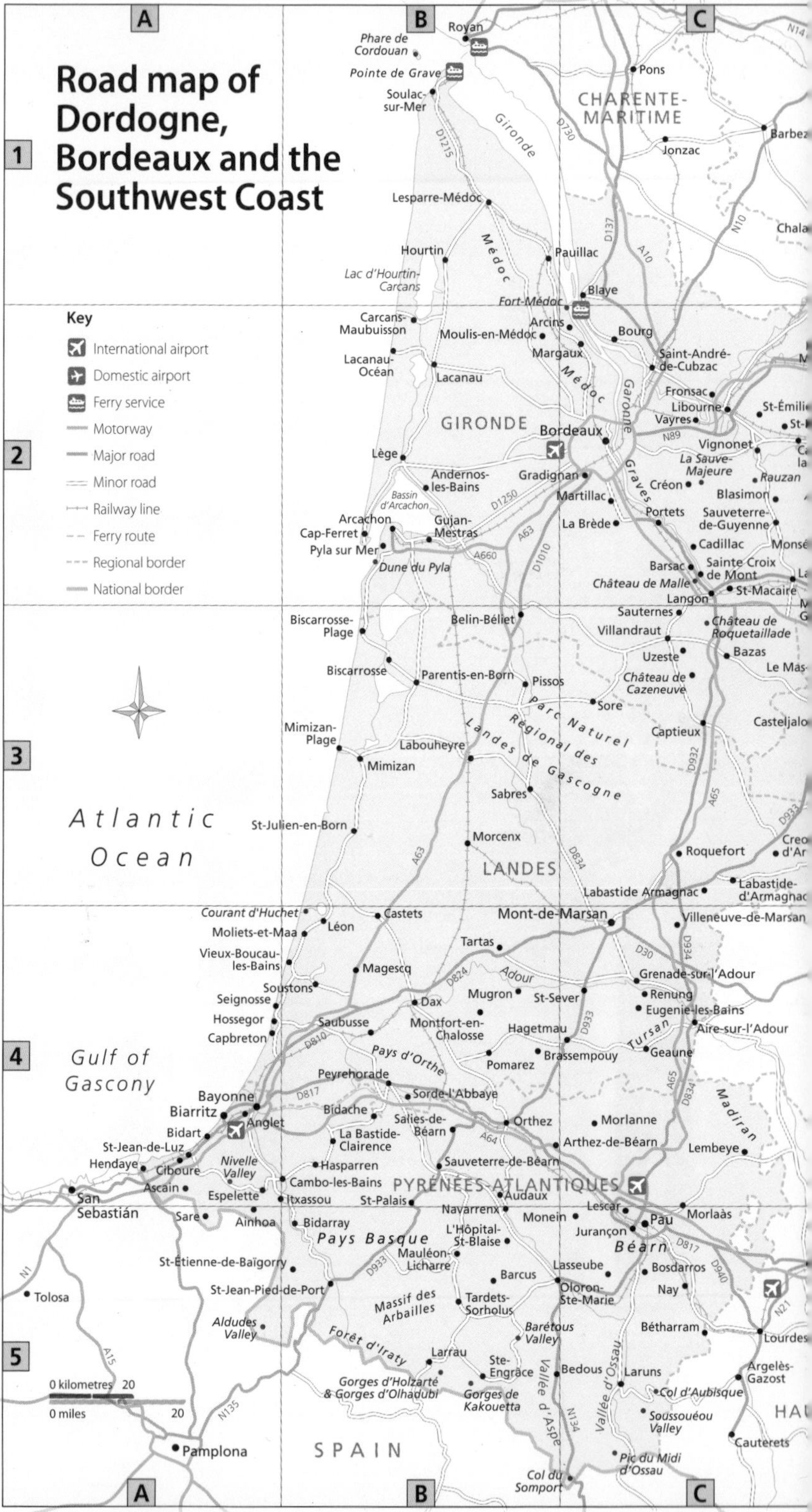